LUCKY STARS
AND
GOLD BARS

To James, a fellow Army Air Corps Officer

Pvt. Lyle V. Sladek 37474253

Lt. Lyle V. Sladek O 872240

Lucky Stars

and

Gold Bars

A WORLD WAR II ODYSSEY

★ ★ ★

KAREN SLADEK

PENLYRIC PRESS

SEATTLE, WASHINGTON

WITH GRATITUDE

To all those Americans who served their country during World War II

To my grandparents for preserving my father's letters

To my father for granting the use of his letters, photographs, and documents for the edification of future generations

LETTERS AND MEMOIRS ARE THE TRUEST TESTIMONY AND THE FINEST MEMORIAL FOR THE MEASURE OF FREEDOM WE ENJOY TODAY

CONTENTS

Preface: A Box of Letters ......   *xii*

1   HOME SEEMS A LONG WAY AWAY   1

2   NO PLACE LIKE HOME   4

3   RUMBLINGS OF WAR   18

4   SWEPT INTO THE MAELSTROM OF A GLOBAL CONFLICT   28

5   YOU'RE IN THE ARMY NOW, YOU'RE NOT BEHIND A PLOW   60

6   ART DECO BARRACKS AND BRONZED GODS   78

7   MEET ME IN ST. LOUIS   128

8   FAMILIAR FACES AND WIDE-OPEN SPACES   164

9   THE CHANGING WINDS OF WAR   174

10   CAROLINA IN THE MORNING   204

11   FOR GOD, FOR COUNTRY, AND FOR YALE   234

12   AN OFFICER AND A GENTLEMAN   292

13   DON'T FENCE ME IN   333

14   PASSAGE TO THE UNKNOWN   348

15   FLYING THE HUMP, SUPPLYING CHINA BY AIR   360

16   THE DAWN OF A NEW AGE   394

17   POSTWAR DUTY IN EUROPE   450

Epilogue: Love and Laughter and Peace Ever After   488

Acknowledgements   511
References   512
About the World War II Letter Writer   520

It is the stars,
The stars above us, govern our conditions.
—SHAKESPEARE, KING LEAR

FOUR HUNDRED LETTERS POSTED FROM FIVE CONTINENTS

A Box of Letters

Those who cannot remember the past are condemned to repeat it.
—GEORGE SANTAYANA

WRITING THIS BOOK was a labor of love, triggered by the discovery of a cardboard box on a closet shelf in the home of my parents. Curious, I cut the twine that bound the carton and rooted through the contents. Inside were hundreds of old envelopes bearing strange imprints—censor stamps, APO numbers, patriotic symbols. Some bore three-cent stamps, others had "Free" inscribed at the upper right-hand corner. I was astonished to learn they were letters written by my father while serving in the Army Air Corps during World War II and posted to his parents back home on the farm in South Dakota.

Somehow, despite many clues in my childhood home—a tapestry from Egypt, ivory carvings from India, embroidered silk cloth from China, cameos from Italy, a mountain goat carved of wood from the Isle of Capri—it had never occurred to me to ask my father about his role in the war and its aftermath.

Like my three sisters and twenty-five cousins, I am a bona fide member of the baby boom generation. During my childhood years in South Dakota I was just another kid on the block, a happy-go-lucky child surrounded by parents, sisters, cousins, grandparents, aunts, and uncles.

Since my father and six uncles served in the armed forces of the United States during World War II, you might suppose war stories dominated the conversation at our dinner table during the frequent get-togethers of our extended family. Not so. Once my father and uncles returned to civilian life, they closed the military chapter and focused on earning a living and nurturing a family.

A cursory exposure to World War II history in a high school class failed to capture my attention. I dutifully read the pedestrian prose and memorized the facts, but important lessons eluded me. Later, I earned a degree at a state university without appreciably adding to my knowledge of the watershed event of the twentieth century. After graduating from college, I traveled throughout Western Europe but perceived little evidence of the destruction wrought by the war.

Shortly after the fall of the Berlin Wall in 1989, my friend and namesake, Karen, suggested we travel to Eastern Europe. We shared the desire to delve into our Czechoslovakian roots. (Sladek is a brand of "sweet brew" in that country.) As we drove through Poland, Eastern Germany, and the Czech Republic, I was struck by the drab surroundings, the lack of joie de vivre, the suppression of the human spirit. Unable to long bear the horrific scene at Auschwitz, we sped away in our rental car. Arriving at Prague, we stumbled upon a three-story boardinghouse in an upscale neighborhood just two blocks from the residence of the president. Vera, the elderly proprietor, warmly welcomed us into her home and showed us to our room.

Each evening, upon hearing the turn of the latchkey, Vera came knocking at our door—under the guise of treating us to tea, pastries, and fruit. Before bidding us good night she would turn and say, "Just one more thing." That ritual completed, the three of us sprawled out in the guest room and talked the night away. Speaking in a mix of German and broken English, punctuated with much waving of hands, Vera related accounts of life in Prague during the war.

Hanging on the wall midst antiques, artwork, and family photographs was a portrait of a beautiful young woman. "Is that you, Vera?" I asked. "Yes, my da'ling," she replied. "Once I was blonde like you, but now I'm an ugly old woman, too unpleasant to be seen." She went on to explain that the picture had been painted by one of her art students shortly before British-trained parachutists of the Czechoslovak resistance descended near Prague to assassinate Reinhard Heydrich, the Nazi Reich Protector at Prague, whom Vera referred to as "Hitler's right arm." The Nazis, seeking a female accomplice to the assassination plot, rounded up young blonde women for interrogation. Vera, having proof she had been outside of Prague on a teaching assignment, was spared her life.

Tears welled up in our eyes as we backed out of the driveway and waved good-bye to Vera. Conversations with her had opened my eyes to an aspect of the war seldom conveyed in history textbooks or lectures—how the global conflict known as World War II impinged on the lives of ordinary people. That lesson was soon reinforced by an incident in another town.

My traveling companion was eager to visit her mother's birthplace. She knew the story of how her German grandparents had been forced to

AUTHOR KAREN SLADEK POSING WITH VERA, PRAGUE, 1990
VERA'S PORTRAIT HANGS ON THE WALL

relinquish their home in Czechoslovakia and leave the country with nothing more than a few valuables sewn into their clothing. I was intrigued by the story. Upon arriving at the place, we parked the car and walked down a dirt path obstructed by cats, dogs, goats, and squawking chickens. Heads turned and eyes became transfixed as we strode up to a house and knocked on the door. When an elderly woman appeared, Karen handed her a letter of introduction written by Vera. Assured we had not come to reclaim the property, the woman sent her grown son to town to fetch a translator. He returned with a woman fluent in German and Czech and with two fancy glasses filled with chocolate pudding—a treat for us that I suspected was beyond the family's means. Tears of healing flowed as we sat in the living room, our thoughts translated among three languages.

When it came time to take our leave, the old woman led us up a steep mountain path. Along the way she picked a large bouquet of wild flowers and handed them to Karen as a token of remembrance. Decades earlier Karen's mother, then an innocent young woman, had made a similar gesture while departing her family home. Deeply touched, we wept as we drove away. I contemplated the resilience of Karen's relatives; how her mother had eventually made her way to the United States and given her children the American dream. Before the flowers wilted, we pressed two of the blossoms between the pages of a book.

Upon arriving at a Polish border crossing in the High Tatras, menacing guards barred us from leaving the country. At that moment, my freedom as an American citizen—a gift I had taken for granted—became very precious to me. Eventually, we gained passage into Germany.

Even after my return to the United States, the economic, social, and political fallout of the World War II era remained abstract and impersonal. My awakening came with the discovery of my father's wartime letters.

My father, after metamorphosing from private to cadet to lieutenant in the Army Air Corps, served as a Cryptographic Security and Intelligence Officer in three theaters of war: China-Burma-India (CBI), European (ETO), and Mediterranean (MTO). As he circled the globe by land, sea, and air, he noted that profound social and political changes were taking place. While stationed in the CBI, he flew "the Hump" from India to China and observed that the Communist forces of Mao Tse-tung were prevailing over the Nationalist forces of Chiang Kai-shek. While walking the streets of Shanghai shortly after the Japanese army had evacuated that city, he was struck by the vigor and modern outlook of its people. Billeted near Calcutta, he witnessed riots as Mahatma Gandhi and the Indian National Congress agitated for independence from British rule. Continuing westward, he encountered political unrest in Egypt and in Greece. Clearly, the British sphere of influence was shrinking. Cognizant of the dictum "The sun never sets on the British Empire," he sensed the sun *was* about to set on that wide-flung kingdom. Arriving in Europe, he found postwar conditions heart-wrenching and chaotic.

World War II brought about wide-ranging political and social changes in Asia, Europe, and Africa; the war marked the transition from the old world order to the new. The desperate struggle between the Allies and the Axis powers led to quantum advances in technology—radar, jet airplanes, rockets, electronic coding devices, atomic energy—as each side sought an edge in the conflict.

Pulitzer-prize biographer David McCullough warns that we are "losing our past, losing our story." Memories of events that took place at Pearl Harbor, Guadalcanal, Midway, North Africa, Anzio, Normandy, Iwo Jima, and Hiroshima are deeply etched in the hearts and minds of "the Greatest Generation." Their children and grandchildren, however, mainly perceive of the World War II era as portrayed in movies and novels.

An ancient maxim asserts, "History is something that never happened, written by a man who wasn't there." My father *was* there, writing letters while serving as a soldier in the World War II army. Upon the death of his parents thirty years after the war, he discovered his mother had saved all of his letters—some four hundred posted from five continents. Written with no thought of posterity, the letters chronicle his observations and adventures from induction to discharge. The letters, while exhibiting the exuberance of youth and old-time values, present "truth" as my father perceived truth.

The letters make no claims of heroics. My father, like the majority of GIs who served in World War II, never fired a shot at the enemy. Fewer than twenty percent of the United States military were combat "trigger pullers." Wartime perils such as accidents and disease claimed more lives than battlefield wounds. Soldiers and sailors lived or died as chance and circumstance ground out their fate. President Kennedy, a war veteran himself, spoke these apt words:

> There is always inequity in life. Some men are killed in a war and some men are wounded, and some men never leave the country. . . . It's very hard in military or personal life to assure complete equality. Life is unfair.

Whether or not veterans have Purple Hearts in their dresser drawers or heroic tales to relate to their grandchildren, they answered the call of duty and deserve our profound thanks for preserving the freedom we enjoy today.

In the course of writing this book, I learned a great deal about the most widespread and destructive conflict in history. I began to understand the genesis of the Cold War, the Korean War, and my country's involvement in Vietnam—a chain of events that overshadowed World War II. For me, World War II is no longer just a topic in a history book; it has affected me emotionally. I admire the American people who made sacrifices on the home front. Most of all, I respect the men and women who served in the armed forces, patriots who risked their lives and postponed personal ambitions while putting down tyranny.

Time colors the past as each succeeding generation becomes further removed from the context of the World War II era. My father's letters, photographs, and documents constitute a primary source apropos to that period. They allow readers to compare and contrast the actual wartime experiences of one American soldier with the mythical constructs espoused by pop-historians and imaginative screenwriters. I am pleased to make this historical treasure trove available to scholars and to the public at large.

Lucky Stars and Gold Bars presents a *living history* of the epochal World War II era. In *King Lear,* Shakespeare postulated the advantage of having the stars in a favorable alignment when undertaking an enterprise of great import. All the stars in the heavens were in the right alignment for my father during those perilous years.

AUTHOR'S NOTE

Many of the letters in this book were written hurriedly and under awkward writing conditions, such as sitting on a bunk with inadequate light, wielding a leaky fountain pen, or when exhausted at the end of a strenuous day. In order to preserve the authenticity, flavor, word usage, and voice of the letter writer, the letters are essentially presented as written, including idiosyncrasies and inconsistencies in grammar, spelling, punctuation, and capitalization. Minor edits have been made for the sake of clarity. Underlined words have been *italicized* to reflect the letter writer's intended emphasis. Some repetitious material has been extracted.

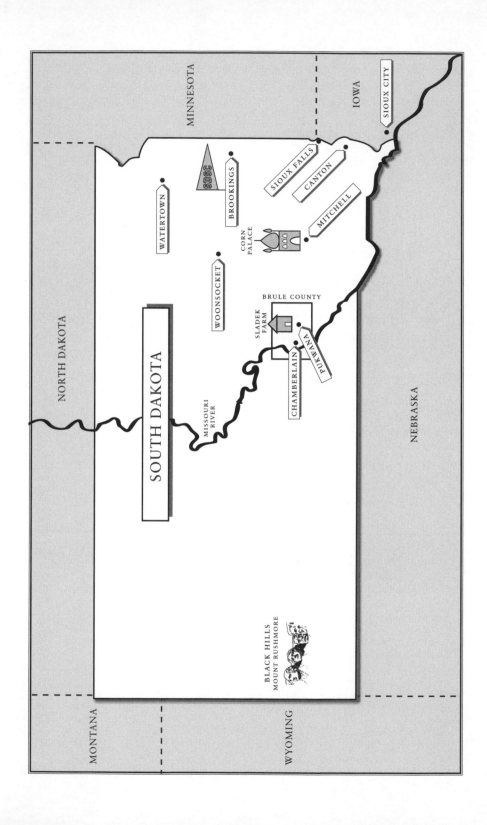

CHAPTER I

Home Seems a Long Way Away

Only mad dogs and Englishmen go out in the noonday sun.
—HINDU PROVERB

STIRRED TO LIFE by the drone of aircraft engines, a drowsy soldier emerged from under mosquito netting as the pink hue of dawn appeared on the eastern horizon—ushering in another sweltering day at the Tezpur Air Base. Pulling on a pair of khaki trousers, he carefully dusted talcum powder between his toes and inspected his GI shoes for green mold; fungus was a problem during the monsoon season in the Assam province of India. Playful monkeys watched from overhanging branches as he washed and shaved from a tin basin on the veranda of the hut. Donning a pith helmet to shield his head from the blazing sun, Lt. Lyle Sladek, 0872240, sauntered off to the bamboo mess hall for morning chow.

While eating breakfast, Lyle thought of his parents and siblings on the other side of the world. Then, ignoring the flies buzzing in and out of the open windows, he sipped GI coffee from a tin cup as he planned his day's activities. Censoring the outgoing mail was first on his list, a task he did not relish but one of his duties as Cryptographic Security and Intelligence Officer for a detachment of the Army Airways Communications System (AACS).

Later in the morning Lyle dropped in at the crypto station to check the settings on the coding machines and to ensure the enlisted men were observing proper procedures in handling classified messages. Not that he anticipated any problems—the men were dependable and knew their work. Still, he was responsible for the operation of the station and did not want any foul-ups. Finding everything running smoothly, he said he would return when new codes were scheduled to go into effect.

Hoping to find something new and interesting to read, Lyle set off for the post library. Although he walked slowly, beads of perspiration dampened his brow and heat rash prickled the small of his back before he reached the bamboo hut. While thumbing through a book of poetry he marveled at how well Rudyard Kipling had captured the India scene. Yes indeed, the heat was enough to "make your bloomin' eyebrows crawl."

After browsing for an hour, Lyle checked out a copy of Shakespeare's *King Lear*. Tucking the book under his arm he ambled back to the crypto station, voiced the password for the day, and gained admittance to the code room.

"How's it going, Sergeant?"

"We can't decode this garbled message, Lieutenant. We're hoping you can unravel it."

"I'll get right at it, Sergeant."

Tenaciously applying several techniques, Lyle succeeded in obtaining clear text. Never, never did he request a sending station to repeat a communication—a grave violation of cryptographic security since cross-referenced messages were a boon to enemy code breakers.

While at the station, Lyle learned Allied bombers had dropped tons of incendiaries on Tokyo two days earlier. Surely, he thought, the devastating firebombing would induce Japanese leaders to admit defeat.

It was dusk when Lyle returned to the basha, a lonely place that evening since his two bunkies were working down on the flight line. Lighting a candle, he pulled a chair up to the native-made table, removed his shoes, and reread a letter from Peggy. Quite a girl, Peggy, plenty cute and danced like a dream. Yes, that last month in St. Louis had been like a fairy tale.

Thinking of another girl back home, Lyle picked up the framed studio photo he kept on the table. Beatrice had a certain touch about her—that dazzling smile and upswept hair, eyes that twinkled with mischief. No wonder she had knocked him for a loop. He thought of their parting at the railroad station a year earlier. She had given him a snapshot, the two of them standing arm in arm by a fountain on Belle Isle. On the back, in lavender ink, she had written, "Till we meet again." God willing, Lyle thought, we will meet again after the war.

Turning his thoughts to home, Lyle filled a fountain pen from a nearly empty bottle of ink and, mindful of censorship, penned a letter to his parents and siblings on the farm in South Dakota:

3 AUGUST 1945 (FRIDAY). Dear Everybody,
For some reason I'm just feeling tops tonite—and I hope it's even better with each of you. Somehow I just hope things always stay on an even keel around home—it will be much easier for us if we come back to

something solid—something dependable. We get used to most anything it seems after about so long but there are times when one feels like how swell it would be to have Mommy tuck him in and bring a glass of water when he's sick. It's a lonely feeling like when they fire a volley and a flag wrapped body breaks the stillness of a tropical sea. Although I guess that's a good way to go. Today I had to censor our detachment's mail which is the worst job in the army. I have enough troubles of my own most of the time without hearing other people's too. . . . Dad, you sure wowed me with that "Fee On Say." You should get on Bob Hope's show. But Dad, you just don't understand the situation here. If you so much as glanced at these Indian gals the MPs would toss you in the guardhouse and quick. You see actually you cannot comprehend this country cause you cannot see and smell it. You cannot possibly realize how absolutely positively it lacks any resemblance to our type of living. Just like trying to tell someone how a carrot tastes. Get me? . . .

Yes, that C-46 picture over the Hump looked natural. While riding the controls through storms I wondered how it would feel to bail out into the dark of the night into the wilds of the world's roughest terrain. Lots have done it—lots don't get a chance to jump. But the life line to China must and will stay open in all weather day and night. August 1 was the anniversary of the air forces. News is good lately isn't it. Got my fingers crossed. . . . It has rained hourly for the past week so it has been some relief from heat. But you have to dry feet and powder well etc to prevent fungus growth. And envelopes must be strung on thread like beads cause they seal if they touch anything. Great country. Really feeling on top of the world though. Be good.

Lyle hoped the war would soon end. Drafted at age nineteen and now nearly twenty-two, he longed to return home and get on with his life. He pictured his mother, Emma, making pancakes on the kitchen range and his father, Charles, returning from morning chores, milk pail in hand. He visualized his three younger sisters, Virginia, Jean, and Wilma, setting the breakfast table. No doubt his little brother, Chuckie, was out on the porch roughhousing with his mutt, Skippy.

Leafing through *King Lear* by candlelight, Lyle pondered the lines: "It is the stars / The stars above us, govern our conditions." Thus far, it seemed, all the stars had been in the right alignment for him, as though some unseen hand had nudged him along a predestined path.

Ready for sleep, Lyle crawled under the canopy of mosquito netting. Clasping his hands behind his head, the young lieutenant reflected on boyhood dreams and world events that had brought him to this strange land—such a long way away from home.

SLADEK FARMSTEAD, PUKWANA, SOUTH DAKOTA, CIRCA 1915
HOMESTEAD HOUSE OF LYLE'S PATERNAL GRNDPARENTS (THE "OLD HOUSE") AT FAR LEFT

CHAPTER 2

No Place Like Home

It takes a heap o' livin' in a house t' make it home.
—EDGAR GUEST, THE PEOPLE'S POET

HOME, FOR LYLE, was a white, two-story house on the windswept plains of South Dakota, a home filled with love and laughter.

In the spring of 1916, Charles Sladek purchased a Sears, Roebuck and Co. mail-order house kit. Shipped by rail from Chicago, the kit came with blueprints, precut lumber, shingles, nails, doorknobs, and paint. Anticipating marriage in the fall, Charles worked feverishly to construct the "new house" just a stone's throw from the "old house" of his aging parents.

The bride-to-be, Emma Swanson, grew up on a pioneer farm just six miles away. Emma was a schoolteacher by virtue of having passed a written examination. One year she taught the "home school" where four of her younger siblings were among the fifteen pupils.

Charles had little formal education; he had attended grade school only in the winter months when he could be spared from the planting and harvesting of crops. After teaching himself to play the violin he became a popular fiddler at community barn dances. On one such occasion, Charles was the successful bidder on Emma's box supper. While sharing the meal during intermission, he offered to escort her home in his buggy, a fancy rig sporting a folding top with isinglass windows and pulled by a matching team of spirited black horses. It was the start of a romance.

The following year while Emma was teaching at a country school near Woonsocket, some eighty miles distant, letters were treasured. Counting the days until the end of the school year, Emma wrote to Charles of her "pipe dream" to travel to New York that summer and of her desire to "wait until the Golden Autumn Days" for their wedding. Charles, while taken aback by Emma's disclosure, accepted the delay.

EMMA SWANSON, 1916   CHARLES SLADEK WITH TEAM AND BUGGY, 1916

CHARLES SLADEK BUILDING A SEARS MAIL-ORDER HOUSE (THE "NEW HOUSE"), 1916

Although Emma was unable to fulfill her dream of going to New York that summer, her wedding to Charles took place as planned. On a mild autumn day the young lovers—the daughter of Swedish immigrants of the Lutheran persuasion and the son of Bohemian immigrants steeped in the Catholic tradition of central Europe—set aside the differences in their religious upbringing and were wed in a private ceremony at Chamberlain. Emma wore a wool jumper over an ecru lace blouse with an upright collar held in shape by a fine wire—later stored with other keepsakes in a trunk her parents had brought over from Germany. Under the heading CHARLES TAKES A BRIDE, a local newspaper reported details of the ceremony and celebration:

CHARLES TAKES A BRIDE

On Tuesday, November 21st, at Columbus College, occurred the marriage of Miss Emma Swanson to Mr. Charles Sladek. The ceremony was performed by Father Lenartz, and the young couple were attended by Miss Minnie Swanson, a sister of the bride, and Mr. Emanuel N. Dudacek. Following the ceremony the bridal party motored to the home of Mrs. J. J. Sladek, where a sumptuous dinner was served to about thirty relatives and intimate friends.

The bride, who is a daughter of Mr. and Mrs. Julius Swanson, is a refined young lady with a cheerful and loving disposition. She taught school several years in this county and has been very successful in her work.

The groom is a son of Mr. and Mrs. V. Sladek, who are known as one of the older pioneer families residing in Cleveland Township. Brule County produces as fine young men as you find anywhere and Charles is one of the best. He is a young man of sterling character who numbers his friends by his acquaintances. He is energetic and progressive and has provided a fine home for his bride on the farm where they will reside in Cleveland Township. They will be home to their friends after December 1st.

The Press-Reporter joins their host of friends in extending congratulations and best wishes.

EMMA SWANSON AND CHARLES SLADEK
MARRIAGE ANNOUNCEMENT, PUKWANA PRESS-REPORTER, 1916

Emma and Charles, mindful of a well-known dance team, Vernon and Irene Castle, named their firstborn son Vernon. There was added joy when a second son, Edward, was born the following year. But, as chronicled by the Pukwana *Press-Reporter,* joy turned to sorrow:

> Edward Charles, the sixteen-month-old child of Mr. and Mrs. Chas. Sladek passed away last Sunday following an illness of three days of bronchial pneumonia. Immediately after the little one showed signs of illness medical aid was called and later he was taken to the sanatorium where all comfort available could be had. Funeral services were held at the M. C. church last Tuesday forenoon, Rev. Framstad conducting the same. Four little girls acted as pall bearers and four young ladies, namely Agnes Weiss, Esther Larson, Esther Lee, and Bernice Geppert, sang. This is indeed a sad blow to the parents and they have the sympathy of all in their sorrow. The little one was laid to rest in the Pukwana cemetery.

The gravestone of baby Edward pictures a lamb and carries the inscription: BUDDED ON EARTH TO BLOOM IN HEAVEN.

Just three months after the death of their son, Emma and Charles welcomed their first daughter. Naturally, they named her Irene. When Lyle was born two years later, Emma clipped a poem from the newspaper and underlined, "So fresh from heaven, he remembers still that God is kind!"

One winter day, at the age of five, Lyle accompanied Vernon and Irene in a horse-drawn sleigh to a one-room country school. Listening to the pupils recite their lessons, playing in the sand table behind the coal-burning stove, and eating lunch out of a Karo syrup pail was high adventure for Lyle that day. He could hardly wait for next year when he would be old enough to go to school every day.

Lyle's first teacher, an elderly man with iron gray hair and steel-rimmed glasses, had moved with his wife and grown son from cosmopolitan Chicago to rural South Dakota at the start of the Great Depression. After settling into an abandoned farmhouse and acquiring two milking goats, A C. Damon purchased a horse-and-buggy for transportation and became the teacher of seventeen pupils in eight grades at the Conley School.

Vernon and Irene, attentive and conscientious pupils, readily learned to read, do their sums, and master the Palmer Method of penmanship. Lyle, less the student and more the dreamer, had little patience for rote learning. But his imagination soared when the teacher read passages from Zane Grey's popular novel, *Riders of the Purple Sage.*

LYLE SLADEK, OUTDOORS ON A MILD WINTER DAY, 1924

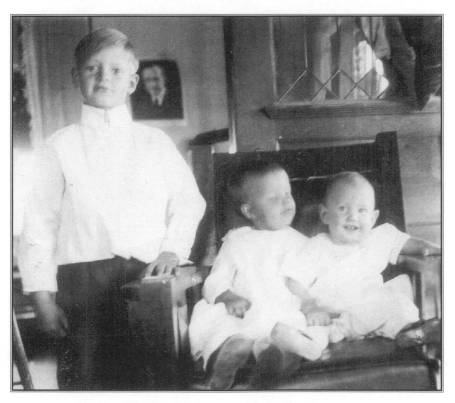

VERNON, IRENE, AND LYLE SLADEK, 1924
PHOTOGRAPH OF PRESIDENT WARREN HARDING HANGS ON LIVING ROOM WALL

On the last day of the 1930-31 school term, a seven-year-old boy, clad in J.C. Penney overalls and scruffy shoes, was called to the front of the room. The kindly teacher placed a little green booklet, *Stephenson's Graded Classical Poems*, in the hands of the proud lad. On the flyleaf was the inscription: "Presented to Lyle Sladek / For 170 days attendance." In shaky handwriting, A. C. Damon had affixed his signature:

The Conley School and the family farm comprised the center of the universe for Lyle. At school he gloried in recess periods filled with snowball fights, "work up" softball, and "playing for keeps" in hotly contested marble games. On the farm he roamed the pastures, fields, and woodlots. Baby chicks, newborn calves and colts in the barnyard, and litters of piglets concealed by tumbleweeds along a fencerow were sources of wonder and delight. And there was all that fascinating farm machinery—contraptions with belts and gears that made clashing, whirring noises. Binders turned swaths of grain into neatly tied bundles. Threshing machines ingested the bundles, poured streams of grain into wagons, and sent clouds of straw and chaff billowing out onto straw stacks. Some days, farm life was enough to make a boy jump for joy with the excitement of it all.

Emma and Charles added another room to the Sears mail-order house to accommodate their growing family. By 1930 their home reverberated with the laughter and activity of five children: Vernon, Irene, Lyle, Virginia, and Jean—later to be joined by Wilma and Chuckie.

Along with cooking, cleaning, and sewing, Emma fostered a vegetable garden and cared for a flock of laying hens. Charles labored in the fields; fed and watered the hogs, horses, and beef cattle; and, in his spare time, repaired the shoes of his seven children. Highly regarded in the community, he made time to serve on both the township board and the local school board.

VERNON, IRENE, LYLE, VIRGINIA, AND JEAN SLADEK, 1930

As clouds of dust and swarms of grasshoppers swirled across the American heartland, Emma and Charles were hit with crop failures and with the Great Depression—a double whammy. Carefree and secure, Lyle was too young to fully understand the struggle his parents faced to provide food and shelter for their children. It seemed the natural order of things that mothers baked bread, canned garden produce, and darned socks by evening lamplight; that fathers worked in the fields from dawn to dusk, tended livestock, and repaired worn-out machinery.

Adventuresome and inquisitive, Lyle loved to explore the spooky "old house" that was once the dwelling place of his paternal grandparents. One day, feeling especially brave, he climbed the narrow, creaky stairs to the second floor. Being careful not to disturb wasp nests stuck to the ceilings and walls, he tiptoed about the bedrooms, imagining his father sleeping there as a boy. Portraits of ancestors in ornate oval frames hung on the walls, and a trunk brought from the Old Country contained hammers, awls, lasts, and other gear of a shoemaker.

Lyle retained just two memories of his pioneer grandfather. Upon returning from town one day, Grandfather Sladek gave him a piece of horehound candy. Expecting the treat to be sweet but finding it bitter, Lyle disposed of it as soon as he was out of grandfather's sight. During last rites for his grandfather in a small, rural Catholic church, the intonations, incense, and liturgical robes were fascinating, but strange.

An old trunk in the basement of the "new house" aroused Lyle's curiosity. Picking the lock, he rummaged through the contents. A photograph of Grandmother Swanson, seated in a rocking chair in the ornate parlor of her

INGRID SWANSON, LYLE'S MATERNAL GRANDMOTHER, CIRCA 1927
EVERY AFTERNOON AT FOUR O'CLOCK INGRID READ HER BIBLE IN THE PARLOR

home, brought back the remembrance of accompanying her to fetch a bowl of butter from a cool, musty cave in the farmyard.

Lyle turned his attention to equipment for developing film and a camera fitted with a lens that moved on a little railroad track. Another item in the trunk, a carefully folded ecru lace blouse, held little interest. Finding a book of poetry by Emily Dickinson difficult to read, he briefly focused on a couple of the letters bound with the book:

24 FEBRUARY 1916 (THURSDAY). Dearest Girlie,
That (Pipe dream) as you called it made me speechless for a spell, but now that I have found my voice, will say—going some. Are you not afraid that some boogieman will kidnap you off broadway? Yes—my sweet I surely could enjoy going there and any where with you. However it will have to be stay here with me as I will sure need all my time and chink [money] in this coming summer. Do you know how much I loved you as I read—that you were making fancy things for *our* house. Beautiful tho they might be, how insignificant would they seem beside you my sweet hope. . . . Emma writing you this letter cheers me up, tho I can not kiss you good night as I'd like to do. I wonder why you are so far away, and girlie I oft times wish, and wish again, that you were here, that we might while away some more happy hours as in the dear old days, to memory sweet. They say, all things come to those who wait, so—be patient. Winter will come and go. Spring time will bring again the flowers and you *dear*. Bye Bye sweetheart. Write me a big-big letter, so big that you will have to send it by parcell post. You might enclose some kisses and a bushel of love as does your loving Charlie.

29 MARCH 1916 (WEDNESDAY). My Dearest Love,
My heart throbbed with joy, when I came home from school tonight and found a letter from you awaiting me. . . . *Charlie Mine*, I feel safe in saying that I love you and think I always shall . . . If we were not meant for each other I'd sincerely hope that we will realize it before it is too late. I have no doubt in the least. (You for me). . . . But, do not hesitate about telling me, if you would feel as tho you would like to change your course. . . . You may break the news whenever you find it convenient (or when you have the courage to). But break it gently. I do not think the Public will be surprised, for I think they are expecting it. And as I have said before I would prefer to wait until the "Golden Autumn Days" are here again. I am still planning on that visit to N. Y. this summer. . . .

Further exploring the contents of the trunk, Lyle uncovered family photographs taken when his mother and father were children.

VENCEL AND JOSEPHINE SLADEK AND FIVE CHILDREN, PUKWANA, SOUTH DAKOTA, 1895
CHARLES, LYLE'S FATHER-TO-BE, FRONT RIGHT

The archbishop claimed a prior lien on the peasant's soul;
the emperor held a chattel mortgage on his body;
and the lord usurped the fruits of his labor.

—T. G. MASARYK

FOUNDER AND FIRST PRESIDENT OF CZECHOSLOVAKIA

Vencel and Josephine Sladek, seeking freedom and opportunity in the New World, bundled up their infant daughter, packed a trunk with shoemaker tools, and crossed the stormy Atlantic on a steamship. Like many immigrants arriving before 1892, they debarked at Castle Garden, New York. From there they continued by train halfway across the continent to the Dakota Territory. Nearing their destination they saw claim shanties and small settlements scattered about on a vast expanse of prairie, a scene worlds apart from the castles, cathedrals, and cultivated fields of their native Bohemia. Undaunted, they detrained at the hamlet of Pukwana in Brule County. Vencel soon applied for citizenship papers, a prerequisite for acquiring land under the Homestead Act of 1862.

While waiting for land to be opened up for settlement, Vencel eked out a living by cobbling shoes and by working on railroad construction in Iowa. Soon after Benjamin Harrison wrested the presidency from Grover Cleveland in the election of 1888, the newly elected president opened a tract of land for settlement. Vencel promptly filed a homestead claim on a quarter section of land in Cleveland Township.

To meet the needs of their growing family, Vencel and Josephine purchased adjoining land and built a two-story addition to their homestead dwelling. Valuing education, they donated an acre of land as the site of a country schoolhouse. They continued to speak their native tongue, the home décor remained reminiscent of the Old Country, and *kolaches* (prune biscuits) were a favorite food. Jovial conversations and games of an intellectual nature, such as checkers, were commonplace in their household.

JULIUS AND INGRID SWANSON AND EIGHT OF THEIR TEN CHILDREN, PUKWANA, SOUTH DAKOTA, 1905 EMMA, LYLE'S MOTHER-TO-BE, FOURTH FROM LEFT

I, Julius Swanson,
do solemnly swear that it is bona fide my intention to
become a CITIZEN OF THE UNITED STATES,
and to RENOUNCE FOREVER, all Allegiance and
Fidelity to each and every Foreign Prince, Potentate, State
or Sovereignty whatsoever, and particularly the King of
Sweden and Norway of whom I have been a subject.

Julius and Ingrid Swanson, natives of Sweden, met and married while working at menial jobs in Germany. Learning that land was still available for settlement in the Dakotas, they determined to improve their lot in life. Along with their infant son they endured a stormy passage across the Atlantic to New York. Once admitted to the country they entrained to Mecosta County, Michigan, where Julius found work and began proceedings to become a citizen of the United States.

Following the birth of a second child, the Swanson family rode the Chicago, Milwaukee & St. Paul Railway to the end of the line at the Missouri River. Julius was fond of saying, "When we got to Chamberlain all we had was two children and fifty cents." He filed a claim on land west of the river and, in compliance with the Homestead Act, built a shanty, dug a well, and "broke the sod" on ten acres. While the family tended the homestead, Julius worked as a fireman and engineer on a steam ferryboat that plied the muddy Missouri, a river with water "too thick to drink, but too thin to walk on."

The water on the claim west of the Missouri River was too alkaline to drink and the gumbo soil too sticky to plow when wet. Learning of an abandoned claim east of the river, the family dismantled their twelve-by-sixteen tar paper shack, loaded their property onto two wagons, and moved to West Point Township. Julius worked as a stonemason in Pukwana on weekdays and trudged nine miles home on Saturdays, carrying a fifty-pound sack of flour or sugar on his back.

After the birth of Emma, their fourth child, Julius and Ingrid added a two-story addition to their claim shanty. Lace curtains graced the windows and a pump organ was the showpiece of the parlor. Additional land was acquired, and Julius purchased one of the first automobiles in Brule County, a one-cylinder machine produced by Brush Motor Car Co. of Detroit.

CHAPTER 3

Rumblings of War

Power corrupts, and absolute power corrupts absolutely.
—LORD ACTON

NINE YEARS OLD IN 1933, Lyle's interests centered on sports figures, aviation heroes, and bank robbers. While somewhat aware of the inauguration of Franklin Delano Roosevelt, he was oblivious to the change of government taking place in Germany, an event destined to shape his life—and to wreak havoc on the world.

Germany was in dire economic straits when Adolf Hitler came into power in 1933. Following a humiliating defeat in World War I—the War to Save Democracy—Germany became a republic. Established in January 1919, the Weimar Republic faced staggering problems. Already burdened by war reparations and humiliated by the "war guilt" clause imposed by the Treaty of Versailles, the new government had to cope with strikes and riots organized by communist factions.

The onset of a worldwide depression dealt another severe blow to Germany. Unemployment and rampant inflation led to social and political unrest. When the election of 1930 signaled that the Weimar Republic was in trouble, Chancellor von Hindenburg seemed unable to cope. The German people looked for a more dynamic leader, someone capable of restoring pride and prosperity to their country.

Hitler, a charismatic leader with persuasive oratorical skills, seized the opportunity and bulldozed his way to power. At his swearing in ceremony on 30 January 1933, he vowed:

> I will employ my strength for the welfare of the German people, protect the Constitution and laws of the German people, conscientiously discharge the duties imposed on me, and conduct my affairs of office impartially and with justice to everyone.

America, like Germany, was mired in a depression. Following the stock market crash of 1929, factories closed down and unemployment soared. Unable to meet mortgage payments, many people lost their homes. When the demand for agricultural products dried up, commodity prices fell below the cost of production, forcing thousands of farmers to abandon their land. Many citizens, in a state of despair, feared that the democratic form of government and the free enterprise system would not endure.

The Democratic Party nominated Franklin Delano Roosevelt (FDR) to oppose President Herbert Hoover in the election of 1932. With the country enveloped in gloom, the campaign waged by FDR came like the sun breaking through a cloudy sky. His smile exuded good cheer as he waved to the crowds from the backseat of an open touring car. His resonant voice was persuasive as he assured the American people he would get the country back on track. Voters caught the vision of a future with sunlit skies when FDR, in a stroke of genius, selected "Happy Days Are Here Again" for his official campaign theme:

> Your cares and troubles are gone;
> There'll be no more from now on.
> Happy days are here again,
> The skies above are clear again;
> Happy days are here again!

FDR was charismatic and urbane. His jaunty air contrasted sharply with the stiff, dour personality of the incumbent president. When Hoover pontificated that "Prosperity cannot be restored by raids upon the public treasury," he sealed his fate. FDR was elected in a landslide. Roosevelt took the oath of office as president of the United States just a month after Hitler took over as chancellor of Germany.

The majority of Americans, isolated on farms and in small towns, were not in close touch with world events. In terms of communication with the outside world the Sladek household was an exception in rural South Dakota. In addition to a daily newspaper and a party telephone line, their home boasted a radio. Neighbors occasionally dropped in to use the telephone for emergency calls or to hear special radio broadcasts. The radio, however, was used sparingly since the 6-volt car battery that powered it had to be taken to town for recharging.

Several neighbors assembled in the Sladek farmhouse on 4 March 1933 to hear the inaugural address of President Roosevelt. They listened intently as FDR spoke these words:

> I am certain that my fellow Americans expect that on my induction into the
> Presidency I will address them with a candor and a decision which the present

situation of our Nation impels. This is preeminently the time to speak the truth, the whole truth, frankly and boldly. Nor need we shrink from honestly facing conditions in our country today. This great Nation will endure as it has endured, will revive and will prosper. So, first of all, let me assert my firm belief that the only thing we have to fear is fear itself. . . .

In such a spirit on my part and on yours we face our common difficulties. They concern, thank God, only material things. Values have shrunken to fantastic levels; taxes have risen; our ability to pay has fallen; government of all kinds is faced by serious curtailment of income; the means of exchange are frozen in the currents of trade; the withered leaves of industrial enterprise lie on every side; farmers find no markets for their produce; the savings of many years in thousands of families are gone.

More important, a host of unemployed citizens face the grim problem of existence, and an equally great number toil with little return. Only a foolish optimist can deny the dark realities of the moment.

Yet our distress comes from no failure of substance. We are stricken by no plague of locusts. Compared with the perils which our forefathers conquered because they believed and were not afraid, we have still much to be thankful for. . . .

Finally, in our progress toward a resumption of work we require two safeguards against a return of the evils of the old order; there must be a strict supervision of all banking and credits and investments; there must be an end to speculation with other people's money, and there must be provision for an adequate but sound currency. . . .

The basic thought that guides these specific means of national recovery is not narrowly nationalistic. It is . . . a recognition of the old and permanently important manifestation of the American spirit of the pioneer. . . .

We face the arduous days that lie before us in the warm courage of the national unity; with the clear consciousness of seeking old and precious moral values; with the clean satisfaction that comes from the stem performance of duty by old and young alike. . . .

We do not distrust the future of essential democracy.

Like many of their neighbors, Emma and Charles found the words of the new president reassuring. His reference to the "spirit of the pioneer" resonated with them. Of pioneer stock, they had encountered hardships similar to those of the resilient settlers portrayed by Laura Ingalls Wilder in *Little House on the Prairie*. Although FDR was of a patrician New York family, they sensed he would relate to the plight of farmers in the dust bowl.

FDR, moving quickly to alleviate the economic crisis, declared a "bank holiday" and called a special session of Congress. During his first one hundred days in office he implemented an emergency banking bill, the National Recovery Act (NRA), and the Agriculture Adjustment Administration (AAA). Over the next four years he instituted a series of New Deal programs, such as the Civilian Conservation Corps (CCC), the Public Works Administration (PWA), and the Tennessee Valley Authority (TVA).

Reform measures encompassed the Works Progress Administration (WPA), the National Labor Relations Board (NLRB), and the Social Security Act. The resulting legislation, denoted by an alphabet soup of acronyms, pleased some citizens and raised the hackles of others.

By the time FDR neared the end of his first term, the economic outlook had brightened in urban areas and increased rainfall had bettered crop conditions in dust bowl states. After winning handily over Governor Alfred M. Landon of Kansas in the 1936 election, FDR acknowledged the need to improve the living conditions of the American people, stating in his second inaugural address:

> I see a great nation, upon a great continent, blessed with a great wealth of natural resources. Its hundred and thirty million people are at peace among themselves; they are making their country a good neighbor among the nations. I see a United States which can demonstrate that, under democratic methods of government, national wealth can be translated into a speaking volume of human comforts hitherto unknown, and the lowest standard of living can be raised far above the level of mere subsistence.
>
> But here is the challenge to our democracy: In this nation I see tens of millions of its citizens—a substantial part of its whole population—who at this very moment are denied the greater part of what the very lowest standards of today call the necessities of life.
>
> I see millions of families trying to live on incomes so meager that the pall of family disaster hangs over them day by day.
>
> I see millions whose daily lives in city and on farm continue under conditions labeled indecent by a so-called polite society half a century ago.
>
> I see millions denied education, recreation, and the opportunity to better their lot and the lot of their children.
>
> I see millions lacking the means to buy the products of farm and factory and by their poverty denying work and productiveness to many other millions.
>
> I see one-third of a nation ill-housed, ill-clad, ill-nourished.

While the Roosevelt administration was coping with the depression, the Hitler regime was circumventing restrictions imposed by the Treaty of Versailles and taking steps to incorporate ethnic Germans residing in neighboring countries. Clandestine rearmament ploys and farsighted domestic projects, such as the construction of the autobahn, improved economic conditions in Germany. Hitler ruthlessly stamped out all opposition, consolidated his power, and by 1936 ruled over the most powerful nation on the continent. Entertaining grandiose plans for the conquest of Europe, he exulted that the Third Reich would last for a thousand years.

The threat of war in Europe reached crisis proportions in 1938 when Hitler demanded that the Sudetenland region of Czechoslovakia be incorporated into the German Third Reich. Seeking a diplomatic solution,

British Prime Minister Neville Chamberlain and other western leaders met with Hitler in Munich. They were mindful of the First World War, a senseless slaughter concluded just two decades earlier. Hoping to avoid another bloodbath, they acceded to Hitler's demands.

The next day, 30 September, Chamberlain stepped off a plane and waved to a jubilant crowd. Then, in front of 10 Downing Street, onlookers cheered as he read:

> We, the German Führer and Chancellor, and the British Prime Minister, have had a further meeting today and are agreed in recognizing that the question of Anglo-German relations is of the first importance for our two countries and for Europe.
> We regard the agreement signed last night and the Anglo-German Naval Agreement as symbolic of the desire of our two peoples never to go to war with one another again.

Chamberlain concluded with comforting words:

> My good friends, for the second time in our history, a British Prime Minister has returned from Germany bringing peace with honour. I believe it is peace for our time.
> Go home and get a nice quiet sleep.

The hope for peace was abruptly shattered in March 1939 when German troops occupied the remainder of Czechoslovakia, ostensibly to avenge war reparations. The ruthless nature of Hitler became apparent in August when he uttered these ominous words to the commanders of the Wehrmacht:

> I shall give a propagandist reason for starting the war, whether it is plausible or not. The victor will not be asked afterwards whether he told the truth or not. When starting and waging war it is not right that matters, but victory.
> Close your hearts to pity. Act brutally. Eighty million people must obtain what is their right. Their existence must be made secure. The strongest man is right.

True to form, Hitler contrived a border incident and powerful German forces attacked Poland by land and by air on 1 September 1939. Two days later, Great Britain and France responded by declaring war on Germany. The posturing and preliminaries ended on that day; once again, Europe was the scene of a full-fledged war.

The United States was in an isolationist "America First" mind-set. In the last stages of World War I—the War to End All Wars—doughboys had experienced the hell of gas attacks and trench warfare in France. Mothers and fathers did not want to send their sons off to fight another bloody war in Europe.

Many Americans watched in disbelief as hostile events unfolded overseas. Although they felt a strong kinship toward the democratic countries of Europe, that conflict was an ocean away. Happenings on other continents were of less immediate concern than national problems at home—bank robberies, kidnappings, and widespread unemployment. Like other farmers on the Great Plains, Emma and Charles continued to cope with crop failures brought about by the unrelenting drought, dust storms, and grasshoppers.

When relatives dropped in for a visit on Sunday, 3 September, Emma invited them to stay for supper. "If there's fresh bread in the house," she always said, "I can come up with a meal." She covered the elongated table with linen, set out her best china, and conjured up a scrumptious spread from the family's own farm produce. After much talk and laughter, the family tuned the radio to a Fireside Chat and listened as President Roosevelt reassured the American people:

> This nation will remain a neutral nation, but I cannot ask that every American remain neutral in thought as well. Even a neutral has a right to take account of facts. Even a neutral cannot be asked to close his mind or close his conscience.

Lyle, a high school junior that year, sought to emulate Vernon and Irene. Vernon had gone to high school, unusual for a Brule County farm boy—many thought schooling was impractical; after all, they knew how to do *real work*. Not only had Vernon graduated from high school, he had earned a bachelor's degree at Dakota Wesleyan University and was studying for an advanced degree at Northwestern University. Irene had graduated at the head of her high school class and was attending college in Sioux Falls.

Interested in mathematics, Lyle persuaded his parents to let him transfer from Pukwana to a larger high school in Chamberlain where the curriculum included Plane Geometry. That placed an extra burden on his parents; they had to find a place where he could stay in town, some fifteen miles distant, since rain and snow often made the dirt roads impassable. Charles found a home where Lyle could sleep in a loft with other boys and helped him secure a job working for his meals at Jennie's Café.

Meanwhile, it was no longer possible for the United States to remain fully insulated from the catastrophic events taking place in Europe. Great Britain, the last obstacle to Hitler's quest for mastery of western Europe, became vulnerable to invasion when German armed forces skirted the Maginot line and overran France in 1940. Quite suddenly, German military leaders—with the aid of binoculars—could see the shores of England from across the Channel. Airfields near the coast of France would soon enable Germany to send waves of bombers over the British Isles.

Winston Churchill, newly appointed prime minister following the resignation of Neville Chamberlain, spoke disheartening words to the

VERNON SLADEK
COLLEGE GRADUATION, 1939

IRENE SLADEK
HIGH SCHOOL GRADUATION, 1938

VIRGINIA, IRENE, JEAN, AND WILMA SLADEK, 1939

British Parliament on 13 May 1940: "I have nothing to offer but blood, toil, tears, and sweat." He vowed his administration would "wage war against a monstrous tyranny never surpassed in the dark and lamentable catalogue of human crime" and declared victory was the aim, "for without victory there is no survival." Endeavoring to rally the British people and seeking assistance from the United States, Churchill spoke eloquently before the House of Commons on 18 June 1940:

> I expect that the Battle of Britain is about to begin. Upon this battle depends the survival of Christian civilization. Upon it depends our own British life, and the long continuity of our institutions and our Empire. The whole fury and might of the enemy must very soon be turned on us. Hitler knows that he will have to break us in this Island or lose the war. If we can stand up to him, all Europe may be free and the life of the world may move forward into broad, sunlit uplands. But if we fail, then the whole world, including the United States, including all that we have known and cared for, will sink into the abyss of a new Dark Age made more sinister, and perhaps more protracted, by the lights of perverted science. Let us therefore brace ourselves to our duties, and so bear ourselves that, if the British Empire and its Commonwealth last for a thousand years, men will still say, "This was their finest hour."

In a Fireside Chat broadcast on 29 December 1940, President Roosevelt made a clarion call to the American people for a national effort to increase production:

> My friends: This is not a fireside chat on war. It is a talk on national security; because the nub of the whole purpose of your President is to keep you now, and your children later, and your grandchildren much later, out of a last-ditch war for the preservation of American independence and all of the things that American independence means to you and to me and to ours.
> Tonight, in the presence of a world crisis. . . .
> We must be the great arsenal of democracy.

Congress devised a stopgap measure, the Lend-Lease Act, allowing the United States to remain neutral while providing material aid to a nearly exhausted Great Britain. When Italy's naval superiority in the Mediterranean threatened the vital Suez Canal, Churchill stepped up pressure for increased American aid.

Lyle was somewhat aware of the rumblings of war in Europe. In the little library above city hall he avidly read two pictorial magazines, *Look* and *Life*. At the local movie house he watched grainy black-and-white newsreels of German armored columns, supported by Stuka dive-bombers, advancing across Poland. He thought the German war machine invincible as it overran France and the Low Countries in a matter of weeks. The swastika, the logo that symbolized the power of the Third Reich, seemed a menacing figure;

its stark straight lines and symmetry, like the *z* in Nazi and the *x* in Axis, exuded rigidity. Whether by accident or by design, Hitler's quirky squared-off mustache and robotic straight-arm salute were of the same motif. It all appeared quite strange and sinister.

By the time the German army had driven to within twenty miles of Moscow, Lyle was apprehensive that the Soviet Union would succumb and that Great Britain would be unable to repel an invasion. Would Hitler's forces seize the Suez Canal? Yet, as an active high school boy, he still had no premonition that the Hitler rampage would soon impinge on his own life. For now, new car models and girls piqued his interest. In addition to working at Jennie's Café and participating in basketball, class plays, and glee club, he found time to read poetry and novels at the city library. One evening he came across Pearl Buck's masterpiece, *The Good Earth*. From that time on, he had a burning desire to see the villages, terraced fields, and cities of China.

Since the farm telephone line connected with a central exchange in Pukwana, calling home from Chamberlain entailed a long-distance charge. Hence, Lyle communicated with his family via penny postcards.

21 JANUARY 1941 (TUESDAY). I couldn't get home last weekend but I *may* get home this one. Jennie was kind of owly yesterday but is in Mitchell today so it will be fine today. We play Ocoma tonight here and expect to win. Chamberlain beat Kimball 31-14 Friday night. Its sure been good January weather lately but it may get worse today. "Boomtown" was a good show. I got a chance to go to it though most of the time I'm too busy. If you come to town Sat. and I don't get home bring my belt, shirts, socks, and handkerchiefs. I can get along without them I guess. If I can't come the 24th, I will come the 31st for sure. It's just about time for noon dismissal.

5 FEBRUARY 1941 (WEDNESDAY). I will be home this Friday night for sure. I had to work last weekend. It sure is warm today. Pukwana beat Chamberlain last night 17-19. It was a good game. Well, I must go to school or I will be late.

2 APRIL 1941 (WEDNESDAY). Don't plan on my coming home for a while. Jennie went to Texas Tues. morning. She will be gone about 2 weeks I guess. We will go to Winner for skip day on May 5th. I reached my peak in typing yesterday. I made 50 words per minute. I don't need anything but shirts and socks. Did Irene get her job yet? We have play practice every night. I've got to go to work now.

Lyle, having no foreboding he would be swept into the maelstrom of a global conflict, continued to pursue his boyhood dreams. On the back of his high school photo, his mother amusingly wrote, "She walked by."

LYLE SLADEK, HIGH SCHOOL GRADUATION, 1941

Clueless as to the rocky road ahead, the Class of 1941 at Chamberlain High School chose for its motto, "Climb, though the rocks be rugged." And, by some quirk of fate, they selected a Hawaiian theme for their senior prom. On prom night they swayed to the soothing strains of "Blue Hawaii" wafting from a phonograph in the city hall auditorium. None envisioned the profound role the Territory of Hawaii was destined to play in their lives in a few short months.

SOUTH DAKOTA STATE COLLEGE (SDSC), CIRCA 1941

CHAPTER 4

Swept into the Maelstrom
of a Global Conflict

Older men declare war.
But it is youth that must fight and die. And it is youth who must
inherit the tribulation, the sorrow, and the triumphs that are the
aftermath of war.

—HERBERT HOOVER

SEVENTEEN and armed with a high school diploma, Lyle looked to the future. Having discovered the "beautiful world of mathematics," he packed a few belongings in a canvas-covered laundry carton and set off for Brookings to enroll in engineering at South Dakota State College (SDSC), a fortuitous choice as it later turned out. He was soon engrossed in academics, debate, and the social scene. Reserve Officers' Training Corps (ROTC), mandatory for all male students, seemed mostly fun and games. He enjoyed the drill, the parades, and the feel of the Springfield rifles. Being short of clothing, he welcomed the fringe benefit of wearing a uniform two days each week. While happily broadening his horizons, he shared his college experiences in a series of postcards and letters to his family.

24 SEPTEMBER 1941 (WEDNESDAY). I have military 3 hours per week and on those days we wear our uniforms. There are 3 hours of English Composition, and 6 hours of Machine shop per week. Freshmen Lecture is 1 hour per week, Algebra 5 hours, Chemistry 6 hours, and drawing 9 hours per week. I did not have enough Algebra and Geometry in high school, so I am carrying more than an average load. We are learning to march, salute, etc in military. In shop, we are running metal lathes. It's lots of fun making bolts. The board is very good. There are

11 students eating here now. The 6 kids that stay here are an extra good bunch.

Did Vernon get deferred? How does Virginia like high school? Could you send me about ($25) twenty-five dollars by return mail. It cost 56 dollars to register, but you get about $15 of that back at the end of a year. This course is the most expensive for books and supplies. Drawing tools and supplies cost $18, but they are used all four years. Shop takes some supplies, and then books for the rest of the subjects. We are always busy. Only been downtown once. More later.

3 OCTOBER 1941 (FRIDAY). I only have 6 hours of classes on Friday so I have some spare time. One of the fellows called me up just now. We're going downtown pretty quick to see if our drawing sets are here yet. We sent to Wards for them. I suppose I could use about five dollars in your next letter for board. Is there any news from Vernon yet? Military is lots of fun and good training.

12 OCTOBER 1941 (SUNDAY). Dulitz and I made 90¢ each here yesterday cleaning and putting on storm windows. I have two tests Mon. Chemistry and Algebra—Algebra is easy. We are learning how to handle military rifle. It is lots of fun.

24 OCTOBER 1941 (FRIDAY). Hobo Day was a success. I was on military duty that forenoon. I was a traffic cop at one of the corners. They said there was 20,000 or more saw the parade.

P.S. I was glad to get the candy and papers.

27 OCTOBER 1941 (MONDAY). Happy Birthday, Irene! I'm financially unable to give you a present and probably not even a letter if you hadn't sent the stamps. It's almost time for supper. I studied hard all day Sat. and some Sunday.

Wednesday.

We sure have lots of fun at the union. Ping pong, checkers, cards, pool, billiards etc. You'd better come up the first time you get a chance. There is always plenty to do. A glass was turned upside down on a table. A drunk came along and picked it up. "This is a strange glass," he said. "There's no hole in the top. He turned it over and exclaimed, "Heavens, the bottoms out." Corney, eh what.

29 OCTOBER 1941 (WEDNESDAY). I've been too busy to write. We had a mid-term test in English this morning. We will have a hard algebra

test in the morning but that doesn't bother me. I got a letter from Vernon and a couple from Irene. Vernon sent me a dollar too. The candy was sure good. It went awful fast. We have Lutheran Student Association (L.S.A.) meetings every other Sunday evening. I just got home from an Engineering film on "Steel." It was very interesting. We don't hardly have time to sleep anymore. Today, I started classes at 8:00 (as usual) and went straight through until 5:15. Then we had another debate meeting. The debate question will be about Strike Legislation. Wes Dulitz and I are one team—he stays here. We have to write a theme for English Friday. The competition here is very keen. There are lots of smart kids. Our military rifles are sure heavy. I wish I had the Savage rifle to carry around instead. I won't have any laundry to send home. I'll bring it at Thanksgiving. We have to wear our uniforms most of the time. It costs quite a lot down here but you get a lot for the money. Good teachers, equipment etc. We have military assembly on Thurs. They march us around in platoons and go through a lot of red tape. (What did the little man who wasn't there have for breakfast) Ghost Toasties, doughnut holes, and evaporated milk. Don't work too hard.

6 NOVEMBER 1941 (THURSDAY). Salutations Irene. The Halloween party at the union was really swell. There were bingo games, ping pong, fortune telling etc. We also had all the cider and pretzels we wanted. Tues. forenoon we have to march around town for Armistice Day. I hope it snows some more because we might get out of it then. Our officers are starting to crack down on us in military. We do some caluthetics once in a while lately.

Friday.

This last week was Farm and Home week here. Lots of people from all over the State. Thanks a lot for the stamps.

8 NOVEMBER 1941 (SATURDAY). It was sure cold at the football game. All the players wore gloves. Donald won a trip to Chicago. He will leave for a week right after Thanksgiving. Some 4H deal I guess. The college debate tourney is just before Thanksgiving vacation.

Sunday.

We sure had a swell dinner today. All the roast pk., potatoes, brown gravy, Cranberries sauce, carrot Gelitine for vegetable, bread and butter, honey, coffee, some good sort of raisin pie, that we could eat. Donald and I played some ping pong after dinner and then I studied debate at the library. Twenty-three percent of the freshmen that register here will graduate according to statistics. The armory is really big. It has a round roof without any supports. There is room for 3 regulation basketball courts on the one floor. On cold days, they march us around in there.

Monday.

I got your letter and 5.00 this forenoon. I'll have to have some more money soon. It costs me 5.25 per week you know. Tomorrow we march. I have shop this afternoon. I will enclose a few clippings from the Collegian.

19 NOVEMBER 1941 (WEDNESDAY). I received your long awaited letter. Jean must have done real well. I got the 5 spot. We are really swamped with work. I will debate at least 3 times in the weekend tourney. Chuckie can print better than I can. How long was Irene and Vernon home. It's terrible how much studying we have to do. I got 88% in a military test. I enjoyed the kids letters.

6 DECEMBER 1941 (SATURDAY). Dear Irene,

It's been another busy week. Monday, we will be able to start practicing rifle marksmanship. Week after this one is test week. Wow! We will be able to go home about Thursday I think. Tomorrow, the 180 voice chorus will sing the Messiah. The military ball was held last night. There were about 350 couples at 2.75 per couple. Red Nickels and his Five Pennies played. They really must have went to town. One girl broke a toe and passed out. I guess someone must have stepped on it. I got so much sleep last week that I woke up in the morning without the alarm. Donald was sleeping the afternoon that he got home from Chicago so we took 3 alarm clocks and wound them up tight. We turned them all on at once and practically blasted him out of bed. About my Christmas list. I really don't want anything but if you *insist*, I'm sure hard on socks and I could use a bottle of hair oil pretty soon. Well I haven't got time to write much tonight.

The next day, Sunday, 7 December, Lyle and his fellow roomers gathered around the table for the midday meal in their boardinghouse at 819 Eighth Street. When the main dish arrived from the kitchen—a casserole of creamed potatoes flavored with sliced wieners—the eleven hungry men dug in with gusto. A popular rendition of "Blueberry Hill" emanated from a radio console in the corner of the room:

> I found my thrill on Blueberry Hill
> On Blueberry Hill when I found you
> The moon stood still on Blueberry Hill
> And lingered until my dreams came true—

Quite suddenly, the excited voice of an announcer interrupted the music—a news bulletin from New York—something about Hawaii and airplanes and bombs and Pearl Harbor. The men sat in stunned silence as they tried to comprehend the import of the message. None were aware of the existence of a naval base at Pearl Harbor. They had never heard of the place.

Unaware of the severity of damage to the U.S. Fleet and aircraft at Hawaii, Lyle, continuing his letter to Irene, alluded to the Japanese strike with a naive one-liner:

> Sunday.
> Well Japan has attacked *Honolulu* but I think Japan will be licked within a week. Later.
> Donald laid down to study military. He always gets real comfortable when he studies and as usual he went to sleep 5 minutes after he started studying. I'll have to wake him up for supper. I beat him 5 games out of 6 in ping pong this afternoon and he's really good. I guess I don't know much to write about.

Lyle did not perceive his country was in grave danger. To him, the United States was a land of giants—Franklin, Fulton, McCormick, Edison, Ford, the Wright Brothers, Firestone, Bell, Lindbergh—and the world leader in technology—Hoover Dam, the Golden Gate Bridge, the Empire State Building. *His* country made the automobiles, the tractors, and the radios for the world. Surely no other country could compete with the United States of America.

On the following day, the SDSC student body gathered at the college armory to hear a radio broadcast. A hushed audience listened as President Roosevelt forthrightly addressed Congress:

> Yesterday, December 7, 1941—a date which will live in infamy—the United States of America was suddenly and deliberately attacked by naval and air forces of the Empire of Japan. . . .
> Yesterday, the Japanese government also launched an attack against Malaya.
> Last night, Japanese forces attacked Hong Kong.
> Last night, Japanese forces attacked Guam.
> Last night, Japanese forces attacked the Philippine Islands.
> Last night, the Japanese attacked Wake Island.
> This morning, the Japanese attacked Midway Island.
> Japan has, therefore, undertaken a surprise offensive extending throughout the Pacific area. . . .
> Always will we remember the character of the onslaught against us. . . .
> I believe I interpret the will of the Congress and of the people when I assert

that we will not only defend ourselves to the uttermost, but will make very certain that this form of treachery shall never endanger us again.

Hostilities exist. There is no blinking at the fact that our people, our territory, and our interests are in grave danger.

With confidence in our armed forces—with the unbounding determination of our people—we will gain the inevitable triumph—so help us God.

I ask that the Congress declare that since the unprovoked and dastardly attack by Japan on Sunday, December 7, a state of war has existed between the United States and the Japanese empire.

Following the attack at Pearl Harbor a wave of disbelief and anger swept across the land. American blood had been shed. American territory had been invaded. The mood of the country changed overnight. Bickering and isolationism gave way to a groundswell of patriotism and national resolve. Playing on the "sneak" aspect of the attack, the words REMEMBER PEARL HARBOR soon appeared on posters and in song, further stirring patriotic fervor. Young men flocked to recruiting stations to sign up for the service.

Although American political leaders were aware that negotiations with Japan were at an impasse, it came as a surprise that Japan was able to strike with force so far from its home islands. Jubilant when informed of the Japanese attack on the United States, Hitler crowed: "Now it is impossible for us to lose the war. We now have an ally who has never been vanquished in three thousand years."

The clamor of the American people for swift retaliation against Japan was worrisome for Churchill, but welcomed by Hitler. He was confident Germany could defeat Great Britain if the United States shifted its military focus from Europe to the Pacific.

Four days later, President Roosevelt asked Congress to declare war on Germany and Italy:

On the morning of December 11 the Government of Germany, pursuing its course of world conquest, declared war against the United States.

The long known and the long expected has thus taken place. The forces endeavoring to enslave the entire world now are moving toward this hemisphere.

Never before has there been a greater challenge to life, liberty, and civilization.

Delay invites greater danger. Rapid and united effort by all the peoples of the world who are determined to remain free will insure a world victory of the forces of justice and of righteousness over the forces of savagery and of barbarism.

Italy also has declared war against the United States.

I therefore request the Congress to recognize a state of war between the United States and Germany and between the United States and Italy.

The United States was plunged into a war for which it was ill prepared: the size of the professional army was akin to that of Portugal; the Air Corps had a dearth of trained men and many of its planes were obsolete; the naval fleet, severely crippled by the attack at Pearl Harbor, was no longer capable of protecting American interests in the Pacific. Nevertheless, following the declaration of war, the American people united in an all-out effort to defeat the primary Axis powers—Japan, Germany, and Italy.

As the country geared up for the war, factories shifted from the production of consumer goods to war materials. Jobs became plentiful and money circulated freely. The government instituted price controls and rationing to prevent inflation and hoarding. Citizens, young and old, immersed themselves in the war effort: children pulled play wagons around their neighborhoods to gather metal, rubber, and other useful scrap—including their own toys; families cultivated *victory gardens* in their backyards or in parks; restaurants and households collected grease for use in making explosives; civilians went out of their way to support "our boys in uniform."

For Lyle, too young to be drafted, the declaration of war was not of immediate concern. The men in advanced ROTC, however, knew active duty was in the offing.

Later in December, when Congress lowered the draft age to twenty, SDSC upperclassmen mulled over their options. Whereas enlistment offered some latitude as to branch of service, draftees generally had no choice. Men assigned the highest draft rating of 1-A by the Selective Service System (SSS) were subject to immediate call. Since food production was essential to the war effort, students who worked on the family farm during the summer months received a lower rating, 2-C Agriculture.

By the time Lyle returned to college after Christmas break, *defense training* and *defense stamps* had become much-used terms. College activities, however, were still his main concern. In a letter home he enclosed clippings from the *South Dakota Collegian* regarding coming events and the rifle team.

14 JANUARY 1942 (WEDNESDAY). I have a full schedule again. Have you heard from Vernon yet? Just got back from a 3 hour workout in Chemistry Lab. There will be a freshman party pretty soon. I got an A in Algebra, a 5 hour course. My schedule is much the same as last time. The enrollment didn't decrease much. I'll write a letter later, maybe.

18 JANUARY 1942 (SUNDAY). It's another nice day in Brookings. I made 35¢ washing windows Fri. p.m. and will get more jobs at that place. We have a test in military tomorrow morning. I'm going up to the

library for debate material and probably stop at the union for a game of ping pong. I have to be corporal of my squad because I'm so tall. Salute the Capt. and take roll.

2 2 JANUARY 1 9 4 2 (THURSDAY). I was sure glad to get your letter. I am enjoying myself immensely and feel fit as a fiddle. We listened to Fibber McGee and Molly the other night. We had caluthetics in military assembly this afternoon. All kinds of exercises including holding that heavy gun at arms length. Tomorrow night is the Freshman pow wow. All it costs is to buy a 10¢ defense stamp. I am making a tap wrench in advanced machine shop.

Friday.

The debate teams go to Sioux Falls a week from Sat. for a tournament with other colleges. I'll get to see Irene. We will have a punctuation test in English Mon. The English Dept. always tries to flunk as many students as possible. Mon. is a Chemistry test. Mr. Burr says it will be a two-hour test with only one hour to write it in. He always says that. Algebra and Geometry are also interesting. We had a test in military last week. They show us films once in a while about maps, tanks, etc. The kids at college are not nearly so war spirited as elsewhere. They all want to dodge the draft.

Saturday.

There is a piece in the Collegian about defense radio training. There will be 9 hours per week of night classes. Must have high school education, and math. I think I will look into it. It will be sponsored by the Gov. because of the need for radio technicians. The party was a big success. I played pool, won a game of bingo for a soft drink, played ping pong, danced, and saw the movie. It was a silent movie of the old days and really funny. Has Chuckie shot up all his BBs yet? I'll bet he makes it hot for the pigeons. Write me more often. Everything is going swell.

1 FEBRUARY 1 9 4 2 (SUNDAY). We left for Sioux Falls at 8:00 Sat and got there at 9:30. There were 8 or 10 schools there. I ate supper at 5:30 at Shrivers. I walked up to the house and Irene got home a little later. We visited until midnight, when it was time to go home to Brookings. I slept late this morning.

I haven't found out about that radio course yet but I may take it. I got 100 in military and algebra tests. I got 80% in an English test. Only 1 other person passed it beside me. Some had as low as 36. I was also pleased to get a C in Chemistry test. School is sure interesting every day. The schedule has been pushed ahead so that we will get out about a week before June. They showed us a film of the coast guard academy at New London, Conn. It looked pretty good.

Monday.

Noon. It's colder today and snowed a little. We had to march in military. I have 3 hours machine shop this afternoon. Donald is going to practice shooting. He made the freshman rifle team. I'm going to see about that radio course this afternoon.

5 FEBRUARY 1942 (THURSDAY). We had military inspection today. I had a pair of gloves in one pocket of my coat. The inspecting officer said, "What's that in your pocket, your overcoat!" I said, "No, Sir." One fellow fainted the other day during inspection. He came up to inspection arms and then he said to the officer, "Pardon me Sir, but I'm going to faint." Then he started falling like a log. A couple of us caught him and carried him out. It took him a long time to come to. We have our first class while it is still pitch dark out.

Friday.

I had my hair cut this afternoon. It was getting pretty long. Another student cut it. He charged me 15¢ and he really did a good job. Clippers and all. I'm not going to take that radio course. It lasts longer than school and they would make me take less credit hours.

Needing money for incidentals, Lyle secured a menial job at the machine shop in the engineering building. Early mornings before classes he swept steel cuttings off the floor and climbed overhead to oil the bearings of pulleys that transferred power through leather belts to the lathes, planes, and metal-chopping machines below. During evening hours civilians, or what Lyle called *defense men,* trained at the shop to become welders and lathe operators for the war effort.

Saturday.

I put the pressure on Dean of Engineering and got a temporary job—it may only last 2 or 3 weeks. I went to work at 10 and will work until 5. I will work each morning from 6:30 to 7:30. It is mostly janitor work.

10 FEBRUARY 1942 (TUESDAY). Intended to write a letter instead of this postcard but—I had my tonsils jerked Fri. Spent 3 days in the hospital. They let me out Mon. morning so I didn't miss any school. Throat is still a little sore. They didn't use ether. I have an hour Geometry test now. Will debate this p.m. Got 80% in Algebra test yesterday. Made

a foolish mistake. Was glad to get your letter and $5.00 yesterday. I can use another 6.00. There were sure a lot who went from Brule Co. to the army, but not many I knew. Write more often in the future. I'm feeling fine. Now for the test.

14 FEBRUARY 1942 (SATURDAY). I worked this afternoon until 5:00. Last night we went over to one of the Methodist's ladies homes for an open house. There were about 25 kids there. We played games, looked through periscopes etc and had a lunch. We had sandwiches, cocoa, and cake. We have to write a 2000 word term paper for English before Mar 6. It sure is a gooey feeling when they freeze your tonsils. They wanted to give me a hypo afterwards but I didn't want one. I haven't missed a class yet this year. We have been testing unknown solutions in Chemistry.

Sunday.

We just got back from church. There was a large crowd. One of the fellows have a pair of boxing gloves so I box quite often. We have some real battles. I think I'll probably put on some weight now that my tonsils are out. I think I feel better already. I got 95 in a geometry test. I guess it's unheard of for an Engineer to make the honor roll here. I'll show them. It seems like just schoolwork keeps you busy here.

We had a swell dinner today. Write soon.

On 23 February, the 210th anniversary of George Washington's birthday, Emma and Charles tuned in as President Roosevelt addressed "My fellow Americans" in a worldwide radio broadcast:

Washington's Birthday is a most appropriate occasion for us to talk with each other about things as they are today and things as we know they shall be in the future. For eight years, General Washington and his Continental Army were faced continually with formidable odds and recurring defeats. Supplies and equipment were lacking. In a sense, every winter was a Valley Forge. Throughout the thirteen states there existed fifth columnists—and selfish men, jealous men, fearful men, who proclaimed that Washington's cause was hopeless, and that he should ask for a negotiated peace.

Washington's conduct in those hard times has provided the model for all Americans ever since—a model of moral stamina. He held to his course, as it had been charted in the Declaration of Independence. He and the brave men who served with him knew that no man's life or fortune was secure without freedom and free institutions.

The present great struggle has taught us increasingly that freedom of person and security of property anywhere in the world depend upon the security of the rights and obligations of liberty and justice everywhere in the world.

This war is a new kind of war. It is different from all other wars of the past, not only in its methods and weapons but also in its geography. It is warfare in terms of every continent, every island, every sea, every air-lane in the world.

That is the reason why I have asked you to take out and spread before you a map of the whole earth, and to follow with me in the references which I shall make to the world-encircling battle lines of this war. . . . The broad oceans which have been heralded in the past as our protection from attack have become endless battlefields on which we are constantly being challenged by our enemies.

We must all understand and face the hard fact that our job now is to fight at distances which extend all the way around the globe.

. . . The object of the Nazis and the Japanese is to of course separate the United States, Britain, China and Russia, and to isolate them one from another, so that each will be surrounded and cut off from sources of supplies and reinforcements. It is the old familiar Axis policy of "divide and conquer."

There are those who still think, however, in terms of the days of sailing-ships. They advise us to pull our warships and our planes and our merchant ships into our own home waters and concentrate solely on last ditch defense. But let me illustrate what would happen if we followed such foolish advice. . . .

Those Americans who believed that we could live under the illusion of isolationism wanted the American eagle to imitate the tactics of the ostrich. Now, many of those same people, afraid that we may be sticking our necks out, want our national bird to be turned into a turtle. But we prefer to retain the eagle as it is—flying high and striking hard.

I know I speak for the mass of the American people when I say that we reject the turtle policy and will continue increasingly the policy of carrying the war to the enemy in distant lands and distant waters—as far away as possible from our own home grounds. . . .

Here are three high purposes for every American:

1. We shall not stop work for a single day. If any dispute arises we shall keep on working while the dispute is solved by mediation, or conciliation or arbitration—until the war is won.
2. We shall not demand special gains or special privileges or special advantages for any one group or occupation.
3. We shall give up conveniences and modify the routine of our lives if our country asks us to do so. We will do it cheerfully, remembering that the common enemy seeks to destroy every home and every freedom in every part of our land.

This generation of Americans has come to realize, with a present and personal realization, that there is something larger and more important than the life of any individual or of any individual group—something for which a man will sacrifice, and gladly sacrifice, not only his pleasures, not only his goods, not only his associations with those he loves, but his life itself. In time of crisis when the future is in the balance, we come to understand, with full recognition and devotion, what this nation is and what we owe to it. . . .

The task that we Americans now face will test us to the uttermost. Never before have we been called upon for such a prodigious effort. Never before have we had so little time in which to do so much.

"These are the times that try men's souls."

Tom Paine wrote those words on a drumhead, by the light of a campfire. . . . "The summer soldier and the sunshine patriot will, in crisis, shrink from the service of their country; but he that stands it now, deserves the love and thanks of man and woman. Tyranny, like hell, is not easily conquered, yet we have this consolation with us, that the harder the sacrifice, the more glorious the triumph."

A hectic schedule precluded Lyle from hearing President Roosevelt's address.

23 FEBRUARY 1942 (MONDAY). Irene was here for the weekend. We had a good time. I even taught her to play ping pong somewhat. Worked 20 hours last week and also this morning 6:30 to 7:30. The work may start affecting my grades. Keeps me on the jump. Got my algebra done during noon. Have shop this p.m. Doc. said my throat was O.K. Well, I must be going.

27 FEBRUARY 1942 (FRIDAY). I worked each morning again and also this p.m. I sure hate to get up at 6:00. I don't usually have time to eat breakfast. I have a terrific appetite lately. Did you hear the radio stations were going to go off the air? They can't get tires for their kilo-cycles! I'm down to my last dime and I mean just that. I guess I'll study for a while now.

Saturday.

Worked again today and then took a bath. I paid my hospital bill the other day. 2.25 for 3 days. The college play was good last Monday nite. It really gave me the creeps. It was a murder mystery in an old church. I got a B+ on my theme "Rattlesnake Pete." It was a characterization. He said I would have gotten an A but too many misspellings. Chemistry Lab is really tough but lots of fun. We have to test to see what we have in a certain liquid. Takes about 4 hours. I got 100%, 100, and 55 so far. Not a bad average.

Do you go by war time? This quarter will be over in about 3 weeks. My English teacher told me I wrote some very pleasing themes. My boss seems to like my work O.K. He said I must had done some janitor work before and that a good janitor was at a premium now days. No one is around when I work in the morning. One Saturday I ran a big metal cutting machine—It chopped off two 5/8 inch bars at a time by brute force. It is the forge and welding shop. School kids work part of the time and defense men the rest. I'll finish that jack screw this week. It's supposed to hold 40 ton. Mine probably won't hold ten lbs. Write again soon.

9 MARCH 1942 (MONDAY). Just laying around studying for Chem test tomorrow. Went to the band concert thurs. nite. Got 90 in an algebra

test. Not so hot. Yesterday I cut steel 5" by 1/4" in a big machine. Just one stroke. Also ground edges on some steel pieces along with other jobs. Looks like the job will last longer than I expected. School will be out about the middle of May as a result of the stepped up schedule. I've been having lots of fun. I would like to come home and sleep for a week. I'll write later.

While Lyle was absorbed in college life, the United States and its allies were facing pressing challenges around the globe. In the vast Pacific, Japanese forces were overrunning the Philippines, Singapore, and much of Burma. Following the loss of the Burma Road, the Flying Tigers of the American Volunteer Group (AVG) were cut off from supplies needed to prevent Japanese forces from knocking China out of the war. In the stormy North Atlantic, German submarines were sinking cargo ships faster than they could be replaced, threatening the very survival of England and Russia. In North Africa, Axis forces were driving toward Egypt and the vital Suez Canal.

Defeating the Axis powers was the objective of Great Britain, the United States, and the Soviet Union, but differences in the social, economic, and philosophical underpinnings of the Allied countries hampered the war effort. Hammering out a cohesive strategy for the conduct of the war required lengthy negotiations and numerous compromises. Furthermore, the domineering personalities of the Allied leaders—a tradition-bound Tory, a freewheeling Democratic president, and a Marxist dictator—created tension. It did not help that two prima donnas, Chiang Kai-shek of China and Charles Andre Joseph Marie de Gaulle of France, were making demands from the sidelines.

President Roosevelt concurred with George Marshall, army chief of staff, that the demise of Japan would bear little consequence with regard to the fate of Germany whereas the defeat of Germany would doom Japan. Despite the clamor of the citizenry to avenge the attack at Pearl Harbor, FDR kept a steady hand on the tiller, declaring Germany, not Japan, the chief enemy.

With the onset of war, geography and availability of resources influenced American policy. Protecting Hawaii and the West Coast from invasion was of paramount importance. Coastal residents, nearing hysteria, feared further attacks on the homeland. In response, government officials in states bordering on the Pacific demanded that people of Japanese ancestry, citizens or not, be isolated in the interior of the country. Exigencies of wartime required weighing the rights of individual citizens against the perceived welfare of the country as a whole. On 19 February 1942, President Roosevelt sanctioned the internment of Japanese-Americans, beginning Executive Order No. 9066 with these words:

Whereas the successful prosecution of the war requires every possible protection against espionage and against sabotage to national-defense material, national-defense premises, and national-defense utilities. . . .

When the realities of the conflict became more evident through reports of harsh treatment of American and Filipino troops captured on the Bataan Peninsula, Lyle realized Japan was a foe to be reckoned with. Still, the war seemed somewhat abstract to a busy college student.

15 MARCH 1942 (SUNDAY). Well, I guess I'll tell of what I've been doing since I wrote last. We had the annual L.S.A. banquet Thursday night. The meal was really swell. Baked ham and potatoes, green beans, rolls, ice cream, cake, and coffee were the main dishes. Met a couple nice girls who are freshmen also. I have been working 15 hours per week. One hour every morning at 6 and Fri and Sat. I have earned about $20 so far but I haven't collected any yet. If you could send me a check for $50 I'll turn the $20 over to the Dr. for my tonsils operation and use the 50 for registration for spring term and board. This quarter ends the 25th and we register again on the same day. Last night I went to a Wesley Club party (Methodist kids) at the church. There were about 50 there. We played all kinds of games. I told the best fish story of the evening.

They pulled the arm badge off my uniform the other day during military inspection just to be ornery. I had to sew it back on again. Some of the students signed up for the marines last week.

I'm going up to the union to see Willie Hopp in a billiard exhibition and then hop to bed.

23 MARCH 1942 (MONDAY). The campanile is chiming some old song which I can't quite remember the name of. It sounds right nice. It often chimes "Sweet Land of Liberty" etc. One time it played a song about spring during a bad blizzard. We had caluthetics in military this afternoon. State has a rating of "Excellence" in military. Hope we retain that rating. Signed up for a sugar ration card the other day. Send letters and clippings.

Lyle completed winter quarter exams on Wednesday and, with the college operating on a wartime schedule, registered for the spring quarter the same day.

29 MARCH 1942 (SUNDAY). I suppose you were in the heart of the blizzard. We had to hand in ten minute speeches for debate. The Prof. said mine was the best. Not bad for being in competition with fellows

who have gone to national tournaments. Yesterday my boss Mr. Bloem bought me a candy bar and told me to take time out for lunch. I cut steel, face grindstones, do odd jobs and clean up. I work whenever I wish and keep track of my own time. I'm going to learn to forge and weld a little this quarter. The enrollment dropped to 1100 this quarter. Thanks for the $60. I sure got rid of it in a hurry. Cost me 44.00 to register but some of that comes back. I haven't collected yet from the college. I will only have to get up at 6:00 on 3 mornings now.

    Monday.

    I played ping pong and whist at the union last night. First nite I didn't study for ages. We will have military outside this quarter. That will be better. I sure get sore when a little squirt of an officer comes around and tells me my belt isn't shined good enough. Theme song of a draftee: In the Navy—my height
                   In the Air Corps—bad sight
                   In the Marines—too slight
                   In the Draft—just right

Noting his diligence in the machine shop, the welding instructor, Professor Bloem, asked Lyle to work on his little farm eight blocks from campus.

6 APRIL 1942 (SUNDAY). I worked for my boss Friday and Saturday. He bought a little farm out on the edge of town and he is getting ready to move in. I worked 17 hours altogether so I made about $7 this week. I did various odd jobs from cleaning to chopping wood. They invited me in for dinner each day so my board didn't cost me much either. Started welding last week. We are using acetylene torches now. The hottest flame known. We melted two pieces together in shape of a V for victory. Later we will use rods and also do electric arc welding and forging. Very interesting.

    We are drawing cylinders, cones and furnace joints as they would look before folded into shape. Pretty rugged. Bates and I are going to church at 10:30 and then we'll eat dinner at the coffee shop. Practically all the students went home. I didn't come home because I didn't have a ride, wanted to work, and didn't want to be all tired out for Monday as I would have been if I had hitchhiked home. We have a military test Monday. Also a military parade.

Participating in a debate tournament in Mitchell, Lyle wrote home on New Navin Hotel stationery that advertised: HOME OF THE FAMED CORN PALACE.

17 APRIL 1942 (FRIDAY). We left Brookings at 8:15 this morning. We got here at 11 and ate dinner at the Widmar at 12:00. We have a north room and I have the big window open. I am going to the show now, "North of Klondike," all seats 15¢. More later.

I was sure glad to get the food in my laundry bag and also the weeklies. As for my clothes I never expected you to get that striped white shirt clean. It was my poorest shirt so I wore it to work and in machine shop for work clothes. As for my other clothes, I always get them dirty on Saturday and then change. You see I usually crawl up about 20 ft. into the rafters and greese pulleys. It is a mixture of greese and dirt. Saw a good show at the union Tues. night for 20¢. It was put on by the film society. "The Thief of Bagdad." By the way, the judge said our debate was better then any she heard at the National at St. Paul. She said my voice and analogy was excellent, but that I should drive harder. I have learned a lot about speaking. Vernon says I should go into defense work, but I wouldn't want to do that until at least next fall. Bates and Hodgson are forced to go to summer school to escape draft. Saw in the Argus Leader that Davis was killed.

20 APRIL 1942 (MONDAY). I am on top of the world today. Just received word that I have been elected to Pi Kappa Delta. Had to have recommendations from Prof. of Speech and vote of members as well as record of debates etc. I have been working toward this. It has been an uphill battle because in competition with experienced debaters. Got a B in English test. One of best grades.

27 APRIL 1942 (MONDAY). The Ags are all wearing overalls today to advertise Ag Barn Dance next Sat. They get thrown in fish pool if they don't. D- in English test. I was one of 3 who passed out of 25. She does it just to be ornery. Got the 5 spot. Haven't collected any more from the college yet. Am taking forge now and working on a grab hook for a log chain.

28 APRIL 1942 (TUESDAY). Just got back from the Pi Kappa Delta recognition banquet held at the union. We had a good supper and speeches. We were each presented with a wooden key by Pres. Lyman Jackson of the college. We had formal initiation Friday night. We had to give an oration blindfolded with the members criticizing etc. My speech was, "A 'Date' Bureau Should Be Established as an Integral Part of the Union's Social Service." Our English term paper is due next week. If you see a light over this way about two o'clock some night, it isn't the campanile beacon. Worked again for Mr. Bloem Sat. Also work ten

SDSC DEBATE TEAM, JACK RABBIT YEARBOOK, LYLE SLADEK AT FAR LEFT, 1941
"VICARS OF VOCABULARY AND WIZARD'S OF WORDS"

hours at shop. Boss would like to talk me into going to summer school, but no ducks. I'm ready to come home. Boss owes me $10 and I have a months wages coming from college. Guess I'll go to bed now and more later.

Next Tuesday.

Am working on my term paper. Don is in the operetta which I am going to tonight. Don and I both slept through the 5:00 alarm this morning, but John Glause came over and woke us up at quarter to six so it didn't hurt any. Expect to work for Bloem's again Sat. You might send me a five spot if convenient. I can't seem to get $20 together at once to pay the Doc.

Just back from the operetta. It was really swell. Very colorful and interesting. Enough for tonight.

13 MAY 1942 (WEDNESDAY). Had a Trig test yesterday. Col. Briggs is here inspecting the R.O.T.C. unit. Am having lots of fun. Finished my shop hammer. Was mad at you for not writing and you same at me. My last test on May 29. I may ship 100 lb by freight. I've got lots of junk. Time for dinner and am I hungry.

16 MAY 1942 (SATURDAY). Worked today for Mr. Bloem. Had a good breakfast, dinner, and lunch. I received a swell offer this week

which needs consideration. Mr. Bloem wants me to stay at their place next year and work for my room and board. He said about three hours per day doing chores etc. Would be a swell room and healthy meals. Also, like most city people, he is misinformed on the amount of time it should take to do a thing. I could probably get the work done in half the time when he wasn't around. Like he said he wanted to have someone around who he could depend on when he had to go to conventions etc. He is head man at the welding department. He sure wanted me to go to summer school so I could work at the shop and for him. Thumbs down on that. I told him I was needed at home which is probably true. I said I wouldn't want to say for sure because I might not be back next fall.

Hope Irene decides to locate in Sioux Falls again. This will be my last letter of the year because I'm out of envelopes.

Wednesday.

Got your letters and 7.00 today and also that 1.00 in the last letter. I just paid 20.00 to Dr. and had my heart checked. Blood pressure is a little high. He also picked up a slight leakage but it's so slight I doubt if he would have found it had I not told him the other Dr. said I had one. He was rather vague as most Doctors are. He doubted if I could get in volunteer branches of the service. As long as I haven't had any infectious diseases other than tonsilitous, he said it might be functional and gradually disappear.

27 MAY 1942 (WEDNESDAY). I'll be leaving here Fri. at ten. Have a ride to 23 north of Mitchell and maybe I can find something better. I have been working at shop and Bloem's. Have a two hour English test today. Went to commencement yesterday afternoon. Worked hard this afternoon. Don and I are preparing to pack our junk. Be seeing you Friday afternoon.

Having completed a year of college, Lyle returned home to help his father with the farmwork during the summer months. Although some war news filtered in to their rural area, Lyle was only vaguely aware of important naval engagements in the Coral Sea and at Midway as the Allies sought to regain dominion of the Pacific. In the Solomon Islands, marines and soldiers were fighting desperately at Guadalcanal to block the Japanese threat to Darwin in northern Australia.

Upon returning to SDSC in September 1942, Lyle accepted the invitation to work for his room and board on the Bloem farm. It was a good arrangement. He had a room all to himself and Mrs. Bloem was an excellent cook. Every morning he was up at a quarter to six to do the milking and other chores before hustling off to class. At noon he returned to the farm, fed and watered the livestock, devoured lunch, and then hurried back to campus for more classes. After evening chores, he occasionally played a couple games of checkers with Professor Bloem before retiring upstairs to study mathematics and physics.

24 SEPTEMBER 1942 (THURSDAY). Last night I was sleeping peacefully at 2:30 when a blinding flash woke me up. I clawed leather to keep from being knocked out of bed. A crash followed which sounded like a locomotive fell through the roof. The reason was that lightning struck the chimney (corner of my room) and knocked out some bricks. It burned out the transformers and telephone and scattered soot all over the basement. That was really a peal of thunder. I went in to see the Dean of Engineering the other day about registering and he seemed to know me to my surprise. He even asked me if I had all the work I wanted which is very unusual. It is usually the students putting on pressure to get a job although jobs are not quite so much in demand this year. The enrollment is much larger than I anticipated. Prof. Gamble—Head of Elect Eng. advised me to steer clear of the Reserves and later join the Signal Corps.

Hitchhiking improved after such a lousy start. Rode with a nice fellow who was related to Susan Smith of Kimball. After 1/2 hr. of hiking and thumbing I got a ride to Union Corner near Sioux Falls with workers from Pavo Project in Black Hills. Another half hour of waiting and a farm couple drove me into Sioux Falls. They stopped a couple times on outskirts but I *stuck* around until I got to the heart of Sioux Falls. I immediately found the highway and walked a dozen or more blocks when a farm family picked me up and took me to about 2 mi. from Dell Rapids. A nice farmer took me into Dell R. after about 10 minutes. He looked somewhat like Uncle Ben and smoked a corn cob pipe. He said he would like to take me clear to Brookings. I next thumbed a hunter who drove an old 1930 car. He was an egotistical pessimist. He operated the Nash-Finch Sioux Falls truck line. He always hit pheasants every time, so he said. He told how he shot 25 shells at geese and didn't get one. They were close to him but the shells were so poor he could hear the shots bounce off their wings. He let me off at the Brookings-Madison Highway. A fellow from Brookings immediately took me to Main Street in Brookings. It was 4:30 by the time I reached the campus. Mr. Bloem drove me up here and I started learning the dairy business. I milk 2 cows in morn. and 3 at night, separate, feed skim milk to a calf, and take care of chickens etc. I get up at 5:45 in order to get to school by 8:00. I check up on water etc. at noon and at night it also takes me about 2 hours. I have an 8:00 o'clock Sat. class also.

5 OCTOBER 1942 (MONDAY). Dear Irene,
This afternoon I have 3 1/2 hr. of Plane Surveying. We take measurements, look through the surveying instrument mounted on a tripod, and lay around on the campus and talk. One girl is taking engineering this year and she is in the class. The instructor told us to let her carry her own instruments.

Wednesday.

I am studying tonight and taking care of the kids at the same time as long as the Bloems went away for the evening. My room is A1, the main features being an innerspring and a dish of apples on my table. The meals are swell. She can really sling the hash. I don't have to work so much either. And she did my laundry already. It is about 8 blocks from the corner of the campus. For assembly today, Jack Rank gave the play "The Merchant of Venice." He played all the parts expertly in costume and voice too. Analytic geometry is tough but I am crazy about math.

Sunday.

Everyone is gone and I am listening to the radio this afternoon while I scribble this. I have been terribly busy partly because a 3 hr. survey came out wrong so it has to be run over. Small matter except that I haven't got 3 hours. As for a birthday present, I think you should spend your money on yourself. You are far too generous. No one around here seems to be very war conscious. We now use the new armory for military. Some fellows could hardly walk a day after Physical Education. It didn't bother me much because I'm in pretty good shape. I have 8 o'clock classes 6 days a week. Sundays I get to sleep until 7. I gave a speech in Speech class on how to tip up a windmill. The student who was in charge of the class told me I was the first engineer he had ever understood while giving a speech. I didn't know if he meant it as a compliment to me or an insult to engineers.

Heard a talk the other day in which the speaker said most parents quarrel over whether a homely child looks like which parent and vice versa. Anyway he said it is lucky that a child never looks quite like either parent because if it did, there never would be any progress on the *face of the earth*. I think I will end up by taking Elect. Engineering and getting in the Signal Corps next year.

11 OCTOBER 1942 (SUNDAY). Another busy week has passed. 1195 collegians have enrolled and in a few weeks the aggies will be here. A drop of about 7%. Had a roast chicken dinner today. Wish I was home for hunting.

The college scene changed abruptly on 13 October when the SDSC president announced the cancellation of two weeks of classes, including Hobo Day and other homecoming festivities. The intent of the moratorium was for students to contribute to the war effort. While some opted to help farmers with corn picking or to go to Pierre to work on an airport construction project, others went home for *mother's cooking*. Lyle decided to stay at Brookings to paint a barn on the Bloem farm. Realizing the war was far from over and that he might be destined for military service, he went to the college health clinic to obtain a medical referral, a prerequisite for enrolling in the reserves. During the physical examination he was devastated when the doctor informed him that a heart murmur would severely limit his future lifestyle. Having just turned nineteen that day, he divulged the shattering news to Irene.

13 OCTOBER 1942 (TUESDAY). I didn't quite get this letter mailed yet. Yes, school closed for two weeks. Went to see the college Dr. after assembly and he told me just how the cards are stacked. No athletics, military, or hard physical labor such as pitching hay for me. No chance of ever getting into the service. However, he told me to come down to the clinic and have a carto— taken. Something like an X-ray I guess. It's not serious only he said it is like this. If you only make $25 a week, you should only spend that or less per week. He said exertion might not take effect for 10 years or more but eventually it will have its effect if I do not follow his advice. Anyway it's a pretty stiff jolt because I am used to being very active and able to keep up with anyone. Hope this didn't burden you Irene. Had to tell it to someone. Mrs. Bloem baked a swell cake for me today. They have three brats. One gave me a handkerchief and the other two each gave me a sock. They treat me swell. I decided not to go home. It takes a strenuous day each way and they wanted me to stay. This will give me a good chance to rest and catch up. I don't think much of this closing school. I doubt if anyone will work. They'll all hunt. Now I don't know why I didn't go home. Mom will be mad at me for staying here. Write and take care of yourself.

In the meantime, weapons of war were streaming from defense plants, thousands of men were being inducted into the armed forces each month, and a presidential campaign was underway with Republican Wendell Wilkie challenging Franklin Roosevelt's bid for a third term.

On the Eastern Front, a bitter battle was raging at Stalingrad. Hindered by the onset of frigid winter weather and the stiff resistance of the Soviet Army, German forces were about to suffer the same fate as Napoleon's troops more than a century earlier.

Writing to his parents, Lyle tempered his optimism.

21 OCTOBER 1942 (WEDNESDAY). The war seems to be going in our favor. Stalingrad and all.

The Bloems left this afternoon for Minn to visit her sisters. They are coming back Fri. night. I stayed here for several reasons. It was too late that day to hitchhike home and it would have taken all the next day. Then, it would take all of Sat. to get back. That would only leave about 9 days. They wanted me to stay to paint the buildings etc. I saw the Doc. the day school closed and he told me military service is definitely out. I will have to quit physical ed. and probably military. I am going downtown and have a cartograph taken before school starts. I got the $10 and it sure went fast. I bought a pair of coveralls for $3 and had a tooth filled for 3.50. Found I had a slight toothache one evening so the next morning I went to a dentist. Irene dropped in Sat. eve. which was certainly a surprise. We went downtown and she bought me a pair of shoes and overshoes. We had a lunch at the Rainbow Cafe afterwards.

The next week, Lyle updated Irene on his latest medical checkup.

25 OCTOBER 1942 (SUNDAY). Had an electricartigram or something taken Sat. forenoon. The nurse developed the film and she told me it looked pretty normal to her. I'm going down Monday to see for sure what the results are. I suppose they will tell me I'm an invalid here and then find nothing wrong with me when I go to the army. When I got your letter yesterday I thought it was the draft board. It had been all over the state and they told me to inform my correspondent of my correct address. Tomorrow we start school again and most of the gang is back already.

Monday.

Boy I could jump clear through the ceiling. The Doctor could find nothing wrong with the elec—. He listened again with ear jiggers and I don't know if he picked up a slight murmur or not. Anyway he said it was not serious enough to ever affect my way of living at all. He did advise me against playing basketball. The film cost me $1.00 and that's all the charge for the whole deal. I had a good rest while the Bloem's were gone but I was glad when my cooking ended. I murder things. Had wieners, eggs and bacon fried together, hot choc. etc. Also other combinations not found in cookbooks. Had a swell time at L.S.A. last night. Also had supper there with a swell girl who I met last year only I'm scared of her. Just think, I can shock and everything. Maybe even get in the army.

Had fresh baked buns for supper. They bought 6 gal honey in Minn. Was going to tell you of some of the good things we have to eat such as pancakes with eggs and sorgum syrup but guess I won't cause it'll make you hungry. I got home that Sun. eve. and they begrudginly gave me some of that peanut brittle you made them. No, they had never eaten such good peanut brittle. We finished what little was left the next eve over a game of checkers. He is a checker enthusiast also. I was lucky to win all 3 games mostly on oversights on his part. Yes, I'm going to get around from now on. More later.

Tuesday.

Just finished my caluthetics. I do some every day in my room which I feel is better anyway than 2 hard workouts per week. And it saves me so much time. Took me an hour to do chores tonight. We had 2 wild ducks for dinner today with dressing, cranberries, and trimmings. No one liked the ducks except me so I ate them. We had pineapple-cherry upside down cake for supper. Very good but I'd rather eat mom's. We put on the storm windows this p.m. This morning I heard talks by officers in the 5 different reserve setups. The Air Corps ground deal sounded best to me. Received a letter containing letters from V, V, dad, and mom this noon. It wasn't exactly a victory letter either. I sure got the war news this time. Fri. eve. is open house for Engr's at the women's dorm. This year with coffee and sugar rationed, it will be a dry night. The lunch the other night was delicious and even Wilkies speech wasn't so bad. He is really very open minded. Here's wishing you a happy birthday. Best wishes is all I've got to send.

Thursday.

Got a letter from Vernon today. He saw General Knudsen at the aircraft factory. Also got a package from home containing popcorn balls, socks, and shirts. In a few minutes I go to military class.

Back home, Emma and Charles were finding the isolation during long, cold winters more burdensome with each passing year. They had planned on retiring to a neighboring town and living in a house with such comforts as electricity, running water, and central heating. But after the outbreak of hostilities they continued on the farm, working long hours to produce food for the war effort. Wilma and Chuckie helped with the daily chores upon returning from the Conley grade school in late afternoon.

In addition to incessant farm chores and housework, Emma prepared food to supplement the diet of Virginia and Jean who were boarding in Chamberlain while attending high school. From time to time Emma sent food packages to Irene, recently transferred to an army base near Watertown and dependent on ration certificates. Occasionally Emma baked an extra batch of cookies to send to Vernon and his wife Vivian, both working at an aircraft plant in Kansas City.

After prefacing a lengthy letter to Irene with weather and family news, Emma expressed her lingering anguish over Lyle's heart condition.

2 NOVEMBER 1942 (MONDAY). Had our first snowfall last nite—several inches of fluffy snow on ground. I am getting so I dread the winters—don't like the cold—hate to leave the fire, also hate to be snowed under and away from civilization.

Have been trying to do a little sewing—but it goes slow. Made Virginia a white rayon blouse with long sleeves (got a pattern so had better luck) and a black skirt out of my old black coat and a jerker from that velvet that Molly gave you. It looked cute on her. The two girls look cute in most any rags. They are so near the same size now and quite a contrast in looks and personality. They enjoy school very much—and manage to keep on top of everything. I enjoy having them come home weekends—something to look forward to. You must be plenty busy if you have to work Sundays too. Maybe Uncle Sam is forming a bad habit like the rest of us. I think if we worked six days like we should there would be no need of working Sunday too. That applies around here I know.

Was about down in bed a week ago this weekend when we had a letter from Lyle mentioning his heart ailment—Had a card later saying it wasn't so bad. (but maybe plenty bad at that) We knew the Dr found a heart symptom at time of tonsil operation, but you know he seemed so peppy and all this summer, so we never gave it much thot. It took the sap out of me—couldn't sleep or eat—but am praying that it will right itself and not hinder his health. Lyle is bubbling over with life and enthusiasm and loves to take active part in everything. I felt that God had answered my prayers—when we got a card from him giving the last results.

The girls don't get any too much fruit or milk in their diet. They like the dinner OK but don't like the other two meals. We may work out something better for them. I feed them up good weekends and send back some food with them—helps a little. School is quite a problem you know, when you live on the farm.

Say that was quite a messy box I sent you—nothing like I planned on (planned on baking you a cake and some cookies on Wed—but I washed clothes and between the rain and some company and chores, I didn't get it done. So next morning between breakfast and mail time (11 AM) I threw the box together—and I mean threw—and of course it looked it. I am sending you another box soon—cookies and a cake—If wishing would do it I would have had the world on wheels at your doorstep. And who wouldn't for a dear girl like you—It has puzzled me how we could have been so fortunate (being blessed with seven of the best children anyone ever laid eyes on—the envy of any childless parents, or otherwise.

Sure hope you find your work pleasant. I knew that after you had been at Watertown a while you would like it. Every town holds some heart that would become dear to you after knowing them.

Had a nice letter from Vernon and Vivian—They were so excited over their new buy—new innerspring mattress—They must have been rather uncomfortable before that and can enjoy perfect rest now. Sure hope Vernon gets his deferment (Maybe I am selfish asking too much.) Vivian said she liked her job—as time keeper.

Aunt Tony expects Dale home on furlough soon—said she was afraid they would send him across soon. Harold is in the Solomon Is. now. Avery is in Texas. Kenneth in Florida. They are scattered all over the world. (If you find time write to some of them. They would all appreciate the letters.) Otherwise no news around here—mostly work and school. The kids sure like school this winter—a big relief to my mind. Wilma plays mother to Chuckie, gives him a little scolding now and then—packs his dinner and sees that he washes clean. Are you going to eat Thanksgiving dinner with us?—If you can't make it home maybe you can visit Lyle, if he can't come either. Send or take some snapshots of yourself at different angles—also of Lyle if you get a chance. Must quit and write Lyle a card and Vernon and V a letter this PM so to mail tomorrow.

Bye Darling.

When Congress lowered the draft age to eighteen in early November, Lyle became subject to being called up for service. In letters home he noted the campus scene was changing rapidly as students departed for the armed forces.

4 NOVEMBER 1942 (WEDNESDAY). Got an Analytic Geo. test back today with 99%. It was the high grade. Anything under 50 flunked which was about 1/3 class. I was chairman of a panel discussion group in speech today. I guess I have received all my mail now until Christmas. Even got a letter from Vernon. The popcorn balls sure didn't last long. Doubt if I'll be home until Dec. 23. The "labor recess" didn't go over good with the students.

6 NOVEMBER 1942 (FRIDAY). I am now in speech class, waiting for my turn. We heard the Deep River singers (a negro quartet) in assembly. Another girl and I have to plan a program for our fall Pi Kappa Delta banquet quite soon. I heard talks by all reserves last week. I'm just going

WARTIME COMIC STRIP LYLE MAILED HOME—ALONG WITH TWO WARTIME JOKES:

FASHION NOTE—THERE'LL BE LITTLE CHANGE IN MEN'S POCKETS THIS YEAR / CAR SALE AD—CAR IS A-1, OWNER IS 1-A"

to wait and see what happens. I rather look forward to joining the army if things end pretty quick. I may not come home at Thanksgiving, but I do not plan on coming back for next quarter. We may have 800 soldiers stationed here before long. We sure had the tests and assignments this week. Speech is quite easy for me. Write all the latest news.

15 NOVEMBER 1942 (SUNDAY). Just taking it easy. Last week they took a vote and decided to eliminate Thanksgiving vacation and start Christmas early—Dec. 18 at noon. I wrote Vernon a letter to get some military advice. Is Dale a pilot? What kind of deal does Lawrence Swanson have? How about the other cousins—were they called yet? Went into Wards about a week ago and the darn salesman sold me a finger tip coat for 13.00. It's worth the money though and I earned the money during the week recess. You guessed it—I've got a guilty conscious. Chores don't take long anymore because I have things down to a science. The enrollment has been decreasing lately due to enlistments. Save some roast duck and grape jelly for me.

22 NOVEMBER 1942 (SUNDAY). Have plenty of money. Maybe I'll go to school next quarter. I'll come home Dec. 18 because of no Thanksgiving vacation. Any more cousins in the service?

While contemplating his future, Lyle came across a brochure posted on the Physics Department bulletin board. The Army Air Corps was seeking college students with a background in mathematics and physics for a meteorology program directed out of the University of Chicago. The blurb explained that in a "global war . . . airplanes and ships cannot be fully effective weapons unless they are aided by the invisible ally, the weather." Estimating the need for an additional six thousand "weather officers" by 1945, the Air Corps was recruiting men for that technology. Lured by the prospect of travel, adventure, and gold bars, Lyle sent away for an application packet.

Lyle updated Irene on his college activities and prospects for military service.

22 NOVEMBER 1942 (SUNDAY). Why have you not written me? Or did your letter get lost? Tues. evening the film society presented "The Howards of Virginia." Have you ever seen it? It was good. I have been in the groove lately. An A in both military tests, 99 and 100 respectively in Analytic geometry tests, B in only Physics test, Bs in History, and I think pretty good in a Survey test Friday. I study very, very little, but plenty of sleep and exercise turn the trick. I'll be glad to get home the 18th. It takes just one quarter of college to make a guy appreciate home where

there is no responsibility, plenty of sleep and food. Are you coming home Christmas? Should I join the reserves? Dec. 31 is the deadline.

Next Sunday.

It's sure a swell day today. You sure are lucky if you go to Calif, Texas, or Alaska. I would sure like to. Thanks for that dollar. Vernon wrote this week and gave me a little advice. I don't know what to do, but I guess I'll see the school military advisor this week. A lady asked for 8 lb. of butter and the clerk asked her what the deal was. She said she just wanted to have plenty on hand in case people started hoarding! There are rumors of butter rationing you know. People are funny, they think more of their stomachs and gasoline than of the soldiers dying out on the battlefields. Almost time for supper and then chores.

After playfully drawing a censor stamp at the bottom of his letter to Irene, Lyle next wrote to his parents.

29 NOVEMBER 1942 (SUNDAY). Just heard Prime Minister Churchill speak. The war is going good. I'm still going strong, but I wouldn't care to get up at 5 very often for a 7 hour forenoon of work, tests, and concentrated math like last Monday. We had a slug of tests this week again, but I'm still above sea (C) level. Vernon thought the Air Corps ground communications would be best. You are lucky, mom, that you have a good cow to milk. I wouldn't own one of these purebred jerseys. They are ornery, finicky, stubborn, and hard to milk. We had goose, and homemade sherbet for Thanksgiving. Very good next to being home.

Write and say whether I should quit school at Christmas and stay home and get deferred for a while, or go to school here and get deferred for the quarter and get in advanced military, or get in the reserves? Look up a birth certificate for me. The reserves close Dec. 31 so I must get action. I'll be home now in less than 20 days. I fixed that sweater right away by tying ends of the yarn together on the inside. Lots of kids got in reserves last summer and now they go through miles of red tape to change to some other reserve etc. They evidently didn't know what they wanted. Sounds like 800 army men will be stationed here starting this month.

The next Sunday, a year after Pearl Harbor, an unfavorable change in circumstance prompted Lyle to lament:

6 DECEMBER 1942 (SUNDAY). Meet a buck private! Heard today that the Pres. closed down all enlistments and reserve enlistments. So here I sit high and dry. Thought I would probably enlist in the Air Corps, go to a gov. meteorologist school for a couple years and get a commission

and bachelor's degree. But if they closed enlistments, that's out. I'm not sorry about not getting in the reserves. I would consider coming back to school next quarter for only one reason—students drafted from college will have a good chance of being sent back to colleges for training. I went back to the health clinic the other day and asked them to state definitely if they would recommend me for the reserves. The Dr. checked my heart and said it was as good as anyone's. There are 3 Doctors here who change off and so now all 3 have checked my heart. I think less of this health department all the time for telling a person he's in such bad shape before they are sure.

Got 100s in my last two math tests. Now I have 99%, 100%, 100%, 100%, 100% in my math tests. I think my professor will have to give me an A which they hate to do around here. I've been helping a kid in Physics lately. He flunked both tests and if he flunks the course he will go into the marines because he is in the reserves. He is an exceptionally practical student and tries hard. I guess he memorizes instead of thinking it out. Anyway, I'm going to put him through the course.

Lyle's parents, more his mother than his father, counseled him to stay out of the armed forces as long as possible. Although he respected their advice, he was convinced he had come across a good opportunity. He secured letters of recommendation from his professors and, despite voluntary enlistments having been closed down due to some branches of the service getting too many men and others too few, prepared an application for the meteorology program.

Monday.

Got your letter this noon and a letter from U. of Chicago concerning enlistment in the Air Corps. The meteorology course would start Mar. 1 at some large college and run for 6 months, and then 8 more months of Advanced Meteorology graduating with a commission and degree. I will see the military advisor about enlisting (which I don't think can be done) and send in my application anyway to get in when drafted.

Excited about the prospect of joining the Air Corps, Lyle returned home for Christmas break. Then, in early January, he was stricken with scarlet fever. While recovering from the illness he waited and waited for a response to his meteorology application, unaware that the program directors were being inundated with some two thousand inquiries per day. Disappointed, he hitchhiked back to Brookings, arriving two weeks after the start of the winter quarter. There, he found several college pals had *joined up* or been drafted. The campus abounded with men in uniform. When his childhood chum Don Swanson departed to join the navy, Lyle felt left out of the mainstream. Restless, but still hoping to hear from "Weather," he wrote impatient letters home.

18 JANUARY 1943 (MONDAY). Send the "Weather" information when it comes. Don went to Sioux Falls today to be inducted into the navy. We had a blizzard Saturday and last night it was 30 below at least and maybe it'll be colder tonight. Hope the "Weather" deal comes through, or I'll try the navy.

19 JANUARY 1943 (TUESDAY). I finished registering today and talked them out of the $2 late registration fee. I'll be caught up before too long. Boy are the cookies good. Now for another session with brain-busting calculus.

21 JANUARY 1943 (THURSDAY). Hope you have heard from "Weather" and sent it along by now. Don is gone now. The enrollment is about 900 and there are 800 soldiers. I have lots of make up work left to do and I'll be glad to catch up. It was a regular blizzard here when I was looking for a room. Guess I'll have to buy a towel or two because we furnish our own. All but this place wanted holiday prices for a room. A chance to charge more as long as the dormitories are used by the soldiers. I picked the right day to come back. It gave me a chance to get going without missing any extra classes. The southern soldiers didn't like the cold weather. It was much colder than I have ever been in before.
Sunday.
I was tired that day when I hit Brookings. I was very fortunate to catch a ride into the heart of Sioux Falls with a farmer who once broke sod with a steam engine out by Kimball. Send me "Weather" when it comes.

Finally, Lyle received a long-awaited letter forwarded by his parents. His heart raced as he ripped open the envelope. Yes, the Air Corps did want him for the meteorology program. The letter from Weather advised him to request his local draft board to include him in its next draft quota and to take the acceptance letter along to the induction station. Hastily withdrawing from classes, Lyle hitchhiked two hundred miles back to the farm and, the next day, visited the draft board office in Chamberlain. Happy to accede to the request of a volunteer draftee, the Brule County Draft Board changed Lyle's classification from 2-C to 1-A.

Several days later, Lyle, tired of the uncertainty, was relieved and ecstatic when he tore open a letter from the local draft board and pulled out an ORDER TO REPORT FOR INDUCTION:

Prepare in Duplicate

Local Board
Brule County

County Court House
Chamberlain, South Dakota

(LOCAL BOARD DATE STAMP WITH CODE)

_____
(Date of mailing)

ORDER TO REPORT FOR INDUCTION

The President of the United States,

To_____Lyle_____Virgil_____Sladek_____
   (First name)   (Middle name)   (Last name)

Order No. _____

GREETING:

Having submitted yourself to a local board composed of your neighbors for the purpose of determining your availability for training and service in the armed forces of the United States, you are hereby notified that you have now been selected for training and service in the___Army or Navy___
         (Army, Navy, Marine Corps)

You will, therefore, report to the local board named above at <u>Chamberlain</u>
         (Place of reporting)
at ___4:00 P. m., on the ___18th___ day of ___February___, 19 _43_
(Hour of reporting)

This local board will furnish transportation to an induction station of the service for which you have been selected. You will there be examined, and, if accepted for training and service, you will then be inducted into the stated branch of the service.

Persons reporting to the induction station in some instances may be rejected for physical or other reasons. It is well to keep this in mind in arranging your affairs, to prevent any undue hardship if you are rejected at the induction station. If you are employed, you should advise your employer of this notice and of the possibility that you may not be accepted at the induction station. Your employer can then be prepared to replace you if you are accepted, or to continue your employment if you are rejected.

Willful failure to report promptly to this local board at the hour and on the day named in this notice is a violation of the Selective Training and Service Act of 1940, as amended, and subjects the violator to fine and imprisonment. Bring with you sufficient clothing for 3 days.

You must keep this form and bring it with you when you report to the local board.

If you are so far removed from your own local board that reporting in compliance with this order will be a serious hardship and you desire to report to a local board in the area of which you are now located, go immediately to that local board and make written request for transfer of your delivery for induction, taking this order with you.

D. S. S. Form 150
(Revised 6-15-42) U. S. GOVERNMENT PRINTING OFFICE 16—18271-2   *Member or clerk of the local board.*

DRAFTEE LYLE SLADEK, CHAMBERLAIN, SOUTH DAKOTA, 18 FEBRUARY 1943
EATING A GRAPEFRUIT WHILE WAVING GOOD-BYE

CHAPTER 5

You're in the Army Now, You're Not behind a Plow

We defend and we build a way of life, not for America alone,
but for all mankind.

—FRANKLIN DELANO ROOSEVELT

AT NOON ON THE APPOINTED DAY, 18 February 1943, Charles backed the fluid drive Dodge sedan out of the car shed. Emma, Wilma, Chuckie, and Lyle piled in for the fifteen-mile drive to Chamberlain. Fortunately, the winter weather was unusually mild that afternoon and the country roads were passable. The family exchanged few words along the way. A certain amount of tension hung in the air at the reality of Lyle's imminent departure for an induction station.

Charles angled the car up to the curb in front of the Red Owl grocery store on Main Street. Emma, taking Wilma along, went to trade a case of eggs for groceries while Charles hurried off to transact business at the bank and county courthouse.

Lyle, with Chuckie in tow, reported in at the office of the draft board. That done, they walked over to their Uncle John's hardware store. While waiting for their uncle to complete his telephone conversation with a salesman they looked over the shiny new tools and hunting gear on display. Finding a moment when Uncle John was off the phone they entered his office, greeted him, and remarked how much they admired the double-barrel, twenty-gauge shotgun in the window. Uncle John agreed, "It's a beauty all right," but added that wartime conditions were making it difficult to procure consumer goods such as guns and shotgun shells. Curious, Lyle asked about the draft status of his cousin Jimmy who was attending the University of South Dakota. Uncle John replied that his son hoped to complete his degree in May before being drafted.

As Lyle and Chuckie prepared to leave, Uncle John asked them to tell their father he would come by on Sunday to deliver a steel grain bin. Shaking hands, he wished Lyle well in his military service and asked him to write a line now and then. Lyle said that since he was just getting over scarlet fever he feared the induction station might reject him. But, in any event, he was looking forward to his first train ride and traveling beyond the borders of South Dakota.

Too soon, it seemed, the sun lowered in the west and it was time for the family to drive back to the farm. Charles arranged the grocery bags in the trunk while Emma retrieved her Kodak box camera. Anxious and dubious about her son's decision to join the army, she snapped a photograph of Lyle as he stood on the sidewalk eating a grapefruit. Then came a mother's tears, final embraces, a father's firm handshake, and vigorous waving as Charles backed the car out onto the street. The waving continued until the car disappeared over the crest of the hill.

Lyle wandered over to the Mussman Hotel, a white, two-story structure fronting on Main Street where the draft board had arranged accommodations for the night. He joined his fellow draftees in the lobby, a room plainly furnished with wooden chairs, a floor lamp, a spittoon, and a desk for the night clerk. With the exception of one fellow, a Sioux Indian, Lyle knew them all; two had been basketball teammates in high school.

Staying the night at the Mussman was nothing special, except for the novelty of occupying a room in a hotel. From a narrow hallway Lyle turned the key in the lock of a darkly varnished door and entered the unadorned cubicle. A transom over the door provided some ventilation from the musty tobacco odor. He settled in and found the shared bath down the hall. Then, along with two companions, he hustled down the street to a pool hall for a couple games of eightball.

The draft board had issued chits for supper at the Derby Café. All the townspeople and tourists who read the billboards along Highway 16 knew Derby's was air-conditioned and approved by Duncan Hines. Even though Lyle had attended high school in Chamberlain, he had never eaten at the prestigious Derby Café. He thought it grand to eat at the town's top-ranked restaurant. His venture out into the wider world was off to a promising start.

Knowing they would be up before dawn the draftees soon retired to their rooms. Having been away from his family for weeks at a time while in high school and college, Lyle was not yet homesick. He slept soundly, anticipating the coming of morning, eager to be off to Fort Crook, Nebraska, in hopes of joining the Army Air Corps. The excitement and glamour of airplanes fired his youthful imagination. Aviation was the stuff dreams were made of—the Wright Brothers, Lindbergh, the Red Baron, Amelia Earhart, and Colonel Scott of the Flying Tigers.

The draftees were at the train depot early the next morning to catch the eastbound Chicago, Milwaukee & St. Paul. The boys waited quietly on the platform, their backs turned to the cold wind, shoulders hunched deeply into jacket collars. They perked up when they saw the stationmaster emerge from the baggage room. He pulled out his pocket watch, squinted at it, put it back in his pocket, and picked up a canvas mailbag. Shortly, the muffled whistles from a steam locomotive announced the approach of the train from the west. It rumbled across the Missouri River trestle and ground to a halt at the Chamberlain depot, belching clouds of steam and smoke.

It was not yet daybreak on that frigid February morning. No band had assembled to play patriotic tunes. No crowd had gathered to cheer those Brule County draftees as they went off to war. More than a year had elapsed since Pearl Harbor; the nation had settled into the routine of the war effort.

The boys transferred to a faster train, the Hiawatha, at Canton, South Dakota. Debarking at Sioux City, Iowa, they boarded a bus for Omaha, Nebraska. Finally, they climbed aboard another bus for the last leg of the journey.

INDUCTION STATION
FORT CROOK, NEBRASKA

A sign along the oiled highway indicated Fort Crook was off to the left. The bus slowed to a near stop as it made the sharp turn onto a narrow road leading to the induction station. The sun, now low in the west, was barely visible through a leaden sky. A chill hung in the air. Tires crunched on frozen gravel as the wheels rolled to a stop at the guardhouse gate.

The mood of the draftees turned somber at the sight of the armed sentries. All that day on the trains and buses there had been good-natured joshing and other shows of boyish bravado. Now, as the bus traversed the entrance to Fort Crook, they soberly contemplated the prospect of wartime military service.

Army staff issued bedding and assigned the newcomers from Brule County to a barracks crowded with strangers. For most, making up their own bed was a new experience. When lights went out at ten, the weary travelers were glad for a few hours of warmth and quiet, each lost in his own thoughts.

A shrill whistle and gruff voice awakened the boys in early morning.

"Rise and shine. Rise and shine."

Breakfast was sparse, especially for those near the end of the chow line— a boiled egg, a slice of cold toast with marmalade, and a cup of lukewarm GI coffee. But the draftees took little notice, for they were thinking of the events about to unfold that day.

The ensuing twenty-four hours seemed utterly strange to those boys from farms and small towns. So arbitrary. So rigid. It would be much later before they realized that, beneath the surface, army ways had a machinelike energy and purpose.

"You are taking your physicals in the gym. Remove your clothing and put it in a bag. Then go through that door over there."

The gym door opened into a scene of frenetic activity. Scores of naked men formed long lines leading to stations with army doctors in white smocks and clerks in khaki uniforms. Procedures were impersonal, but efficient.

"Step on the scale. Let's measure your height. Move on to the next station."

"Have you ever had a seizure? Open wide and say, 'A-a-a-h.' Bend over. Next station."

"Step on the blotter. Your arches are fine. No flat feet here."

And so it went throughout the morning.

Keyed up by the excitement of it all, Lyle's pulse rate and blood pressure shot up every time he came within three feet of a medic. Perhaps because of his recent bout with scarlet fever, a medic drew a blood sample and told him he would have to wait until Monday to learn the result.

That Saturday, Lyle retrieved one of the penny postcards his mother had placed in his hands at the time of their parting. Wiping a tear from her eye, she had admonished, "Write when you get there." And write he did, the first of some four hundred letters and postcards posted from five continents:

20 FEBRUARY 1943 (SATURDAY). All of the best fellows in Physical Exam can have choice of army or navy. I was one of them but I must first hear from the blood test. Had to lay down to get under the blood pressure. Fort Crook is 7 miles S of Omaha. The ride was very tiresome. Andresen did not pass. I would have been sworn in today if the blood test had come through. The meals are O.K. only we had to get up at 5 o'clock.

Following the attack at Pearl Harbor, newspaper and magazine advertisements became saturated with pictures of men in uniform. Lyle did not want to remain on the sidelines. Although he loved his country, he had given little thought to such abstract notions as patriotism or democracy when considering his options. Travel and adventure beckoned. In response to a letter he received from Irene before leaving home, he adamantly replied:

20 FEBRUARY 1943 (SATURDAY). I definitely was not drafted! They would not have taken me for at least 6 months—had a 2-C classification. But you know, I thought I was missing something. When fellows like Don started leaving I got restless—and here I am. Those fellows at 819 Eighth Street were an O.K. bunch. I certainly have no regrets about joining. I sent an application to the air corps to get in Meteorology school. Yes, I went back to school for the 3rd and 4th weeks of the second term and one night I got a letter from home saying that I had been accepted in the meteorology deal. That night I talked with different people and decided to go home and probably volunteer for induction. The next morning I tore around like a mad man—paid my room rent, cashed my meal ticket, got a military certificate, arranged to leave my clothes, took a screening physical test to see if I could pass, and arranged with each instructor to temporarily withdraw from classes. I wanted to come back to school if I decided not to join, or didn't pass. I hitchhiked to Sioux Falls arriving before noon. There I interviewed the navy and army recruiting boards and hitchhiked home. It was fun hitchhiking that day. Had the draft board reclassify me 1-A so they could draft me with the next group—Feb. 19.

The chow is good next to home cooking. Of course they don't care whether the food suits you or not. We read, play cards, ping pong, pool, and touch football. I haven't been beaten in ping pong. I'm tickled pink to be in the army. Was afraid I couldn't make it. When they call you at 5 in the morning it makes you wonder why you enlisted. The sleeping is swell. Nice and cool and clean bedding. I'm one of the few here that will get in the air corps or navy.

Out of stationery, Lyle hunted around for more. Consumer goods such as paper had become scarce since most of the country's resources were going toward the production of war goods.

Well, I found some more paper so I'll continue this letter.

A Sgt. just asked, I mean told, a bunch of us to volunteer for sweeping so we spent over an hour sweeping sidewalks. Planes are continually roaring around overhead. Be sure and write me as soon as I get some sort of an address. A Red Cross lady treated us in Sioux City. She had a box of gum, apples, oranges, and candy bars. Went to a show yesterday. They have a theatre right at the post here, and charge only fifteen cents. We are well supplied here with magazines, games, and coke machines. I'll be kind of glad to move along again. Had a good time when I was home for two weeks. Hunted some pheasants, visited Thompsons etc, and slept until I got hungry enough to get up. I hope they don't make us get up at five o'clock all the time in the army. It seems rather strange to really be in. I had to do some fast talking and three rechecks to get my blood pressure down. It's really normal but when they start testing it the pressure goes up. Maybe more later.

The next day Lyle scavenged United Service Organizations (USO) stationery that carried, in bold red letters, the reminder: IDLE GOSSIP SINKS SHIPS. Expecting a normal reading on his blood test, he anticipated moving on to an army reception station in Kansas.

21 FEBRUARY 1943 (SUNDAY). I'm playing ping pong just now. Won easily from 2 guys but the third was tough. I will be at Fort Leavenworth for about 2 or 3 days and then sent away. I expect to hit a meteorology school before March 1. Played 3 games of pool in Chamberlain and won 2. Ate a good supper at Derby's with Reimer. Stayed at the hotel and boarded the train at 5:00. Slept between White Lake and Mt. Vernon. Got to Mitchell before 7:00 and left for Canton in 10 minutes. Ate a *very* hasty breakfast at Canton and took the fast Hiawatha to Sioux City. Arrived at Sioux City at about twelve but didn't have time to eat dinner. It's a smoky city. Took the bus for Omaha and arrived at 4:30. Ate a poor steak supper and boarded a bus for Fort Crook. All buses and trains were very crowded. Arrived at highway on west side of Fort Crook as the sun was near the west horizon. It looked like a large military academy or West Point. Lots of buildings something like a campus. Walked over to the induction building and waited for something to happen. We were issued bedding at 7:00 and made our cots. I got a lower cot. We took showers and went to the show at 8:00. Went to bed at 10 and slept until a quarter to five. When they called to get up I began to wonder why I enlisted. Had to clean and mop the building and had chow at 7 o'clock. It was not bad but not so good as the soldiers get.

Physical Exam lasted until noon and was *very* strict. Heart was O.K. and my eyes perfect. Could not read a 4 on a color blind chart but got about 90% right. Couldn't see two dots. Quite a few fellows were rejected. Gene Steckleberg had to stay two more days to have his nose X rayed for sinus. Don't know if he will pass. Andresen was sure disappointed. His nose had a hole in it somewhere. All those with almost perfect exam were given a choice of army or navy. I was one of them and had to see the navy room man. He took one look at my Air Corps letter and said there was no use trying to get me to join the navy. He wished he had a deal like that. All the others go into the regular army. The navy is the very best men. About 150 were sworn into the army yesterday afternoon. I will be sworn in Monday. Kind of late to write home for a deferment isn't it. We are right adjacent to the Omaha plane factory. They are continually roaring around in test flights. It's a huge factory.

It became apparent that airplanes were potent weapons of war when German ground forces, supported by dive-bombers and paratroopers, swept across Poland, France, and the Low Countries in 1939 and 1940. Defensive positions, such as the Maginot line in France, failed to slow the German *blitzkrieg* (lightning war). Previously, most American military leaders considered battleships to be the epitome of power. When Billy Mitchell, a prominent aviator in the Great War, returned to the United States in 1919 and became Director of Military Aeronautics, he raised the hackles of navy admirals by asserting that bombers could sink the huge dreadnoughts. In 1925, after his public criticism of the Navy and War Departments, General Mitchell was court-martialed for insubordination. Subsequently, the United States had neglected the development and production of military aircraft.

Addressing Congress in May 1940, President Roosevelt made a surprising statement: "I should like to see this nation geared up to the ability to turn out at least fifty thousand planes a year." Upon hearing of that production target, Hermann Göring, the leader of the German Luftwaffe, scoffed, "The Americans can't build planes, only electric ice boxes."

Göring was wrong. Aircraft production increased dramatically and thousands of young men, intrigued by newsreel shots of the air war in Europe, volunteered for flight training. In less than two years the Army Air Corps expanded from fourteen hundred officers and enlisted men to more than two hundred thousand, eventually burgeoning to nearly two and one-half million personnel.

By February 1943 thousands of planes were streaming off the assembly lines, many of them four-engine bombers. At Fort Crook, Lyle watched B-26 Marauders, also known as *Widow Makers*, roar over the field base in test flights. Although not so sleek or adaptable as the B-25 Mitchell, named after Billy Mitchell, the B-26 could fly higher and carry a heavier bomb load.

Thinking of Vernon and Vivian working at a B-25 plant in Kansas City, Lyle recalled when the two-engine bombers with tricycle landing gear had raided Tokyo in April 1942. Led by Colonel James Doolittle, sixteen B-25s launched from the aircraft carrier *Hornet* had bombed selected targets in Japan before flying on to China. With the Vs on his mind, Lyle continued:

I may go through Kansas C. on way to Fort Leavenworth. I'll try and talk to Vernon. I'm just taking it easy and glad that I'm in. We got to sleep until 6 this morning but I went to bed at 9 last night. How is the hog business coming? One kid tried to correct a sergeant on his name pronunciation and sure got told off. They don't care how *you* pronounce your name. This is quite a change for some fellows. I sure slept good and am feeling swell. Hope I continue to like it.

Lyle retained vivid memories of his last hour at Fort Crook. Late Monday afternoon a sergeant barked:

"You have passed your physical. You are qualified for both the army and navy. Which do you want?"

"Uh, army I guess. I think I would like the Army Air Corps. What do you think, Sergeant, about—"

"If you want the army get in that formation over there. The lieutenant is about ready to swear them in."

"Raise your right hand. Repeat after me, I swear to . . . Sergeant, take over."

"You are to take the next train to Kansas City."

"Sergeant, uh, will we have time to—"

"Come on, move it soldier, move it. Don't you know there's a war on!"

Men rejected for service returned home. Those who passed the physical and psychological screening had the option of a furlough or of going directly to a reception station for classification tests, interviews, shots, and uniforms. Lyle, one of a motley group of boys still clad in civilian slacks, sweaters, and oxford shoes, boarded a night train for Fort Leavenworth.

RECEPTION STATION
FORT LEAVENWORTH, KANSAS

Faint lights from farmhouses flickered through the frosted windows as the train sped through the countryside, swaying and bouncing on wartime tracks. Three hours later the sleepy men debarked at a siding and marched to a barracks area.

The following morning Lyle could see MPs, armed with shotguns, marching denim-clad prisoners from the adjacent detention barracks to work details. Observing that grim scene he vowed to shape up and conform to army regulations.

Herded around a cheerless army camp of drab wooden buildings and muddy grounds, Lyle and the other recruits anticipated three days of "hurry and wait" as they made the transition from civilian to army life. An overcast midwinter sky added to the dreary atmosphere.

23 FEBRUARY 1943 (TUESDAY). We got here as members of the army. I'm feeling healthy—and fairly wealthy and wise. Rows of barracks and about half are colored boys. It feels good to be really in after all the red tape, etc. I can't hardly believe it. Got tired of not much to do at Ft. Crook and yet sort of hated to leave it. No use writing me yet.

The army encouraged letter writing. It was good for morale. Thanks to GI franking privileges, posting a letter did not cut into a soldier's meager budget; he simply wrote his name, serial number, and address at the upper left and the word "Free" in place of a stamp. Lyle teased Irene:

23 FEBRUARY 1943 (TUESDAY). Don't feel so important. You wouldn't be getting this letter if the postage wasn't free. Ha. We were sworn into the army yesterday at 6:00 in the evening and left immediately for Leavenworth. We arrived at 9:00, took blood type test, and went to bed. We had to get up at 4:30 and sweep the floor and make the cots. The army does things funny. You spend a lot of time making the cots, but you must take them apart and make them over different before you can sleep in them. Then we had breakfast chow, rested for an hour, and took about 3 hours of written tests. By that time it was light out. We were shown army films this afternoon. Tomorrow we will probably have interviews, take shots, and get uniforms. Do not attempt to write me until I settle down. I think I will like the army. Even if I don't, I will be glad I joined because I would have always thought I was missing out on something. The Leavenworth penitentiary is located by this army post. We are about 30 mi. N.W. of Kansas City. I might call up Vernon sometime. I was beaten in ping pong tonight in 2 out of 3 games. Maybe revenge tomorrow. Kansas is a lot different than South Dakota. It was cloudy all day. I hope to advance soon to better than a buck private. Played pool a little at Fort Crook and won quite often. One fellow was a poor loser so I poured on the heat and beat him worse the next time. About half here are colored soldiers. In my roster of 8 are 5 Indians from South Dakota. They are funny. One said the colored soldiers should be used on night blackout and he (Indian) at dusk blackout. Color scheme you know!

The United States was far from a superpower in 1940 when Congress enacted the first peacetime draft in American history and called up seventy-five thousand men. The first conscripts, later called draftees, found themselves in an army with a severe shortage of facilities and equipment. Some made do with leftover supplies and uniforms from World War I and, during training maneuvers, used broomsticks for rifles and trucks to simulate tanks. Thanks to superb leadership, conditions and equipment improved rapidly. In his memoirs Churchill credited General Marshall with building a mighty army and referred to him as "the architect of victory." Resuming his letter to Irene, Lyle observed:

> They are really inducting men fast now days. I sure felt good about being eligible for any branch of the service physically. I kept my fingers crossed until they swore me in. One kid thought there might be 50,000 men here but I sure doubt there is half that many. Fort Crook was sort of a picturesque place. And to think I almost passed up this chance and stayed in school. Boy, the cokes sure disappear around here. Even if I didn't have this deal lined up I think I could get into something pretty good. Two out of the five draftees from our county were rejected. I did not take the usual 7 day furlough because I did not see any sense in it. Maybe our paths will cross one of these days. Now for a good nights sleep.

The next morning while undergoing aptitude tests Lyle encountered a series of questions such as, "Pictured is a pile of blocks. How many blocks are there in the pile?" Visualizing the three-dimensional images from all angles, he quickly counted them. As a voracious reader and worker of crossword puzzles, his language skills were better than most. Having completed a year of college engineering, the mathematics section posed little challenge. Likewise, his familiarity with farm tools and machinery made mechanics a snap. Later, a noncommissioned officer (noncom) told Lyle he had scored very high on the Army General Classification Test (AGCT) administered to all recruits. Not surprising, since inductees, on average, had completed just one year of high school.

The Air Corps, needing trained personnel to operate and maintain the planes pouring off the assembly lines, had first priority in the selection process. Recruits who scored well in qualification tests were deemed potential pilots, navigators, bombardiers, mechanics, radio operators, photographers, or technicians in a host of specialties such as radio and meteorology.

Lyle was perplexed, however, when his letter of acceptance from the Air Corps meteorology program appeared to be a meaningless piece of paper. When presented to interviewers, it drew a blank. Perhaps his mother had been right all along when she suggested that the brochure was just a "come-on" to induce college students to join up. It did not occur to him that some confusion was inevitable as the army sought to channel millions of recruits into suitable training slots during the rapid buildup.

Next, the men were herded into a barnlike building permeated with a rich aroma of mothballs and oiled leather where their civilian clothing was replaced with Government Issue (GI) gear. Brusque clerks, demanding height and waist measurements, piled an assortment of new and recycled olive drab garments on outstretched arms. Except for clothing and footwear, the wartime army did not cater to individual differences; soldiers slept on standard-size cots and adapted to standard-issue equipment. The last items doled out were a woolen overcoat, a pair of GI shoes, a canteen, eating utensils, and a barracks bag stenciled with name and serial number.

The next step in the process was unpleasant but brief. As the men paraded by single file, medics administered injections in machine-gun fashion. When the aroma and the banter about square needles caused some to fall over in a faint, the hardier souls let out derisive hoots and catcalls.

Finally, each recruit placed his personal belongings in a cardboard box labeled for shipment home. That procedure completed, Lyle took time to examine the inscription on his dog tags: SLADEK, LYLE V. 37474253 B. Apart from his name, serial number, and blood type, the letter *P* for Protestant was imprinted on the bottom right of the metal rectangles.

That evening, Lyle updated his parents.

24 FEBRUARY 1943 (WEDNESDAY). We got up again at 4:30 this morning and made up our cots. In the dark, we marched to chow at quarter to five. Then we swept and scrubbed the barracks and waited for something to happen. About 9:00 we went up to a building and were interviewed to determine branch of the service you were to go into. I showed them the meteorology letter, but for some reason or other the deal was fishy. Meteorology apparently had closed down or something on Feb. 1.

However, after lots of questions etc, they decided they could put me in the air corps either as a surveying computer, a draftsman, or a lathe operator. Then they told me to show the meteorology letter after I got to the training place. Anyway, they seemed to think I would get into it. The Air Corps, you know, is the best in the army. Then I met William Bohannon from New Jersey who had been going to college somewhere out here and was in the same kind of a mess. But it will turn out alright. Then we were issued complete equipment and is there ever a mess of it. We went to another building and were given three shots representing about 10 different vaccines. We came out of there feeling like a porcupine and smelling like a drugstore. Then we had chow again at 11:00 and sent home our civilian clothes. Later we were marched over to another part of the camp located over a hill. This is really a big outfit. At 4:00 we marched back for supper and now here we are. So this is the life of a buck private. Don't attempt to write me here. I may get shipping orders tomorrow. But I don't have the least idea where I will be shipped. The army is about 100% better after the first couple weeks are over. My arms are stiff from the shots but I'm feeling good. If you ever want me to get an emergency furlough go to the local Red Cross because it will save time rather than call me. Take care of yourselves.

After three days at the reception station the order came down to "Pack your barracks bags, you are shipping out this afternoon." Lyle was glad to be moving on. After only eight days in the army he was disgruntled. The regulations and regimentation had already made the personal freedom of civilian life nothing but fond memories. He noted that the younger fellows accepted the loss of individuality more readily than the others. Writing on a piece of outdated USO stationery inscribed with SEASON'S GREETINGS, he hastily informed his family:

26 FEBRUARY 1943 (FRIDAY). It is now 2:30 and at 3:00 I leave here—destination unknown. I have no regrets leaving here. I did not particularly enjoy my stay at this part of Fort L. I will go through Kansas City and might get an hour or two lay off. I ate chow twice at noon and got by with it. I had about two hours of sentinel duty last evening after a full day otherwise. The landscape is rolly here with solid ridges of trees. To the north can be seen the bright red brick buildings for officers quarters etc. In another direction over a hill is the reception center where I spent first couple days. In another direction is Leavenworth Penitentiary and then this old CCC camp here now used to hold soldiers until you get your shipping orders. The climate is too cloudy and biting chilly. I got pretty sore at the army yesterday but I'm over it now. It must be an awful pill for an older person. But the worst is over now and we'll be settling down. My serial number is 37474253. Always use it along with my name. Almost time to leave. I'll shoulder my 70 lb. barracks bag and go out to the street to be shipped.

A shrill whistle signaled it was time to *fall out* and get into formation in front of the barracks. Clad in regulation uniforms with clodhopper GI shoes, the men looked more or less alike. Already the green recruits were acting like soldiers—falling in line, responding to orders, and seeing themselves as part of the group. They marched to a bus station, rode to the Leavenworth train depot, boarded a troop train—and waited to move out, curious as to where they were going.

TROOP TRAIN

Clueless, the men speculated as to their destination. Posters inscribed with admonitions such as A SLIP OF THE LIP CAN SINK A SHIP did not slow the rumor mill. Lyle could take his pick of several guesses flying about the train:

"Looks like Alabama to me."

"No, I was told Texas."

"Well, I saw some orders stamped Fort Ord which is in California."

Knowing his mother and father had never journeyed outside of South Dakota, Lyle highlighted the sights to give them a vicarious travel experience.

Later.

We went by bus from Ft Leavenworth to Leavenworth where we boarded this fast sleeper special troop train. It soon got dark so the porter and us made up the beds. This is swell. I'm all eyes and ears and very thrilled. We have crossed the muddy Missouri and are headed east. Train just stopped. On our way again. This is apparently a car of Air Corps men. They are swell fellows I think. Air Corps is tops. Looks like Florida is where we are going. We may travel for a few days. We are headed east past a medium sized river. Guess I'll take my Lil Abner army shoes off. It is easy to see that this Kansas soil would blow. Seven oil wells by the track here.

We are along the Missouri R now? We are going south now. We are by oil refinery and a large railroad center. I guess it is Kansas City. Kansas City is big and smoky. Hope I can call Vernon. We are crossing a river bridge and I guess into K. City. Ozarks, here I come. We are under a trestle. John Deere plow Co. factory. Miles of smoke and railroad tracks and slums. Conductor says we ride for two weeks. He's bluffing.

The train progressed slowly as it chugged through the Kansas City area, making frequent stops on sidings. Lyle watched as other trains rumbled past in either direction. A crucial element in the war effort, freight and troop trains crisscrossed the country day and night as army transportation planners set priorities for trains competing for passage on the main lines.

Strangers at the start of the journey, the soldiers clustered together exchanging tales about their families and home states. Lyle enjoyed hearing firsthand accounts of lifestyles in other parts of the country. Even though the army had replaced the "Air Corps" moniker with "Air Forces" in 1941, he and his newfound friends still thought of themselves as being in the Army

Air Corps. After all, they were still singing the song with the Air Corps refrain at the end of each verse:

> Off we go into the wild blue yonder,
> Climbing high into the sun;
> Here they come zooming to meet our thunder,
> At 'em boys, Give 'er the gun! (Give 'er the gun now!)
> Down we dive, spouting our flame from under,
> Off with one helluva roar!
> We live in fame or go down in flame. Hey!
> Nothing'll stop the Army Air Corps!

The Air Corps patch and fancy uniforms worn by pilots had caught Lyle's eye—silver wings gleaming above a row of ribbons, three brass buttons above the belt buckle, a khaki tie knotted in regulation fashion and tucked into the front of the shirt. He liked the way pilots crushed and indented their visor caps, not according to regulation but in the *hot pilot* mode. Lyle surmised that the Air Corps, due to rapid expansion, would offer more training and travel opportunities than other branches of the service. Hopeful to see the world, he thought he was off to a good start. As the train resumed its passage, he continued:

> About an hour stop in K.C. but here we go again. We are heading south or east out of K.C. Met a nice kid my age from Missouri here who is going same place as I. He hunts squirrels etc. Mo. has lots of scattered trees. Apparently we are going to Florida, Texas, or Carolinas. It's exciting not to know. Boy, it is thrilling. I heard a rumor we are going to the best camp in U.S. Hope it is true. The army has its good and bad points. Glad I joined because I want to see the world. We are going south. Maybe it's Texas. We are on the last car on the train and a Pullman, hence, it looks like a couple days and Florida.

When conversation waned, card games and reading became the diversions of choice, until drowsiness set in and the intermittent lights from towns fading in and out lulled the men into fitful sleep.

Awakening Saturday morning, Lyle discovered that the train was passing through Arkansas, the state where some of his cousins lived. The countryside was as he had "always imagined with an occasional sawmill or fairly nice shack—pretty with the sun shining through the trees." When the troop train commander announced it was time for their car to go to breakfast the hungry soldiers made their way along the aisles to a dining car, an ordinary baggage car fitted out with a regular army stove. There, as

Kitchen Police (KP) dispensed chow, Lyle stood by the open door and took in the passing landscape.

Morning.

We are now in Arkansas. So this is Arkansas. Land of evergreen timber, hills, shacks, little saw mills, and now and then a little corn field. We got up and had a very delicious breakfast in a sort of diner. Scrambled eggs, bacon, bread, coffee, butter, jelly, and apple. In the meantime we were roaring past beautiful pines and sycamores on rolling hills. They had cases of eggs and crates of fruit. They told us we would eat this way all the time so maybe we go a long ways. I'm learning lots of geography. Homesick and going farther away. We are going south. I would like to camp in this wild country in summer. They fed this whole train of soldiers this morning. We'll have pork chops for dinner. Have seen no razorbacks yet. Sure wish I had a U.S. map now.

Red soil and rocks. Tree stumps where timber has been cut. We have our own silverware. Sun is coming up through timber. This is the life. Here is a spot like Black Hills but more gradual slopes. They left one carload in Fort Leonard Wood, Mo. last night I heard. Beautiful little pine seedlings. If I see Uncle Earl I'll wave. This is terribly interesting country. A few nice houses in the woods. Passed a nice oiled highway. It froze here last night evidently. This is a beautiful country. Five railroad tracks here. De Queen, Arkansas. A scattered town. 3004 people. We are on the last car of a 10 car train and are talking out of the window to a boy. We are going east to Texas and then at *least* to Louisiana. That's an inside tip. Here is a cotton field of all things. Less timber here. Can see Arkansas mules over there and oil storage tank 50 ft diameter. Some nice brick buildings here. Some open spaces. An Ark. girl wouldn't wave back. Here is a river in southern Ark. We are traveling S.E. toward Texas I guess. Winthrop, Ark. Allene, Ark. Wilton, Ark. A saw mill and big factory along road. Ashdown, Ark. Must be the Ark. river we just went over. An apple orchard here and some fairly large fields. An ugly red sand river that must of flooded terribly at one time. A green winter wheat field. Negroes plowing with mules. We'll probably travel for 3 or four days yet.

The soldiers gazed at the fleeting scenery through a haze of cigarette smoke and smudged windows. Shortly the piney woods of Arkansas gave way to the oil fields, swamps, and cypress trees of eastern Texas and western Louisiana. Later in the day cotton fields came into view, a strange sight for those from the Midwest who were accustomed to fields of corn and oats. In the third grade Lyle was fascinated when he read *Bunny Brown and His*

Sister Sue in the Sunny South by Laura Lee Hope, but he never expected to be in "the land of cotton."

> We are now in Texarcana, I think Texas. This is a lot of fun. We wave and talk to people and they wave back. More colored than white people. We are headed due south and some signs of oil country. Sharp red sandy formations. A green watered lake with pines in it. They think we'll hit New Orleans by midnight. Bloomburg, Texas. We are cutting through N.E. Texas and will soon hit Louisiana. This is above all expectations. North Rhodese, Ark.—land of oil wells. Now back in edge of Ark.
>
> Vivian, Louisiana. Oil City, La. A giant lake or river with an oil derrick out in it.
>
> Mooringsport, La. La. is a wilderness of swamps, sage grass, scattered with trees—no life. A huge lake swamp miles across.
>
> Shreveport, La. We ate chow here. Steaks, peaches, spuds, etc. La. is getting better scenery. Warm enough to have your head out window. We go south now until morning until we get to coast and New Orleans. Then I think to Florida. Now we're getting into prosperous La. and it sure is beautiful. Green grass—red soil. We are getting into wooded areas again. Talked to another meteorologist again in a car up ahead and we are going to try and put that deal over when we get where we are going. He is *really* smart. Write me when I send my new address or I'll get mad. We are still rolling fast south in La. These air corps men are much above average. A few cotton fields and millions of pine trees and seedlings. They have lots of dykes here to separate swamps from highway and fields.
>
> Have you heard from State College about my tuition reimbursement? Alexandria, La. 183 mi to N. Orleans.
>
> Almost sunset now and we must be near New Orleans. I think we go to Miami, Florida. That suits me fine.

Approaching Baton Rouge just as it was getting dark, the train lumbered up a grade to reach the level of the giant bridge spanning the Mississippi River. Lyle continued:

> In the distance the glittering lights of New Orleans surrounded by oil derricks and tanks. We are approaching the mighty Mississippi. We are on the bridge hundreds of ft above water. This is thrilling. More than a mile wide. My mistake, this is Baton Rouge, La.

Rolling on to New Orleans, the train was shunted to a railroad siding for a good portion of the night. By morning it was approaching Mobile,

Alabama, one of the coastal cities where workers fabricated ships twenty-four hours a day as the Allies strove to replace those sunk by *Unterseeboots,* German submarines known as *U-boats.*

Sunday morning.

We are rolling east in swampy Mississippi and I guess quite near the Gulf of Mexico. Orchards now. The chow was excellent. We have not been off the train. We are now in Alabama. Grand Bay, Ala. Red and Orange soil. Pines, fruit trees. Swamps of Pines. The Sgt. announced we travel today, tonight, and yet tomorrow. Next town is Mobile and we get 10 minutes off train. I'll write more later when we arrive at our destination. I'm feeling good and enjoying it immensely.

During a brief stop at Pensacola, Lyle grabbed two colorful postcards before the train continued east along the Gulf Coast to Jacksonville, Florida.

PICTURE POSTCARDS, PENSACOLA, FLORIDA, 1943

RECRUITS ARRIVING AT ART DECO HOTEL BARRACKS
MIAMI BEACH, 1943

NEW ARRIVALS SHOULDERING BARRACKS BAGS
MIAMI BEACH, 1943

CHAPTER 6

Art Deco Barracks and Bronzed Gods

Moon over Miami
Shine on as we begin
A dream or two that may come true
When the tide comes in.
—EDDY DUCHIN

THE TROOPS STIRRED TO LIFE as the train came to a halt under the station shelter at Jacksonville, Florida. Told they could debark but to stay in the vicinity, most, after seventy hours of confinement, relished another chance to stretch their legs and breathe fresh air.

When the conductor sang out "All aboa'd, all aboa'd," the soldiers dutifully scurried back to their seats. Soon the train began to move and a raucous cheer went up as it rolled south along the Atlantic seaboard.

The men settled into comfortable positions as the train gathered speed for the night run down the east coast of Florida. The air was balmy and the sweet scent of orange blossoms drifted in through the open windows. If only my parents could be here to enjoy this ride, Lyle thought.

At the Miami terminal the men, groggy and somewhat disoriented after several days' travel, shuffled off the train. It was well past midnight by the time they climbed aboard army trucks for the ride over the causeway to Miami Beach. The trucks pulled up to a hotel where the new arrivals were issued blankets and assigned to cots.

When he awoke in the morning Lyle could hardly believe his good fortune. He remembered seeing advertisements in *National Geographic* extolling Miami Beach—colorful layouts picturing a wonderland of palm trees, sandy beaches, and art deco hotels. Wow. Here he was at one of the leading winter resorts in the whole world. Eager to share his adventures, he mailed a postcard to Irene.

VICTOR HOTEL, MIAMI BEACH, 1943

LINCOLN ROAD, MIAMI BEACH, 1943
ARMY TRUCKS PARKED ALONG THE CURB

2 MARCH 1943 (TUESDAY). After a 3 day train ride and knowing very little about the future, we arrived here Mon. night at a Hotel in downtown Miami Beach. It is warm, sunshiny, and palm trees outside big bay windows. The chow was delicious and I'm feeling swell. 3 blocks from swimming beach. We won't have any free time for a while yet though. We are in the U.S. Army Air Corps. We have 5 days of processing. About a month of basic training here I guess. Write me cause I'm sort of lost for a while. I'd be homesick but I know it wouldn't do any good.

Shortly after the United States entered the war the army, at the urging of General Hap Arnold, leased several hundred hotels on Miami Beach, available because of the curtailment of leisure travel. Replying to critics, Undersecretary of War Robert Patterson remarked, "The best hotel room is none too good for the American soldier." The warm climate and open spaces made the area a desirable training site; over the course of the war a half million service people would pass through "the Beach."

The art deco hotels that served as barracks were of an architectural style that came into vogue in the 1920s. Characterized by geometric lines and pastel shades of stucco, they featured open lobbies and generous windows. Standing out in sharp contrast to the multi-hued hotels was a mess hall, a nondescript structure erected by the army on an empty lot. Perched on stilts above the sand and with exterior walls of unpainted plywood, the building looked sadly out of place. And the interior décor was nothing to write home about, just crude benches and tables fashioned from planks.

Writing on colorful red-white-and-blue stationery picturing a flag, Lyle expressed his delight at being "where summer spends the winter."

MIAMI BEACH, 1943

2 MARCH 1943 (TUESDAY). We arrived here at a swanky resort hotel at 3:00 a.m. and got up at 5:30 in the morning. We ate chow and wonder of wonders were allowed to rest all forenoon. Chow this noon was delicious, but I ate too much. Pk. chops, cake, fruit salad, small bananas, sweet potatoe, soup, tomatoe sauce, bread and jam, and ice cold nectar. It is very warm here and there is a little breeze. This is by far the prettiest city in U.S. Green lawns, flowers, Spanish style houses and small hotels, along with palm trees. The soldiers go marching along the streets singing all kinds of songs such as the one about the national colors flying over Berlin and Tokyo. The fellows are all deeply suntanned. They are a nice bunch I think. Guess I'm about as far from home as I could get. Saw groves of orange trees and grapefruit trees on way down here. I think I'll really like it here although at first it is new and strange and you don't know anyone. Did you get my cards and letter written on train? Let me know because they were sent free. I've been in 12 states now and still going strong. The Gov. sort of broke faith with me on the meteorology deal, but I'll still work on getting into it. Anyway, this might be just as good. Don't send me any food or anything cause I have more than plenty. But let me know how things are coming in the wide open spaces. Is it cool there and have you had any more snow? I came through the train trip in very good shape although some were pretty tired and sick. It's a heck of a long way down here. We followed the Atlantic coast through Jacksonville, St. Augustine, West Palm Beach etc. It doesn't seem possible to me that I am in Florida at the swankiest resort area in U.S. It won't be all sunshine either though. You can make sure of that. But I can take it if they let me have 8 hours sleep. I'm looking forward to a good time and hope you take it easy too.

Whenever the order came to fall out, the men raced down the stairs and assembled on the street in front of the hotel. They stood at attention until a noncom bellowed, "All present and accounted for, sir." That formality finished, the soldiers marched off to the mess hall or to a designated training site.

On day two Lyle scribbled a note to Irene describing life in a resort hotel.

3 MARCH 1943 (WEDNESDAY). We are confined to quarters in this third floor room in the Kenmore Hotel. There is an elevator but we are not allowed to use it so we run up and down the stairs many times each day when called out for formations. My five roommates are from Kansas and Missouri. Their names are Dunham, Vestal, Yokum, Pollock, and Peck. I am the youngest of the bunch and they make fun of me because

FALLING OUT FOR MAIL CALL, MIAMI BEACH, 1943

KENMORE HOTEL, MIAMI BEACH, 1943

I am from South Dakota. They think South Dakota is at the end of the world. We have orders to keep the door and all five windows open at all times so we have fresh air and ocean breezes. The bathtub is our laundry tub. We soak our fatigues in the tub and tramp out the dirt with our feet. At Fort Leavenworth there was a screwed up deal. But my classification test scores were high enough for the Air Corps so they sent me here.

Just two months earlier during a meeting at Casablanca, Allied leaders had decided to use B-17 Flying Fortresses for round-the-clock strategic bombing of Germany. Consequently, the Air Corps needed more tail gunners. Unlike one of his roommates, Billy Vestal, Lyle was too rangy to fit into the plastic bubble at the rear of the plane. Lucky for him—because B-17 bombers, lacking long-range fighter escort, were incurring heavy losses.

After exchanging information with two other trainees possessing meteorology letters, Lyle was hopeful of getting into the program.

4 MARCH 1943 (THURSDAY). It got much cooler last night and we almost froze with the windows open and only one blanket. It seems now that we will get into meteorology but we may have to wait quite some time for an opening. Chow was good this morning, and I ate a whole Florida Grapefruit. It tasted same as in South Dakota. At least when I'm done here they will have to ship me nearer home cause I'm about as far away as I can get now. I'm ready to come home anytime now so I hope the war ends soon. Hear we won another naval victory. When Sunday comes, maybe we will get some freedom. Some things about the army I hate such as making beds just so, getting up early, and hanging clothes etc. just so. Altogether it's going to be good experience and worth the chips. At first a person doesn't know anyone or his surroundings and then it seems pretty dreary especially when they tell you your every move. How is everything coming on the farm etc. You know it seems like a year since I left home. I've stayed now at 3 camps and in two places in the one camp. I'm too tall for an aerial gunner, and I'd rather stay on the ground anyway.

Later in the day, after performing well on additional classification tests administered by the Army Air Forces Technical Training Command (AAFTTC) at Miami Beach, Lyle expected a technical assignment related to mathematics—if he failed to get into the meteorology program.

Afternoon.
We had tests on math, mechanics, and telegraphy. The math was very simple. I'll have no trouble getting classified into something good

I hope. You can use this new abbreviated address until told otherwise. Yes, I think my stay here will be a lot of fun. I'll do my writing in the afternoon when I feel optimistic. In the morning when you get up tired it's different. Are there any pheasants left? I'm going to get a G.I. haircut—so it sticks up all over. We are furnished razor, toothbrush, socks, hankies, etc. In fact too much makes it tough to pack around.

Having limited access to newspapers, magazines, and radio broadcasts, Lyle mostly heard about war developments through the rumor mill. In his next letter he alluded to an important naval battle fought among the Bismarck Archipelago in the Pacific; the Allies had sunk four Japanese destroyers and eight transport ships. He also indicated the family farm was still the center of his world.

5 MARCH 1943 (FRIDAY). Dear Irene,
It is nice here and will be better in a couple days when we are no longer confined to quarters. Guess I'll go swimming and to a show soon as I get a chance. See where we won another naval battle from Japan. How do you like your apartment by now? We stay in a Hotel in the fashionable district of one of our most popular resorts in the U.S. I'm getting darker all the time and they say after 18 days we'll be in better condition than ever before. Regular hours of sleeping, eating, and exercise. Some of the Corporals, Pfcs, and Sgts. sure try to act tough. The food is good although it's not like eating at home. Hope I hear from civilization soon cause no letters since I left home on Feb. 18. The trip was very interesting. Kansas, Missouri, Arkansas, Texas, Louisiana, Mississippi, Alabama, and then Florida. There was one other too that I can't remember. We had lots of fun. At first a camp seems strange and they herd you around into barracks like cattle. Then you get homesick. I think the army will be good experience and lots of fun. U.S.O. etc are good, but lots of times people take advantage of soldiers. We have to keep our rooms spotless. Guess I don't know any news. Write me when you have time.

Army planners faced a daunting logistical challenge as they classified thousands of recruits from every corner of the nation and with diverse backgrounds. Nevertheless, Lyle and his two cohorts were channeled into meteorology as promised. The program was of such importance to the Air Corps that program directors had been given authority to overrule other assignments.

6 MARCH 1943 (SATURDAY). Just back from another shot. Pretty soon we will be all processed and pickled. Three of us here at camp

had meteorology letters and we were classified as Meteorology students yesterday. We will finish basic training here in about 20 days and then we should be shipped to a school. That is really the way the letter read too. When we had difficulty at Ft. L. one fellow wrote to "Weather." Today he got a letter back from headquarters with authority to overrule anything here in case we couldn't get in. According to the letter it seems we should have gotten basic training in Mississippi though. It's working out just like planned. Played bridge last night. It's a lot of fun and we won easily. We may be confined to the hotel yet tomorrow. Expect to hear from you by Monday but maybe letters take longer than that. What's happening around there lately? Next week we start drilling and caluthetics which will be more interesting. A band is marching by somewhere out in a street. The troops sing songs as they march to keep in step and it sounds nice. We still haven't seen much of the layout around here. Of course there are lots less socialites than other years. The coconuts are still quite green up in the Palm trees. Have you had any more snow or rain? We had a short fast rain the other day and got sort of wet. Would like to drop in on you for a while but it'll probably be at least 4 months. Take it easy and write me the news.

Letters were the primary link with family and friends back home. The army ritual known as *mail call* was the highlight of the day for soldiers living among strangers in a regimented army camp. Upon hearing the signal the men hurried outside and stood at attention. A noncom approaching with a bag of mail shouted, "At ease," and began hollering out names. When a GI heard his name called, his face lit up and he briskly stepped forward to grab his mail. It was a glum day for those who received none, especially those away from home for the first time.

7 MARCH 1943 (SUNDAY). We are still confined to quarters so all we did today was eat, sleep, sign for paychecks, and have mail call. The 3 or 4 fellows who got mail were certainly looked upon with envy. No one felt too good today on account of the vaccination. Played a little bridge again last night. It's more fun than any other card game that I know. It's breezy here today and nice and cool when out of the sun.

At the first opportunity, Lyle headed for the beach to see the wondrous ocean.

Monday.
We were allowed to leave this evening and hereafter and it sure feels good to know that you can leave if you want to. I went downtown and

bought some laundry soap, a washcloth, a glass of coconut milk, and a G.I. haircut. So now I washed my hair and put out some clothes to soak until morning. Went down to the ocean for the first time tonight. It's more vicious than I imagined. A funny greenish blue with really white caps. And of course there is an awful undertow wash back from the waves and tide. It's really quite a thrill to see the mighty Atlantic. You can't really see out very far, or else you can't judge distance. Anyway, it proves that the earth is round. Very little mail has reached this group yet from Missouri and Kansas where everyone but me is from. Soldiers like letters better than anything else except for a furlough. It's nice sleeping with cool ocean breezes blowing in. Heard it was below zero in Kansas City but it doesn't seem possible when it's hot here. We got $10 today as our first pay. Hope everything is O.K. over there and that you all take it easy. I'll be having lots of fun and exercise and experience. You know, a person really has to be in the money to live here a winter. Fruit is almost as high as home in stores because of high rent, salary, etc.

Social life at the Beach was nil. There was a scarcity of young civilians around town and the training regimen kept the soldiers on the run from early morning until evening chow, after which they mostly did laundry, wrote letters, and fell into bed. However, while marching in formation along the streets the soldiers whistled and hooted whenever they sighted young women, unless the noncom forbade it. More often than not, girls appreciated the interest of boys in uniform, or so the soldiers thought. Lyle recalled a saying he had heard: "Little boys like tin soldiers and little girls like rag dolls; but when they grow up, the girls like the soldiers and the boys like the dolls."

Still without mail, Lyle complained to Irene.

9 MARCH 1943 (TUESDAY). Dear Sis,
This is no fun writing letters since I left home and yet receiving none in return. But of course I realize it can't be helped. Now we can go out nites if we want to until 10:00. Today we saw some more training films, and had lectures. From now on we'll get plenty drilling, and caluthetics. The chow is good especially in the morning although I guess it'll soon get so it always tastes the same. Boy I could go for some home cooking. Last nite I had my hair cut off to about an inch or less long all over. It's thick and sort of lays down and sure feels swell. About 17 days more in Florida and away I go to new experiences. Yes, there are lots of personal pronouns but what else can I write about? Had a glass of cold coconut milk and it was good. Right by and above our window is a palm tree with green ones.

Wednesday.

Did a little laundry and I'll send the rest to a laundry. Instead of me asking questions, you just write and tell me about everything that's happening. I might accidentally get jerked out to meteorology before Monday. We have been here 8 days and still very few letters even from Kansas City have gone each way. That's how slow mail connections are down here to this isolated region. Guessed my weight last nite at 160 but it went to 166 so I didn't get my penny back, boo hoo. The food must agree with me at that rate. After a few days of caluthetics, it'll be about 130. We have to do lots of seemingly useless things to learn discipline and coordination but altogether it's O.K. I'm healthy, wealthy, and even feel fairly wise about joining.

On the cover of a pocket-size songbook compiled by the Operations and Training Section at Miami Beach, Lyle recorded the names of his barrack mates along with the names of hotels and streets. Several of the marching songs listed in the booklet had been sung by American doughboys while serving in World War I. Among Lyle's favorites were "A Grand Old Flag," "Working on the Railroad," and "The Caissons Go Rolling Along."

No.	Titles	Page
	TABLE OF CONTENTS	
1	Star Spangled Banner	5
2	God Bless America	5
3	Battle Hymn of the Republic	6
4	A Grand Old Flag	6
5	Pass the Ammunition	7
6	Spirit of the T.T.C.	8
7	The Army Air Corps Song	9
8	Working on the Railroad	10
9	Vive La Companie	11
10	British Flyers' Ballad	12
11	She Wore It For A Soldier	13
12	Oh! It Ain't Goin' to Rain	15
13	The Caissons Go Rolling Along	17
14	Over the Sea	18
15	Pack Up Your Troubles	18
16	K-K-K-Katy	19
17	The Marines' Hymn	19
18	Mech's of the Air Corps	20

POCKET-SIZE SONGBOOK, ARMY TRAINING COMMAND, 1943

Twice each day, while in formation along the palm-lined streets, the men sounded off the cadence—hup, two, three, four. As they marched back and forth between the hotels and the drill grounds at the Flamingo Park golf course, they belted out songs. The lively serenading was a boon to keeping in step, eased the boredom, and helped homesick boys forget their worries. As they proceeded down the avenues in the early morning hours the mischievous soldiers turned up the volume so as to awaken sleeping vacationers.

No sign of grass remained on the Flamingo fairways and greens. Thousands of GI shoes had trampled the surface into a fine powder that swirled with every breeze. As the tropical sun beat down mercilessly on the formations, trainees who made the mistake of locking their knees while standing at attention toppled over like so many tenpins. There were better moments, such as when the drill sergeant barked, "Take ten," the signal for soldiers who smoked to light up while the others just rested their weary feet. Perspiring in the hot sun, Lyle remarked to a buddy, "Would you believe that just three weeks ago I was tramping through snowdrifts hunting pheasant on our farm in South Dakota!"

When marching with rifles some of the rookies turned left when they should have turned right, resulting in the clashing of steel barrels and walnut gun stocks. Given time, the soldiers would learn to act as a unit, neatly interchanging ranks and files so their flight could pass through gates or along narrow roads. Lyle had no problem performing the maneuvers; ROTC training in college had primed him for close order drill.

9 MARCH 1943 (TUESDAY). Another day of drilling, lectures, and training films—and no letters. Is that 20 gauge doublebarrel still in Uncle John's store? Send me clippings about State College too. Drilling is easy after taking R.O.TC. We may have a bad day tomorrow so to bed I go.

The following day the trainees marched to the beach to begin the hardening-up process. Men versed in physical training directed the recruits through push-ups, sit-ups, and other exercise routines. Perched on platforms above the white sand, the muscular, suntanned instructors appeared to Lyle as bronzed gods.

Thursday evening.
Yesterday we had caluthetics for the first time. One fellow passed out on account of it was hot and fairly strenuous. It did not bother me nearly so much as most. Made me fairly mad today not to get a letter even from Vernon as close as Kansas City is. Most everybody from that

MORNING DRILL, MIAMI BEACH, 1943

BEACH ENTRANCE FOR CALISTHENICS, MIAMI BEACH, 1943

area have gotten letters from there. We had an easier day today but tomorrow will be rougher. It's early to bed for me again tonight. 5:30 every morning, but it's not bad when you get used to it. Most everybody has coughs and colds here due to change of climate or something. I'm a little bit sunburned on the back of my neck. Over to west of us is the larger city of Miami proper. I sleep on a Simmons innerspring as does one other fellow in the room. The rest have cots which really are just as good as far as I'm concerned. I like breakfast best. Slice French toast, Bacon, Milk, orange or half grapefruit, is a typical one. It's not to be compared to a home cooked meal by a long ways at least if you are homesick. Of course I don't know where the other Brule County boys were sent to. Andresen and Steckleberg didn't pass you know. I sure wouldn't trade places with them. There are two other fellows here who will be sent to the same place as I when we leave here, so I'll know someone when I get there. How is the hog crop? Get the corn shelled? Who goes to army next month?

Three weeks after leaving home and at his third army camp, Lyle heard the corporal call out, "Slay—deck." Ecstatic to receive a letter, Lyle cared not a whit how his name was pronounced. He eagerly stepped forward and grabbed his mail. That very same day, he replied to his sister who had written immediately upon receiving his address.

12 MARCH 1943 (FRIDAY). Dear Irene,
We arrived back to the hotel after a hard drill workout this morning at 11:30. The big event of the day was at hand—mail call. Everyone else in Flight D—now Flight L had gotten letters before because they live in Kansas or Missouri. So you see being it was my first army letter, it was no wonder my mouth flew open when the Corporal called my name. You certainly were thoughtful to get that letter off right away to a lonely soldier. Wonder of wonders, I also got an airmail letter from Dad containing duplicate letters from Meteorology. It hardly seemed possible at first to be in Miami Beach staying in a fashionable hotel which I cannot name.

Suddenly, Lyle's writing was interrupted by an order to black out the hotel windows to prevent city lights from silhouetting ships off the coast of Florida, making them easy targets for enemy submarines. In a six-month period German U-boats had sunk sixty-one ships off the East Coast, including two cargo ships torpedoed in full view of sunbathers on Virginia Beach. Before Lyle drew down the blinds, he saw anti-submarine balloons patrolling the sky and tanker ships on the horizon.

Had to lower the Venetians just now cause they want no lights reflected out to sea. Yes, we are about 4 blocks from the mighty Atlantic. It sure looks pretty and inviting on a hot day. I'm going swiming one of these days. As yet we have had no daylight time off for swiming. Does *swiming* have two m's? As far as we know we stay at this hotel until basic training is finished and we are shipped away. It's about two blocks from the mess hall. It certainly seemed strange to see brown skinned people, palm trees, and pretty hotels with flowers and lawns. The soil is sandy and can become very dry and dusty soon after a rain. You never know when there will be a downpour followed by a hot day. Send all the pictures you can. I have plenty of money, food, sleep, and exercise. As for exercise, this afternoon we drilled, had caluthetics, ran the obstacle course including hurdles, walls, etc, and did some cross country running. I'll have difficulty lifting my legs on the bed. All I need now is letters to keep me happy.

Compared to the depression-era meals served at the boardinghouse at 819 Eighth Street in Brookings, the food at the mess hall seemed lavish. A poster on the wall admonished soldiers to TAKE WHAT YOU CAN EAT / EAT WHAT YOU TAKE. For Lyle, the message was superfluous. Burning calories and growing rapidly, he packed in the food.

Irene, I really eat too much. For instance at breakfast I went through twice and ate—2 boiled eggs, 2 slices of toast, a box of cereal with milk, two helpings of bacon, and 3 oranges. Also went through dinner chow twice. No wonder I'm gaining, and it takes lots of energy each day. You hit the A.A.F.T.T.C. on the nose. B.T.C. is Basic Training Center, and Flt. D was our flight number that now is L. A flight is the same as company in army. Miami Beach does not have very high buildings but covers quite a little ground. Will tell you more about it after Sunday. Wish you could hop a plane and visit here. It's a very pretty place. But don't think it's a paradise. Sounds funny to hear of snow. Have no idea when we'll be sent but expect we might get shipped out of here before too long. Notice how definite that sentence is. You must be really having a swell time. Bet there is more entertainment etc. in a smaller training center than here. We are getting very dark and you won't be able to tell me from an Indian except my hair is lighter. We also have lectures each day. It's always, "Joe, get on the beam," or "double time, Mac," with the Corporals and Sgts. They always hurry you and then keep you waiting. The discipline is good for people though. You get up whether you want to or not, eat what they serve, and scrub floors along with everyone else. They'll certainly toughen us up with a few more days like this. Boy, will civilian life feel good again after the war. Guess I'll go to a show tomorrow night. In the meantime I'm enjoying each day as it comes and hope you do the same. Don't worry, I can take care of myself. R.O.T.C. comes in handy, as does the long hikes while hunting. Boy, there is nothing like hunting pheasants in S. Dak. Sure appreciate your letter—it really gave me a lift. Keep writing if you have time, and I'll be able to raise my 10 lb. shoes much more snappily—

The next day, following a strenuous workout on the beach, the instructor permitted the perspiring men to swim in the cool ocean water. Cognizant his cousin Tracy Sladek—the son of Uncle John and Aunt Blanche—had drowned in just a few feet of water in a stock dam, Lyle tenuously approached the waves.

When the signal came to fall into formation the swimmers lacked sufficient time to clean all the wet sand from their feet before pulling on their heavy leather shoes for the march back to the barracks.

That evening, in response to the first letter from home, Lyle replied:

13 MARCH 1943 (SATURDAY). Was sure glad to get your letter dad and hear from civilization again. How are the pigs coming along? We have now started doing caluthentics along with stiff drilling, and lectures. After getting all tired out from exercises, they had us run the obstacle course. Ordinarily it would be easy but everyone was on his last legs in the *hot* sun, so the wall, climbing a rope, and jumping hurdles were all we could do. But to top it off they made us run and walk some more around the golf course where we train. Today we did exercises on the beach and then went swimming in the Atlantic. It was really swell. Warm, salty, with a nice sand floor. The salt water tastes good—I know cause some waves washed over my head. I'm going in again tomorrow and as often as I can in order to lose fear of the water and learn to swim better. My legs are dead tonite, but we are all getting tougher. I can take it better than most. Sunday (tomorrow) we have it easy so I'll probably go to a show. Things are sky high here—grapefruit 3 for 19 and not so big as the 5¢ ones at home.

I had written to "Weather" before I got your letter to let them know my address and circumstances. Three of us are in the same deal. This meteorology program is not much known about by the army. We took and successfully passed weather observer tests before we were classified. Now that we have the new letters of different type, I believe we could have overruled them anyway. Seems that we most likely will be here until April 5 but the class starts March 15. We talked to several officers and they thought new classes start all the time and we might also get orders from "Weather" anytime. At least we are in but don't know when we start.

It's hard to get up in the morning. Some fellows failed to pass inspection this morning and will have to wash windows part of time tomorrow. We saw a small convoy go by today and a blimp also following the coastline. The Corporals, Sgts. etc act tough but they don't scare me. Did you get any pheasants before the season ended? You probably don't realize how hot it gets here during the day. We learn first aid, about rifles, chemicals, health, and marching. They are all really quite elementary. The fellows here always try to scare new recruits by telling of vaccinations with square needles, needles with hooks etc. In reality they run you through a line like cattle and you hardly know when they stick you. It makes you sick after some shots for a while. Maybe I'll write more in the morning but it's 8:30 and time for bed.

15 MARCH 1943 (MONDAY). Just back from the field and waiting for mail call and chow. Yesterday a fellow and I went swiming in the clear, salty Atlantic. A wave comes in and you swim right over it. I'll soon feel at home in the water. We had the best dinner yesterday since being in the army. Roast Pork with apple sauce, cake and ice cream etc.

Monday evening.

Back to our rooms after a long day which included two shots. Your arms sure get stiff about a minute after they stick you. We get up at 4:00 in the morning tomorrow for Kitchen Police (K.P.). We'll live through it. Got a letter from Irene today and one from V and V yesterday. Talk about a hot day—wow!

After days of physical training, guard duty, and close order drill, assignment to KP came as a welcome change of pace. Still, KP detail, frequently the subject of cartoons and complaints, could be exhausting. That Tuesday night Lyle fell into bed. When he awoke, he finished his letter before marching off to breakfast.

Wednesday morning.

We survived 17 hours of K.P. in a large hotel on the shores of Biscayne Bay where "Moon over Miami" was filmed. It's almost time for 6:30 chow. We have guard duty tonight. We didn't get mail yesterday, but heard there was a letter for me. Enclosed a picture of a typical home here. We have another rough day ahead, but at least we have recovered from those shots. That's all I have time for now. Write me the news.

Still recouping from the mega stint of potato peeling and pot scrubbing, Lyle's day, in addition to the usual training regimen and guard duty, included a retreat parade. He found the spectacle exhilarating. The squads, marching to martial music and exhibiting as much spit and polish as they could muster, passed in review before the commanding officer and his aides. Lyle recalled newsreel images of "goose-stepping" Nazis, soldiers who had honed marching to a high level of perfection. He began to understand how discipline and drill fostered esprit de corps. It was common lore that German boys took to soldiering more readily than American boys. Now a soldier himself, Lyle pondered whether the strict regimentation imposed on the German army by Hitler's professional officer corps was a strength or a weakness. In any event, he doubted the American public would accept such harsh treatment of a militia composed mainly of citizen soldiers.

RETREAT PARADE, PASSING IN REVIEW, MIAMI BEACH, 1943

At the end of the taxing day, Lyle summoned enough energy to do his laundry and write to Irene.

17 MARCH 1943 (WEDNESDAY). Yesterday we had K.P. duty. We got up at 20 to 4:00 in the morning and worked until past 8:00 at night. I was on the chow line which fed about 2200 men each meal. The rest of the time I worked in the Kitchen. We had lots of food including cake and ice cream. Boy were we tired when we got home. Today we had lectures, drilling, caluthentics, and running. Then we had a retreat parade. They are toughening us up pretty fast. Did I tell you we had 2 shots again Monday? Enough of the dark side of life. It really is not a bit bad though. We have very good eats all the time and I'm gaining weight. During the week we are too tired for entertainment. But Sunday, Oh Boy. There is nothing to compare with swiming in the salty Atlantic.

Warm and clear. I think your airmail took 3 days including here at the post office. I believe we are very fortunate to be stationed here. They try to teach us in 18 days what the infantry learns in 13 weeks, so they say. The Sgts. and Cpls. all yell around in disgusted tones but after the first week they don't scare you any. I put out a good sized washing tonite. Most things can't be sent to the laundry cause they can't be back in time. I doubt that Vernon would like the army. We'll have more time later on in training and we will not tire so quickly. Glad to hear you are having a good time. On Sunday you can see a palm tree, a girl in the shade of the tree, and all soldiers who can comfortably stand in the same shade. Saw the show "Casablanca" Sunday. It was pretty good and ended rather different. Some southern non-coms pronounce Burns as Boines etc and wonder why you don't understand.

Lyle recognized that army cooks, contending with regional differences in food tastes and preparation, had a thankless task. It was impossible to please everyone. While boys from Sioux Falls and San Diego did not relish grits for breakfast, boys from New Orleans and Charleston were not keen on oatmeal. Like other trainees, Lyle sometimes grumbled about getting up early, standing in line, and performing seemingly senseless tasks. Thus far, however, the travel and adventure outweighed the heavy-handed discipline and physical discomforts. Along with hard cash, the army was providing him with food, clothing, and shelter. Overall, he was finding army life easier than college life, when he had taken a heavy load of classes, worked on the side, and made do with bare necessities. Regarding the personal belongings he had left behind at college, he concurred with his mother:

19 MARCH 1943 (FRIDAY). Yes, I'll have to write to have my clothes sent home. Also to see about the tuition refund. Well, we had an easier day today and have completed 9 days of Basic. It is terribly dirty and dry here the last few days. The soil is sandy and the drill grounds are tramped on by thousands of feet. Anyway, clouds of dust roll by as you sweat. All day as I sweltered in the heat, I thought of the little salty pool so I'm going swimming now. Then to a park for boxing matches. We had a big retreat parade this afternoon. We are very suntanned and getting tougher. Lots of fellows are a little disgusted with army life. They think food should be cooked just as they like it, don't like so much work, hate to be bossed around. In other words, they would like to be babied. I'm sure glad I'm in cause I wouldn't be content anywhere else until the war is over.

Above all, the soldiers hated those nights when they were jolted out of sleep and had to fall out for a formation. Nighttime drills that cut into their meager rest, especially when used for disciplinary purposes, were *not* appreciated.

Saturday.

We have now completed 10 days of basic. We did calthentics on the beach and then swam. I can now swim in 4 or 5 ft. waves for a while. We signed the payroll tonite so we'll get some money this week. I put out quite a large washing just now. It's hot here every day. Always about 80 to 90 is my guess. That cold spell was before we arrived here. It has never gotten below about 60 that I know of. Last night at 1 o'clock we were awakened by 3 blasts of a whistle. We put on shoes, grabbed a blanket, and headed for the proper stairs. It turned out to be a fire drill. Last week we were terribly stiff and tired when we got up at our usual 5:30. It's tough to be tired and know you have a strenuous day ahead too. But now we are more caught up on sleep and get less tired during the day. We had Pk. chop for supper with sweet spuds. I'd get a dishonorable discharge if they knew how much I ate. I haven't weighed for over a week but will when I get a chance. School must be a lot of fun now for Chuckie and Wilma. We really had a full moon over Miami last night. I know quite a few in the draft list you sent. Glad I'm not in their shoes for the first 3 weeks. The new recruits always hear rumors about vaccinations with square needles and all that stuff. It really was fun and interesting though. Any new calves? How is the cane holding out? Did you ever get a B ration card?

Aware of wartime rationing, Lyle knew his mother sometimes substituted Karo syrup for sugar and made burnt-wheat powder to replace coffee. Of course there was no easy substitute for gasoline and tires. Thinking of the family car, he continued:

Fluid drive dodges are quite noticeable around here. Someday I'll go over to the city of Miami. It's early to bed for me again as usual. Most fellows don't feel too much like going out after a day like this. It's sure outrageous the price that these hotels rent for during the season which is just ending. We have some delicious breakfasts here—at least I think so. The fruit is hardly as good as at home, although maybe the army doesn't buy the very best.

Well, take it easy. I'm having a very good time here and enjoy the toughening up process. Oh, Oh. We have guard duty tomorrow nite for two hours.

Guard duty at Miami Beach had its hazards; after falling coconuts injured several soldiers the order came down to wear helmets while standing guard. Although the routine of two hours on (walking the post) and four hours off (resting) over a period of twenty-four hours was no hardship in the mild Miami climate, it disrupted sleep and was a lonely assignment that many loathed. When confronted by the officer of the day and told to recite general order number two the guard, having memorized all eleven general orders, was expected to flawlessly recite: "Sir, I will walk my post in a military manner, keeping always on the alert and observing everything that takes place within sight or hearing."

When training activities lightened up on Sunday, Lyle attended church services held at the band shell. Lack of time and transportation made it inconvenient to leave the base to go to civilian stores, but the nearby Post Exchange (PX) offered toothpaste, soap, sewing supplies, candy, writing paper, canned chocolate milk, insignia for uniforms, and other supplies. Lyle spent the latter part of the free day relaxing at the popular recreation pier for servicemen, as he indicated to Irene in a short note.

21 MARCH 1943 (SUNDAY). I have two hours of guard duty from 4 until 6 in the morning. I went to Protestant services in a park this morning and then had a very good dinner. This afternoon I swam for a while and laid around on the beach. That's really fun to swim the waves. Some waves are about 4 ft high and you can swim up over them or with them as they break. At least I got my mouth full of saltwater at times and a slight sunburn. I could ride the waves a short time if shipwrecked. Friday nite I saw 10 good boxing matches between soldiers from all over the U.S. An overflow crowd. I had a cup of ice cream at the P.X. tonight.

RECREATION PIER, MIAMI BEACH, 1943

Weighed myself in summer dress and got my penny back. 170 pounds of bone and skin and muscle. We now have 8 days of basic left here not counting Sunday. Everyone entering the air corps takes this training and then they send you to special schools.

After completing basic training at Miami Beach the soldiers moved on to specialized technical schools, such as aircraft mechanics, gunnery, radio, or meteorology. They filled vital roles in what was to become the largest and most formidable air force in the world.

In his next letter, Lyle thanked Irene for a gift that satisfied his curiosity about the geography of the United States.

23 MARCH 1943 (TUESDAY). Was sure glad to get your letter today and the map. Would have given a lot to have had a map on my way down here. We had a fairly easy day today. In the morning they took us in large trucks a few miles north along the coast to a rifle range. We fired .30 rifles at a target. 15 shots altogether. That rifle sure kicks if you don't have the sling tight. It was more to get us used to the gun than marksmanship. It got cool here for about the first time last night. This afternoon we drilled, had a lecture, and then went to the beach for exercises. We did not get a chance to swim as usual because the ocean was too rough.

We were just looking at the map and discovered that we are a long way from home. It must be a lot of fun in the apartment. Cook what and when you want and clean only when it needs cleaning. Here we clean the room every morning. I've been very fortunate not to get special detail work for not passing inspections etc. Usually several scrub the lobby every night. Some fellows including a big red head sure get into trouble even it they try to stay out of it.

Just took time out to polish a couple pair of shoes. These G.I. shoes are terribly heavy but they don't blister your feet. I stood guard yesterday morning for two hours. So getting up at 3:00 this morning made it a long day. We really are very fortunate even if the field is terribly sandy dusty. The meals sure taste good to me and we have all we want. It got down to 64 F and everyone was froze up all day. That's a fact—it's usually at least 80 during the night. Where did you say that Sgt. is from? We sing such songs as hang all Sgts. to a sour apple tree, and throw all Cpls. to the bottom of the sea. A fellow had his eye exam for army and he pretended he couldn't see the sight card. He went to a movie and found himself sitting next to the Doc. He said, "Pardon me, is this the bus to Chicago?" Keep those letters coming.

The few civilians encountered by the soldiers, whether in town or at the beach, were mainly retirees from the New England states who had come to escape the cold winter months in the north. Their attire and city ways seemed strange, almost foreign, to those who had grown up among country folk in the Midwest. Remembering snowstorms at home, Lyle appreciated waking up to warm winter days.

23 MARCH 1943 (TUESDAY). We shot the rifles on the range this morning and I can put them in pretty good. Those guns are really vicious. We had our last vaccination for a while yesterday. Saw a cartoon of a soldier being shot in several different places at once. That's the way it was at Ft. Leavenworth. I did not enjoy my stay at Ft. L., Kansas. My legs are tired again tonight. We played touch football after caluthentics. I now weigh 173 in summer dress. Hope they lay off on us this weekend so I can go to Miami or something. I would hate to leave Florida without seeing more of it. Met another Meteorologist today. There are four of us here that I know of. Where did you plant wheat? How much cane is left? You often hear the expression here, "I'll be glad to get back to the U.S." The city is mostly foreign element. It's nice to get up every morning with the temperature at about 70°. But boy when the Sun beats down during the day. We now have gas masks.

Aware poison gas might be used by the enemy, the army provided training in the use of gas masks. While drilling on the dusty grounds and ordered to don the masks, each trainee pulled the rubberized appliance down over his perspiring face and labored to breath through the protective canister.

The next morning, Lyle awoke with thoughts of life back home on the farm.

24 MARCH 1943 (WEDNESDAY). We are starting our 13th day of basic. The ocean was too rough for swimming yesterday. How are the pigs doing and are you going to shell corn soon?

Evening.

Got your Saturday letter this evening. You do right well on the letters cause I know it isn't so easy to write out there. Or has the mailman been going 5 minutes later than usual. We had a real workout again today including the obstacle course. In fact the bed always looks too good to want to go to a show or anything nights. We almost had a minor revolution at noon waiting in the chow line. There was an argument as to which flight was to go in first. Nothing happened though and we went in first.

25 MARCH 1943 (THURSDAY). Dear Irene,
Might as well start answering your letter now. We had big steaks for supper and as long as we were the last being served, we got seconds also. We had caluthenics on the beach but the weather and water conditions prevented any swimming. Guess I'll go down to the beach now though for about an hour. I was paid $20 today so money is no object for a few days. We have completed our 14th day of basic so we are getting near the end. Of course some of us might not leave for a long time. They can leave me here a while if they want to.

I went down to the beach but the water was rough and there was no one else there so I didn't go in. We sure sleep with 5 windows and a door open. The air blows through in several directions cause this is a corner apartment. Six of us in a room, small adjoining room, and adjoining bath. Plumb full of cots and shoes. One of the fellows name is Yokum so we call him Lil Abner. He and another fellow are going to eat a jar of olives tonite. 4 of us are young (19) and 2 are married and quite young. We have to dust the venetians before Saturday as well as clean the rest of the room every morning. There is a group singing a popular song in the other wing, "You are my Sunshine."

ART DECO HOTEL ROOM, MIAMI BEACH, 1943
DUSTING VENETIAN BLINDS, FLOOR, AND BEDSRPINGS

Almost everyone knew the leading songs aired on the *Hit Parade*. Whenever someone banged out a tune on the piano others, perhaps thinking of sweethearts in distant towns, gathered around and broke into song. Extolling the advantages of an intimate social setting, Lyle continued:

You must have good recreation facilities in Watertown, Irene. Better than in a large place like this. You probably don't realize how big an outfit this is at this base. This weekend maybe we'll have more pep nights and get out more. I actually hear from home quite often. When I was home Mom and Dad tried to write to you for about a week. Finally Mom said she must write but Dad told her to wait until the next day so he could copy his letter over. The next morning we missed the mailman and the next day it stormed. It was nip and tuck but we made it the next day. It's really quite a struggle at home when it comes to letter writing. I sure had fun at home before I left. Nothing like pheasant hunting. Pretty nice to sleep late and do as you please at home. Suppose you know we bought a steel grain bin from Uncle John. We are starting to get scattered all over the country but someday we'll have a big reunion, won't we?

26 MARCH 1943 (FRIDAY). Well, we completed our 15th day of basic. It was a dusty tiresome day and tonight our flight drew guard duty. They started at the first of the alphabet and ended with R so I escaped by the skin of my teeth. Very fortunate indeed cause my feet hurt for the first time. I was paid $20 yesterday so I'll send some more home. About 8 from our flight of 100 or more got shipping orders this morning. We'll be leaving pretty soon, at least most of us. We just put some clothes in the tub to soak and pretty soon we'll tramp them. I have hopes that sometime before I leave here I'll feel ambitious and see some shows etc. There are boxing matches in the park tonight. As it is the bed is altogether too inviting. Every morning it's 5:15 and if you are sleepy you hate to start another day of training. What I wouldn't give to sleep until 7 some morning. It must be fairly warm up there most of the time now isn't it? Have the ponds filled up yet or hasn't the snow melted? Did the land deal ever go through?

Back home, Charles had submitted an offer to purchase a tract of land adjoining the farm. He recognized it was a good time to buy land that banks and insurance companies had foreclosed on during the dust bowl years. With climatic conditions improving, the once barren soil was again capable of producing grass for the herd of cattle.

Continuing his letter, Lyle attributed respiratory ailments to temperature changes. At some point during basic training many recruits fell ill and were hospitalized, perhaps because thousands of men from all over the States congregated in close quarters. Along with prematurely boasting of good health, Lyle mentioned defense activity along the seacoast.

> One thing about Florida climate is that about every 3rd morning everyone wakes up with a cold although it sort of goes away soon. We had gas mask drill this morning. The field is terribly sandy dusty. Thousands of marching feet and no rain for a couple weeks. Well, I've been in the army over a month already and still going strong. I haven't been on sick call once yet and most everybody else has. Wish you could take my place here for a while. Every couple days a Blimp goes along the coast on patrol. Also lots of planes diving around. Guess I'll write more later in the week. Can't think of any news just now.
>
> Enclosure $10. Too much to have around here. No use buying anything here, cause it's high and just makes more stuff to drag around when we ship.

Remembering Vernon had earned a dollar a day shocking grain for a neighbor, Lyle's army pay seemed big to him. Except for haircuts and incidentals he had no particular expenses, and he knew better than to lose his money playing poker or craps with city slickers. Having no place to keep cash, he frequently sent the excess home. Saturday night, however, he wandered downtown and spent some of his loot.

27 MARCH 1943 (SATURDAY). Dear Irene,
This morning we went to the field with raincoats and at 9:00 it started to rain. A real tropical rain that filled the streets to the sidewalks. We came back to the hotel, changed clothes and had a lecture. This afternoon we went to the beach and really had a workout. Guess I'll go downtown for a while and maybe to the show. We also practiced artificial respiration on the beach. Our flight is being slowly shipped out. I imagine practically all of us will leave by next Sat. Seems to me I'll go either west or north, doesn't it?
Sunday.
I'll enclose some typical snapshots that I bought at a drugstore. Went to the show "The Crystal Ball" last night. It was really pretty good. We had cakes, bacon, oranges, cream of wheat, milk, and jam for chow. We also drew guard duty again tonight.
Back from Protestant services at the bandshell. You might send a couple of those pictures home. They are of course the brighter side. For instance the one with new arrivals. We arrived at midnight tired, carried our barracks bags a few blocks, stood around until two o'clock, were

issued a blanket, and were able to sleep until 5 o'clock. We also crossed the causeway at night but maybe I'll get to see more on the way out. What are you doing today? Hope they leave me here at least another week cause it's swell now that it has rained and settled the dust. I'm all caught up on laundry for once. Don't mind my writing—we write on the bed cause there are no tables and only 2 chairs for 6 of us. Guess I don't know anything to write about.

Having gained more than ten pounds in the five weeks since waving good-bye to his family at Chamberlain, Lyle was now considerably heavier than the average GI. To his mother, he proudly reported:

28 MARCH 1943 (SUNDAY). I weighed 171 last night with summer dress. That is not fat either. Had a delicious breakfast this morning, went to Protestant services, watched a softball game and here I am. Expect to go swimming this afternoon, see a baseball game, and report back here for guard duty tonight. Hope I get an early shift. Wish I was home for a while—but I've always wanted to come to Florida and I might as well be this far away as in Brookings. It's a swell day here. If you don't hear from me for a while, I'm on shipment.

ADVANCED BASIC TRAINING

Some soldiers completed basic training before other Air Corps commands were ready to accommodate them for specialized training. Not wanting the men to be idle, the army shuffled them into advanced basic training—just more of the same with a fancier name. Lyle found himself in that circumstance as he waited for the next meteorology class to begin. His buddy Billy Vestal was also put on hold.

1 APRIL 1943 (THURSDAY). We ran smack into a week of guard duty and detail work. I scrubbed floors yesterday evening and had guard duty the night before. We have finished basic and have started advanced training. Yesterday we had caluthentics, ran over to the obstacle course, ran the obstacle course, and played volleyball. Heard from "Weather" and they said all who missed the March 15 class would be taken in the May 17 class. Looks as though I get to stay here for quite a while yet. "Lil Abner" Yokum got shipping orders today.

Interrupted, but not easily dissuaded, Lyle signed off:

They just came in and caught us writing letters instead of cleaning the room, but I'm going to write anyway. Write and tell me how things are coming. I'll write to State College again about that R.O.T.C. uniform reimbursement.

The next day Lyle was surprised to learn his father had traveled to the western part of South Dakota to see Mount Rushmore and other attractions in the scenic Black Hills. Because of the unrelenting farmwork, Charles, like other Brule County farmers, seldom traveled more than a few miles from home. Several years earlier Emma had gone to "the Hills" while Charles tended the farm. Under Emma's supervision, eleven-year-old Wilma and eight-year-old Chuckie were able to handle the chores for a few days. Tired and not feeling well, Lyle responded in a muddled letter.

2 APRIL 1943 (FRIDAY). Boy, oh boy! What a newsy letter. So Dad finally got jarred loose. He probably thinks he is a terrific distance from home. Show him a map and then he'll realize how far I am. It makes me homesick—the calves, grass, and spring in general. School must be really interesting for Wilma and Chuckie. I feel better today cause we haven't had guard duty for two nights. Is Kenneth Lunn in the Air Corps? He sure is seeing the country. How can you handle the chores? The weather has been damp and much nicer. The temperature is not so terribly hot—but the sun is directly overhead and at least as hot as July at home. It sunburns you much easier here than at home. Both Jean and Vernon wrote me a letter. My roommates and I are having an awful argument about land values over the U.S. and it really gets heated. Did you have a sick cow and calf? We had a retreat parade this afternoon. Somehow the terrific heat this afternoon caused me to lose my appetite. It's hard to believe that Dad went to the Black Hills. They are really prettier than any scenery I have seen although Arkansas was very nice. My nose has peeled a little. Did you know that coconuts have a green inch thick husk on the outside? You peel that off and get to the hard shell like they are in stores. Apparently they will leave me here until May.

Out of energy, Lyle stretched out on his bed and wrote a note to Irene.

2 APRIL 1943 (FRIDAY). It was awful hot when the sun beat down today. Been having a hard time getting enough sleep lately. We are working on a crossword puzzle. We have had guard duty and details lately. We have completed 3 days of advanced training. Tuesday we fired 17 rounds from a Sub-machine gun. Did you hear that Vernon got a deferment? I doubt he would like the army as well as I do. What have you been doing for entertainment lately? We have a crossword puzzle genius in our bunch. Don't mind my writing. I'm tired and laying on my bed. My brain doesn't function much tonight. Guess I'll quit and write

some more letters Sunday if we don't have K.P. I want to swim some more before I leave here.

6 APRIL 1943 (TUESDAY). Sat. we had our regular field day including exercise and swimming at the Beach. We then went on K.P. at 6:00 in the evening and worked until 7:00 Sunday morning. There were 3 of us K.P.s at that mess hall and we cut up the morning's bacon and snapped 6 bushel of tightly packed string beans. So you see it was a snappy job! We had cake, bananas, milk, etc to eat. Slept off and on Sunday and got up for evening chow. They got us up at 3:30 the next morning (yesterday) and we worked K.P. in another mess hall until 7:30 last night. And of course they got us up at 5:00 again this morning as usual. My morale is low when we don't get enough sleep. Maybe we will have it easier for a couple days now. I have a little cold and cough and I'll get some vapor rub if I get up ambition to go downtown. Heard from Irene yesterday. She seems to be having a good time. There were lots of happy fellows to get shipped out of this place. About 2/3 of our flight has shipped out now. The rest are anxious to leave except me. They would rather get nearer home, the grass looks greener over there, and we've been too busy to do anything here. Weighed 186 on the mess hall scale but it must weigh at least 10 lb. too heavy. Almost time for morning chow. Bye.

The following day Lyle felt unusually fatigued. Continuing his letter, he informed his parents he had elected to allot a portion of his pay for the purchase of war bonds, a commitment encouraged by the government since it helped finance war expenditures and decreased the competition for scarce consumer goods.

Wednesday.
There will be some bonds sent home from time to time. Another Sunday is very welcome after a strenuous week. We had steaks last night.
Did you get the 10, 6, and 5 dollar letters? We have finished 3 days of advanced now. Guess I'll hit the hay cause I'm sure tired. We should wash windows tonight but we might skip it. I'll enclose $5 cause I just signed the payroll again. Glad to hear that Vernon is sitting pretty.

Since Vernon was working at an aircraft plant, an occupation deemed vital to the nation's security, the draft board had granted him a temporary deferment.

In his next letter Lyle complained to Irene of sleep deprivation and the dearth of social opportunities.

6 APRIL 1943 (TUESDAY). Your letter last night was most welcome. Yes, we can go downtown practically every night and Sunday but—with a schedule like this we are seldom able to walk that far after hours. For instance we had regular drill, exercise, and swimming at the Beach Saturday. We went on K.P. that evening at 6:00 and worked until 7:00 the next morning. We staggered home and those of us who didn't get shipping orders went to bed. I slept off and on Sunday until evening chow and went to bed again immediately after chow. We were awakened at 3:30 a.m. for day K.P. Well we worked until 7:00 in the evening and of course they got us up at 5:00 again as usual. We had drill this morning, and after drill this afternoon we have our first shot. Guess it hits you pretty hard at first. Tomorrow we go out to the Rifle range again which I like. There are no regular recreation halls.

Wednesday morning.

We go to the rifle range in a few minutes. That shot yesterday was bad for a few minutes. Guess it is about the last one we get. I was plenty sleepy this morning. Weighed 173 pounds in summer dress last night. They say you always gain 10 lb. the first week. Two lb. from shots and 8 lb. from shoes. We had no more shipping orders this morning. Hope they don't move me to a different hotel. This sort of seems like home to me now. We have to take raincoats this morning. Most of the fellows are looking forward to getting back in the U.S. again. There is a lot of foreign element here and we hear a lot of jabber. Hope to have some time this weekend to see a show or something. This is a good place to be if you have any spare time. This is about the most expensive place for a soldier to be stationed.

To Lyle and his buddies, the prices seemed excessive at Miami Beach, a community that catered to wealthy New England vacationers. The presence of civilians lolling on the streets, in the shops, and on the beach affronted the men in uniform who had relatives working long hours in factories and on farms.

Three days later Lyle was pleased to get a letter and a copy of his hometown newspaper, the *Chamberlain Register*, forwarded by his mother. Apropos to his father's trip to the Black Hills, he commented:

9 APRIL 1943 (FRIDAY). The highest elevation on Miami Beach is 22 ft. You see this is really a large built up island or something. Glad to hear it rained there even though you didn't say how much. We have moved again to another hotel. This time it is the swanky 415 Training Group headquarters. Vacuum cleaners for the carpets and even a writing desk. Two roommates are from N.Y. State and the other from

Missouri. We haven't had K.P. for two days so we are lucky. We are half through advanced. The ocean was very warm and rough yesterday. We had another retreat parade this afternoon. Tell me when you get my college clothes and if they were sent collect or not. I think they will send tuition refund soon too. I'm feeling very healthy all the time and getting tougher. Seems like I have to go to bed early every night though in order to get enough sleep. I sure do enjoy the Register and clippings. Keep the letters coming.

Just two days after assuring his mother of his good health, Lyle grumbled:

11 APRIL 1943 (SUNDAY). I lost weight last week. Now weigh 172 lb. My appetite and the food have gone down hill. Hope they ship me a long way north. I'm tired of standing in line in the burning sun. We stand in line for chow, for a drink, for mail call, shots, to go to a show, for payroll, and every other imaginable thing. Those 15 hour K.P. days of scrubbing floors, washing dozens of greasy pots and pans etc. is not much fun. But by driving us K.P.s they are able to keep those mess halls unbelievably clean. The army is an awful pill for fellows who are used to having their own way and just what they want to eat etc. I'm in very good humor this morning because they let us sleep until 6:20. It's nice and cool for a change. Yesterday we sweated in the morning, during the day, and even in the evening. Had my hair cut last night and it's less than 1/2 inch long in the longest places. There are two of us in this new hotel room. Our other roommate shipped out. We certainly ran into a mess last week. Plumb full of K.P. and other corruption. We had a blackout and gas mask drill Fri. night so that cut down on our sleep too. Have you sold any horses or anything?

Sure enjoyed reading the Chamberlain Register. Why was Uncle Mike in the hospital? How much are you farming and where are you planting what? It's pretty nice for me to have the whole day off. $21 enclosed.

Feeling rundown, losing weight, and fed up at forever standing in line in the hot sun, Lyle indicated to Irene he was eager to ship out to a cooler locale.

11 APRIL 1943 (SUNDAY). After a very rugged week of K.P. and other things, we hit the jackpot and got the day off. Our flight was once a proud ornry army of 100+ but now by morning we will be about 15 strong. I suppose pretty soon there will be 4 or 5 instructors for us three meteorologists who will be here for about a month yet. It has been much

too hot for comfort lately. I scurried for the beach where I had a fine time sunning and swimming. I have lost most of my fear for water now. Pretty nice to have a day off in the playground of the millionaires. The sun shines much more brightly here than it ever does in S. Dak. This is a nice little room with closet and private bath. Easy to clean too. It's always nice to think of being shipped and seeing more of the country. Hope it is New England or Great lakes. I don't like such a hot climate. Chow.

Two Hollywood productions released in 1939, *The Wizard of Oz* and *Gone With the Wind*, were instrumental in defining the golden age of movies. Lured by film idols and seeking diversion from war tensions, some ninety million Americans, a number exceeding half the population of the country, went to the box office each week.

For Lyle, as with many moviegoers, the preliminary cartoons and newsreels were as much of an attraction on the silver screen as the main feature. In one memorable scene a jubilant Hitler could be seen dancing on the street following the June 1940 signing of surrender documents in Compiègne, France. It was revealed later that Allied propagandists had doctored film footage of Hitler stepping backwards to make it appear as though he were dancing a silly jig. Once the United States entered the war, however, developments favorable to the Allied cause dominated the twice-weekly newsreels.

As with many wartime films, *Hitler's Children* promoted public support of the war effort. The movie pictured Nazis as evil fanatics, obsessed with burning books in public bonfires and brainwashing German youth into reporting their parents for espousing anti-Nazi views. After seeing the show, Lyle became more concerned about the German threat to the democratic nations.

Even though Lyle had no knowledge of atrocities committed by the Nazi regime, his feelings about Germany were more negative than his feelings about Japan, a minority view; a 1943 survey indicated that the majority of Americans viewed Japan as the chief enemy.

Whether soldier or civilian, citizens were seldom privy to the overall war strategy of the Allies. Wartime news was limited and sometimes slanted. Good news was exploited and bad news suppressed. Generally, the American people just put in their best efforts and trusted their leaders. In unity with his companions, Lyle soldiered on.

Just got back from the show "Hitler's Children." Irene, it certainly makes one realize what we're fighting for. Heard that we have detail work tomorrow. It's hot in the room tonight. Luckily I sleep by an open double window. It would feel good to get real cold again. Hope I get a letter tomorrow. Are you going to send me some snapshots sometime?

Wish I had a 3 month furlough now. Don't we all. Billy Vestal leaves at 5:00 in the morning. Guess I'll get me another roommate.

Writing on stationery depicting the standard army insignia, the crested emblem found on the fronts of army visor caps, Lyle expressed his readiness to move on to a meteorology school for some mental stimulation.

U. S. ARMY

14 APRIL 1943 (WEDNESDAY). We were rudely awakened at 4:00 this morning and told we had K.P. The address was wrong so we marched a mile or two extra before we got to the correct mess hall. We worked fairly hard all day and got through a little before 8:00 tonite. We always have all we want of the best of food when on K.P. Took a warm bath and did my laundry so I'm all done for today. Had an agreeable surprise of 4 letters yesterday. Irene sent 4 snapshots. Also heard from Royce Bates. He was one of the roomers my freshman year. Guess I'm in the best physical condition ever, at least I can climb ropes easily. I have learned a good deal about floating and swimming also. You may have to send me a few dollars at times because pay is very uncertain and it doesn't pay to keep much money around. Did you truck the two hogs to Sioux Falls? Did you ever shell corn? Have you lost any calves? Almost time for lights out which is 9 o'clock. It will be nice to get to school again if the deal comes through as it is supposed to. Hope I can get in on a harvest furlough.

In the morning, having heard about epidemics breaking out in army camps, Lyle dutifully swallowed prescribed medicine before finishing his letter and marching off for mess.

Thursday.
They caught me with lights out last night. It's very cool and breezy for a change this morning. We took a couple more pills for spinal-meningitis again this morning. The room is all cleaned and we are waiting for chow. This will be our tenth day of advanced training on the drill field.

Saturday evening, feeling a need for relaxation after another week of training, Lyle went to the post theater to see *The Moon is Down*. Based on a propagandist novel by John Steinbeck, the movie depicted life in a Norwegian town occupied by Nazi troops.

Lyle was somewhat aware of the variety of roles played by the Scandinavian countries in the war. Following the conquest of Poland in April 1940, Hitler ordered German armed forces to occupy Denmark and Norway, a bold move designed to prevent British encroachment on Scandinavia and the Baltic.

The German attack on Denmark, accompanied with the promise that political independence would be respected if the country offered no resistance, lasted just a few hours.

Norwegian patriots fought to repel the surprise invasion of their country but were handicapped by a Quisling-led government sympathetic to Germany. Nazi troops quickly occupied Norway and imposed their rule on the populace.

When the war broke out in 1939, Finland declared neutrality. But after refusing to meet territorial demands it was attacked by Russia and forced to concede ten percent of its territory. In 1941, when Germany attacked Russia, Finland declared war on Russia in hopes of recovering its prior loss. Ironically, six months later Great Britain declared war on Finland.

Sweden, zealously protecting its neutral status, refused to allow England and France to transport troops across its borders or on its railways, yet permitted Germany to do so.

The Moon is Down reinforced Lyle's view that German soldiers were akin to robots, devoid of emotion, and that Germany was a ruthless foe. Thoughts of the movie lingered on his mind.

I 8 APRIL 1943 (SUNDAY). My luck runs in streaks. Received no mail for a couple of days and then got 2 letters and the Register today. Vernon sent snapshots. He now works outside. We had a really good breakfast and dinner today. Went to services in the park this morning. Then I took about an hours nap. Last night I saw the show, "The Moon is Down." It was a story of German occupation of Norway and the underground movements that followed. I really enjoyed it. Now I'm waiting for a while after dinner to go to the Beach with another Meteorologist who is just as short as I am tall. He's sure a nice fellow. One of my roommates at the last couple hotels is the meteorology student I ran across at Leavenworth. The weather has been swell the past week. Aren't we lucky to get our Basic training here especially now that shots etc are over with. I enjoy the Physical Training program very much. Yesterday we ran the obstacle course twice. Then a couple of us went over the board wall 4 times more for practice. I tore a shoulder muscle just a little. It's a little sore but no damage done. The wall is of very smooth boards about 9 ft tall and in loose sand.

Monday.

I sure swallowed up the Register. It doesn't seem possible that so much water could ever go down the Missouri valley so deep. I'll bet they need those dykes on the Miss. in Louisiana now too. People must be awfully enthused about chicken raising. I assure you, Wilma, tramping these fatigue clothes—

Quite abruptly, Lyle put down his pen; in the morning he went on sick call. At the infirmary a medic listened to his breathing with a stethoscope and found congestion in his lungs. After two months in the army Lyle found himself at a base hospital, a converted hotel. Fortunately, respiratory diseases were treatable with recently discovered sulfa drugs.

Two days later, except for unsavory soup, Lyle had no particular complaints about his hospital stay. For lack of stationery, he wrote home on the back of a hospital memo that read:

N O T I C E

TO: All Patients, Station Hospital, Miami Beach Training Base.

1.   The Inspector General, 5th District, AAFTTC, will make his annual formal inspection of the Station Hospital, Miami Beach Training Base on Friday, April 23, 1943. All patients who are in the hospital as of that date have blanket permission without reference to any Medical Department enlisted man, member of the Army Nurse Corps, Ward Officer, etc., to register any complaint they may have with Inspector General on that date.

2.   The procedure for registering complaints to the Inspector General will be as follows:

> Bed Patients – Patient concerned should notify the Ward nurse that he desires to see the Inspector General. The Inspector General will then visit the patient sometime during the day.

> Ambulatory Patients – Room No. _____, Floor No. _____, _____ Hospital, will be set aside from 1 P.M. through the afternoon for the exclusive use of the Inspector General for interviewing any patient who desires to register a complaint. All patients who so desire to be interviewed should go to room No. ____ at 1 P.M., Friday, April 23, 1943.

W. F. HALL,
Colonel, Medical Corps,
Surgeon.

22 APRIL 1943 (THURSDAY). It has been a very dull day for me. You see, I'm in an army hospital. I have had a chest cold for some time and Monday night I got a fever. Went on sick call the next morning and they decided at the dispensary to send me to the hospital. Arrived over here about noon. They took blood samples and the first couple times they sort of missed the vein so they stuck me 3 times with a dull needle before they got some. Small matter though cause this is the army. Finally got to the hospital about 2:30 and they X-rayed my chest. By that time they had taken my temperature several times too. So I finally arrived at the hospital feeling considerably worse than when I started. You must never be in a hurry in the army or you'll always be het up. They say I have or had a touch of pneumonia. At first my diet was lots of pills and little food. The soup looked like tea but was saltier. It's nice here only tiresome. I think they'll let me out pretty quick. Maybe I did the right thing to go on sick call cause it might have gotten worse instead of better. If I meet up with the mess Sgt. after the war who is responsible for this soup, I'll try and put him in a hospital. Two months since I was sworn in. Sometimes it seems like two years and sometimes like two weeks. Maybe I'll start getting mail again tomorrow. They had me sign the payroll tonight. Guess I'll work on a crossword puzzle. Most of the nurses here are Lieutenants. My suntan won't last this way. In fact most of it has already reddened the sheets. My pet peeve is soldiers who complain about the food at the table. The army doesn't care if they like it, the other soldiers don't care, and I don't care so why don't they dry up? One of the two fellows in this room had pneumonia plenty bad but he's recovered now.

Friday.

With a borrowed pencil and Red Cross envelope, I'll finish this letter. I'm feeling fine and expect to be out soon. Got your card and a letter from the girls today. My lungs feel like after running a long way in cold weather. Guess we have a short movie downstairs this evening. Expect to get shipped about May 10. Hope I go through Carolinas up to New England states. I'm glad the decision of where I go to school is up to them. It would be too difficult to decide. All caught up on sleep now, so I'm anxious to get out.

24 APRIL 1943 (SATURDAY). Dear Irene,
Your long newsy letter was extra welcome this afternoon. You see, I am in an army hospital. They treat me nice here. A Corporal hunted me up a pencil and some paper—seems like I never have stationery when I want it. At present I am sitting by an open window desperately trying to salvage a little suntan. They didn't give me a pajama top so they can

hardly object to my sunning myself. After a lot of red tape they said I had a spot of Pneumonia. They quit the pills. Now I am allowed to eat downstairs in the mess hall and actually get some food. What have I been doing for entertainment? I go to bed early, sleep late, take a nap in forenoon, take a nap in the afternoon, and the rest of the time I eat, read, and help clean the room. Last night we had a movie downstairs which was funny but dumb. Don't know what the name of it was. My lungs have cleared up now and I feel swell. As it is I'm already slept out and getting tired of laying around. The windows look out on one of the main drags. Now to answer some of your questions. They move us to a new hotel when some get shipped out so as to make room for new groups called Flights to be altogether in a hotel. You are lucky to have a radio. I do not get a chance to listen to a radio very often.

Lyle recalled cold winter evenings when the family gathered around the radio to listen to favorite shows, enthralled at the mysterious, but exciting, transmission of music and voices emanating from WOW Omaha and WNAX Yankton.

One evening in 1936 several neighbors came to listen in on the prizefight between the American Joe Louis and Max Schmeling of Germany. Louis suffered his first defeat in the ring when Schmeling knocked him out. In a rematch two years later, Louis destroyed Schmeling in the first round, a severe blow to Hitler's Aryan supremacy belief.

In addition to a radio, party telephone line, and local newspaper subscription, Charles and Emma added another household luxury in 1940 with the purchase of a Windcharger and a set of 32-volt batteries. During periods of normal wind, the Windcharger produced enough electricity to power a lightbulb and a small refrigerator. For radio broadcasts, however, the family still depended on their old 6-volt set.

WINDCHARGER STANDING TALL BEHIND SLADEK FARMHOUSE

After pondering what made a radio work, Lyle continued his letter to Irene.

The folks should get a 32-volt radio soon. You certainly seem to keep on the move. It's more fun to be in a small place like Watertown for soldiers and you working gals than a large place like this. There is a recreation pier quite a long way up the Beach. The P.X. here charges even more than the business places. Recreation is rather scarce except for the beach and theatres. The beach is enough for me. The soldiers come and go here pretty fast and are kept busy so they don't worry much about providing Recreation. You see, I'm staying about twice as long as the average waiting for school to open. I am classified to go to Meteorology school in the class opening May 17. We expect to be sent to one of several large universities. My fingers are crossed—first started working on the deal in November and I'm not there yet. Why should everyone get in an uproar about my college clothes? Everything is under control. They will be shipped home soon unless my letters to Brookings got lost. I have a few shirts and books at Bloems. Everything else is at Lee's in a big box or on hangers. Mrs. Lee said she would ship them home if I wrote her to. You remember the pen you gave me? They ruined it at home before I left, but maybe I can fix it. I'll be spending Easter here I guess. What are you going to do? Don't send me anything here. I'm well fed etc. I'll be closer you know pretty soon now. Don't you envy me looking forward to another cross country trip with all expenses paid. Sure would like to see New England. It may be U. of New Mexico, U. of So. Calif, Mass. Inst. of Technology, U. of Iowa, etc or one of several other large schools. Jean and Virginia write to me occasionally. Also V and V. I'm glad Vernon can stay in Kansas City for a while. I'll mail this if it is possible to buy, beg, or borrow an envelope.

During his childhood years Lyle was surrounded by thirteen sets of aunts and uncles and fifty-five cousins. Three sets of cousins were double cousins, the offspring of three Sladek sisters—Antonia, Mary, and Minnie—and three Korzan brothers—Mike, John, and Frank. Lyle frequently corresponded with his cousin Dale Korzan, a military policeman (MP) in Europe. In response to the news regarding another Korzan cousin, Lyle commented:

27 APRIL 1943 (TUESDAY). Got your letter this p.m. a week after you wrote it. Surprised to hear Gladys Korzan is engaged—not too surprised though. *If* I hit New York for school, I'll take in the wedding! I'm still in the hospital but not for long I hope. They keep you plenty long so as to prevent a relapse from the sulfa drugs. In the afternoons

we can go out on the beach. Played shuffle board and darts. I worked 2 puzzles that the nurse said hadn't ever been worked here before. Took a little patience and confidence. We also get magazines, books, and games from the Red Cross room. Altogether I had a good time today. Tonight there is a variety show downstairs. I have new roommates because I moved to another room. One has a radio. Billy Vestal from Kansas was shipped to Las Vegas, Nevada, where he is training to be an aerial gunner. He says it's hot in the day time and cold at night and even a jackrabbit would starve out there. He is a nice fellow. I miss swimming—the ocean looks so inviting. I'll enclose a profile drawn by my Italian friend from Brooklyn. Save it for me. Maybe I'll get a chance to swim wherever I go. I have ambitions to become a good swimmer. Bet they send me to Mass. Institute Tech. I can hardly wait to go even though it's nice here. One main objection here is the cost of everything. Not many special deals for soldiers like other places. Have not seen any State College fellows. Would be like running into someone you know in Kansas City or Chicago. Is the grain up yet? This Florida weather has thrown my seasons of the year all mixed up. There is a James H. Sladek somewhere in this Hosp. They brought me 8 letters yesterday. It was an agreeable surprise until we saw they didn't belong to me. Read a good Scotland Yard Mystery yesterday. Never again will I lunch between meals. It feels too healthy to eat only regular meals. Maybe I'll change my mind when I get home. Take it easy at home. You didn't say if Chuckie won the spelling contest.

30 APRIL 1943 (FRIDAY). Dear Irene,
They let me out of the hospital this morning. Ten days was plenty for me. Now I am relocated in another room of the same hotel. I sneaked up to the roof in order to sun myself and write letters. Just so they don't catch me cause I'm supposed to be puttering around the room. It's warm and breezy up here. Planes are almost continually overhead and there are usually ships on the ocean horizon. You can usually hear several groups of soldiers singing as they march on the streets. They have cut down on the food at the mess halls lately. I think they are short on transportation to ship all that food down here. They will never get me to a hospital again unless on a stretcher. However, I did enjoy the sleep, games, reading, etc. I did enough caluthentics right along to stay in shape. Pretty nice to get out in time for the weekend. We have spent exactly two months in fabulous Miami Beach. After being stuck 5 times for blood tests at the hospital, I am beginning to feel like a pin cushion. Have you ever played shuffleboard? They have a very nice court at the hospital. They also had some very difficult puzzle games. Everything seems to be going O.K. at

LYLE SLADEK, NICKNAMED S.D. FOR SOUTH DAKOTA, 1943
PROFILE DRAWN BY MIAMI BEACH HOSPITAL MATE FROM BROOKLYN

home. We have a new colt as well as kittens, etc. I seem to have put on weight again lately—at least my belt is getting short. One of my former roommates, Billy Vestal, is in Nevada. He had a 108 hr. train ride. I am looking forward to being shipped too. It's exciting to not know where you are going. Saw a WAAC driving a truck this morning.

WAAC, the acronym for the Women's Army Auxiliary Corps formed in 1942 as the first women's wartime service, was later shortened to WAC when the Army of the United States (AUS) incorporated that civilian organization.

Still basking in the sun on top of the roof of the hotel, Lyle scribbled a letter home.

30 APRIL 1943 (FRIDAY). This pen is evidently ruined. It sure feels good to be out of that hospital. I have gathered up my belongings and have moved. We still have 14 left in our flight. We expect to leave in about a week for meteorology school. We arrived here two months ago. It will be less of a change in climate now than if we had left a month ago. Is the colt from the horse we broke last summer? We seem to have a hard time cutting down on the number of horses. The Register was very welcome at the hospital. I came out in good condition because of all the sleep, suntanning, and moderate exercise. There is actually some fat on my ribs. Won 3 games of checkers yesterday from an Italian who thought he was pretty good. Another fellow skinned me nicely in two games the day before.

Just got back from sunning myself on the roof. Hope the Sgt. doesn't catch me writing a letter. I am confined to quarters today on account of having been in the hosp. and am supposed to be cleaning up the room. It's against rules to write letters during the day. What color is the colt? Do you have the horses home too? You forgot "Beach" when you addressed the Register. It is important that army addresses be exactly as we send them. Miami alone is a separate city. Guess I don't know any news just now.

1 MAY 1943 (SATURDAY). We were paid again yesterday so I'll send home some money. Being in the hosp. set me back behind our flight so I had to move again today after being in that room only one day. They told me the wrong hotel so I had to pick up my stuff and move on to another hotel. I'll be glad to get out of Miami Beach. I'm tired of packing and lugging around those barracks bags every few days. This move will also stop my mail for a day or two. One main objection to the army is that when some higher ranking officer tells you to do something—you've

got to do it no matter what. If it was something unreasonable he will be punished later, but that doesn't help you any. However I haven't run into anything unreasonable yet. Too bad about the coal strike.

The war effort was disrupted when labor leader John L. Lewis ordered a half million coal miners to strike for higher wages. A shortage of that vital commodity hampered rail transportation and the production of war goods. Just a month earlier President Roosevelt had issued the order to "hold-the-line" and freeze prices. Hesitant to alienate a labor union that had supported him in three previous election campaigns, FDR, hoping to end the strike, resorted to jawboning in a Fireside Chat on 2 May:

> I am speaking tonight to the American people, and in particular to those of our citizens who are coal miners. . . .
> I have just returned from a two weeks' tour. . . .
> Everywhere I found great eagerness to get on with the war. Men and women are working long hours at difficult jobs and living under difficult conditions without complaint.
> Along thousands of miles of track I saw countless acres of newly plowed fields. The farmers of this country are planting the crops that are needed to feed our armed forces, our civilian population, and our allies. Those crops will be harvested.
> On my trip, I saw hundreds of thousands of soldiers. Young men who were green recruits last autumn have matured into self-assured and hardened fighting men. They are in splendid physical condition. They are mastering the superior weapons that we are pouring out of our factories.
> The American people have accomplished a miracle. . . .
> I want to make it clear that every American coal miner who has stopped mining coal—no matter how sincere his motives, no matter how legitimate he may believe his grievances to be, every idle miner directly and individually is obstructing our war effort. We have not yet won this war. We will win this war only as we produce and deliver our total American effort on the high seas and on the battle fronts. And that requires unrelenting, uninterrupted effort here on the home front.
> A stopping of the coal supply, even for a short time, would involve a gamble with the lives of American soldiers and sailors and the future security of our whole people. It would involve an unwarranted, unnecessary, and terribly dangerous gamble with our chances for victory.

Despite a flood of criticism from the press, John L. Lewis shunned FDR's plea for national unity. The public thought Lewis anti-American, and some communists referred to him as "America's greatest enemy." In the end, Lewis won higher wages for the coal miners.

Wartime tensions were common. While relaxing at the beach Lyle observed pleasure boats offshore—standing out in sharp contrast to cargo ships and to aircraft patrolling for enemy submarines. Back in his room, he wrote to Irene on stationery that portrayed palm trees in blue ink.

Miami Beach, Fla. May 2

Dear Sis,

Army life has

2 MAY 1943 (SUNDAY). Army life has been swell today. Went to outdoor Protestant services this morning and then played ping pong in the hotel lobby. They did not give me too much competition. We had a delicious army dinner today although we had to wait quite a while in the sun to get at it. Mashed spuds with gravey, string beans, stewed tomatoes, a hot biscuit and slice of bread, lots of stuffed olives, sauce, a square of ice cream in waxed paper, and lots of cold lemonade was the menu. I forgot the 2 slices of roast Pk. It was cooked just right too—must have been some mistake somewhere! Naturally after a meal like that I had to come home and take a nap. Also did a little washing. Then I headed for the beach where I had lots of fun practicing floating and swimming. Saw a beautiful fish about a foot long and thin as a goldfish. It was light green and silver. It certainly does not take much saltwater to make a person sick. There were steamers and sailboats on the ocean and planes and a blimp overhead. I climbed up the rope before coming back. Received your interesting letter today and also a letter and card from home. Mason Dixon Line is the division between "You all" and "Youse guys." Ain't it the truth.

When at the hospital they put all my stuff in the barracks bag and took it to a hotel and then to another hotel. I located it and lugged it back to the hotel room I was in before going to the hosp. That same afternoon they told me to move to a room upstairs. I packed my stuff and moved. The next day (Sat.) they put me in a different flight and had me move to the hotel we stayed in the first night here. It was a mistake so I moved to this hotel where we stayed for a month and a half before. So now I am in a room all alone and it has 6 beds and bath. I'm in a flight in 9th day of advanced whereas I was in 13th day of advanced about two weeks ago. It's not so nice or handy and I don't know anyone here. I'll be packing my stuff and carrying it back to that hotel when I go on shipment pretty soon. Why does everything happen to me?? But I've really got nothing to squawk about. Hope I get sent to some place fairly permanent pretty soon where I'll have time to hang my clothes up. Haven't seen any shows except "Happy Landing" at the hosp. It was lousy, the machine didn't work, and it was hot in the room—and not enough chairs. Went to town (2 blocks) this evening to choose one of two proofs for Mother's Day. One colored 8x10 and 2 cabinet size.

Having patronized a photography studio so the folks back home could see how he looked in uniform, Lyle fretted over whether he had selected the best pose. On the back, he proudly inscribed, "Private Lyle Sladek, 37474253."

PRIVATE LYLE SLADEK, 1943

3 MAY 1943 (MONDAY). Received your letter and card yesterday and a card again today. Don't send me any money cause I'm well supplied. Hope you get the pictures O.K. I just came to the conclusion that I chose the wrong pose. In order to save red tape and time I sent them all to you. You can give one to Irene if you want to. They didn't do such a hot job coloring the big one did they? If they are too late for Mother's Day blame it on the Pneumonia. It took a little pressure and first class mail to get them there as soon as they did. Is everybody over their sickness at home? Irene sure gets around. Hope I land in a small town for a while. You probably don't realize the number of soldiers here. Everything is crowded—and this is a big place. The army will make a person appreciate civilian life after the war. Lights out—it's 9:00. I'm sure glad though that I joined up. Guess I'd like to finish college too if all the kids haven't graduated by then.

Tuesday.

The Register was most welcome again today. Seems like the last few days the news has been that the war will end quicker. Hope it is true. Did you get the $40 in that letter? Meant to register it but the P.O. closed too soon. Guess I'll enclose the two proofs so you can tell me I chose the wrong one. Tomorrow is gas alert day so we carry masks all day. We had another lecture on Ju Do this afternoon. Those aerial gunners deserve a lot of stripes. You do not get any rating (stripes) when here in training. *Maybe* I'll have a stripe before too long when I ship.

"DON'T COME TOO CLOSE, DEAR,
YOU'RE LIABLE TO MESS UP MY NEW STRIPES"

For a GI, getting a stripe (promotion) meant an increase in pay and something to write home about. Lyle thought his buddy Billy Vestal, training to become an aerial gunner at Las Vegas Army Air Field, warranted all the promotions he could get. However, most aerial gunners and radio operators were enlisted men whereas pilots, navigators, and bombardiers generally were commissioned officers or flight officers, receiving more pay and wearing fancier uniforms. Regardless of their rank, aircrew members just wanted to survive their twenty-five combat missions and return home.

The next day, Lyle updated Irene.

4 MAY 1943 (TUESDAY). I have a new roommate tonight. He is from Colorado. We had swimming and floating at the beach this afternoon. The tide was out and the water was swell. Chow was not so hot tonight. Wrote to Brookings this evening in order to get a 1943 Jack Rabbit yearbook. Sent those three pictures home last night for Mother's Day. I think they'll send you one to help fill up empty drawer space. Received the Register from home today. It is too warm for sleeping this evening. Here's hoping I start heading north pretty soon. Minnesota, Maine, or Colorado. Not a bit choosy am I? I have a hunch we will get K.P. in the morning. If we do I'll make an X on the outside of the letter. We always catch up on our eating when on K.P.

6 MAY 1943 (THURSDAY). Last night they made me move to this room downstairs. They got us up at 3:30 this morning for K.P. But wonder of wonders I was on shipping. We had clothing checks this a.m. and we meteorologists will no doubt leave within three days. So don't write anymore to this address. I can hardly wait to be on the road again. There are no regrets about leaving Miami Beach even though I had a good time here. Hope there is not too much change in temperature all of a sudden. It's almost time for noon chow. Maybe I'll write again before we leave.

Three years earlier in June 1940, Hitler had urged Mussolini to launch an offensive from Libya for the purpose of driving the British out of Egypt, seizing the Suez Canal, and gaining control of the Mediterranean Sea. Hitler aimed to cut off British access to the Middle East and the Far East except for ships sailing all the way around the Cape of Good Hope.

A year later German troops, under the command of Erwin Rommel, reinforced the Italian army in North Africa and the Axis forces drove toward Cairo.

Troops from the United States joined the fray in November 1942 when Allied forces staged a surprise invasion on the coast of Algeria and Morocco. After months of fierce fighting, the Allied forces prevailed.

Lyle, like other Americans, was elated when the Axis forces in North Africa surrendered. He thought the Allied victory was a major turning point; surely the capture of thousands of Axis soldiers would cause Italy to lose heart for the war.

Upon learning their father had bartered their well-worn Underwood for a household comfort, Lyle wrote a lighthearted note to Irene.

9 MAY 1943 (SUNDAY). It must be a lousy bathtub if someone would trade it for our typewriter! I'm still waiting for final shipping orders. The ping pong table in the lobby is kept going all the time. One opponent this a.m. said he beat the state champion of Michigan. He was rather an egotist and so sure he could beat me that I buckled down and trimmed him. He won the second game though. There is plenty of fast competition here. We are supposed to be at our destination by May 12 so we should be leaving soon. My roommate is from Mississippi and expects to be a cadet. He is smart and almost as tall as I. It will be tough for the Axis now that we won in Africa. I have 7 unfinished crossword puzzles in front of me and once in a while I get an inspiration. Wonder what the folks are doing on Mother's Day? Someone is usually playing the piano in the lobby. When we are restricted to the hotel for not having the rooms clean, someone is sure to play, "I don't get around much anymore."

Guess I'll go to bed early cause they will get our flight up early for K.P. in the morning. I won't have to go on K.P. because of being on shipping.

10 MAY 1943 (MONDAY). We just got back from detail work and are now going swimming at the beach. I was paid 25 today and will send some home by registered mail. I'm in a hurry. Thought I would get a letter today but no ducks. Now for a nice swim at the beach.

SUNNY DAY AT MIAMI BEACH, 1943

Upon returning from riding the waves in the "little salty pool," Lyle learned he would be shipping out in half an hour. While scurrying about and packing his belongings he ruminated about the Miami Beach experience. He felt no regret about leaving behind the potato peeling and pot scrubbing but vowed to return someday to the white sands of the beach.

The blue-green water glistened and the sun bade farewell as the army trucks passed over the causeway to Miami. Lyle did not know where he was going, but he welcomed the prospect of new adventures.

CAUSEWAY LINKING MIAMI TO MIAMI BEACH, 1943

TROOP TRAIN

11 MAY 1943 (TUESDAY). Evening. Here we are in Sylvester, Georgia almost to Atlanta. It is cool and rainy today. We left in a hurry last evening and went by truck across the causeway to Miami. It is a series of islands and bridges. We slept in a Pullman and got to Jacksonville at 2:00 where we switched to this Georgia train. We are traveling in civilian trains and think we are going to Washington U. in St. Louis, Missouri. We eat in the dining car but meals are not so good as army chow. Georgia is much the same as North Florida and Alabama. Once in a while you can see green peach orchards and fields. Most of it is wooded and the trees are tapped for tar. All the houses are shacks in a clearing along with small fields and gardens. Now we are really getting in the peach country. Boy, it sure feels good to be heading toward home again. Feels good to be back in civilization. They plant crops in among the trees in orchards here. Peach trees are nice and shapely like elms and have a delicate green colored foliage. We had a short game of bridge this afternoon. Sure feels good to get back in a cool climate.

Wednesday.

We awoke this morning in Nashville, Tennessee. We are going to St. Louis by way of Evansville, Indiana. Here we have heavily wooded hills with an occasional eroded field on the side. It is very pretty here. They are getting to be as big as the outer Black Hills. Blackout?

We were in a tunnel for about 3 minutes. We are still in Kentucky and haven't had any breakfast. I think they are putting on a diner car now. Kentucky is also very pretty. Red soil and hills covered with trees. Crossing the Ohio River. Just as dirty as the Missouri. There is an outfit out in the middle of the river dredging. They have a fairly large shipyard here in Evansville on the Ohio River. This trip is very educational. We heard a rumor that St. Louis is one of the best cities for a soldier to be stationed in. Enclosed is a paper bird. Place the wings straight out, hold the front, pull the tail, and the wings flap.

While making their way to the dining car the soldiers engaged in good-natured bantering designed to capture the attention of the navy WAVES (Women Accepted for Volunteer Emergency Service) and army WACS on board the train. One WAC, with wavy blonde hair, reminded Lyle of his sister Virginia. When she noticed him glancing her way, he managed a bashful smile.

After returning from morning chow, Lyle continued:

We have a couple cars of WAVES and a couple cars of WACS on this train. The highlight of the morning of course was going through their cars to the dining car and getting to eat before they did. Later the soldiers sang "The WAVES and WACS will win the war, so what the hell we fighting for?" etc etc

We are crossing the flooded Wabash River. We have now crossed the River into Illinois. Southern Indiana has lots of oil tanks etc. You have heard of the banks of the Wabash, haven't you?

The words from the song "On the Banks of the Wabash, Far Away" had intrigued Lyle when a child. He was thrilled when he saw the sign WABASH RIVER as the train passed from Indiana to Illinois.

Next stop, St. Louis.

CHAPTER 7

Meet Me in St. Louis

Meet me at the fair,
Don't tell me the lights are shining any place but there.
—MUSIC FROM THE ST. LOUIS WORLD'S FAIR

"ST. LOUIS, ST. LOUIS, NEXT STOP, ST. LOUIS." The train approached
the Mississippi River, rumbled across Eads Bridge, and pulled into Union
Station.

St. Louis, the Gateway to the West. St. Louis, a city rich in history.
Mississippi riverboats unloading cotton along the wharf in the 1800s. Dred
Scott standing before the bar at the Old Courthouse in 1847. Throngs of
Americans taking in the sights at the Louisiana Purchase Exposition of
1904. Dizzy Dean and the Gashouse Gang immortalizing baseball in the
1930s.

After many fits and starts, Lyle was in the Air Corps Pre-Meteorology
program and he was exuberant. He could hardly wait to tell his family he
was stationed on the campus of Washington University in St. Louis.

12 MAY 1943 (WEDNESDAY). We arrived in St. L. union depot
at 5:30 and had free cookies and sinkers at U.S.O. while waiting for
an army truck. We were packed in and couldn't see anything cause
the truck had the canvas top on. We arrived out here at Wash. U. on
the outskirts of St. L. It is very nice and has a 155 acre campus with
a baseball field, tennis courts, trees, etc. Can you imagine anything so
nice. Toward the north side is a row of 3 story brick fraternity houses
which will be our quarters. It's beyond all expectations! Heard a rumor
that there are 8 girls on the campus per soldier and that they are very
friendly. The Sgt. said they would invite us out more than we would have
time for. Our classes do not start until May 31 and we will go through a
toughening up practice and review until then. The fellows are all former

OLD GLORY BY FRATERNITY HOUSES USED AS BARRACKS
WASHINGTON UNIVERSITY, ST. LOUIS, 1943

college students and a lot of the pre-flight soldiers are from the Dakotas, Minn, Nebr. etc. This appears to be too good to be true. The officers are swell and don't treat you like dumb animals. Things are arranged so you don't have to stand in line for a long time to eat etc. The weather is swell and cool. The soldiers all looked unhealthy here—until we remembered that they hadn't come from Miami Beach. They are sure white compared with us 33 who came from Fla. The only good thing about Miami Beach is the ocean—and why not swim in a pond as long as you can't use it all anyhow? Until May 31 we can stay out until 2:00 in the morning. Lights are out at 11:00. We have to get passes to go to St. Louis.

Army Air Corps aviators, relying on visual reference points, needed to know weather conditions along flight paths and at airfields. Moreover, accurate weather forecasts were vital to forces fighting on land and at sea.

As military operations extended around the globe the need for weather forecasters grew exponentially.

In order to ensure a steady stream of meteorologists the Air Corps established a committee of scientists at the University of Chicago to direct a meteorology training program. The committee formulated a curriculum, constructed tests that set a national standard, recruited young men with an aptitude for mathematics and physics, and selected applicants. Three levels of training—A, B, and C—were instituted at eight universities. Washington University conducted Class C and Class B Meteorology. Although Lyle had completed a year of college engineering, he needed additional study before being eligible for Class A Meteorology.

The training command at Washington University informed Lyle and his classmates that Class B Meteorology, stressing mathematics and physics but including English and geography, would be the most demanding of any army training in the country. By admitting more men into the course than needed and by grading on the curve, they aimed to spur the students on to their best efforts.

Though expecting an intense six-month academic program, up before dawn and busy until lights out, Lyle intended to socialize and do the town while in St. Louis. After strolling about the campus and shyly eyeing the coeds in front of the Women's Building, he returned to his room and leafed through an entertainment guide. While combing for fun ideas, he continued his letter.

Just saw where service men could get free tickets to St. Louis Cardinals baseball games. This is going to be one big merry go round. We have a recreation pamphlet here that tells of all the free entertainments for service men in St. Louis. Roller skating, dancing and everything. A coed now strolls past the French windows. Meteorology students who came from Miami B. include a Yale graduate and son of a famous Judge etc. The course is tough and competitive but I'll get tough too. They give you things here in St. L. rather than trying to steal your shirt. The address on the envelope is accurate enough so a letter will reach me. Wasn't I lucky to come to Mo. in the springtime? One of these days I'll take a steamboat excursion on the Mississippi. Yes, I'm going to get around down here. You might send 5.00 in next letter if handy? St. L. is 8th ranking in U.S. There are really only 3 cities much larger. I can't get over how nice the cool weather feels. The course lasts 6 months here and we will remain privates while here. Hope they really shoot the physical training to us—competitive games etc. Send me a little sewing kit—needles and thread—in a little jewelry box if you have one. Maybe a jar of vapor rub and some of my best white handkerchiefs. Also the pair of basketball socks if you have them. My new shoes when they come from Brookings. A white towel if you have one to spare. I might want math books later on. That makes about 17 or 18 states for me so far. We can get weekend passes etc. I'm pretty enthused about this deal. Keep those letters coming.

Lyle ended his letter with an optimistic, but naive, prediction: "In my opinion Germany will fall in 1943." He was aware of the severe losses Germany had suffered in North Africa and Russia. And while crisscrossing the country in trains he had noted the vast volume of war goods pouring from the factories. Failing to reckon Hitler had absolute power and nothing more to lose, Lyle supposed Germany would concede once defeat was inevitable.

A headline in the college newspaper caught Lyle's attention: "Joe Campus Is Now Man in Khaki." Yes indeed, he thought. The sight of soldiers marching across the campus quadrangle had become commonplace as the Air Corps utilized college facilities for Pre-Flight and Pre-Meteorology training. Faculty members had adjusted their schedules and civilian students had accepted changes in housing and dining services to accomodate the men in uniform.

Although the soldiers were allotted more food stamps than their civilian counterparts, the university cafeteria competed in the same wholesale markets as eateries catering to the general public. Cafeteria managers were hard-pressed to fulfill a model menu prescribed by the army:

Breakfast:	Fruit, sweet rolls and butter, eggs and bacon, milk and coffee
Dinner:	Soup, beef stew, diced carrots, spinach, mashed potatoes, vegetable salad, rolls and butter, milk, apple pie
Supper:	Soup, roast veal, potatoes, peas, rutabaga, salad, milk, cake
Sunday:	Chicken

Still elated the day after his arrival, Lyle wrote to Irene.

13 MAY 1943 (THURSDAY). We had a swell 45 hour trip through Fla, Ga, Tenn., Kentucky, Ind. Ill., and into St. Louis at 5:30 yesterday. Five hundred soldiers here of whom 130 will be Class B Meteorologists. We actually had milk for supper and you pick up food cafeteria style. They don't splatter food all over your tray. The course will be rough and competitive but I'll get tough too. They might flunk me out—but they'll get an awful battle.

The weather here is cool and perfect. No more sweating 24 hours a day. They said the coeds would invite us out and entertain us royally. "I'm not going to sit around much anymore." The Profs are civilian teachers who have written their own college textbooks. Don't you envy me? This will be somewhat like a military academy. We will get up at 5:30

and be on duty until 5:30. It will be physical training, classes, and drilling. I forgot to tell you that I'm enthusiastic about this! Couldn't buy film in Miami Beach but I'll try here. We get no furlough during the 6 month course here. You'll come to Mo. this summer for a visit though, won't you? You scc I'm pretty close to K.C. too. I believe this will be beyond all expectations. Hope you write and tell me what you're doing.

Saturday afternoon Lyle viewed Forest Park from the archway of Brookings Hall. Heeding the siren song "Meet Me in St. Louis, Louis," Americans by the thousands had gathered at the park to attend the Louisiana Exposition of 1904. Lyle envisioned the fairgoers enjoying the verdant setting, a beautiful expanse of grass and trees. Four decades later St. Louis was still basking in the afterglow of that extravaganza. It was a fascinating city for a country boy. Trolleys plied the streets. The steamboat SS *Admiral* docked on the Mississippi waterfront. The Browns and Cardinals played major league baseball at Sportsman's Park.

While marching off to class on Monday, the soldiers belted out songs—exhilarating for Lyle. It appeared that army life on the campus of Washington University would be the best of all worlds. The professors seemed intelligent and urbane, his fellow soldiers lively and sociable. Not only would he be earning college credits, the army would be picking up the tab. Swimming in the indoor pool and running on the Francis Field track, two campus facilities constructed for the Olympic Games of 1904, would be thrilling. As he read the plaque over the entrance to Francis Field—*Per Veritatem Vis* (Through Truth Comes Strength)—he anticipated a great blend of academic, physical, and cultural activities.

18 MAY 1943 (TUESDAY). It is a beautiful early morning in St. Louis and the air is crisp. Yesterday I got your card and a Register that had arrived at Miami Beach too late to catch me. Also a box of delicious cookies and marshmellows from Irene. My roommate and I promptly disposed of them. Yesterday we started our review classes and as we marched to class for the first time, naturally we sang, "School days, school days, dear old golden rule days." Most of our instructors are really good. They are definitely "on the beam" as the army puts it. In the afternoon we drilled and then went to physical education class. A half hour of exercises really made us sweat. Such as lying on our backs and bringing our feet back of the neck to the floor. Then we were divided into 3 groups—one group to the swimming pool, another taking track, and us to the gym. We practiced climbing 20 ft. ropes. The instructor showed us a method of locking our feet on the rope so as to be able to rest on the way up. In this way a person can climb a rope of indefinite

BROOKINGS HALL
WASHINGTON UNIVERSITY, 1943

FOREST PARK FROM THE ARCHWAY OF BROOKINGS HALL
WASHINGTON UNIVERSITY, 1943

height. There was only 1 or 2 persons in our group of 10 who could go up faster than I. Then we took quick showers and fell out for supplies. Later we had chow and mail call. We certainly put away the grub. That Physical T. program is really going to be O.K. The class of 140 is small enough so we can get individual attention. The only difference between this and college is that we can't go home when we want to, they pay all expenses and a salary here, we have a better Phys. T. program, and the teaching should be at least as good. I'll admit it sounded fishy at home—but here I am. Having never been in a city before, traveling on streetcars is very perplexing. It must be 5 or 6 miles from here to the main business district by the river. Sat. afternoon was spent at the park museum, and Sunday afternoon I saw the St. L. Browns and Philadelphia Athletics split a pair of baseball games at Sportsman's park. The field is very pretty with its green infield and outfield surrounded by huge stands. I think the champion Cardinals play this weekend. Whenever you don't hear from me every 4 or 5 days you think floods and everything have gone wrong. Too bad it rains too much here and none at home. Are the pastures coming without rain? How many calves have we got now? Are they nice marked white faces? How many chicks did you get? Have you got any duck eggs setting? I can't imagine school being out already. Chuckie hasn't written to me for quite a while but I suppose he is pretty busy with his cats?

This is quite a spiffy looking group on average. Everything is done in routine here. We get up at the same time each morning and on certain days we air the beds. Shoes must be kept shined and under the bed and clothes hung a certain way in the closet. We have the same schedule of classes and Phys. Ed. every day. They loan out tennis equipment so we will be able to go out to the courts in front and play tennis. This campus is sure pretty. All buildings are quite old and of the same material and general design. There are long elm shaded walks etc. Wish you would drive down here this summer. Irene, Vernon, and I will soon end up at the same air base if we keep moving. At least we are getting closer. St. Louis is not crowded with soldiers like other cities. Jefferson Barracks is about the only camp near here and they can't come to St. L. much except weekends. For that reason this is an ideal city to be stationed in. Guess it's almost time for 8 o'clock classes. We have review Physics, English, and Math this morning. There will be plenty of competition in this group of 140 fellows cause the requirements were quite high.

I can imagine the awful floods cause I saw the levees in Louisiana, Miss. etc. They are 10 to 30 ft. above the level surrounding country and so when one of them breaks it really pours out water.

This is even G.I. paper.

Still bubbling with enthusiasm and marveling at the splendid grounds and the beauty of Brookings Hall, Graham Chapel, and other buildings fashioned of brick and stone, Lyle wrote a long letter to Irene.

GRAHAM CHAPEL, WASHINGTON UNIVERSITY, 1943

23 MAY 1943 (SUNDAY). This will be a 6 month vacation with all expenses paid if you ask me. They issued us $40 worth of textbooks such as Calculus, Physics, Atlas, Mechanics, English, Geography, and others. The Physics book is same edition as I was using in college. We hope these books are for ornamental purposes only. They also issued slide rules, notebooks, and other supplies. This U. is very beautiful with its large brick and stone buildings, shady walks, trees, athletic fields, birds, squirrels, etc. It is chiefly an engineering school and has huge Physics Labs, etc. It would be hard to find a healthier life. We get up at 5:30 and have revellie. Then we wash up, clean rooms, and march to chow where we eat a hearty breakfast. Two of us live in this second story room with French windows on the south and west, and double deck bed. Physical Ed in shorts and tennis shoes will be from 8 to 9 a.m. Classes will last until about 4:30 and then an hour of drill. We are free from Sat. 2:30 until Sunday night. The Goon platoon consisting of soldiers who did something wrong will drill Sat. afternoon. Mail call is at 6:30, and there are lots of mailboxes handy around the campus. There is a set monthly fee for laundry, and pressing and mending jobs are done free. We have less regulation than most army posts. The fraternity houses have two-way radio sets to Headquarters for messages. This morning they called "Get up right away if you want to go to chow at 7:00—if you want it served in bed see Sgt. Reynolds." We eat only when we want to on weekends and do not have to go over in formations. These fellows are

nice to be around—the typical enthusiastic college fellows. This campus is located next to St. L. largest park with its skating-dancing arena, and world famous zoo, etc. I have a free ticket to this afternoons baseball game if it doesn't rain. I always did want to see major league teams play. The officers treat us swell and things are made pleasant as possible. There is more individuality here. This deal is beyond all expectations. I don't know how I happen to rate a deal like this.

Monday.

Thanks Irene for those delicious cookies. I guess they were about the best I've ever eaten. There is a rule here that we must not leave food laying around the room very long—so my roommate and I promptly ate them. Of course we needn't have taken that rule so literally. We had drill and Physical Training yesterday. We go through all sorts of exercises and contortions. After that we either swim, go to the gym, or have track. This Physical Training will really build us up if we live through it. This sure is a swell set up. We even get paper and pencils. The streetcar problem is very perplexing for a country greenhorn. There is no system of streets and avenues—just a jumbled mess of crooked streets. I'm glad they are going to leave us here 6 months cause it will take me that long to see everything. You and Vernon and I are sort of converging aren't we? You could come down here quite easily some long weekend. This campus is like you read about but never expect to see. I won't send this letter until I get your Sioux City address.

When the War Department made reductions in force at the air base in Watertown, Irene opted to transfer to the air base at Sioux City. There, sharing an apartment with cousin Gladys Korzan who worked at the same airfield, Irene wrote to Lyle describing the circus of cockroaches scurrying for cover whenever a light was switched on in the kitchen. He responded:

Wednesday evening.

Now that I have your address I'll mail this letter. I think you will soon like Sioux City. Of course it is a lot different from Watertown or even Sioux Falls. I'll bet you will like it there before long. At least I hope so. I have been enjoying myself very much. Think I'll like the Profs although math will be tough. They say this is the toughest course in the army and I agree. However, I have always studied to learn something rather than for grades and I think now will be the payoff. Some will flunk out right along. Please write.

Lyle knew if he *washed out* of the meteorology program for any military, physical, or academic deficiency, he would be sent to Jefferson Barracks (JB) for reassignment. JB, a long-established army post outside St. Louis, mainly served as an Overseas Replacement Depot (ORD), the last station for many soldiers before shipping overseas.

In responding to his mother's concern about the floods along the Mississippi River, Lyle chided her for fretting and assured her he was in no danger.

26 MAY 1943 (WEDNESDAY). Fine thing—you don't hear from me for a week and then you start worrying. The flood has not affected me although they have been sending soldiers from Jefferson Barracks to help. The river is going down now. I didn't get a letter from you for about a month but it wasn't your fault. The letter with the $5 must have gotten mis sent. Did you get my $40 letter from Florida? Guess I have never felt better in my life. This weather is very invigorating. Let me remind you that a chest cold is called Pneumonia. If I had gone on sick call about a week sooner I wouldn't have gotten it. No harm done though. You should have gotten a letter the day you mailed this one to me. I can tell now that the math will be tough—there is some terrible competition here. Just review so far. Tues. we ran around the race track in stretches for about a mile or more. Today we did chin ups and then ran 300 yds in 60 yd laps around poles. I led my group of 8 until the last lap and then 1 or 2 passed me. My time was 51. The best was a 47 running up to 65 seconds. Guess I was in the top 20 or 30 of the 120 fellows. They keep records. Guess I'll run a little Sunday before breakfast too because we don't have Phys. T. on Sunday. We really eat after a schedule like this. I am getting lean and healthy. This is a wonderful chance for a fellow of my age. Just what I needed. We go to Jefferson Barracks tomorrow forenoon for physical examinations. I expect to pass perfectly again. Some are scared their eyes won't pass. My eyes and ears are perfect but I'm not perfect on color blindness. Very few people are. Expect to put in a big weekend again. Where did you plant the cedars? Wish we had a vacation during June or anytime for that matter. Vestal is still in Las Vegas, Nev., and Peck is in Denver. Another fellow is in Gulfport, Miss. Flight L is now scattered all over the U.S. Irene sent me a letter today. Her first impression of Sioux City isn't so good. The railroad station didn't appeal to me either. St. Louis—once the smokiest city in the U.S. is now the cleanest. They have smoke traps on the chimneys.

28 MAY 1943 (FRIDAY). Everything is going swell here. We start our regular schedule on Monday. There are students here with doctor's, master's, and B.A. degrees taking this course. They lacked some math for taking the A course. We had caluthentics and cross-country running this afternoon. I've stayed in all week so this weekend I'll get around. The day I left Brookings, I talked about meteorology with Dean Doner—the

registrar's son. He had been inducted into Class C Meteorology. This noon I heard the name during mail call and sure enough it was him. We got clean sheets tonight. We have most of tomorrow afternoon off. You might send me that package of handkerchiefs, etc when it is handy. Are the kids out of school already? We must pass standard tests from the U of Chicago or we wash out.

Passing the Chicago tests was crucial for Lyle. Washing out of the meteorology program meant reassignment to a less desirable role in the army with little prospect of promotion. He expected the competition to be formidable; many of his rivals had attended large high schools in urban areas and several already possessed college degrees.

On Sunday, taking advantage of the lull before the start of regular classes, Lyle visited the downtown USO. The United Service Organizations—created in 1941 by uniting the efforts of the YWCA, the YMCA, the National Catholic Community Service, the Salvation Army, the Jewish Welfare Board, and the National Travelers Aid Association—maintained more than two thousand "home away from home" facilities stateside and abroad.

While socializing at USOs, young women from the local communities mingled with servicemen from all around the country. The words of an oldie song expressed the wishful thinking of the girls back home and the boys away from home:

> Don't sit under the apple tree with anyone else but me,
> . . . .
> Don't give out with those lips of yours to anyone else but me.

The admonition did not apply to Lyle since he had no girlfriend back home in South Dakota. Before stepping out onto the dance floor he helped himself to coffee and cookies, sat down at a corner table, and wrote a letter.

30 MAY 1943 (SUNDAY). This has been a busy day for me. I thought maybe it would be the last time I'd have spare time. Went to the University City Methodist church this forenoon. Then I had a delicious chicken dinner. I was unable to get a ticket to the ball game so I went swimming at a Y.M.C.A. pool. We played tag in the water etc. Then I started for the U. I must have gotten on the wrong streetcar cause I soon found myself in the slums. After changing cars several times and wasting a lot of time I got home. I bought an all day car ticket (25¢) so I came downtown tonight. I looked across the flooded Miss. River to smoky east St. Louis, Ill. Now I am at a U.S.O. There is no scarcity of nice looking girls here. These U.S.O.s are pretty nice. We only have 10:00 permission

now. This is a swell deal so far. And we'll know some mathematics if we make the grade. They have some mixed singing around the piano now along with several other attractions. Guess I'm plenty lucky to get in on a deal like this. Why don't you write more often—what have you been doing lately?

On the first day of regular classes Lyle and a fellow soldier noted their family names were of Bohemian origin. Both were proud of their heritage. Lyle extolled his father as a man of prodigious endurance and innate intelligence, a self-taught man who, as the son of immigrants, had enjoyed little opportunity for a formal education.

That evening, Lyle solved the most recent brainteaser received from his mother, a kindred soul who shared a love of learning and poetry. In her letters, Emma frequently enclosed puzzles and poems clipped from newspapers and magazines.

31 MAY 1943 (MONDAY). I hit the jackpot today. Ten letters finally got to me. Most of them had been sent to Florida and then Jefferson Barracks. So I sorted them according to dates and had a very enjoyable hour. Also worked the puzzle on the 8 and 5 gallon containers. That is a good puzzle. Heard a *rumor* today that we would get furloughs in 3 months. This morning another fellow and I were caught talking while marching so we are on the goon platoon Sat afternoon. Four hr. of marching while others have the afternoon off. We had it coming—we shouldn't have got caught. Tonight there is a free excursion for service men aboard the "Admiral" on the moonlit Mississippi. It is a very large expensive boat—but guess I'll study a while. Our Physics teacher is a little weak but the rest are A+. One witty Prof. said, "You are very lucky to be able to get 4 years of college in one year." Some of the fellows are from Vanderbilt U., U. of Chicago, U. of North Carolina, and many other famous schools so there is real competition. It is a pleasure to live with fellows like these. Our Phys. Training has been same as usual. We have been running quite a lot. I'm a little below average on endurance in distance running. This is really delux to be stationed here. This city and campus already seem very familiar. We will have records made in English speech to improve our speaking. A Bohemian (Hubba) from Lincoln, Nebr. is in this house. These fellows are from all corners of U.S. and have lots of different accents. Don't take me serious when I write bad news home—there is always some mistake. I've always got a foot in hot water. It's early to bed and early to rise for me. I'm not going to let school interfere with sleep and entertainment. You folks are more up on your shows than I. There seems to be plenty happening out there all the time. Hope we get a furlough before this course is over.

Strapped for time, Lyle jotted two missives on the YMCA postcards he had acquired while enjoying the downtown facility the previous Sunday.

2 JUNE 1943 (WEDNESDAY). I'm a little bit sleepy this morning. A general will inspect us this weekend. I've got Physics and Calculus done for this week. The Register says you got a rain at last. They keep me on the run here. We swam once yesterday.

5 JUNE 1943 (SATURDAY). We are about to start another busy day. Yesterday we had class from 8:00 in the morning to 8:30 in the eve. A general is here this weekend. This p.m. about 30 of us will march off gigs on the "goon platoon." Tomorrow is a free day.

PICTURE POSTCARD OF DOWNTOWN YMCA, ST. LOUIS, 1943

7 JUNE 1943 (MONDAY). This was a wet weekend for me—and the rain even helped me out at times. They were really giving the goon platoon the works Sat. afternoon when a rainstorm came up quite suddenly. The Sgt. had on his good clothes so he had to dismiss us. I went swimming at the pool here on the campus after that. It was clear in

the evening so I went to a show over at University City. It was a double feature—Hello, Frisco, Hello, and a murder mystery. Entertaining and that was all. Of course it was raining when I got out and me without my raincoat. I went to church Sunday morning and in the afternoon a bunch of us went to the ball game. The champion Cardinals and the Phillies were tied 1-1 when it started to rain. They rolled canvases on the infield and finished just as the rain quit. They started playing again and soon came a shower. The Phils had 2 men on base and the field was getting very wet. The last Phil to bat knocked in two runs just before the umpire halted the game due to rain. It was supposed to have been a doubleheader. There was almost a capacity crowd. The green ballpark looks rather small because of the stands and fence surrounding it. It's easy to see that the Cards are champs. It was cool and cloudy today for a change. They are covering ground fast in this course—but I'm a jump ahead of the instructors. Some fellows have trouble keeping up. I'm glad I worked some in college—now I know how to do assignments in a hurry. The days here are long and busy. We are going from 5:30 a.m. to 6:30 p.m. and then we usually have to study.

Hope Uncle John gets well in a hurry before he gets too far behind in the store. Must be pretty nice for the kids to be out of school. The Class C Meteorology students get 8 day furloughs starting Sat. and they have only been here 3 months. My roommate is very smart—between us we work all problems they throw at us.

Learning that a former college boardinghouse mate had been admitted to Officer Candidate School (OCS), Lyle hoped his friend would survive the grueling ordeal. OCS, the butt of many jibes and jokes, was a rigorous training program for select enlisted men. Candidates who completed the three-month regimen became commissioned officers, referred to as *90-day-wonders* or *shavetails*.

Tuesday.

Royce Bates wrote from Officer Candidate School in Georgia. He likes it there. One of these days my Jack Rabbit for '43 should come. It will be nice to see pictures etc of this school year. I'm not gaining weight here as yet. Our table faces the west window where the sun disappears into the treetops in the evening. This will probably be a busy week for you if the gang all comes home. Wish I was coming too. Can you make the ice last until August?

Anticipating a furlough in August, Lyle recalled summer evenings when he had fetched ice from the icehouse and cranked the handle of the ice-cream freezer, earning the right to lick the dasher once the mixture was frozen. He thought of his mother returning from the garden with peas to shell and ground-cherries to shuck; of his father showing off a newborn calf or colt.

There were unpleasant memories as well, such as in 1934 when giant tumbleweeds rolled across the land, piling up against fence lines. Hordes of grasshoppers destroyed crops in the morning and clustered on the shady side of fence posts in the heat of the afternoon. A neighbor family, unable to meet mortgage payments, loaded their belongings into a car and set out for Seattle. Older now, Lyle realized how discouraging the dust bowl years must have been for his parents. But they had persevered. With the depression years over and the weather pattern returned to normal, life in Brule County was good once again.

A letter awaited Irene when she returned from the farm.

8 JUNE 1943 (TUESDAY). Have you recovered from your vacation by now? Those vacations usually leave a person all in. You have very good train connections home though. You can plan right now (I hope) to go home with me when I come through Sioux City on my furlough. You should be able to get a few days in about 3 months. Hope that deal goes through and you and the Vs come to St. Louis some weekend. Of course my time is limited to Sat. at 3:00 p.m. until Sun. evening at 10:00. St. Louis is a rather old city and is therefore spread out and poorly planned. It has nice parks and other attractions, but the city does not seem very large. We have been concentrating on Physics tonight. Some problems are really rough. There are lots of groans and consultations with one another. One of our math teachers is really a card. We have a regular picnic in his class—and learn quite a lot too. One math teacher talked about 4th dimension so we asked this Prof. what he thought of it. He said every time he thought about 4th dimension he went down to Garavini's Beer Parlor and had 5 beers! We are treated much like other officer training schools. A cap more than an inch over the right eye, or an unbuttoned button means the goon platoon. That is reasonable enough except that they sometimes call you out for drill before you are back from Physical T. You take a fast shower and dress desperately because if you are late—it's the goon platoon. We are on the run from morning until night. This week Flights A and B are on furlough so we get to sleep late—6:00. However, we wake up at 5:30 anyway from force of habit. Calculus is real stuff. We are already integrating. I do not own a Garrison Cap but we are allowed to wear them off the post here. Maybe I'll buy one sometime. We do not have leather belts either. That's a good idea to get a ticket to the Y.M.C.A. Wish I had a chance to swim more often. I enjoy this very much. The army has done lots for me and I'm very glad I joined. Hope I didn't give the impression that I didn't like

Miami Beach. As a whole I enjoyed it lots and wouldn't give it up for anything. Chessin just brought me a hunk of good cake. These fellows here are swell. This is a regular 3 ring circus.

His thoughts wandering back to the farm, Lyle inquired of Irene:

How were Mom and Dad and the kids? They said Jean was getting plump. And I suppose Chuckie was very much embarrassed with all the company. They probably showed you the bathtub about 3 times the first hour—or have the kids changed. Is the radio working? I will be glad to get away from city and crowded camp life after the war. Does the fluid drive still work or is it all used up in the Dodge? Did you get a chance to drive much while home? Just think, I'll be home during cane cutting time and when hunting season is on. I am a very poor but lucky hunter. Does Sioux City agree with you any better now? I know how you feel—every time I got acquainted with my roommates at Miami Beach they would tell me to pack my barracks bags and stagger under them to a new hotel or room and start all over again. You get so you don't care what happens—you do what the army says and sleep in the handiest bed. The main thing in the army is to never be in a hurry. We now wear fatigues to class—they are cooler and easier to keep clean. We have a Calculus test tomorrow but I never let studying interfere with sleep. Our drill Sgt. is the typical army Sgt. He is more bark than bite though. Take it easy on your job. You always feel sorry for the Gov. like I do. Your letters raise my morale 99%.

Two days later Lyle continued to juxtapose farm and army life and complained that the command, on a whim, had curtailed the detachment's freedom.

10 JUNE 1943 (THURSDAY). A new post order just came out that we can't leave the post except on weekends. We are moving along fast in our studies but I have no trouble keeping up. You might send my tennis shoes in that package if handy. Pretty nice to have the pond full up north. Has the corn come up yet and where did you plant cane? We have been running cross-country lately as well as exercises. We have a Physics test tomorrow—our first one. I'll have no trouble with it. Vector Mechanics has us pretty much in the dark so far. It's almost time for the day's classes to start. We have a very busy day here but it is very interesting.

Four months after departing college Lyle was still chasing down his personal belongings. In updating his mother, he also glossed over his most recent exam results.

11 JUNE 1943 (FRIDAY). Today we had the usual day of 5:30 until 6:30—but on Friday evening we also have 2 hours of Physics Lab. We had a Physics test this morning and I did poor mostly through coincidences but it doesn't matter. We recorded our voices in Speech class today and the instructor really thought my speaking was O.K. There are lots of different accents and speech defects here as they come from all over the country. We had exercises, ran around the race track, and then went swimming during Physical Training. I weighed 171 lb stripped which represents a gain of at least 15 lb of muscle since getting into the army. We drilled an hour after that. It was hot today so we'll be tired by the time Physics Lab is over. We will get about a week furlough this fall—the news of the month. Got a letter from a roommate at 616 7th ave. He said Seidschlaw picked up my clothes soon after I quit. They are probably in Alpena, S.D. I'm sure glad I made a fast decision and joined the army. It has done lots for me. I'm looking forward to a big weekend. My 1943 Jack Rabbit came yesterday and is very interesting. I find that State College turns out students who can easily compete with students of the large Us. About the best college there is I guess.

14 JUNE 1943 (MONDAY). Got a nice long letter from Irene today. She evidently had a swell vacation while it lasted. We are future officers here and like other officer schools we really get the works. For instance after exercises they ran us around the track 3 times. We had about 10 minutes to get back, take showers, dress, and fall out again. We marched for an hour and had mail call and chow. Save this opera program for me. The opera was magnificent. Beautiful scenes, lighting, and singing. The Cardinal-Pirates game Sun. had some spectacular plays. These major leaguers play desperately. They slide into base men to prevent double plays etc. The umpire threw out a couple players. St. Louis is a sweatbox in the summer. I could go for a cold drink of well water. We have lots of things going on around the barracks here. These fellows are cards. I'm going to beat the sun to bed tonight.

16 JUNE 1943 (WEDNESDAY). I'm tired tonight. We had a tough workout in P.T. and drill afterwards. Also a surprise Math test in which I did very poorly. I'll get in gear one of these days though. What are you doing these sunny June days? Did the grain survive the drought and the garden too? We ran an obstacle course this afternoon. The sweat pours off you and just as you get back to the barracks they start to call you out for drill. So you take a shower and dress in no time flat and shiver for fear you left a button unbuttoned or don't get out in time. Such is the army. There is never an excuse in the army. Is the grass growing pretty

good this year? Irene said Uncle John was on his feet again. Guess I'll go to bed now.

Thursday.

It's a little cooler this morning. In a few minutes we march off to class again. Only a couple more days of classes before the weekend. Some are going on an excursion steamer on the Mississippi this weekend. It's the largest river boat in the U.S. or world I guess. Might accidentally go myself. Write when you have time.

Meanwhile, the commanding officers—a major, two lieutenants, a warrant officer, and two sergeants—were enforcing discipline at the meteorology detachment; two soldiers who had missed bed check were destined for Jefferson Barracks.

19 JUNE 1943 (SATURDAY). Just time for a very short letter. My roommate just talked me into a blind date on the river boat "Admiral" tonight. My roommate and his wife are going too. You know, dancing etc. We had a rather strenuous week just past. Last night about midnight they called us out on fire drills so they could take roll or something. I guess maybe they suspicioned some were off post after hours. At least they said a couple were going to get shipped down the river. We have rigid room inspection Sat. morn so we have scrubbed, dusted, and made up the beds without a wrinkle. We had Physics Lab until 9:00 yesterday evening. The weather has been cooler lately making studying easier. Three hours of classes and then afternoon inspection and we are done for the week. I'll have to study some this weekend though. The Register came yesterday. That big rain makes me homesick. Guess there's nothing like S.D. when it rains. Did the new dam live up to expectations? Are there any grasshoppers yet?

P.S. We haven't forgotten Dad on Father's Day.

23 JUNE 1943 (WEDNESDAY). Well, I'll try again this morning. We've been playing a little baseball in the evenings so I didn't get around to writing a letter. We are busy as ever. They sure took the pep out of us in P.T. yesterday. Seems like they sort of concentrate on the stomach muscles. You lay on your back and slowly raise and lower your legs etc. When you get this we will have completed a month of our course here. Guess I'll have to turn in my laundry now. We took a moonlight trip on the Mississippi last Sat. night. The boat is very nice and has air conditioned ballrooms etc. We had a good time dancing etc. I'll have to hit the books harder from now on. We're going to organize platoon baseball teams. We are going to have a meteorology dance downtown

some Sat. night. We are counting the days here until furlough. Almost time for class again. Calculus is fun but Vector Mechanics is over our heads so far. Hope I hear from you today.

24 JUNE 1943 (THURSDAY). We marched back from class this afternoon in a big rainstorm. We had P.T. in the gym and no military drill afterwards. We played some catch after supper and are going to work on Calculus now. I did quite poor on the Geography test this afternoon. I forget that it really has to be a good test in order to rate here. Everyone here is pretty good so there is always some who have everything about right. Guess I could study more too. Calculus is my easiest subject. It is really a wonderful science. You can compute things that could not be done by any other principle. I'll finish this in the morning.

Friday.

So you are cultivating corn already. Is the corn as high as the banks yet? My idea of the seasons is all turned around because I've been in summer climate since the last of February. My roommate was C.Q. (Charge of Quarters) last night and this morning. That is, he is at headquarters and wakes us up over the loudspeaker, etc. We are all sleepy this morning. Guess I'll mostly sleep this weekend. It's almost time for our platoon to go to chow. The mess hall is civilian and therefore the food at times is not as good as army chow. Today we aren't through until about 9:00.

26 JUNE 1943 (SATURDAY). My idea of an interesting afternoon. We had a kittenball game as soon as we were done at 2:00 and our team was beaten. I got a real suntan because we play in shorts. Then we went swimming in the pool. We had a rough game of water ball. When a person gets the ball the rest pile him and he either lets go of the ball or gets a ducking. I also progressed in swimming. Almost half the meteorologists were on the goon platoon today but they didn't have to march for long. For once I didn't have any gigs. Those pictures and the paper came yesterday. Those pictures are sure good and clear. Jean and Wilma have changed a lot.

We just had a discussion as to what to do tonight. Guess we'll go to chow first and then maybe to a U.S.O. or something.

Sunday morning.

Four of us went to the municipal U.S.O. last night. We danced, played pool, and fooled around. Of the four of us—one from North Dakota had received congressional appointments to West Point *and* Annapolis, but turned them down for Meteorology. His brother is a Major in the army and a West Point graduate. The other from Florida

CHARLES AND CHUCKIE SLADEK BUILDING A DAM, FAMILY FARM, 1943

CHARLES SLADEK CULTIVATING CORN, FAMILY FARM, 1943

VIRGINIA, JEAN, AND WILMA SLADEK, 1943

turned down a West Point appointment in order to study meteorology. His dad is a Colonel with the army. So you see it would be no disgrace to wash out of here. The Class C Meteorologists are pretty much high school graduates and not picked over much. I don't think many of them will make the grade. Guess we'll study Physics until church time. We slept until 8:00 for a change. I guess there is a really good chess and checker player downstairs. He challenged me to a game sometime. Some people like army and navy life and some don't. Those who don't have my sympathy. It's a dog's life at times in some camps. Later.

Sunday evening.

We had a fine day. Church, a good dinner, and then off to the ball game in an army truck. The St. Louis Browns beat Detroit in an exciting game. We came back to the campus and found an unlocked door in the swimming pool building. Six of us had the pool all to ourselves and we had lots of fun playing water polo. When a person won't let go of the ball you sink him to the bottom of the pool until he lets go. Some of the fellows are going to church to a Junior League again tonight. There were some comments just now that it might be because of a critical Physics test in the morning. These fellows are a witty bunch. On Sundays we don't have inspection so the room gets all messed up. But Monday morning it's neat as a pin again—or else. Everybody is counting the days until furlough. We are going to have a P.X. here starting this week. After one month here, I have come to the conclusion that this is the best the army has to offer. We work hard but it's a lot of fun. A vacation would certainly be welcome though. Hope you write real often.

1 JULY 1943 (THURSDAY). How is everything in South Dakota? We were paid yesterday. From now on they will buy a bond a month out of my pay. We are going on a picnic at Forest Park on the 4th. What are you going to do? We have had it easier in P.T. for some reason or other. I sure have been sleepy lately. I've not been doing much studying evenings cause seems like 6 hours in the classroom is enough. It gets to be a strain to study all the time and get no recreation. I hit fairly high in a Physics test and low in a Geography test. I'll enclose a sheet of Vector calculus notes like we try to digest every day. We understand it but we can't seem to apply it in problems. I guess it's just that it's new to us yet. Almost time for another day of classes. I'll send you some postcard pictures of some of the buildings soon. Enclosure $10.

3 JULY 1943 (SATURDAY). Saved by another weekend. I worked until 10:00 last night and came out very close on another physics experiment. Three more hours of classes this morning and we are done. It's lucky

that rain was no bigger. The new pond must have been plenty big when that high. Did it wash any? We put on clean sheets Sat. mornings. One fellow was sent to Jefferson Barracks with a nervous breakdown. I'm feeling fine and enjoying myself.

Following a big Fourth of July celebration the command disrupted the sleep of the men, summoning them outside for a frivolous diatribe about the difficult road ahead.

5 JULY 1943 (MONDAY). Another busy weekend is past which included swimming, shows, a picnic, and a fireworks display in our stadium last evening. There were many beautiful rockets and displays. About 11 o'clock, they called us out for fire drill and lectured to us. He lectured about how tough our course is, that we didn't get enough sleep, that one fellow had a nervous breakdown last week—and that 21 fellows were to wash out today and 25 more Friday. In the meantime we were losing sleep while he blowed. They ran us around the field and dismissed us. This morning they washed out 21 Class C men for scholastic reasons. They will be reclassified and some sent overseas. The military part of it hasn't been so rigid lately. They are right about some more will probably break down. It's all right as long as there is no pressure on you about washing out if you go down on another test or something. But they won't get me—I always get enough recreation so it doesn't get to be a strain. Every day I realize more and more the competition that is here. We had a Vector test this morning and I was again below average. I again made a couple foolish mistakes—but I realize you can't make foolish mistakes when it's your say as to whether a plane can go up safely or not. Maybe that's what makes me like it here so well—I have to really scratch to compete. I'm not the least bit worried though cause I think I know the stuff.

Tuesday morning.

Well, we won our ball game last night. I'm sleepy again this morning. Wish I was sleeping under a haystack in South Dakota. Did much of the cane drown out? And do you mean to tell me that the grain is headed out already? So my college clothes are at last starting to wander home. We will be cadets with cadet pay when we finish the Class B course here.

11 JULY 1943 (SUNDAY). What a ball game! At first the game was quite even between the St. Louis Browns and Boston Red Sox. With the score tied at 4 apiece, a St. Louis player hit the ball in left field to the top of the wall. The ball apparently went over the wall and into the stands and then bounced back out to the field. The umpire called it a home run.

Joe Cronin—the Red Sox Manager—got in a heated argument with the umpires about it. In the first 1/2 of the 9th inning the Red Sox scored three times to tie it up. One was a terrific home run to the stands in center field. In the last half of the 9th the Browns loaded the bases with one out. The ball went to the shortstop who threw to second for one out. The second base man threw to first to get the other runner but the runner going to second blocked the ball with his hand. In the meantime the player came home from third with the winning run. Joe Cronin convinced the umpire that the winner had interfered with the ball so the decision was reversed. That made the third out so the run didn't count leaving the game tied. The manager of the Browns didn't like the reversed decision so he got into an argument with the umpires. Then the St. Louis fans started pouring out onto the field to get at the umpire. The police turned the crowd back. In the meantime a Boston player had to duck a beer bottle thrown from the stands. About a dozen men with baskets picked up the bottles thrown from the stands onto the field. Neither team scored for a couple innings until a St. Louis player hit a home run down the left field line. It went into the stands about one foot from being a foul ball. So the Browns won 7 to 6 in 11 innings.

Tuesday morning.

We had a physics test again yesterday. I managed to get a B out of it. If I get through here I'll have almost enough math for a major. After we finish calculus we take a course called Higher Mathematics. Vector Mechanics is plenty deep for me. Among other things last weekend, about 70 of us meteorologists were invited out to Shaw Park in Clayton last Sat. evening. Clayton is a good residential suburb of St. Louis. They had outdoor dancing. The first girl I danced with is engaged to a soldier in Florida who lived in the same fraternity house I'm now in—in fact in the same room. Then I met Elizabeth. She attended this U. last year and is working in a defense plant this summer. We danced and went swimming in the best pool I've ever been in. The chief hostess brought a couple of us back to the U. in her car. First time I've ridden in a car since leaving home—that day I decided to venture out into the world. Altogether I had an extraordinary time at the party. We lack one thing here—and that is sleep. Seems like sometimes when I try to go to sleep, I'm subconsciously trying to solve problems. It's rather a shock to those who used to be at the top in college when they get low grades at times here. I should study more but enough is enough. I don't plan too much on ever getting a commission—there are too many things that can happen. Wish I could come home. Just to not have to shine shoes, and march in step, and get up at 5:30 every morning. I forgot and wrote on the envelope part of the letter too.

Writing on a sheet of stationery designed to fold into an envelope to save paper and shipping weight, Lyle finished his letter.

Wednesday morning.

We turn in laundry on Wed. mornings and we have a calculus test this forenoon. They woke us up at 5:15 instead of 5:30 this morning. Guess it was a mistake. They sure lower our learning efficiency by giving us so little sleep. If things get worse I'll simply stay in weekends and rest up instead of staying out late. We will go out to Jefferson Barracks for target practice in a week or two. J.B. is probably the least liked camp in the U.S. It's an overseas replacement center. Do you have any grasshoppers to bother the cane? I suppose the barley is about ready to be cut. Don't send my tennis shoes—but send the dress shoes as soon as they come—if they come. Guess I'd better study for the Calculus test. This course would be a snap for me if it weren't for Vector Mechanics.

16 JULY 1943 (FRIDAY). There is a car with a S.D. license plate out here today. The color of the plate happened to catch my eye. Yesterday we ran the obstacle course after caluthentics. First over a horizontal bar about chin high, then jump onto a table, over a wall about 8 1/2 feet high, over a couple hurdles, climb up framework back of the grandstand, up and down the steps in several places, climb up a pipe, and then hand over hand on a horizontal bar. Some of the fellows can't make it. The sun is bright and we really sweat. Today we play touch football after caluthentics. The other platoons get to play volleyball or go swimming. I got 3 letters yesterday. I had a notion to put a couple away for later in the week. Another weekend is almost here. Time for class now.

Saturday morning.

The war seems to be going in our favor. Maybe it will be over soon. Everyone was terribly sleepy this morning. You can go to bed early but at 10:00 when it's time for lights out they yell in the loudspeaker and blow whistles as a signal for lights out. This weekend I have nothing planned. I'm going to sleep, swim, study, and do just what I feel like doing. This morning I awoke tired and sleepy and just wished I was home. I was going to maybe take Betty to the opera tonight but guess I'll stay home. I sure hate to miss those operas. They are world famous. We have our rooms all scrubbed and cleaned because Sat. is the main inspection day. They are making improvements all the time. We now have a pool table, pianos, phonographs, couches, and a player piano in one of the recreation rooms. I recommend that the girls go swimming every chance they get. My swimming has improved a good deal. Harvey Hall and I have been working out on the horizontal bar and track a little every evening. He is very good at athletics and so I pick up quite a little from him. There is always something interesting happening in our platoon. Seems like Dale Korzan gets a furlough quite often. Gerald Korzan has really been going up in rank if he is a Captain already.

News from home that a Korzan cousin had received yet another promotion made Lyle, still a lowly private, even more eager to advance in rank. The brochure advertising the meteorology program had implied it would lead to an army commission. In his mind's eye, Lyle could see gold bars glittering in the distance. But the competition was fierce and the army was looking for the best. He knew the laggards and the unlucky would fall by the wayside.

Lyle continued his letter after returning from a photo session of the Class B Pre-Meteorology soldiers. Now that things were evidently going his way, he could not resist crowing, "See Mom, I knew just what I was doing when I joined the army to get into meteorology." He realized luck played a role, but thus far he had prevailed.

Saturday still later.

I must finish this letter. We had our usual Sat. afternoon inspection and they took a few group pictures. There are several parties tonight but guess I'll just stay home. I had a nice swim this afternoon. Some are playing ball and tennis and others left the campus. I think this is a wonderful deal for me. Do you still think, Mom, that it isn't much good or I wouldn't have gotten in? One problem they worked out in vector mechanics this morning was about a crank and connecting rod such as a mower pittman. It's pretty deep but in every accurate machine you figure mathematically just what is needed for efficiency. In higher mathematics, numbers are very little used. Some of this stuff is pretty much over our heads at times. They are shooting it to us pretty fast. They have a special physics class for those with poor grades while the rest of us have inspection. The weeklies and postcard came today. I haven't gotten a refund on college tuition but I'll tend to that myself cause I know what the deal is. Maybe I'll see them personally sometime. Where did you plant those evergreens? The trees in the garden should be doing good with all the rain. The army is a great melting pot. Some fellows don't get adjusted to it very good. They are used to being waited on and taking their time. If anyone has any special faults he gets bluntly and brutally told about them cause everyone says what he thinks. We signed the payroll today so I'll send a bill in this letter. Hope you take it easy at home. Did the cistern get filled up—or didn't you get the troughs cleaned quick enough during the rainstorm?

CLASS B PRE-METEOROLOGY, SIXTY-FIRST TECHNICAL TRAINING DETACHMENT, CENTRAL TRAINING COMMAND, ARMY AIR FORCES
LYLE IS THE TALLEST SOLDIER IN THE BACK ROW ON THE RIGHT-HAND SIDE OF THE ARCH

The cistern, located underground by the corner of the farmhouse, stored rainwater from the roof. Hand pumped into the kitchen sink, the runoff provided a convenient source of soft water for washing and bathing. Drinking water, however, was carried pail by pail from a farmyard well. While enjoying city conveniences, Lyle never ceased to monitor the activities of his family or to inventory the seasonal management of the farm.

20 JULY 1943 (TUESDAY). Are you actually ready to harvest already? Are the grasshoppers cutting any heads? I had a nice quiet restful weekend. Got a B on my last English paper which surprised me. We played volleyball part of P.T. yesterday. I could go for some home cooking. I wanted very badly to go to the opera this Sat. evening—but there is a dancing-swimming party at University City. We play ball tomorrow evening which we enjoy. I sure like it here. Never a dull moment—in fact I wish there were a few. Calculus in 11 weeks—wow. Take it easy on the harvest.

22 JULY 1943 (THURSDAY). The P.X. opened up yesterday and I heard they sold 700 pints of milk. The food has been rather lousy lately. They sure can murder some of it. Mom would like their onions. They have about 10 times as much kick as any I've ever seen. Those cookies sure hit the spot. Those filled ones are especially good. Keep those letters coming and tell me how the harvest is coming. Does the potato crop look pretty good? Guess I'll get ready for class now. We have a new part time math prof. We call him "machine gun Bill" because he lectures so fast. About three weeks of study left on this half of the course. My grades are coming alright and I'm learning plenty.

Immersed in military duties and academics, Lyle and his fellow soldiers had little awareness of the course of the war, perhaps less than most civilians. With little access to war news they mainly heard word-of-mouth reports of the most important developments. Such was the case when Mussolini was deposed in July.

In 1936 Germany and Italy had issued a statement of common interest. Three years later Hitler and Mussolini expanded the coalition into a formal military alliance called the *Pact of Steel,* later known as the *Rome-Berlin Axis.* The media picked up on the word *Axis,* and the adversaries of the Allies, including Japan, came to be known as the *Axis powers.*

It was an important juncture in the war when, after initial setbacks, the Allied forces prevailed in North Africa. The surrender of the Axis forces in May ended the threat to the Suez Canal and resulted in the capture of a quarter million German and Italian soldiers. Exploiting the victory, the Allies invaded Sicily in July and overran that island in spite of stiff resistance. Following the conquest of Sicily, Churchill and Roosevelt, in a joint broadcast, issued an ultimatum to the Italian people: "Die for Mussolini and Hitler—or live for Italy and for civilization."

Disillusioned with the course of the war the Italian people sought new leadership. In its first meeting since the conflict began, the Fascist High Council passed a resolution to depose Benito Mussolini and replaced him with King Victor Emanuel III. The following day Mussolini was arrested and Marshal Pietro Badoglio was appointed prime minister of Italy, marking the end of the Rome-Berlin Axis.

The trainees were glad to learn that Badoglio had immediately dissolved the Facist Party.

25 JULY 1943 (SUNDAY). News has come through that Mussolini has quit. Things may move fast from now on. Any drastic change in government like that makes me think the war will soon be over. I was going to the ball game but decided to stay here and sleep. It's a long hot streetcar ride to and from Sportsman's park. I've got to work on Calculus and English a little this evening. I'm having trouble with integration in Calculus. About half of the fellows have had it before. Had a very nice time at the party last evening. They had dancing and soft drinks at the tennis courts followed by swimming in the nice big pool. This party was at Heman Park in University City. The girl I went swimming with and I spent most of the time diving. I've never dived before. I'll bet we dived 30 times if once. Eventually I got so I could dive a little anyway, although I lit on my stomach once off the high board. Good thing my stomach muscles are tough. Wish I could come home. I'm tired. We have 3 weeks of studying, a week of review, and a week of tests before this half of the course is over. The Lieut. sounded as though we might not get a furlough during our week break—but instead go to the gun range. If they do that the morale will be seriously impaired here. Everyone is living for that furlough. The food is getting worse. They have a peculiar habit of serving old milk on weekends. It was a little sour this noon but I drank it. It was totally sour this evening. Guess I'll sneak out to the Ozark Mts and sleep for a week. The weekends pass too fast. I think we actually put in more time than any other branch of the service. Every day those Physics problems must be worked. Every day we cover a new mess of Calculus and Vectors. Just to illustrate that we use mostly letters in math I'll enclose this paper with an equation that I took off the board in my notes. It is not really as difficult as it looks. Some little integral problem like this will stop me though. By the end of the week I had better be able to do it.

$$\text{Show that} \int e^{ax} \cos bx \, dx = \frac{e^{ax}(a \cos bx + b \sin bx)}{a^2 + b^2}$$

27 JULY 1943 (TUESDAY). The C.Q. overslept this morning so they didn't get us up until 6:00. It has a good psychological effect to get up when it is light out rather than not quite light. You never did say how many calves there were. Did the tomatoes recover from the flood? Are people going to get caught combining grain this year or are there more combines? Almost time to go to class again. My roommate hit orderly room detail this morning. Maybe I'll get the Register today. Take it easy on the harvest.

Continually on the run and lacking newspapers and radio, Lyle failed to hear President Roosevelt's 28 July Fireside Chat on the status of the war:

> My fellow Americans:
> Over a year and a half ago I said this to the Congress: "The militarists of Berlin and Tokyo started this war. But the massed, angered forces of common humanity will finish it."
> Today that prophecy is in the process of being fulfilled. The massed, angered forces of common humanity are on the march. They are going forward—on the Russian front, in the vast Pacific area, and into Europe—converging upon their ultimate objectives: Berlin and Tokyo.
> The first crack in the Axis has come. The criminal, corrupt Fascist regime in Italy is going to pieces.
> The pirate philosophy of the Fascists and the Nazis cannot stand adversity. The military superiority of the United Nations—on sea and land, and in the air—has been applied in the right place and at the right time.
> Hitler refused to send sufficient help to save Mussolini. . . .
> And so Mussolini came to the reluctant conclusion that the "jig was up"; he could see the shadow of the long arm of justice. . . .
> So our terms to Italy are still the same as our terms to Germany and Japan— "unconditional surrender.". . .
> In every country conquered by the Nazis and the Fascists, or the Japanese militarists, the people have been reduced to the status of slaves or chattels.
> It is our determination to restore these conquered peoples to the dignity of human beings, masters of their own fate, entitled to freedom of speech, freedom of religion, freedom from want, and freedom from fear. We have started to make good on that promise.
> I am sorry if I step on the toes of those Americans who, playing party politics at home, call that kind of foreign policy "crazy altruism" and "starry-eyed dreaming."
> Meanwhile, the war in Sicily and Italy goes on.

Emma and Charles, all too aware that many pioneer aviators had died in crashes, viewed airplanes as dangerous flying machines. Even though their son was in the Air Corps they had counseled him to stay on the ground. Lyle respected and listened to their views but made his own decisions, capitalizing on any perceived opportunity that came his way. Anticipating a potentially touchy reaction, he wrote:

29 JULY 1943 (THURSDAY). Just back from Jefferson Barracks. The army seems to have a jinx on me at times. If there are any mistakes to be made they make them on me. There was some mix up so I had to take physical exam "63" which is for officers. I had to have some teeth fixed so they put me in the Dental Chair. A big husky Lieut. put the drill in full gear and really went to town. Wow! I rather enjoyed it though he was so fast and efficient. I breezed through the exam which made me very happy. A nice Lieut. suggested that I take physical "64," which is the very toughest there is to pass in any branch of the service. It is given to Aviation Cadets and includes the Snider test for pulse, heart, blood pressure, and how fast the pulse returns to normal after exercise. The eye test had about 20 different parts to it including color-blindness tests, how fast they focus etc. Depth perception is tested by pulling strings to line up two little poles. Mine passed easily. So I ended up by passing the toughest test of the bunch without any question or doubt. They check you very thoroughly. I weighed in at 169 lbs. and am 6 ft 2 inches tall which is just right. In other words, I could get into cadet flight training. I was terribly surprised to pass the test. You probably don't realize how exact it is. Fellows often spend days trying to pass it if their blood pressure or something is a little off. The Lieut. was sure nice to me.

Your letter came this evening. Chuckie must get a puppy by all means. Our detachment is having a picnic this Sunday out by some river resort away from St. Louis. There will be swimming, beer, picnic dinner, etc. I can't make up my mind whether to get a date for it or not. The Cards and Dodgers play this Sunday too and I hate to miss that. From all indications part of the World Series will be played here in St. Louis. We lost our sixth straight ball game (by 1 point) this week. The fourth platoon has physics lab tonight. We have it Friday evening. We have to carry gas masks everywhere for the rest of the week. We have a physics test in the morning. We are counting the days until our week furlough. The barber cut my hair strictly G.I. last night. About an inch or less at the longest. Sure feels good though.

Don't get me any shoes at least for a while. So a bond finally arrived? Lyman (from Boston) and I played a game of checkers the other evening. He has not been beaten in the army. By luck I got him down to 4 to 3 checkers in my favor and then traded him to 3-2. I failed to corner or trade him in the next 50 moves so it ended a draw according to the rules. I found out afterwards that it is possible to force a trade at 3-2. I ate dinner at a mess hall in J.B. which was good for a change. I could go for some home cooking. Is there a good crop of young pheasants? We sure have it nice here although I believe I have had just as much of army life in 5 months as anyone else. I hit orderly room detail the other morning. Harvey Hall and I are going out for our evening workout pretty soon. He is an example of perfect physique. I guess he has trained all his life.

Lyle thought his friend Harvey Hall, the son of an army colonel, had it all. Harvey was well traveled, personable, intelligent, and athletic. Lyle was certain his buddy would make a mark in the world, assuming he survived the war.
Still reveling over passing exam "64," Lyle finished his letter.

Friday.
It's cool and cloudy this morning so the Physics test won't be so bad. I'm still surprised and elated over passing that physical exam "64." They checked me for everything except dandruff. I'm up on all my work and probably about average or better in grades. I'll have to study pretty hard though to learn this integration. I'll enclose a little folder about St. Louis. I didn't get the last Register you sent. It's probably around somewhere though. Be sure you address them exactly right.

Regularly assigned to details, such as cleaning facilities, policing the area (picking up trash), and clerking at the PX, the men became wary of volunteering for anything. More often than not, what appeared to be a good deal turned out to have a catch.

30 JULY 1943 (FRIDAY). Just back from Physics Lab. On Friday we are on the go from 5:30 to 9:30 so we really put in more hours than any other army post. I'll enclose a clipping about O.C.S. We are lucky though cause we learn something while they go through just as much and don't learn anything that will ever be of any use. I have been getting good grades in English. My last theme, "The Gamble of Wheat Farming," brought me an A. He wrote that it was interesting, instructive, and well paragraphed. I probably couldn't do it again but it takes something "on the ball" to get an A in that competition. One fellow has a doctor's degree. We read them over the microphone from another room. The Pirates are playing the Cards here tonight. I'm ahead of assignments now. I want to finish early and spend a lot of time on calculus. The tests will be mostly facts rather than ability to work problems which doesn't suit me. The Sgt. today asked who knew anything about water. Everyone immediately got suspicious that he wanted to catch a couple suckers for a cleaning detail so no one would raise their hand. Then he said that someone wanted a couple fellows to go on a weekend camping trip to a lake in the Ozarks or somewhere. It still sounded fishy. Finally a couple volunteered and it turned out to be straight stuff. But then I want to

stick around and study anyhow this weekend. I have to clean this hall on the second floor in the morning. Orderly room detail is cleaning and mopping up the headquarters offices. Every so often your name is picked for that or a mess hall or P.X. detail. Our platoon went swimming part of the time in P.T. today. Guess I'll go to bed now.

On Monday, Lyle and three other soldiers were ordered to report to post headquarters where they were briefed on possible training opportunities and told to state a preference. Aiming to be diplomatic, Lyle informed his parents of an intriguing development.

2 AUGUST 1943 (MONDAY). You might not like this. You know I passed the army physical "64" last week. In fact 4 of us out of the 130 here passed it. I guess everyone who thought he could pass took it. They asked us today if we wanted to transfer to flight training, or radar, or remain in meteorology. I had half an hour to decide. I never had any intention of transferring from meteorology when I took the physical. I chose radar—that new science of electrical engineering, radio, and electronics or something. I don't know anything about it. Here's a little about the deal. I'll remain here for the other 4 months of the Class B course—and take the rest of this with a grain of salt—a six month course at Harvard and then a commission followed by 8 months at Mass. Institute of Technology. I have never seen Boston and Cambridge so that is what influenced me. I take it that the course is tougher than Class A Meteorology. It is a new field and certainly not crowded. The requirements are so stiff physically and scholastically that I thought it must be a good deal. What do you think? Besides, I can always study meteorology myself after finishing this math. I'm all enthused about this deal. Lots of fellows would like to get into radar. I'm sure it will be much more interesting and specialized than Class A Meteorology.

Aircrew training was alluring to Lyle. Airmen, frequently regarded as the pampered darlings of the army, often led a more comfortable existence than soldiers in other branches. However, he had been in the army long enough to know there were no guarantees—army brass would assign him to whatever best suited wartime needs.

Later that Monday the meteorology detachment learned of a tragic accident. While they had been enjoying a Sunday picnic out in the country, the mayor of St. Louis, the commanding officer of the Washington University post, and eight other passengers had perished when the wing of their Waco glider collapsed in a flight over Lambert Field. Unfortunately, quality control problems had arisen when, in an effort to speed up production, plants began assembling gliders from components produced by multiple companies.

SITE OF SUNDAY PICNIC, MISSOURI COUNTRYSIDE, 1943

Strange, Lyle mulled, that the opportunity to transfer to flight training, the glider crash, and yet another letter from his parents urging him to stay on the ground should all occur within twenty-four hours. Attempting to minimize the anxiety of his parents, he added a breezy note in which he sandwiched the glider accident among scattered news.

Your letter came today. You got the harvest out of the way in a hurry. Chuckie can take my place. We are going to have a 24 mile hike sometime. They try to scare us but I always figure I can walk as far as anyone. Among other things at the picnic, we swung out over the river on a rope and dived in. Also suntanned a little. My next job is to hit this math for the next 4 weeks. The food is really lousy lately except breakfast. But I don't mind—at least it's healthy. I'll be home pretty soon, so don't bother to send cookies unless it's handy. Had the Doc put a splint on my little finger. It got bent back in a ball game a while back. The Major was killed in a glider crash yesterday. Take it easy on haying. Maybe you could just leave it in rake piles. You would have to farm with a hoe and axe from what I've seen of Missouri. We had a 2 inch rain Sat. to break the drought. I'm enjoying it here and waiting for furlough.

5 AUGUST 1943 (THURSDAY). We had a good game of volleyball yesterday. I haven't gotten a Register for a long time. I have made no plans for the weekend as yet. Maybe I'll go to the opera. Chicago tests start in 3 weeks. I'm getting more confident all the time of passing. Almost time to fall out for class. I've gotten a lot done the past couple days. Lots of fellows would like to get into radar. The grass always looks greener somewhere else.

Nearing the end of the first three months of study, Lyle hunkered down and focused on passing the first set of Chicago tests. No way was he going to remain a buck private and ship out to Jefferson Barracks for reassignment.

Five days later, scribbling on a postcard carrying the watchwords BUY U.S. SAVINGS BONDS, Lyle instructed his parents:

10 AUGUST 1943 (TUESDAY). By return airmail send me that $50 bond. It evidently was some mistake. I will be getting a bond from now on but this one must be returned at once. The weather is too hot for study. We are in Geography class now. One hour of class after this, P.T., drill, and then we are done. Everyone's shirt is soaking wet. There was a big water fight in the barracks last night.

Another outlet from the stilted routine was a juvenile, but harmless, "hot foot" prank. While one soldier distracted another in conversation, a confederate deftly wedged a match between the sole and upper of the victim's GI shoe. When ignited by a second match, the sting of hot leather invariably caused the unsuspecting soldier to jump and yell "Ouch!" Practical jokers, however, did not mess with a fellow soldier unless they knew him well. Because of academic pressure, some of the trainees had short fuses.

15 AUGUST 1943 (SUNDAY). This has been a rather strenuous week. Yesterday afternoon some of us worked out on the horizontal bar and track after inspection. Harvey and I usually run two laps and we are going to increase it a lap after furlough. Then we played basketball and went swimming. I learned a lot in the pool. Chessin and I dived for a bolt in the deep end of the pool. We also exhaled air and sank to the bottom and sat down. One fellow pretended he was drowning down under the water and I tried to rescue him. He tried to drown me at the same time. Neither one of us would have gotten out that time. The next time I got him from behind, locked his arms, brought him to the surface, and towed him in. The pool sure felt good after a week of sweating. One day after P.T. we had a combat trying to take a hill from a couple other platoons. There were some real wrestles. Last night I went right to bed after chow. Guess I'll continue to stick around here pretty close weekends until after furlough. We expect to finish here on noon of Sat

the 28th. Most of our tests will be 3 hours long. In 3 hours they can find out what we know. We are graded in competition with meteorology classes in the other 8 schools. It will be rough if they are all as good as the bunch here. Is the wheat really running better than the barley? Everyone is thinking in terms of "two weeks from today" around here. It gets tiresome day after day to march to class and half step and listen to lectures and eat the same kind of meals and get up at the same time etc every day. So cousin Dale Korzan is a Sgt. now. I wouldn't care to be an M.P. though. About time for church now.

18 AUGUST 1943 (WEDNESDAY). Just time for a few lines. We will be issued cadet uniforms in the near future along with the emblem, etc. We are not officially cadets yet though. We beat the 4th platoon in soccer. One fellow in our platoon cracked a rib. We are days in review. About ten more days and here I come. I have to give a short speech in English this afternoon. I'm breaking in a pair of G.I. shoes this week.

20 AUGUST 1943 (FRIDAY). Just got my shoes polished. It sure has been a nice cool week—our blankets are being cleaned so we have to sleep in wool underwear. I'm getting pretty confident about the tests. The latest fad is a 3 dimension tic tac toe game. We made recordings of speeches in English this week. I have a cleaning detail this morning so I have to get busy now. Don't know what to do this weekend. I may just stay here and sleep and study a little. I doubt that many will wash out in our group. I don't know anyone in our platoon who isn't plenty good. I'll try and let you know when I'm coming.

22 AUGUST 1943 (SUNDAY). Just finished taking a shower after a workout. Also played a little pool and badminton. The captain inspected the rooms yesterday morning and found them in poor shape so we had a G.I. party yesterday after inspection. My roommate and I had our gas masks hung wrong on the bed and we sure got told about it. They inspected again at 4:00 and then let us go. Last night Weiss and I went to the opera, "Ali Babba and the Forty Thieves." It sure had lots of pretty scenes. We got on the wrong bus and ended up at the highlands amusement park. He didn't want to ride the roller coaster cause he had ridden it before but he waited while I rode. I thought I could take it. Wow! You go through a pitch dark tunnel and suddenly plunge almost straight down. Then a cable automatically hooks on and pulls the rocket up to about 100 feet or more. You take an almost vertical plunge to the bottom. A weak person would pass out. It's a sickening sensation to suddenly go straight down. At the bottom it tears around some

curves and goes up again. It was beyond my comprehension that there is anything so vicious in an amusement park. It is a little beyond being thrilling. We finish tests at 11:00 Saturday but the Captain announced the other day that we couldn't leave until 5:30. Some fellows had already bought early tickets. We expect the order to be changed though. Some fellows would lose over a day if they missed the early train east. I studied a little today. I'll pass the Chicago tests alright but they will be plenty tough. Be sure and fan that ice a little so it will last. One Register came Thurs. The next day they called us out for packages and papers mail call but I didn't go cause I knew there would be none for me as long as the Register came the day before. It so happened that there was a Register for me and I almost got into trouble. Rather a coincidence. One Register never did come though.

24 AUGUST 1943 (TUESDAY). This morning I dreamt I was home when they called us so we almost overslept. Looks like we won't be able to leave until Sat. at 5:30. Played catch and studied Calculus last night. It's surprising how much calculus we learned. We had apple pie for dinner yesterday. Two fellows in the house are going to get married while on furlough. Guess I'll go down to the station tonight to find out when the trains leave. Almost time for class again. It's hard to study this week because it's review of stuff we've had before. This is the week that counts.

25 AUGUST 1943 (WEDNESDAY). Spent last evening at the train station. Service to Mitchell is lousy. And we still don't know when we can leave. The order of 5:30 still stands. It will sure mess me up unless changed. If Irene comes we will most likely need you to meet us in Mitchell because we will have no way out. Can't get to Sioux City early enough for the Hiawatha train. Don't expect us till we get there. Class call.

During the ensuing two days Lyle and his classmates wrote the first set of Chicago tests. They would not, however, learn the results until they returned from furlough.

After seven months of army life, Lyle was elated to be going home. Once the leave authorization was duly signed and in hand, he hopped a streetcar downtown to Union Station and boarded a night coach to Kansas City. Upon arrival in the morning he caught a northbound train to Omaha and then a bus to Sioux City. Irene was waiting at the station. Together they traveled homeward on the westbound train, eager to renew family ties.

SLADEK FARM FROM THE NORTH LANE, PUKWANA, SOUTH DAKOTA, 1943

CHAPTER 8

Familiar Faces and Wide-open Spaces

The cultivators of the earth are the most valuable citizens.
They are the most vigorous, the most independent, the most virtuous,
and they are tied to their country and wedded to its liberty and interest by
the most lasting bonds.

—THOMAS JEFFERSON

MINDFUL OF GASOLINE RATIONING, Lyle and Irene took the train all the way to Pukwana, the stop closest to the family farm. Unlike the clamor and jostling crowds at the stations in St. Louis and Kansas City, all was quiet and peaceful at the little depot; brother and sister were the sole passengers stepping down onto the wooden platform. They hurried over to the telephone exchange by Jones Store and asked the operator to ring three shorts and one long.

"Hello."

"We're here. Can you come get us?"

"Sure. But you'll have to wait a bit. Dad is just getting home with a load of hay. He'll have to unhitch the horses and such before he can get started to town."

"Great. Tell him we'll be waiting in the lobby of the Larson Hotel."

An hour later Lyle was taking in the familiar landscape as he drove the fluid drive Dodge down the north lane to the farmhouse. Emma and the girls waved from the doorstep as Skippy, barking excitedly, raced across the yard with Chuckie in close pursuit.

Everyone was talking all at once. Virginia and Jean, attractive and vibrant high school teenagers, peppered Irene with questions about life in the city. Wilma, a precocious eleven-year-old, tugged on Lyle's arm, eager to show him the new bathtub. A bashful Chuckie asked, "How old do you have to be to get in the army?"

The aroma of freshly baked bread emanated from the kitchen. Emma, tending pots and pans at the cookstove, opened the oven door and removed two crusty loaves. Meanwhile the girls, as Lyle called his younger sisters, stretched the table to its full length and covered it with a red-and-white checkered cloth. Dishes clattered as they set places for eight.

Except for Vernon and Vivian, the entire family was reunited. Chatter and laughter filled the room as they savored home-canned beef with mashed potatoes and gravy, garden-fresh peas and carrots, watermelon pickles, and whole-wheat bread smothered with chokecherry jelly. There were "ums" and "ahs" when Emma served dessert, her special-occasion "Saturday cake" topped with burnt sugar.

Following the meal, Charles tuned the Philco to *Major Bowes' Original Amateur Hour*. Despite static and a sometimes fading radio signal, the family enjoyed the performers and their lighthearted banter with Major Bowes. The room was nearly dark before they switched on the lightbulb hanging from the ceiling; the electricity generated by the Windcharger, stored in 32-volt batteries, was readily exhausted.

The family would be up early in the morning. Farmwork would await them as on every day of the year. Lyle was glad to retire to the familiar upstairs room with the blue walls and chintz curtains. It seemed heavenly to stretch out on a full-size bed swathed in sheets fresh from the clothesline. The faint scent of clover drifted in through the open windows, and a chorus of frogs courting in the pond back of the house lulled him into a deep and peaceful sleep.

Awakened in the morning by sunlight streaming in through the windows, Lyle jumped out of bed and slipped into work overalls. Safely away from rigid military regulations, he purposely left a shirt button undone. After greeting his mother busily stirring pancake batter at the stove, he strode across the farmyard in search of his father. Chickens were scurrying about, picking up kernels of grain and chasing down unwary grasshoppers. Young roosters were making feeble attempts at crowing; few had yet mastered the art.

Early each spring Emma ordered a hundred chicks from a commercial hatchery. Upon receipt of the order the hatchery placed newly hatched chicks in cardboard boxes with round peepholes for ventilation and shipped them Rural Free Delivery (RFD). The mail carrier, knowing the chicks might perish from the cold if left at the roadside mailbox, delivered the cartons to the farmhouse door. Emma immediately set the containers on the kitchen floor by the stove. There the snug chicks peeped happily, eating mash and sipping water from fruit jar lids. Once the fluffy, yellow creatures feathered out enough to withstand outdoor temperatures, they were moved to the chicken coop. The roosters soon grew to fryer size and the pullets replenished the flock of laying hens. Emma traded surplus eggs for fresh fruit, sugar, coffee, flour, and other staples at the grocery stores in town.

IRENE AT MORNING CHORES, 1943

IRENE HORSING AROUND, 1943

Lyle found his father down by the toolshed, vigorously cranking a grindstone as he sharpened a sickle for the hay mower. He had already milked the cows, distributed a ration of oats to the workhorses, and watered the Hampshire hogs, a cash crop. Except for one or two butchered for family consumption—pork chops, roasts, and lard—the hogs were trucked to Sioux City in the fall and sold at the stockyards.

The family did not linger long over their breakfast of fried eggs alongside buckwheat pancakes drizzled with dark Karo syrup. For Charles, "Make hay while the sun shines" was a maxim to be heeded. It was necessary to mow the thick prairie hay on dry days when it would not clog the sickle bar. Once cut and raked into windrows, it had to dry in the sun before it could be stacked in the field or stored in the haymow of the barn.

Since the men would be working in the fields all day, Emma and the girls packed lunches. While Charles prepared to start the John Deere tractor, Lyle told Chuckie about the exciting day in 1931 when he first saw the green-and-yellow machine coming down the lane, perched like a giant grasshopper on the flatbed of Uncle John's Chevrolet truck. The rear wheels were tall and spindly, their rims bristled with gleaming steel lugs. And the smokestack and air-intake pipes reached clear to the sky. Later, when a neighbor bought a Farmall tractor with a four-cylinder engine that ran with a steady purr, Lyle was embarrassed when schoolmates made fun of the two-cylinder John Deere, calling it a "Poppin' Johnny."

Charles, ready to start the engine, opened a petcock on each side, advanced the spark, and rotated the big flywheel by hand. The engine popped a couple times, backfired, and then burst into a loud PHOT-fut PHOT-fut. Although the tractor was dependable, its tricycle design and high center of gravity made it susceptible to rolling over. And the steel lugs, though good for traction, caused a back-wrenching crunch whenever they hit a large rock buried in the soil.

As their father drove the tractor up the lane toward the hay meadow, Lyle and Chuckie prepared for a day of fence mending. They harnessed two workhorses, Ted and Beauty, and then hitched the team to a wagon stocked with a posthole digger, wire stretcher, hammer, pliers, and other fencing tools. After loading a bag of oats and a barrel of water for the horses, Lyle and Chuckie stowed a lunch box and a burlap-wrapped water jug for themselves and set off for the land their grandfather had dubbed "Klondike." Located four miles from the homestead, the half section of land had seemed far, far to the north when horses were the only mode of transportation.

After an hour of travel, Lyle and Chuckie reached the Klondike land and went to work repairing the three miles of fence that confined the cattle to the pasture. They reset wooden posts that had rotted off, reconnected strands of broken wire, and tightened fence lines with a wire stretcher. Fencing was a pleasant task on such a nice September day. Fleecy, white clouds dotted the blue sky; bumblebees hummed across the meadow in search of flowering plants; a soft breeze rustled the prairie grass. Although the work was strenuous, Lyle found it satisfying because he could see immediate results from his labor.

While traversing the fence lines Lyle and Chuckie looked over the white-faced cattle, some two hundred head, including the calves, grazing on three hundred acres of native prairie. Lyle did not attempt to count the herd, just noted it appeared to be intact. The older animals looked up as the wagon rattled by, then returned to cropping and munching on grass. The calves, unaccustomed to the sight of humans, were skittish and wild-eyed. Two huge Hereford bulls, vying for dominance, were rumbling, pawing up clouds of dust while eyeing each other warily.

Although the beef cattle operation was relatively easy during the summer grazing season, Lyle was well acquainted with the daily grind during the cold winter months. Before the first blizzard hit, Charles, riding on horseback, would drive the herd along country lanes to the homestead where they would have feed, water, and shelter. Needing more shelter, he had purchased an abandoned barn three years earlier and moved it two miles to the farmstead. As with other showy red horse-barns, once the pride of neighboring farmers, the structure had become outmoded when tractors replaced horses for pulling farm machinery. In earlier days the barn loft, floored with hard rock maple, had served as a dance floor and roller-skating rink. Now, it stored hay.

Every fall when the cattle returned to the farmstead, Charles weaned the calves and sold the yearling steers to cattle buyers from the Sioux Falls stockyards. Every winter day, no matter how inclement the weather, he loaded a hayrack with hay or sorghum, hauled it to an open area covered with clean snow, and dumped the feed into piles for the animals to eat. During prolonged periods of freezing temperatures, he axed ice from the stock tank to allow the cattle to drink. When the Aeromotor windmill was inoperative during periods of calm weather, he labored with a hand pump to supply water from the well to the stock tank. Lyle viewed his father as Superman, strong but gentle, and capable of dealing with almost any adversity.

While Lyle and Chuckie were returning from the Klondike in late afternoon, Virginia and Jean were digging under a layer of straw in the icehouse, collecting two pails of ice from blocks sawn from the pond the previous winter. Emma and Irene were filling a six-quart freezer with a custard concocted from eggs, whole milk, canned pineapple, and sugar.

As Lyle and Chuckie drove down the lane they could see the girls cranking the ice-cream freezer, a welcome sight. Once the milking and other evening chores were done, the family enjoyed fried chicken, baked beans, and bowls of refreshing pineapple ice cream. Following supper, Chuckie asked Lyle to show him an army routine of push-ups and sit-ups. Charles still had enough energy to tune his fiddle and play a favorite number, "Turkey in the Straw."

Lyle asked about the grain harvest completed earlier in the summer. Thanks to plentiful rain and a good growing season the yield had been well above average. As in other harvest seasons the old McCormick-Deering binder, pulled by the tractor, had spewed out neatly tied bundles of grain as it circled fields of barley, wheat, and oats. In Lyle's absence the girls had helped shock the grain, arranging the bundles into conical piles. Though they had not minded shocking the oat bundles, the scratchy beards of wheat and barley had relentlessly penetrated their clothing.

Lyle wished he could be home in late fall when the neighborhood threshing crew would swing into action. He recalled the childhood thrill of watching the threshing machine ingest bundles, pour streams of grain into wagons, and blow clouds of straw and chaff onto stacks that shimmered like gold in the autumn sun. Most of the harvest was stored in steel grain bins to provide winter feed for the livestock, with the surplus sold at the grain elevator in Pukwana for shipment to flour and feed mills. The straw supplied winter bedding for the horses and cattle.

A field of sorghum would be ready to harvest in October. More drought resistant than corn, the cane was bound into bundles, stored in shocks, and fed to the cattle during the winter months. Shocking cane was a man-sized job, for the bundles were heavy and some were more than six feet tall. Lyle regretted he would not be around to help with that chore.

For Charles, corn picking was the last and most tedious task of the harvest season. Hour after hour, while walking alongside a wagon pulled by a team of horses, he snapped mature ears of corn from the stalks and tossed them against the bangboard until several thousand filled the cart. All the while, he set aside choice ears with plump kernels to shell for next year's seed corn. It was imperative he finish reaping before the fields drifted full of snow.

Although much remained the same at home, the pantry off the kitchen now housed the newly acquired bathtub. For Lyle, bathing in a tub was no great treat; he had enjoyed the luxury of running water, warm showers, and bathtubs since going away to high school. Still, he could understand why his mother and sisters thought the elongated, cast-iron tub was a fine improvement over the round, galvanized washtub.

Preparing to take a bath, Lyle pumped water into a copper boiler at the kitchen sink; had the cistern been dry, he would have carried water pail by pail from the farmyard well. Keeping the kitchen range well stoked, he heated the water for two hours before transferring it to the tub. *Voilà*, the bath was ready. When describing the process to an army roommate from Brooklyn, Lyle had joked, "Your home has *running* water, mine has *walking* water."

Several years earlier Emma and Charles had replaced the scrub board and hand-cranked wringer with a washing machine. Hot water for the washer, however, was acquired in the same manner as for the bathtub. If lucky, a vigorous yank on a cord wrapped around the flywheel started the gasoline engine. Once clean, the clothes were rinsed in a separate vat and hung on the clothesline to dry. In the summer they dried quickly, but on cold winter days the garments froze stiff and danced about in the wind like scarecrows.

One day while home, Lyle helped his mother tend her garden. Emma's garden was not a wartime *victory garden* per se, since she planted a garden every year. During the dry days of summer she irrigated the rows of plants with water from a nearby stock tank. Her labor of love never failed to produce a bountiful crop of vegetables and berries. While his mother gathered carrots, onions, and tomatoes, Lyle picked ground-cherries and blueberries. Supplemented by the chokecherries, buffaloberries, plums, and wild grapes gathered by the family on their annual pilgrimage to the Missouri River bottom, jars of jams, jellies, fruit, and garden produce would line the basement shelves come fall.

While Irene prepared the garden vegetables, Virginia and Jean husked the yellow ground-cherries and cooked them into a sweet sauce to spoon over bread. Lyle thought the sauce even better than the cherry jam served at the Miami Beach mess hall.

The following day Lyle accompanied his father and sister Virginia to the hay field. The windrows of hay cut earlier in the week had dried sufficiently for stacking. Riding on a hay bucker, Lyle drove a team of horses along a windrow until a large pile accumulated and then hauled it over to the hay stacker. Charles, using a second team of horses, elevated the pile of hay and dumped it onto the stack, where Virginia spread it evenly with a pitchfork. Building a symmetrical haystack with straight sides was a prideful thing in the neighborhood.

STACKING HAY, VIRGINIA ON TOP OF THE STACK, 1943

Late in the afternoon a bank of dark clouds appeared on the western horizon. Ordinarily the stacker horses were content to stand and rest until the next load was delivered. But hearing a distant roll of thunder, they began to shake their bridles and stomp the ground with their hooves. Wary of getting caught in the thunderstorm the family haying crew worked frantically to top out the last stack. The horses needed no urging on the drive back to the farmstead. Once unhitched from the wagon, they bolted for the barn just as the first hailstones rattled off the roof.

On his last day of furlough Lyle helped his father assess a problem with the windmill tower. Then they repaired the binder for the upcoming sorghum harvest. After replacing a worn gear and adjusting the knot-tying mechanism, they put a shim in the bearing of the pitman that drove the sickle in the sickle bar. Lyle liked mechanical contraptions and working with his hands. As a child he had amused himself by constructing toy cranes, wagons, and combination safes. Gears, levers, and pulleys were second nature to him. Were it not for the war, he mused, he would be in college studying mechanical engineering.

While working side by side Lyle and his father talked about the livestock, grain prices, and other aspects of the farm-ranch operation. Asked why he had purchased a quarter section of land that summer, Charles replied he expected land values to increase because "they aren't making land anymore." He went on to say it was the prospect of owning land that had brought his parents from Bohemia to South Dakota. "Besides," he added, "with a couple good crop years and these wartime commodity prices, the land could pay for itself in three or four years."

Later in the day Lyle, armed with the .22 caliber, pump-action Savage rifle, tromped off with Chuckie to inspect the newly purchased quarter section to the west of the house. Running through the land was a creek bed with a dense growth of reeds, sunflowers, and thistles—an ideal habitat for pheasants. Due to the wartime shortage of ammunition and plentiful grain in the fields, the pheasant population had exploded. Lyle bagged two birds for the family table while, true to his scruples, shooting only at cock pheasants.

A familiar aroma awaited Lyle and Chuckie as they trudged through the door. The previous evening Emma, using her own fermented starter and home-ground wheat flour, had mixed a dishpan of dough. Although the oven of the cookstove had no heat control, she knew just how to stoke the fire with corncobs while baking six loaves of bread and two pans of cinnamon rolls. Lyle and Chuckie helped themselves to slices of warm bread topped with freshly churned butter and wild-plum jelly. "When I was your age," Lyle remarked to Chuckie, "I envied schoolmates who came to school with sandwiches made with store-bought bread in their lunch buckets. Now I'm older and more discriminating."

The family was somewhat subdued during the evening meal. After five days at home, Lyle would be donning his uniform in the morning and returning to army life. Irene would be staying two more days. When asked what kind of sandwiches he wanted to take on the return trip, Lyle, thinking of the *Blondie* comic strip, quipped, "Dagwood sandwiches would suit me just fine." After a few last games of checkers with his father and Wilma, Lyle retired upstairs.

In the morning a misty drizzle turned to rain. Apprehensive the dirt roads would become too muddy for passage, Lyle bid a quick farewell to his brother and sisters. Hurriedly placing a lunch box in his barracks bag, he assured his mother he had all of his belongings and kissed her good-bye.

Lyle and his father were not long at the Pukwana depot before the train chugged in from the west. As the train bumped along toward Kimbal, Lyle's thoughts shifted to St. Louis and the meteorology program. Had he passed the first set of Chicago tests?

ALLAHABAD BANK
LIMITED
ESTABLISHED IN 1865
Affiliated with the Chartered Bank of India,
Australia & China who conduct the Bank's
London and other Overseas Business

HEAD OFFICE : CALCUTTA
6 & 7 Royal Exchange Place

OTHER OFFICES AT :

Agra	Jhansi
Agra, Johri Bazar	Jubbulpore
Ahmedabad	Jullundur City
Aligarh	Kalpi
Allahabad	Kasganj
Allahabad City	Khatauli
Amritsar	Kosi Kalan
Auraiya	Kunch
Bareilly	Lahore
Bareilly City	Lahore City
Benares	Lucknow
Bindki	Lucknow,
Bombay	Aminabad Park
Bombay,	Lucknow City
Kalbadevi Rd.	Lyallpur
Buxar, Bihar	Meerut
Calcutta	Moradabad
Calcutta,	Moradabad City
Burrabazar	Mussoorie
Cawnpore	Muttra
Cawnpore City	Muzaffarnagar
Chandausi	Nagpur
Dehra Dun	Nagpur City
Delhi	Naini Tal
Dibai	New Delhi
Etawa	Orai
Firozabad	Patna
Fyzabad	Rae Bareli
Gadarwara, C.P.	Raipur
Ghaziabad	Sangla Hill
Gorakhpur	Shahjahanpur
Gulaothi	Siswa Bazar
Ispur	Sitapur
Hardoi	Tahsil, Deoria
Hathras	

W. LOTHIAN BROWN
General Manager

BIRTHS.
GILES—On the 25th July, 1943, at B.M.H.,
Deolali, to Gloria, wife of Capt. Norman
Giles, Royal Artillery, a son.   de
KIRKBY—On the 17th July, 1943, to Cynthia
(née Catley), wife of Capt. T. Kirkby,
R.I.A.S.C., the gift of a son, William
Richard. (English papers, please copy.)
RUSSELL—On the 18th July, 1943, at 13,
Municipal Rd., Dehra Dun, to Kathleen,
wife of James Russell, I.C.S., a daughter
(still-born).   de
THOMAS—On the 25th July, 1943, at Miss
Riordan's Nursing Home, Calcutta, to
Kathleen, wife of Henry Noel Thomas,
a son. Both well.   de

FORTHCOMING MARRIAGE.
The engagement is announced between
Major Ferdinand James Behets, Royal
Signals, younger son of Mr. and Mrs. R.
Behets, of Finchley, London, and Heather,
only daughter of Major and Mrs. B. J.
Robertson, of Mossley Hill, Liverpool and
Simla.   dfi

MARRIAGE.
MEALIN—CANNIFF—On the 21st July,
1943, at St. Thomas' Church, Middleton
Row, Calcutta, Edmund Maurice, son of
Mr. and Mrs. E. C. O. Mealin, to Molly
Margaret, daughter of Mr. and Mrs.
J. W. Canniff.   dg

DEATHS.

SIC TRANSIT GLORIA
1922—1943

EPITAPH

*"In an unreliable
world there is
only one thing
that can be
relied on, and
that is the
unreliability of
Mussolini."*

ADOLF HITLER
1937

Balmer Lawrie & Co., l

THE STATESM

CALCUTTA, JULY 28,

EXIT A TYRANT.

MUSSOLINI has gone. This
great news, perhaps the gre
news of the last two
for no event since Hitler's a
on Russia has seeemed
tined to exert weightier influ
on the fundamentals of wo
politics. Mussolini is the init
and architect of Fascism.
21 years he has wielded tyranni
power over the Italian people;
served as inspiration and mentor
Hitler in that now greater tyrann
early days; he was the first Europea
statesman since Versailles to derid
and (within the limits of his reach
to suppress the democratic way
life. His doctrines postulated th
war is good in itself, he assiduo
prepared his own country for
and to the historical eye is
even guiltier than Hitler

CHAPTER 9

The Changing Winds of War

In an unreliable world there is only one thing that can be relied on,
and that is the unreliability of Mussolini.

—ADOLF HITLER

WHILE HOME ON FURLOUGH, enveloped in the serene setting of family
and farm, Lyle had thought little about the war raging in distant lands.
But on the train trip back to St. Louis he was jolted back to reality by a
newspaper headline: ALLIES INVADE ITALY.

The formation of a new government in Italy had brought about large-
scale defections in the Italian military. As a countermeasure, Hitler had
immediately sent additional troops to Italy to resist the expected Allied
invasion. Meanwhile, the Badoglio government signed a secret armistice
with the Allies and directed the Italian navy to sail for Malta to prevent the
fleet from falling into German hands.

The Allies were on the offensive once again. The changing winds of war
stimulated the flow of adrenaline on the home front and helped placate
Stalin, who had been pressuring Roosevelt and Churchill to invade Europe
to alleviate German pressure on the Eastern Front.

Judging by the size of the newspaper banners, the invasion of Italy was a
decisive blow. Like in a boxing match, Lyle thought, we will knock the Axis
out.

5 SEPTEMBER 1943 (SUNDAY). Got back to the campus in time
for breakfast this morning. I had the super duper luck of getting a seat
all the way. Got to Sioux City at noon and had to take a bus half an
hour later to Omaha. A Red Cross lady came through the bus and
gave us treats so I had an orange on the way to Omaha. That makes 3
times in Sioux City and each time a Red Cross treat. Arrived in Omaha at

4:30 and took another train to Kansas City right away. We passed the
Golden Spike Railroad Monument near Omaha where the east and west
railroads met. A man on the train gave me a stick of gum and two new
Chicago newspapers. They sure had inky headlines about the invasion of
Italy. Got to Kansas City about 9:30 and had to wait two hours for a St.
Louis train. While waiting at the station a man gave me a new Saturday
Evening Post. Said he had it memorized already. When they opened the
gate to the St. Louis train, people really poured on. The seats were filled
and the aisles full of standing people. Managed to sleep a little at times.
One standing soldier got so tired he just laid down in the aisle and
stretched out and slept. There were officers around too but I guess he
got by with it. While waiting for a streetcar to come up from the station
a man in a car came along and said he was coming this way. He insisted
on driving up on the campus a ways so I wouldn't have very far to walk.
After sleeping all forenoon I feel pretty good. Two more soldiers just
came up the hill with their suitcases. Did you make it home all right on
the muddy roads? I don't suppose it rained any more that morning. I
sure pulled a dumb boner in forgetting those 4 articles of clothing. Just
forget about them at present.

Back on campus after furlough, Lyle and his classmates anxiously awaited
their scores on the first set of Chicago tests. Fearing they had botched one or
more of the physics, calculus, vector mechanics, or geography exams, they
dubbed Washington University *Wash Out U.* Meanwhile, the second half
of the Class B Meteorology course got underway with the usual daily and
weekly tests.

7 SEPTEMBER 1943 (TUESDAY). A cold wave hit here last night.
The air looked frosty in the valleys. My cold is getting better. Guess you
had better send those four articles of clothing as soon as convenient.
Don't see how I forgot the whole mess. We were paid yesterday. Got a B
in English. There were a couple A- and a lot of Bs and Cs. Guess we all
did poor on the Physics test. A lot of tricky questions that did not test
a knowledge of Physics. Did the kids all get started to school again? I
should finish before they do if things go right. Time for class again.

In a radio broadcast on 8 September, the day before the American Fifth
Army landed at Salerno, President Roosevelt reported:

> Today, it is announced that an armistice with Italy has been concluded.
> This was a great victory for the United Nations—but it was also a great
> victory for the Italian people. After years of war and suffering and degradation,
> the Italian people are at last coming to the day of liberation from their real

enemies, the Nazis. But let us not delude ourselves that this armistice means the end of the war in the Mediterranean. We still have to drive the Germans out of Italy as we have driven them out of Tunisia and Sicily; we must drive them out of France and all other captive countries; and we must strike them on their own soil from all directions. . . .

The great news that you have heard today from General Eisenhower does not give you license to settle back in your rocking chairs and say, "Well, that does it. We've got them on the run. Now we can start the celebration."

The time for celebration is not yet. And I have a suspicion that when this war does end, we shall not be in a very celebrating mood, a very celebrating frame of mind. I think that our main emotion will be one of grim determination that this shall not happen again.

9 SEPTEMBER 1943 (THURSDAY). Your card came today. It's in the wind tonight that a new commanding officer (C.O.) is coming tomorrow. The Top Sgt. is going to O.C.S. so we have a new Sgt. He is going to start a "new order" starting Monday. It will be put back on a "gig" basis like the aircrew with weekend marching for punishment. The Class C Meteorology students are taking their tests and have a furlough next week. We had a fire drill the other night and the warrant officer said 30% might flunk out now. I don't believe he knew what he was talking about. My name is about due for orderly room detail in the morning. Had a house detail this morning. My cold is improving and I feel good. We are having First Aid lectures by a Red Cross man during drill periods.

Couldn't you take all the braces out of the windmill tower below the stand and spread the legs to meet the anchors? Italy's surrender seems to be quite a decisive event in the war.

Friday morning.

I missed detail this morning but I'll likely get it tomorrow morning. They got the name next to mine. Physics isn't a bit interesting just now. Wouldn't be surprised if I got very low in the Physics test. It was full of catch questions rather than a knowledge of Physics. I'll try and buy a World Series ticket soon. They probably cost plenty. The Cards have a 15-game lead and 22 games left to play. This weather here certainly must not be normal. There must be a cold wave from the north. I'll send my ration certificate if you want it. Don't know what I'll do yet this weekend. Today is our day for swimming during part of P.T. Take it easy.

12 SEPTEMBER 1943 (SUNDAY). A rather rainy day today. Wrote that line and then played 3 games of pool. I've been taking it too easy on the studying so far. The grades are back from Chicago and we'll soon find out who flunks out. We had some good games of touch football

and basketball in the gym yesterday afternoon. Also went swimming afterwards and dived a couple times. Yesterday evening I went to a doubleheader show. "Five Graves to Cairo" and one about Texas A and M. The latter was sadly illogical and overdone but the first one was good. Slept too late for breakfast this morning. I was really hungry by noon cause breakfast is my biggest meal here. Three of us walked over to church this morning in the rain. A major has replaced the Captain as C.O. of this post so there'll be some changes made soon.

Lyle resumed his letter after learning of a favorable war development reported by the media. In typical British understatement, Admiral Cunningham had announced: "Be pleased to inform Their Lordships that the Italian battle fleet now lies at anchor under the guns of the fortress of Malta."

It seems that the Allies now have the Italian fleet. That is a very decisive blow. The clothes came Saturday. Don't see how I could possibly forget so many at one time when I left! The lunch box etc seemed to make the barracks bag about the right size. They gave us a check for about $4 for furlough rations. Do the girls like school again? The regular college will open here soon. I'm improving a good deal on the obstacle course. It's really juicy out just now. Am sending a little clipping. Gail Myers was on the opposing team the first time I ever debated at State College. We were defeated very decisively. Guess I'll study a little Physics before going to bed. We had a fire drill the other night—they usually wait until a rainy night like tonight. I'm glad I'm in the army because most everyone else is and it's building me up too.

As the war progressed, General Hap Arnold and his staff made policy changes and fine-tuned plans. In accordance with military forecasts, Air Corps training programs were accelerated, slowed down, or shut down. Apparently army planners had overestimated the number of men needed for weather analysis. Rumors were circulating that the Class B Meteorology program would soon be terminated. The news was upsetting for some of the students, but not for Lyle. He foresaw new opportunities, perhaps in the new technology known as radar—ra·dio d·etecting a·nd r·anging. For those soldiers with test scores below the standard set by the Chicago Board, it meant the end of the Air Corps technology training line.

17 SEPTEMBER 1943 (FRIDAY). Eighteen men washed out Wednesday which was one in every six. A couple of them just didn't have it, a couple didn't work hard enough, and the rest were just a little lower than the rest. It sort of took out the stragglers just like taking

the odd colors out of a herd of cattle. None of them were outstanding physically either. I got 55% in Geography. 50% was passing and the high grade was 85%. Thought maybe I had flunked that one. The champion checker and chess player washed out. The other grades will be out soon. We had a good game of touch football last evening. Our side won by two touchdowns due to better teamwork. Tonight we have Physics Lab. We are going to the rifle range in a week or two which will be fun. They are going to break up our 5th platoon because they only need 4 platoons. Our platoon was quite outstanding. Only one washed out of our platoon and we had the highest class average, etc.

Several fellows got letters this week from other meteorology schools saying that Class A and B Meteorology schools were being dissolved. We have heard nothing official yet and we hope to finish the B course here but there seems little chance of going on to an A school. The fellows were disappointed by this. You often hear fellows saying they don't like it here, but when it comes face to face with going they change their tune. They are stricter with us now but they are reasonable.

20 SEPTEMBER 1943 (MONDAY). Another nice weekend is over. The Class C Meteorology students are back from furlough and there are more rumors in the air. They announced Sat. that us Class B Meteorology students definitely would finish the course here and go on to A schools. It sounded fishy to me because meteorology students in other schools are being reclassified. I expect we'll finish here but it wouldn't surprise me if the thing blew up any day. The washouts were shipped to Jefferson Barracks Sat. p.m. They are being reclassified as aerial gunners and weather observers it seems. We played basketball Sat. afternoon after inspection and also went swimming. I went to bed early Saturday evening. Some of the fellows saw the movie stars in the U.S.O. on their way to the Bond Cavalcade performance. They said Mickey Rooney was a sad sack. Saw the Cubs beat the Cards in both games of a doubleheader yesterday. The Cards have already cinched the pennant though. Did you start cutting cane already? Are you done with putting up hay! A new wisdom tooth bothered me a little last week. I should be working a little Physics right now. The Gestapo regime starts today. They are going to start giving out demerits etc so I'll have to be careful.

Seeking to make his presence felt, the new commanding officer of the meteorology detachment tightened up on discipline, increased the dispensing of gigs, and shipped more washouts to Jefferson Barracks.

With the meteorology program scheduled to close in November, Lyle and his fellow soldiers went before an officer review board for reassignment. After being interviewed, Lyle was told his academic record made him eligible for communications cadet, but that he would likely go to aircrew training since he met the strict physical requisites for that assignment. Not wanting to distress his parents, he soft-pedaled that possibility.

22 SEPTEMBER 1943 (WEDNESDAY). In a few minutes we go to class and have a physics test. I was unlucky enough to hit P.X. detail this morning. I told you about the rumors we had been hearing around here the past couple weeks. Ten officers from a Colonel on down arrived here by plane from Fort Worth, Texas, yesterday. They told us that only Class B Meteorology students who graduated before the middle of October would be sent to an A school. So we had personal interviews and were reclassified with very little choice of classifications. My first choice was Communications Cadet and secondly aircrew. I presume Radar is out because it's doubtful they need Radar students anymore as long as they have a surplus of meteorologists. We stay here for the rest of the course which is about two months. The classifying officer said I would probably go to aircrew. However that involves another physical exam and all sorts of balancing and coordination tests. I wouldn't mind taking just a few flying lessons but that's a long way off too so just forget about it. The fellows are rather disappointed, but I figured it was too long a course to ever get through Class A Meteorology. We signed the payroll yesterday. Still haven't bought a World Series ticket, but I'm going to a game by some hook or crook. The cane isn't so hard to shock as last year is it? How are those watermelons coming? Hope we get a furlough after finishing here. I'll have to pack up now for class.

Apprehensive and upset by the latest news about aircrew, Lyle's mother folded the letter, placed it back inside the envelope, and wrote on the backside:

> Life is a trust
> that must be accounted
> for to God,
> the soul of the universe.

While mulling over his options, Lyle wondered, Do I have the *right stuff*? Were he to wash out of flight school, like many would-be pilots, he would revert to buck private and be assigned to some other role. Were he to make it all the way, likely he would become a bomber or transport pilot since only the very best aviators became fighter pilots. Or he might end up as a flight instructor and never have the opportunity to go overseas.

Wishing to ease the anxiety of his parents, Lyle pointed out in his next letter that the president's wife frequently traveled by plane. Thinking some aircrew assignments might be more acceptable to them than others, he sounded out possibilities.

23 SEPTEMBER 1943 (THURSDAY). Boy, was I lucky tonight. I forgot to sign up for a haircut this evening but the next fellow in line for a haircut was a few minutes late so I hardly had to wait at all. We'll have to get haircuts practically every week—or else. Wonder of wonders, we had apple pie for dinner! The food has been better since the major came. We have a geography test on African cities, rivers, and mountains tomorrow. About 100 or more strange names to memorize. Guess I'll just learn enough to get by which is a poor attitude. But I don't like geography and I think it's relatively unimportant. We played field basketball part of our P.T. period today. I could sure go for a plum jelly sandwich, or a Dagwood sandwich with peaches and plums. It is funny how mail call is the high spot of the day. Pete Smith gets so mad when he writes to people and they don't answer the very next mail.

Some of the fellows feel pretty sour about meteorology closing up. They don't realize that the army doesn't have to make them any promises. I'm pretty enthused about going into aircrew (if they do take me in aircrew) although it's a long rough training period. I see that Mrs. Roosevelt just got back from a couple hundred thousand mile plane trip. Do you know anything about whether pilot or navigator would be best? Aircrew has a good tough physical program that would build me up. Guess I'll go to bed. I feel blue in the morning if I get up sleepy and it's still dark out.

Friday morning.

I swiped an extra banana at chow this morning. My roommate is on hall detail. I'm glad the weekend is almost here. But we had better have our rooms just so tomorrow morning or we will get restricted. It's a nice bright cool morning and we have orders to wear flight jackets to class.

24 SEPTEMBER 1943 (FRIDAY). We are up quite a while before daybreak these days. We have Lab tonight but we'll try and get that over with in a hurry. I'm not particularly ambitious in the books lately. Got a C on the Chicago Physics test. The two math grades were maybe better.

Now that the meteorology program was shutting down, Lyle's motivation was dwindling. He was content to stay in the middle of the pack while reserving enough energy for the next challenge, whatever that might be.

In the interim, Lyle received a letter from his parents urging him to see about the possibility of the Army Specialized Training Program (ASTP). But he foresaw no glamour or excitement in specialized training at some college while the army decided where he was needed. In response he thoughtfully, but resolutely, replied:

27 SEPTEMBER 1943 (MONDAY). Was glad to get your letter. Those fellows are maybe rather lucky to be sent back to their home college but I wouldn't want to be in A.S.T.P. Besides, I think there is a little clause in fine print that you have to sign up for overseas duty after the war is over. I'm satisfied with what's going on. The army doesn't make you any promises you know. And you can't control your destiny in the army. They put you where they need you. If they put me in aircrew, I'll try and be a navigator rather than a pilot and definitely not a bombardier. A navigator only gets basic flight training and then goes to navigator school. Bet I could fly a plane as good as any of them though. The war will likely be over though before I would ever finish that. And I have two months here before they even decide at all if I go to aircrew. You can't tell anything about Radar. Seems like there might be a chance as long as my application is in. I sure enjoy it here and I'm proud of my physical improvement. I can go over obstacles, etc much better than the average. About 50 to 70 Class C Meteorology students will wash out this week. That will make things much roomier around here. Some of us are going ice skating this evening. No, it's not that cold here yet. There is an indoor rink downtown a little way. Saw a couple shows and a doubleheader ball game this weekend. The Cards beat the Phils. It is easy to see that the Cardinals are world champions. I expect they'll easily beat the N.Y. Yankees in the World Series a couple weeks from now. Maybe Germany will fold up before Christmas. It's rather doubtful they will fight after they know they are beaten. Do you really think it would be foolish for me to get in aircrew? Mrs. Roosevelt flew all over the world you know.

Did my drawing set come with my stuff? That black case with all the instruments in it? We had a real good dinner today. Sweet potatoes, ham with candied pineapple, etc. Of course I had to go through the line twice for a meal like that. Seems like we have to get haircuts every week here but a haircut on Friday will last for two inspection Saturdays.

Tuesday.

Well, we skated at the Winter Garden last night. It is really swell with nice music and people flashing around on the ice. Neither Harvey nor I had skated before but neither of us fell down all evening. The main trouble is weak ankles. We were going plenty good by the end of the evening. He was skating a little better than I at the end—he is the best athlete in the flight. So we had a nice time but now we pay the penalty cause we're awfully tired this dark morning. I'm going skating quite often I guess. A couple of our subjects are not interesting just now but they'll be getting better. Why don't you get rid of some of the calves like last year? Too big a bunch of calves get wild and break down the fences. Time now to do my housecleaning.

In light of gasoline rationing, Lyle wondered if his family would be making the seventy-mile drive to Mitchell for the annual harvest festival. He supposed the Corn Palace—a showy building with gaudy turrets and exterior walls decorated with grains, grasses, and colorful ears of Rainbow Flint corn—would feature patriotic mosaics again this year, perhaps planes in aerial combat and other war scenes. He was unaware that the swastika, an ancient good luck symbol used by native Americans, had appeared along with other decorations on the Corn Palace in 1927. Each year the Palace featured top entertainers, such as Jimmy Dorsey in 1938 and Paul Whitman in 1939. Russ Morgan, known for his *wah-wah* trombone style, was slated to be the star attraction in 1943.

CORN PALACE, MITCHELL, SOUTH DAKOTA

Not having seen Vernon and Vivian during his nine months in uniform, Lyle was looking forward to an upcoming reunion. In his letter home, he included his official scores on the Chicago tests that he finally received a month after returning from furlough. Before inserting a photo of a friend standing atop a decorative stone, he jokingly wrote on the back, "The only time Pete Smith was ever on the ball."

PETE SMITH "ON THE BALL," 1943

30 SEPTEMBER 1943 (THURSDAY). Just a few words before—Friday night.

Was going to write before going skating last night but didn't make it. The skating was fun but I didn't improve much over the other time. Guess my ankles are a little weak yet. Just got back from Physics Lab this evening and washed out a couple pair of socks. Suppose you went to the Corn Palace today. How was the show? Were the concessions and carnival rides going full blast? Did the kids skip school too? Vernon wrote last night that they were coming from Kansas City for a weekend visit so I suppose they'll get here in the morning. However, my weekend doesn't start until the middle of Saturday afternoon but from then on until 10:00 Sunday evening I am free. So I'm especially looking forward to this weekend. Had to give a speech in English today and got a B without putting in too much time.

I'll put here a little table of my scores from the Chicago tests:

	Calculus	Vector Mechanics	Physics	Geography
Passing	55	90	52	50
Mine	86	120	72	56
Wash U. average	80	117	70	61
National average	83	117	74	64

So I ranked a little above the average and especially in the important math courses. But some fellows were way above me. I had a narrow squeak in Geography. We had physical rating tests Wednesday including sit ups (73), chin ups (11), and 300 yd shuttle race (50 sec). My rating was in the Very Good class but short of Excellent. Our assignments are rather long and tough lately. This was registration day for the college freshmen so there were swarms of coeds around. Someone said there would be 3000 girls attending the U. this fall. School starts Monday. We have some horseshoes around now and I find I can play with the best of them. In fact three times I put on double ringers.

We also play a little hardball and we played field basketball part of P.T. today. Things are very interesting around here. Kenneth Lunn wrote yesterday. He was home on a 3 day pass from Ohio. Royce Bates is still in Georgia and I suppose Jimmy Sladek is still there too.

Saturday morning.

I hit mess hall detail this morning. We are really cleaning our rooms for the big inspection today. Each sock must be rolled just so. Seems like they can always find some little thing wrong with a room.

5 OCTOBER 1943 (TUESDAY). No letter in the mail today! We're doing a little reviewing this evening for a big calculus test in the morning. It's mostly double and triple integration for areas and volumes. Vernon and Vivian came to St. Louis on the Saturday morning train and got in touch with me late in the afternoon. Vernon's roommate at Northwestern University, Paul Moore, and his wife, Flo Alice, live here in St. Louis so they called them up from the station. Paul was out of town on his Red Cross job but Flo Alice met them at the station in her car and so they made her apartment their headquarters. The Apt. is not very far down the same car line as I live on, which was a nice coincidence. We had a spaghetti supper at Garavellei's (where one of my Math Profs. has too many beers). We talked and walked a little and drove around in Flo's car. I came back to the U. for the night and went back for late breakfast. Flo made the most delicious bacon and eggs and toast. Guess her cooking was very popular at Northwestern too. We spent Sunday driving around to points of interest and had a nice meal at a hotel. V and V had to get to the train station early in order to get a chance for a seat. Hope they made it cause they had to go to work early the next morning. We had a nice weekend. What did you do? Did the melons and tomatoes freeze and how many spuds did you raise? Thanks, Mom, for the peanut butter marshmellow squares. They came and they went. They sure were good. Would like to have gotten in on more of that cake. I didn't know Wilma was having a birthday. The papers came today. How was the

Corn Palace? It sounded like a good program. Did you see that fellow dive with a noose around his neck? The World Series started today and I won a dime on the Yanks although I really thought the Cards would win. Some of the fellows are going to stand in line all Saturday night to get a Sunday World Series ticket. Don't know if I'll do it or not. I could sleep for a week although a couple nights will probably do the job. We are now wearing our woolen clothing cause the weather is getting cooler. It's very doubtful now that I'll go into aircrew.

Thursday morning.

Forgot to mail this yesterday. The mornings are very dark and rather chilly. The Cards evened the series yesterday. I'll try desperately to get into the game Sunday although some say the line for the bleacher tickets will form 24 hr ahead of time. All the good seats of course have been sold for some time. We may go to the rifle range this Saturday. Guess I did poorly on the calculus quiz—seems like I know it pretty good too. They changed us to Squadron 3, Flight E, a few days ago. The room is in order so I'll study a little.

10 OCTOBER 1943 (SUNDAY). Wow! Today I saw the World Series game between the Cardinals and New York Yankees. I was very lucky to get in a servicemen's line about 9 o'clock and get a seat out in the left field bleachers. Lots of people including some of the fellows here stood in line all night to get in. Some people stood in line several hours and didn't get tickets. There were about 40,000 packed in the park and even standing room was packed. I wanted to see the game at any price and feel very lucky about getting in. Had to wait about 3 hours in the hot sun packed in with people all around before the game started. Even great stars like "King Kong" Keller of the Yankees who played in left field a few feet from where I was sitting was nervous as the game was about to start. The Yanks are very powerful and Gordon, Keller, and Dickey put several home runs in the stands during batting practice. Joe Gordon made some spectacular plays at second base. The Yankees won by a score of 2 to 1 which was disappointing to St. Louis.

Yesterday morning we got up at the usual time, ate chow, cleaned our rooms, and left for Moss Hollow small arms range at seven o'clock. It was cold in the open trucks so we stopped to warm up a little. By the side of the road was a pear tree with little pears that were really delicious. Moss Hollow is like it sounds—a little valley out in the hills about 35 miles S.W. of here. We shot first with the sub-machine gun for practice and then spent the rest of the forenoon cleaning Garand rifles. At noon we had two sandwiches, half pint of milk, and a couple cupcakes. After being outside all morning it tasted good like when you are in the hay field or picking corn in the fall. Or like after taking a long walk hunting and finding fresh cookies when you get home. After dinner we shot a few rounds on the carbine for practice and then started firing it for a record. The range is 200 yds and the black spot doesn't look very easy to hit. It went something like this. First fire 4 shots standing, put in another 4 and shoot them from the prone position all in 40 seconds. I did fairly poor on the first 8 shots cause I shot them faster than necessary. The next four shots were standing followed by 4 more sitting, all in 40 seconds. I got 5 bullseyes, a four, and a three, and missed the target altogether once in that batch. The next 8 were all shot from prone. I squeezed off the first four but messed up changing the clip. It jammed up and the forty seconds was over so I lost 4 shots or a possible 20 points. The four that I did shoot that time were all bullseyes. The other 16 shots were about the same. Altogether I got about 150 points out of 200 possible which was marksman and almost sharpshooter. I could do better if I could get another chance—at least I was improving. We got home about 8:00 in the dark and didn't get any mail or supper so I had a malted milk at the drugstore. A couple of the fellows went down to the ballpark as soon as they got back last night so they are really tired now. I'm satisfied now even if I never see another World Series game. I just played it on a hunch—and won. Of course it was uncomfortable sitting all crowded together in the hot sun and I would have had more fun playing football or shocking cane but it's nice to have seen the game. I'm getting tired of studying and this part of Physics about electricity is hard for me. I think you're right about me buying some shoes here cause those are probably too small. No cattle buyers yet? I can hardly wait for that cake to get here—don't let Wilma get a hold of it first. Boy, that bed looks good to me tonight.

The following Sunday, Lyle and his buddy Harvey Hall were warmly greeted when they attended a church service in University City. Wartime posters encouraged civilians to SUPPORT OUR BOYS. Such reminders were unnecessary since nearly everyone had relatives, neighbors, or friends in the armed forces. Civilians went out of their way to help the men in uniform. Women baked cookies and handed them out to soldiers passing through on troop trains; motorists with empty car seats usually stopped to pick up hitchhiking GIs; parishioners invited visiting soldiers to their homes for Sunday dinner following church services. Mothers did not mind a bit when their daughters became acquainted with servicemen, ordinary citizens from farms, towns, and cities.

Having turned twenty on 13 October, Lyle expressed appreciation for birthday treats from home.

18 OCTOBER 1943 (MONDAY). Thanks, Mom, for that swell birthday cake. I guess that was about the best ever. And my favorite frosting. It sure made a hit here on the second floor gang. Don't see how you find time to bake a cake like that on top of canning and everything. Irene sent me a nice billfold which I needed and V and V sent me a shoe shine kit and tie. I was surprised to get all the presents. We had inspection in the barracks Sat. p.m. and got out about 3:00. Some of us had fun playing touch football until supper time. I went downtown and hunted for a pair of shoes Sat. eve. It's hard to buy anything in a city like this cause the business districts are all scattered out. Found a comfortable pair of military style shoes that were really wide enough for their length. Cost me $6 dollars. Then I just had a malted milk and came home. Sunday morning I woke up in time for chow and then studied. A few minutes before church time Harvey suggested we go to church so we got ready in a hurry and dashed over. After services a lady stopped us at the door and asked us over to her house for dinner and to spend the day. Harvey had an engagement for the afternoon but I didn't have anything very definite and she had a good looking daughter so I gladly accepted. It was a family of four and they lived in a nice residential section of University City. He has some sort of livestock finance business and they evidently are quite wealthy and very nice. We had a good dinner including two pieces of apple pie. Shirley and I played ping pong, played the victrola and radio, went walking, etc. She is a senior in high school and plans on going to Stephen's College for girls.

27 OCTOBER 1943 (WEDNESDAY). An announcement just came over the speaker system that a Kappa fraternity wants ten soldiers for a Sat. night dance. Six of us had a little game of football this evening but the season is about over cause it gets dark too early. Guess I like the outdoors too well. We had to write a theme today for English. Guess I'll go downtown this Sat. eve. and try and buy Irene a present for her birthday—maybe a box of candy as a last resort. I hit a detail this morning too. Also got my hair cut this evening and today was laundry day so I've been busy. I've gained five or six lb since furlough—over 175 now. The freshmen had a bonfire back of our barracks this evening but we weren't invited. We'll likely be here about a month yet and then maybe a while at Jefferson Barracks. It will be good to move along again. Don't eat too much confetti at the carnival. Have you gotten any bonds from me? You never told me how you fixed the windmill legs. I'm tired so guess I'll make up my bed. On Wednesdays we fold up the sheets etc for airing out so now we have to make the bed. Take it easy on the work.

Knowing Irene had been contemplating taking a weekend jaunt to visit former coworkers, Lyle wondered if she had made the journey. He expressed admiration for his sister.

29 OCTOBER 1943 (FRIDAY). Happy birthday, dear sister. We sure are proud of you. Us younger kids are lucky to have a brother and sister to set an example for us. Did you make the Watertown trip last weekend? Would you still rather be there or in Sioux City? This morning at revellie they called Roy Agner's name for a detail. He hollered 3 times when his name was called before the Sgt. heard him. When the next name was called in our flight we all yelled together. The Sgt. got mad so we may get restricted this weekend. But I doubt it. We had a real game of soccer the other day and finally beat the 4th platoon 2 to 1. There is a lot of rivalry cause we live in the same house. Some of the games get pretty rough. We usually play a little while after dark just for fun. Turned in a pair of pants for exchange a couple weeks ago and they still aren't back so I'm short of clothes. Guess I'll borrow an iron and press these. I should be studying but my homework is done. It's a good thing we'll be leaving soon cause most of us are getting pretty dull on the studying. Bet I'm a better goldbricker than you are.

Feeling somewhat burned-out as the meteorology program wound down, Lyle was keener about the rivalry on the athletic fields than in the classrooms. He related to soldiers who took a certain amount of pride in getting by with the minimal amount of effort, especially when doing menial tasks. A skilled goldbricker went through the motions of peeling potatoes while on KP but did not peel very many; better yet, an experienced army goof-off went on sick call to get out of work details altogether.

On Halloween night, Lyle wondered about the activities of his family.

31 OCTOBER 1943 (SUNDAY). What did you do today? It was an extra nice day here. We had a parade yesterday afternoon instead of the usual inspection. Then some of us played basketball in the gym. Saturday evening I fooled around downtown and ended up by going to a double feature. "Passport to Suez" was a good show but the other one, "The Youngest Profession," stunk. It was raining when I got out and it kept raining harder and harder so I got a little bit wet coming home. Managed to wake up in time for chow this morning. Used to be that Sunday morning breakfast lasted until 9:30 but they have moved it up to 8:30 in order to save on food. Maybe there was some other reason. Harvey and I managed to make it to church this morning. It's about a 5 block walk from here over north in University City. We have absolutely

no idea of our next assignment. Suppose we'll go to various places. Kenneth Lunn is going to California soon for a short course on one of the bombers. He apparently has some sort of maintenance training or something. He sure is lucky to go out there for the winter. Slept a couple hours this afternoon, played pool and ping pong, and worked out a little on the track; so now I'm ready for supper. That semi-colon is there as a result of the last theme we wrote for English. I got a B- which isn't so bad. Our math is getting pretty theoretical lately. We are studying out of a book by Solkmkoff now. Guess I'll go over and eat now. Wish I could get in on some of that hunting.

4 NOVEMBER 1943 (THURSDAY). Maybe I'll have time to scribble a letter. We have formal graduation exercises on Nov. 26. Chicago tests start Nov. 12. We just had revellie. Everybody is sleepy and my roommate crawled back in bed. I haven't gotten a letter all week. Maybe it's just as well with the new system of mail distribution they put into effect yesterday. Our flight won our game of touch football yesterday and soccer the day before. We are undefeated in 4 games. I doubt if any of the flights will beat us for a while. We have a physics test in the morning. We are now working differential equations in math. We got about a year of college here at least. It's almost our turn to go to chow. Our breakfasts are usually pretty good. Sometimes I drink a whole qt. of milk. Have you finished picking corn yet? Pretty fast if you have. Hope they put me in something with more time outdoors when we finish here.

CHARLES SLADEK UNLOADING CORN, FAMILY FARM, 1943
CHUCKIE, SKIPPY, AND FRIEND LOOKING ON

6 NOVEMBER 1943 (SATURDAY). It was raining at revellie this morning. This is the morning to really get our room in shape for inspection. Had a letter from Vernon yesterday. He is busy cleaning up the apartment. We won our 5th straight game yesterday in touch football with another platoon. Maybe I'll hear from you today. My mail has been very scarce lately.

9 NOVEMBER 1943 (TUESDAY). You can easily see I'm down to my last piece of stationery. It was windy and chilly yesterday and snowed an inch or two in the evening. Everybody is froze up. Yesterday I had PX detail and a house detail—at least I got rid of most of my details for the week. Last evening at 6:30 we had to go to Brown Hall for a couple short talks by army chaplains. One was just back from the Aleutians. After that we had a math review lecture so it was a full day. Got your card yesterday—the first for quite a while. I should be helping you get ready for winter. We start Chicago tests this weekend. They will last all day Friday and Saturday. I might not make the grade but I think I will. Last week we had our usual 18 question Physics test and I got only 4 right instead of my usual 14 or 15. But that can happen to anyone. We lost our first touch football game yesterday to the 1st platoon. Guess I had better get busy now.

Although confident of hurdling the first two Chicago tests on Friday, the second pair scheduled for Saturday gave Lyle cause for concern. Assuming he would pass and expecting to stay in the mainstream, he informed his folks:

11 NOVEMBER 1943 (THURSDAY). This is the night before the Chicago tests. Tomorrow we have a 3 hr. Calculus test and a 3 hr. Vector Mechanics test. That will be rough but I believe I can make them easy enough. But the Geo. and Physics tests Sat. may get me. We were told today that 62 out of the 98 go on to Communications Cadet so that will include me. We will go to a regular army camp and leave here about Nov. 27.

The mail just came in but none for me. I haven't gotten any mail except your card for a long, long time. I haven't heard from Irene for a couple weeks—have you? Guess I'll study Calculus for an hr and go to bed. The main thing is to be clear headed and work fast. We had a good dinner today including strawberry shortcake. Things have been rather uneventful lately. Everyone is more or less reviewing quite a lot. I'm anxious to be leaving here. Maybe get rid of that—Pvt.—and also have a change of scenery. It may be rough like Officer's Candidate School though. We really learned plenty here. I'll really be mad if I don't get a letter from home tomorrow. Getting any pheasants lately? Keep a watch out for a chance to buy a few shells. Time to hit the books. I'll have to borrow an envelope.

Later.

Latest rumor is that we will be Communications Cadets at Yale U. in about a 12 week course leading to a commission. I've got my fingers crossed.

Friday.

Just back from the 3 hr. Calculus test. They hit my weak spots but I'm confident I made it. Don't broadcast this letter cause it may not turn out for sure.

Vectors test was easy.

While attending a party in University City, Lyle met a girl named Peggy. Too addled to learn her last name, he plotted to meet her again.

14 NOVEMBER 1943 (SUNDAY). Yesterday was rather a long day for me. I had the detail of cleaning up the basement in the morning. Then we had our three hour Physics test and it was pretty difficult—for me. That's the trouble here. There are specialists in practically every subject. This eye doctor knows everything about light and lenses in that part of Physics. In the next room a Harvard grad. knows geography inside out. Everywhere you turn there is someone who knows all the answers in some particular subject. My roommate can listen to a geography lecture and remember the name of every Russian or Chinese town mentioned. These were the first tests I ever took that I thought maybe I wouldn't pass. It's rather a funny feeling. We took the Geo. test in the afternoon and I passed it providing the class average is low enough! There were questions on all the continents except Australia. I can't remember which South American town exports coffee and in what part of India is Jute raised. But I can work out math problems.

After a day of tests I felt rather stuffy so I worked out a little on the track and in the gym. Was rather tired but decided to go to the dance for soldiers at University City. I wouldn't have missed that for anything. Danced first with a girl who is a freshman at the U. here. Her name was Merriam something and she was a good dancer. Then they had a mixer and I met a girl who had been to Miami Beach this spring. She knew some of the same places as I. She thought it was quite the city but I disagreed with her there. Then I was lucky and got a dance with Peggy somebody. She danced like a dream. She's a high school senior and awfully nice. Never knew I could dance til I danced with her. But after several pieces someone cut in. I was tired but the next partner showed me how to jitterbug etc. She was really a live wire. Her dad was hunting in South Dakota just last week. I think they should raise the license for out of state hunters. She was amazed to find out I had hardly ever danced before. Then they had a La Conga line. It has wild African music with drums etc and gets faster and faster. There is a picture of a Conga line in the 1942 yearbook. We drank lots of cokes, ate cookies, sang songs etc. Managed to get some more dances with Peggy but one of my housemates cut in (the bum). The party broke up about midnight and I had lots of fun. Peggy goes to the same church so maybe I'll get to see her this morning. I've had lots of fine times here at Washington University. I didn't burn up any books but I did learn to swim, etc.

At last a letter from you yesterday. Also the Register and a letter from Irene. I don't see where Irene gets her pep. She has more trips, dates, etc. Don't see how you get the work done so fast around there. That apple butter sounds good. Wish I had been there for that big feed. Among other rumors, I heard that there is a communications school at the Sioux Falls base. It might be tough especially with all that stuff you get in officer training. Guess the usual requirements are an amateur radio license, etc so maybe I'm biting off more than I can chew. But I'd like to take a shot at it. I don't even mind getting up at 5:15 anymore cause I just go to bed that much earlier. We continue our schoolwork until graduation November 26.

With some careful sleuthing, Lyle acquired Peggy's telephone number. Quite suddenly, six months of disciplined study and attention to military detail gave way to a flurry of social activities and dreamy meanderings.

Sunday evening.

By a round about way I found out Peggy's last name so I called her up and got a date for the concert by the St. Louis Symphony orchestra. We got seats in the third row from the front so it was really O.K. The conductor was a funny fellow—a true musician. The piano players go through all sorts of contortions and you think they will jump through the ceiling. We had a nice time and got back a little after 6:00. Her mother invited me over for supper on my night off. Just found out that it is Tuesday night. Really quite a girl. Maybe I'll hate to leave St. Louis. Got back ten minutes too late for supper so I'm dieting tonight. Also got beat in a couple games of ping pong tonight. Guess I'd better get to bed fairly early. Went to church this morning. A rural electrification man picked me up and gave me a ride home. What did you do today? Not one book did I open all weekend!

Monday.

We had a physical exam today instead of school. I breezed through again. My roommate had flat feet and is color blind. Got both cards from you today and even a letter from Chuckie and Velora Lake. Glad to hear that cookies are on the way. Don't see how Mom gets all the birthday cakes and cookies baked. Latest rumor is North Carolina.

Responding to Irene's invitation to rendezvous in Kansas City, Lyle replied:

18 NOVEMBER 1943 (THURSDAY). Nice to get your letter this noon. Had my bag almost packed before I reread your letter and found out you meant next weekend instead of this one. I might have been able to make it this weekend but not next—we graduate the day after Thanksgiving and expect we'll ship out about the day after. At least it is almost certain we go before the end of the month. But if you came over here Saturday there is a good chance I might still be here. I know you'll have a nice time in Kansas City and I wish I could come over. If I hear that we won't ship out before that Sunday, I'll write and you can come over here. Why don't you prepare to take a couple extra days off if necessary. If neither one of us makes it I'll expect you to come and see me very soon at my new station. I'll even pay your fare so you'll have no excuse for not coming. You see I expect to go east and I think you would like a trip east better than here. The trains are fast there and I might have more time. We had lots of good news today from the major's office. We get all Thanksgiving Day off. If our school doesn't start immediately we will get a travel enroute furlough and report to our new station. We will not have to go through Jefferson Barracks if we passed the tests? A General will speak at our graduation exercises at 8:00 Friday evening. We get diplomas and the Class C Meteorology students have to come and clap for us. We now have lectures on Field Theory which is Post Graduate Math work. However we are not supposed to learn it—we are just being exposed to it so it won't seem so hard if we ever get it again. Mom sent me some good cookies too.

As the sojourn at Washington University was drawing to a close, the post command was making arrangements for a celebration on Friday evening at a hotel on the King's Highway. Lyle wasted no time inviting Peggy to accompany him to the grand affair. Continuing his letter to Irene, he harked back to a wonderful time at Peggy's home at 797 Yale Street in a trendy neighborhood of University City.

Thursday night.

Sure had a nice time last Tuesday evening including supper at Peggy's house. Even had a piece of mince pie and a piece of lemon pie. There are 5 kids in the family including an older sister Jean. Peggy's real name is Margaret. She looks a good deal like Jean and is like my sisters. She had to go to a church rehearsal and after that we went over to Delmar and had malted milks. I'll hate to leave St. Louis now. We are going to the big meteorology powwow at the Kingsway hotel tomorrow evening. I never was particularly crazy about dancing until I met her. Had a talk with Dean Doner this evening. He had been back to Brookings on furlough quite recently. One of my fraternity brothers is in an Oregon conscientious objectors camp. He is a swell fellow—hope he is making out O.K. Got beat in ping pong this evening. Nice to get the snapshot. You will have to show me how to bowl sometime—I've set pins but never bowled. You can see it's impossible for me to come to Kansas City but I think you should come to St. Louis and go back by way of Chicago. But be sure and take plenty of time off if you do that. I'll let you know if I'll still be here. I sure get more than my share of the breaks. I'm all enthused about communications and everything. Can hardly wait for tomorrow night.

Our student group leader is too thorough with his work to suit us. For some reason he had to make the bed check instead of a noncom. We put two fictitious names on a hall closet door and tied the inside handle to a pail full of water on the shelf. He shouldn't have opened that door anyway! Nothing doing so I'll go to bed early. Wish I could be seeing you in Kansas City. You will like that city.

Lyle showed up at Peggy's home on Friday evening with a fragrant, white gardenia wrapped in cellophane. Together they rode a streetcar to the hotel on the King's Highway.

The gala at the Kingsway revealed another side of the officers and noncoms. Stiffness and formality gave way to cordiality. Quite suddenly, the martinets who had imposed military discipline on the meteorology detachment were seen to be warm, friendly human beings.

In the morning, Lyle dreamily wrote:

20 NOVEMBER 1943 (SATURDAY). It's a dark sleepy morning in St. Louis. Most of us got in about 2:00 last night and it's a little after 5:30 now cause we just had revellie. Had a wonderful time last evening. I'll never forget that evening at the Kingsway. Practically all of our faculty was there as well as all of our officers. I took Peggy a gardenia last night

and her mother said she should have had me over for supper. Her dad
gave us a streetcar pass and I had bought one so we boarded about a
dozen streetcars very cheaply. It's a dime every time you get on a car
unless you have a pass. We danced and danced and talked and met
people. I tell you she is really swell. Never knew anything could hit me
so hard and so fast. Hope it's mutual. At least I keep getting more dates.
I'll have to be coming back to St. Louis for a visit especially if I get a gold
bar on my shoulder. That dance really topped off a wonderful stay here
in St. Louis. We have formal graduation Nov. 26. Better come cause there
will be at least one general there. We even get diplomas. I rather expect
to go to North Carolina. It will be tough like all officer schools but I can
take it. Guess I can even hold my breath for 3 months if I have to. I've
got to exchange sheets now and make up the bed real nice for inspection.
Got the floor mopped etc. Had detail yesterday morning so won't get
that for a while again. Had speeches in English lately. Only a couple of
us didn't use notes or read them but they rated mine in the top bracket
anyway. Besides I want to learn to speak—not get grades. What are you
doing? Wish they would let me come home and help out for a month or
two. Got a big douse of vinegar in my water at chow last evening when
I wasn't looking. Tasted horrible. Got to get to work now.

More travel and adventure loomed on the horizon. Newly rated a cadet,
Lyle was about to ship out to the South.

22 NOVEMBER 1943 (MONDAY). We are in the homestretch now.
We had a few weeks left here and then all of a sudden it's just about
ended. Saturday we were officially informed of our new assignments.
About 50 of us go to Seymour Johnson Field, North Carolina, and will
arrive before the end of the month. All other assignments except us get
a furlough! We went up before that Officer Board that time and some
fellows who wanted it didn't make Communications Cadet—not officer
material. I'm afraid it will be strictly O.C.S. at North Carolina—they
want to find out who can take it. I came very very close to going into
aircrew—that bunch gets a furlough and go straight to Pre-flight. Others
go to A.S.T.P. and Weather Observer school, etc. I have the best deal if
I make the grade. Some of us went to the Symphony Concert yesterday
afternoon. It was good. May send a bunch of papers home to be kept
for future reference. Also caught up on sleep over the weekend. Don't
know whether it would be worthwhile to have Irene slip over here from
Kansas City Friday, or not. We graduate that evening and ship out the
morning after. I've always wanted to see North Carolina. Does anyone

want to go along for the winter? I'll gladly trade places—I know what O.C.S. is like. Spent a while last evening tearing up old letters etc—really had a ripping good time as they say in England. Almost time for chow if we can find our way over in the pitch dark. Better let me hear from you when I get down south.

Three days later, words written by Irving Berlin came to Lyle's mind as he contemplated Thanksgiving Day:

> While the storm clouds gather far across the sea,
> Let us swear allegiance to a land that's free,
> Let us all be grateful for a land so fair,
> As we raise our voices in a solemn prayer.

> God bless America,
> Land that I love.
> Stand beside her, and guide her
> Thru the night with a light from above.
> From the mountains, to the prairies,
> To the oceans, white with foam
> God bless America, My home sweet home.

25 NOVEMBER 1943 (THURSDAY). Guess we sure have plenty to be thankful for today. To be living in America for one thing. We finished our work yesterday and so some of us played football in the afternoon. Went to bed at 6:00 last night and we didn't have revellie this morning. Didn't feel like getting up at 6:00 for breakfast so I waited until 7:30 when I knew the aircrew would be about through eating. Sure enough, the line was empty so I had a swell breakfast. Grapefruit, 1/2 pint milk, two boxes grape nuts, French toast with bacon, etc. Guess I was the only one to pull that deal this morning. They almost washed out 3 fellows from Communications Cadet yesterday on account of Chicago tests but decided to let them through. They took about the 2/3 highest here for Communications and aircrew so I'm one of about 75 out of the original 150 who made cadet. I think there were only about 3 or 4 farm boys here. All other classifications get 10 day furloughs so I was out of luck there. Sure would have liked to come home. You could use some help and I could get in on some hunting too. Part of the game, I guess.

Interrupted by a phone call and suddenly on cloud nine, Lyle hurriedly finished his letter.

The best news of all is that Peggy's father called me up and invited me over for Thanksgiving dinner. Wow! So I'm to be over there about 11:00. Have a date with Peggy tonight too. Boy, I'm sure getting the breaks. One of the fellows has been trying to date her too but hasn't succeeded. Sure keeps me on my toes though. Hope you tell me what you are doing today. About Sat. we will start a two-day train ride east. Hope we go via Washington, D.C. rather than Tennessee. Goldsboro, North Carolina, with the lowest recorded temperature of 2 above zero.

On graduation morning, Lyle wrote:

26 NOVEMBER 1943 (FRIDAY). Was I surprised when I woke up this morning and found I had a letter from Irene yesterday. I'm glad she is taking a vacation.

Gus made me laugh. He said when he gets home on furlough the first thing his mother will say is "John, you've got a cold"—as though he didn't already know it. Gus is really a card and one of the extra fine fellows here. Boy, did I ever have a day yesterday. Turkey dinner with Peggy's family and some of her relatives which was really delicious. Peggy and I went to a football game in the afternoon and then we stopped at the Jewel Box in Forest Park on the way back. It was beautiful—just like an enchanting spot in the woods. I'll have to tell V and V about it cause they saw the Jewel Box with different decorations in effect. We went home and had a lunch and then went roller skating at the arena. It's one of the few places I hadn't been to before. We couldn't skate very long and even then it was past my time when we got back to her house. I covered that almost mile over here in about 5 minutes and beat bed check by a narrow margin. Very fortunate. She is coming up to graduation this evening and then we have until midnight to get back to the barracks. It's going to hurt tomorrow when the other fellows head home on furloughs and we ship for a new camp instead. I'm glad Irene will be home for a while. Well, I'll be back home again before too long. Bye now.

Although Lyle never received official scores on the second set of Chicago tests, he knew he had passed by virtue of assignment to communications cadets. Upcoming graduation exercises and another date with Peggy were the important things now.

For most of the soldiers in the meteorology detachment, the graduation ceremony was just another must-attend military event. Not so for Lyle. When he saw Peggy enter the hall accompanied by her mother and father, he was walking on air. In the short time he had known them, they had become like family.

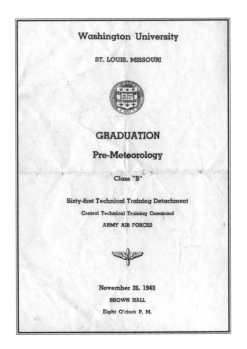

Washington University

ST. LOUIS, MISSOURI

GRADUATION

Pre-Meteorology

Class "B"

Sixty-first Technical Training Detachment

Central Technical Training Command

ARMY AIR FORCES

November 26, 1943

BROWN HALL

Eight O'clock P. M.

HONOR GUESTS

MAJOR GENERAL FREDERICK L. MARTIN
Commanding General, Central Technical Training Command, A.A.F.

LT. COL. THOMAS M. CARTER, Chaplain
Central Technical Training Command, A.A.F.

UNIVERSITY STAFF MEMBERS

DR. GEORGE REEVES THROOP
Chancellor

PROFESSOR ERNEST O. SWEETSER
Academic Administrator of Pre-Meteorology Programs

DR. FRANK W. BUBB
Professor of Mathematics

DR. GEORGE E. M. JAUNCEY
Professor of Physics

DR. LEWIS F. THOMAS
Professor of Geography

DR. DONALD C. BRYANT
Associate Professor of English

ASSOCIATE PROFESSOR WILLIS H. SUMMERS
Supervisor of Army Physical Training

POST COMMANDANT
LT. COL. CHARLES H. STEWART, C.A.

DETACHMENT OFFICERS

MAJOR BURT D. FERRIS
Commanding Officer

2nd LT. CLAYTON L. HOLM
Adjutant

2nd LT. ROY H. KOCH
Supply Officer

GRADUATION EXERCISES

Prof. E. O. Sweetser
Presiding

MUSIC...Air Forces Band

THE GENERAL'S MARCH........................Air Forces Band

INVOCATION.............................Chaplain Thomas M. Carter

OPENING REMARKS..................Chancellor George R. Throop

GRADUATION ADDRESS...........Major General Frederick L. Martin

AIR CORPS SONG...................................Air Forces Band

PRESENTATION OF DIPLOMAS.........Chancellor George R. Throop

BENEDICTION.........................Chaplain Thomas M. Carter

THE NATIONAL ANTHEM............................Air Forces Band

MUSIC...Air Forces Band

GRADUATION PROGRAM, CLASS B PRE-METEOROLOGY, WASHINGTON UNIVERSITY, 1943

The ceremony was carried out with the appropriate formality. The army band played an opening musical number followed by "The General's March." Then came the invocation, opening remarks, and graduation address. Afterward the band sounded off the Air Corps song and diplomas were presented. Following the benediction, voices rang out with the national anthem, "The Star-Spangled Banner":

> Oh! thus be it ever, when freemen shall stand
> Between their loved homes and the war's desolation!
> Blest with victory and peace, may the heaven-rescued land
> Praise the Power that hath made and preserved us a nation.
> Then conquer we must, for our cause it is just,
> And this be our motto: "In God is our trust."
> And the star-spangled banner forever shall wave
> O'er the land of the free and the home of the brave!

Lyle would be shipping out the next day. There was time for one last date with Peggy. Following the graduation reception they hopped a streetcar to the Candlelight Inn where, lost in time, they sipped hot chocolate at a corner table.

There was a tender moment of parting on the steps of Peggy's home at 797 Yale—and a promise to return.

"It's been fun. I hope we'll meet again."

"Oh, we will, we will. I'll come back to see you after the war."

The next morning, still reveling in the highlight of his stay in St. Louis, Lyle wrote to his parents.

27 NOVEMBER 1943 (SATURDAY). I just have to tell someone what a swell time I had last night, so it might as well be you. The commencement program went off very nicely and included a talk by General Martin. He is a two-star general, but he was just as nervous giving that talk as you or I would have been. Peggy and her parents were there so it was nice to know someone. There was a reception afterwards which was a pain in the neck. The tea and cookies were good though. I'll enclose my diploma. I'm rather proud of making it here and I guess I'm filling a spot in the army and going when and where they tell me to.

Peggy and I went out to the Candlelight for the evening. It's sort of like a rustic English inn and as you guessed, they have candles for lights. Peggy is about the nicest, sweetest girl in the world. I'm sure you would like her. Guess I'll have to come back here again soon. I had to be in by midnight but the buses only run every 1/2 hour and we missed one so we had to come the rest of the way in a taxi—and then I came back over

WASHINGTON UNIVERSITY

This certifies that

LYLE VIRGIL SLADEK, 37474253

has satisfactorily completed the course of study in

Pre-Meteorology -- B

as prescribed by the

Army Air Forces of the United States

and in testimony thereof is granted this certificate.

Given at St. Louis, Missouri, November 27th, 1943.

LT. COLONEL, C. A. C.—COMMANDANT

CHANCELLOR

MAJOR, A. C.—DETACHMENT COMMANDER

ACADEMIC ADMINISTRATOR

DIPLOMA, CLASS B PRE-METEOROLOGY, WASHINGTON UNIVERSITY, 1943

CLASS ROSTER

Pvt. Agner, Roy Augusta, Jr.
Cpl. Ahern, Charles Joseph
Pvt. Alm, Ross Creighton
Pvt. Baldwin, Jr., Earl Frederick
Pvt. Batts, Jiles Larry
Pvt. Beach, James Elliott
Pvt. Belin, Jack (NMI)
Pvt., Bierer, Jr., Charles Dana
Pvt. Binder, Harold (NMI)
Pvt. Birchfield, Thomas Elmer
Pvt. Blanchard, III, Samuel Edson
Pvt. Bohannon, William Maxwell
Pvt. Bragdon, Douglas Estes
Pfc. Brannon, Samuel Rex
Pvt. Brightwell, Ernest Jackson
Pvt. Brooks, Sidney (NMI)
Pvt. Brown, Philip Irwin
Pvt. Burke, Jr., Edward James
Pvt. Campbell, John Edward
Pvt. Chessin, Hyman (NMI)
Pvt. Clark, Martin Burns
Pvt. Curtin, William John
Pvt. DeLong, Glenn Robert
Pvt. Egan, Jr., John Paul
Pvt. Ely, Jerome Hirsh
Pvt. Exstein, Louis Hausmann
Pvt. Friedland, Lawrence Norman
Pvt. Gupton, Connie Dale
Pvt. Gustafson, John Maurice
Pvt. Guthrie, William Veitch
Pvt. Hagemann, Richard Frederick
Pvt. Hall, Harvey J.
Pfc. Hausman, Howard Jay
Pvt. Henisch, Donald Everette
Sgt. Higgins, Richard Hamilton
Pfc. Hill, Orlando Amos
Pvt. Holbrook, Herman Lindsay
Pvt. Holman, William Sherwood
Pvt. Hurst, Ted Daniel
Pvt. Jordan, Lucius Green
Pvt. Kaplan, Arthur Lincoln
Cpl. Levin, Abraham Leo
Pvt. Lockwood, Kenneth George
Pvt. Marquard, Paul Lawrence
Cpl. Nitsche, Carl James
Pvt. Martin, John Joseph
Pvt. Moldow, Alexander Sidney
Pvt. Montgomery, Francis (NMI)
Pvt. Morris, James Harris

Pvt. Osterhout, Russell Dean
Pvt. Paschall, Jr., Albert Buford
Pvt. Pease, Robert Flagg
Pvt. Platt, Jr., Robert Swanton
Sgt. Pollock, Melvin Martin
Sgt. Pomerance, Eugene Charles
Pvt. Powell, Jerome Millard
Pvt. Powers, Robert Allen
Pvt. Puksta, Charles Peter
Pvt. Ratner, Stanley Irwin
Pvt. Reitler, Henry Louis
Pfc. Rochman, Robert (NMI)
Sgt. Rose, Raymond Robert
Pvt. Ruark, Walter Franklin
Pvt. Ruesch, Earl Gordon
Cpl. Rybak, Joseph Zigmund
Cpl. Sachs, Philip (NMI)
Pvt. Shorey, Jr., Clyde Everett
Pvt. Sively, Garland Bidwell
Pvt. Sladek, Lyle Virgil
Pvt. Smith, Lester Lloyd
Pvt. Smith, Pete Ward
Pvt. Spielman, Philip Burnett
Pvt. Stevick, Earl Wilson
Pvt. Stewart, Clark Berry
Pvt. Stolnitz, George Joseph
Pvt. Stubbe, Earl Clinton
Pvt. Summers, Jr., Thomas Wilbur
Pvt. Sundell, Richard Howe
Cpl. Sutter, Lewis Floyd
Pvt. Tamm, Richard Lewis
Pvt. Timms, Robert James
Pvt. Tyler, Franklin Jaynes
Pvt. Urban, George Harry
Pvt. Vargo, Jr., Frank Gerald
Pvt. Waite, John Robert
Pvt. Walch, Raymond Edward
Pvt. Walnut, Jr., Thomas Henry
Pfc. Waples, Robert S.
Pvt. Weeks, Jay Landon
Pvt. Weiss, Martin Joseph
Pvt. Westhaver, Clyde Joshua
Cpl. White, Calvin Hardy
Cpl. White, Carl Larue
Pvt. Wilson, Jr., Hugh Hayes
Pvt. Zaremba, Theodore J.
Pvt. Zesmer, David Mordecai
Pvt. Zonis, Morton Stanley

ROSTER, CLASS B PRE-METEOROLOGY, WASHINGTON UNIVERSITY, 1943

here in the same one. Got here about 12:15 and beat bed check! Just about ready for bed when they gave the alarm for fire drill so we piled out and marched around outside a while. It was about their last chance to get a crack at us. We leave this p.m. for Goldsboro, North Carolina. Seymour Johnson field—we won't like it there maybe. Guess we go by way of Nashville, and Atlanta. The other half of the group assigned to aircrew leave on ten day furloughs. If I ever need anything, please send it promptly cause getting through this school will really require that we be "on the beam." I'll be buying lots of shoe polish. A letter now and then will help a lot down there. Take it easy and I'll be home one of these times sooner than you expect. I hate to start out southeast instead of northwest but it can't be helped.

Once again it was time for Lyle to part with fellow soldiers. Brimming with confidence in his mental, physical, and social abilities, he felt he had reached the pinnacle, that he could be whatever he wanted to be. The next phase of training would test his resolve.

CHAPTER 10

Carolina in the Morning

Oh! How I Hate To Get Up In The Morning,
Oh! How I'd love to remain in bed
For the hardest blow of all is to hear the bugler call:
"You've got to get up, you've got to get up,
You've got to get up this morning!"

—IRVING BERLIN

BOARDING A TRAIN and setting off for a distant part of the country was still the ultimate adventure for Lyle. He delighted in visiting cities and states he had read about.

The two-day train trip to North Carolina included a stopover at historic Atlanta. Now grumpy, as well as downhearted from parting with friends in St. Louis, Lyle hurried off to a hospitality center. After freshening up, he acquired stationery with the heading ATLANTA SERVICE MEN'S CENTER and settled into a quiet corner.

28 NOVEMBER 1943 (SUNDAY). We had a stuffy ride in a day coach all the way up here. We are taking advantage of this couple hour layover by taking showers and resting up. I don't like Atlanta—it is a smoky city. In fact I don't care about "the land of cotton" at all. They can have all of it.

Upon hearing the boarding call, the soldiers quickly returned to their seats. As the train resumed its passage through Georgia, Lyle continued:

We go northeast now to Seymour Johnson field, North Carolina and arrive at 5:00 Monday morning. It will be rather hard on us if we don't get a Pullman tonight—but so far I'm standing the trip in excellent shape. Will see some new country this afternoon. Have been through Atlanta before. Peachtree street is the main drag here. We came on the Chattanooga Choo Choo through that city and Nashville, Tenn. I sure hated to leave friends in St. Louis. You know you will never see some of them again. Virginia's letter before we left saved the day for me yesterday. Guess I'll send V and V a postcard just to be doing something. We will be having dinner pretty soon. Bye now.

Raindrops spattered the sooty windows of the train as it rolled onto a siding at Seymour Johnson Field (SJF). The cadets, tired and disheveled after two nights of travel in a day coach, did not relish leaving the familiar warmth of the car. But the men were soldiers. When the order came to fall out, they dutifully gathered their few belongings and fell into formation on the platform.

The cadets were ill prepared for the chilly December weather in North Carolina; their overcoats, along with their baggage, had been shipped on another train. Hacking coughs broke the early morning quiet as they shivered in the cold rain while waiting for something to happen. Ten minutes later, they marched off to the cadet headquarters area. Tar paper barracks, connected by muddy paths, stood scattered among trees and stumps in the piney woods.

Seymour Johnson Field was named after a native of Goldsboro, a navy lieutenant who had died in a plane crash two years earlier. Accessible to railroad lines and the seacoast, the sprawling base served as an Overseas Replacement Depot (ORD) and training site. Pilots roared P-47 pursuit planes on and off the runways as they honed their flying skills. Rangers trained on rugged obstacle courses as they developed physical prowess. Aviation cadets in Pre-Flight School (pilots, navigators, bombardiers) and Pre-Technical School (communications, armament, photography) vied to survive the regimen as they strove to become officers.

Lyle, envisioning the gold bars of a lieutenant, was eager for the communications course to get underway. He knew Pre-Tech training would be challenging, but he aimed to give it his best effort.

After three days at SJF, Lyle found time to write home.

2 DECEMBER 1943 (THURSDAY). How is everything at home? Things look better here all the time. Our barracks bags came today so we will be able to dress properly. We would have gone on a forced march the other night if our overcoats had been here. Today was gas alert day. We only had one gas alarm and usually they turn loose some tear gas. This post has many advantages over Washington University in the way of barber shops, army stores, post theatres, and supplies. Spent an hour the other night in the crowded P.X. buying a towel. By

the time I got it, it was too late to take a shower. I have a very good appetite here and we will be outdoors a good deal. We will get kicked around a lot but at cadet school they give you a good deal of confidence. Altogether I'm sort of looking forward to this. It is just like you see in newsreels of O.C.S. Wish I was home for a little hunting. Also catch up on eating and sleeping. It's hard to get up in the cold barracks at 5:30 every morning. A couple of our fellows ended up in hospital with colds or something—it was a rather hard trip. Saw the big Chesterfield and Lucky Strike factories and warehouses in Greensboro, Durham, and Raleigh on the way through. Also noticed Duke U. and N.C. State College. This course will be something like this—week at gun range, week of K.P., week of guard duty, week out on bivouac, etc etc. It will be a healthy deal anyway. They haven't started gigging us here. A week or more first to find out what they want. I don't anticipate any trouble getting through here. Better they should have given me a couple weeks off. Let me hear from you.

The eleven-week course at SJF commenced with "hell week" as the army began to weed out cadets short of determination, stamina, or military bearing. Lyle intended to be among the survivors. No way would he wash out and revert to his former status of buck private.

4 DECEMBER 1943 (SATURDAY). Well, everything is rosy again. I weathered the storm and am feeling good again. Yesterday was hell! I had a bad cold and was sick and we rushed around all day. I'll never go on sick call if I can stand up cause you go through about half a day of red tape, marching, etc and if you do ever get to a Doctor, they treat you either for athletes foot or indigestion. The trip and lack of proper clothing our first few days here was hard on our bunch from Wash. U. Two are in hospital, several have gone on sick call, and several are droopy. All have colds. But don't mind my griping. You don't expect to enjoy cadet school. There will really never be any time off in our stay here but the actual training will be pleasant at times. You just have to close your eyes to it. We had a big barracks inspection this morning. Most fellows got gigged a couple times. My bunk mate has 4. You walk a tour on one of your couple hours off weekends as soon as you get 5 gigs. I don't have any so far and my fingers are crossed. In O.C.S. you shine your shoes as good as you can. You get gigged and shine them better. Lucky that I dusted the corner braces in under my bunk. Maybe I'll get some mail soon. That will help a lot. Guess we go to the range about our first week after "Boot Camp." The food isn't too bad only we can't talk or anything and have to eat "square" meals with one hand

only above the table. This won't be bad and the time will go fast. We go to Yale U. after here.

The cadets moved to a permanent squadron barracks, a large, open space with a spartan layout. Six bare lightbulbs hung from the ceiling. Two rows of double-deck steel cots covered with olive drab blankets lined the walls. A wooden clothes rod extended from the wall near each cot. Fire extinguishers clung to the structural posts. Sand-filled cans provided a parking place for butts. At one end of the building was a washroom and latrine. A potbellied stove, the only source of winter warmth, occupied the center space.

There was little time for bickering or quarreling among the forty cadets assigned to a barracks; every cadet was penalized when a barracks was not properly cleaned or in regulation order. Any shirker or troublemaker incurred the wrath of the group. When "Lights out!" blared over the loudspeaker, the cadets immediately stripped to underclothing and crawled in under their blankets.

Patterned after West Point, the cadet corps at SJF was big on military protocol. In late afternoon the flights assembled on the parade grounds and passed in front of the reviewing stand as an army band played "Stars and Stripes Forever," a stirring march composed by John Philip Sousa. The March King had played at the Mitchell Corn Palace festival in 1904 and again in 1907. While in high school, Lyle had memorized the patriotic lyrics:

> Let martial note in triumph float
> And liberty extend its mighty hand
> A flag appears 'mid thunderous cheers,
> The banner of the Western land.
> The emblem of the brave and true
> Its folds protect no tyrant crew

On the second anniversary of Pearl Harbor, and in his sixth army camp, Lyle wrote:

7 DECEMBER 1943 (TUESDAY). Another nice day today and fairly interesting. Mostly drilling and lectures. The coursework really starts about the 17th of the month. The food here is about the poorest in the six camps I've eaten at. But by going back for seconds it isn't bad. Got good seconds on salad and pear sauce tonight. There are rumors of a forced march tonight so I've got my fingers crossed. We moved to our permanent squadron barracks yesterday and are settled again. A letter from Vernon caught up with me from St. Louis yesterday and also got

one from one of the fellows home on furlough in Boston. We have to spend quite a lot here for incidentals. Tomorrow morning is our laundry day. I should get a letter from you tomorrow.

We had a retreat parade this evening which was quite impressive with a band, officers, and lots of cadets. I haven't been gigged yet—yet. This will really be an interesting course, and they change us from enlisted men to officers. There is a big wide line in the army between enlisted men and officers and they even discourage us from associating with enlisted men. We can't go to U.S.O.s or Service Clubs. Necessary for discipline I guess. Rather tough on us to be shut in after the entertainment we had in St. Louis. No chance for me to get home for several months. Rather a tough break. Can a couple squashes and hide a couple shotgun shells for me cause I'm getting hungry.

Lyle and the other cadets from Washington University had already learned the rudiments of military bearing and were well conditioned. They did not anticipate any trouble with the regular obstacle course, alleged to be less difficult than the ranger course, or with other facets of the physical training at SJF. However, the academic aspect due to commence after three weeks of orientation was an unknown. The potential officers merely knew that the intense, week-long courses were designed to acquaint them with the basics of running a military establishment.

10 DECEMBER 1943 (FRIDAY). The temperature dropped almost to zero last night but the sun is melting some of the snow. Yesterday there was too much snow for regular caluthentics so they took us out in some woods for some cross country walking and running. The pine trees and bushes in leaf were very pretty covered with snow. We could see the obstacle course on the way back and it looks pretty rough. They also have a ranger course somewhere. Got a box of delicious candy from V and V this week and it didn't last long. Last evening we had a squadron party at the chapel with talent from within the squadron. We have some sort of training films after mess tonight. Latest rumor is that we have Christmas Day off and the next day is Sunday. They say these cadet schools are tough—but so far it appears to be much easier in many ways than at Wash. U. We don't have so many details, etc and not so much studying.

There was a big train wreck here in Carolina yesterday. We have a big inspection in the morning—guess there is a visiting General. It's tough to roll out of bed in the dark in the morning when the barracks is cold. But we get to sleep late Sunday morning. Hope the weather isn't too severe in South Dakota. The humidity and wind make the cold very noticeable here and you aren't always dressed right. Bye now.

12 DECEMBER 1943 (SUNDAY). This has been a very pleasant day—in fact, about the first enjoyable day since I've been here. The sun is shining brightly and the temperature is about 60°F. We were allowed to sleep late which we enjoyed very much. We missed mess so saved $.25 cents and then practically everyone went to Catholic or Protestant chapel in the forenoon and then to noon mess. It was rather poor. I sure would have liked to tear into an upside down cake at home. No mail came through in this mail call for me yet. I may score about tomorrow or Tuesday. We always hate these periods of no mail. I'm kind of wondering what you are all doing today. Probably pretty busy with chores—and I'll bet you had company. We had a nice game of volleyball this afternoon too. Things will be interesting and fast moving after we get started on regular classes. Physical training will be easy cause most of the cadets have only been making about "good" on physical fitness ratings (P.F.R.). We got about an average of "very good" in ours at Wash. U. I am high up in the "very good" class near the top rating of "Excellent." Our P.X. is always crowded but things are pretty cheap. Let me hear from you.

While responding to his mother's inquiries regarding military terms and procedures, Lyle interjected an optimistic view about the course of the war. He knew his mother, like other Americans, yearned for the day "when the war is over," a phrase frequently used in everyday conversation.

14 DECEMBER 1943 (TUESDAY). A rather chilly cloudy day today for North Carolina. Wilma's letter came today telling about your trip to Mitchell. Now to answer a few questions. I am an Aviation Cadet in Aviation Cadet Pre-Tech School—the only one of its kind in the U.S. A cadets or officers word or honor cannot be questioned because we are "gentlemen by congressional appointment"—very indirectly of course. The next eleven weeks here are equivalent to O.C.S. which turns out the 90-day-wonders you hear about. However, we have technical skills and will go on to Yale and become technical officers. They apparently expect the European war to be over before summer but the Pacific war will last longer, so they say. Even a buck private if placed over us could tell us what to do but in some ways we outrank the highest Sgts. Some things in the army are very queer such as the big line between officers and enlisted men. Technically speaking I am no longer a soldier. We had P.T. today and it has symptoms of being very tough. There are rumors of a forced march tonight. Hope not. We have lots of stuff to swallow such as having to come back and change into our best uniforms before going into the P.X. We are still restricted but should get out soon. Mom had better plan on wearing that new outfit when she comes to see me at Yale next spring. Sounds like a good deal on the calves—better sell

some more stuff before winter. We live in a long (airy) tar paper barracks in rows set in among pine trees. A temporary sort of camp built up recently. Not nice like some such as Ft. Crook and Leavenworth. Lots of planes flying around all the time. I missed being in aircrew by a very very narrow margin—although that might have been best for all I know. Take it easy.

Throw away any pessimistic letters cause things usually aren't so bad as I write.

Whining was considered undignified and elicited short shrift in rural South Dakota. Keeping a "stiff upper lip" and downplaying adversity was more the norm.

Still intrigued at the sight and sound of airplanes roaring on and off the tarmac, Lyle continued to ponder "the road not taken." Now an aviation cadet in Pre-Technical School, not at all glamorous, he could have been an aviation cadet in Pre-Flight, preparing to soar into the *wild blue yonder*. Nevertheless, the Pre-Tech and Pre-Flight uniforms were similar.

17 DECEMBER 1943 (FRIDAY). I've been waiting all day for a mail call but no results yet. Rather expect a letter from you tonight. We have been issued our service caps and hardware and extra shirts so are now aviation cadets in full uniform. We took a physical exam again today— seems like we get one every couple weeks. Rather fun though as long as they never find anything wrong. Some of the fellows will wash out on account of it. These first 3 weeks of orientation before classes start are not very tough—just a little boring. I am one of few who hasn't been gigged yet. We have a big inspection in the morning. The food seems to have picked up a little. Wilma's letter came yesterday. I'm glad Mom got lots of Birthday presents. Good thing everyone isn't forgetful like me. No mail call until tomorrow morning—just announced. A poor thing for the morale to not have a mail call—

Just then, a signal for mail call interrupted Lyle's letter writing. In a letter forwarded from St. Louis, he learned Irene had taken a new job with the War Department in another city. Cheerfully resuming his letter, he began with an apology.

Beg your pardon—a fellow just brought mail in the barracks—a card and letter from you. They were the ones mailed to Washington U. Good to hear from home after a couple weeks of no mail. So you shelled the corn last week. Guess you must be plenty busy. Doesn't surprise me that Irene got a good job. She will like Omaha—I think it's a busy little city. Wish I could have gone to the junior class play. I'll bet it was good. The general said our cadet corps retreat parade the other night was the best he had ever seen. Almost time for our evening bracing session and I'll have to get to work cleaning up my bunk.

The cadets lined up for an evening bracing session in front of the barracks. Usually taking place after a long day of physical training, military drill, and lectures, bracing helped identify cadets who reacted poorly under stress. When ordered "Hit a brace, Mister," the hapless cadet pulled in his chin and abdomen, stood rigidly at attention, and stared straight ahead. While Lyle was standing in that exaggerated posture, an upperclassman tested his demeanor and inspected his uniform; insignia out of place, belt buckle not shined, inability to correctly shout one of the military orders, or any other perceived infraction, real or imaginary, would result in gigs to walk off during free time on Sunday. The army was looking for potential officers, men who exhibited military stature, composure, and grit.

Those cadets who survived the first three weeks of orientation, physical training, and military exercises proceeded on to eight weeks of academic courses: Gunnery, Military Law, Mess Hall Management, Aircraft Recognition, Guard Duty, First Aid, Administration, and Supply.

19 DECEMBER 1943 (SUNDAY). We have a few minutes before noon mess. It got plenty chilly last night but the bright sun soon warms up the air. Of course we slept late this morning which seemed good for a change. Most everybody went to church and the Protestant chapel was packed full. Everybody is hungry after skipping breakfast. We have retreat parade at 4:30 this afternoon followed by mail call. In our spare time we sort of study aircraft identification and other things which we will need to know. Altogether this should really be easier than the course at Wash. U. Received a letter from Martin Weiss which he wrote on the train on his way from furlough in Boston to Chanute Field, Illinois, where he will go to weather observers school. We will get out of "restrictions" Tuesday so we can go to a post theatre or something once in a while. They have recorded concerts at the chapel on Sunday evening.

Had plenty to eat by going back for a second—although nothing like dinner at home. This is indeed a small world. Happened to be standing by a cadet and saw by his serial number that he was from same service command as I—the 7th. He looked slightly familiar so I asked him where he was from. He said Kansas City and it turned out that his brother was on the same shipment troop train to Miami Beach and was in my flight in the same hotel. He is now overseas. Never happened to know him too well but after living around him for a couple months, this face caught my eye—and out of thousands of soldiers I've seen. My old roommate met a cadet who lived next door to him for ten years in Westfield, N. J.

Most of these cadets have had at least as much college as I because it will be a technical course at Yale. We won't learn much here but they stress posture, military bearing, and leadership. It will be three months of forgetting about social affairs but I won't mind much. I'm afraid the physical training won't be as good as at Wash. U.

The cadets at SJF related to the words of a song written by a World War I soldier, Irving Berlin: "Oh! How I Hate To Get Up In The Morning / Oh! How I'd love to remain in bed." But woe to any cadet who was late for reveille. When the morning whistle blew, the men bounded out of bed, pulled on clothing, slipped into woolen coats, and dashed outside. One gutsy fellow, desperate for extra sleep, dared to linger in his sack. At the last second he raced to join the formation. Due to the early morning darkness the sergeant failed to notice the cadet was out of uniform, unclothed beneath a long overcoat.

Finding the first week of instruction, Gunnery, to his liking, Lyle wrote:

23 DECEMBER 1943 (THURSDAY). We have been studying guns and firing them on the range this week. Yesterday we fired the Sub-Machine gun for practice. If we had been firing for record, I would have gotten "expert" cause I had 96%. Expert is 80% and other qualifications are lower. Today we fired the caliber .45 army pistol for record. Managed to make 80% which is "sharpshooter" for the pistol. Expert starts at 86%. Some fellows shoot as low as 30%. So I could wear medals for the carbine and pistol. Tomorrow we fire the carbine for practice. Altogether it is a very interesting week for me. Tomorrow evening some of the fellows will be taking off for home—if they live within 300 miles such as Wash. D.C. I'm going to stick around and take it easy. The Register came today and seemed to have a lot of news. It's funny SDSC finally sent the tuition refund. Our revillie is really something. About 5:20 they blow a whistle to awaken us. We pull on stiff shoes and an overcoat before the second whistle blows a few seconds later. We have one minute to go a couple blocks and fall in at parade rest. So we dash wildly through a maze of trees, mop racks, stumps, sidewalk construction projects, and lumber piles in the dark. It is worse than an obstacle course and if you don't make it you get gigged. Later.

Following morning reveille the cadets, all present and accounted for, rushed back to the barracks and went to work on the morning cleanup.

They removed ashes from the stove, mopped the wood floor, made up the beds, and hung their clothing in regulation fashion. Somehow, before dawn on a cold winter day, Lyle found time to scrawl a few more lines before marching off for morning chow.

Went to a short G.I. movie last night. Walt Disney's "South of the Border." A travel picture of Latin America which was very interesting. Temperature dropped almost to zero last night. It will be chilly shooting this morning on the range. Funny it stays so warm out there—hope it keeps up. Irene sent me a nice sterling silver dog tag chain which is something I needed. You missed a change in my address about a week ago. It's Sqdn. H now instead of U. Time for mess now.

After breakfast the cadets piled into trucks and headed off to the gunnery range to fire carbines. Most were in good humor, for it was the day before Christmas. Those from North Carolina or neighboring states would be going home for a couple of days. That evening, FDR addressed the nation from the White House:

My Friends:
On this Christmas Eve there are over ten million men in the armed forces of the United States alone. One year ago 1,700,000 were serving overseas. Today, this figure has been more than doubled. . . .
That this is truly a World War was demonstrated to me when arrangements were being made with our overseas broadcasting agencies for the time to speak today to our soldiers, and sailors, and marines and merchant seamen in every part of the world. . . .
But everywhere throughout the world—through this war that covers the world—there is a special spirit that has warmed our hearts since our earliest childhood—a spirit that brings us close to our homes, our families, our friends and neighbors—the Christmas spirit of "peace on earth, goodwill toward men." It is an unquenchable spirit.
During the past years of international gangsterism and brutal aggression in Europe and in Asia, our Christmas celebrations have been darkened with apprehension for the future. We have said, "Merry Christmas—a Happy New Year," but we have known in our hearts that the clouds which have hung over our world have prevented us from saying it with full sincerity and conviction. And even this year, we still have much to face in the way of further suffering, and sacrifice, and personal tragedy. Our men . . . know, from their own experience and knowledge of modern war, that many bigger and costlier battles are still to be fought.
But—on Christmas Eve this year—I can say to you that at last we may look forward into the future with real, substantial confidence that, however great the cost, "peace on earth, good will toward men" can be and will be realized and ensured. This year I can say that. Last year I could not do more than express a hope. Today I express—a certainty though the cost may be high and the time may be long.

Since the family farm was several days' travel far to the northwest, Lyle spent Christmas Day at the camp. The sun was shining, the air was clear and crisp, and there was a turkey dinner at the mess hall. Enjoying a rare day of leisure he strolled over to the flight line where, for the first time, he heard the uplifting words from the new Broadway musical, *Oklahoma*:

> Oh! What a beautiful morning.
> Oh! What a beautiful day.
> I have a wonderful feeling
> Everything's going my way.

Continuing on to base Chapel No. 4, Lyle attended a Protestant service for cadets. In his letter home that day, he enclosed the service bulletin, which contained an apt poem attributed to the inspirational poet, Maltbie Davenport Babcock:

> Be Strong!
> We are not here to play, to dream, to drift;
> We have hard work to do and loads to lift;
> Shun not the struggle: face it, 'tis God's gift.
> Be Strong!
> Say not the days are evil—who's to blame?
> And fold the hands and acquiesce—shame!
> Stand up, speak out, and bravely, in God's name.
> Be Strong!
> It matters not how deep intrenched the wrong.
> How hard the battle goes, the day, how long;
> Faint not, fight on! Tomorrow comes the song.

Dear Folks,   *Christmas day*
Just another soldier in an
army camp on Christmas day. But

25 DECEMBER 1943 (SATURDAY). Just another soldier in an army camp on Christmas day. But really a rather enjoyable day—slept late, a good dinner pretty soon now, and the whole day off. Of course there are a couple places where I would like to be now. Before I forget—when I first got in the army I took out $5000 insurance costing me about $3.50 per month. When we came here they wanted us to all take out the full $10,000 but I didn't see any use putting in that much for this type of insurance so I had to sign a refusal form which you got. It saved a lot

of red tape. In the Cadet Corps they can put on pressure and make you sign a fool thing like that refusal form. You should be getting a bond per month right along. We haven't been paid yet here but will get paid soon. The army always sends write ups to our local papers when appointed Cadets—noticed any yet? We have nothing to write on here in the barracks. Yesterday we went to the range again in trucks and fired the carbine. We got out there before sunrise and the temperature fell almost to zero the night before so it was awful cold with a stiff wind blowing. We fired 40 rounds (shots) with each bullseye counting 5 points so you have a possible 200 points. Marksman starts at 120, sharpshooter at 150, and expert at 175. We weren't shooting for record so we didn't even have practice shots to zero in the sights. We were cold and had to shoot and change clips with overcoat and gloves on. You have 40 seconds to shoot 4 shots, change clip, change firing position, and shoot 4 more shots. My best batch was drilling in 7 bullseyes, and a 3 in about 30 seconds—which you see didn't leave me any time to fumble while changing that clip. I ended up with 170 out of 200 points which was high sharpshooter. With decent shooting conditions I would have had an easy expert. Too bad it wasn't officially for a record. A carbine is really a sweet little gun. So I really believe I can now shoot expert on the army's small guns. You would be surprised at the number of fellows who miss the whole target at times. That big .45 pistol really barks and bucks. Pretty tame compared with shooting at a pheasant. Lots of these fellows sure can't stand the cold. There is a cadet dance in Goldsboro this evening. Poster says lots of food and women but I'm not going. You see I turned my blouse in for one 3 sizes larger and they sent me back a wrinkled one so I turned it in to the cleaners. Too hard to get back and forth from town anyway. Also had to exchange my shirts for a size and a half bigger neck. My bunk mate from Miami is really an unorthodox likeable fellow. He likes to talk and let on that he does everything different than the rest of the world. Almost time for dinner and I really have an appetite.

We had a very good dinner—turkey, dressing, sweet spuds, pie, ice cream, celery etc. And the best part of it was that there was not too much of it so that we would feel stuffed all afternoon. Guess I'll go to a post theatre. Wish there was something to do to get some exercise this afternoon. Such as a five mile walk hunting around the country. One day last January I walked over to Collin's Flat, north to Klar's, into north pasture and over on Baileys. Just as it got dark a rooster flew up but the gun failed to fire!

Saw a fair show this afternoon. Would have gotten more fun out of even working—at least I wouldn't feel so dull. It's nice to have these two days off to catch up on sleep and rest. Hope you have the work caught up in case of storms. Don't see how you get all of the work done. Is the radio working?

I do hear from Peggy but it's not too serious—after all I only knew her 13 days—wish I was walking down Yale St. to her home right now.

29 DECEMBER 1943 (WEDNESDAY). Just a sort of a break in a busy day. I'll give you a little sketch of our schedule. Wake up at 5:20 and have revillie, clean barracks, and go to morning mess. At 7:20 we fall out for an hour of class followed by an hour of drill, and then 2 more hours of class. We have noon mess immediately followed by two hours of class. Then we have an hour and a half of physical training packed full of caluthentics, hand to hand combat and running. We dress up and have retreat parade until supper time. Then we have time off until bracing period in the evening. Tonight we still have classes starting at 7:00 and it's time to go to that now.

The cadets faced hours of instruction and numerous exams. At the end of each week, test results determined whether a cadet went on to the next course or dropped back to the following section number and repeated the class. Those who washed back were separated from their buddies and jeopardized their chances of surviving the program.

Class is over and we are done for the day. We have been studying Military law this week. The Lt. who teaches us was a civil lawyer and he keeps lectures interesting by telling some experiences in civil cases. The test will probably be tomorrow and it is one of the hardest courses here. Hope I pass it.

Just got an insured package card so went to the mail room after it. Guess what—a nice concealed stitch billfold with a bill in it from V and V. But I'll still vote Dad's letter and the box of treats as my best presents. I've been rationing out the cookies and didn't discover that some of the candy was homemade fudge until tonight. Anyway I'm sure enjoying the cookies and candy. We moved to a different barracks yesterday and are now a little closer to revillie. Expect K.P. sometime toward the end of the week. This weather is something. One day zero cold and windy, next day about 60° and sunny, next day several inches of rain, then turned cold and driving sleet storm this morning. This place is a muddy mess right now. Some of our fellows have to march a tour Sunday but I've been lucky yet. I seem to do the right things when the gigging officers are around. I'll enclose a couple of little clippings out of the camp paper. They are treating us O.K. here—3 squares a day and a fairly interesting schedule. And we are looking forward to Yale of course.

During his first weeks at SJF, Lyle had been subject to field rations, a centralized procurement and food distribution system prevalent at most military bases. Early in the war the Quartermaster Corps had found it necessary to institute the field ration system as the army expanded to millions of troops dispersed around the globe in varying climates and conditions. With SJF reverting to a garrison ration system, a subsistence program wherein the base purchased its own food, Lyle anticipated better meals. As a cadet he received a salary plus a daily food allowance for meals at the mess hall. Although the payroll deduction increased, he was upbeat about the change in the ration system that went into effect on New Year's Day.

Back from noon mess, Lyle reacted to a sympathetic comment in his mother's most recent letter. Out in the world and full grown, he whistled in the dark, aiming to give the impression he could take whatever came his way.

1 JANUARY 1944 (SATURDAY). Just back from a very good dinner. Starting today we are switching from field rations to garrison rations. It will cost us a little more but the meals will be better from now on. I object strenuously to Mom calling this an ordeal. So far it has been very interesting and good training. We were paid yesterday and we netted about $85 after all deductions because we got a throwback from food allowances. I bought a bond yesterday and I'll probably send a little home at times. There is nothing to spend it on here but will probably be able to use it at New Haven, Conn. There is a rumor floating around that this cadet corps may be moved before Febr. but I doubt it. The fellows who went to Jefferson Barracks from Wash. U. for aircrew are still there and will be there for a couple months. So it looks like they won't even get up in a plane for several months yet. Heard from Kenneth Lunn a while back and he spent most of December in Los Angeles. He visited Ole Nelson's Hollywood Canteen etc. Here is a little extract from a magazine article— "Tom Lockard had lived in twelve camps, but Camp Davis, in N. Carolina, had impressed him most. He said it was the only place he ever saw where you'd be standing in mud up to your knees and have sand blowing in your face."— He hit it about right.

The Military Law test was not too hard as far as the principles concerned but some questions were hard to interpret. I drew K.P. for tomorrow (Sunday) and next week is "mess management" week so I'll be spending some time around the mess hall. Went to "North Star" at the post theatre last night. Enjoyed it very much although the last half was over dramatized. After all one man can't deliberately shoot two men with a pistol—if they both jump him he'll only be able to get one. It rather pleased me to get my first gig last week for a dusty bed. I didn't get time (or take time) to dust in under the springs. I'm glad to hear Wilma is skating. I think Wilma is feeding me a line on that fortune. Some of the fellows are going to Wilson (about 20 miles) to a dance tonight. I should go just to get out of camp once in a while—but I'm not. When I get to Yale maybe I'll get around. That's pretty near New York City you know. I plumb forgot your wedding anniversary. As for being sick I have hardly had a sick day since at Miami Beach and that was my own fault for not going on sick call. We had a physical condition test the other day. I did 70 sit ups easily and could have gone the army's limit (114) but wanted to leave room for improvement. Of course we aren't in good shape as though we had been working all day. After all we only get an hour and half a day of exercise. Royce Bates (Mitchell) graduated from college in R.O.T.C. but is still a corporal taking A.S.T.P. in Georgia. Dale Korzan might be shipped to some island a long way from the war. It would be kind of nice to take a boat ride to some place like Hawaii. It's a beautiful day here in North Carolina—warm enough for just a shirt. I never saw such changeable weather. Enclosed $10.

During the third class at SJF, Lyle drew dining room orderly (DRO) detail, entailing on-the-job training at the mess hall while simultaneously fulfilling the need to feed the cadet corps. One day, when the pecking order was reversed, the underclassmen were permitted to harass the upperclassmen. Despite that opportunity to let off steam, it was a trying week.

5 JANUARY 1944 (WEDNESDAY). This is our roughest week so far. Sunday I had K.P. but it was easier than at other mess halls and only lasted 9 hours. This week we are studying Mess Management which includes such things as nutrition, army stoves, meat cutting, etc. Every morning a bunch of us are on D.R.O. and are awakened at 4:00 in the morning. It was my turn today so we spent a couple hours each meal at the mess hall on the serving line. We were very lucky though—for dinner they served fried chicken and pie—and you can bet we really went to town on them while working around there. I'll be on D.R.O. again about Saturday and also have K.P. again later in the week. I got gigged again yesterday for not hanging up my overcoat before going to P.T. They sure can rake us over the coals in an hour and half of Physical Training. Our squadron took first place in the retreat parade this afternoon. Yesterday was "turnabout day" so we braced the upperclassmen last evening—they will really be out to get us tonight. I passed Military Law without too much of a margin of safety. Top ranking men from places like the radio school at Sioux Falls come here to cadet corps. Most fellows who have been at Sioux Falls are very favorably impressed with South Dakota people. There is a rumor of a forced march tonight—that would be the

end of a long day. We are tired on account of being awakened at 4:00 every morning by the bunch going on D.R.O. so most of us will hit the hay right after bracing period. Did the horse snap out of the sick spell? I'm glad you are having nice weather.

8 JANUARY 1944 (SATURDAY). Yesterday was a super special. We got up at 4:00 a.m. and cleaned our barracks, and then marched to the mess hall for D.R.O. After serving mess all morning we got back in time for 7:30 class. Then we had an hour of drill followed by class. Then we went on D.R.O. again for a couple hours at noon getting back in time for class. Then an hour and half of Physical Training followed by retreat parade. Then mess followed by some drill in the dark for our drill team competition today. Back just in time for evening bracing period. Then most of us had some assignments to do for Mess Management. In between times everybody was shining shoes and scrubbing floors for this morning's big inspection. So we were ready to hit the hay when lights went out at ten o'clock. We really slicked up our barracks for inspection this morning but my bunk mate got gigged. He may be due for marching a tour tomorrow. I was lucky enough to miss D.R.O. for Sunday so I'll have the day off until 3 o'clock parade. I'm glad they keep us busy though—

It was sort of ironic that the work Sgt. should come in just then and volunteer us for a cleaning and moving job in another barracks. We were in dress uniform so we had to change into fatigue clothes. Every time you change a shirt or pants or something, you must button every button on it and put it on a hanger in a certain place. Sad sack! Now we have to change back into Class A uniforms for class. It must be the balanced meals that keep us well cause nobody ever gets sick much. You stand in wet feet, dress warm or cold (whichever they tell you to wear)—but never get sick.

I passed the Mess Management test by a narrow margin. It was a stinkaroo test. But it doesn't matter cause your grade is either satisfactory or unsatisfactory.

Sunday.

Got Mom's newsy letter yesterday and the Register for Dec. 23. By the way, the end of this course is at Yale U., not Harvard. If things go as planned (which is doubtful) I will be here about two more months— more or less. This field is an overseas replacement training center and it's sometimes rumored that washouts here start training for overseas—but I doubt it. A couple cadets were discharged last week from the army to go back to essential aircraft jobs they held before coming in army. Of course the army never promises us anything—they could give us a boat ride tomorrow if they wanted to. Our meals have been very good since going on garrison rations—I'll be getting fat.

We are having a wet snow this afternoon. We solved some of the puzzles on the jeep board you sent but couldn't get one of them. Our worst week here will be guard week—two weeks hence. You march long stretches day and night and often go without sleep for a while. But it probably won't be so bad either. In officer schools they want you to get tougher training than the men who will be under your command— otherwise they wouldn't have much respect for an officer if he didn't get his bars the hard way. I kind of thrive on this stuff though except there is nothing very exciting to do in spare time.

Peggy wrote that Mr. Robert Casadesus, a pianist we heard at St. Louis Symphony, was the featured guest artist of Philharmonic Orchestra from Carnegie Hall last Sunday.

In his next letter Lyle expressed apprehension about the fourth course, Aircraft Recognition. Identifying American, British, German, and Japanese planes from images projected onto a screen for a split second was daunting. Many of the American planes were christened with fanciful names:

Boeing	B-17	Flying Fortress
Consolidated	B-24	Liberator
North American	B-25	Mitchell
Martin	B-26	Marauder (Widow Maker)
Curtis	C-46	Commando (Dumbo)
Douglas	C-47	Skytrain (Gooney Bird)
Douglas	C-54	Skymaster
Vought	F-4U	Corsair
Interstate	L-6	Grasshopper
Lockheed	P-38	Lightning
Bell	P-39	Airacobra
Curtis	P-40	Warhawk
Republic	P-47	Thunderbolt (Jug)
North American	P-51	Mustang
Northrop	P-61	Black Widow

The letter *B* stood for bomber, *C* for cargo/transport, *F* for fighter, *L* for liaison, and *P* for pursuit. The P-38 Lightning, a long-range fighter with an innovative twin-boomed design, was one of the fastest planes in the sky. Attaining speeds up to 390 mph, the German Luftwaffe called it the *Forked-Tail Devil*.

Hurricane and Spitfire denoted two important British fighter planes. German planes, such as the Messerschmidt, carried the name of the manufacturer. Oddly, the name of the Japanese Zero originated from the zeros in 2600, the year of the old Japanese calendar at the time the plane was designed. Fast and highly maneuverable, it was the premier fighter plane early in the war but lost its preeminence when the P-38 Lightning and F-4U Corsair made their debuts.

The Corsair fighter, a single-engine, low-wing monoplane, was easily recognizable because of its inverted gull wing, a design that allowed the propeller to clear the ground. With its long nose and speed exceeding 400 mph, the Japanese nicknamed it *Whistling Death*.

12 JANUARY 1944 (WEDNESDAY). Just time to catch a breath and write a short letter. We are studying Aircraft Recognition and really keeping busy. Friday we will have a test on about 40 planes which are active in combat areas. They will be flashed on the screen in 1/5 second and you have to tell what plane it is. If your eyes aren't focused on the screen in the right place, you won't even see it at all. Of course that is too short a time to see any particular part about the plane but it just strikes you as being for instance a B-25 or Messerschmidt. Just like you might recognize a person you have seen once before without being able to tell the shape of his nose or mouth. A Corsair plane was doing barrel rolls and loops over our barracks yesterday. We certainly see a lot of different kinds of planes flying around here all the time. Lots of planes look very much alike and some are simply later models. I doubt if I'll pass—but my luck might pull me through—and I'm improving all the time.

I drew K.P. for Sunday again so that means getting up at 4:30 Sunday morning. If I survive next week which is guard duty, it will be sort of a turn in the tide cause after that I'll be an upperclassman. The Register and postcard came yesterday. I see they made a pretty bad mistake in the article. They have Basic *Office* Training—should be *Officer*. Could look pretty bad unless people know that there isn't such a thing as Office training. Royce Bates wrote today. He is still in Georgia and is going home this week on a 15 day furlough.

Lyle continued his letter from the squadron Day Room, a place of refuge from the noisy barracks. Instead of sitting on a cot, he sat in a comfortable chair at a table and wrote at a leisurely pace while listening to the *Lucky Strike Hit Parade*. Sponsored by the American Tobacco Company, the popular program featured tunes most frequently played on jukeboxes and at radio stations around the country. As a clever advertising ploy, a tobacco auctioneer feigned selling tobacco leaf at an auction house, always closing his chant with *Sold American*, implying American Tobacco Company bought the highest-grade tobacco leaf for its Lucky Strike brand of cigarettes.

Bracing period has just ended so we are through with another day. The cadet chorus is broadcasting over the tobacco network just now. Quite a few fellows were gigged enough for tours this week but I'm still in the clear. We had a combination rain, sleet, and snow storm the other day all at once. Seems like we just go from one day to the next here without any breaks in the monotony—but we'll be leaving here before too long. Sleep an extra hour for me.

15 JANUARY 1944 (SATURDAY).   Managed to pass Aircraft Recognition and by a pretty fair margin. Quite a few flunked. We will see planes buzzing around in our sleep for a week. It was a nerve wracking course to say the least. I had a two hour cleaning detail last evening and a really good workout in Physical Training yesterday. First caluthentics and then at least an hour of ranger and obstacle courses in the woods. I enjoy that outdoors stuff even if it did leave me stiff this morning. It rained last night and today leaving a few islands of yellow mud—we have lots of almost freezing rains here—just the kind that you don't like. And with no sidewalks you really wade around. Don't know whether to go to an early show this evening—or go to bed early for 4:30 K.P. in the morning. We also start guard duty tomorrow (Sunday) and have it for a week. You will find us marching our post on and off day and night—rain, snow, or sunshine. The food has been excellent—but it's terribly risky to eat cause so many fellows get gigs or tours when caught talking, not sitting right at table, or for not cleaning trays properly when leaving the mess hall.

Following a bracing session, Lyle returned to the Day Room. No doubt his family back home was listening to the *Hit Parade*—provided the batteries had sufficient charge to power the radio. Now more than halfway through the eleven-week regimen at SJF, he looked forward to the final phase of training at Yale University, envisioning pinning gold bars on the shoulders of an officer's uniform.

We had a two-hour bracing period today. Lots of fellows will walk tours tomorrow but they didn't get me. We stay surprisingly healthy and I've never felt better—but Oh, that getting up at 5:20 every morning—if not earlier. I always did want to see if O.C.S. was tough—it isn't bad considering they used to get a commission for what we take here. Irene seems to be getting settled in Omaha. I'll bet it helps not having calves around. Dad may work harder than I but no one tells him where to put each forkful of hay, when to water a calf, nor does he have to wait in line half an hour for dinner. We don't have too much longer here though.

Which coast is Dale Korzan going to? He may come here cause this is an Overseas Replacement Center. Is the radio going yet? Maybe you could get a 32-volt job. The Hit Parade Tobacco Auctioneers live here in Goldsboro. Wrote two letters and now my weekend is gone—Great life here. But we have our fun off and on during the week.

Fun fell by the wayside with the start of Guard Duty, the fifth course during week eight. When guarding army installations it was mandatory to be on the alert at all times, even when fatigued. The country was aware of the danger of sabotage. Several English-speaking saboteurs, deposited on the East Coast by German submarines, had been captured by the FBI before they could carry out their mission.

19 JANUARY 1944 (WEDNESDAY). Just a few lines before hitting the sack. Was sure nice to get the cookies yesterday and it was nice to sink my teeth into a good cinnamon roll. This week isn't so bad in some ways except that it's sort of tough getting out of bed all times of the night. Spent my shifts last night guarding a big warehouse. Nothing happened except officers drove up to see if we were "on the ball." Sometimes they try to trick the guards or sneak up on them just to see if they are alert. Feel pretty good right now after a shower and a hair wash. We expect a fire drill this evening but it may be a rumor. Got an interesting letter from Kenneth Lunn—he is back in Ohio again. Guess I'm pretty lucky to be here for the winter and then go to Conn. in the spring. It isn't bad to be in the army if you are going to some sort of school and learning something. It will be wonderful to get out of this army red tape when we do. Hope to be able to go to a show or something this weekend. We do get time for a game of pool or ping pong once in a while. Our meals here are very good now. Of course they are costing us more now—we still get about $80 per month. But we will need it just before and after getting commissioned. They don't wash out many cadets here but at Yale U. the mortality rate is pretty high. Let me hear from you. Don't let the guns get rusty. In the army you have to clean them every time you lay a hand on them. Throw all alarm clocks in the junk pile. I pity the first person who tries to get me up before sunrise when I get out of this army. Make Chuckie drink lots of milk. We drink all we can get here.

While Lyle and his buddies were coping with the rigors of cadet life, the Allies were striking a blow at German forces in Italy. On the morning of 22 January 1944, British and American troops stormed the beaches near Anzio, a resort town between Naples and Rome. Following the surprise landings the Allied forces moved inland and consolidated their positions. In the meantime, German Field Marshall Kesselring, attempting to contain the beachhead, moved in troops from Rome and other sectors of Italy. During the ensuing four months Allied troops, in their quest for Rome, fought desperately to repel the German counteroffensive.

UPPERCLASSMAN

After achieving upperclassman status, Lyle was free to move about the base and could occasionally get permission to leave the confines of the camp when not on duty. Unfortunately, it was his turn for orderly detail—taking messages, awakening the men in the morning, watching out for fires, and performing other chores. While on the night shift he composed a long letter during the early morning hours. Having grown up with the strong work ethic and laissez-faire mind-set of Dakota farm people, he complained about inane, time-wasting aspects of army life. Surprised to learn Vernon was likely to be drafted in the near future, he sounded off that the armed forces had enough men to defeat the Axis. Conscripting more men would just cut further into production, making consumer goods ever more scarce.

23 JANUARY 1944 (SUNDAY). It is now 3 o'clock Sat. night or should I say Sunday morning. I'm on my second 6 hour shift as orderly so this is another weekend shot. I'll try to get a little sleep during the early part of the day. Who knows, might even get next weekend off. Weekend here means Sat. evening and Sunday until 3:00 p.m. when we have retreat parade. Am an upperclassman now so things will be better from now on in. The bright spots here are the meals and the recreation room. Since we started kicking in 90¢ per day for meals, the mess hall has started keeping us supplied with oranges, apples, and tangerines—and we sure do hit them hard. It's a good deal cause it keeps some fellows from eating too much candy. We now have a pool table, ping pong table, radio, magazines, and a piano which some of the fellows can really make music with. Ping Pong is a game in which you can always find a better player. Almost beat Vargo yesterday in a vicious driving game. I'm not much good at pool but a couple of us beat a pair of pool sharks by strategic playing. It keeps this deal from being sour grapes altogether. We study First Aid under good doctors this next week. Word comes back from Yale U. that lots of fellows wash out in the communications branch in which I'm classified. Most fellows who come here have taught radio or radar in other camps or have radio licenses. All I know about a radio is that it has a dial. Maybe I won't make the grade—and maybe I will. Rather envy Pips Coler in Hawaii. They make it plain to us that we will have a P.O.E. (Port of Embarkation) address

soon after graduating from Yale. My section (49) may get out of here in late Febr. or in early March. Sections 43 and 44 are already shipping. We had fire drills on two nights last week. It's a sign they are beginning to weaken when they have to use something as old and outworn as a fire drill to get us out of bed nights. You run outside with a sand can or fire extinguisher and run into cadets and half-built sidewalks on the way to the building where the fire is supposed to be. It's a good example of the army's organized confusion! Usually you get back in bed only to discover that it was a false "all clear" signal. The workings of the army are very strange. Makes one realize that what makes this country great economically is freedom of enterprise—just opposite of what you have in army. Haven't heard from Vernon lately, but by your letter it seems he may be called in soon. Don't know who is to blame but someone has badly bungled the manpower situation. Maybe the whole mess will end soon. You can bet we'll be glad to get to Yale for a change and the sooner the better. Should have some really good times up there if we even get any time off. I know we will be restricted the first 3 weeks. One of our Wash U. boys washed today on account of sinus trouble.

The 4:00 to 6:00 shift is now going out to relieve the old guard relief. A cold damp fog rolled in the other morning when I had that shift—it was so thick that you had to chew it in order to breathe. I'm growing all the time but haven't weighed for a couple months. And feeling very peppy right along. I'm getting rather stale from the continuous routine so had better go to a show or dance soon.

Sunday evening.

Feel pretty good right now. By skipping dinner and taking a few chances, it was possible to attend a show. Was about the Seabees and sort of stunk. But it was entertaining and broke the monotony. We just finished retreat and will have mess in a few minutes. Take it easy.

Now in the ninth week at SJF, Lyle and other upperclassmen harassed the underclassmen, *dodos* in army lingo. During evening bracing sessions they singled out cadets and ordered, "Hit a brace, Mister!" A series of questions, orders, and responses followed:

"Do you like it here?"

"Yes, sir!"

"Do you speak French?"

"No, sir!"

"Recite general order eleven!"

"Sir, I will be especially watchful at night, and during the time for challenging, to challenge all persons on or near my post, and to allow no one to pass without proper authority!"

"At ease, Mister!"

26 JANUARY 1944 (WEDNESDAY). Was nice to get your letters yesterday. I hit the jackpot again—K.P. on Sunday for the 3rd Sunday this month. But you just wait and see—I'll get a Sunday off one of these weeks. We are going to have a mock battle Friday night out in the woods somewhere which should be interesting. This week we are studying First Aid—training films and captains in the medical corps giving lectures. Really picking up lots of information. Played 3 games of pool this evening before bracing the new dodos. We lost the 3rd game thereby losing the table. The meals today were swell. Weighed on the P.X. scale yesterday dressed in light dress without a coat and it said 195 lb. But they say it weighs 5 lb. heavy—and each G.I. shoe weighs about 8 lbs! Our Physical Training is pretty rough and a Sgt. gigs everybody who doesn't do the exercises just right or who gets tired on an exercise and quits. I'm enough above average so it doesn't bother me. They sure are passing out gigs—There will be a big bunch marching tours this weekend. Guess I'm thriving on this although in the morning at 5:00 we feel pretty frazzled. Last evening we saw the World Series movie for servicemen. With a telescope, you could have seen me about a 1/2 mile back in the left field St. Louis bleachers. I could go for one of those pheasant suppers—you furnish the pheasant. Wonder if I could get one with a box of shells? Would really be something to enjoy the comforts of home again. The cadet I told you about who washed out was called to take an overseas physical exam the next day. Enough wind for the radio yet? Do you ever have a flat tire? Be seeing you next summer about July—with or without bars on my shoulder.

A mock skirmish out in the countryside on Friday evening furnished a change of scenery and a diversion from the rigid routine. Lyle found the army rations palatable. The C rations, meant to provide nutrition for combat soldiers with no access to a field kitchen, came in two cans. One can contained stew, hash, or meat and beans; the other contained large biscuits along with candy, sugar, fruit juice, or coffee—and cigarettes. The K ration, containing breakfast, dinner, and supper units, came in three small cardboard boxes heavily waxed for preservation. Lyle especially liked the D ration, an emergency chocolate-flavored bar (weighing four ounces and containing six hundred calories) that was meant to supplement C and K rations.

29 JANUARY 1944 (SATURDAY). I'll try and write a letter while waiting for the pool table. Got 88% on the First Aid test yesterday. At 4:00 we got into our leggings, canteen, gas mask, etc and went out in the country in trucks. It was sort of better than a picnic and fun to get away from camp. The battle area was about a mile square and full of cotton

fields, corn fields, streams of water, old deserted houses and buildings, woods, and dense undergrowth. We ate our supper of C, K, and D rations—about twice as much calories as we are supposed to eat and got all ready for the fight. At dusk we organized in patrols and started capturing prisoners. A man was dead as soon as you got his name tag. An amplified phonograph of battle sounds and tear gas attacks made it very realistic. In the dark you get all turned around in directions and you feel very funny when the enemy suddenly jumps out all around you. Our squadron won the battle and we quit at 10:00. Then we hiked the 7 miles home and were lucky enough to get home by 1:00. It was a beautiful night and very warm and we had a good time singing songs on the way.

Some of the cadets at SJF wore metal emblems shaped like bottle caps on the shoulders of their uniforms. Those cadets, referred to as *bottlecaps*, had authority to enforce discipline in the cadet corps. Caught in the middle, bottlecaps were viewed as martinets by their fellow cadets yet were subject to the same regimen and threat of washing out.

Guess what—I have all evening off. Don't know whether I need the sleep or a show most. Lots of fellows have tours to walk this weekend—some have 10 hours of them to walk. Heard one deal—a bottlecap inspecting barracks moved the end of a bed to see if the floor had been mopped under the legs. That left the shoes underneath a couple inches out of line and the next bottlecap gigged the man for having his shoes out of line. They get you coming and going. They can pull deals on you here that won't go in the G.I. army. Nothing is so hard but we put in a terrific number of hours per week. We are like newly hatched butterflies—we droop around early and pep up as the sun comes out. By evening we are full of vim and vinegar again.
Sunday.
Make any connections at the land sale? Grassland should be the best bet. Got a V-mail from Pips Coler from Hawaii. He had a leave in Honolulu. Guess I should have gotten in the navy in some ways. "Don't get around much anymore." My correspondence really covers the U.S.

Now in the tenth week and expecting to ship out soon, Lyle wrote:

2 FEBRUARY 1944 (WEDNESDAY). A whole half hour with nothing to do except write this letter. We are having a sort of sad sack course this week in Administration but I'm a little above passing in it so far. We had a true false test in it Tues. If you didn't answer a question you had

the usual percentage taken off. If you answer it and answer wrong, it is taken off double. I'm a gambler so answered some I shouldn't have. K.P. Sunday wasn't bad except that it ran the weeks together again. We spent lots of time snitching choc. cake by clever maneuvering—not because we were hungry but more for the sport of it. Got gigged a couple times already this week but may not get enough for tours. We have very rigid table manners—only one hand above table, etc. Gets to be a habit so if one hand comes up above the table top, the other automatically goes down like pistons in a motor. Hardly worth the risk of tours to eat a poor meal—but most of them are good meals. There is a keen rumor that some of us 49 Section may ship a week from Sunday. We will know early next week. At least we'll go the week after. The battle of Seymour Johnson is almost over—and won. We will be restricted the first three weeks at Yale U.—and have evening parades 7 days a week. In the cadets you don't live, you just exist counting off each of the 18 hours every day—glad when another day is done. Wilma had better practice up on her solitaire cause I'll sure beat her. Is Chuckie growing too? Had turnabout day yesterday and the dodos raked us upperclassmen over the coals. Had to attend a dumb program last night until about 11:30. Got paid again the other day. We earn that extra cadet pay. Almost time to go and brace the dodos now. Take it easy. Looks like a clear weekend ahead for me.

Granted permission to leave the base, Lyle and four buddies took off for a weekend excursion to a neighboring town. Enjoying his first social opportunity since leaving St. Louis in November, he wrote home on Hotel Cherry stationery, scribbling "balony" next to the advertisement: ABSOLUTELY FIREPROOF.

5 FEBRUARY 1944 (SATURDAY). Sixth floor, 1 o'clock, and all is well. Five of us managed to get out of the coop this evening and came over here in one of the fellows "merry oldsmobile." We checked in at the hotel here and then had supper. I had tenderloin of trout, rasin pie and so forth. Sure felt good to be able to eat without a bottlecap standing over your shoulder to see if you break your bread in four pieces. The 5 of us are from Maryland, Fla., S.D., Ga, and Mass. We went to a dance at the community building with a jukebox for music. The girls were badly

outnumbered and sometimes you could only get 4 or 5 steps before someone cut in. Bet I cut in 60 times altogether. Of course we had a good time. These N.C. gals are alright but rather hard to understand. "Take me back to St. Louis." Boy, am I tired. Wilson, N.C., is a small town (typical southern) and the largest bonded tobacco market in the world. Our last test in Admin. was the same type as the first one—double off for a question wrong. I was overly cautious and left 26 questions blank. It was almost fatal. The 3 tests totaled 1000 points. I got 746 points—passing was 745 points. So I passed with a margin of one point in a thousand! For a grade of 74.6 or 75 which is passing. But here one point is as good as a hundred—but that was too close. And the funny part is that my bunk mate passed by 2 points. Some of my Section 49 communications will go on shipping Monday and leave next Sunday. Doubt if I'll be on it—but for sure next week. I'm anxious to leave. Just think, no fire drill or revillie tonight. Is Vernon home yet? He ought to take a sort of rest before going in if possible. Hope the navy deal comes through. Don't mind the inkblots. I'm sort of tired and sleepy.

If you can't read this, you can at least look at the pictures.

Embarking on the last course, Supply, Lyle learned his parents had placed a second star in the front window of their home, signifying they had two sons in the armed forces. Vernon had been inducted into the navy.

6 FEBRUARY 1944 (SUNDAY). Found a letter from you and one from Irene when I got back here this afternoon. Feel like starting another week now after the splurge in Wilson. So we now have a little army-navy rivalry in the family. Wish I could drop in on you for a while—but the army says no. We should get a leave in about 4-5 months. A letter back from Yale U. told how a fellow got 8 gigs for not polishing the door handle on his room. Sounds interesting though. I could go for one of Mom's vegetable dishes. Feeling tops and having a pretty good time of it.

8 FEBRUARY 1944 (TUESDAY). On Squadron C.Q. (Charge of Quarters) for today so I'll have some time to write a letter—I hope. My job is to take care of the office for all business of the day. Easier than going to classes and formations—but I'll be responsible for the material they cover in class anyway. Everything is under water and it's still raining hard. Rather dull around here—drab barracks and mud puddles. Three of our Wash. U. cadets went on the shipping list Monday and will likely ship Sunday. Our Sec. 49 is large so they may not get me next week yet—but I'll be out of here before the end of the month. Some of the fellows who have flunked a course won't ship quite so soon. We had a

very good chicken dinner today—in fact all the meals are good. The first month they were poor and skimpy. Have been pretty tired and sleepy mornings this week as is everybody else but the weekend will soon be here. Looks like I'm safe on tours again too. One fellow walked 9 hr. of them last weekend—can't seem to do things quite right. We had boxing in P.T. a couple days and wish they would have it more often. Had time for a couple games of pool last night but it was an "off night" in that game. The easy way out in the army is to remain a buck private—but it's natural to want to go up. Let me know what's going on around there. Bye now.

Lyle received news that Vernon had passed through the reception station at Fort Leavenworth and was now in boot camp at Farragut, a landlocked navy base near Coeur d'Alene, Idaho.

12 FEBRUARY 1944 (SATURDAY). Just got your card—you don't know how nice it is to hear on the same card that a sick person is well again. Sort of a funny thing to have happen to a person. Another busy week has ended—and this is really my lucky day. First I found out that I passed this weeks Supply course by a score of 82. Thought maybe I flunked—usually manage to melt into the average of a group. So my record here is clean. And today (wonder of wonders) they put me on shipping and I definitely leave Sunday the 20th—so stop all correspondence. There is one little catch—the Guard Squadron is short so we will be on guard duty this week. Just as easy as classes though and no test to pass. I'm going to bed early tonight cause my first shift starts at 2:00 Sunday afternoon. The weather has been windy and chilly but may clear up by then. Just think, we go way past N.Y. City—and maybe through there. No tours to walk this weekend either. My bunk mate and some other pals are shipping at the same time.

So Vernon also went through Ft. Leavenworth. Hope he doesn't get stuck in that old CC Camp by the detention barracks where I was those last couple days. That was rough—and I do mean rough. How come he didn't have a longer stay at home? I'm glad he's in the navy cause they are more apt to recognize ability than army. You have lots going on around there—this was sort of an even grind. What I wouldn't give to wake up with the sun shining in my window and feel rested in the morning. But it doesn't hurt us any cause we are plenty peppy by afternoon. Will be nice to hit Yale cause the surroundings are very nice there. Bet it keeps you plenty busy around there but you would all be busy even with a dozen hired men anyway. Suppose my mail will drop to half now—but you do remarkably well at that. Wish they would let us come home once in a while. Ever listen to the Hit Parade—I like the songs that are popular now. I could go for some corn fritters. We got good training here and pretty rigid discipline—and I saved enough energy for the homestretch at Yale. Take it easy out there where the Sun sets.

13 FEBRUARY 1944 (SUNDAY). Supper whistle.
We had a swell supper including fried chicken and rutabegas and now I'm over at the chapel listening to recorded music. Pretty soon they will have vesper services. It's a nice place to write letters and I'm way behind on letters anyway. We were so busy last week that one fellow didn't have time to read a letter until the next day. One evening we had to go to a lousy cadet program. About 11:30 everyone was tired and it was absolutely a stinko deal so everyone started singing "Show me the way to go home, I'm tired and want to go to bed" etc. The officer probably didn't like that. The Carolina countryside is sure funny. Scattered as though by the wind are old clapboard and log buildings some of which are occupied. Tree stumps, trees, drainage ditches, odd shaped fields, etc. It's really a "has been" place. We are having a blustery rainstorm now. If you think bowling is an up and down proposition just try pool. Sometimes you can't sink a ball no how. Our laundry is pathetic too— open up the bundle and buttons and pieces of buttons shower out. Then they gig you for having a button off of the clothes you have hanging up! Out of paper so I'll sign off now.

During a tour of guard duty, two hours on and four hours off over a period of two days, the only way Lyle could get a three-hour stretch of sleep was by crawling into bed fully clothed. He had neither the time nor the inclination to write home for several days.

17 FEBRUARY 1944 (THURSDAY). Maybe if I write some letters I might get some. My mail has been as scarce as waffles in an army mess hall this week. This is by far the nicest week I've had here at Seymour Johnson. Here is the deal—some of us shippers are on guard duty and when we are off duty, we do as we please. However, early in the week we had a 48 hour tour of guard duty and ordinarily they won't put you on more than a 24 hour tour and it was raining some of the shifts. One shift it was raining and sloppy and nighttime and I was guarding a lonely warehouse. The O.D. (Officer of the Day) came around in a staff car and tried to mix me up. He didn't succeed. Also challenged a couple soldiers armed with carbines but they turned out to be field guards and should have been mentioned in the special orders. Decided to be reasonable with them cause their guns were loaded—and mine wasn't! We were really in tired shape when we finished so we hit the sack all afternoon and then went to the show "Lifeboat." We walk over to the mess hall and eat just

about whenever we feel like it. Got a haircut yesterday afternoon and played pool. Took a P.F.R. yesterday morning in order to clear up all my records before shipping. There are 5 classes—poor, fair, good, very good, excellent—and I was in the very good class.

Saturday.

Last night the squadron that was best for the week had a party near Wilson at the country club. We have some friends in that sqdn who pulled some strings so my bunk mate and I got to go. We went in army trucks with the usual singing. The country club was very nice and they had a hot little soldier orchestra. As usual it was a few steps before someone cut in. Lots of nice girls but of course none to compare with Peggy. And they had a nice lunch too. You don't have the drinking at these parties like at home. One reason of course is that N.C. is a dry state. The party busted up about midnight and we headed back to camp. Seems funny that in a giant camp like this there is a certain barracks that is home to you. Have been in the army for a year now and certainly have no regrets. Had to look on my map to see where Vernon is. Didn't know Idaho was so near home. Imagine he may like navy life better than he anticipated. Slept until 9:00 this morning so haven't had breakfast and am I hungry! Guess we'll skip over and eat pretty soon. When you first get here until you leave you always envy the shippers—and now it's hard to realize that I am one now. They kept us so busy that the course passed very quickly. Just think, Sunday we board the train for Wash., D.C, Baltimore, Phil., N.Y., and all points North. In about two seconds I'm going to put this leaky pen on the floor and tramp on it. We start another 24 hr. guard tour this afternoon and it's raining. But it will be our last. About 1/2 or 1/3 of the Wash. U. group will be on my shipment. The rest will come later. Flunking a course is one thing that holds you back.

Assured he could compete in the physical, military, and academic arenas, Lyle was ready to move on to Technical School Yale, the last obstacle standing in the way of a commission.

Sunday afternoon.

We were very lucky to end our stay here with a week like this. Leaves a good taste in our mouths. Am glad I went through this course—everyone should take it. The chores are probably pretty hard now that winter has struck. But I suspect everything is under control around there. You have enough barn room too. Remember the winter that each barn was a different degree of hospital—with the horse barn for extra special cases. Hope Dad's eye is alright by now. Have you heard from Vernon yet? One shipping officer put it very nicely the other day. He said, "Well, you will soon have your feet out of the mud, your hands out of the soot, and—

Lyle abruptly abandoned his letter writing. Given just a few minutes to pack his barracks bag, he marched off to the railroad siding in a pouring rain—a year and a day since joining the army. He was thrilled at the prospect of entering the hallowed halls of Yale.

TROOP TRAIN

21 FEBRUARY 1944 (MONDAY). We are in Pennsylvania Station, New York City, and have been sitting here in the dark station a couple hours playing bridge. Of course they never let us out. We marched over to the field station at 4:00 Sunday and headed north in Pullman cars. Had a light box lunch and had the porter make up the berths real early—I can just barely stretch out full length. Woke up at 2:00 in the night when we hit Wash., D.C. Went through Virginia, Maryland, and hit Baltimore in very early morning. Got up early in morning and came to Philadelphia and almost immediately hit Trenton, N.J., East Orange, Linden, Jersey City, and several others. The east is so highly industrialized that one city merges into another. New Jersey is one stretch of railroad yards, factories, skyway across the river—and slums. I was terribly disappointed in N. Jersey. Through the smoke and haze we saw the Empire State Building just before going into the tunnel under the Hudson River. It sticks way up above the rough level of the other buildings. We are sitting a couple blocks from the Empire State Building—but can't see it. Saw some subways between N.Y. and N.J. We should leave here soon for Conn. I'm glad we are going up to New England—hope it isn't so terribly industrialized as this. Are moving again now—in a dark sub-passage. We are feeling good and will come out of this short trip in excellent shape. It was a cold rainy day when we left N.C.—just like the day we got there. One fellow in this car—my Wash. U. roommate—has been on every shipment that I have been on starting at Ft. Leavenworth.

Wow! Stood on the platform as we went on Long Island and had a wonderful terrific 15 minute view of the New York skyline. It's really something. Rockefeller Center Bld. is the biggest but the Empire State Bld. is taller cause it has a peak on it. The Chrysler Bld. is something too. We went through the Bronx and saw Manhattan, Queens, Brooklyn, Long Island Sound and mazes of bridges and buildings. Almost too much to grasp. Never expected a view like that. It's bumpy as we roll toward—

NEW HAVEN FROM THE GREEN, YALE UNIVERSITY, 1944

PHELPS GATE, YALE UNIVERSITY, 1944

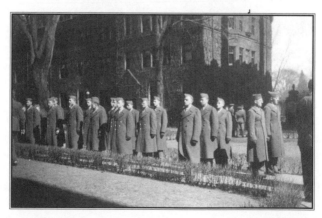

"POOR SUCKERS—JUST IN FROM SEYMOUR JOHNSON FIELD," 1944

For God, for Country, and for Yale

School days, school days,
Dear old golden rule days,
Readin' and 'ritin' and 'rithmetic,
Taught to the tune of a hick-ry stick.

—WILL D. COBB

THE TRAIN PASSAGE from North Carolina to Connecticut was an eye-opener for Lyle. He found the industrial density of the Atlantic seaboard astounding and the skyline of New York City awesome. Nearing New Haven, he could hardly wait to set foot on the campus of Yale University, a storied place he had read about but never expected to see.

Upon arrival at the station the aviation cadets detrained and fell into formation on the platform.

"All present and accounted for, sir."

Off they marched along narrow streets bordering the New Haven Green and on to Phelps Gate, the arched entry to Old Campus. Lyle felt a tingling in his spine as he passed through the portico and read an inscription carved in stone: FOR GOD, FOR COUNTRY, AND FOR YALE.

The reception at the Yale Army Air Forces Technical Training Command (AAFTTC) was a portent of the months to come. Greeting the dodos with "You'll be soooooorry," the upperclassmen lined the new arrivals up on the campus quadrangle facing Connecticut Hall.

"Head up! Chin in!"

"Suck in your gut, Mister!"

"What's your serial number!"

"Now—right—face!"

Knowing how to play the hazing game, Lyle blended into the group so as to avoid undue scrutiny. While standing at attention he eyed the sidewalks

BRACING NEW ARRIVALS (DODOS), TS YALE, 1944

YALE UNIVERSITY FROM NINTH FLOOR OF BINGHAM HALL, 1944

NEW HAVEN FROM NINTH FLOOR OF BINGHAM HALL, 1944

lined with stately elms, the modern stone structures in Gothic architecture, and the old brick buildings. In front of Connecticut Hall stood a statue of Nathan Hale, the patriot who spoke the oft quoted words: "My only regret is that I have but one life to give for my country." The Yale campus, so old and steeped in tradition, radiated an aura of timelessness.

Following the bellicose bracing session, the cadets marched off to a beautiful building near the Sterling Law Library. What a surprise. Inside the cavernous dining hall with a vaulted ceiling was a musical ensemble, dressed in army uniforms, playing popular tunes.

"Wow. They can really play those golden trombones."

"Yeah, and those mellow saxophones."

"Can this be the army?"

"Sure beats the mess hall at Seymour Johnson."

Assigned to a plain room in Bingham Hall, Lyle viewed the campus and the New Haven skyline from a window on the ninth floor. Then he hurriedly scribbled:

22 FEBRUARY 1944 (TUESDAY). Arrived about noon in New Haven and marched a ways to the campus and mess hall. It is a big building seating hundreds and the food is prepared and served by civilians. The food is excellent and they have a little orchestra too—but it costs more than at S.J. field. The U. is located near the heart of N. Haven—in fact the building we are quartered in looks out over a city street on one side and part of the campus on the other side. We are in Bingham Hall. This is a large outfit but I doubt if it is as pretty as the Wash. U. campus. The course is tough and lots wash out. But I'll work hard enough to go through. Better get in gear here and start unpacking. If you don't hear from me—I'm busy.

Except for a few necessities, such as razor, toothbrush, toothpaste, and shoe polish, the cadets were forbidden from keeping personal items, not even stacks of letters, in the dormitory rooms that served as barracks. Any unpolished leather or hardware, any trace of dust, resulted in gigs for all seven men who occupied the room. Once again, roommates affected Lyle's prospect of surviving the program; passing room inspection hinged on the performance of them all.

A photograph posted in Bingham Hall showed the regulation way to "break a bed" on bed-airing day. In compliance, the cadets neatly hung their barracks bags, tied in a precise manner, on the rails at the end of each bed. They placed their shoes in the proper order on the floor with toes aligned evenly with the edge of the bed. Whenever there was a change in command, the incoming officer modified the patterns, conveying the subtle message, "I'm in charge now."

INSPECTING CADET QUARTERS, TS YALE, 1944

PROPER WAY TO "BREAK A BED," TS YALE, 1944

The upperclassmen at Technical School (TS) Yale substituted the word *tough* for technical. In addition to physical training and military bearing, TS Yale aimed to turn out officers capable of directing the enlisted personnel who kept aircraft operational around the globe. Each aviation cadet studied one of five specialties: aircraft maintenance, engineering, aircraft armament, aerial intelligence photography, or communications.

Lyle's hometown newspaper, the *Chamberlain Register*, soon received a form letter:

PUBLIC RELATIONS OFFICE
Headquarters Technical School
AAFTTC
Yale University   For IMMEDIATE RELEASE
New Haven, Conn.

     NEW HAVEN, CONN., <u>FEB 22</u> - - <u>LYLE V SLADEK</u> , son of
                     (date)   (full name)

  <u>MRS CHARLES SLADEK</u> , of <u>PUKWANA SD</u>
                                 (city and street address)
has begun training as an Aviation Cadet in the Army Air Forces Training
Command School at Yale University. His training will prepare him
for the duties of a Technical Officer in Communications, and upon
completion of the course he will be commissioned a second lieutenant.
West Point traditions and discipline are in effect at the Training
Command School at Yale.

     According to Col. Raymond J. Reeves, Commanding Officer of the
School, courses he will take here include study of transmitters, receivers,
the radio compass, radio and wire equipment, and portable ground
stations. In addition to classroom work, much of his schedule will
include intensive training for physical fitness, toughening him for terrain
and temperature found in fighting fronts around the world. Part of his
time will be spent in the field under simulated battle conditions.

     After being commissioned he will be placed in charge of a crew of
enlisted men specialists at flying fields in the United States or overseas
where he will maintain the plane-to-ground and plane-to-plane
communications so essential in the aerial campaign over Europe.

-30-L-N-H-

(Fill in the above blank. In the address box on the reverse side,
print the name and address of your favorite hometown newspaper.)

Leafing through a booklet issued by the Public Relations Office, Lyle read a blurb about his area of specialty:

> Communications is the nerve center of all Air Forces activities, and we who are learning to be officers in this branch will be serving at vital posts. . . .
>
> Radio is probably the most widely used method of communication in the Air Forces, for, as Col. David Sarnoff of the Army Signal Corps says, "It is radio that helps to coordinate the infantry units and planes, and the Marines and Sailors on the Seven Seas. . . ."
>
> Therefore, we have to learn a great deal about radio. . . . During our course of study we learn how to send and receive international Morse code, which is, in itself, an achievement worthy of note. We have our own sending and receiving sets which consist of headphones and key, and we are able to talk to one another just as we will soon be doing from ground stations.
>
> Maintenance of equipment, though, is probably the most important work that we will be doing, so that much of our time here is spent in the laboratory, where we begin at the bottom by building small receivers and work up through to a point where we can construct larger sets, including transmitters. . . .
>
> Aviation has its own peculiar type of radio equipment. . . . Therefore, our course of study is quite different from that of the conventional type. It is also more complex and includes information that is of a restricted nature. . . .
>
> Every white starred ship that heads into hostile or friendly territory depends on a communication officer for information and navigation. . . . We send out homing signals to friend and create static for foe. Not only are we "on the beam"; we are the "beam"—.

Stepping up production on the home front was crucial to the Allied cause. Factories idled during the depression were reactivated and new plants of unprecedented size constructed. Erected in just thirteen months, the Ford bomber plant at Willow Run, Michigan, was the "world's largest room." In many factories, men and women kept the production lines humming around-the-clock.

With Great Britain and Russia heavily dependent on American output, it was necessary to transport the great mass of goods pouring off the assembly lines to distant shores. Early in 1942 the U.S. Maritime Commission urged the W. A. Betchel Company to build a shipyard in the San Francisco Bay Area. The organization went into action. Just three months later a shipyard named Marinship, operating day and night, began turning out a completed vessel every thirteen days. Likewise, employees working in shifts at the Kaiser Shipyards in Richmond, California, turned out a staggering 747 boats over the course of the war.

At TS Yale, the training command ran three shifts to make optimal use of the classrooms and other facilities. Lyle learned his weekly schedule would run from Thursday to Wednesday. When daily lectures and tests ended at midnight, he would have a few minutes of free time before marching off to breakfast. Expecting the swing shift to conflict with his natural biorhythms, he realized he faced a herculean challenge. Nevertheless, he optimistically wrote:

23 FEBRUARY 1944 (WEDNESDAY). Two days completed at Yale U. and it looks like the course will be O.K. We start classes at 6:00 tomorrow evening—you see I was unfortunate enough to get the swing shift. There are 3 six hour shifts of academic classes and mine is from 6 until midnight. Then we will have breakfast at 1:30 and sleep until 9:00 in the morning. Then you have some rugged P.T. and drill etc during the day. The wash out rate is apparently very high so I may not make it— have never had any work with radios, etc except some of the theory. But it will probably be all right—at least I'll know in a few weeks. It rained a little yesterday and we had a two hour bracing line in which they try to beat you down. Not bad though. We are settled now in a comfortable but bare room. We don't sleep in our beds cause the sheets and pillow case would wrinkle—so we sleep on top in a comforter. After three weeks we can leave the post theoretically—but they say you don't have time—and some fellows get as many as 22 hours of tours to walk before their first 3 weeks are even over. That will take up weekends all the time a soldier is here. But we will know a good deal about communications if we make it. About 5 months worth if we make it at all. I'm planning on making it. The competition is quite terrific here. The meals are swell and the surroundings very pleasant. For years students have leisurely strolled along the walks under the elms—but we must run except when in formation. Below my window in the quadrangle is Connecticut Hall built in 1750 where Nathan Hale, Noah Webster, and many others roomed. It is now a dispensary for the cadets. They say that tomorrow will be a day we will long remember—5:30 until midnight or later. But altogether this will be a pleasant stay here. And we will get some mail in about a week now. How is everything going at home? Signing off.

Using the carrot-and-stick mode of education, TS Yale spurred the communications cadets to rapidly absorb the coursework. The carrot was the dream of winning gold bars. The stick was the threat of washing out, reverting to previous rank, and being reassigned—perhaps to infantry. To escalate the competition, more candidates were selected for the program than were needed. Regardless of how well they performed, the laggards were destined to wash out. It was heartless, but effective. Cadets who survived the mental, physical, and military rigors would become, by act of Congress, Officers and Gentlemen.

The communications training consisted of seventeen weeks of study:

Direct Current (electricity) I and I I	4
Vacuum Tubes	1
Transmitters I and I I	2
Receivers (radio) I and I I	3
Very High Frequency (V.H.F.)	1
Command Sets #287, #274, #522	3
Radio Compass	1
Wire (telephone and telegraph)	1
Ground Sets	1
	17 weeks

In addition to electronics, the curriculum included the study of cryptography, Morse code, and duties classes that dealt with the basic responsibilities of officers. Cadets who passed each weekly test, two-week test, and comprehensive exam would go on to the next unit of study. Three washes eliminated a cadet from the program.

While marching at Washington University, Lyle had sung "School Days." At Yale, he soon learned the true meaning of the line: "Taught to the tune of a hick-ry stick." The regimentation was more stringent than any he had previously encountered. Still, he took pride in printing *Yale* as part of his return address. On Saturday evening, after the first two days of Direct Current and Cryptography classes, he took time to write home.

26 FEBRUARY 1944 (SATURDAY). We are having a nice quiet snowstorm just now which started just while we were eating supper. This New England climate is really swell. Seems sort of funny to write a letter cause so far I haven't gotten any mail yet—but it should start coming through pretty soon. The first few days while you are getting settled and don't get any mail go sort of slow. But we've been here almost a week already and are still kicking. Once in a while I get discouraged—and then again I decide to go through with it "come hell or high water." For one thing you are under strict regulation and discipline almost 24 hr a day and some stuff is hard to swallow. We don't take to regimentation like the Germans. In the Cadet Corps they really have you over the barrel cause they can gig you and wash you out. But you can see those little gold bars glitter in the distance leading you on. And of course the competition is terrific cause everyone is determined to go through. Everyone here is very capable and yet they wash out a lot to keep the standards high. I'm not a bit confident of making it—but the chips are down and the stakes are high and I love competition. We

have class straight through from six in the evening until midnight and then eat breakfast—or supper? Has been sort of hard on us until we get used to the schedule. This week we are studying basic electricity and cryptography—and can already break down easy codes.

Apart from the tough academics and strict military regimen, the cadets were required to improve the physical records they had set before entering the program. Raised in a hardworking farm family, Lyle was above average in strength and physical endurance. Even so, he found the physical training demanding.

This afternoon we went over to the "Torture Chamber" again—I'm referring to the immense (7 story) Payne-Whitney gym which cost an estimated 12 million dollars and was built in 1931. It's about the world's best and largest—They say a cadet got lost in there and was A.W.O.L. (Absent Without Leave) for a couple weeks. Today they weighed us and then we took a P.F.R. test again. I weighed 182 lbs net and am getting fairly muscular? Chinned 10 times with palms forward on the bar, 90 sit ups, and 300 yds on a poor indoor track in 44 seconds. Did about my best cause it might save the day in case of academic failure. Monday we take the Brushe test where you step up on a 20 in. pedestal for 5 minutes at 30 times per minute. Then they take your pulse rate at intervals to determine how fast you pick up again. If your heart is O.K. then they take no pity on you in P.T. This test really knocks you down and some can't go the 5 minutes. Try climbing a ladder fast for 5 minutes! The P.T. program will be excellent here. We will get swimming instruction from the famous Yale coach who turns out world champions, boxing, tumbling, wrestling, and such. This gym has everything in it but football fields. This Yale U. is really a giant outfit and has lots of large buildings. For a large city the people are more on the easy going small town order—in fact just as you would expect New England people to be. The city seems very clean and well built up. The main thing here is to try and forget about graduating and take the attitude that you are lucky for each hour you can spend in this high powered university. Even then it will be a terrific grind but I'm easy going and won't worry about passing too much. We actually work with electrical equipment here. If at all possible I'll try and get out a little too. Do you ever hear from Vernon? Guess there's no use asking questions though cause I'll probably hear from you soon. Wish I could lay around out there for a nice rest. If I get through here about the 1st of July, I should get a short delay en route to a new station. If I wash out, I might get a furlough very soon. But I'm not going to wash out cause I'm too near the goal. Let me hear from you.

While being introduced to the rudiments of cryptography, Lyle learned that both the Allies and the Axis had ciphers of great complexity—some employing substitution, transposition, and fractionization algorithms simultaneously. Germany possessed a highly sophisticated coding device, the Enigma Machine, that exchanged one letter for another with no logical repeat before two hundred trillion subsequent depressions on the keyboard. German leaders believed that messages converted to code by their Enigma Machine were unbreakable in *real time*—that is, in time to be of any use to the enemy.

Although a closely guarded secret, mathematicians, chess players, and crossword addicts working at Bletchley Park, a mansion near London, succeeded in breaking the German code and changing the course of the war. Some aspects of war history and Allied strategic planning had to be rewritten when, decades later, their secretive work became publicly known.

Lyle reported home on stationery embossed with the shiny gold wings insignia and the words: UNITED STATES AIR FORCES.

March 1, 1944

Dear Folks,

1 MARCH 1944 (WEDNESDAY). Just back from the sweat box where we really had another good workout. But we are tired out and the day is just starting for us. It's not a bit fun to drag yourself to six straight hours of classes—especially night classes. I'm sick of this place as is everyone else—not of the U. but rather what goes with it. These first few weeks they deliberately try to break down the morale—and they succeed. Show me the way back to Seymour Johnson Field! It's hard to get adjusted to our hours but it will be better when we get used to it. It costs us $1.40 per day for food—and we only get a $1.00 per day allowance for food. And with haircuts, cleaning, laundry, etc, we aren't making much. This week we studied Direct Current I and Cryptography and we have the last tests in them tonight. I'm about the dumbest guy in Crypt. but I'll put on enough pressure to make it. But in electricity (the important one) I'm near the top. I'm getting that old feelin' of breezing through. There is lots of pressure on all the time—you can wash out for not saluting an officer. I've got some gigs but may not get enough to walk tours yet. Your card and the Register and a letter from Irene came yesterday. Irene is going to come up here next summer and we'll go to New York City for a day or two—if I'm still here. It really isn't so bad here—this was just

an extra bad day and got me kind of sore—which is probably what they want to do. Wish they would let us go home once in a while.

Restricted to the campus for the first three weeks, Lyle did not have a single picture of New Haven in his mind's eye, except for the city skyline from his dormitory window. He could see, all in a row on the New Haven Green, three landmark churches: United, Center, and Trinity. He thought their grandeur was really something, the spires so tall and white, the bricks so red. Center Church, the Georgian masterpiece of architect Ithiel Town, was indeed splendid. On the back of a photograph, he inscribed, "As straight as a New England church steeple."

CENTER CHURCH, NEW HAVEN GREEN, 1944

Knowing his brother Vernon—possessing a master's degree from Northwestern University—was due to become a commissioned officer in the navy, Lyle revealed his competitive spirit.

5 MARCH 1944 (SUNDAY). A rather nice chilly morning in Connecticut—but we are still restricted so we are sitting around studying and loafing. Sunday is a long day cause we have revillie at 7:00 in the morning and don't get back from class and breakfast until well after

midnight. We are getting used to these night classes now though and don't mind them. I'm getting confident again—passed Cryptography and got 100s in tests in Direct Current I. Of course it will get tougher and will soon be stuff I haven't had before. We have good workouts in P.T. in caluthentics and usually run a mile to finish off—and yet I'm gaining weight. No, this place is not too tough for me—but you know there is a difference between something being tough—and something being exasperating. It's getting better though and after this week we'll have a few free minutes. My mail really came through last week—Your letters, one from Irene, Vivian, Peggy, Kenneth Lunn, Royce Bates— guess that's all. Still don't know if Vernon got a commission. It's really something if he did. Don't see how the navy can do that—unless they train them after being commissioned. If he did then that means I've got to make it cause one can't let a big brother get too far ahead. There is an awful lot of responsibility and prestige that goes with being an officer. We certainly have good meals here—milk morning and night. Pleasant surroundings except for the military and academic pressure. But enough said about that—we asked for it. You are probably going somewhere for dinner today. I imagine it's a rather nice day out there with a few signs of spring around. Wish I could drop around for a while—but then I'd hide in a haystack and they wouldn't get me back again. Irene sent me a few good snapshots. Chuckie is growing fast now. Where did Dad get that zoot hat? No use mentioning my stay at Yale—sounds like a soft deal—a person would have to go through this to understand it. We do have some good times though and it won't be bad when we get to be upperclassmen. Be sure and keep the news coming through when you find time. Pretty lucky—never expected to be going to Yale—even if it is T.S. Yale. Time for mess now.

Elated to learn Vernon had been commissioned an ensign in the navy, the rank equivalent to second lieutenant in the army, Lyle wrote:

8 MARCH 1944 (WEDNESDAY). Had a letter from Vernon yesterday and almost jumped through the ceiling to hear he got that commission. He's coming out here somewhere and I suspect N.Y. or Mass. so I'll get to see him probably. Really a lucky break. We had a good workout in P.T. this afternoon and I do mean a workout. Then we came back here for our booster shots. You see when you have been in over a year the shots run out. They gave me 3 shots and a smallpox vaccination. My arms hurt a little. The army sure keeps you well fortified.

We eat supper now and then have class and 2 week tests in Direct Current I until midnight—then a short wait until breakfast and bed. We sure drag by that time. Yesterday we climbed the 20 some flights of stairs in the gym followed by a mile and half of running. Sure nice to get your letters. Used to always be the big event of spring when the ice broke and the creek ran for the first time. Bet you'll be glad when the grass is green again so the cattle will be gone. Of course this isn't too tough for us—was just that they kept shouting "wash out" at us all the time and had a psychological effect. We have come a long way and want so badly to get through it. You don't know how badly we want to make it unless you've been in the army a year yourself. If I get through tonight I'll tell you now to expect me in July with bars on my shoulders. They've been beating us down so far but from now on it will get better and better. The first possible chance I'll throw my books in the corner and head for N.Y. City for a day. We are really learning electricity so far and I'm doing all right in that part of the course. They're calling us out again. Never quite get a whole letter written.

When the first two weeks of study ended Wednesday at midnight, it was a tense time for Lyle and his classmates. Those with passing grades in Direct Current I and Cryptography would move on to the next course, Direct Current II. Those with failing grades would become members of the *Thursday Morning Club*. Washing back was a severe setback. It meant repeating the course and diminished prospects of getting through TS Yale.

Thanking his lucky stars for clearing the first hurdle, Lyle replied to a letter from home.

11 MARCH 1944 (SATURDAY). Was nice to get the letter and clippings yesterday. Our squadron gets some new dodos from S.J. Field so things will be much better from now on. We get to go off post tonight too at last—we don't have class Sat. night but we do Sunday. Don't

CADET (DODO) HITTING A BRACE, TS YALE, 1944

know whether to study, sleep, or go somewhere? I'll end up by going to a dance or something. Yes, I passed the first two weeks with 86 in Cryptography and 88 in Direct Current I. Got a 100 in the final so was near the top in Direct Current I—the highest grade given out was 92. Some of the upperclassmen were able to go to N.Y. City today and can stay until tomorrow noon. Vernon may be out here by now but haven't heard from him. We got paid today but it takes quite a lot to keep us going it seems. The P.T. is very good here and they really work on the shoulders, arms, and stomach muscles. This is really a layout—I'll send you some pictures sometime. But for a nice place to go to school, S.D. State College or Wash. U. would probably be nicer in many ways. I suppose people are starting to get their machinery lined up for spring planting. Everything is doozy here now and will be swell if we don't wash a couple courses. Don't work too hard out there and soak up a little sunshine for me.

Despite dissimilar backgrounds, an athletic farm boy and an urbane city boy, Lyle and Phil Spielman were fast friends. Pete Smith, another member of the Washington University gang, was a mutual friend. At the first opportunity the three cadets left the campus for a change of scenery. While Lyle and Phil conversed with a coed, Pete snapped a photo. On the back, Lyle wrote, "Wolves at Larson Girl College."

CADETS PHIL SPIELMAN AND LYLE SLADEK, 1944
LOOKING TO MEET COEDS AT LARSON GIRL COLLEGE

Sunday evening it was back to the academic and military routine. Oftentimes guard duty, work details, harassment, and other military "stuff" cut into class and study time. But that was no excuse for a low grade.

15 MARCH 1944 (WEDNESDAY). Everything is going pretty swell in New Haven. They weakened last Sat. evening and let us out of the walls so we did a little shopping and went to a YWCA dance. The girls seemed a little foreign but we had a pretty good time. Sunday afternoon we took a little bus ride out of town and spent a couple hours bumming around a small girls college—and were invited in for a couple hands of bridge. Our 3rd week of work ends tonight and us 3 are still riding high and dry. There are 20 out of our 27 still up to schedule. I go on 24 hr. guard duty starting this evening so will miss some classes. If you miss out on something and flunk—"that's tough old fellow." Bought a ticket today for a water carnival Sat. evening—several world champion swimmers and divers are in it—including Yale's Allen Ford. It will be in the amphitheater pool in the gym where we will swim a little later on. Should really be a good deal. Irene wrote and said Vernon was going to end up in N.Y. State at some small place—it's about 100 miles west of here and sort of in line on the way to the big city. Maybe we can have a little party there some weekend if I get a chance to leave here. He sure is lucky to get to stop in at home on the way and to travel so much in that short time—guess he has already covered more miles than I have. It's good to hear the ice house is full and there had better be some grape juice and canned pumpkin left. Looks now like my chances here are good of making it but not on schedule. Hardly anyone ever goes straight through. If I wash out I'll tell them, "If my pa was here, he could do it." Got a letter from a fellow who was at Wash. U.—he is on a 13 day furlough—the second one since we left there—but he is still a buck private. About time to get our white gloves out for retreat parade followed by mess.

Every afternoon, following a strenuous day of duty and physical training, Lyle went through a careful routine. He buffed his shoes to a high gloss, polished the brass buttons on his blouse, unwrapped his service cap, and checked his white gloves for blemishes. When the whistle blew, he joined his fellow cadets and marched through Phelps Gate for a retreat parade on the New Haven Green.

Hundreds of townspeople gathered to watch the cadets, decked out in service caps and white gloves, brass buttons flashing and shoes glistening in the sun, as they paraded to the martial music of Glenn Miller and his band.

CADET DRILL ON FAMOUS "OLD CAMPUS," TS YALE, 1944

CADET RETREAT PARADE ON HISTORIC NEW HAVEN GREEN, TS YALE, 1944

Glenn Miller, a nationally acclaimed musician of the big band era, was too old to be drafted when the war broke out. Later, however, he received an army commission and assembled outstanding instrumentalists from army bands throughout the nation to form the 418th Army Air Force Band. The fifty-member group performed for reveille, taps, entertainment, and cadet parades at TS Yale until the spring of 1944.

Noting the respect of the civilian onlookers as the cadet corps paraded to the snappy rhythm of the "St. Louis Blues March," Lyle felt he was part of an important enterprise.

19 MARCH 1944 (SUNDAY). Should hurry and get this written and start studying cause we have retreat parade in a little while. The civilians swallow these parades hook, line, and sinker. One month already since leaving S.J. Field. This is the critical week ahead cause of a two week test plus a couple comprehensive exams in Direct Current I and II which prove fatal to so many. If we make it we take Vacuum Tubes next week—you know, those glass tubes in radios and of course that involves electronics. After that the going will get tougher. Last night I went to the water carnival at the gym and saw some top notch diving, comedy acts, Ballet by girls from Smith College, and a new world's record in the 100 yds by Yale's Alan Ford. He swam it in 49.7 sec which is comparable to that dreamed of 4-minute mile in running. Time for retreat parade.

Resuming his letter, Lyle complained about the duties classes that dealt with the basic responsibilities of officers. He had to master Army Organization, Military Law, Military Correspondence, Air Forces Supply, Combat Orders, Tactical Procedures, Interior Guard Duty, Military Courtesy, Service and Customs, Officer of the Day, Court Martial Board Officer, Censor Officer, and Mess Management Officer.

I'm about the dumbest cadet in our duties classes which is a lot of rot anyway. Lot of memory work etc on army procedure along with the main course. We finish them this week though. But in the main course of electricity etc I hold my own easily so far. Guess I can get the duties stuff too if I want to lower myself to studying it—my highest ambition in that part of the course is to get a 75 for a grade—to pass efficiently. Haven't heard from Vernon yet. We should be able to get together out here once in a while. So Dale Korzan ended up in England. As an M.P. he likely won't be in a very hot spot. At least for a while. Had guard duty one night out at Coxe's Cage where the engineers work with planes and motors. It is a giant building full of thousands of dollars worth of equipment. Temperature changes cause the girders and windows to

a spooky place where I stood guard one night.

THE BEAVER

PRIZE PICTURE of the exhibit in Street Hall is this exceptionally clear view of Coxe's Cage taken from the rafters by Lt. James Taylor. The original

COXE'S CAGE, NEW HAVEN, CONNECTICUT, 1944

make all sorts of weird noises and echo back and forth and it was really dark and spooky out there. The Officer of the Day didn't come around though to try and cross me up cause my pistol was loaded. In a situation like that we would shoot first and ask questions afterwards. Just in two hour shifts of course. We had a swell turkey dinner today with apple juice—they feed us good here. Now weigh 185 lbs net and gain about a lb per week. Seems funny with all the sweating we do in P.T. Suppose you are glad spring is just around the corner. Be sure and plant a few squash if nothing else. Or is the garden still under water. I envy you out there with no one chasing you with a whip all the time. The gestapo system here is pretty vicious. Lot more fun though than laying around some camp not learning anything. Jean must really be able to toot the tooter now. Chuckie hasn't written me a letter for a long time. Can't put off that studying any longer. Be sure and tell me all the news. I'll be safely through the first month by the time you get this.

23 MARCH 1944 (THURSDAY). This was sort of a hectic week up until now. Had four duties tests Tues night and two comprehensives in Direct Current I and II and a weekly test in Direct Current II last

night. As far as I know the three of us got through. We'll know at least by tomorrow. That makes 1 month completed raising our chances to about 2 in 3 I guess. We start Vacuum Tubes along with Morse code now although we will never be too good at receiving Morse code. Gradually we are picking up what makes a radio tick—really not too hard. Most fellows who come here are Sgt's etc and graduates of radio schools like the one at Sioux Falls and some were teachers in various camps but so far us meteorologists who know the mathematics have been able to compete successfully with them. We are having a drizzle which is finishing melting the 4 inch snow of the early part of the week. The seven of us in this room have been very lucky about gigs so far—we really clean our room up too. This is sort of turning into a pretty interesting stay here and I think that from now on we might as well take a little more carefree attitude about passing. Either you make it or you don't. One of my roommates, Ted Hurst, is from a ranch in Oklahoma and owns some of that Domino Hereford strain. He is one of the few fellows here who isn't from a large city. Had a letter from Vernon last Sunday— I'm glad he can get an apartment and live off posts. Quite a coincidence that he and I would end up at Harvard and Yale at the same time. But keep things cookin out there in S.D. so we can have a soft nest to fly home to when the going gets too tough outside for us. Be sure and get that camera out once in a while. What are you planting and where this year? Did you get the school section of land? We go to P.T. pretty quick now—we always enjoy that.

At TS Yale, as at Seymour Johnson Field, a cadre of cadet officers enforced discipline. A cadet officer bearing three bottle cap emblems on his shoulder was referred to as a *three-diamond bottlestopper*.

Cadets who accumulated a number of military infractions, real or imaginary, marched back and forth, back and forth, across the campus quad on Sunday. Not only was marching with a rifle on the shoulder tiresome, it also cut into study time and increased the risk of washing out. A combination of good luck and attention to detail enabled Lyle to avoid walking tours during the crucial first month at TS Yale. Washing out and regressing to his former buck private rating after more than a year in the army was unthinkable. But army worries never eclipsed his thoughts of home.

26 MARCH 1944 (SUNDAY). Has spring arrived in South Dakota like it has here? The grass on the green is actually getting green and it's nice and warm. Heard some fellows marching outside my window and

looked out and there was about 150 men marching tours for gigs. One of my roommates will do some walking next weekend. You've got to stay on the ball around here. Some fellows accumulate so many tours that they won't have time to walk them all off in the time they are here so they wash out. Of course that is in rare cases. Some fellows love this place! Last week the faculty and tactical boards had open season and really washed out a slug of cadets including a 3 diamond bottlestopper. Most of them are Cpls. or Sgts. though so it isn't so bad as for me to revert to a private. Phil, Pete, and I successfully completed the first 4 weeks and are 5th week men now. We have an hour of Morse code and 5 hours of Vacuum Tubes nightly. The first time we got to class the instructor threw a test at us—but luckily we were all primed and loaded for bear so we got off to a good start. It seems kind of hard to understand and then I get kind of dull after 9:00 anyway but I think we'll make it through this week. Then we start Transmitters I. Stayed home last night in order to catch up on some work and sleep. You always figure a little more study might make the difference. And too if you are tired Sunday morning it makes a long day from 7:00 in the morning until 1:30 at night so it's always a hard decision as to whether to go out or not. And too I want to save a little energy for the homestretch and in case we get a 200 mile pass later on to go to N.Y. or Nova Scotia. Phil and I are going to go to church now—usually kind of hard to get started. Then we'll have a good dinner. I'll bet you are having upside down cake for dinner. Yum Yum. How does the Dodge work—it's quite a car. Planting any trees this year? Fan that ice a little—I'll be home in July.

Since static often interfered with radio voice transmissions, Morse code was common in army communications. At first Lyle had difficulty discerning the combinations of *dits* and *dahs* that represented the letters of the alphabet. Additionally, in a matter of weeks, he had to master the principles of electronics and learn how to construct radios and transmitters. Typically writing a letter during the short break between the end of class at midnight and marching off to breakfast, he responded to his mother's suggestion that he ease up a bit. Although appreciative of her concern, he was still on track and determined to make the grade.

29 MARCH 1944 (WEDNESDAY). Tonight I'm thoroughly disgusted with this place. A good place, Yale, only no one likes it here. It's after midnight and we are waiting to go to breakfast. Just finished another hectic week but we passed Vacuum Tubes and start Transmitters I tomorrow—the sixth week. Never have I had to really get down and

dig so hard as this last week in order to pass it. Phil led his high school class of a couple hundred and it's even tough for him. One of the fellows who was an instructor in radio receivers at Sioux Falls said he didn't see how we could learn it so quickly. He had trouble too. Luckily I was sharp a couple nights during the week. Tonight I'm in a fog from lack of sleep and from studying so continuously. It's times like this that we would gladly sign on the dotted line for overseas to get out of this hole. Don't mind me—I'm just tired from an extra bad day of military stuff. Now for the brighter side. We are getting a high powered education in radio—they practically have us building them already—we will in a couple weeks. Guess it will mean staying in again this weekend. I've decided to go through here at any cost and that's part of the price. Wish they would call breakfast so we could go eat and get to bed. This is worse than a concentration camp. Morse code is coming good already. They will soon have us receiving about 8 words per minute. Phil is on guard tonight. It sounds alright to take a carefree attitude about this place but you can't relax and still make it.

Having written a complaint at midnight, Lyle felt the need to tone it down the next morning before posting the letter. True to his upbringing, he was predisposed to seeing the cup as half-full rather than half-empty. He readily related to the words of a hit song popularized by Bing Crosby and the Andrews Sisters:

> You got to ac-cent-tchu-ate the positive,
> Eliminate the negative,
> And latch on to the affirmative,
> Don't mess with Mr. In-Between.

Thursday.
Gee whiz, I must really have been bitter last night. Kind of a bad sign cause it shows I'm weakening. What's the matter—can't I take it? Pete and I have been gunning on transmitters. How to impress audio waves (voice waves) on radio frequency waves so they will carry. This is very interesting stuff and you should see some of the deals we set up in the laboratory.

On Saturday Lyle scurried over to the main PX to purchase a can of shoe polish and a bottle of ink. Seeing a jukebox, he inserted a coin and punched the selector button. While relaxing to the soothing melody of the "White Cliffs of Dover," he sipped a Nesbits orange soda and gazed at the gold bars

POST EXCHANGE (PX), TS YALE, 1944

displayed in the uniform accessory showcase. If his lucky stars held out, he would be back in three months to buy gold bars.

Of the five barbershops on the post, Lyle patronized the one at Phelps Gate because it was closest to the barracks. Sanitary measures were enforced at the shop. As set forth by the Public Relations Office: "Barbers don't escape regular Army inspections either. Also, they are prohibited from using brushes of any sort on soldiers' heads, hair or faces."

His GI haircut completed, Lyle took his laundry to the cleaners. Then he hurried over to a neighborhood drugstore a couple of blocks beyond the Green where he picked up photos and purchased a roll of film. Returning from his Saturday errands in good humor, he sat down to write a letter and enclosed a few snapshots. On the back of one, he gloated, "186 lbs.—same as Phil Spielman and same height too."

I APRIL 1944 (SATURDAY). Say, everythings O.K.—at Yale. We finished another week so it's an evening all to ourselves. My pen is going dry. How do you like the spring weather by now or are you still traveling around in boats? It was really a beautiful day here in Connecticut and we had a white glove inspection and retreat parade on the Green again. This evening I took some clothes to the cleaners and stopped at the drugstore for some prints we took last Sunday. I'm keeping the best one and also sent some to Irene—the better ones. Guess you don't rate! We

CADETS LYLE SLADEK AND PHIL SPIELMAN, NEW HAVEN, CONNECTICUT, 1944

really got a good teacher for the next two weeks in Transmitters I and I I. He is really hot. This is a really good course in transmitters and radio—we don't just learn how to make them—we know why each piece goes where and what it does. We will each build a complete transmitting set this next week so keep your radio tuned. We can slap a mouth piece to a headphone microphone in a few minutes. It's sure a mess of wires, tubes, condensors, resistors, batteries, and choke coils. Pretty simple to do though when you know how it works. I think now I've got a 50-50 chance of graduating if I work hard. Today we had swimming in P.T.—first we swam 200 yds and then went up to the balcony to jump into the pool. It's 16 ft. from your feet to the surface of the water. (Guess I'll go in the circus and dive into tubs of water.) Went in feet first nicely and for some reason somersaulted under water and lit on the bottom—about 12 feet under. Great sport. One cadet got scared the last minute and didn't jump. Then he almost toppled forward head first but caught his balance. I'm afraid he would have plunged head first against the edge of the pool below if he had fallen. Cadets are expendable! One cadet on guard was a victim of circumstances and got 30 hours of tours and 15 gigs for something not really his fault. It happens quite often—Will take all the weekends he is here to walk them off. What it means is that if something like that happens to happen to you, it's the same as washing out. You wouldn't stand a chance cause it would already be two strikes on you. So that's what I mean—if things go well I'll make it—if they don't, I won't. It isn't bad here—except once in a while little things get on your nerves.

Shouldn't have been leaning against the rail in that picture—makes my legs look about 3 ft too long. Don't let your camera get dusty. See you in June or July. Time to plant wheat isn't it? Bye now.

5 APRIL 1944 (WEDNESDAY). Midnight. Just to let you know that we finished Transmitters I and most of us passed. Must have been close. This is quite a strain cause they won't tell you what you get in any tests—just passed or not at the end of the week. Eleven more weeks to go. Got a long letter from Vernon today with a couple snapshots. Almost 1:00 and time for breakfast now. I'm plenty tired too. We had a little snowstorm today but it has stopped now. So we start sweating out another week but very interesting—we build a transmitter among other things. Hope you are O.K.

The next day, when two roommates graduated from TS Yale and departed the post with gold bars on their shoulders, Lyle increased his resolve. Having successfully completed another week of classes and duties, he faced week seven. Following a full day of military and physical exertion with negligible free time, he wrote home before marching off to a crowded, dimly lit classroom for the start of Transmitters I I.

6 APRIL 1944 (THURSDAY). We moved last Monday over here to Edwin McClellan Hall. Two fellows from my room graduated and were commissioned today. They were of course kind of happy and woke us up a little early this morning. They said of course that they would never go through here again for anything—but you don't mind it so much the first time. The main thing is if we stay well and keep passing. The trouble with this place is that you are tired at the end of the day and don't even care if you go to bed or not cause you get up in the morning just as tired and another grind to go through.

Was nice to get your letter this morning. Really sounds juicy out there with all the rain and melting snow. There is a rumor that we may get a couple days off at Easter—I doubt it. Luckily another weekend is almost here so we can hit the sack early Sat. eve. We had a top notch retreat parade Sunday afternoon with the entire cadet corps on the Green. Don't worry—we all get sort of disgusted here about every so often.

A survival tactic resorted to by some cadets at TS Yale was to go on sick call and be hospitalized for a week of rest and study. The downside of that ploy was falling a week behind classmates and delaying graduation, which increased the odds of washing out.

8 APRIL 1944 (SATURDAY). Pete went on sick call with an imaginary ailment in order to not take the comp last night. He and Phil will get it Sunday night. Phil definitely has the edge on us but he is no athlete. I can clean him in boxing, wrestling, swimming, etc. We had swimming yesterday which was fun as usual. Of course we have to swim just the way they want us to so you really don't get a chance to learn things like when swimming on your own. It's really early in the sack for me tonight—sleep is one thing we lack here. But for physical condition they are getting me fairly tough. In the regular army you don't get hardly any Physical Training but for over a year I've been in basic training, meteorolgy school, and cadets—all of which had good P.T. Guess I'll go to church tomorrow—found a really nice Methodist church last Sunday and the minister is just as good as Dr. Cashy in St. Louis and Rev. Hanson in Brookings. They showed us the film "Battle for Britain" again today. You've really got to hand it to the English people for what they did in the dark days. I wonder if we Americans realize how near the brink we were.

Lyle lauded the Royal Air Force (RAF) for its heroic effort in turning back the attempt by the Luftwaffe to bomb England into submission. He agreed with Churchill's words: "Never in the field of human conflict was so much owed by so many to so few." Had Great Britain capitulated, there would have been no base from which to launch attacks on Hitler's Fortress Europe.

Empathizing with a friend and other soldiers sweating out their service on small islands, waiting, waiting for possible invasions, Lyle continued:

> Had a letter from Pips Coler from the Pacific somewhere. Said he had it pretty soft with lots of sunshine but not too much excitement. Was thinking about maybe asking Mom to come out here for a visit but the way transportation is and living conditions—a person is much better off at home for the duration. Take it easy.

As much as Lyle wished his mother could visit him in New England, he realized it was impractical. While riding on trains and buses he had seen people standing for hours at a time, even mothers with small children in tow. The government, in light of overcrowded conditions and wartime conservation, discouraged unnecessary travel.

On Easter Sunday, Lyle observed cadets below his window marching off gigs.

9 APRIL 1944 (SUNDAY). Just a short letter before it's time for church. It's a nice cool morning here and the sun is starting to peek through the clouds. Pretty much just another Sunday for the army. Cadets were walking tours as usual out here in the old quad and others were unlucky enough to have guard duty today. We will have retreat parade this afternoon and then back to class again tonight. Our present teacher in Transmitters II is very good—he is just as interested in teaching us something as in testing us. Didn't think it was possible to learn radio so fast. If you have an incentive and enough pressure and competition you really learn it or else. These fellows are pretty keen—makes me really dig to keep up with them. Got 81% in last weeks Transmitters I course. This is a critical week cause we take 3 oral comprehensive exams—but I'll get my 75% or more. We are about half done building our transmitters—could broadcast all over the world by putting on an aerial wire—but it might interfere with other stations on the same frequency. Very interesting stuff. We are already taking 10 words per minute in Morse code which is about twice ahead of schedule. You have to go into a trance sort of in order to get 10 words per minute. Guess I'll be an amateur radio ham and have radios and transmitters hanging all over the walls. Just

a bunch of wires etc. If all goes well I may get home the last of June if I can hold this pace for a few more weeks. Last Easter I was in the Hosp. in Miami Beach having a pretty good time. Bet you are going visiting today somewhere. This isn't so hot sitting around stuffy old buildings with someone cramming radio down your throat. How much did that new quarter section of land cost? Hope you are all feeling as peppy as I am—except no stiff neck from standing on your head. You see, we had tumbling at the gym yesterday. Chimes, church bells, and clocks keep up quite a clatter around here. Saw a robin today. Time to sign out in the orderly room and go to church.

Here is a picture of Peggy—please send it back.

Though safely through week seven and Transmitters I I on Wednesday at midnight, Lyle faced a daunting three-week study of Receivers I and I I. Then, on Friday night, an unwelcome surprise caused him added stress.

15 APRIL 1944 (SATURDAY). Another week finished and a nice quiet rain outside. The most exciting thing this week was the box from home. Really made quite a hit around here. Mom's filled cookies are still tops. Don't see how you got around to making several different treats, Mom. Or did Wilma have a hand in it too. Had a long letter from Vernon telling about their N.Y. weekend. As for Mom suggesting me going to Nova Scotia some weekend—Ha ha. In the G.I. army you have a little freedom but here—worse than a prison. And even if they did let us go we couldn't spare the time. Maybe as an upperclassman we may get a 200 mile pass sometime. Skimmed through Transmitters I I with a grade of 81% last Thursday. My teacher in Receivers (Radio) is a sort of henny lady. She may teach us plenty but it's going to be plenty painful. I'm sure polishing the old apple though. Send me a basket of apples—I'll need them cause I have her for 3 weeks—She will make me or break me.

Last night they jerked us out of class rather unexpectedly to take oral comprehensive exams on Vacuum Tubes, Transmitters I and I I. A different instructor gives you each comp. It was like running into a stone wall. I was sleepy and lots of the questions we had never covered in class at all and there is lots of pressure on you. And I was off the beam so it was pretty disastrous. I may have washed all 3, maybe just 2, maybe only 1, and a bare possibility (about 1 in 6) of having passed them all. It's only counted as one wash whether 1 or 3 so it's not too bad. Just maybe sort of the beginning of the end. But most fellows wash a course before they get this far so it's only one strike on me. You are out on the 3rd strike. This course was designed for fellows who have had radio before. One fellow who has taught radio for two years in the

ENSIGN VERNON SLADEK AND WIFE VIVIAN, 1944
OBSERVATION TOWER OF ROCKEFELLER CENTER

army was sweating them out too last night. They sure wash out plenty in this course—fellows who really learn fast too. This place is loaded with Harvard, Yale, and N.Y. U. graduates. It's really good for a fellows ego though. This is the first time I've ran into something I couldn't pass no matter how hard I tried. I'm kind of out of my class here—but the more competition the better I like it. They've just irritated me enough so I'm going to get through just to show the army I can do it. But even if I graduate I'll agree with everyone else—it isn't worth the nervous strain just to get a little gold braid.

Three days later, Lyle learned his worries and rationalizations had been for naught.

18 APRIL 1944 (TUESDAY). Good news! By some miracle I passed all 3 of those comps—I was sure I failed. They must have given me a

break. I'm telling you I sure sweated them out, guessing, psychology, steering off the subject, and luck. Still don't see how it happened. My roommate flunked, my Wash. U. roommate flunked and several others. And he is one of the smartest fellows I've ever run into when it comes to Physics. Depends a lot on who gets the breaks. This place stinks for all of that. A civilian would never understand though. It's not tough physically or like in a foxhole but a different sort of toughness. But I don't mind it as much as most. This means my chances of getting through here are very good. Am passing Receivers I even if the instructor is an old hen. We build a radio next week. We can slap a little receiver together and pick up a local station in a few minutes. Can also draw the schematic of a radio. Today we took a physical exam to see for sure that we qualify to be officers. Never passed one better than today. Weigh 188 lbs. Almost time for mess. Will be an upperclassman in 1 week so things will soon be coming our way. Beautiful spring days here lately. Two out of our room are in hospital. They drive us pretty hard and a lot get sick. Never felt better though. One cadet was accidentally shot by a .45 pistol in the lung a couple days ago. Some fellows still can't handle a gun. Mess!

Lyle thanked his lucky stars for surviving the first two months at TS Yale. Here he was, one of the few from Washington University still on schedule to graduate. Nearing upperclassman status, he was feeling upbeat about his chances.

23 APRIL 1944 (SUNDAY). Midnight. A nice quiet rain this evening to march to mess in. Had an exceptionally enjoyable evening of classes tonight. Have my super-heterodyne radio about 2/3 done now. I'm slow though cause some of the fellows already are getting stations and tinkering around tuning them up. Passed 12 words per minute in Morse code tonight which is way ahead of schedule—That's as high as we have to go to graduate but you keep working higher anyway. Got Mom's and Wilma's letters today. Mom, you should hop on the train and come up here for a few weeks in New England. How about it? Won't be too expensive and anyway everything else is in proportion. But it can't be one of those hurried affairs where you hardly know you got there and wonder why you went. Of course Wilma and Chuckie are *too* little to be left alone and they couldn't get along without your cooking. Let me know. Just think—I'll be an upperclassman Wednesday if I pass this week. Miss Britton (my present teacher) is from Nebraska and really a pretty nice person. I keep my mouth shut and my ears and eyes open and really polish the apple. I got an 82% last week in Receivers which was average so I should pass this week too. You know I thought I flunked those comprehensive exams. Well I got 75% in Vacuum Tubes, 75%

in Transmitters I, and 80% in Transmitters I I. Was on the ball in Transmitters I I wasn't I. Ha. Anyway it was a miraculous escape and the difference in making it here or not. About half a dozen out of 50 of us from Washington U. are all that's up to schedule. The rest have fallen by the wayside either academically or hospital. Seems like they would catch on that the hospital rate here is much too high. It's been to my advantage though cause it has taken lots of the smart birds out. We take the last comprehensive exams a week from today in Receivers I and I I. If I get through it means a direct ticket to a commission. All I ask though is to get out of this place in one piece—with or without a commission. Haven't heard from V or V since their trip to N.Y. They may come up here in a couple weeks. I've got to stay in one more weekend though at least. This course was a case of putting in all your effort or none at all cause halfway wouldn't have been enough. Guess I had better get to studying a schematic of a super heterodyne receiver. They can ask you some awful embarrassing questions about what would happen if a wire here or there came loose or something. To answer the question right doesn't mean much. They always want to know why.

How did Wilma come out in spelling? Hope she had better luck than I used to have. Guess you must be pretty busy if the stock is still home. Bye now.

26 APRIL 1944 (WEDNESDAY). Midnight. Passed Receivers I tonight and am now an upperclassman—half done here and no washes yet. And I have the same instructor in Receivers I I next week and she is really O.K. The best yet. Everything is going good and will be much better from now on. Had a letter from Irene today. About time for mess.

UPPERCLASSMAN

Attaining upperclassman status was a giant leap forward for Lyle. He no longer had to run everywhere and could occasionally leave the base. He looked forward to working with his hands constructing radios and transmitters. However, the upcoming comprehensive exam for Receivers I and I I was a crucial hurdle. Passing would leave just seven weeks until graduation; failing could spell disaster.

30 APRIL 1944 (SUNDAY). The Sun is shining brightly and you can almost see the leaves grow on the trees. A nice day to be playing baseball, in fact, doing anything besides studying radio. Radio isn't so hard in itself but the little refinements like delayed action volume control really get you. They have a large board—about 4 x 6 ft—with

a 7 tube radio built on it so everything is out in the open. They have 36 switches so by switching one, something will go wrong with some part of the radio. Sometimes it goes dead, sometimes howls, or is so low you can barely hear it or something. It usually takes 5 or ten minutes to find out what's wrong. You can sort of tell by the symptoms where to start checking. I don't have the aptitude or ability to learn radio as fast as the rest of the fellows in my class and I really have to be careful not to show my ignorance in class. On paper my record here of no washes looks good but I know in my own mind that it's just that I got the breaks. I'll try and steer the instructor off the subject in this last oral exam and try to give him the impression I know enough about radio to pass. I remember the good old days when I knew enough about the subject that I didn't care what kind of tests they gave. These night classes don't agree with me either—but it can't be helped. Note change of address—doesn't mean anything—just typical army. In an hour we have retreat parade on the Green again. I guess our parade is as good as any the West Point cadets put on. This is a dog's life but it can't be helped. I'll try not to stay cooped up anymore after this weekend—I'd hate to leave New Haven without meeting any people. Guess you are getting ready to plant corn now too. You've really got it pretty nice to be able to work around in the sun and fresh air. Those dark factories and smokestacks and underground railroad stations of Jersey, N.Y., and Penn. make me sick. Back to the grind again. It's O.K. if I can just keep passing. Will have to buy an officer's uniform in a couple weeks. We get $150 when we graduate to pay for them. If all goes well in a couple months I'll be discharged from the U.S. Army and commissioned a 2nd Lt. in the Army of the U.S. This is the week that will tell the tale.

If the stars remained in a favorable conjunction for another two months, Lyle would be discharged from the *wartime* army and granted a temporary appointment as a lieutenant in the *regular* army. In military parlance, the commission would "continue in force during the pleasure of the President of the United States for the time being, and for the duration of the war and six months thereafter unless sooner terminated."

Because of assignment to other duty, Lyle was excluded from taking the Receivers I and II comprehensive exam on Wednesday night.

4 MAY 1944 (THURSDAY). I've been C.Q. for the past 24 hours and don't have anything to do for a few minutes before it's time to awaken the squadron for revillie. This is one of the jobs that you get once in a while as an upperclassman. My class took the comprehensive in Receivers last night—Phil said it was easy but some say it was hard— sort of depends I guess on whether you know your stuff or not. I'm not

a bit confident about passing it but I'm sure going to try. This place is altogether unreasonable but as long as I'm getting through there is no kick coming. Another nice bright day and warm enough so we don't wear coats much anymore. We have swimming at the practice pool today which is better than most of the other PT even though we have to swim one behind the other in order to get the maximum use out of the pool. About the only thing they don't regulate here in cadet school is how you brush your teeth. You get mighty sick of doing everything according to someone else's whims all the time but I guess that is the only way it could be run. Time to awaken the squadron—only we use a nerve jangling whistle instead of a bugle.

The closer Lyle got to the goal line, the more determined he was to succeed and the more he abhorred the thought of washing out. Then, on Thursday, he learned of a setback. Not wishing to worry his parents, he glossed over his misfortune.

Friday.

Well, I joined the Thursday Morning Club last night. I took the Receivers Comprehensive and washed it with a grade of 68%. It was very easy and they gave me the impression I was really doing O.K. Thought I would get about an 85% in it but I really must have messed up somewhere. Only a couple others flunked. I can't complain cause I sure got the breaks before last night. Would have been time to order a uniform if I had passed. So I take Receivers I I over which drops me back a week. But I did pass 14 words per minute last night in Morse code. Some of the top men in radio haven't passed 10 words yet so will probably wash on account of that. And some like Phil can't swim a hundred yards so they will have trouble there. Anyway I've still got a much better than average chance of getting through here but it wouldn't break my heart if I didn't. We have a new tactical officer for our squadron now and he is a worm of the first class. It has got to the point where we can't even keep a few personal things like old letters or an extra can of shoe polish. Had a good time swimming and learned to swim pretty fast on my back by just frog kicking my legs once in a while. We really have some beautiful spring days here at Yale. Once in a while a gray squirrel comes up the elm tree by the window and nibbles some of the new tiny leaves.

Just got a card from Wilma. So Chuckie just has 3 weeks of school left. Bet he'll be glad to get out and be able to spend all his time building rafts. It's almost time for mess and after that I'm on cleanup detail. Phil got a birthday cake today from his mother in Maryland. We are going to carve it up. Later.

Phil's cake was promptly devoured. Cadets were not allowed to have food in their rooms, for, as expounded in an article released by the Public Relations Office, "food attracts vermin and vermin attracts germs."

SANITATION AT ARMY AIR SCHOOL

Sanitation at the Army Air Forces Training Command's Technical School at Yale is no different from sanitation anywhere—there's just more of it!

A survey, conducted with medical and mess officers at the school, reveals that the attention paid to all phases of cleanliness is continuous, and that no details are spared to safeguard the health of Enlisted Men, Aviation Cadets and Officers.

A soldier may sometimes grumble at constant inspections, at officers insisting upon attention to details, at frequent G. I. parties. But all this attention to order and cleanliness is for that very soldier's own health.

Daily inspections assure each man's responsibility for clean quarters and clean latrines. . . .

Inspections are even stricter . . . at the four Mess Halls. . . .

Kitchens and Mess Halls are the height of cleanliness. Ice-boxes are scrubbed from top to bottom and from left to right daily with hot water, lye, and a good, strong G. I. scrubbing-brush. Stoves and rations pans undergo steel wool attacks after every meal, with a cleaning powder added for chasers. Stock rooms are scrubbed daily; serving rooms undergo similar treatment after every meal.

Trays, silverware and cups are accorded special treatments. Each metal tray is first scrubbed with scalding germ-killing solutions and then put into a regulation washing-machine. Cups and silverware, covered with big, white sheets whenever not in use, get the same sort of germ-killing treatment, with a thorough rinsing added as an extra course between the scalding water and washing-machine routines. Sugar bowls are emptied after every meal, washed, dried, then refilled before the next meal. Dining room floors are swept after each meal, and cleaned with a special fluid, then waxed at least once every week.

A New Haven Department of Health directive observed: "The alert young men in their trim uniforms . . . are in the pink of condition, and it is the Army's intention to keep them that way."

Upon returning from cleanup detail at the mess hall, Lyle ended his letter on a positive note.

Guess I'm pretty lucky to go to school here even if it is a dog's life. Guess we can stand a couple more months of it. In a week or two we start studying radio and transmitter sets used on planes—spending a week on each set. Bye now.

The final stretch at TS Yale required total concentration. Survival was the watchword as each week passed in a blur. Humor was nonexistent. Free time was a rarity. Diversions were few. Even so, Lyle and Phil indulged in a stroll around New Haven on Sunday afternoon. Back in his room in

CADET LYLE SLADEK, NEW HAVEN, 1944

SUNDAY AFTERNOON, NEW HAVEN, CONNECTICUT, 1944

McClellan Hall, Lyle apprised his family of the result on his retake of the Receivers comprehensive exam.

14 MAY 1944 (SUNDAY). Salvaged a few minutes to write you a letter before parade. Hope you are all feeling as peppy as I am today and that the weather there is as perfect as here today. Managed to get up in time for church this morning and then had a good dinner at the mess hall. What did you do today for excitement? Passed the Receivers Comp after taking that week course over. It really makes me dig here and it will be close to make it at all. A Harvard law graduate washed out last week along with others. I have a good teacher this week in Very High Frequency (V.H.F.) and am all through with the theory of radio communications. Now I start on actual aircraft sets. In some ways this is interesting but you get tired of working with things you can't see. Electrons in the cathode ray tube travel at 5000 miles per second! Time to fall out now. Will have to finish this tomorrow.

Monday.

Sure feels good to be wearing suntans again. It was awfully hot in woolens at retreat yesterday. Phil hasn't washed yet so he has ordered part of his officer's uniform. Jim Rather graduates Thursday morning. He is from Louisiana. Pete and Wayne are back from the hospital and they said it was so nice and restful out there that I'm anxious to get sick for a rest. Right now I don't feel like it would be possible to get sick. Gee, I sure envy Chuckie getting out of school now. Bet his dog likes it too.

CHUCKIE SLADEK BATHING SKIPPY, 1944

We had a hike in P.T. the other day and it really was nice to walk in the grass again. We are pretty much cooped up here. Captain McNally is lecturing cadets on the pistol below my window. He is trying to teach them how to handle a gun so less cadets will get shot around here. Some fellows never saw a gun before getting in the army. Another of our Washington U. fellows goes before the board today to be washed out. They wash out a lot here. Time for mess now. Don't try to farm the whole country. Maybe see you in July I hope.

It shook Lyle up when a roommate, after months of hard effort, washed out and reverted to buck private—a brutal blow. Ordered to report before the Officer Review Board, the ill-fated cadet marched into the room, saluted, and received official word he was shipping out. Finding a newspaper article that struck a chord, Lyle tore it out and wrote, AMEN:

> When I was called for cadet training I was overjoyed, but now like 1,000 other cadets, am quite unhappy. It's "hell." It's just for men and "hellers" that can take a lot of discouragement, bawlings out and so forth. I have taken it and I can. But it's the truth.
> They can wash us out anytime, and that's why a cadet is worrying all the time. Never for one minute is he free to enjoy himself. We get out once every other Sunday until 9 p.m., and have to be in bed every night at 10.
> It's a hard life, but a good one, unforgettable and priceless experience for discipline and education.

Having fallen a week behind Phil, one of two cadets from Washington University still on schedule, Lyle was about to commence week thirteen. With another roommate about to have gold bars pinned on his uniform, Lyle vowed to hang tough for another five weeks. Yet graduation day seemed far, far into the future.

18 MAY 1944 (THURSDAY). Jim Rather gets his gold bars this morning in about an hour. Another week ended last night. I passed the V.H.F. course. We really had a stinker of a final test in it. They are altogether unreasonable on how much they expect you to learn in a week. A former radio instructor at Truax field in Madison, Wisconsin, washed. I happened to hit it pretty good and probably got a pretty good grade for the week. Now I take the #287 aircraft transmitting and receiving set. Phil passed the tuning check in it but two others from Wash U washed it. That leaves a couple from Wash U still in front. It would be unhealthy for me to wash it. These sets are much more complicated than a home or car receiver because they operate on bands of higher frequencies and even temperature changes from altitude are

very important. Last night took the cake. We got to bed at 2:00 and then they woke us up and called us out at 4:00 in the morning for an hour. We are short on sleep anyway so we are kind of droopy. The bad thing about this place is when they give a hard test about 11:00 when you are asleep on your feet. There is so much about this place that doesn't show up on the surface. And of course the lower part of the class has washed out so I'm sort of near the bottom of the heap. I really stuck my neck out when I got in here. A good deal if I get through. My gig average is still low enough for a Boston trip later—maybe.

Friday.

Glad to hear everything is O.K. out there. Bet the kids are glad to be free again. The Register came yesterday and Wilma's card and letters from Peggy and Kenneth Lunn. Probably my quota for a couple weeks. It's time for supper (our breakfast) in a few minutes. It really is pretty nice around here if you take it easy and don't let things bother you. Be seeing you in July.

On a photo of the radio set he was currently studying, Lyle notated, "The 287." Using a blank page of the AAFTTC pamphlet, he wrote:

21 MAY 1944 (SUNDAY). Here is a little of the glamour side of cadet life at Yale. But it doesn't tell about the nervous breakdowns, or the 150 men below my window this Sunday afternoon getting instruction

CADETS TUNING A 287 RADIO SET, TS YALE, 1944

in the pistol as punishment, or blurry eyed cadets at midnight trying to learn radio from some sad apple instructor who doesn't know what the score is himself. But altogether it's an experience that couldn't be gotten anywhere else. When you get out in this cast iron world you have to look out for yourself cause no one else will. I have a good instructor (a civilian) this week in the #287 but he expects altogether too much. Guess I'll get through the academic part of it but the tuning check washes lots of cadets. It's like a giant jigsaw puzzle. You set dozens of controls etc in tuning the transmitter and receiver in ten minutes and a mistake or tuning to a harmonic means a wash. A former radar instructor washed last week as did several others. I'll make it. Made it to church this morning. Really a beautiful day here in Conn. Did you go to the concert? Back to the books.

Although the academics at TS Yale were not so deep as at Washington University, the hurried pace and relentless pressure made the program more demanding. About to start week fourteen and the study of the #274 Set, Lyle anticipated winning gold bars.

Cadets nearing graduation, however, had to clear another hurdle, an Appointment for Commission Physical Examination. Certified as having met the physical requirements, Lyle mailed home the two-page report that detailed myriad measurements such as:

Posture __good__	Figure __stocky__	Frame __heavy__
(Excellent, good, fair, bad)	(Slender, medium, stocky, obese)	(Light, medium, heavy)
Temperature _98.6_	Height _75_ inches.	Weight _188_ pounds.
Chest: Rest _39_ inches;	inspiration _41_ inches;	expiration _38_ inches.

Abdomen _32_ inches.

A letter from home brought news that a cousin stationed in the Solomon Islands had been stricken with a tropical disease.

26 MAY 1944 (FRIDAY). I'm glad you are having nice weather and plenty rain. Sure too bad Harold Swanson got messed up with Malaria cause unless it's very light you can't get rid of it. He certainly has done his share. At least they will send him back to the States. Well, I passed the #287 set with an 84 which isn't bad cause it's one of the hardest courses here. Also passed the tuning check in it. I'll have to pat myself on the back for that cause the pressure was really on and the chips were down. You have ten minutes to tune it up and one little mistake will mess

you up. My receiver picked up a transmitter station on the frequency I was tuning on so I had to zero beat my frequency right out from under it. Air Corps uses very high frequencies which is same as shortwaves on home receivers. By the way, that electric eye on the radio is a lot of bunk. I'm in the #274 Set now which is easier to tune but the stuff really comes fast and furious. The competition is terrific and sometimes you wonder if you can last another week. Not just me but all of us. A big bunch washed out last week including one of my roommates. Phil is before Commissioning Board now and I go next Friday—sort of a mere formality preliminary—or something. He is a week ahead of me on Radio Compass. I've got to order an officer's uniform this weekend. Will barely have time to have one tailored if I decide to.

Saturday.

Yesterday we went on a hike and run out north of town in P.T. I'm restricted this weekend on account of flunking an Infantry Drill Regulation test. Just another of the little things that they use to try to beat you down. The joke is on them cause I was not going out this weekend anyway. Usually go to bed at 6:00 and sleep until 10:00 the next morning. I have to work harder to get through here than lots of the fellows—but then some others aren't getting through here at all. This takes in a lot more territory than a year of college. To wash out of here is usually a furlough and then right overseas. But if I pass the #274 this week I'm definitely in the money. I see Don Swanson was home and he must still be going with Lois Palmer. They are tops. By the way don't think I'm going crazy just cause I complain. That is a chronic ailment that everyone has here. Maybe we can't take it very well. You can't let any one bad day (like yesterday) get you down.

31 MAY 1944 (WEDNESDAY). Tonight we finish another academic week with a test in the Command Set #274 and a tuning check on it and a final in Tactical Procedure. All week I've really been in there tough trying to pass the 274. A couple of the fellows in my class are washbacks from last week taking it over, one is a former Radar instructor, and about 3 of the others are graduates of Sioux Falls radio school or such and have studied the set before. So you see what I'm up against. It is really going to be close but I believe I'll make it. If I do it means that I have learned as much here as some of the fellows learned in both G.I. radio school and here. But I wonder too if I can hold out at this pace for a couple more weeks. You can put in your best for a short time but eventually you are apt to crack up. But if I pass tonight in everything then they won't wash me out hardly no matter how I do from now on. I got a 100 in the #287 tuning check last week so it really must have

been tuned up. My instructors this week are really a bunch of sore thumbs—just another of the things we put up with that you can't see on paper. It even comes to the point where we wonder if it's worth it to stick it out the next few weeks. What would be nice would be to pass tonight and then get a little bit sick and get hospitalized for a week. Wish I knew something about psychology. I can't understand what it is that gets everybody down around here. For one thing they have been driving us for about 7 months with never a full day off. I'll stick it out. Phil, Pete, and I got measured up for uniforms last Sat. at a reasonable shop. I hope someone heads me off quick if I get to be an officer and act like some I know. Some take advantage of their rank now but they will find out to their regret that this war is going to end one of these days.

Guess if I get out of this strain I'll shake this off and get back to normal. We have our fun. Today we are going on a hike or run out in the sun. Got paid today too. Irene is due here in a couple weeks and my gig average is still O.K. so I may break away to N.Y. for a few hours with her. Sometimes this just seems like a long dream. Maybe I'll get to come home for a few days in July. Just depends on where I go from here for one thing. Got a letter from Vernon yesterday and a couple snapshots. They will be Boston bound pretty soon. Bet Harvard is nice but probably not quite so nice as Yale. You know Yale certainly has nothing to compare with the Union Building at S.D. State College for social activities. Guess I would prefer State to Yale for a place to go to school. So you finally contoured the east field into corn. Should be a good deal. How is the pheasant crop this year? Are the cattle at Klondike now? I remember how I used to tear down that canyon past the wash outs on the bicycle on the way to the dam.

When it came to dealing with unseen electrons coursing through radio circuits, Lyle had to strive diligently to compete with his peers. The hands-on aspects of radio were his forte, however, since he had grown up using screwdrivers, wire clippers, and soldering irons.

Wednesday midnight.

I passed again. We had four fellows wash in my class. But I never want to go through another night like this. First we had a final test on the #274 which was not only tough but also a guessing game as to what they wanted. Then a 2-week test in Tactical Procedure. Then a tuning check on the #274. I really tuned it up. One of the fellows who washed it had blood dripping from a thumb from trying to turn too fast and was dripping wet. He couldn't get it to load. You have 7 minutes to do it in. Then from 11:00 until midnight they got us up to the board and grilled us. I'm mighty sick of this place. But now I'll get through here almost for sure. Almost time for mess. We get to sleep about 2:00 a.m. and the day shift cadets usually awaken us in the morning singing outside or something. This week will be just as tough I guess. Again I wonder if it is worth while to go through here. I can take anything they want to dish out but a fellows got to have some pride and I wonder if I can crawl any lower on the ground. Don't mind my moan and groan. There won't be so much pressure on me from now on. Don't get too ambitious out there.

On 5 June, Lyle's parents tuned the radio to hear President Roosevelt's Fireside Chat. FDR had good news to report:

> Yesterday, on June fourth, 1944, Rome fell to American and Allied troops. The first of the Axis capitals is now in our hands. One up and two to go!
>
> It is perhaps significant that the first of these capitals to fall should have the longest history of all of them. The story of Rome goes back to the time of the foundations of our civilization. We can still see there monuments of the time when Rome and the Romans controlled the whole of the then known world. That, too, is significant, for the United Nations are determined that in the future no one city and no one race will be able to control the whole of the world.
>
> In addition to the monuments of the older times, we also see in Rome the great symbol of Christianity, which has reached into almost every part of the world. . . . It is also significant that Rome has been liberated by the armed forces of many nations. The American and British armies—who bore the chief burdens of battle—found at their sides our own North American neighbors, the gallant Canadians. The fighting New Zealanders from the far South Pacific, the courageous French and the French Moroccans, the South Africans, the Poles and the East Indians—all of them fought with us on the bloody approaches to the city of Rome.

The titanic struggle between the Axis and the Allies reached a climax two days later when Allied forces stormed the beaches at Normandy. Early in the war, Allied leaders concluded that they could not achieve the unconditional surrender of Germany without the use of ground forces. With England serving as the "platform for invasion," a massive buildup of troops and war materials preceded the planned offensive across the English Channel. In early June, following years of preparation and diversionary tactics, General Eisenhower, supreme commander of the Allied forces, made the decision to launch what he later termed the *Great Crusade*. When assured by meteorologists of a break in the weather, Eisenhower said, "OK, let's go," and the greatest amphibious operation in history was underway.

Upon hearing of the assault on Fortress Europe, Lyle, full of youthful bravado, expressed regret at not being in on the action; then, regaining his senses, he reflected on his good fortune.

7 JUNE 1944 (WEDNESDAY). The invasion should be in full swing by now—maybe we will hear some news at the mess hall about it. Must be pretty tough over there especially for their side cause we've got the air power. Wouldn't mind being there in some ways though I guess an hour of it would be enough. You can't realize what it is unless you've been there. Sort of funny how things work out. If they had left me classified as draftsman at Ft. Leavenworth or if I had washed out somewhere along the line I would very likely be in England now. Hope it gets over with fast now—should be able to tell in a few weeks what the score is. We finish another academic week tonight and this is the first time for a while that I'm fairly sure of passing. Am in the Radio Compass (a 15 tube set that is much more complicated than an ordinary radio). You see it automatically tells you the direction to any station you tune in so that by shooting a bearing on a couple stations you can tell where you are. Also used for flying the beam. We saw a training film of a flight from Nebraska to Minneapolis in which they tuned to 570 and "This is WNAX, Yankton, S. Dak" came blaring in. They used Yankton, Omaha, and Mason City to get a fix. Very simple procedure. Will leave me 3 academic weeks if I make it tonight.

Back from class with week fifteen completed and Radio Compass test results in hand, Lyle quickly scribbled:

> Wednesday midnight.
> Knocked another one over tonight so that leaves 3 weeks of academics to go. I'm getting back in the groove again. One of my troubles here has been lack of confidence—but maybe for a good reason. We go to mess in a few minutes now and I'm hungry. Seems to me you could study radio for years and still not be too sure of what's going on cause you can't see what happens. It has been a pleasant week for me cause I had good teachers. I was Corporal of the Guard one day and night so missed some class too but made it. Guess Irene and I will visit N.Y. about June 24. By having a low gig average, writing a military letter for pass, they will give me a 200 mile pass good for 24 hr. but of course class work goes on.

In a broadcast on 12 June, President Roosevelt linked aircraft production with the Fifth War Loan Drive:

Of course, there are always pessimists with us everywhere, a few here and a few there. I am reminded of the fact that after the fall of France in 1940 I asked Congress for the money for the production by the United States of fifty thousand airplanes per year. Well, I was called crazy—it was said that the figure was fantastic; that it could not be done. And yet today we are building airplanes at the rate of one hundred thousand a year.

There is a direct connection between the bonds you have bought and the stream of men and equipment now rushing over the English Channel for the liberation of Europe. . . .

While I know that the chief interest tonight is centered on the English Channel and on the beaches and farms and the cities of Normandy, we should not lose sight of the fact that our armed forces are engaged on other battlefronts all over the world, and that no one front can be considered alone without its proper relation to all.

It is worth while, therefore, to make over-all comparisons with the past. Let us compare today with just two years ago—June, 1942. At that time Germany was in control of practically all of Europe, and was steadily driving the Russians back toward the Ural Mountains. Germany was practically in control of North Africa and the Mediterranean, and was beating at the gates of the Suez Canal and the route to India. Italy was still an important military and supply factor—as subsequent, long campaigns have proved.

Japan was in control of the western Aleutian Islands; and in the South Pacific was knocking at the gates of Australia and New Zealand—and also was threatening India. Japan had seized control of most of the Central Pacific.

American armed forces on land and sea and in the air were still very definitely on the defensive, and in the building-up stage. Our allies were bearing the heat and the brunt of the attack.

For Lyle, it was just another day in another week with another course to master.

1 2 JUNE 1944 (MONDAY). We just finished tearing into Virginia's cake and have just enough left for a little lunch this evening. Vernon and Vivian are sort of settled in Cambridge already. Don't let them kid you—Harvard isn't as nice as Yale! Today I go to the carbine range for instruction and tomorrow I'll try and show them how we shoot in South Dakota. This is instead of P.T. and drill. Am doing O.K. in this weeks course (the #522 which is remotely controlled and sounds like you are hitting a pinball jackpot when you press a button). They have some really good equipment here and I'm learning lots these last few weeks. If I pass the tuning check and academic part then I'll be in Wire next. I have uniform inspection a week from Saturday and I'm about lined up on it. There is a rumor of a two week extension on the course but I doubt if it will catch me in time. If it does I'll just keep working a little longer cause I'm so near now nothing is going to stop me.

Wartime competition hastened the development of new weapons. While Germany was perfecting jet airplanes and rockets, the United States was crafting the B-29 bomber, dubbed Superfortress because it was capable of carrying heavy bomb loads at high altitudes and boasted of advanced technical features. Equipped with pressurized compartments, remote-controlled guns, and radar, the B-29 was ideal for bombing targets in all weather conditions.

Since radar was an offshoot of radio technology, Lyle, slated to take the physical examination mandatory for flying officers, expected an assignment involving radar on B-29s—if and when he made it through TS Yale.

> Tuesday.
> Might as well give you a little inside dope now and you can tell me what you think. It looks now like those of us who can pass the flying physical are apt to go direct (2 days to get there) to Boca Raton Field in Florida for secret Radar training. I think we are being investigated by the FBI now. I think it would involve some flying in B-29s—giant bombers. But nothing at all sure yet. A very few will go to Boston to Mass. Institute of Technology for Radar training. This radar involves Mathematics + radio which is more in my line so there is a chance there too. Otherwise the rest will go most anywhere. I'm lower than average in my class so Mass. I. T. is not much chance for me. No leave at all if I go to Florida and I'm sick of army schools anyway and it will be hot down there—but I wouldn't have to assume any responsibility yet that way and it's good training. I'm glad that not much of the decision will be up to me. I've been in over my head for a long time. They washed out 1/3 of us in meteorology school and didn't get me. Then they washed some out at Seymour Johnson and didn't get me, and here almost a half wash out but I squeezed through. I worked a little harder than the rest. These fellows here are a bunch of brains and can memorize something right off. But some of them can't use their hands and don't have any native intelligence. Anyway I'll have to admit I couldn't learn radio as fast as the rest of them. I don't much give a hoot for radio anyway—no one knows exactly why some things work like they do. Electronics involve sizes and speeds that are far beyond the comprehension of the eye or ear. Let me work with something I can see. Things are going smooth for me lately and I'm sure everything will turn out O.K. I've been saving up energy for N.Y. for 15 weeks now and am raring to go. Time now to go to Phelps Gate to go to the range. I'm going to enjoy this afternoon outside.

When continuing his letter two days later, Lyle was exuberant. Having made it through week sixteen, he had just two courses remaining. Meanwhile, the high washout rate had received the attention of the Office of the Inspector

General. Following an investigation, the length of the communications course was extended from seventeen to nineteen weeks. Luckily for Lyle, he was too near the finish line to be affected by the change.

Thursday.

Fooled them again last night by passing the #522, Tactical Procedure, and the tuning check. Really sweated it out last night especially on that tuning check. I'm in Wire now—telephones, switchboards, and telegraph. They have eased up here the last few weeks as far as washing fellows—a general was nosing around here a few weeks ago wondering why the wash out rate was so high. They just slapped two more weeks on the course starting a couple classes behind me so that was too close for comfort. I'm in now as far as the academic part of it goes but could be washed out otherwise yet. Phil is in his last week here now. Had a couple pleasant afternoons at the range. Shot a high sharpshooter with 168 out of 200 but it was rather poor cause I messed up on a couple batches. Marksman starts at 120, sharpshooter at 155, and expert at

CADETS OPERATING A FIELD TELEPHONE, TS YALE, 1944

175. Started out good but didn't have my gun zeroed in good on the 300 yd range.

Just got a card—my uniform is ready for a fitting. But there is still work to be done in Wire so here goes. Hope everything is O.K. with you too. If you have any suggestions, comments, or questions let me know.

Ten days after the Allied invasion at Normandy, Lyle mailed home an article from the post publication, *The Beaver*, regarding Operation Overlord:

WHAT'S NEW WITH THE AIR WAR

Allied air support of the French invasion kept up a ceaseless battering at German positions during the week, despite deteriorating weather conditions. Following up the record 12,500 sorties on D-Day, American and British aircraft swept across the Channel day after day and night after night, singling out French bridges and road junctions, hurtling down their bombs on Nazi troop concentrations, airfields and reinforcements rushing to bolster the German defense lines on the Cherbourg Peninsula.

The word "greatest" continued to be the most used word in newspaper headlines and on-the-scene accounts by correspondents. This week it was the "greatest daylight heavy bomber attack of the war", with over 1400 U.S. Fortresses and Liberators in a grand assault on 16 enemy airfields and six strategic bridges.

One week after D-Day, official records of flying missions revealed that 56,000 Allied sorties were flown and 42,000 tons of bombs were dropped on Nazi-held France and Germany. Allied aerial support to the Cherbourg Peninsula battle was heightened by strong formation flights of bombers and fighter escorts all over western Europe. Singled out for a mass attack by 1500 heavy bombers of the Eighth Air Force was a big oil refinery at Emmerich in northwest Germany and rail bridges in France, Belgium and the Netherlands.

From Italy other planes smashed at targets in Munich four days in a row, blasted oil refineries and other oil installations in the Balkans. The RAF, using part of its huge bomber fleet on separate missions not connected with the invasion of France, hammered away at Gelsenkirchen in the Ruhr and paid other visits to much-bombed Cologne.

From the Pacific came other news of mass air warfare. This time it was Admiral Nimitz' carrier task forces in a large-scale attack on the Marianas Islands, hitting with all their might at the important enemy bases of Saipan, Tinian, Rota and Guam. In a two-day battle 140 enemy aircraft were destroyed, 13 Japanese ships were sunk, and sixteen other surface vessels were damaged. Of the Jap ships sunk, one was a destroyer. American losses amounted to 15 aircraft destroyed and 15 flight personnel lost in action.

Whereas his buddy Phil was pleased to be selected to take the test devised by Massachusetts Institute of Technology (MIT) for possible radar training at Harvard, Lyle was relieved his name was not on the list. He did not want more technical study.

Fate brought about happy twists and turns just as Lyle was on the homestretch at Yale. With Vernon stationed at Harvard and Irene due for a leave from her duties with the War Department in Omaha, the stage was set for a Sladek mini-reunion in New England.

Irene's office chums presented her with a corsage of gardenias and escorted her to the railroad station. Finding all of the seats occupied, she stood in the aisle until two GIs in the same predicament found three seats in another car. She enjoyed their companionship all the way to Chicago. From there she proceeded on to the nation's capital, where friends gave her a grand tour of the city. Then it was off to join Vernon and Vivian in Boston.

IRENE SLADEK, 1944

18 JUNE 1944 (SUNDAY). Midnight. Just back from Sunday night classes and waiting for mess. Guess Irene is in Wash D.C. by now. She should just about hit here Sat. morning when I have uniform inspection—complete officer's uniform minus the gold bars. This (if I get through) will be a big day for me—sort of came up the hard way through the ranks. The only bad effects from this rat race is a little nervous tension which will soon disappear. Wire is interesting. For one thing we had 5 switchboards set up with about a dozen telephones and we would put through calls equivalent to home to Mitchell through stations etc. Sure keeps you busy when several calls come through at once. Also have more than one telephone and telegraph on the same line at the same time. This telephone stuff is simple after radio. Army uses practically same telephones as at home. Guess I'll get a job as Central in Pukwana after the war. Was lucky to hit the test wide open tonight too. Two more weeks and 3 more days! Here's hoping to come home in July but nothing sure. Been almost a year now. They will surely give me a leave before leaving the country anyway. Phil takes the MIT exam tomorrow. If he passes he will go to Harvard. My grades here are too low to get a shot at it. I could probably pass it cause it's mostly Math which is up my alley. I don't want it. I had an 86 average for the week in the #522 but got a 75% for a final grade. Guess I must have gotten the 30% grade in the final. Can you imagine getting a 30 in a test where you guess 25% anyway? Sure took the wind out of my sails. They passed me but few teachers would have. However 2/3 of the class got below 75% in it. Whoever made up the test had a foul sense of humor. We are falling out for mess now.

With continued good luck, Lyle would don an officer's uniform in two weeks. Phil, one week ahead, was scheduled to embark on the last week of training at the airport. *Going to the airport* was tantamount to completing the program and winning the coveted commission, a document issued by the President of the United States conferring authority to military officers.

21 JUNE 1944 (WEDNESDAY). Midnight. Fooled them again and passed Wire so now I'm over the hump and have it downhill from now on in. Phil goes to the airport in the morning and I go a week from today. My uniform is ready and I'm rarin' to go. This week is mostly outside and the course is called Ground Sets. I get to eat first in the squadron all week too. I'm going to get through here but could never do it again. Irene is likely in Boston now—had a card from her in Wash D.C. We will take a shot at N.Y. on Sunday and take a chance of passing anyway. I've sure had the luck—getting kind of excited now that it's pretty close to me. Phil isn't going to Harvard. About 10 best fellows took the test and

only the 5 best go. I'm surprised that he wasn't at the top even though the competition was terrific. He has a touch for this scientific stuff and is about the brightest fellow I've run into. Three of our Wash U. gang get their bars a week from now out of 50 who came to cadets. Then another bunch of us a week later. It takes more than a uniform of course but it does sort of give a fellow a feeling of having accomplished something. How is everything in S. Dak? The cows and horses won't even know me pretty soon to say nothing about the cat. Gerald Korzan has sure gone up in rank fast enough for being in this country instead of overseas. We will tell you all about our blowout in N.Y. Will sure be good to get to see someone I know. We will have a good time. See you soon.

Vivian met Irene at the Boston train station and whisked her off on the subway to Cambridge. Lyle wrote to Irene at that address to coordinate their long-awaited excursion to New York City.

22 JUNE 1944 (THURSDAY). Hello everybody. Is everything under control in Boston? According to a card from Irene from Wash. D.C. she should be in Boston now. Are you there Irene? Just want to give a little dope on this end of it. Fooled them again this week and passed Wire. Probably got one of my better grades here. So now I'm in Ground Sets which is mostly outside work and go to the airport next Thursday. So this weekend I think we should hit New York. I'll tell you what I'll be doing Saturday and you can arrange to get here whenever it suits us both best. Revillie at 9:00 and uniform inspection from 10:00 until about 11:00. My Class 36 will be inspected by a 1st Lt. to see if our uniforms are O.K. But this is inside the old quad and it takes a pass for a civilian to get in to this part of Yale. At 11:00 we eat and my class eats first now so I could be back to Phelps Gate by 11:15 and see you until 12:00 providing we can get our room and things ready for inspection. Then I'm busy until 3:30 when we get ready for inspection and retreat on the lower Green. Wish you would take in our parade. Then we go to mess at 5:00 from there and I could be free at 5:15 to tear out for N.Y. So if you would look up schedules and see how quick we could get a train after 5:15. I have a pass already. I'll draw a little map of the area here. Looks best for you to meet me at Phelps Gate at 11:15 or the Taft Hotel lobby. Come when it suits you best. Might as well stroll around Yale—you will be on your own. I've got plenty cash. Try and let me know what the score is if you can.

On Saturday, upon debarking at the New Haven station, Irene and Vivian made their way to the Taft Hotel. Vernon, arriving on a later train, joined them in the lobby. When Lyle breezed in he was surprised to see V and V. Following warm greetings, Irene chided Lyle that the "couple blocks from the station" in his letter turned out to be a mile. Lyle sheepishly admitted he had barely seen the streets of New Haven since arriving from Seymour Johnson Field in February. Preliminaries fulfilled, the four family members departed on the next train for New York, arriving at dusk in a pouring rain.

The stay in New York was brief. The next day, Vernon caught the one o'clock train to Boston and Lyle boarded the two-thirty train for New Haven. Irene and Vivian lingered in New York for a few more days of sightseeing.

On hotel stationery, Lyle described the "city with tall shoulders" to his parents, beginning with the headline:

26 JUNE 1944 (MONDAY). Yes, we stayed at the Roosevelt in New York City. Irene and Vivian arrived here from Boston about noon Saturday and Vernon got here about 4:30. It rained Saturday so we had inspection in the barracks instead of out on the Green so I got out a few minutes early and met them at the Taft Hotel. We grabbed a taxi and got to the station in time for a 5:30 train and were in New York in about 1 1/2 hours. Vernon got rooms at the Roosevelt which adjoins Grand Central Station through a tunnel. Irene and I had rooms on the 16th floor and V and V on the 5th floor. We dined out at a nice restaurant on 45th St. near Madison Ave and took plenty of time eating. It rained a little off and on during the evening and Sunday morning. Later in the evening it dried up a little and we strolled all around upper Manhattan in the area of Empire State, Rockefeller Center, and Times Square. The streets around Times Square were packed solid with people but other streets in New York seemed rather deserted. One thing that impressed me about N.Y. is the number of taxis and the speed they go tearing up the streets. If you are crossing the street and the light changes, it's too bad! At night you about break your neck to try to see the top of a tall building and they look like they are hanging right over you and are going to tip over. The skyscrapers seem to sort of close up on you. Of course we saw Macys and the Astor Hotel and the Chrysler Bld. We didn't get to bed too early and got up about 8:00 and went to the Mayflower for breakfast—waffles and doughnuts on Times Square by the Times Building. Then we went to Rockefeller Center and looked

through the Hall of Motion and Irene and I went on an N.B.C. tour in the building. We saw different programs being put on the air and learned a lot about how it is done. Was especially interested cause a lot of it is in the same line as I've been studying. Then we went to the television rooms and Irene broadcast over television to another room where the rest of us in the tour watched. Irene is the right type for television—came over very good and also her voice came over good. We listened in on Prince Matchabelli Perfume program of Stradivari Orchestra and then the weather cleared so it wouldn't be too foggy to go to the top. Irene and I got tickets and shot up 70 stories to the observation roof—and then you really see N.Y. A trip to N.Y. is at least half going to the top of a skyscraper. We were right in the middle of Manhattan. To the south about a mile was Empire State Building like a fence post in tall grass. Away to the south in the distance we could see the Statue of Liberty

CADET LYLE SLADEK AND SISTER IRENE, 1944
OBSERVATION TOWER OF ROCKEFELLER CENTER

and Staten Island and New York Harbor. To the west the Hudson River spanned by the George Washington Bridge pours into the harbor and also East River to the east of us. To the north in the center between the river edges of Manhattan is Central Park—a rectangle of about 3 square miles. In the west on the blue horizon 60 miles away were the mountains of Penn. and just across the Hudson is N. Jersey. Brooklyn is east across East River. And so it goes. Irene and I had our picture taken with Empire State in the background. Then it was time to get back to the hotel and catch a train to New Haven. Irene and Vivian are staying in N.Y. for about 3 days and then Irene is going up the Hudson to upper New York State. Irene was looking super duper and really knows how to travel. V and V were looking good too and seemed to feel at home in New York. Vernon is a snappy looking Naval Officer and fits the part of an officer much better than I will ever be able to. What really strikes one about N.Y. is the miles and miles of close packed tenement houses. New York isn't the skyscrapers of Manhattan that you see in the movies—it's the crowded desolate slums where you see a tree about every 3 miles and dwarfed from lack of sunlight at that. It's good to see N.Y. if for no other reason than to appreciate where you live. Getting lost in Central New York is almost impossible.

Say, that makes me jealous—Jean drives the car and I don't think Mom would even trust me with it yet! Just think, they may let me come home in about 10 or 12 days. If I pass this week. Don't know where they will send me. Nothing sure I'll pass this week either. Two more days at Yale and a week at the airport. Got to study now. Passed the tuning check last night. Be seeing you.

On Thursday, Lyle and the other cadets nearing graduation rode to the airport in the back of a truck. According to a blurb released by the Public Relations Office, they would train "under simulated battle conditions, from sleeping in a plane to working on its wireless system at night with the aid of black-out lanterns." Lyle found "simulated battle conditions" to mean nothing more than living in tents, eating army rations, and working on actual airplanes at the airport—no hardship at all. Although he anticipated a furlough upon graduation, he cautioned his family not to count on it.

30 JUNE 1944 (FRIDAY). Greetings from the airport! I'm through at Yale U. and am now at that mythical place you never expect to get to—6 days away from a commission. It's wonderful to be away from Yale. This is life again—just like being in the regular army. They treat us decent and don't try to scare us all the time and even give us some time to lay around. Of course yesterday was a rather bad day cause we had to

get up at 5:00 to come out here so only had 3 hours sleep. They couldn't drag me back to Yale with a dozen tractors. It will take a while to get back some confidence. A look at all the communication equipment in that B-26 made me feel very helpless. They should have put me in something mechanical instead of this stuff. Our assignments may come through tonight or tomorrow. I think I'm too low to even be picked for Boca Raton—a good deal cause no one wants to go there anyway. Just think—if they pass me this week I'll likely be home next weekend. Of course they grade you this week too but it's very seldom anyone washes back. But I'm through as far as studying goes. They can wash me back a week if they want to cause I like it out here.

If I go to Boca Raton to B-29 radar school I'll have to report there immediately. Any other assignment means a 10-day delay en route plus traveling time to the next station. It's rather warm here today in Conn. Our barracks is in a nice wooded area and you have to cross a little footbridge to get to it. Nice and quiet and fresh out here. Phil was commissioned yesterday and they changed his assignment to MIT instead of Atlanta, Ga—so he got a good deal. Now is when the responsibility starts and I'll really have to get on the ball from now on. No use writing to this address anymore. Don't expect me though until I get there cause you can't make plans in the army. Just start oiling up that freezer and mixing some bread dough. I'm afraid I'm letting myself get too enthused here and then be disappointed if it went haywire the last minute. But at least I went through this school so I'm satisfied no matter what. Guess I had better get a haircut now for inspection tomorrow. Keep your fingers crossed.

Lyle's uncertainty about receiving a furlough increased when he read a directive issued by the base commanding officer:

CADETS TO RECEIVE FURLO INFORMATION

Bent on clearing up the question of furloughs which confronts many graduating Cadets, Col. Raymond J. Reeves, Commanding Officer, this week disclosed that all men would be informed of their furlough status at least a month before they are commissioned. *Fooey*

they haven't told me anything.

DEPENDS ON 'EXIGENCIES'

"It may be impracticable to authorize leaves and furloughs in some individual cases due to exigencies of the Service such as meeting commitment dates and training schedules," the Colonel said.

"Graduates will be advised that every effort is being made to authorize leaves and furloughs for each graduate in accordance with existing policy."

The Colonel stated that no promises could be made as leaves and furloughs are granted not as a matter of right but as a matter of convenience to the Government.

Meanwhile, Lyle eagerly anticipated graduation day. In typical army verbiage and format, a by the numbers Schedule for Graduation Procedure was placed in his hands:

HEADQUARTERS, DEPARTMENT OF MILITARY TRAINING
3510TH AAF BASE UNIT (TECHNICAL SCHOOL)
Yale University　　　New Haven, Conn.　　　9/ahb

28 June 44

SUBJECT:　　Schedule for Graduation Procedure

TO:　　　　All Concerned

　　1.　The following Graduation Day schedule for graduating cadets is published for the guidance of all concerned. Cadets will follow this procedure in order to enable departure from this station with the least possible delay.

0500	– Reveille (Airport)
0510-0530	– Bedding turn in (Airport)
0600	– Breakfast (Airport)
0630	– Entruck for South Barracks Area
0700	– Report to Cadet Supply, basement of 28th Division to turn in equipment. Cadets will run clearances after equipment has been turned in to Cadet Supply
0900	– Cadets to graduate will form for graduation parade in South Barracks Area
1000	– Graduation Parade
1045	– Cadets to graduate will report to Sterling Law Auditorium
1100	– Graduation in Sterling Law Auditorium
1200	– Final Pay in Room 1088, Cadet Headquarters. Pay all civilian obligations and complete clearances
1300	– Receive orders, turn in completed clearances, room 1088, Cadet Headquarters
1500	– Departure processing at Sterling Law Auditorium. Officers will bring all orders, 201 file, and allied papers when reporting.
1700	– Sign out after processing has been completed

　　2.　Each graduating cadet will be responsible for the proper allocation of his time in completing clearances, etc, to insure strict compliance with the above schedule.

ERIC C. NICHOLIS
Captain, Air Corps
Commandant of Students

- 1 -

2 JULY 1944 (SUNDAY). My duty station assignment came out and what a break! Ten day delay en route and report to Santa Monica, California (near Los Angeles) for A.A.C.S. (Army Airways Communications System). I'm tickled pink. Was too low in my class to have to go to Boca Raton to school with no delay. Have guard duty starting at noon. This is swell out here and we are getting some good experience. May come by way of St. Louis and Omaha but doubt it. Don't expect me til I get there.

In the interim, the Public Relations Office at TS Yale sent a congratulatory form letter to Lyle's parents:

HEADQUARTERS TECHNICAL SCHOOL
ARMY AIR FORCES TECHNICAL TRAINING COMMAND
YALE UNIVERSITY, NEW HAVEN, CONNECTICUT

DEAR MR AND MRS SLADEK:

Some time ago we sent you a letter and newspaper story about your son's progress in the Army Air Forces Training Command. It is our pleasure once more to tell you about his further success in the AAF.

Please accept our congratulations on your son's accomplishments. We know that you are proud of the work he is doing, and we would like to add that we also share your pride.

As you may recall, we send an identical copy of the story about your son to the newspapers mentioned at the head of the enclosed page, so that it will not be necessary for you to take your copy to the editors. Generally, newspapers will publish stories like this, but the war situation has placed a premium on space and sometimes an article may be shortened or omitted from the columns entirely.

In the event you do see it published, however, we would appreciate it if you would send us a clipping of the article. If you care to communicate with us concerning this story, please do not hesitate to call on us.

Cordially yours,

CHARLES J. NELSON
Captain, A. C.
Public Relations Officer

Touting his achievement and alluding to his future role in the Army Air Forces, the Public Relations Office issued a news release to the *Chamberlain Register*. The outside of the envelope bore the sketch of a lieutenant along with an announcement:

LOCAL BOY !
MAKES GOLD.

PUBLIC RELATIONS OFFICE
Headquarters Technical School
AAFTTC   For IMMEDIATE RELEASE
Yale University   CHAMBERLAIN REGISTER
New Haven, Conn.

NEW HAVEN, CONN., 6 July -- Aviation Cadet   LYLE SLADEK   son of
MR AND MRS CHARLES SLADEK   of   PUKWANA, SOUTH DAKOTA
was awarded the gold bars of a second lieutenant today at graduation
exercises of the Army Air Forces Training Command School at Yale
University. Graduation ceremony was held in the auditorium of the Sterling
Law Buildings before a large audience of classmates and friends.
    Rated as a Technical Officer in Communications, he is now prepared to
assume duties with tactical units of the Army Air Forces, according to Col.
Raymond J. Reeves, Commanding Officer. His training has included study
in the use and operation of transmitters, receivers, the radio compass, radio
and wire equipment and portable ground stations. For two weeks prior to
graduation the new officer has been trained under simulated battle conditions,
from sleeping in a plane to working on its wireless system at night with the aid
of black-out lanterns. In addition to the classroom work, much of his schedule
has included intensive training for physical fitness, toughening him for terrain
and temperature found in fighting fronts around the world.
    Lieut. SLADEK   will shortly be assigned to a tactical unit where he will
be in charge of maintaining the communications of his outfit. He will head a
group of enlisted men specialists. It is groups such as these that are enabling
the AAF to operate in a well-knit campaign over Europe.

- 30 - L - N - H -

Emma clipped the article, LYLE SLADEK GRADUATES—2ND LIEUTENANT, from the *Register* and later stored it with his graduation program and enlisted record showing: "1 year, 4 months, 15 days service for longevity pay."

On graduation day, Lyle awoke with a feeling of elation mixed with disbelief. Some of his roommates had survived the TS Yale regimen, pinned on the gold bars of a second lieutenant, and proudly departed the post. Others had washed out, their dreams shattered. Now this is my day, Lyle thought, whether due to determination or to lucky stars, this is my day.

At 1045 hours, Lyle and other graduating cadets marched to the Sterling Law Library for a commissioning ceremony. The event was businesslike and brief. Discharged from the United States Army, each cadet received a certificate bearing the words: "As a testimonial of Honest and Faithful Service to his country." That formality completed, they were sworn into the Army of the United States. Each newly hatched officer pinned gold bars onto his uniform and received official documentation:

HEADQUARTERS
ARMY AIR FORCES EASTERN TECHNICAL TRAINING COMMAND
455 LAKE AVENUE, ST. LOUIS, 8, MISSOURI

In reply   6 July 1944
refer to AG 201 Sladek, Lyle Virgil

SUBJECT: Temporary Appointment.

To   :   2nd Lt. Lyle Virgil Sladek, 0872240,
              Army of the United States

1.   The Secretary of War has directed me to inform you that the President has appointed and commissioned you a temporary Second Lieutenant, Army of the United States, effective this date. Your serial number is shown above.
2.   This commission will continue in force during the pleasure of the President of the United States for the time being, and for the duration of the war and six months thereafter unless sooner terminated.
3.   There is enclosed herewith a form for oath of office which you are requested to execute and return. The execution and return of the required oath of office constitute an acceptance of your appointment. No other evidence of acceptance is required.
4.   This letter should be retained by you as evidence of your appointment as no commissions will be issued during the war.

        By command of Major General FICKEL:

                                          ROY R. WALKER,
Inclosure   Captain, Air Corps,
      Form for oath of office.   Actg. Asst. Adj. Gen.

A lowly cadet one hour, an officer the next, Lyle signed an oath of office and followed procedures prescribed by the commandant "to enable departure from this station with the least possible delay." There was a war on. Training space was needed to accommodate newly arriving cadets.

At 1700 hours, sporting the gold bars of a second lieutenant, Lyle exited the Yale campus. Pausing for a moment at Phelps Gate, once again he read the inscription: FOR GOD, FOR COUNTRY, AND FOR YALE.

LIEUTENANT LYLE SLADEK, 1944
OFFICIAL ARMY IDENTIFICATION PHOTOS

CHAPTER 12

An Officer and a Gentleman

What is outside yourself does not convey much worth;
Clothes do not make the man, the saddle not the horse.
—ANGELIUS SILESIUS

TWENTY YEARS OLD and clad in the uniform of an officer, Lyle departed the familiar surroundings of the Yale University campus. While inwardly the same person, the outer world perceived him differently. Though novel at first, the frequent salutes of cadets and enlisted personnel soon became burdensome.

During the preceding year and a half Lyle had traveled to military bases in the company of fellow soldiers, boarding trains as ordered and getting off when so directed. Now he was responsible for making his own travel arrangements at congested railroad stations.

Although the ten-day travel allotment for the trip from Connecticut to California seemed generous, nearly three days elapsed before Lyle reached the family farm in central South Dakota. His family was overjoyed to see him but took little notice of the brass on his uniform. Rank had its privileges in the military, but clothing did not make the man in rural America. However, when he opened the cabinet of a malfunctioning radio, analyzed the problem, and restored the set to working order, his parents were impressed.

Glad to be freed from army protocol, Lyle eased back into farm life. He enjoyed the sight of Hereford cows, white-faced calves at their sides, grazing on grass lush from melting snow and soaking rains. He gazed at a field of ripening barley, the bristled heads waving with every passing breeze. Barring a summer hailstorm, the field would yield a good crop.

Four days passed quickly as Lyle helped his father tune up the tractor, clean the storage bins, and ready the grain binder for the harvest. Realizing it would require three days of travel time from the farm to southern California, he wired AACS headquarters in Santa Monica requesting a two-day extension. He received a terse telegram in reply:

On the eve of Lyle's departure a fierce thunderstorm turned the dirt roads into a quagmire impassable for the family car. Charles, ever resourceful, hitched two horses to a buggy while Emma packed a lunch. In the dark of night father and son set off for Pukwana seven miles distant, arriving at the depot just in time for Lyle to catch the eastbound Chicago, Milwaukee & St. Paul.

Although California was far to the west, train connections mandated that Lyle travel two hundred miles east to Sioux City and then south by bus to Omaha. After a short visit with Irene, he continued on by train to Kansas City where he boarded the Golden State Limited.

Lyle was enchanted by the scenery of the Southwest. However, on a picture postcard from Tucumcari, New Mexico, he scrawled: "Train derailed in Texas so one day late here. Will wire ahead. Nice down here in N.M. Time here to eat lunch—the first today. Bye now."

PICTURE POSTCARD, TUCUMCARI, NEW MEXICO, 1944

The next day, Lyle followed up with a travel narrative:

20 JULY 1944 (THURSDAY). Greetings from the glittering sunshine of noon in Tucson, Arizona. We stopped here long enough so I could wire ahead to the Commanding Officer that I was coming late. Had a nice cool ride to Sioux City and talked with a cadet nurse who was a visiting senior at our high school on Winner skip day. Rather warm bus ride to Omaha and no Irene to meet me. Was just ready to grab a taxi to a train station when Irene came around the corner. She expected me at the other bus station. We went to the station and found out that an 11:45 train was the best bet so we went to her apartment and I showered while Irene cooked a good steak dinner with lemonade, carrot jello salad, etc. and really filled me up. Then we listened to the radio and went for a walk and bought a qt. of ice cream. Got an old crowded coach to Kansas City. Had a two hour stopover and succeeded in getting a reserved Pullman to Los Angeles on the Golden State Limited. That "limited" must mean the speed cause it's plenty slow. You should see Kansas. Miles and miles of wheat fields all evenly combined and here and there long piles of wheat on the ground especially near the panhandle of Oklahoma and Texas. Must have been a terrific crop and they really got all of it clean with combines. At 10:30 Tues night twelve cars left the tracks near Delhart, Texas. No one hurt except a couple older people badly shaken up and taken to the hospital. We sure came to a screaming halt. They backed the couple hind cars still on the rails back to a junction and it took us 16 hours to bypass the spot. So yesterday we came through New Mexico with its vast acres of sage brush, mesquite, cedar trees and rocky hills and dry river gorges with an occasional herd of Herefords. Traveled with a major who told me a few of the details about the country. This forenoon we traveled through the more dry cactus country until getting to Tucson. This trip has by far the nicest scenery of any I've taken. The sun is really bright and warm. Did the big rain hurt the grain too badly?

SANTA MONICA

Arriving in Los Angeles late at night, Lyle made his way to Santa Monica where he located the headquarters of Army Airways Communications System (AACS), the outfit that maintained control towers and a network of message stations throughout the western region of the United States.

While awaiting official word on his duty assignment, Lyle went sightseeing.

21 JULY 1944 (FRIDAY). I'm somewhere in Los Angeles in a drugstore. Sort of tired after the 80 hour trip from Omaha but having a

good time. Got here at 3:00 a.m. and the streetcar and bus connections are so poor that it took me until 7:00 to get to Santa Monica to a small inconspicuous building where I was supposed to report. The way it looks we will ship out of here today or tomorrow—probably for Seattle or somewhere. Anyway we are apt to be in the States for at least 3 more months and I think 30 days of school in Michigan. Don't ask me cause I don't know. Sure is pretty out here—have been through Beverly Hills etc but it covers so much territory that it's hard to get around. May get a chance to look around a little more before we leave—would like to stay a while here. Leaving now—got to be back at Headquarters by 1:30. Things seem awfully favorable in Europe now—may bust up this week even.

Six weeks after landing at Normandy the Allied forces broke out of the coastal plain of France and advanced toward Paris. The second front, long sought by Stalin, was now a reality. The Allies were pushing toward Germany from the west and Russian armies were approaching from the east.

Lyle, not understanding the mind-set of Hitler, thought the German dictator would recognize the futility of continuing the war and negotiate a peace treaty. However, as later explained by Albert Speer, minister of armaments and war production in Nazi Germany, Hitler linked the future of the German people with his own bleak fate; if the German people failed in the quest for mastery of Europe, they deserved annihilation.

Meanwhile, in response to the destruction of its industrial centers, Germany launched *Vergeltungswaffes* (vengeance weapons) toward England. The twenty-five-foot V-1 bombs, nicknamed *buzz bombs* or *doodlebugs*, terrorized the British people.

Three days after he arrived at AACS headquarters, Lyle and three peers were offered some latitude as to their duty station. Lyle opted for an air base in Nevada where his Miami Beach roommate, Billy Vestal, had taken gunnery training. Knowing his parents were familiar with the location of Boulder Dam, but not of a neighboring town with less than ten thousand people, he wrote:

24 JULY 1944 (MONDAY). Just a few lines to tell you where I'm going. The four of us had a choice of 4 places—one of us to each—Long Beach (near here); Tucson, Arizona; Fresno, Calif; and Las Vegas, Nevada. Guess which I chose. I'm leaving at 7:30 in the morning for Las Vegas which is near Boulder Dam. What do you think of the choice. Just a shot in the dark. Went swimming and sunning at the beach this afternoon. Seems to be just as salty as the Atlantic and not quite so nice a beach as Miami Beach. So now I've about seen what I want of this

section. Spent Sunday afternoon in Hollywood including a stage show. Too expensive around here living on your own. Your letter and Peggy's came today. You are doing right well on the grain cutting too. This address will do—

Lt. Lyle Sladek 0872240
Det, 101st AACS SQ.
Las Vegas AA Fld,
Nevada

Sort of hard to get used to this after cadet school. It is just opposite treatment. And you can bet I'm taking full advantage of everything. Bought two grapefruit on my way home—cost 36¢ for two of them! Of course they were as big as watermelons. Take it easy out there as I'm doing.

Have to report "as soon as practicable"—very nice!

LAS VEGAS

Las Vegas was just another dusty watering stop for steam locomotives making the run between Los Angeles and Salt Lake City. Three casinos with garish neon signs, the Nevada Biltmore, Last Frontier, and El Rancho Vegas, fronted an oiled road to the south of town. Nestled in a valley, the little town was surrounded by four mountain ranges: Spring Mountains to the west, Sheep Range to the north, Sunrise Mountain to the east, and Black Mountain to the south. The view was spectacular. After making his way to the airfield north of town Lyle unpacked his belongings and went for a stroll around the base. In the cool of the evening, Las Vegas Army Air Field (LVAAF) seemed like paradise. Later that night, he wrote:

25 JULY 1944 (TUESDAY). "Don't get around much anymore." Left L.A. this morning at 7:30 and just barely made the train. It was a 10 hr. trip across the Mts and desert. You never saw such a hot dry bare country. Got to Las Vegas at 6:00 and saw an army truck by the station ready to leave and sure enough he was going out to camp. So he drove me the 7 miles straight north out of town to what looked like a mirage in the desert. All around are small Mt. peaks and out here away from everywhere is the neatest cutest little army camp and airfield you ever saw. Signed in at Headquarters and then came to B.O.Q. (Bachelor Officers Quarters) and showered and changed. Still had time to eat at B.O.Q. mess hall and what a treat to get plenty of good solid army chow after a week of skimpy meals on trains and at restaurants. Only 50¢ a meal and plenty of milk. Looked around camp for about an hour. Kind of embarrassing always getting saluted every little ways. It's a rather

small camp and consists of gunnery school and a phase of flying so most here are cadets and officers (many flight officers which are just below my rank). Right close is an outdoor pool and you should see the nice P.X.s and theatre etc etc. Better entertainment than a city. Of course I guess I can go to town anytime I want to. Anyway I think this will be a very pleasant stay. More later.

In the morning Lyle walked over to the flight line and presented his official identification to the officer in charge of the AACS communications station and control tower. On the card were his photo, name, designation (2nd LT AC), signature, countersignature, thumbprint, and specific physical data along with a warning:

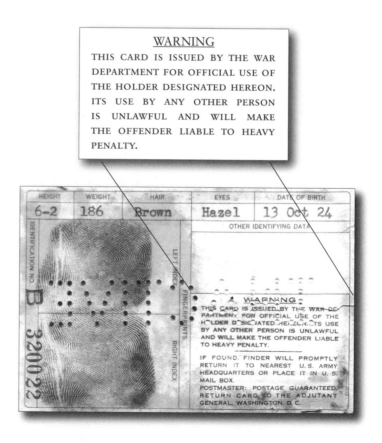

The check-in formality completed, Lyle was free to explore his surroundings. The flight line was abuzz with activity. Swarms of mechanics were servicing airplanes in the hangars. P-47s and P-51s were roaring on and off the runway as pilots qualified to fly the single-engine planes. Four-engine bombers were taking off for training missions above the desert range, where aerial gunners practiced shooting at targets from gun turrets.

Situated on public domain wasteland valued at one dollar per acre, LVAAF was an ideal site for aerial combat training. The mild climate made for year-round flying, with dry lake beds for emergency landings and barren hillsides for absorbing machine gun and cannon fire. Approximately two hundred pilots and six hundred gunnery students passed through the base every five weeks. Lyle could see LVAAF was a no-nonsense field with less emphasis on spit and polish than older permanent posts. Finding the base facilities and recreational opportunities to his liking, he recorded his first impression.

Wednesday.
This is a swell place—more like a health resort than an airfield except for the planes overhead. Sure is hot here—The earth is entirely bare except for two cactus plants in front of the Officers Club. Feels like S.D. in 1934 all the time. Was swimming this afternoon in the outdoor pool—I'm brown as an Indian. Write cause I don't know a single person here.

Life as an officer at LVAAF was a different world from the hectic pace and austere existence of cadet school. Dining with captains, majors, and colonels at the Officers Mess and socializing with them at the Officers Club seemed strange at first. And being the same rank as the lieutenant who commanded the AACS detachment and accountable only to AACS headquarters in Santa Monica, Lyle enjoyed considerable freedom. Still somewhat incredulous after three days of duty, he expressed his sentiment to his family.

28 JULY 1944 (FRIDAY). This ain't the army! Boy what a soft life this is. You see my headquarters are in Santa Monica several hundred miles away across the desert. No one at the field here hardly knows I'm here—or cares. And they would have no particular control over me even if they did know I'm around. There are four of us 2nd Louies and several enlisted men in our A.A.C.S. station in one of the hangars. One of the 2nd Lts. is really the Officer in Charge but he is the same rank as I so naturally he wouldn't try to tell me what to do either. We run 24 hr per day and it's really sort of just for me to get a little experience before going to cryptography school in Michigan for a month. It still surprises me what a little gold bar will do. And I never saw a post where everybody is so eager at saluting. My poor weary arm! I can't quite get used to this—it's so different from cadet school. Of course this post is so

largely composed of flying officers that it's different than others. Pilots are eleven cents a dozen now days. The meals are good—lots of milk, raw vegetables, and fruit juice. I'll soon gain that weight back I lost on the trip. Awfully hot here but it gets nice and cool by morning. Am in the Officers Club and just finished shooting some pool. Too bad I can't help you out with some of the work out there. Have been swimming for exercise. Have a golden brown tan now. Got the oats cut yet—how did it turn out? My mail may start coming through soon I hope. I'm having a very enjoyable time and hope you are too. The strangest thing happened the other night. It was dusk and a flying cadet saluted as we passed. Then he recognized me and it turned out to be Stanley Pierson—one of the best debaters to ever hit S.D. State. He has a couple months to go before commissioned a navigator. Bye now.

With the AACS station operating around-the-clock, Lyle, one of four lieutenants, supervised enlisted personnel during an eight-hour shift. He found them to be well trained and dependable. Message center staff communicated by radio and telegraph with other stations in a network throughout Nevada, Utah, Arizona, and California. The crew in the control tower monitored and directed air traffic. From his vantage point in the communications station in a hangar alongside the flight line, Lyle could see heat waves shimmering off the runway as planes took off for practice flights over the desert. Having time to spare, he sat down at a typewriter and described his leisurely life.

3 AUGUST 1944 (THURSDAY). Station WYWH. Today I'm working the evening shift until about 2:00 in the morning and tomorrow I get to loaf. This is sure a soft life compared with some in the other camps. As yet I don't know how much longer they will keep me here but the longer the better—at least a couple more weeks would be nice. Usually get in some swimming every day and about 60 sit ups so I'll SOON be getting in shape again. Is Chuckie still doing his sit ups and push ups or has he forgotten about them already? We had some dust storms around here a couple days ago and it really got pretty bad—this is the dryest place I've ever seen and I doubt if it has ever rained here. Engine heat sort of hangs around a plane or car like on the tractor on a hot still day. The latest dope is that we are getting a couple WAC operators here in our station—guess we'll be spending more time around here from now on. Haven't seen them yet but some of the fellows have. Should be spending my spare time taking a correspondence course or something but so far it has been swimming, pool, and reading. The Officers Club here is really nice. One thing though about the army—the more they pay you the more it costs to live so it sort of always balances out. And if you had any

to spare you could sure get rid of it in a hurry gambling in Las Vegas. Haven't been there yet except to drive down the street to the station. I'm going over to Boulder Dam one of these days and also probably to a Mt Charleston resort if it works out. Might as well take advantage of things at the same time. Saw an article in the paper the other day that more Americans have lost their lives in auto accidents since Pearl Harbor than in the theaters of war. Hard to believe but I guess it is true. Had some nice ripe red watermelon for supper tonight and they sure have lots of green vegetables and stuff. And it cools off good at night for good sleeping so this is really a healthy place. Guess you have the grain in the shock now if the binder held out. Must be quite a relief to not have to think about shocking, isn't it girls?

Lyle mused about his sisters working in the harvest field, struggling with bundles that weighed nearly as much as they did. Thinking of pheasant hunting and refinishing the wooden stock of his Savage rifle, he signed off: "Better be getting some varnish cause I may be coming through there in a month or two and I'm going to put it on or else."

A week later Lyle seized an opportunity to go up in an airplane. Upon landing, he went to the message station and typed:

9 AUGUST 1944 (WEDNESDAY). Today I got the idea that I wanted to fly—so I went over to the hangar and beat on them for a ride. Maybe it was just to find out if it would scare me or not or to see what it was like or something. Anyway a B-17 Flying Fortress was due to go up in a few minutes and they said I could go along. The pilot and copilot and crew chief wanted to take some checks on the engines—turned out his name was Sladek too and he is from Chicago. So we crawled in and taxied to the end of the runway for the take off. In taking off you get it up to well over a hundred miles per hour and pull on the stick and up she zooms off the ground and away you go. We gradually gained altitude and it was rather like riding in a truck and no particular sensation and it seemed much safer than in a car with a reckless driver. There was not much more sensation of height than when on the windmill and it rides pretty smooth except for an occasional air pocket. At first you can see all the features of buildings etc below and the camp in neat little rows of play houses and the painted desert with an occasional pencil mark for a road and a train that looked like a mechanical worm. Then we finally got up to about two miles and you could see the curvature of the earth and outlines of Mts. like in a sand table and a few miles away the blue water of Lake Meade. The pilot was a good Joe and he agreed to take me over to Boulder Dam and Lake Meade. We were pretty high up but the water spread out and backed up farther than you could see and

the concrete structure looked like some child's toy workings in a sand table. The little line of blue passing over its spillway was the turbulent Colorado River. Then the pilot laid the ship over on its side and we could look right down on it and see the little curve of concrete from one side of the canyon to the other and the miles and miles of Lake Meade. Really a sight and you could see it from the air so much better too than from the ground. Then the pilot grinned at the copilot and knowing it was my first time up they decided to try to scare me by pulling into a dive—and they succeeded! Anyway I was wondering if I would ever find my stomach again. It was quite a trip and thrill altogether and I highly recommend that everyone do likewise cause it is different than anything else. Anyway I came to the conclusion that I could fly one of those tin cans as well as the next fellow.

I'm on duty this evening so consequently the letter. Got a letter from Royce Bates today from Arkansas. I expect orders any day to report to Selfridge Field in Michigan but it may be over a week yet. This is a soft life after Yale. But I do my sit ups and pull ups and swimming every day so I'm getting strong and healthy—but not wise nor wealthy. My pool is improving though! Boy you folks are doing alright on the work—too bad I'm not there to help with the haystacking. We could roll up some big ones again although I guess the only reason people make big stacks is just to show the neighbors. Where did you cut the hay this year? Was there any trouble with rocks with the outfit? How did that piece on the shank of the sickle hold out on the grain binder? Did it get loose or wear down? Surprising that the binder held together again. Guess I'll stick in a bill that I don't need just now. Everything is going swell here and I hope it is out there too. Bye now.

Aware that AACS officers frequently traveled by air to bases on other continents, Lyle speculated about his own future. He supposed, following a stint of advanced training in communications and cryptography at Michigan, he would fly overseas—perhaps to China? After telling his mother not to worry so much, he wrote of his pending orders.

15 AUGUST 1944 (TUESDAY). I'm sorry you haven't gotten my letters cause I'm pretty sure that I wrote at least two since you said you hadn't gotten any. And I think there was a twenty dollar bill in one of them. But you should take the positive attitude rather than a negative one—assume that everything is OK unless you hear to the contrary. Cause things are going well for me here in Nevada even though this climate is not fit to live in. Hot every day and night and often the dust blows. Am expecting orders to go to Michigan any day now cause I think it starts about the

22 Aug but I'm not sure. Am looking forward to those Lake Michigan breezes and a whooping good time in Detroit. A fellow in the barracks wants me to look up his brother there—says he will really show me the town. The deal looks about like this—orientation in Michigan for about a month and then probably back here and then overseas to the Pacific Theater. Most AACS men fly over so I could be here one day and in China 48 hours later. The war will likely end about that time but I will be stuck overseas for some time cause they may demobilize about like this—taking into consideration age and dependents, foreign service, length of time in the army, rank, etc which will leave me near the bottom of the barrel. But there are lots of strings that can be pulled too and if it happens I'll just make the best of it. Did you get a letter telling of my plane ride? Have been getting my daily swims and would really be in shape if they left me here for about a year. The other forenoon I went out to Sunrise Mountain and fired the pistol just to be doing something. Didn't improve any over the other time. The food is good, the weather is bad, and the work and recreation are good so altogether it has been a pleasant stay here in Nevada. My typing isn't really that bad except when writing a letter out of the head and trying to type fast. You sure are going to town on the haystacking. The corn must look nice—bet it will really make money for people this year cause there is not so much expense to harvesting it. When is our time to thresh? Have the kids got a place to stay yet in town or are they waiting til the last minute. Did you ever get a letter from my roommates at Yale with my diploma in it?

We were fairly busy here at the station for a while this evening but it is a little quieter just now. The other evening I visited with Stan Pierson (in my debating society at S.D. State College and really a swell egg). He is a cadet in navigation here just now and about where I would be if I had gone in flying like I almost did after Washington U. He was in meteorology at University of California Los Angeles (UCLA) until it busted up. He knew a cadet in the next barracks from Chamberlain. It was Chuck Laustrap in my class in high school. Sure funny how you run into fellows you know. They are taking gunnery here and have several months of navigation left but they say it is easy compared with meteorology. Expect to hear from you tomorrow saying that you did get those letters. But let's not be for thinking the wrong things when you don't hear. Just coax those tomatoes along and keep that rifle clean.

Young, restless, and tired of being on hold, Lyle contemplated transferring to another branch of the army in hopes of increased pay and an earlier discharge. He was pleased to learn his cousin, Kenneth Lunn, had finally been at one base long enough to be eligible for a promotion.

20 AUGUST 1944 (SUNDAY). It is another warm day in Nevada and I'm on duty this Sunday for a change. In a few minutes I'm going after the mail and if orders don't come today it will look like that Michigan deal is all off cause I expected to leave before this. May hear from you today cause you haven't written for a couple days now. Still don't know if you ever got my letters. Had a letter from Kenneth Lunn yesterday and he has been promoted to corporal at last—he hasn't been getting any breaks on promotions. Lots of places in the army promotions get frozen and it is impossible to ever get a boost. About half of it is luck. Anyway the army is just opposite of civilian life in this country. It is a stagnant thing cause there is no individual enterprise and it kind of goes against the grain. I want to get out as soon as possible after the war before I get lazy permanently. Pass the buck, shoot the bull, and make seven copies of everything. That is the army. But it does manage to get things done although very inefficiently. I'm ready to move along anytime now. That is one thing about fellows in the army—if they ship to a new camp every week they would be happy but after about a month in one place they want to move along. Guess I'll go after the mail now.

Monday.

Your letter came this morning—everybody seems to have deserted the haying except Dad. No orders came for me today so maybe Michigan is out. Might mean several different things. But of course I'm not positive just what date the deal was supposed to start either. I kind of think I could transfer into the infantry or paratroopers if I wanted to but have no intention of doing it at least not yet. Might get out of the army quicker in the infantry than in the air corps. Guess I'll go up and eat now. Our meals are good here but I'm not getting fat—haven't weighed for a couple months. Has been getting a little cooler here nights—would be a nice place to be in the wintertime. Don't know any news so here's signing off.

Two days later, Lyle lamented:

23 AUGUST 1944 (WEDNESDAY). Sladeks are really getting popular now days. In fact you will likely see my picture soon on the walls of all post offices in the U.S. While swimming on August 16, someone went through my room and snatched my wallet—full of cash, papers, pictures, and that officers identification book you saw. Made me kind of mad cause he could just as well have taken the bills out and left the papers and identification, etc. What I hated most was that I've never had anything stolen from me before and I didn't think anyone would ever do a thing like that. I kept it quiet except to report it to the Military Police

and got new identification. Today, a week later, I received a telegram from el Rancho Las Vegas (a big gambling joint where movie stars go when in Nevada) that my two checks had bounced. I had never been out there and had never written any checks so I knew right away that my name was being forged so I went to the Provost Marshal (Military Police) and told them the story. A little later two more checks came back from Hotel Last Frontier (another gambling joint). The fact that I had reported the theft a week earlier helped save me an awful lot of explaining. In the meantime the M.P.s had picked up the checks and we went out to these places and to a cashier's home. The M.P. of course really wanted to check me as much as anything so he quickly asked the cashier if she had seen me before. She immediately cleared me. The 2nd Lt. (or fellow in a Lt.'s uniform) is only about 5' 3" tall and we have a fair description of him from two cashiers. His forgery of my name and serial number is good but not perfect—a little shaky and tightened up. He also slipped up on a couple numbers. Apparently he is one of the copilot officers from my barracks except an officer has too much to lose on a deal like this. An officer's uniform was stolen a couple days earlier and it is faintly possible he is in uniform only. It is a big enough and serious enough deal so I believe the F.B.I. is or will work on the case. They would get him but I doubt the military will push it enough to get him. If we do I'll try and put in a claim for my cash. Everything is quiet and we have tipped off all places in town. If he lays low he is O.K.—if he forges one more check here he will serve a long stretch. I have no respect at all for the people of Nevada. They have nothing better to do than throw thousands of dollars on the gambling tables in these air conditioned joints while the rest of the world fights. They have ruined many a young fellow here—clean him out of money so he'll have to steal to get back on his feet.

Cognizant of wartime sacrifices, Lyle was peeved with the Nevada gaming industry, deeming it a drain on the war effort. While service people were risking their lives in the armed forces and many civilians were working overtime in factories and on farms—making do with outworn cars, clothing, and machinery—casino patrons were gambling in air-conditioned comfort. Impatient to receive orders and move on to further training, he continued:

Oh yes, good news—was told unofficially that in a couple days I will go to Michigan—but it will be too late to be there the same time as Peggy. Oh, well. Had a letter today from Phillip Coler. He is still bored with being on a lonely Pacific island. I'm studying Spanish a little now and also do a little diving. Guess I'll go get in a game of pool. I'll tell you how this all turns out.

Writing to Vivian the next day, Lyle joshed about being the victim of identity theft.

24 AUGUST 1944 (THURSDAY). The Sladeks are on the warpath again. Soon you may see my picture in your post office—but please don't try and get that reward. Oh, it isn't that bad. You see this officer was using my identification and forging my name on checks. He apparently is not very bright. He made enough with the cash alone and could have gotten by with that much of it for sure but he is apt to get caught for this forgery. He is an amateur but he signs my name in front of the cashier good enough so that no one would ever question it as being mine unless they were looking for something like that. He apparently has changed the height and weight and has evidently put his picture in it. But he is pretty dumb cause changing all that leaves only the signature and the official looking booklet that is any good to him. He should have just gotten a booklet, put his picture in it, and written in some fictitious name, and then it would be easier for him to sign the checks and also it wouldn't have been found out nearly so soon. I've got a personal score to settle with the fellow cause he could have gotten me into serious trouble and he has a picture I want. He probably isn't using my picture for identification unless he looks like me (I wouldn't wish that on even a crook) so if they get him before he goes to another field my name probably won't get spread around too much. Would have been rather embarrassing if I had tried to cash a check in one of those places a couple nights later. More darn fun. Probably this fellow ran up a gambling debt and took an easy way out. I hope the joints are never able to collect—they have probably ruined more airmen than the flak over Germany. This fellow will serve a long stretch for forgery and theft while those bums in white shirts in those gambling rooms clean up on some more servicemen. Pardon me if I blow my top. I'm going to answer this Last Frontier's letter and tell them a thing or two in plain language.

You know for the last two weeks I had been expecting orders to go to Michigan but they never seemed to come. Peggy was spending a couple weeks with her grandmother in Michigan and it looked like we would be there about the same time—but no ducks. But Vivian, you know a fellow can't really cook with gas only seeing her a day every year—but there is no hurry either so. She is starting school in a few days at Washington U (Wash out You we called it in the old days) so I think she is pretty lucky. Wouldn't mind too much going there myself after the war for a year. But you know it looks like I'm apt to be in some foreign place for a year or two after the war cause I'll be at the bottom of the list for discharges. Was thinking of joining the paratroopers cause they might get out sooner but I doubt if they would release me from AACS and I'm too tall and heavy. Might be a good deal at that. How does it feel to be a working gal again Vivian? Are you going to keep working at that same place—you mentioned you weren't too enthused about it. How much longer will you two be in Cambridge? I'll bet Vernon has to work a lot more than I have here. It sure will be good to get back in civilization again and I'll bet Michigan is tops. Don't forget to drop me a line after the 5th of Sept:

> 78th AAF BASE UNIT
> AACS SRC
> Selfridge Field, Mt. Clemens, Mich.

The way things are going in France we may see S.D. again before too long—will be good to be civilians again won't it? Bye now.

Lyle had reason to be optimistic about the progress of the war. Desperate to stop the Allied drive from the west, German leaders redirected troops from southern France, weakening their position in the Mediterranean region. Sensing an opportunity the Allies assembled an invasion force at Naples in preparation for assaulting what Churchill coined the "soft underbelly" of Fortress Europe. After securing a beachhead, Allied troops aided by paratroopers drove north to Grenoble.

In the Pacific theater American troops were completing the conquest of Saipan in the Marianas. Of strategic importance, an air base on that island would put B-29 bombers within striking range of Japan.

Finally receiving a telegram from AACS headquarters directing him to report to Selfridge Field, Lyle alerted his sister he might be passing through Omaha.

24 AUGUST 1944 (THURSDAY). You made a mistake when you invited me to dine with you again—cause I think I'll take you up on the deal one of these days. At last my orders came today to report to Michigan no later than Sept 5 and I'll try to get released from here a little early so as to have a couple days to stopover somewhere depending on the route I take. I'm sure looking forward to getting back to civilization again after being here for over a month. Guess I'll probably come by Salt Lake, Denver, Omaha, Chicago—does that sound like a good route to you? You hit it about right when you said neither—in fact, I got so hard up for something to do that I'm now studying Spanish grammar and one of the fellows here was helping me with the pronunciation. Not hard to read Spanish but rather hard to speak it. If I learn the grammar it will be easy to learn to speak it when I go south of the border.

Say, I beat a fellow in pool who is really a champion. Pool like lots of other things is dependent on breaks and how you happen to be clicking at the time. And sometimes in stiff competition you play over your head.

But he beat me in the second game. How are you on the diving? I do a little once in a while. So far all I can do is fall off the low board without getting hurt too much at any one time. Say do you know anything about the paratroopers? I'm thinking about asking to be transferred into them after this Michigan deal is over. Would be a hundred dollars more per month and lots of good tough training and maybe a chance to get out of the army sooner after the war.

A B-24 just called in that one motor is out and it is circling for an emergency landing. Sure is taking a long time about it. Here's signing off—see you later.

Like many civilians, Lyle's mother had little knowledge of how the army chain of command functioned. Having grown up in a pioneer community, she supposed people always did vital, productive work, such as growing crops, teaching school, or clerking in a store. Now that her son had completed extensive training she expected his work to be essential and noteworthy. She pointedly asked, "Just what do you do there?" Lyle, although responsible for the operation of the AACS station during his eight-hour shift, admitted his duties were not *real* work.

26 AUGUST 1944 (SATURDAY). Got a couple letters from you yesterday with lots of news. Also a letter from Vernon—they seem to be on the go most of the time to various resorts etc. Went to town for a couple hours last night and what a town. Every building has a bar and all sorts of gambling and I do mean every one of them. Some are really hotels and stuff but they all have a bar and gambling machines. There is lots of money around and it is nothing to lose a couple thousand in a few minutes of gambling. Altogether Nevada is the poorest or I should say the least likable state I have seen. It is unofficial but I expect now to leave in a day or two for Michigan which doesn't make me feel bad at all. May go by plane so I might even beat this home although it is doubtful I'll get home this time. In the meantime you will find me swimming once every afternoon. Yesterday the commander of the WACs—a Captain from Iowa—married a Lt. pilot. She outranks him by two grades and is taller so he will probably get stepped on plenty. One of our new WAC radio operators is on the job now and is doing OK. You asked just what I do here???? Let's not ask embarrassing questions. To be real truthful I don't do much of anything. Just sort of a fixture so that if something went wrong or there was some decision to make then I would be here to absorb the shock. You don't understand the army and I guess no one does.

Later.

Was snagging passes in a little football practice this afternoon and a couple fellows asked me who I had played for. They said I was a natural football end and they told me to go to a big ten college and play. Guess I will probably try it—will probably play the end of the bench. Have been in strict training now for two years and another year would top it off. Felt rather flattered when they asked me where I got my shoulders! More fun.

Hot and dusty in August, the Las Vegas environs offered little in the way of recreation other than gambling. After more than a month in Nevada, Lyle was glad to be leaving for the cooler, greener clime of Michigan. Stretching travel time a bit, he stopped over at the family farm in South Dakota. Proceeding on, he jotted a note while switching trains in Chicago.

4 SEPTEMBER 1944 (MONDAY). Arrived in Chicago at 9:30 after a rather easy trip. Walked down toward the loop and saw the Chicago Exchange etc—guess I was in the main part. Chicago is a busy, cold, dirty city. My train leaves at 11:50 for Detroit arriving at 7:20 in the morning which will give me time to get settled. Mom played a trick on me—both apples had worms in the inside!—but the most of them was O.K. Met an Irish girl from Chicago on the way in. Better hunt up my train now.

DETROIT

Upon arriving at Selfridge Field, Lyle learned the origin of the base name. One September day in 1908, Orville Wright and Lieutenant Thomas J. Selfridge climbed aboard the Wright Brothers *Flyer 3* for a demonstration flight. After the engines were started by cranking the twin propellers, a catapult sent the flimsy machine down a monorail to gain airspeed. When one of the wooden propellers split and caught a wing guy wire, the plane tumbled a hundred and fifty feet to the ground. Orville Wright survived; Thomas Selfridge died of a fractured skull.

Lyle strolled the grounds of Selfridge Field, a permanent post with a golf course flanking the shore of Lake Saint Clair. He admired the brick buildings set among trees. The grass and the cool breeze off the lake contrasted sharply with the sand and summer heat of Nevada. He found the change exhilarating. And when he reunited with friends from cadet school, it seemed like old home week.

5 SEPTEMBER 1944 (TUESDAY). Just time for a note before going to a show here in downtown Detroit. It is raining a little and if it stops we will slip over to Canada for a few minutes. It's just a 3 minute ride *South* of here. The field is swell and about a dozen of the Wash. U. gang

showed up for the course as well as some others. Classes start tomorrow and the whole affair promises to be a picnic and thensome. The field is on the shore of Lake St. Clair and you can just barely see across it. The air is cool and crisp and it's fun to meet up with fellows you know. Came from Chicago with a car of Italian people who had spent a big weekend in Chicago. Tony had an accordion and they had some harmonicas so they really made music. Italians are happy-go-lucky. They really take care of us here in Detroit and don't even charge on streetcars. It's quite a ways from the field though. Guess we will go now.

On Wednesday, Lyle and the other officers, all with FBI clearance, began receiving instruction in codes, ciphers, secret cryptographic devices, and security procedures to prepare them to operate overseas message stations.

When the first week of classes ended at noon on Saturday, Lyle and three buddies, free to leave the base until Sunday evening, caught the first bus to Detroit. After exploring the downtown area and taking in a vaudeville show they gravitated to the Officers Club at the Tuller Hotel. Quite suddenly, they were invited to a wedding reception in another part of town.

The celebration was in full swing when the lieutenants entered the hall. The wine was flowing, the music was lively, and the girls were eager to dance. A lithe, vivacious bridesmaid accepted the invitation to jitterbug with a twenty-year-old army lieutenant.

Lyle and Beatrice danced and danced until the night grew late. When it was time for the party to break up, Beatrice escorted Lyle over to where her parents were seated.

"How will you get back to the base?" her father asked. "The buses don't run after midnight."

"You are welcome to come to our home for the night," interjected her mother.

The aroma of coffee and bacon awakened Lyle in the morning. While refilling his glass with milk, Beatrice's mother offered another breakfast roll and urged him to eat a second helping of bacon and eggs.

Following church service, Beatrice's father escorted his wife, daughter, and Lyle out to the car. Happily puffing on a big cigar, he chauffeured them on a tour of the city. They took a spin around Grosse Pointe. Then they sped over the Douglas MacArthur Bridge to Belle Isle. Late afternoon they dined at a café on Woodward Avenue.

At the end of the day, Beatrice's parents offered to drive Lyle back to Selfridge Field. Along the way there was some holding of hands in the backseat of the car.

As the Buick rolled to a stop at the field gate, Beatrice's mother invited Lyle to stay with them the following weekend. Beatrice whispered, "Please do, Lieutenant."

Sharing the weekend episode with his parents, Lyle joshed about being dressed in the attention-grabbing attire he had seen teenage boys wearing in Los Angeles.

10 SEPTEMBER 1944 (SUNDAY). Just back from a big weekend in Detroit. Was shooting pool at the Officers Club in Tuller Hotel sort of waiting for something to develop when one of the fellows dashed in and asked if we wanted to go to a wedding—and the next thing I knew we were in a car dashing across Detroit. It was really some powwow with at least a hundred people, lots of food and lots of liquor. I had on my reat pleat, with the drape shape, zoot suit, winter uniform—and of course I started flirting with the bridesmaids immediately. Then the dance started and I had just enough wine so it didn't take me long to learn to jitterbug and rumba etc. The dance lasted until 2:00 a.m. with time out for lunch at midnight. Everyone was very friendly and I had a good time—and monopolized the cutest bridesmaid and as long as I had no place to stay for the night, her parents invited me to their home. They are well enough fixed to have a new Buick 8 and a swell home in a nice residential section—and the mother was a Michigan farm girl and she fussed around a lot to get things just right for me—and cooked a big breakfast, etc etc etc. We all went to Catholic Mass at 12:00 and in the afternoon went driving in Detroit and over to Belle Isle in the Detroit River (pride of Detroit) which is a sort of large park like American Island in the Missouri River at Chamberlain and went to aquarium, flower gardens, toy motorboat racing etc. It was very pretty and huge ore boats go up and down the river. I've got a date for next Sat evening—but getting more convinced that the sooner I get back to St. Louis the better it will suit me. We had dinner at a restaurant before they turned me loose.

The other day we went to Windsor, Canada, and had supper over there. You would be surprised how much different the people and customs are for being just across the river. Went to a stage show featuring Lena Horne who sang her two famous songs, "Stormy Weather" and "Honeysuckle Rose," and also a couple other dog acts etc. Took a rumba lesson at the club and that's about it. They are not putting any pressure on us here at all—I'm glad they aren't. Seems like they just about cracked me up mentally at Yale and I'll never take things seriously like that again regardless. It wasn't worth the chips.

Say, I didn't really drink enough last night to affect me at all so don't be jumping to conclusions. We shot a roll of film this afternoon. Michigan is just a nice friendly place to be with its green countryside and blue lakes. Be sure and write and tell me how the work is coming and how the kids are getting along in school. I'm having a swell time here.

14 SEPTEMBER 1944 (THURSDAY). Don't know why I'm writing at all cause I don't know anything new. This morning we saw a demonstration of our incendiary and smoke bombs but otherwise it is lectures and some practical work in our line. Went to a show at the Post theatre last evening—a story about Gypsies but more like a cowboy show. This is an old army airfield—all well built brick buildings and somewhat like a little city—homes for permanent personnel too. Gee, my mail has sure been scarce lately—one from Irene yesterday. Guess I'm getting by with that little detour home but it doesn't seem likely that another one will be possible. I'll sure hate to go back to the desert. Just heard that a good friend of Seymour Johnson F. days washed out at Yale. He had almost a degree in Law. That Yale course didn't separate the men from the boys. Why don't you drop me a line and let me know what's doing. This is too soft—they even make our beds for us! But it won't last much longer. Enclosed $20.00.

It was evident the parents of Beatrice did not mind that their only daughter was keeping company with a soldier. On ensuing weekends, when traveling by streetcar was impractical, her father handed the keys to the new Buick 8 over to Lyle. Beatrice pointed the way as they wheeled the chic, two-toned vehicle about the city.

17 SEPTEMBER 1944 (SUNDAY). Back from another strenuous weekend in Detroit. Well, maybe not so strenuous but a lot of fun. Beatrice and I went to a show downtown (hour and half each way)—"Double Indemnity" and had a lunch afterwards etc. It was a very puzzling show and different than any previous. Her folks insisted on my staying at their place which didn't hurt my feelings any. Very ritzy house and they have plenty dough but are down to earth people and very friendly. And she is a good cook like Mom so I don't care if I eat again for a week. We had chicken for dinner. Beatrice is an only child and darn good looking and spoiled. Guess we will go dancing next Sat. evening. We may have some snaps to send you sometime. Well, I always have a place to hang my hat when in Detroit. Are you working on the cane yet? Too bad I'm not there cause a little exercise with the bundles wouldn't hurt me any. Got a teacher yet?

Lyle was aware teachers for rural schools were hard to find in the wartime economy and enrollment at the Conley School had dwindled. Still, he was surprised when he learned his mother had become the schoolmarm to Chuckie and three neighbor boys, Bobby, Buddy, and Mike. His father had moved a section of the original homestead dwelling to a site adjacent to the farmhouse to serve as their schoolroom. While thinking of the plum thicket in the lower woodlot and craving a plum-jelly sandwich, Lyle continued:

> Seemed to me that there should have been more than a bushel of plums down there. This course is pretty tame but interesting as I predicted. Less than 3 weeks left here now. Had a letter and some snapshots from Vernon the other day. I'll put in a bill to get rid of it—tell me when you get it. Went bowling the other evening and did good enough for a first time. It's a good game. Getting your quota of pheasants lately? They better watch out next time I come after them. Better not try to set records on that cane harvesting and take time to drop me a line.

> 25 SEPTEMBER 1944 (MONDAY). Been too busy having a good time even to write to you. Saturday night Beatrice and I double dated with another couple (friends of hers) and danced at the ballroom in the Graystone Hotel. Afterwards we went to another place to eat before going home. Had an awful lot of fun although my dancing is pretty poor.

While watching a movie, Lyle felt that Hollywood productions, heightened by special effects and beefed up by the generous use of literary license, gave a distorted view of the war. The actors were ten to twenty years too old, the dialogue was stereotyped, and only enemy soldiers got killed.

> Went to the show "Since You Went Away" and just got back. Don't know if I liked it or not. In fact it was kind of poor like most of Hollywood's attempts to dramatize the war. Sure gets cold here in Michigan nights. Every morning is like a corn picking morning. Surprised me that you got the cane done in such a hurry. Sometimes I wish they would make us do a day's work for a change. But I sure am thriving on this climate compared with Nevada.
>
> Back to the weekend again. I feel kind of like a bum practically living at their place every weekend but I date the daughter and they insist on my staying. Of course it is a couple hours at the best back to camp. So I sleep until I feel like getting up and then Mrs. R makes me eat huge quantities of bacon and eggs and rolls and always refills my milk before the glass is empty. And she thinks I don't eat enough even though I'm stuffed. We went to late church and then Mr. R and I drove across town to Briggs Stadium to the ball game—Detroit beat Boston in a good game full of home runs and everything. Our large cities are all the same—square miles of crooked streets—rows of tenement houses and blocks of old houses all exactly alike—and streets full of people who have probably never seen anything clean and spacious. Of course there

are nice homes and a better downtown section but I'm talking about the big majority. About 40 thousand in the ballpark—kind of nice to feel that you can get away from it when you want to. And then they had a big supper ready when we got back. Saw the Packard Plant and many other parts of Detroit.

Tuesday morning.

We had a little test this morning. Ted Hurst from Oklahoma is stationed at this field. He went to weather school from Wash U. Will look him up sometime. I'm enclosing a bill that I don't need now. Only one more weekend left here—will be glad to move on again. We get restless with such a soft time of it when we feel we should be overseas. Sooner we go the sooner we'll get back.

Fretting to go overseas, Lyle mirrored the frame of mind of most GIs, thinking the sooner they got the job done the sooner they could return to civilian status and a normal way of living.

Along with telling of a last date and weekend of hospitality before returning to Las Vegas, Lyle enclosed a photo of Beatrice.

1 OCTOBER 1944 (SUNDAY). Just back from Detroit. Another big weekend! As you can see by the picture there must be a manpower shortage in Detroit or I wouldn't be taking her around! Last night we went dancing at the Vanity Ballroom and had a nice time. It is a swell place. They don't come any nicer than this girl and Nevada will seem kind of dull. By the way don't send any more mail here cause I'm leaving. Saturday noon the Major ended his lecture by saying we were a good class—and let us scram until Monday again. So we took off in a hurry—trying to get to Ann Arbor for the Mich-Indiana football game. But transportation is so poor it took 2 hours to get to Mt. Clemens (world famous for mineral baths) so we didn't make it. So I went to the baseball game instead. Sunday afternoon Beatrice and I drove to Oakridge to the Shrine of the Little Flower built by Father Caughlin with stone etc from all over the world including a stone contributed by S. Dak. You have undoubtedly heard of it. We had a big chicken dinner with lemon pie. Oh yes, we had pie for breakfast too. As you have guessed I practically live there and run the place.

Got Dad's letter—they are singing "Goldmine in the Sky" on the radio now. Do you remember it? How come you aren't putting up cane and hay for the neighbors seeing as how you have so much spare time. Would like to be helping you but you folks seem to be getting the work done faster without me. Only please go a little easier on the corn picking. Did you raise any melons? It wouldn't really be like corn picking without a couple little melons and the shotgun along. Don't you worry about getting rid of your canned stuff Mom—we may all drop in on you one of these days and really clean up. Are you kidding Mom, about stopping over on the way back! The major spoke the other day about such stuff. And with my guilty conscience I thought he was looking at me. He made it sound very dangerous to stop even a day more than traveling time. They may find out some day I stopped home on the way here cause they check a lot of records but I doubt it. Don't ever say Yes or No if ever asked out there. Luckily I came on my own transportation so they can't trace that. But I'm sure it will be O.K. Plumb forgot Wilma's birthday. I remember the morning she was born. Did you go to the Corn Palace? You probably saw Vivian's parents if you did. Please send the one snap back. Maybe you will meet her someday. I'm glad to have a mom and dad that I'm proud to introduce my friends to. Guess I'll hit the sack now—away out here in Michigan.

When instruction at Selfridge Field came to an end, Lyle went to the railroad station for the return trip to Nevada. He was surprised and delighted when Beatrice and her parents showed up to see him off. After farewell embraces, there was a poignant moment and some tears as Beatrice whispered, "Till we meet again, Lieutenant."

LAS VEGAS

As with other soldiers, Lyle carried his sturdy GI shoes to the base repair shop whenever the leather soles wore out. In exchange, he was issued another pair of used shoes. Resoling millions of GI shoes required vast amounts of leather. By 1944 the United States faced a shortage of that vital commodity. Seeking to alleviate the leather problem, the Office of Price Administration (OPA) requested commanding officers to ease up on the dress code for shoes at army posts. Upon his return from Michigan to LVAAF, also known as McCarren Field, Lyle was surprised to find an unusual order:

> Due to the shoe shortage, the OPA requested, and the LVAAF headquarters approved officers and GIs wearing civilian shoes of various styles, both on the post and in town. Cowboy boots are okay, provided they don't have the fancy inlay tops, and provided the trousers are worn over, not in, the footgear.

9 OCTOBER 1944 (MONDAY). Already feel at home again way out here in McCarren Field, and it is still warm enough to wear suntans. Had a nice trip out here. Stopped about 3 hours in Chicago and saw everything around the loop including the Boston Store where Vernon worked while at Northwestern. Ate supper at Taffenettis. Got to Omaha at 7:30 and called Irene at her office at 8:00 a.m. She came down to the station and we visited for half an hour. The prettiest scenery I have seen was in northeastern Utah with its mountains and sunlit green valleys. Got out here to Las Vegas at midnight and was lucky enough to find an army truck at the station so they brought me to B.O.Q. for the rest of the night. Am already almost through getting settled including a desert fever shot etc. Reported into the adjutant and he recognized my name and asked me if I got the telegram. I shivered in my boots thinking of that little deal a month ago and said "no." He took me into legal claims and they produced my wallet with all pictures and papers. Only the cash missing. This fellow was a young flying officer my age from N.Y. He was dishonorably discharged and is serving 5 years. I'm going to get permission to see him but I guess there is nothing I could do to help him. Guess he got by pretty lucky considering the offense. But I still think the State of Nevada is equally guilty. Guess I'll finish getting settled today and go down to the radio station in the morning. This place is a letdown after Michigan. Am in a B.O.Q. right next to the swimming pool so that is handy. And I hope to leave before the end of the month. Enclosed $20 for a bond or something. Write right away and let me know what's cookin.

11 OCTOBER 1944 (WEDNESDAY). How goes it in South Dakota? Yesterday I took an overseas physical exam and sent it into Hdq. at Santa Monica. Maybe they will take the hint. Also am getting my shots out of the way. Not working too hard and plenty of time to swim and sun. Have lost weight since Yale so this soft life must not agree with me. The food is swell here compared with at Selfridge and actually costs less. Guess they were making a profit at Selfridge. At Salt Lake City a couple of us walked fast away from the station for 12 minutes and got as far as the Mormon Tabernacle—looked for a minute and walked fast back 12 minutes and just got back in time to catch the train. It has beautiful grounds and seems to be a group of buildings. The station in Salt Lake is quite a ways out from downtown. Had a nice trip and arrived in good shape. Got acquainted with a SPAR from Akron, Ohio, on the train. [SPAR, *Semper Paratus* Always Ready, a division for women serving in the Coast Guard].

There is some kind of a powwow at the Officers Club this evening. Didn't get any mail the last few days at Selfridge so it makes quite a stretch. Some of the fellows went from there to schools—Harvard, Washington and Lee University, etc. Guess I'll go eat supper now. Actually was partly cloudy here today. Still got my fingers crossed about that 5 days last month—guess it is alright though.

Still a fledging army officer, Lyle remained apprehensive about possible repercussions for an unauthorized stopover at home while en route to Michigan.

On his twenty-first birthday, Lyle wrote:

13 OCTOBER 1944 (FRIDAY). I've got a new roommate now—from New York—a Fordham graduate—so things are more lively. In a few minutes it will be time to go and get a couple more shots. Very surprised that no orders have come for me yet. Got the letter with snapshots a couple days ago along with one from Irene and a card with a couple bills from V and V. Irene sent me a hairbrush. Also a letter from Mom today—Don't you ever get done canning? Swanson boys must have been on their toes to pick off 4 pheasants. How did the tomatoes turn out— must have been pretty good. Are Vs going to get home from Harvard or are they just guessing? Probably won't be quite so convenient for them in a regular base. Wish you would send me the negatives of a couple of those snaps of me so I can have a couple reprints made to send to a couple of the fellows I write to. Nothing like getting pictures in the army. I'm getting quite a pile of pictures. Am going to buy a real good camera after the war. This is sort of a recreation-health camp as far as

I'm concerned. Lots of sleep, good clean air, and lots of physical training but of course it will get dull again after a month. Things are smooth at the station—a couple more WACs now too. Maybe there will be a cake for me tomorrow? Could skip out and go to Los Angeles some weekend but it's quite a long way to go. Nothing very exciting here—just nice and relaxing. You better take it easy too.

Later.

Got my shots. The one for typhus (not typhoid) kicked like a mule. Brought back memories of Miami Beach where we stood in long lines in the heat waiting for shots and the smell of vaccines was sickening. Some fellows would come out into the sun and promptly keel over. Some things are so absolutely pathetic in the army that they are funny—so you laugh them off and gripe and it keeps soldiers from going stark mad. Some can't laugh and do go off the beam.

Sheer logistics precluded the army from catering to the whims and fancies of individual soldiers; nevertheless, it amused Lyle when procedures were done by the numbers, such as switching from suntans to woolens on a prescribed day even if the temperature was ninety degrees outside. Having grown up in a large family, he took minor irritations in stride. By now he was resigned to the fact that there were three ways of doing things: the right way, the wrong way, and the army way.

Surmising AACS headquarters intended to mold him into a Cryptographic Security and Intelligence Officer, Lyle wrote:

15 OCTOBER 1944 (SUNDAY). Greetings. Really a nice day here in Nevada. Managed to get up in time for breakfast this morning and here is what I et—Two fried eggs with ham, two glasses of orange juice, glass of milk, box of grapenuts, toast and jam, and cup of cocoa. The meals here at BOQ mess are really good and very reasonable. Went to services at the chapel and then picked up our station's mail and came down here to the joint to see what was going on. You see we run continuous and so I just come down when I feel like it. There isn't too much else to do so I spend quite a little time down here. Makes it nice cause that way I get up when I feel like it and there is no set time to have to be anywhere. Once in a while I work one of the nets even though it really is not my job—I'm not supposed to be a qualified radio operator. We have a good bunch of fellows and three WACs and are one happy family. Won't tell you what but rather expect something is developing at headquarters for me and it is pretty good but so far it is just a guess in the dark. At least it sounds like a good deal. Got your forwarded letter of October 3 yesterday which was the first for quite a while. Glad to hear everything

is going good. Was a lucky break to get to talk to Irene in Omaha. Didn't have her telephone number but contacted the 11th floor WOW bldg and got her right away. Got any corn picked yet—guess you really must be hard up for work out there if Dad spends his time stemming blueberries. Wouldn't hurt me a bit to do a day's work once in a while even though I do get enough exercise swimming etc. Sort of miss the companionship that you have as an enlisted man and don't have as an officer. It is kind of stuffy always trying to keep up appearances and saluting all the time. You salute so much more as an officer cause there are so many more enlisted men than officers.

Yesterday I got permission to talk to that kid in jail and was rather surprised. Last time I was here I stayed in a BOQ with flying officers cause the permanent officer barracks was full. My schedule was so different from theirs that I never really got to know them at all. But one fellow I did get acquainted with though I didn't know his name. When I first found my billfold missing I happened to think that he had been swimming at the same time and had quit earlier. But at a time like that one mustn't jump to conclusions cause he is apt to suspect most anybody. Well it turned out that he is the fellow. He was friendly and as you might suspect seemed a little bewildered. He let me read the recording of the trial and he pleaded guilty to six specifications with full knowledge that it carried a maximum of life. He stole my billfold, forged my name, stole a billfold at another place at a later date and forged a check in another name etc. But they really gave him the advantage of the doubt with only five years cause one would have to assume that it was premeditated as long as he practiced the signature and also did the same thing at a later date. As had been brought out in the trial he had been drinking very heavy at the time or I should say period of time. He made no attempt to destroy the evidence, told me he didn't need the money, and agreed that he had done a very poor job of it. He had to have plenty on the ball to get through flying school so I'm sure it isn't that he just doesn't know what the score is. Guess maybe he sort of cracked up mentally—young and just commissioned an officer and more money than ever before, lot of spare time on his hands with nothing to do but drink and gamble. A sad case if you ask me. As far as the army is concerned there is nothing lower than a fellow who will steal from his barracks mates and especially an officer. Getting about time to go eat again and then a little swim after dinner. There is a golden-faun Great Dane dog here on the field who always likes to suntan with me. He weighs 180 lbs and built rangy so you see he is big as a horse and very playful only he plays kind of rough like a big bear. His name is Desperate and he is sort of an institution around here. The same blue sky and the continuous drone of planes around here. Bye now.

24 OCTOBER 1944 (TUESDAY). Last night it got cloudy here and an electrical storm came up and somehow shorted out the power from Boulder Dam so all the lights went out. Then the wind blew and we had a real sandstorm for a short time—and it actually rained a few days. This forenoon I went out to the range and fired the carbine and really did miserable—guess I'll try again soon. We have had quite a little business around the station lately—the Officer in Charge is on leave so there is more responsibility just now. My birthday cake came yesterday and is going fast. It's really good and stayed almost fresh out of the oven. Some canned tomatoes would go good with it. Got a letter from the girls yesterday too. Don't see how they pull down the grades while being in so many things and working at the same time. Vivian said they were planning on going to Florida. Did they make it home—I doubt it. No orders for me yet—guess maybe that month of school in Illinois was a wrong hunch. But surely they won't leave me here much longer. We are going to have a costume Halloween party Sat. evening here at the Club. Won't be too much though cause of the shortage of girls. I get up a little before sunrise each morning in order to make it to breakfast. But the catch is that the sun comes up behind a Mt. so it's really pretty late. Guess I'll go get in a game of pool now. Haven't been to the big-little city yet but can see the bright lights from here. And also the red lights of our transmitter antennae on the way to town. Bye now.

Due to personnel turnover at the AACS station, Lyle assumed more responsibility.

29 OCTOBER 1944 (SUNDAY). Last night we had a Halloween party at the Officers Club—a costume barn dance and it really was rare. Really amazing the variety of funny costumes—In fact the best I've seen and a big crowd too. I was a poor imitation of Lil Abner—Stuffed shoulders in fatigues and huge G.I. shoes. The walls are still standing this morning but the inside is a mess. Mostly officers wives, WAC officers and nurses and a few WASPs and etc. Met a girl—MaryAnn Somebody—she works here on the field and her brother is an officer. She is from Oklahoma. Anyway we sure did jitterbug and I have a heavy date for next Sat. Of course they will ship me out now that things are improving. Our niftiest WAC operator got back from furlough in Rhode Island today. Did I tell you I am now the "Officer in Charge" of this detachment so it is up to me to keep things clicking and keep Santa Monica off my neck. Have good personnel so everything is smooth so far. Put my name on a lot of stuff now and I go down some every day including a couple hours Sunday to keep track of things. Peggy's older sister, Jean, was married

last week in St. Louis or I should say University City. Went to a high school football game in Las Vegas the other evening with a couple of the fellows. Found the top two Registers and then found the bottom two after eating the cake! Got a letter from Irene this morning and one from Pips Coler. At best this isn't much more than just marking time out here although I do try to make as much as possible out of it. Have fun in P.T. etc and it certainly is a soft place. Am getting much stronger too right along. Finished all my shots now. What are you doing today. Don't be too surprised if I drop in before too long—never can tell. More later maybe. Be sure and write.

Praising the Air Corps for its stupendous achievement in training multitudes of personnel to operate and maintain some three hundred thousand aircraft around the globe, Lyle, in a particularly good mood, detailed his latest adventure.

4 NOVEMBER 1944 (SATURDAY). The field is really buzzing with activity this morning and I guess there will be a couple generals on the field sometime today. It is a cool cloudy morning for a change so you can walk without so much glare in the eyes. Everyone around here seems to be in pretty good spirits this morning. Yesterday afternoon this WAC radio operator and I decided to go for a plane ride so we found a Flying Fortress that would take us along—piloted by a couple of WASP flyers (women pilots not of army status). So we hopped in and fooled with the radio equipment while they warmed up the engines. After we took off we tuned up a transmitter and a receiver to a frequency of our station guards and called them in code. And right away they answered so we asked them for the weather for various parts of the country and shot the breeze with them. Was very agreeably surprised to be able to get the equipment going after having been away from it for 5 months. Rode in all parts of the plane—tail, radio compartment, pilots compartment, and up in the glass nose where there is glass under you, and all around you, and the earth nine thousand feet below. Almost as bad as being up on a windmill tower! The desert is really rugged around here with an occasional peak of eleven thousand feet. The field looked very nice with its lines of barracks and hangars and the neat rows of planes. We were up for three hours so were glad to get our feet planted on good solid ground again. Those girls do a good job of handling that huge plane with its thousands of controls and instruments. Really is unbelievable how the army keeps its thousands of planes in flying condition. The secret is that there are technicians for every part—engines, armament, turrets, electric system, oxygen system, radio equipment, hydraulic lines,

and precision instruments. It all makes up a team that is hard to beat. These planes are so much more complicated than one would realize.

Went to the show "An American Romance" last night and enjoyed it very much. Story of an immigrant who came to this country and made good in the steel industry. Have a date tonight but there is a catch to it cause my blouse is in the cleaners and they are closed today. Was going to get it yesterday afternoon but didn't get down in time. We heard from one of the officers who was here last August—he is in Egypt near Cairo. I am long overdue to leave this place so orders may come soon. Will be something like this—either to a school for a month in Illinois and then to a processing center, or direct from here to an overseas processing center, or maybe a delay en route in one or the other. So the Vs are in Florida now but how long will they be there? How is the corn turning out—as good as expected? May get a letter from you today with a few of the details. Guess that is about all and in fact maybe too much.

Grateful to be living in a democratic country, Lyle expressed his thoughts about the presidential election. FDR was running for a fourth term against republican Wendell Wilkie.

7 NOVEMBER 1944 (TUESDAY). Well the election returns are starting to come in. Guess it doesn't matter too much who wins—the important thing was that we could have an election in wartime with two names on the ballot. Vernon wrote from Florida and they seem to be doing O.K. Was afraid it would be so crowded that apt's would be scarce. Went out to the carbine range today and did lousy. Had expert on the 100 yd range but hit bottom on the 200 yd. Had the shots grouped but not on the bullseye. No excuse for that cause there are practice shots to see how the sights are. Was pleasant out in the open anyway cause we had a *rain* over the weekend. Not much but cooled things off and settled the dust. There is snow on Mt Charleston now and the clouds were hanging right on the peaks. Took a physical fitness test today and did O.K. Ran the 300 yd shuttle run in 49 sec., ten pull ups, and a hundred sit ups. Saturday night was a waste of time. Got to my date's apt. and there were two other couples there and a pt of whisky—so we killed the whisky the first thing. Then we went to Last Frontier and drank, and to the Nevada Biltmore and drank, and to the El Rancho Vegas and ditto. Never was so bored and disgusted before. You know how it is—they naturally assumed I had come to drink and so I strung along and drank a little too and left as quickly as possible. Guess it wouldn't have been right to be in Nevada and not live as the Nevadans do for at least an evening. What goes in S.D. Do the girls get home weekends? Got the

Register yesterday. Hope you are busier than I am. Just keep digging up as much excitement as possible to keep busy. Have been reading a little—amateur photography, weather etc. You should see my awful G.I. haircut. They call me burrhead. May drop in on you one of these days—a chance anyway.

A month after returning to Las Vegas from Detroit, Lyle was pleased when the order came to proceed to Chanute Field near Champaign-Urbana, Illinois, for a month-long course in cryptography.

SALT LAKE CITY

12 NOVEMBER 1944 (SUNDAY). Boarded the train Sat. evening at Las Vegas and slept the clock around and woke up in Salt Lake. Had breakfast at the station there. The scenery is beautiful in Utah—All snowcapped Mts with green valleys and lots of thrifty farms and good stock. Will get to Omaha Monday eve and will stay over at least a day with Irene. Then on to Chicago and down to Chanute Field (Rantoul, Illinois). Will sign in there and then hope to go to St. Louis for a day or two before things start cookin in that cryptographic course. Will be there a month and then back to Nevada unless they change my orders. It's a very pleasant trip so far. Couldn't quite see the way clear to come to S. Dak this time cause of several reasons. Lose so much time too cause of the poor connections. Am sticking my neck way out as it is. When I travel now it is not miles but days of distance. But it is fun to keep on the move. And of course nothing could be better than Chanute cause it's near St. Louis. Any snow in S.D. yet? Sure would like to stop around there. You can write to that outside address and it will get to me. Guess I'll stroll around the town a little now.

OMAHA

15 NOVEMBER 1944 (WEDNESDAY). Greetings from Omaha. Irene is cooking some liver and onions for supper and also baked some chocolate chip cookies. My train leaves at 7:30 for Chicago and gets there early in the morning. Then I change trains for Rantoul, Ill. Will sign in there and try to take off for the weekend in St. Louis! Classes start Monday and the course will be interesting. Got here Monday evening and managed to get to Irene's apartment on a streetcar. Was sure glad to get off the train even though the trip was pleasant. Lots of women and young kids on my car and in that long of a trip you find out why the third child's middle name is Cornelious and how often little Susie has

stomach trouble. Irene and I went to a show, Bob Hope in "Princess and the Pirate" which was killing. Went bowling yesterday afternoon and cooked steaks for supper. This noon we had dinner at Paxton Hotel. Sure was a lucky break to get back here to the Midwest. Irene says she is going home at Christmas. Looks like I'll have to head straight back to Las Vegas. But boy St Louis here I come. Irene has it very nice here—nice job and good living conditions. She is looking very chic and healthy. It is cool in Omaha. Hope things are going good at home. But I know they are except probably too much work. But you folks thrive on work so no sympathy from me. Bye now and love from apartment 701.

Lyle signed in a day early at Chanute Field. Anticipating a visit with Peggy, he hopped a city bus into Champaign-Urbana and transferred to a crowded Greyhound for the trip to St. Louis.

ST. LOUIS

A year had elapsed since Lyle had departed Washington University for Seymour Johnson Field. His return to St. Louis came on a chilly, gray November day. On the long ride out to University City, what had once seemed an enchanted place now appeared to be just another noisy, sooty urban area through the window of the streetcar. Stepping off the car, he hiked briskly along Yale Street to 797 and rapped on the door.

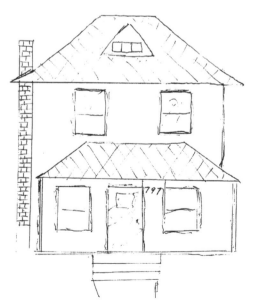

SKETCH OF PEGGY'S HOME, UNIVERSITY CITY, MISSOURI, 1944

Peggy and her mother warmly greeted Lyle. Over coffee and cookies, he expressed how much he had enjoyed Thanksgiving dinner at their home the previous November.

As they strolled about a neighborhood park, Lyle and Peggy shared events of the past twelve months. Now enrolled at Washington University and aspiring for a career on the stage, Peggy was enthused about her dramatic arts classes. Lyle, a soldier, had no definite plans for the future.

The enjoyable afternoon came to an abrupt end when Lyle apologetically made a hasty exit. Due at Chanute Field early in the morning, he had stretched the visit with Peggy longer than intended. On the streetcar ride back to the station, he worried that all the bus seats would be sold out.

For lack of a camera, Lyle sketched an image of Peggy's home as the Greyhound bus wound its way out of St. Louis and gathered speed on the open road. Though the interlude was brief and parting for a second time bittersweet, he was glad to have made the sentimental journey.

CHAMPAIGN-URBANA

Chanute Field, a large permanent post named after an early aviation pioneer, seemed drab to Lyle, perhaps because it was the winter season. He joined other officers with FBI clearance for in-depth training in cryptographic security. Already familiar with the rudiments of cryptography and message station management, they were at Chanute to learn coding techniques designed to make it difficult for the enemy to break messages and procedures for safeguarding cryptographic material. Since the Army Airways Communications System (AACS) operated a global network, compromise of security at a single station jeopardized cryptographic security throughout the entire world.

One evening, on stationery bearing U.S. ARMY AIR FORCES in blue ink and a picture of a B-17 bomber superimposed in faded blue clouds, Lyle wrote:

28 NOVEMBER 1944 (TUESDAY). Well cryptography hasn't driven us completely off the beam yet. We are a third through the course now and breezing right along. To get too low a grade here would hold up promotions so we work fairly hard and the stuff is interesting and maddening. Got a letter from Vernon and we will leave the same day

for the West Coast but I doubt if I'll get to stop at home although they haven't said "no" yet. Would be too lucky to get ten days at Christmas. I'm counting on not getting it so as to not be disappointed. If only they OK my delay en route. Am still surprised at getting by with the last couple deals. But they still could get me. Any snow out there yet? All it does here is blow and rain. Sat. eve a bunch of us went to a party at the U. but weren't impressed. Guess I'll go to a mixer dance at the Union or else to Chicago this weekend. The Union Bldg at the U. of Ill is not as nice as S.D. State's. In fact, SD State is the best college I've seen although I wouldn't want to go back there cause all of the old gang would be gone. Am studying a biology book and learning a little shorthand now. It's fascinating writing shorthand. Saw some boxing last evening and one was a knockout—just one blow laid him cold. This fellow just let him keep swinging and waited for an opening. Is everyone peppy at home? I can't seem to get sick anymore. Guess getting in the army was the best thing I ever did cause it sure has helped me out. The next best thing will be to get out of it cause we have had enough. This is definitely my last training—when did I say that before. Mom, you better get some tomato soup and roasted vegetables ready just in case. I'll furnish the duck. Pretty quiet around the barracks tonight. Drone of planes once in a while cause we are right on the end of one landing strip. Everything is swell here. Goodnight now.

Those officers who successfully completed the training at Chanute Field would be classified as Cryptographic Security and Intelligence Officers; the others would retain their former status. Lyle anticipated the personal freedom inherent in running a cryptographic station. Code rooms had double sets of locked doors, no windows, and only cryptographic personnel with FBI clearance could enter that private domain. He enjoyed the puzzle-solving elements and the need for creativity and mature judgment.

When the day's instruction ended, the officers were free to sign out and leave the base; Sunday provided additional free time. The University of Illinois became the center of the social scene for Lyle and his buddies. They caught the bus to the Champaign-Urbana campus where they soon became acquainted with coeds.

6 DECEMBER 1944 (WEDNESDAY). Got your letter today and at least you aren't snowbound yet. Am surprised that Vernon is going to Minnesota. They will be chilly for a while cause there is an awful difference between S. Florida and Minn. Expect to hear this week regarding my delay en route—will go west from here the 16th so can squeeze a day or two somewhere on the way. I guess a couple of the

fellows washed out of the course here. This leaning over a desk most of the day digging around in jumbled up letters and numbers doesn't appeal to me. And this job will be very touchy to handle. Got exactly in the middle of my class for grades so far. Never can get out of the average rut but who cares. These fellows are alright—most of them are pretty smart scholastically and rather studious. Not much imagination or practical ability in some things. But they sure make me look sick in books. One of the fellows fractured an arm in P.T. the other day but he is up and around. Did I tell you last Sat eve I went to a basketball game at the U.—Chanute Field vs U of Illinois. They beat Chanute pretty bad but it was a good game. Went to a dance at the Union afterwards and then spent a lot of time waiting for a bus to get home. We lead a hard life—if only we knew enough to stick to the barracks and take it easy instead of chasing around in taxicabs and buses in strange cities. It's at least a mile to even get to the gate to wait for a bus. We are going bowling and dancing Sat evening instead of to the Junior Prom cause my date couldn't get her formal from Chicago. It's more like old times here living in an open barracks etc. Last night a Chinese-American Lt and I broke a newspaper cryptogram to be doing something. He is from California. Only one poor defenseless popcorn ball remains from that swell box. Those cookies were the best ever and the candy couldn't be beat. It came off the wax paper easily. Thanks, Mom. They must put vitamins in coffee now days for Mom to get everything done and make candy besides. Got a package from V and V to not be opened until Christmas. This place is really deserted this evening. Mom, you said something about sending that Detroit picture back but it wasn't in that letter. I don't want it but was wondering if you sent it and it got lost or what. In Nov 27 Life magazine is a story on "Clifton's"—that beautiful cafeteria in Los Angeles where I ate once. Really not much doing here except the usual routine. Will drop you a line if the delay en route should come through. So hold down the fort.

11 DECEMBER 1944 (MONDAY). Just got back from the show "Meet Me In St. Louis," and liked it very much. A story about the Louisiana Exposition of 1904. We have 9 inches of snow and icicles all over but not very cold. Bet you got some in South Dakota too. Had a big weekend again. Friday night was the Junior Prom complete with a blonde senior, corsages, and a good orchestra. Had a very nice time and got back at 3: 00 so was really a dull tool in Saturday classes. Then Saturday night a date with this other coed bowling, dancing, and billiards. She beat me in one line of bowling but my 125 took the other. And some evening this week maybe a date with the other one again cause she is definitely

interesting. Boy how the money goes! Always good to get back to Nevada and catch up on sleep and dough again. Still no answer to my letter to H.Q. but I'll probably wire if they don't answer in a day or two. Am leaving this week you know. Would like to stay here a little longer. We got grades again Saturday—I now stand a little below average in the class but am confident I can do the work.

One of the fellows is reading an excerpt from a letter from his girl— it seems he casually asked her if she had any particular dislikes as to the kind of engagement ring. She came back saying she visited a jeweler and found just the thing—a 1 karat $700 ring, and boy he sure is going to tell her a thing or two. He couldn't raise that if he hocked everything. That wealthy girl—poor boy stuff isn't so good.

Will kind of hurt to sail right past home again but I sure have no kick a coming. Will stop in Omaha a day if it works out. I'll enclose the Chamberlain High School clipping that came in the Register from Irene today. Wilma has one of her usual *intelligent* answers in it. Guess I'll practice a little shorthand now and then into those woolen blankets. Certainly a soft life here—maybe too soft. We should trade for a while. Goodnight now.

Having marched to the martial music of Glenn Miller at TS Yale, Lyle was saddened when he heard a news report that the renowned bandleader had disappeared while on a flight over the English Channel.

After nearly two years in the army, Lyle anticipated shipping overseas. He yearned to spend Christmas at home but was still waiting for a reply to his request for a delay en route on his return trip to Nevada. At the depot, he opted for a route through South Dakota.

HOME FOR CHRISTMAS

Remembering a lonely Christmas spent in North Carolina the previous year, Lyle made his way home. Setting aside army cares he slept late, played checkers, and chopped wood for the stove. When questioned about his work in cryptography he was vague and noncommittal, as instructed at Chanute Field, but talked freely about his recent social life at the University of Illinois. Other than indicating he expected an overseas assignment in the near future, he was unable to satisfy his mother's inquiries regarding his prospective military role. He savored his favorite dishes—a pot of roast beef with vegetables, tomato soup, and custard made from home-canned pumpkin. Hoping for a pheasant feed he tramped through snow-laden fields with a twelve-gauge shotgun. Returning after a successful hunt, he showed off the game to his sisters.

LYLE SLADEK, FAMILY FARM, 1944
PHEASANT HUNTING DURING CHRISTMAS FURLOUGH

JEAN SLADEK, FAMILY FARM, 1944

VIRGINIA SLADEK AND LYLE SLADEK, FAMILY FARM, 1944

WILMA, VIRGINIA, IRENE, AND JEAN SLADEK, FAMILY FARM, 1944

JEAN SLADEK, FAMILY FARM, 1944

LAS VEGAS

On the trip back to Las Vegas, Lyle narrowly escaped a serious train wreck. Using stationery he had squirreled away from The Roosevelt in New York City, he wrote:

1 JANUARY 1945 (MONDAY). Stepped off the train in Las Vegas at midnight just as the people were ushering in the New Year and it sounded like a civil war was on. Got to Omaha in good shape and found out they couldn't get me a reservation on that train so I went to Irene's apt. They called me and said I could go on the Challenger in the morning so I stayed at a hotel for the night. Irene fixed supper and then we went to the show, "Our Hearts Were Young and Gay." The next night I got to Cheyenne, Wyoming, and hit Ogden, Utah, Sunday morning. Heard that the train just ahead of us—the San Francisco Challenger cracked up pretty seriously. Got on the field very smoothly and am already quietly established. A general just walked into the club here! Hope he stays a long way from me! The sun is shining brightly and it is only a little bit cool here. My roommate from N.Y. is still here so my footlocker was still in his room. He is away on a troop train now. Was a good thing I had that food along cause this train seldom stopped. Will enjoy it out here for a while again cause this is a nice field in some ways. Found a couple letters waiting when I got here and most of the gang is still at the station. Will toss this in the box so you'll know I got back here O.K. and feeling good.

Shortly, Lyle received orders to report to Sheppard Field near Wichita Falls, Texas. The five months stationed at Las Vegas had been an ideal venue for honing his communications skills and learning to conduct himself as an officer. After two years of military, physical, academic, and cryptographic training, the army deemed him well groomed for an overseas project.

CHAPTER 13

Don't Fence Me In

Oh, give me land, lots of land under starry skies above,
Don't fence me in.
Let me ride through the wide open country that I love,
Don't fence me in.
Let me be by myself in the evenin' breeze,
And listen to the murmur of the cottonwood trees,
Send me off forever but I ask you please,
Don't fence me in.

—COLE PORTER

AFTER TWO NIGHTS IN A DAY COACH while en route from Las Vegas to Wichita Falls, Lyle decided to lay over in Albuquerque. He entered a hotel near the railroad station and joined a line of civilians and soldiers waiting to speak to the desk clerk. When he finally reached the counter and asked for a room, the clerk merely shrugged and pointed to a NO VACANCY sign. Disappointed, Lyle turned to pick up his flight bag—only to find it missing. Someone had carried off his luggage! When the Albuquerque police recovered his bag, all of the valuables and personal effects were missing, including a silver identification bracelet and a priceless stack of photographs.

Chagrined, tired, and hungry, Lyle proceeded on to Texas with just the clothes on his back and an empty bag. Upon arrival at Sheppard Field he signed in and settled into a BOQ, glad to be off the road.

The huge base, a permanent post that sported a bowling alley, assembled *projects* for overseas deployment. But due to wartime secrecy, Lyle was not privy to the nature or destination of his project. Once again, he waited for army brass to grind out his fate.

13 JANUARY 1945 (SATURDAY). Still sweating it out in Texas. Guess everyone in the Air Corps eventually ends up in Texas for a stretch. But I kind of like it here cause the climate is perfect and they certainly don't work us too hard. Today I was roped in on being a Pay Officer. We paid a large group of soldiers so we handled several thousand dollars from large bills to pennies. And when we paid the last man it came out exactly to the penny. Of course it was out of our pockets if it didn't so we were rather careful. Looks like it will be a month or more before I get out of here cause they have to decide where to send me etc. But if I get discouraged I just look out the back window at the guardhouse where the prisoners are fenced in. I always say a fellow is alright if he stays out of the guardhouse cause that is really a dog's life. One of the fellows in the barracks has a radio he built. It looks like a pile of junk but is really a good one. Still no mail. Had better be a letter from home in a day or two. The war news sounds pretty good just now. Two evenings a week I go to Spanish and photography classes in one of the buildings. Play basketball, horseshoes, football, volleyball, eat, and sleep. It's a rough life alright. Bowled a couple lines this evening and saw a poor basketball game in which Sheppard Field got beat. Enclosed a bond and a ten spot. Where is Vernon now? If I were to walk toward the North Star I would hit very close to home. I'm a long way south of you though. Guess I'll go to bed now.

Sunday evening.

Had a rather pleasant Sunday. Got up at 9:00 and had a light breakfast and 3 of us went to town to a Methodist church. It seats 1700 people and the pastor is very sharp and witty. And a Texas accent of course. Then we went to the Officers Club cafeteria and had pork steak, milk, pie, carrot salad etc. Played horseshoes and football a little while this afternoon. Am going to Dallas next weekend. What are you folks doing.

On OFFICERS MESS stationery, gooey and sticky from food spills, Lyle wrote:

17 JANUARY 1945 (WEDNESDAY). It rained today and sure is gooey out here. The soil is sort of reddish gumbo and sticks to your shoes. Saw a pretty good show tonight, "Can't Help Singing," in Technicolor with nice scenery and music. But at times it was corney and they sure whoop it up at times in a G.I. theatre when it is obviously fake stuff. Some of the fellows are shipping out tomorrow for points unknown. They are glad to get out of here. They don't keep us busy and to let soldiers be idle is the worst thing they can do. Better to make us dig ditches and fill them in again. One of my friends may get me a date for Friday eve with a sister

of the girl he met last weekend. Guess I'll go to Dallas this weekend. May hitchhike with someone. It's three or four hours away. All your letters caught up with me at different times. How did Dad get the impression I was going the south route? You go straight west from Omaha to Ogden, Utah. This is really enjoyable here at least until you have been here too long. I could sure go for that supper Wilma described. Chuckie, have you been training your dog any? Can't see how a battery would ever give up all of a sudden. Was it broken or froze or maybe just run down? Can't understand how it could get ruined all at once. A nice Christmas card from Beatrice and her parents in Detroit caught up with me today after chasing me all over the country. They are swell people. Am surprised and etc that they didn't approve that 5 day extension. No repercussions from stretching it a little though. Got in just after midnight but signed in as of before midnight so as to cut the days down by one.

Upon earning a commission Lyle felt a keen sense of accomplishment, yet he recognized that luck and circumstance had played a significant role in his achievement. Cognizant that army personnel of all ranks would be lumped together as veterans in postwar America, he pontificated that officers were merely juiced-up citizens clad in brassy uniforms for the duration.

I sort of lead a charmed life by the breaks I've been getting right along. One of the original fellows of Wash U. is here too and most of us were in Yale at one time or another. Don't ever make the mistake of judging a serviceman by his rank. I'm not a bit proud of mine and less and less so. Really doesn't mean a thing as to ability or character or anything. Nice to have the extra privileges though. I hope we all get set for the letdown we'll get when this thing blows. This field is kind of stuffy. You can't walk a half block without saluting or getting saluted a dozen times. And rows of big barracks as far as you can see to the top of a little hill. And of course a high fence around. It's O.K. if they don't fence me in on weekends. Irene was lucky to go to Denver but she should have stayed longer.

We have a basketball game at 1:00—just a bunch of us amateur players but fun. Should get some mail today too.

Lyle confirmed that standing alongside a road with a thumb turned out was the fastest way for a man in uniform to get from one city to another. Usually the first car with an empty seat stopped.

20 JANUARY 1945 (SATURDAY). Greetings from downtown Dallas fifth floor of second largest hotel. We hitchhiked over here Friday afternoon and had good luck. It's only about 150 miles from Sheppard

Field. This seems to be a pretty nice city but so far we haven't had any particular fun. Last night we went roller skating after having supper. Prices are sky high here for some reason or other. The skating rink is out at the park where the Dallas Exposition was held a few years ago. The Cotton Bowl is also there. This is a busy town with crowded sidewalks and full hotels. But there are no Officer Club facilities so it really isn't so hot in some ways. Doubt if I'll come back here again. It rained a little this afternoon so that didn't help matters any either. Saw a little more of Texas on the way down here. Mostly ranch country and a little cotton with mosquite bushes and persimmon trees. These cities are all alike. Sure hope Virginia's ear is alright by now.

Monday.

Got your card today and a bunch of Christmas cards and letters caught up with me. We had fun hitchhiking back. Got on the wrong road and found ourselves on the way to Ft Worth. Caught rides with interesting people. One car had a daughter just out of finishing school but she was too short for me to date. Guess maybe the convertible car would go with it! Spent a lot and had a poor time in Dallas. May go to Tinker Field at Oklahoma City this weekend. Hitchhike of course cause that is fun. Last night some firebug set fire inside four of the chapels on the field here. Guess he ran out of matches cause there are several other post chapels. Did a lot of damage inside all of them and caused lots of commotion in the night. Went to Spanish and photography classes again tonight and learned a little. Played basketball this afternoon with an officers P.T. class and one asked me to play on their section team tomorrow night. Boy Mom, that mincemeat sounds good. Food in the cities is really terrible now days. You can't imagine. Pay two dollars and still not get much of a meal. Still no news about moving out of here. May be a month yet. I refuse to fret about it cause this is fun. It's really time for lights to go out in this barracks. My Chinese friend got here today. Guess I'll finish this in the morning.

Tuesday.

Last night one fellow insisted on leaving his light on after the rest of the barracks wanted to sleep so we took his lightbulb out and took his bed apart in small pieces. Once in a while someone has to learn the hard way. Got your letter and snapshots today. Have to do some processing tomorrow morning.

Following a week of filling out forms and taking shots in preparation for an overseas project, Lyle took to the open road again. Upon returning from the weekend jaunt, he learned his cousin Jimmy Sladek was missing in action in Europe.

By November 1944, five months after the Normandy invasion, Allied forces had advanced across France and the Low Countries and were poised to carry the ground war to German soil. With Russian forces advancing toward Germany on the Eastern Front, Germany appeared to be on the verge of collapse. Sensing victory, some American troops were speculating, hoping, that the war in Europe would be over by Christmas.

Hitler was aware that Germany could not afford a war of attrition; the supremacy of the Allies in manpower and in the production of armaments was too great. Unless he could find a way to alter the course of the war, Germany was doomed to defeat. Hitler ordered his generals to plan a surprise offensive with the aim of driving a wedge through Allied lines and retaking the Port of Antwerp. He projected the offensive would disrupt Allied plans, buy time to develop new weapons, and lead to a stalemate in the war.

The surprise German move, aided by a severe winter storm, succeeded in breaking through Allied positions in the Ardennes. The Allied lines gave way, or bulged, and thousands of American GIs were killed or captured during the onslaught. After the initial confusion, resistance stiffened, the weather cleared, and the Allies overwhelming air superiority turned the tide. Hitler's gamble to take Antwerp failed. The desperate struggle of December 1944, later termed the *Battle of the Bulge*, ended the delusion of German leaders that they could win the war.

With his usual optimistic outlook, Lyle replied to the worrisome news about his cousin.

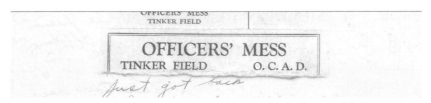

OFFICERS' MESS
TINKER FIELD

OFFICERS' MESS
TINKER FIELD   O. C. A. D.

Just got back

29 JANUARY 1945 (MONDAY). Just got back from Oklahoma City and got a big batch of mail—two Registers, letter from Vivian, you, the girls, a girl in Champaign, a friend in Kansas, business letter, and a letter from Irene. Was sorry to hear the news about Jimmy but he still may be alright as you know a lot were captured in the German drive. The news is better now in Europe and maybe it will end. Guess you are having sloppy weather like we are but you don't know what mud is until you come to Texas. Really gooey and doesn't dry up. Hope you don't have too much trouble keeping up with work around there. Of course that beefsteak should give you lots of pep. Last Friday this Chinese officer friend of mine hitchhiked with me to Oklahoma city which is in central

Okla. We had phenomenal luck averaging forty-five miles per hour and it was a beautiful day so we enjoyed it. Went out to Tinker Field which is several miles out of town and got a room at the visiting Officers Club Quarters and ate at the Officers Club. They had delicious meals there. We went to an Operetta, "The Gypsy Baron," at the Municipal Building. It was good even if the critics didn't like it. Also went to a couple dances and a Symphony concert etc and came back today "Monday" which was stretching our stay past the limit. Had a good time but didn't meet anyone to rave about. The amazing thing about the city is that people have oil wells in their backyards instead of flowers. There actually are more big oil derricks in the city than trees! And we were lucky hitching back too. May go back next weekend if I don't ship out soon. A couple of us wanted to go to Mexico City but there are too many border complications. My Spanish class meets tonight again. It is fun but I'm not learning very fast. Seems like most of the fellows have shipped out. One of the fellows just told me my sisters were cute. I agreed with him. I'll send that fifty dollar bond home one of these times.

Heard that they put me on a project now which means they know where they want to send me. Bet it's over a month yet before I see water. Guess you know by now too that Vernon will likely put out to sea soon. Will be disappointed if he beats me out of the country.

Having learned Vernon was being transferred to a naval facility at Long Beach, California, Lyle assumed his brother was destined for sea duty. He was glad when more details about the Vs arrived, along with a special package of baked goodies from his mother.

9 FEBRUARY 1945 (FRIDAY). Was sure glad to get your letter this morning with all the news. Vernon was lucky to get to stop at home. Guess they are in Calif by now. Guess I'll ship out from the east coast. And thanks a million Mom for the box. Guess those filled cookies were the best ever. My bunk mates went for them in a big way too. The orange nut filled ones were really delicious only they didn't last long enough. We live in ordinary big barracks here and eat in a G.I. mess hall which doesn't compare with home cooking. There are lots of rumors going around about my project as to where we are going, when, and how. But I won't pass them on to you cause if they are true they shouldn't be told and if they aren't then it doesn't do any good to tell them anyway. I'm very anxious to go cause when I get there I can start figuring out a way to get back. And I do want to get back in a hurry. In fact I plan to start flying lessons tomorrow to get interested in something so as not to fret

here. Also take a good workout each day. My basketball may be good enough for a college team someday. Didn't go any place today cause I'm just staying here this weekend and taking it easy. Took a couple booster shots today—take them every year for some diseases. Want to be all full of everything before going overseas. Went to a dance etc at the Officers Club last night. When I get out of Texas they can put that big fence around it cause I don't ever care to come back. The climate is beautiful in winter though. Warm and balmy for shirtsleeves today. I'll enclose a snapshot of the girl I took to the Junior Prom etc at U. of Illinois. Blonde, interesting, and from a fruit farm in southern Ill. Wasn't doing so bad there was I but sort of missed the boat. Also hear from the other one there. The shorter girl is her roommate and also a senior. She will likely marry my Chinese friend after the war and it is a very good match. Got a letter from Irene and the Registers today also. Sure would like to be home instead of passing time around here. How does Dad get roped in on all of those parties? I sure do a lot of chasing around just to keep the ball rolling and not mope around wishing I were someplace else. Just got talked into a bridge game.

In retrospect, Lyle realized opting for communications cadet over aircrew had been a fortuitous choice. Whereas he had achieved a commission, his Washington University buddies assigned to aircrew had yet to see the inside of a plane. Apparently the Air Corps had overestimated the need for pilots and other flight personnel. Still intrigued by the thought of becoming a *hot pilot*—one of the glamour boys—he wandered over to a small airfield near the base and inquired about flying lessons.

Saturday morning.
Got up for breakfast and walked clear across the camp to the dental clinic and had my teeth checked. All O.K. and wisdom teeth alright too. Also made arrangements to start flying Monday. Will get in about 5 hours which isn't quite enough for a license. It's real windy here today. About time for dinner now. What are you having to eat? Another troop train went out with some of my friends. I stay here forever. Can't complain though. Did the cane freeze down yet? Hope you aren't getting as lazy as me. Will put in a bill that I don't need. Bye now for a while.

Lyle was careful to adhere to military protocol, such as saluting high-ranking officers passing by in staff cars. Early on in his army career he had learned a humorous dictum: "If it moves, salute it; if it doesn't move, pick it up; and if you can't pick it up, paint it."

16 FEBRUARY 1945 (FRIDAY). Just got your letter and might as well answer it. No, I'm not going to Okie City this weekend. Have got a date for the Sat. night dance at the Club with Doris. She goes to Junior College here and lives in Wichita Falls. Also took her to the play, "Abie's Irish Rose," last Monday evening. It first hit broadway in 1922 and has been going ever since. It was very funny. Was sure glad to get those clippings. What I wouldn't give to drop in on the Senior Ball cause I know all those kids. Can't see how some of the fellows stayed out of the army. The war sure has taken a good turn the last couple days. Maybe the Axis will quit soon. Our project still isn't too warm so we may be here at least a week more. It is pretty bad around this field just now. Sort of a purge on about saluting etc. I was sure glad I saluted a staff car yesterday. It turned out to be a full colonel in it and he sure looked eager. Haven't gotten into any trouble yet. It is over done here. We sure have beautiful weather here. Am getting my suntan back. Play lots of basketball in P.T. We had a P.T. test the other day. My stomach muscles are sore yet. Always get in the very good class which doesn't mean too much. Yes, I'm at least partially a hot pilot now. Have been taking a lesson about every day. Yesterday I took off (was glad the instructor was along) and we flew for over an hour. It was really rough and I had to fight the controls all the time. Flying in these little cubs is like flying on a paper kite after riding the big bombers. I feel a little safer in these planes than in an automobile. In good weather they fly themselves and you can easily land them even when the motor stops. But you sure have to be on your toes to keep enough air speed, go straight, keep proper altitude, watch out for other planes etc. It is a lot of fun and someday I'm going to get a pilot's license. There is too low a ceiling to fly this afternoon. At least it is something interesting to do here. And it is cheaper than most places and more convenient. Was surprised to hear the creek ran so early. Guess that makes the work a little harder though when you can't cross the creek. Wish I could help with the work instead of loafing here but the army says no.

May go to the show this evening here on the post and maybe play bridge afterwards. I had a card from Vernon from his new address in California. They sure are lucky to get a deal like that. But it would be better for me overseas. Where did Raymond Sharping end up or hasn't he gone yet?

Guess I'd better get this in the mail now. And I owe lots of letters now too. Hold down the Fort everybody.

While families were doing their part on the home front, marines were engaged in seizing a strategic island located halfway between Tokyo and the Marianas. The Japanese, realizing an American air base on Iwo Jima would enable fighter planes to escort B-29 bombers all the way to their homeland, fought desperately to hold the island. Fighting from underground fortifications, each Japanese defender was charged with killing ten American invaders before dying himself. Japanese leaders hoped that by inflicting severe casualties, the United States would be deterred from launching further ground attacks on Japanese territory.

On 23 February 1945, triumphant marines planted an American flag on Mount Suribachi, the highest peak on Iwo Jima. News of the event, augmented by a stunning photograph, received immense fanfare on the home front. But it would be late March, after suffering heavy losses, before the Allies would succeed in capturing Iwo Jima and making the island an "unsinkable aircraft carrier" in the Pacific.

Aware of the passage of time, Lyle was thinking of the spring season back home on the farm.

23 FEBRUARY 1945 (FRIDAY). Well, here it is in the third year of army life for me. In less than a year I'll draw longevity pay but I hope to be out before then but likely won't. And it is the third spring too. Mom will get baby chicks too early and plant the garden too late. And you, Dad, will plant some wheat even if it hasn't paid out for several years.

The first two years certainly had their ups and downs but altogether things have been pretty swell. The most important thing was to come in with a good attitude instead of with a chip on the shoulder. And second to have good times and learn things instead of wasting time to be regretted later. One thing we all seem to have a hard time learning is to forget about always wanting to ship out of a field cause one place is about as good as another. We had about 4 days of rain and this place really got gooey. But now the weather is good again so I have gotten in more flying. Sometimes it seems very easy and other times it takes lots of effort. If the air is smooth and very little wind it is easier than driving a car. But landing in gusty wind is difficult and also taking off. The other day we did stalls. In a power off stall you shut off the throttle and point the nose up. Your speed decreases so you lose control of the plane. Then it breaks in the air so you put the nose down and gun the motor and pull out of the dive when you have enough flying speed again. Lots of fun and easy. If they leave me here too long I may go on and get a license. I'm taking Link training on the side here on the field. It is the air force training device which has the controls and instruments of a plane and teaches you blind flying. Every afternoon we have a good basketball game at the gym so we are staying in good shape. Most everyone who got here even after me has left but my project stays here. We still don't know where we are going but have some hot rumors. Guess it's been about a week since I've written. Not busy but just didn't get around to it.

Last Saturday night Doris, Betty, Bob and I came out to the Club for the dance and had a swell time. Then we invited ourselves into Doris' home for breakfast at 3:00 in the morning and had everything from boiled eggs to cookies to eat. But I slipped up badly and didn't date her early enough in the week for tonight so I'm out of luck. However, another deal is cooking now. Rather expect a letter from you today. Pips Coler is in Hawaii now and likes it better. Lots of planes buzzing around here lately. We are going to the mess hall to eat now. Once in a while we play bridge here in the barracks. Saw "A Tree Grows in Brooklyn" and thought it was good.

Still lacking a few hours of flight training before being ready to solo, Lyle learned he was about to ship out to Fort Douglas, an overseas staging area in Utah. Nevertheless, the flying lessons would prove useful later on.

2 MARCH 1945 (FRIDAY). Don't write to me here anymore unless you hear from me again. The melting snow around here is really messy and there was a heavy fog this morning. Got your letter yesterday with the snaps and thought they were very good of the girls. Also a letter from Vernon in Long Beach. I've still got to get in 40 more minutes of flying before leaving and get packed etc. Have just gotten back from a hangar where I take Link training every morning. Have in about 7 hours of Link now. The latest fad here is playing bridge. A couple of our bunk mates took second place in a tournament the other night. Will tell you sometime about a big deal here that almost came through. A special volunteer project for only a few specially qualified fellows. But I'm sort of glad it folded up cause I hate to volunteer for anything in the army.

By the way you will hear from me again somewhere in the States for a short while. I'm glad to be on the way too.

Will be a rough summer if you don't get that ice house filled. Guess you aren't having any particular trouble around there with chores. You haven't mentioned any particularly bad storms either. Harold Swanson sure got to the Philippines in a hurry.

Continuing his letter with a thinly veiled message, Lyle cleverly skirted censorship at Sheppard Field and revealed his destination to his parents.

In your first letter send me the address of Alice Pazour (the one with twin girls) so I can look them up or maybe I can get it from a directory. But I've forgotten the last name. Just got back from taking a walk and now I'm going to bed. So "so long from Texas."

TROOP TRAIN

5 MARCH 1945 (MONDAY). Aboard a troop train headed for Amarillo, near Denver, Salt Lake City, and on to an Overseas Replacement Depot (O.R.D.) at Kearns Army Air Base near Ogden, Utah. It is late afternoon and the sun is shining brightly but seems to be in the wrong direction. The winter wheat is green in the fields and some fields have unpicked cotton. In the distance are a couple long hills that could be a couple of the Bijou Hills south of our farm. In a few minutes we will have supper in the kitchen car. I am O.D. of the train from 4 a.m. until breakfast and will have to awaken the K.P.s (some of the enlisted men) in time for them to cook breakfast. They have army stoves and cook pretty good meals and it reminds me of the other troop train from Kansas to Florida. My companion is from upper Massachusetts and we get along good so it's pleasant. Have been reading the Register that came today and a new Readers Digest. Also got your letter this morning.

This train is sort of rough. Friday I ended my flying lessons by taking spins. You go up to at least three thousand feet and shut off the throttle and put the nose up so the plane stalls. As it breaks you kick a rudder all the way in. The plane drops out from under you and heads noseward toward the earth and spinning like a top. As you look forward out of the windshield you see rivers, roads, and fields spinning and you wish you had never left the ground. And without parachutes you would feel embarrassed if a wing floated past you when pulling out of it. After about 5 of them I had enough. Got As in 7½ hours of the Link trainer too. Don't know how long our project will be at Kearns. May visit Salt Lake City. Send me that address soon as possible. More later.

Tuesday.

We are nearing Pueblo, Colorado, now and soon should approach the Rockies. Salt Lake will be about as near home as I've been in the army. Address:

AACS ORD

Kearns Army Air Base

Utah

It's dinner time but no dinner in sight yet and I'm starved. You sure get hungry on trains. May only be at Kearns for a short time to draw equipment before moving to a Port of Embarkation (P.O.E.) on one of the coasts. This is a lot like Nebraska around here. Flat and trees only on the low ground. Guess I'll toss this in a box at Pueblo. Don't know how long I'll stop there. We may march the men around a little for exercise. More from Kearns.

From the plains here we suddenly see snowcaps ahead so we are now getting near the Mts.

It's Pikes Peak about 60 miles in the distance.

SALT LAKE CITY

8 MARCH 1945 (THURSDAY). Am enclosing a receipt for Class E allotment and a bond. In a few days I'll send home a box of clothes etc. Our project is already getting hot—in fact it is cooking with gas. So far, our processing has been quite painless. We got to Kearns Army Air Base in early afternoon and were taken in buses to the Officers Club for dinner and then we cleared the post, cleaned up, and got settled. It is amazing how quickly we can feel at home in a new place. Our barracks here are tar paper but better and more convenient than at Sheppard Field. All around this level plain are very high snow covered mountains. Yesterday afternoon the upper half of them was covered with light blue clouds which gave a beautiful effect. The climate here seems very nice but a little windy and chilly this morning. The trip up here was the most scenic for me. Soon after leaving Pueblo we started up the Royal Gorge following a cold blue stream of mountain water rimmed with snow and ice. As we climbed, the walls got higher and higher until we came to the Royal Gorge where a suspension bridge waved in the breeze hundreds of feet overhead. All afternoon we climbed and finally were over 10,000 ft up. We are less than 20 miles from S. L. City—may go in tonight. My stay here will be short but pleasant. If you don't hear from me for a while you will know what's up. But it may be a couple weeks—we don't know.

OFFICERS' CLUB   KEARNS, UTAH

Army Air Forces Overseas Replacement Depot

Dear Folks,   *Sunday eve*

---

11 MARCH 1945 (SUNDAY). Henry and I are waiting to take on the winners of this pool game. We can clean up on most games of eightball. This has been a very pleasant weekend for me. Saturday afternoon I went to town and met another of the fellows while looking around the grounds of the Mormon Tabernacle. Then we went up to the Utah capital building which is a copper domed affair high on a hillside overlooking the city. We looked in on the House and Senate and looked over some exhibits. Then we had supper at the Utah Hotel and bumped into a

couple other fellows and decided to go to a dance at the Plantation Club. It is a very nice ballroom and had a good orchestra. And early in the evening I met a very cute little blonde. You guessed it—she turned out to be of Mormon faith. It seems to me very few people know just what the Mormon religion is all about. I didn't either but she straightened me out a little on it. We went to a little Chinese restaurant and had chow mein. She said she had never tasted tea or coffee and of course liquor etc is taboo also. I would like to be here another week and go to their church once. Anyway we are going out tomorrow night which will be my last chance in Salt Lake City. Will also look up those people if that address comes tomorrow from you. Utah seems rather like a foreign country like Holland or something. Just gives me that impression but I don't know why. Was rather late getting in last night but got up this morning anyway to go skiing. Special Services furnished skiing equipment and buses which took a convoy of us about 40 miles into the Mts for an all day ski outing. It was a very warm pleasant day and I enjoyed it immensely—and no broken bones but a sun wind burned face. At first I took spills but at the last I tore down the steep slope without getting battered up. They have a towline for pulling you back up the slide. It is a good sport and I want to do some more sometime.

We have drawn our equipment now—from mosquito netting to helmets. In a few days you will get a footlocker by freight. Also a change of address card on which they will stamp my P.O. number. Yes early this week we will board a troop train in full battle dress and head for a P.O.E. but of course we don't know which one. May get to see Vernon but rather doubt it. You may not hear from me for a month or two. Expect to see a little of the world now.

On his last day before shipping out to a POE, Lyle responded to the good news that his cousin Jimmy Sladek was alive, albeit at a German Prisoner of War (POW) camp.

15 MARCH 1945 (THURSDAY). Just got your airmail letter Mom. Sure made me happy to hear Jimmy is O.K. Took a long time for the news to come through. You sure were "on the ball." This gave me a chance to call Mrs Case and she invited me out to her place for supper. Isn't that perfect. I'll have to leave fairly early for my date. Will mail this now and go and eat.

15 MARCH 1945 (THURSDAY). My last day in Salt Lake City was really OK. Your letter came at noon so I called Mrs. Case [Alice] and was invited up for supper. So I went to town and caught a bus out to

their house which isn't very far. Mr. Case [Joe] had just gotten home from work—he does carpenter work for various projects. Alice had just baked a cake cause it was hers and [her twin sister] Stein's birthday. But she said she had thought it would be an eventless day as far as having any visitors. Joe and [their daughter] Sally took me sightseeing in their car—we visited a museum of early Mormon stuff including Joseph Smith's wagon that came across the plains and a photograph of Brigham Young's wives. We drove through Fort Douglas, University of Utah campus, the beehive etc and got back in time for a swell supper. It was a very enjoyable visit. The twins [of Alice and Joe] are cute as ever and peppy. They go to kindergarten and they have them in different rooms at school to get them used to being separated. After supper I had to go for a date with this girl—her name is Alice too. We decided to go dancing at the Rainbow where they had a good orchestra and a cozy atmosphere. There we met some friends and had a pleasant time. Afterwards we had a lunch at a cafe and met a marine Lt from Colorado who went to Iowa Teachers college and played football against S.D. State. Anyway it was a most enjoyable evening. Alice is very lively and doesn't put on any airs and plenty cute. Maybe it's a good thing they didn't leave me at Kearns very long. Guess I've got to get up in the morning so it's sack time.

Write 6¢ airmail if handy:

Casual Sq A-2 APO 19176 A

c/o Postmaster

N.Y., N.Y.

Due to security restrictions, Lyle was unable to divulge his POE. He signed his name on the lower left of the envelope, over which a censor stamped a seal of approval:

During his short time in Utah, Lyle had packed in a ski trip, toured Salt Lake City, visited relatives, and dated a blonde. Still with no inkling of his destination, he filled out a CHANGE OF ADDRESS card with an overseas Army Post Office (APO):

A SUPPLY OF THIS FORM WILL BE GIVEN TO EACH SOLDIER WHEN HIS ADDRESS IS CHANGED.	NOTICE — CHANGE OF ADDRESS	INSERT DATE HERE *13 March 45*

MY NEW ADDRESS IS: ☆ GPO   16—41863-1

GRADE	FIRST NAME—INITIAL—LAST NAME	ARMY SERIAL NO.
2d Lt	*Lyle V. Sladek*	*0872240*

COMPANY OR SIMILAR UNIT	REGIMENT, GROUP, OR SIMILAR ORGANIZATION
Casual Sq. A-2	

A.P.O. ADDRESS OR *(Complete one only)* → POST OFFICE ADDRESS OF INSTALLATION IN UNITED STATES

A.P.O. NO. **19176-A** % **P. M N.Y. N.Y,**

% POSTMASTER

NOTE: WHEN THIS FORM IS SENT TO PUBLISHERS OF MAGAZINES AND NEWSPAPERS COMPLETE OLD ADDRESS BELOW.

SIGNATURE *Lyle V. Sladek*

MY OLD ADDRESS WAS:

W. D., A. G. O. Form No. 204   This form supersedes W. D., A. G. O. Form No. 204, 1 Nov. 1943,
15 September 1944   which will be used until existing stocks are exhausted.

When Emma and Charles received the censored letter from Utah and the change of address card with a New York APO, they feared their son was on his way to Europe.

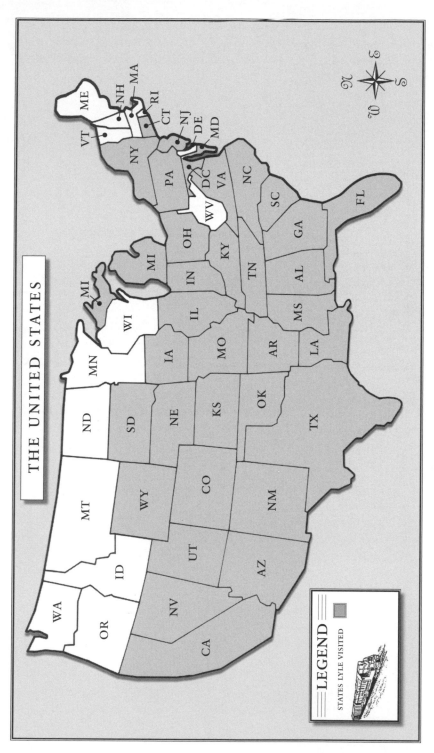

THE UNITED STATES

LEGEND

STATES LYLE VISITED

NEVER BEFORE OUTSIDE OF SOUTH DAKOTA, LYLE CRISSCROSSED 35 STATES BEFORE EMBARKING OVERSEAS

CHAPTER 14

Passage to the Unknown

Roll on, thou deep and dark blue Ocean,—roll!
Ten thousand fleets sweep over thee in vain;
Man marks the earth with ruin,—his control
Stops with the shore;—upon the watery plain

—LORD BYRON

THE TROOP TRAIN CHUGGED through mountains and desert until it reached Camp Anza, located inland between Riverside and Arlington in Southern California. Upon arrival, the billeting officer took charge of the soldiers as they detrained at the siding and noncoms conducted the men to their assigned tents. The camp, an overseas staging area with a capacity of six thousand men, was bustling with activity.

Processing began immediately. Physical inspections were carried out to detect infectious and contagious diseases. Medical and dental problems were treated. Inoculations were completed. Eyeglasses were furnished to those in need. Payrolls were prepared and wage payments made current. Personal matters—such as insurance, pay allotments, powers of attorney, wills, taxes, and aspects of domestic relations—were handled by specialists.

As soon as he completed processing, Lyle set off to find the Vs in Long Beach. Although they had no telephone and he had to rely on public transportation, he succeeded in locating their apartment. The opportunity to visit with family members before shipping overseas was an unexpected boon.

Upon returning to camp in the evening, Lyle joined several thousand soldiers for an outdoor stage show featuring Bob Hope and his troupe of entertainers. From a seat at the fringe of the crowd, Lyle could see Shirley Temple and Jerry Colona jitterbugging backstage while Bob Hope was delivering one-liners up front.

At overseas staging areas, the military intensified its effort to maintain secrecy in troop movements. At Camp Anza, the soldiers were cautioned about leaking information that might be useful to the enemy. Nevertheless, speculation was rife regarding departure dates and shipping destinations.

Meticulous planning preceded the movement of the troops from the staging area to the pier. Each soldier bore a number on his helmet to indicate his place in the passenger list. The same order was maintained upon arrival at the dock. When it came time for a unit to board the ship, the soldiers lined up single file and the unit commander identified each man as he passed by the embarkation desk.

While Lyle was waiting to board the USS *Calahan,* a member of the Gideon Society presented him with a pocket-size New Testament. Inscribed on the flyleaf were the words, A SACRED TOKEN. A reminder of wartime regulations appeared on the inside cover:

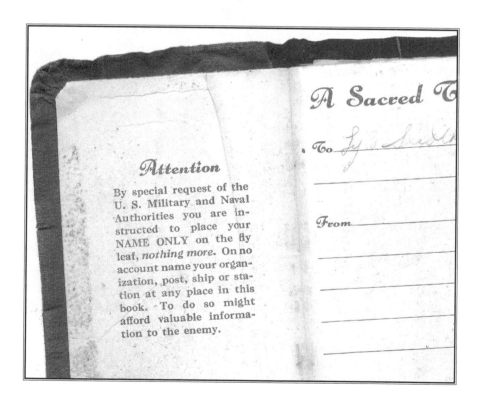

Among the contents were The Lord's Prayer, Well-Loved Hymns, Where to Find Help When, and What Jesus Taught About Some of Life's Problems. The flag, bearing forty-eight stars, was pictured opposite a letter from the president of the United States:

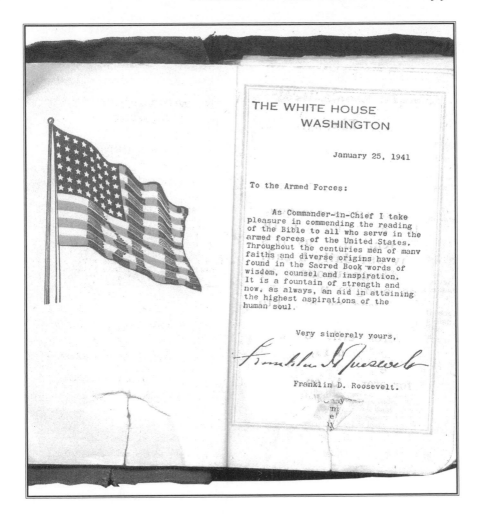

THE WHITE HOUSE
WASHINGTON

January 25, 1941

To the Armed Forces:

As Commander-in-Chief I take
pleasure in commending the reading
of the Bible to all who serve in the
armed forces of the United States.
Throughout the centuries men of many
faiths and diverse origins have
found in the Sacred Book words of
wisdom, counsel and inspiration.
It is a fountain of strength and
now, as always, an aid in attaining
the highest aspirations of the
human soul.

Very sincerely yours,

Franklin D. Roosevelt.

Hearing his name called, Lyle shouldered his bag and climbed the gangplank to the deck, where he was told his compartment number and handed a life preserver. He was instructed to wear the flotation device whenever outside his quarters and, in case of emergency, to inflate the belt by triggering two gas cartridges.

The compartments of the troopship were fitted out with rows of canvas bunks stacked four tiers high. As men entered the cramped spaces they were directed to crawl into their bunks so as to allow those following to squeeze through the narrow aisles with their barracks bags.

No crowd had assembled to wave good-bye and no band played patriotic tunes as the USS *Calahan* edged away from the pier. For security reasons, the military banned unauthorized persons from approaching the docks as troops embarked for overseas.

Lyle had mixed feelings as the troopship got underway. It was a melancholy moment to depart for distant shores not knowing where he was going or for how long he would be gone. On the other hand, two years had elapsed since his induction and he was eager to be on his way. Like most GIs, he just wanted to "get the war over with" so he could return to civilian life.

The ship sailed out of the harbor and into a tempestuous sea, with wind and waves more violent than any the boat had previously encountered. No one, not even a crew member, was allowed on deck. With the rolling vessel barely able to right itself, the captain changed course to head more directly into the waves, a maneuver that intensified the pitching motion. As the propeller alternated between water and foamy air, grinding noises and shuddering vibrations permeated the stricken ship. Most on board were seasick within the hour. The stench of vomit added to their misery.

The rolling, pitching motion continued for two days. Realizing his life was in danger, Lyle's philosophical thoughts gave way to survival instincts and coping mechanisms. He forced himself to be up and about during the daylight hours, climbing the stairwells for exercise and eating meals even though food held no appeal. Not all of the men fared as well. Some stayed in their bunks, refusing to exercise or eat, and became weaker and felt ever worse. Several lost the will to live and were taken to sick bay to be fed intravenously. Nevertheless, seasickness took its toll. A somber burial at sea remained forever etched in Lyle's psyche.

Because of crowded conditions and minimal crew, the galley provided just two stand-up meals per day, sufficient sustenance for men expending little energy while sitting on their bunks or playing craps in the aisles. Lyle thought the liquid dispensed from a machine that mixed a powdered dairy ingredient with water to be a poor substitute for fresh milk, a popular and nutritional element in the diet of most GIs.

Once the sea calmed and the roll of the ship lessened, Lyle felt like living again. He frequented the deck where he could view the ocean from the prow. Sucking in fresh air was a welcome relief from the heavy, sweet aroma emitted from the ship's vents, an amalgamation of cooking odors, perspiring bodies, and exhaust fumes from the engines.

Traveling without escort the USS *Calahan* relied on speed and a zigzag course to elude enemy submarines. Subs were not fast enough to overtake the ship and, not knowing her route, could intercept only by chance. The troops were prohibited from lighting matches during night blackout, and they were warned to stay clear of the rails. The ship, an easy target if stationary, would not stop to search for anyone falling overboard. Startled the first time he heard the deck guns being fired, Lyle was relieved to discover the crew was merely practicing gunnery.

Several days out of Los Angeles, Lyle saw the Hawaiian Islands on the horizon, bringing back memories of swaying to the soothing strains of "Blue Hawaii" during his high school senior prom. As the ship continued on midst calm, tropical seas, he whiled away the time playing bridge or checkers, reading, and conversing with new acquaintances. Coming across a saxophone in one of the compartments, he entertained himself blowing notes. Now and again he tended to assigned duties, such as keeping watch at night in a compartment of enlisted men. Being an officer, he carried a service revolver that he cleaned twice a week, perhaps more often than necessary.

Day and night the USS *Calahan* plowed onward as it crossed vast expanses of the Pacific Ocean. Like the prairies at home, the curved vista of the watery plain stretched to the horizon. Lyle felt suspended in time and isolated from the real world. Family and friends seemed far, far away. He put letter writing on hold since there was no way to mail a letter until reaching port. There was little to write about anyway, as each new day blended in with yesterday and the day before. There was one memorable exception, the day he suffered stomach cramps after eating a meal of fried, perhaps tainted, oysters. Sunday service on deck marked the passage of each week.

After two weeks at sea, keen rumors circulated that the ship would be putting in at a port in Australia. Though not permitted to disclose the route, Lyle wrote a letter he intended to mail from that continent. Wishing to allay the anxiety of his parents, he let them know when to expect the next missive. He knew it would be at least two weeks before he could mail another, and it would have to travel across the Pacific Ocean and halfway across America before reaching the family farm. He failed to mention the loneliness in witnessing a flag-wrapped body break the stillness of a tropical sea.

4 APRIL 1945 (WEDNESDAY). How are you getting along way back there in Dakota. My mail will be strictly censored yet for a while so I can't tell you where I am or anything and besides it doesn't matter. We have been out to sea for a long time and still have a long way to go. This is no pleasure cruise either. Oh happy day when I get another breath of cool clean air and some good solid food. But at least I will have seen as much of the world as I will ever care to see. And maybe more. After seeing so many days of water one realizes that these continents of ours are just islands. The ocean was rough the first couple days out and everyone was seasick. What a miserable feeling it is to be even a little sick. But now except for the heat and monotony everything is O.K. There is nothing so lonely as the sea at twilight when the wind is blowing and the waves pound on the side of the ship. Often we have singing sessions on the

deck in the evening. Also some bridge games, reading etc. I have a few hours of duty daily which helps keep me busy. I suppose someday I'll wake up and be at home again and hardly realize that I even was around the world. We get radio news and it sounds good on the European front. Hope I don't have to spend too much time where I'm going. You won't hear from me for a month or two after you get this. By that time mail should start coming through again. You keep things under control there and it'll be O.K. here too.

Cool, refreshing breezes swept over the troopship as it neared Melbourne. Lyle acquired a *V-mail* form to send a second letter home from that port. Regarding the *V* sign, Prime Minister Churchill had sent a radio message to the people of the occupied countries shortly after the German armed forces had overrun much of Europe:

> The V sign is the symbol of the unconquerable will of the occupied territories and a portent of the fate awaiting Nazi tyranny. So long as the peoples continue to refuse all collaboration with the invader it is sure that his cause will perish and that Europe will be liberated.

The letter *V* began to appear everywhere—buses, cars, sidewalks, streetlights, windows, and walls. As an act of defiance, oppressed Europeans tapped out *V* in Morse code—three dots and a dash—with knuckles, toes, fingers, forks, beer glasses, pencils, and spoons.

Churchill popularized the *V for Victory* sign in the United States when, upon completing an address to Congress on 26 December 1941, he held up two pudgy fingers in the form of a *V* while departing the congressional chamber midst thunderous applause.

Patterned after an innovation used by the British, the United States instituted the V-mail system to streamline postal delivery to and from troops overseas. Letters were photographed, miniaturized onto microfilm for shipping, enlarged upon arrival, and delivered as regular mail. The V-mail process enabled a cargo plane to carry more than a hundred thousand letters in a single mailbag. Not only did the technology reduce the communication time between the home front and distant outposts, it reduced the risk of the enemy intercepting mail.

Lyle hoped his V-mail letter would reach the family mailbox in a couple weeks.

8 APRIL 1945 (SUNDAY). Here it is another Sunday at sea and now we are nearing our first stopping place. Last Easter Sunday they had services up on the deck. Tell me how much longer it took for this

to get there than the airmail letter. I'm sure you are all well and happy and of course with a good dinner about now. Far away places have lost their allure for me—they can ship me home anytime. It is a little more comfortable now and I'm feeling good. Don't you get too ambitious this spring up there in Dakota. Maybe there will be mail soon when we get there.

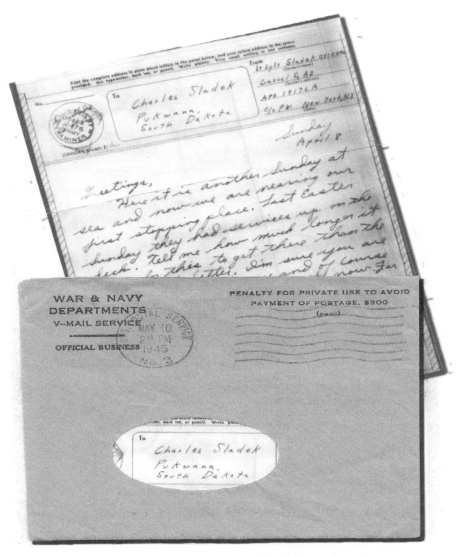

MINIATURE ENVELOPE CONTAINING V-MAIL LETTER MEASURING 4 1/4 BY 5 1/4 INCHES

Red-tiled roofs were a welcome sight when the ship approached the dock at Melbourne. Although the troops had been at sea for several weeks, they were not allowed to debark. Upsetting as that was, Lyle understood the necessity of keeping the men on board. Loading several thousand troops under controlled conditions at Los Angeles had been a formidable task. Had the command allowed the men to roam the port city, likely some would have disappeared.

While at Melbourne the USS *Calahan* took on supplies and dropped off mail. After two days it sailed out of the harbor and continued on its westward course. By that time Lyle was quite sure the destination was India, poles apart geographically and culturally from South Dakota. He jotted another V-mail.

13 APRIL 1945 (FRIDAY). We stopped at a port but it turned out to be a big disappointment cause they wouldn't let us off. It was hard to take after being on this crowded ship so long to not be able to get off and look around the city for a few hours and drink some of their beer. So now we sail again for a few thousand more miles. Guess school will be about out when you get this.

We just heard that President Roosevelt died. It is a tragedy that it should happen at just this time when our country needed him most. But he likely had the peace plans already drawn up. Bye now.

News of the death of the president cast a pall of sorrow and disbelief over the troops aboard the USS *Calahan*. Recently elected to a fourth term, FDR had been president for as long as most of them could remember. Even those Americans who opposed his domestic policies had come to see him as having a steady hand on the tiller of the ship of state during the war years.

As the USS *Calahan* continued its passage the men speculated about the leadership qualities of their new commander in chief. Only the politically minded were aware that Harry S. Truman, who had replaced Vice President Henry A. Wallace on the democratic ticket in the 1944 election, was now president of the United States.

The ship proceeded along the southern coast of Australia before turning northward into the Indian Ocean. As it approached the equator for a second time, the seas became smooth as glass with no movement of air except from the forward motion of the ship. Each evening, when the steel deck cooled down, Lyle went topside to observe, in the words of Rudyard Kipling, "the flyin'-fishes play."

Writing to Irene, Lyle alluded to *Our Hearts Were Young and Gay,* a book in which Cornelia Otis Skinner and Emily Kimbrough related humorous episodes encountered during a voyage to Europe. On his last visit in Omaha he had accompanied Irene to a movie by that name. He knew she would deduce he was somewhere on the vast Pacific since passage across the Atlantic to Europe would require less time.

15 APRIL 1945 (SUNDAY). Dear Sis,
At breakfast time they blew church call and suddenly I realized it was Sunday again. Seems like the days come and go and time has no meaning on the ship. Sort of out of this world. They had services up on the deck and sang lots of favorite hymns. When the choir sang "Church in the Wildwood," it took me back to the days we had church in the schoolhouse and went in the buggy. Remember? We stopped at a port but they wouldn't let us off. Would have given anything to look over the large city—a last chance to see some civilization before getting to the place I'm going to. Gee, it's been a long time since hearing from you and home. But I'm sure everything is O.K. I'm feeling swell and find it fairly interesting. Have some good checker games with a couple fellows. Oh yes, "My Heart is Young and Gay" too. But they only traveled a few days. Write.

As the days and weeks passed, Lyle found things to do to ease the boredom and discomfort. From the fantail he viewed the phosphorescent water of the ship's wake stretching back to the horizon. He watched for sea life and observed the variations in color of the seawater. At night he studied the unfamiliar constellations in the southern sky, noting the Pole Star no longer appeared above the northern horizon. Thinking of Mother's Day coming up in May, he wrote a letter that included a broad hint he was in the Southern Hemisphere.

18 APRIL 1945 (WEDNESDAY). Dear Mom,
Here it is about time for Mother's Day again and I just want you to know, dear mother of mine, that though we are many miles apart our thoughts are just that much closer. Last night I woke up and for a minute I thought I was home—but the roll of the ship bumped me against the side of the bunk and soon changed that notion. We have been on here so long and the time is so meaningless that you have the feeling of expecting to be on the boat forever. But I guess another week or two will complete the voyage. Right now, at least we can't get any farther from home. A couple days ago we saw a whale spout several times but he was too far away to see anything but the spout. This morning about a mile from the ship a school of some porpoise (or other large fish) kept jumping out of the water and splashing. The sea is very calm today and it's rather pleasant up on the deck. The sunsets are pretty and usually the stars are

quite bright. Of course here we see some constellations and planets that you can't see up there and vice versa. When you take a shower here it is really something. The hot water tank is on one side of the ship and the cold water on the other. When the ship rolls starboard you scald—when it rolls portside the water is cold.

While novel at first, showering in saltwater and lathering with a specially made soap soon gave way to wishes for something less abrasive. Swallowing pills as a precaution against disease was also discomforting, as was the intense heat. Lyle longed for the cool April climate of South Dakota.

> Sunday.
> Just got through cleaning my gun to get the dust out of it and keep it from rusting. Was surprised to find it was Sunday again when someone mentioned that fact at breakfast. They had services up on the deck as usual. It's so hot today that we are dripping wet with no clothes on. The sun is a scorcher and it is about as hot as I ever want to be. In less then a week now we will be getting off this tin tub. They already have us full of atabrine to keep down malarial symptoms. Boy, what a spot I'm getting into. But I'm sure it will turn out O.K. Have been playing some checkers lately. Manage to hold my own most of the time. There is a chance of having mail waiting when we reach port. Sure hope so. Seems hard to realize it is cool springtime up there. School will be about out when you get this. Some days this boat rocks so you are walking on the walls about half the time. Sometimes you find yourself running downstairs to keep from falling. Well, I'm not going to fret over here. Might have some interesting times over here and it certainly will be different. This voyage has been an education for a landlubber like me. Be sure and tell me what's going on around the farm. Oh for some of that ice cream right now. Just about as hot as on top of a haystack in August!

The ocean water took on a brownish hue as the ship sliced deeper into the Bay of Bengal. Lyle's first glimpse of life on the subcontinent of India astonished him. Midst a green field, a native in white garb was acting as a human scarecrow to protect the crop from birds.

The ship proceeded up the Hooghly River, a channel of the Ganges Delta, and tied up at a dock. After thirty-eight days at sea Lyle had arrived at Calcutta, the chief seaport for war materials destined for China.

It took nearly a day for the military personnel to debark. Lyle, among the last to step ashore, was relieved to be on solid ground. Along with the others he milled around on the quay, fascinated by the strange scene. Slender Indian porters carried heavy loads on their heads. Children begged for food, candy, and gum. Cripples pulled themselves along the ground on their elbows. British troops chased away natives taking up space on the dock.

Glad for the pith helmet that protected his head from the intense rays, Lyle recalled the phrase, "Only mad dogs and Englishmen go out in the noonday sun." That saying made sense to him now. Although he knew better, he succumbed to temptation and purchased a glass of lemonade. Sipping the drink, he marveled at finding himself in India. Exotic India, crown jewel of the British Empire!

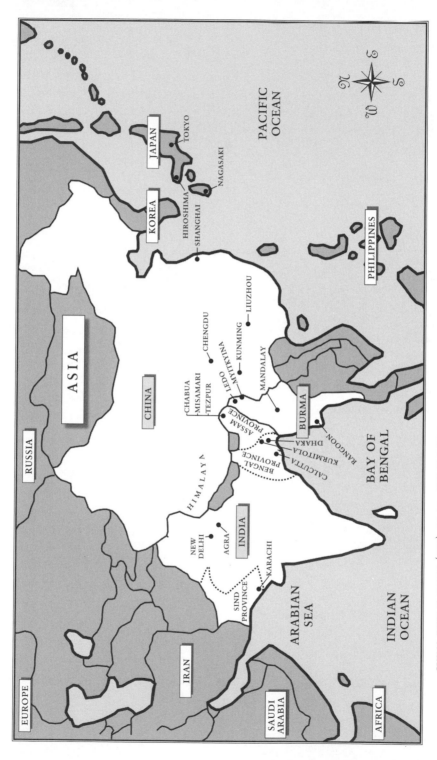

CHINA-BURMA-INDIA (CBI), 1945 — INDIA LATER COMPRISED OF PAKISTAN, INDIA, BANGLADESH, AND SRI LANKA

CHAPTER 15

Flying the Hump,
Supplying China by Air

OH, East is East and West is West, and never the twain shall meet.
—RUDYARD KIPLING

WHILE TRAVERSING THE INDIAN OCEAN the troops aboard the USS *Calahan* were told something of what to expect in Calcutta. Still, Lyle encountered cultural shock as he rode through the city in the back of an army truck. Rail-thin Brahma cows forlornly meandered about streets teeming with people. Flies swarmed around chunks of raw meat hanging in front of food shops. A cacophony of blaring horns, oxcart wheels grinding on pavement, vendors hawking their wares, and beggars pleading for food assaulted his ears. The scene was disconcerting to a farm boy accustomed to the clean, peaceful Dakota prairies, where sleek Hereford cattle grazed on gently waving grass, meadowlarks sang melodic songs, bumblebees softly hummed in search of flowering plants, and the horizon could be scanned without seeing a single building or person.

Overwhelmed by the barrage on his senses, Lyle penned these lines for his family:

> Calcutta—city of shoeless feet,
>   of starving people in a crowded street.
> The tragic look in the beggar's eyes,
>   as midst the filth he plaintively cries,
> "Baksheesh, Baksheesh," in endless chants—
>   humanity passes with scarcely a glance.

Sacred cattle roaming the street,
    often trodding on the lifeless feet
Of cholera victims who died that day,
    soon the 'gatherer' will cart them away.
The dust, the death, the opium smoking—
    a blend of centuries, stifling, choking.

Swarms of urchins with somber faces,
    older than children of other places.
Too busy to laugh and run and play,
    quest for food is their life each day.
Untouchables resigned to their fate,
    indifferent alike to love and hate.

India, awaken from lethargic sleep,
    don't accept that life is cheap!
Religion should lead to a happier life,
    not to poverty and hopeless strife.
Let all be equal—abolish the caste,
    how much longer will this darkness last?

CHARACTER STUDY OF AN INDIAN, CALCUTTA, INDIA, 1945

Once the army trucks reached the outskirts of the city, the troops boarded railroad cars and were transported to an army camp out in the jungle. Assigned to a tent, Lyle rolled up the sides, sat on a bunk, and read long-awaited letters from family and friends.

Writing on AIR MAIL stationery that featured a picture of the globe, Lyle informed his parents he was in the China-Burma-India (CBI) theater of war, a region that had received little attention in the newspapers back home. Although censorship precluded him from directly revealing he was near Calcutta, he enclosed his poem together with a snapshot labeled, "Character study of an Indian."

29 APRIL 1945 (SUNDAY). So you thought I went to Europe! Tish! Tish! Didn't you know I was in California? But of course I couldn't tell you that. And it is closer to here by way of Europe than the way we came. Yes, it was good to set foot on land again after more than a month on a hot, crowded troop transport. Maybe it was better on the boat than this will be but so far it's O.K. We got to the port and I was one of the last to get off. So we got off this morning and got on a crazy little Indian train and rode several hours out to this camp. I'm in the C.B.I. (China, Burma, India) theater and am at this camp only temporarily. Well we got out here and were glad to wait in line for our mail. And I hit the jackpot. We were a happy bunch to get stacks of mail. I got 3 letters from you, one from Lt Pete Smith, one from a fellow in Kansas, two from Vs, 5 from Irene, 6 from Beatrice, 4 from Norma in Champaign, and two from Peggy. Guess I'll be going back to Detroit soon after getting back—and other places. This isn't very easy to write on my lap sitting on a bunk in a tent—at least it will be hard to read. You don't know how good it was to hear you are all O.K. and everything is under control. Of course it makes me want to come home to hear about gardens, spring plantings, new calves, and everything. I wonder if you realize what a paradise we have up there in Dakota or anywhere in the States for that matter. There are 400 million people and 200 million cows in India. The cows are sacred and treated well—the people aren't so lucky. You never saw so many people—just can't imagine it. They beg continually—"Beufill, Reiopee" is what they say. Today (Sunday) they were washing clothes and bathing in the filthiest water. Soon it will be the monsoon (rainy) season here. In fact a storm seems to be coming up now—so we put the sides of the

tent down. Also put the mosquito netting around the bunks. It was hot today but we got used to that on the trip. But it is quite comfortable here and cool this evening. And I'm just as near home here as in Nevada for all practical purposes so I'm really quite content. Cause now I can start thinking of coming home instead of leaving. That will be the day. Oh say, you can open that footlocker with a matchstick or hairpin—I've still got the key. Just tin. Don't lose the papers in the footlocker—some are important.

Asia was a faraway land when travel was by ship. A song popular in the thirties, "Slow Boat to China," epitomized a voyage to the Orient. Americans traveling to the Far East were mainly sailors, missionaries, and members of the diplomatic corps. Lyle never expected to journey to the land of enchantment and knew his parents would be flabbergasted when they received a letter from India.

Feeling somewhat queasy, Lyle retired at nightfall. Having been cautioned about malaria, he lowered the mosquito netting draped over the canopy of his bamboo cot and carefully tucked in the edges before stretching out.

That humming sound—was it his imagination, or was there a mosquito inside the net? The growling in his stomach was certainly real. Already he regretted drinking that glass of citrus on the dock.

Jackals were making an eerie racket as they called to one another in the jungle night. It was all very interesting. But as he drifted off to sleep, Lyle yearned to awaken in the room with the blue walls and chintz curtains—and to the aroma of pancakes floating up the stairs from his mother's skillet.

Alas. An attack of dysentery jarred Lyle back to reality. Frequent trips to the latrine made his first night in India a memorable one. Glad when morning came, he reread letters from home before jotting more lines. For the sake of his mother, he omitted mention of discomfort and continued to downplay his distance from home.

You certainly would be wasting your time to do any worrying about me. Was surprised that you made it to Omaha, Mom. It was sure nice that you made it. Irene said you weren't too impressed with the city so we agree. Harold Swanson was in a hot place but sure a lot nearer home than I. Also Phillip Coler is practically at home. Don't ask me how I know! It doesn't seem possible to be in India. A word of explanation about the poem—Calcutta left an impression in my mind never to be forgotten. If this poem can give you a shock too, than it is a success. It cannot give you a true picture of Calcutta cause no picture is complete without the sweet sickening odor, the heat, the tiny child with one hand behind and the other held out to you with pleading eyes. The begging word "baksheesh" means give anything—the first word every Indian child learns. We take our life at home for granted—until we see India. First bear in mind that this is the oldest civilization known, that people do die from famine, and that they do have cholera epidemics—the dead left lying until evening when all are gathered up. A multitude of religions that at one time may have taught brotherhood, love, and how to live— but which have degenerated until now a very curse. There seems to be no solution to the problems of India—I see no hope for a better India of the future. I predict with a burning shame, a hundred years will find it the same. Maybe Virginia could read the poem like I mean for it to be read. Gee I sure appreciate your coming through with those airmail letters. Snapshots would be very welcome too. Don't work too hard and don't forget to eat ice cream real often. More later so bye now.

Snippets of news from the European theater reaching the troops in the Bengal camp indicated Germany was on the verge of defeat. Russians from the east and Americans from the west had met up at the Elbe River sixty miles outside Berlin. The Luftwaffe, short of pilots, airfields, and fuel, had ceased to be an effective defensive force. Mussolini, while attempting to flee to Switzerland from German-held northern Italy, had been captured and shot by revengeful Italian partisans.

As Russian troops drove toward his bunker in Berlin, Hitler signed his last will and testament. On the day Berlin fell, Lyle responded to news from home that his cousin Jimmy Sladek had been freed from a German POW camp. Relieved, he supposed Jimmy and another cousin, Dale Korzan, would soon be returning stateside.

2 MAY 1945 (WEDNESDAY). Just went to the post office to get some stamps and it sure made me hot and tired even though it really wasn't a long walk. We get enough to eat but it's mostly eating to live and besides one shouldn't eat much in a hot climate. I like it here for one reason—we can run around in shorts and sandals during the day. My suntan is coming good and we sleep under netting in the open air so it's a healthy life in some ways. You should hear the jackals and hyenas at night—a silly racket out in the woods. Your letter of April 20 got here yesterday which is good service. Guess Jimmy and Dale will be home soon. They can make it in a short time cause Europe is close to home. I'm a shellback—having crossed the equator twice. You are pollywogs. Also crossed the International date line—order of green dragon. May move soon. Hope I go where I requested.

The tent camp in Bengal was not Lyle's final destination. After four days he began a journey deep into the heart of Asia, to what seemed the farthest corner of the earth.

ASSAM PROVINCE OF INDIA

A trip across India on the Bengal and Assam railroad was a comical, yet arduous, experience. The rickety train reminded Lyle of a newspaper comic strip, the *Toonerville Trolley*. The cars were packed full. Some of the natives rode on the roof and others hung out the windows or clung on to the sides. Occasionally, all of the passengers disembarked and stood in the hot sun for several hours while waiting to ferry a river or transfer to a train with a different gauge track.

All along the way native children appeared in every village and from behind every bush to beg as the train went by. Standing alongside the track they chanted, *Baksheesh! Baksheesh!* as they clamored for coins, candy, and leftover *K* rations. The soldiers soon ran out of treats to toss into the outstretched hands of the urchins.

Whenever the train stopped at a station the thirsty soldiers filled their canteens with tap water, added two iodine tablets, and let the mixture stand for two hours. Once purified and with the sediment settled to the bottom, the water was ready to drink. The tepid liquid kept them alive but did not quench their thirst. On the second day, the train reached a British army camp where the men were treated to lukewarm tea laced with condensed milk. Lyle had never acquired a taste for tea, but he found it a satisfying drink that day.

Meanwhile, Admiral Karl Doenitz, having been named by Hitler as his successor, sent General Alfred Jodi to Supreme Headquarters Allied Expeditionary Forces to seek terms for the end of the war. On 7 May, General Jodi signed for the unconditional surrender of German forces effective the following day.

On 8 May, President Truman and Prime Minister Churchill proclaimed victory over Europe (V-E Day). In the United States, there was dancing in the streets, fireworks, and parades when President Truman broadcast the victory to the American people from the Radio Room in the White House:

> This is a solemn but a glorious hour. I only wish that Franklin D. Roosevelt had lived to witness this day. General Eisenhower informs me that the forces of Germany have surrendered to the United Nations. The flags of freedom fly over all Europe.

For this victory, we join in offering our thanks to the Providence which has guided and sustained us through the dark days of adversity.

Our rejoicing is sobered and subdued by a supreme consciousness of the terrible price we have paid to rid the world of Hitler and his evil band. Let us not forget, my fellow Americans, the sorrow and the heartache which today abide in the homes of so many of our neighbors—neighbors whose most priceless possession has been rendered as a sacrifice to redeem our liberty.

We can repay the debt which we owe to our God, to our dead and to our children only by work—by ceaseless devotion to the responsibilities which lie ahead of us. If I could give you a single watchword for the coming months, that word is—work, work, and more work.

We must work to finish the war. Our victory is but half-won. The West is free, but the East is still in bondage to the treacherous tyranny of the Japanese. When the last Japanese division has surrendered unconditionally, then only will our fighting job be done.

We must work to bind up the wounds of a suffering world—to build an abiding peace, a peace rooted in justice and in law. We can build such a peace only by hard, toilsome, painstaking work—by understanding and working with our allies in peace as we have in war.

The job ahead is no less important, no less urgent, no less difficult than the task which now happily is done.

I call upon all upon every American to stick to his post until the last battle is won. Until that day, let no man abandon his post or slacken his efforts. And now, I want to read to you my formal proclamation of this occasion:

A Proclamation—The Allied armies, through sacrifice and devotion and with God's help, have wrung from Germany a final and unconditional surrender. The western world has been freed of the evil forces which for five years and longer have imprisoned the bodies and broken the lives of millions upon millions of free-born men. They have violated their churches, destroyed their homes, corrupted their children, and murdered their loved ones. Our Armies of Liberation have restored freedom to these suffering peoples, whose spirit and will the oppressors could never enslave.

Much remains to be done. The victory won in the West must now be won in the East. The whole world must be cleansed of the evil from which half the world has been freed. United, the peace-loving nations have demonstrated in the West that their arms are stronger by far than the might of the dictators or the tyranny of military cliques that once called us soft and weak. The power of our peoples to defend themselves against all enemies will be proved in the Pacific war as it has been proved in Europe.

For the triumph of spirit and of arms which we have won, and for its promise to the peoples everywhere who join us in the love of freedom, it is fitting that we, as a nation, give thanks to Almighty God, who has strengthened us and given us the victory.

Now, therefore, I Harry S. Truman, President of the United States of America, do hereby appoint Sunday, May 13, 1945 to be a day of prayer.

I call upon the people of the United States, whatever their faith, to unite in offering joyful thanks to God for the victory we have won, and to pray that He will support us to the end of our present struggle and guide us into the ways of peace.

I also call upon my countrymen to dedicate this day of prayer to the memory of those who have given their lives to make possible our victory.

In Witness Whereof, I have hereunto set my hand and caused the seal of the United States of America to be affixed.

Tired and sweaty, Lyle finally arrived at a jungle camp in rural Assam. A country boy at heart, the quiet, verdant landscape calmed his senses. Mindful of censorship, he merely disclosed:

13 MAY 1945 (SUNDAY, MOTHER'S DAY). I am still in India but have moved up to the Assam province if you know where that is. This seems like paradise after the stay at the other camp. It is not so terribly hot here and the food is better and this is a more rural area, hence much cleaner. It rains a lot here so everything is a lush green including the tea plantations.

As for the trip up here—it was really a trip to end all trips. It certainly was not an easy trip but so interesting that I didn't mind it a bit. It involved trains, boats, and trucks.

You simply have to see that other region before you could believe it. One has to have a strong stomach. We slept nights on the wooden seats of the train and ate K rations. We were allowed to buy bananas from the natives providing the skins were unbroken. They will sell 16 medium sized ones for a rupee—about 30¢. It's a strange feeling to awaken in the night and find yourself on a train rolling across India. After getting more out in the rural area we could watch the natives working in the fields and we saw elephants, strange birds, etc. We came through some jungle areas too. We met one boy aged 14 who could speak English fluently and was very bright. His parents are Hindu but he said he was Christian. These people are friendly and of a good disposition and would likely progress except for their religion and being too crowded. In one village a magician and snake charmer put on a show and then passed the hat. He had a couple snakes including a big cobra in a basket. One native tried to sell me a red ruby and two cut diamonds but they were just a good grade of glass.

We haven't gotten any mail now for several days and it will probably be a week yet before it comes through. When I get to my station I'll send my permanent A.P.O.

I just barely made it to chapel this morning. Of course the chaplain gave a Mother's Day talk and they had a good servicemen's choir.

I'm wondering how you are all getting along and what you are doing today. I hope Mom has a good garden this year. Have you tapped the ice cream yet? Chuckie should be about through school by now and the gals too. Got a long letter from Irene last week. She seems to have it very nice there now and does lots of interesting things. She plans to go home for a while this summer. Is everyone farming big again this year?

Curious as to how a grade school classmate was adapting to service life, Lyle asked, "Does Duane Olson mind being in the army? He can take it much better than most." Concerned about his college chum who had contracted malaria, he wondered, "Is Don Swanson out of the hospital?" Lyle reassured his mother:

I expect to get out of here without catching anything too serious. So far I'm feeling good and am anxious to get settled and get to work. Haven't been able to hang my hat for about a year. Last week I got a very cute picture from Beatrice. She still has that twinkle in her eye. Wish you would send me some snapshots when you can. Did you get my $100 allotment for April? No use sending me the Register cause I doubt it would ever get here. Send clippings in letters instead. They have assigned me to a field near here as a Crypto Officer and I'll be there in a day or two. I had hoped to fly the Hump into China but didn't get assigned there. Guess it's better here anyway. More later.

While at the Santa Ana staging area Lyle had supposed he was destined for a post somewhere in Asia, perhaps China. While in high school he had read *God Is My Copilot* by Colonel Scott, one of the Flying Tigers. Scott described his feat of flying a supercharged P-40 Warhawk over Mount Everest. Intrigued at the prospect of flying *the Hump*, Lyle, after arriving at Bengal, had requested an assignment on the China side of the Himalayas. Instead, he was ordered to report to an air base in Assam used by the Air Transport Command (ATC) in ferrying supplies over the Hump from India to China.

In 1937, when Japan invaded and occupied the coastal region of China, the Nationalist government of Chiang Kai-shek retreated to the interior of the country. There, while resisting the Japanese army, the Nationalists relied on a trickle of supplies that reached Kunming via the Burma Road, a winding mountain road barely passable for trucks even during the dry season.

Shortly after the attack at Pearl Harbor, Japan invaded Burma and seized a section of the Burma Road, cutting off that overland supply line. A feisty general by the name of "Vinegar Joe" Stillwell directed the construction of another road to link Ledo with the northern portion of the Burma Road. But the Ledo Road, originating near Assam, India, proved ineffectual due to mountainous terrain and monsoon rains.

The Allies were concerned by the prospect of Japanese forces overrunning China; if that were allowed to happen, millions of Japanese soldiers and hundreds of planes would be freed up for use elsewhere in the Pacific theater. Further, Allied leaders envisioned China as a staging area for the final assault on Japan. But, with no access to China by land or by sea, the only possible means of supplying the Nationalist forces of Chiang Kai-shek was by air transport over the most formidable mountain barrier in the world, the mighty Himalayas.

Near the terminus of the Bengal and Assam railroad, at the crossroads of Asia where China, Burma, and India all come together, British bulldozers carved little airfields from the jungle at places bearing strange names like Misamari, Tezpur, and Chabua.

On the China side of the Hump, at Kunming, Chengdu, and other remote places in the interior of the country, Chinese laborers, carrying wicker baskets of rock and yellow clay, leveled tracts of land. Then hundreds of coolies, pulling on ropes attached to huge stone rollers, packed the earth and rock to form runways.

MISAMARI, ASSAM, INDIA

Three weeks after docking at Calcutta, Lyle arrived at Misamari, an air base consisting of a narrow airstrip and a smattering of bamboo huts. After reporting in he settled into one of the bashas on the perimeter of a small clearing. Second in command of a detachment of twelve men at the message station, a well-guarded bamboo shack, he was charged with supervising the encoding and decoding of classified messages and with the safeguarding of cryptographic machines and materials. Coded messages arrived in five-letter groupings with no punctuation and no differentiation between capital and lowercase letters.

Four days later, Lyle and two companions drove a jeep through tiger-hunting country to inspect tower and transmission equipment that enabled navigators to get their bearings when their planes got off course. Along the way they happened upon a dead tiger and stopped to snap a photo. Wanting to impress the family back home, Lyle annotated: "This tiger was shot in the jungle here. This is the Bengal tiger, the biggest and fiercest of them all." Recounting the outing and still captivated by the strange surroundings, he described the sights from within the four walls of his basha, a hut with open windows, fissured, bamboo walls, and a thatched roof.

20 MAY 1945 (SUNDAY). It's rather pretty here looking out the window. It is just getting dark and the trees about a mile away are

BENGAL TIGER FOUND SHOT IN THE JUNGLE, ASSAM, INDIA, 1945

siluetted against the faint pink of the sky with a few blue clouds above them. The birds are making quite a chatter, probably happy cause it has stopped raining. The air is fresh and cool and not a breath of wind. Yesterday we had to go out to one of our installations in a jeep and after fording a couple shallow rivers and following jungle trails, we finally got there. It was interesting to see the bright colored birds such as parrots and pretty flowers here and there. Most places the bamboo and other plants are so thick a snake could hardly crawl through. Saw one banana tree with a big cluster of green bananas. It's very interesting seeing how this other half lives. Seems unbelievable that so many of the natives could live all their lives in such poverty. Cause the soil seems rich enough and the jungle is clean except where the native villages are. The whole family and their goats, brahma cows, pigs, and flea-bitten dog live in the same bamboo hut! And they never seem to work but just sit cross legged on the floor and stare into space.

I'm in another camp in Assam now—came up here by plane from the other place. This is the best place I've been in India and this is where I'm assigned so will stay here a while. It's wonderful to unpack your stuff after living out of a handbag for 3 months. I am now working as a Crypto Officer with a 1st Lt over me but he is a nice fellow and we get along good. He is showing me the ropes. If you were to try to break into our locked room you would find yourself looking into several sub-machine guns, pistols etc. It is the most secretive work in the army and not even a General could come into our room without the proper pass. It is fascinating work but will probably get boring after a time. This field even boasts of a little library. Just now I'm half through, "The Robe," and it is very interesting. Also read "Goodbye Mr. Chips." In late afternoon I work out a bit, sun a little, and shower for supper. They have plenty water here so that's another good thing about this place. Note new address:

Detachment A.A.C.S. Station #207

APO 489

c/o Postmaster

New York, N.Y.

Haven't gotten any mail lately but did get your letter of May 1 a few days ago. Glad to hear cousin Jimmy is on the way home. I hope to come back by way of Europe—it's a little closer that way and might see a couple more ports. But that may be several months away. I'm optimistic about this end of it. You should have the corn in now and most of your garden. Wouldn't mind being home to do a few days work—haven't worked up a good sweat for quite some time by real work. Things will really hum around there when school is out. Be sure and take some pictures soon. Yes, I wish I were home this Sunday evening. The next time I get home at least I won't have to go chasing off to some distant camp at 4:00 in the morning. I'm fed up with army life—but at least over here it's more casual and easy going on things that don't matter. Wonder what kind of deal Vernon is in by now. Sure hoped they would stay longer in Long Beach. It's a nice little city. We had a nice time but we sure had difficulties getting together. They had no phone and I had no address that could be given out. But we made it.

I'll be expecting to hear all that goes on around there. It's a cool night and good for sleeping so I'll say "Goodnite" now and hit the sack.

The men slept on native-made cots with bamboo strips for a mattress and four posts that supported a mosquito netting. When water dripped through the thatched roof during the monsoon season, Lyle placed his GI raincoat over the netting to divert raindrops onto the floor. As for the food, he thought it remarkable that the Quartermaster Corps—despite limited cargo space, great shipping distance, and the hot, humid climate—was able to provide the troops in India with packaged supplies that not only retained nutritional value but were palatable. Although aware that the dehydrating and powdering of food products were necessary innovations, he craved fresh milk and fresh vegetables.

After two more weeks of jungle life, Lyle lightheartedly described his surroundings.

3 JUNE 1945 (SUNDAY). This has been a very pleasant day for me. Last night and this morning it rained as usual and now it is fresh and cool. There is different layers of clouds and it is cloudy enough so there is a very pretty effect on the mountains in the distance. They are a couple shades darker than the grey blue upper clouds and part way up the sides are bunches of fluffy and very white clouds. And the vegetation here is very green and lush from all the rain. The water grass grows six feet high and the trees are pretty much of the tropical variety. In fact it is pretty much jungle around here. The birds are much different than those at home and I believe they sing louder but most of them are not so pretty. Now if this were a tourist camp in the States it would be worth a fortune cause it is what you might call rustic with the native buildings of bamboo and grass and the natives themselves wandering around in their funny clothes. Some of the men have long grey flowing beards that match the tattle tale grey cloth they wear. Some have long hair worn in a knot or braid and occasionally you see one with naturally curley hair that many a coed would envy. They are about the same chocolate shade as the colored people at home but their features are Aryan like ours. However up here some of them are of the Mongol race and have features more like the Orientals. When you ask them a question they want to be polite so the answer is always yes. "Is the field this way?" and the answer is yes. If you point the opposite direction and ask another native the answer is still yes. If you are trying to explain to them some work to be done it is always, "Nai moullo, sahib." Meaning they don't understand. But they can understand what you mean if it is to their advantage. I just noticed a lizard on the wall in front of me but he is a little one and minding his own business. As for the food here it seems to be sufficient. Never have such things as milk. All the cows are tubercular so of course no milk. But really except for a day of dysentery at the other place I have never felt finer. Contrary to what some people would have you believe the army does a fine job of taking care of us. Especially when you consider that all the water has to be purified and insects controlled and all the food brought in. Food spoils very quickly here cause of the heat and dampness. Today was a good day for mail cause some had accumulated where it has to be forwarded to my new

address. Among them was the letter from Virginia and the V-mail from Jean. I was rather pleased to hear that Virginia was second instead of first. This way people remember that she was active in things rather than the girl with the 97.6 average. I'm in favor of colleges where there are no grades given out. And fooey on compulsary military training. Our soldiers are best because of training on the football fields instead of a lot of foolish parades on the drill field. What we need is a few more places like West Point to turn out highly trained officers. Now that is off my chest.

On the positive side, Lyle was appreciative that the commanding officer at the Misamari base had a relaxed attitude about dress code. Shorts, open collars, and rolled-up sleeves prevailed. Still, the men suffered from a painful rash brought on by the oppressive heat and excessive perspiration.

After washing in a basin outside his hut, Lyle hung his damp clothes in the sun to dry. Feeling refreshed, he began a letter with an upbeat line.

9 JUNE 1945 (SATURDAY). I feel so good tonight I'll just have to write you a letter. For the last couple days it didn't rain a bit and it was almost cloudless skies and bright sun. And I do mean bright sun. The temperature doesn't get any higher than the hottest days at home cause of all the rank green vegetation—but the sun is murder. One simply couldn't do any work like shocking grain out in the sun here. In fact if a dark-haired person stands bare headed in the sun he will likely get sunstroke. If you so much as walk a short distance in midday you get so heated up that you almost pass out. So of course we avoid being out of the shade and we don't do any work. It was hot every day in Calcutta— "the black hole." I read a book, "The Royal Road to Romance," about an American's world travels. His part about India interested me. He arrived in Calcutta in April and he said it was one of the 3 hottest places on earth—the other two places being suburbs. The cholera epidemic kept me from getting into town on my own—but the less you see of that the better.

Anyway what I was getting at is that last night I moved my bunk out under the stars but there wasn't a breath of air. When I went to bed about 11:00 the sweat ran off me. Not just drops of sweat like at home but streams of it. Towards morning it cooled off comfortably but today it was awful again. By wearing few clothes and showering daily I have pretty much avoided heat rash.

Tonight when I was at work a storm came up and was it ever welcome. And when I got home I took a shower so that is why I feel so good tonight. The coolness sure picks a fellow up after the hot days. If you drink plenty water and take salt tablets it doesn't hurt you any.

LYLE SLADEK SHAVING OUTSIDE HIS BASHA, ASSAM, INDIA, 1945
NATIVE COT MOVED OUTDOORS TO SLEEP UNDER THE STARS

You will get $80 soon probably in the form of a check. Seems to me you should hold on to the old Dodge. When new tires come out I might want to take it off your hands.

Upon receiving letters from home, Lyle read a newspaper clipping his mother had enclosed about his cousin Jimmy Sladek, now home from a POW camp in Germany:

CORP. JIM SLADEK, VERMILLION,
CAPTURED IN LUXEMBOURG, DECEMBER 18,
HAS UNPLEASANT MEMORIES OF BAD ORB, KASSEL PRISONS

Vermillion, S.D., May 21.—Memories of vermin infested barracks, sour black bread, and greasy soup are lucidly entrenched in the mind of Corp. Jim Sladek, who was confined to German prison camps for nearly four months.

The young infantryman, formerly of Chamberlain, captured in Luxembourg on December 18, two days after the German breakthrough, was sent to Bad Orb, Germany, and later transferred to another camp near Kassel.

LIBERATED ON GOOD FRIDAY

Liberated by the American First army on Good Friday, Corp. Sladek was evacuated by plane to France and from there by ship to the Untied States where he was granted a 60-day furlough. . . .

Upon graduation from the State University in 1943 . . . Corp. Sladek entered the service. In August, 1944, he was sent overseas with the 28th division, joining the First army in France.

FOODLESS ON TWO-DAY MARCH

Immediately following their capture began a two-day march, during which the prisoners were given nothing to eat and had to get water by eating snow. At Garoldston they were loaded into boxcars where they were actually "packed in like sardines."

Terrific American air raids kept the trains from traveling during the daytime; consequently it took them five days to reach their destination 100 miles away.

AIRMEN DID GOOD JOB

"Our air force was always on the job and I might add, it was always a good job. The bombing was heavy near Frankfurt and one of our cars was overturned."

At Bad Orb they found Russians, Poles and Frenchmen—many of whom had been there for five years. The prisoners were segregated as to nationalities and were not allowed to communicate with each other. Corp Sladek, along with other non-commissioned officers, was later transferred to a camp near Kassel.

CRAWLING WITH INSECTS

Conditions in both camps were about the same—deplorable. The barracks were crowded, filthy and crawling with insects, and there was always a constant dread with the prisoners and the Germans alike of typhus.

"Most of us Americans were lucky, however, in that we were never beaten or forced to work," remarked Corp. Sladek.

The daily ration, meager and unpalatable, consisted of a pint of greasy, watery soup at noon and one-sixth of a loaf of black bread at night.

"It might be interesting to know what we did to pass the time," he volunteered. "Within our group were men of all different types of trades, professions and occupations—bakers, engineers, lawyers, college students. Each man would take his turn and recount his various experiences. It was really informative as well as entertaining."

RELIGION PLAYED PART

That religion played an important part in these camps was stressed by Corp. Sladek, who pointed out that although there was no American chaplain with them, rosary was held once a day for the Catholics and Bible classes were organized by the Protestants. Nightly prayer services were conducted.

"It was on Good Friday that our white flag was hung out just after a nearby town had fallen. By this time most of the camp staff had fled, leaving only a few to guard us. We were confined to our barracks when the First army arrived to liberate us. But the sight of the first GI who entered the gate was too much for us—we ran out and mobbed him, laughing and crying at the same time."

A combined church service for Americans and British was conducted in the camp on Easter Sunday between the barracks by an American chaplain with the liberating division.

Although freed, the men were not allowed to leave the camp for 10 days. Corp. Sladek explained that the delay was caused by a tie-up in transportation. He will report to Hot Springs, Ark. July 17.

Lyle was thankful his cousin Jimmy had survived the war. Judging by the enclosed photographs, however, it appeared his health had been impaired.

Sunday.

Today Wilma's V-mail and Mom's letter of May 28 found their way to me. I must say Virginia certainly got the looks in our family and that photo certainly doesn't flatter her either. Guess she has beauty and brains on account she did so well in school! She should always fix her hair like that.

Did you plant cane on the same field again this year? What is Mom going to do with all her chicken money this year?? Mom looked full of pep in the picture like she must have had a couple cups of coffee before the banquet even started. You girls don't sound too enthusiastic about school being over. I'll bet Chuckie is though. If you ever get a chance to buy a popular size roll of film you could send it to me airmail. Film and blonde girls are both very scarce items over here. Jimmy didn't look too much like I remembered him. Will he be discharged now? That will be the day. If this doesn't drag out too long over here I'll be able to look back on it as a real experience. The food is surprisingly good here and I like my work. Once in a while I feel I pull a sharp one out of the bag—but then that is what I'm getting paid for. I want to get to China if possible and a few other places while over here. And when I get back I'll never want to travel again.

They had a track meet this afternoon and some good competition. I would like to have tried the half mile but it was hot enough so I was content to be a spectator. It's hot this evening. A shirt gets wet right away—I'm sweating without any clothes on. India is hardly fit for people to live in. One of the fellows has a little pet monkey the size of a cat. I've been reading poetry trying to get rid of some time before going to bed.

When the China airlift began, planes searched out routes over the Hump from India to China. Whereas many of the Himalayan peaks rose to more than twenty-six thousand feet, the fully loaded transport planes attained altitudes of less than twenty thousand feet. Only by staying on course could the planes make a safe passage through mountain saddles. Severe thunderstorms, sleet, hail, icing, clouds, fog, and turbulent winds that "tossed aircraft like leaves" took a heavy toll. Engine failures, navigational errors, running out of fuel, explosions from gasoline fumes, and Japanese Zeros lying in wait to lure the unarmed two-engine planes off course or into enemy airfields were other pitfalls. Aware of the loss of hundreds of planes, the men who flew the Hump dubbed the route *Aluminum Alley*, a term not permitted in letters home because it was bad for morale on the home front. But while on duty the next morning, Lyle alluded to some of the hazards.

Monday.

Our AACS outfit uses equipment to radio the planes to a landing when the ceiling is zero. Sometimes a field may be closed in by weather so that a dozen planes may be stacked over the field at different altitudes circling—when one lands they all come down a step. Our tower calls out the crash crew when a plane is in danger when landing. When a few tons of aluminum is moving around from 200 to 400 miles per you have to have things regulated cause it makes a big bang when things go wrong. A complex business. Obviously this letter has gone far enough.

A week later Lyle revealed his intention to fly to China in one of those giant tin cans. While in high school he had spent evenings reading literary gems in the one-room library on the second floor of the Chamberlain City Hall. Along with the poetry of Rudyard Kipling he had discovered a book, *The Good Earth,* by Pearl Buck. Being a farm boy, he had related to the heroine, Olin, and her family as they struggled to wrest a living from the soil of China. Buck's description of the villages and terraced fields had fascinated him. Now, by some twist of fate, two of his wildest dreams were about to materialize.

> 17 JUNE 1945 (SUNDAY). Tomorrow I plan to go in for a little excitement or something. For the past few years it has been my ambition to "fly the Hump" and I believe tomorrow I'll get the chance. Will be fun to see a bit of China too. Want to go along? Haven't heard from you for over a week. Maybe it has been raining so the roads are blocked or you are busy. Had a good time playing bridge last Saturday night. One of my men and I played partners against a couple other fellows. We clicked and gave them a drubbing to remember. It's a fascinating game—you have to remember every card, figure the playing of the whole hand out before even taking the first trick etc. A couple good players can walk all over a couple of average players. I guess bridge is one of the few things I do well in.

On the return flight from China, Lyle chatted with the pilot and copilot while viewing the treacherous terrain from the cockpit of the plane. Once descended to a lower altitude the copilot removed his oxygen mask and went to the cargo section to relax. Lyle moved to the vacated seat and followed along on the controls. Shortly, the pilot got up and made his way to the back of the plane for a smoke; the fifty-five-gallon drums of high-octane gasoline—sometimes hoisted into the planes by trained elephants—had been unloaded in China.

Lyle rode the controls, keeping the plane level and on course through murky skies and darkening twilight. Like other boys flying the Hump in million-dollar planes, the three lieutenants thought themselves invincible.

Having fulfilled his dreams of flying the Hump and seeing terraced fields and villages of China, Lyle described the experience for his parents.

> Monday night.
>
> Just back from China. "Don't get Around Much Anymore." It was as interesting as I had anticipated too. It's nice to look down on the clouds and once in a while there is an opening so you can see the rugged Himalaya Mts just itching to get you in their grasp. And then you see the smaller Mts and hills of China with green patchwork patterns of the well-tilled fields and the terracing which is the work of centuries. Then when you get lower you can take off the oxygen mask and then you see the little Chinese villages each with about 50 houses all piled together to save valuable land. No one lives on their little farms—they live in villages and walk out to them. The soil is reddish and the slipperiest mud I ever saw. The climate is nicer there but the food isn't so good as

in India. On the way back (this is unofficial) they let me fly the plane by my lonesome for over an hour. When you can't see the ground cause of clouds or darkness you have to "fly on instruments." I took some link training in Texas so I know what I'm doing. "Hot Pilot Sladek" they call me. Anyway I really got cold for the first time in months and feel ready to settle down to a nice quiet existence for a while. When I got back your letter was waiting. It was a super duper letter all full of snapshots etc. I guessed right about it raining there. Things will really look prosperous when the water goes down so you can see the fields again. Is the cane on the low field again this year? Irene's package hasn't arrived yet. Don't send me anything except snapshots, clippings, and letters telling me everything is under control at home. These sure were newsy letters. Wish I had been there for the fish feed and the picnic. Dad and the girls I can tell really enjoyed the picnic cause they are busy eating. In the ice cream picture Dad looks like he has had ten cups of ice cream and is seriously pondering the advisability of just one more. A momentous decision. Where were you Mom? Your camera technique is improving right along. Do you mean Chuckie actually shoots some game with the rifle? Did he train the dog or was it just the turning over of a new leaf? I always said he was a good dog. Yes it does rain about 30 feet in some parts of India but that couldn't be here could it. Or could it? Every soldier here is issued a pair of hip boots and a rowboat. But the rain keeps it reasonably cool. I hear from Irene quite often. Can't help but notice how enthusiastic her letters are—just bubbling over with zest for living. Guess she'll be home before long. I'll enclose the key to the locker. Don't throw away any of the papers. Must be awfully nice around there this summer. You are probably cultivating corn by now.

Interrupting his letter, Lyle checked in at the message station to monitor the activity. He liked the code room personnel. Being younger than most of the enlisted men, he was tactful in his interactions and complimentary of their work. Nevertheless, he ensured they were vigilantly following proper procedures. A miscue on the part of a German cryptographer had helped the Allies fathom the workings of the Enigma Machine. Another careless German operator had used the first three letters of his name and the first three letters of his girlfriend's name when setting rotors on the machine. Such human failings had provided invaluable clues to the Allies.

After unscrambling a garbled message, Lyle returned to his basha and finished his letter.

My work is still interesting and tricky enough for a little mental browbeating at times. My C.O. is a nice fellow. And I take my pills and have no ills. Well I'm tired and it's time to crawl in under that netting for a good nights sleep. Don't you envy me—you have to get up about now.

26 JUNE 1945 (TUESDAY). How is everything in the Sunshine State— if the sun were shining? The Draft Board sure has their eye on the young fellows around there don't they? I sure would hate to be coming into the army now. I recognized lots of names in the State College grad clipping. Irene said Virginia might work in Omaha. Might be O.K. to work a year and then go to college next year. Of course I am very much in favor of college for people who want to go—not so much for what you learn but rather the social life and good times. What does she think? I'll enclose a Chinese bill. Chinese money is so inflated that it takes a basketful to buy a meal. No news here—feeling good—keeping fairly busy. Always glad to hear things are going smoothly at home. It seems too far to ever get back there but I guess some morning I'll awaken and see the blue walls with the sun shining in the window. How often are my letters censored by a censor higher up? You should see the bats here—a little bigger than a crow. How would you like one of them in your hair?

Come morning, the fiery red sun foreshadowed another day of perspiration and dull routine. As usual Lyle joined friends at the mess hall, another shelter that featured walls of bamboo screens and a thatched roof. Suspended from the ceiling were three rectangular bamboo flaps attached to a rope that extended through the wall at one end of the building. A native, seated outside on the shady side of the hut, pulled on the rope to move the flaps, stirring the air inside. While chowing down on the usual breakfast fare—canned grapefruit juice referred to as *battery acid*, powdered milk, powdered eggs, dehydrated potatoes, Spam, bread, and a rubbery substance that came in a tin labeled CANNED BUTTER—the soldiers chattered about news from home, the progress of the war, and their prospects of shipping home.

As measured by some wartime assignments, serving in the CBI was not hard duty. Yet most of the men would have opted to serve elsewhere. During the *hot*, muggy days from May to October, one in five fell ill with malaria. Some days, when it did not rain, it was so hot the mechanics had to wait until night, when the metal cooled down, to service the planes. As for entertainment, organized recreation was a rarity and there was no physical training program. The tiny PX offered little in the way of supplies. Some men, unable to cope with the extreme heat, tedium, and isolation, suffered psychological problems termed *jungle fever*. Even for a boy "with cheeks of tan" who had sweltered in the harvest fields, the intense rays of the sun were a bane.

One day, just for a lark, Lyle wrapped his head with a Sikh turban, wielded a Gurkha knife, and posed as a tiger hunter while his basha mate snapped his photo. Jesting, Lyle wrote on the back, "Watch out tiger!"

LYLE SLADEK, ASSAM, INDIA, 1945
DRESSED AS A TIGER HUNTER

1 JULY 1945 (SUNDAY). Today was another scorcher and it's pretty hot yet this evening. In the morning you wake up and see the bright sun on the green trees and dew covered grass and the birds sing—beautiful country—then about 9:00 it is getting hot and the leaves curl up, the birds and Indians find a shade to sleep in, and you wish you were any other place on earth. The rain makes your clothes mold and even the bedding gets pretty bad on account of sweating so much. Undoubtedly this climate takes something out of you but I don't know how much.

Seems to me to be rougher on you mentally than physically, but so far I can't complain about either. For one thing in late afternoon I take some light exercises and run just a bit. That really makes the sweat run and then when you take a shower your skin is clean and open. So far it has kept me from breaking out with much heat rash. A shirt gets wet in a few minutes—but our outfit is behind locked doors so we work in just shorts. And they aren't too particular about what you wear around here.

Don't take this as being pessimistic cause really I'm in pretty good humor. Just letting you know a little about the place—I realize there are lots of rougher situations to be in. We take atabrine (no quinine) for malaria so I'm yellow as the Chinese. The food comes out of cans—I think it is a pretty good diet except for no green vegetables and calcium. Can't tell you anything about this field or about my work in particular. It is a job where you keep your tongue from wagging—better than most jobs. We run continuously—sometimes I work in the early part of the night—worked quite a bit today. Pleasant fellows to work with—plenty sleep.

Last night we had a band concert. That is always a big event for me but much too rare. I miss music here. No, Irene's package hasn't arrived yet—should be here in a week or two. It surprised me if Irene did actually go to Boston. I'm sure she will have a nice time there. What I wouldn't give to go swimming in the ocean—or anywhere. Gee, I sure hope Harold Swanson gets out soon. He has taken a lot—I don't see how he stood up under it so well. Just been four months and I'm ready to go back anytime.

Resuming his letter, Lyle longed to hear details about the animals and crops. Even after being away from the farm for two and a half years, he was still interested in the activities.

Was sorry to hear Mrs. Hlouka passed away. She was one of the early pioneers out there I bet—and so peppy even a couple years ago. I guess the world just keeps moving on. Guess the crops are a little slower this year but last year at this time we were already getting the binder lined up for the barley. Why doesn't someone corner Dad when he hasn't got any excuse and put a pencil and piece of paper in his hand? Mom you cover most things except what is planted in which field and why etc. Did the pony fatten up pretty good again this spring? I could go for a drink of cool clean well water. And some of that garden would go over big. The fabulous riches and wealth of India? I haven't seen them. Well it's getting late—about midnight here—twelve hours earlier there—let's see, that would be about noon—someone should be finishing the breakfast dishes about now! Anyway Good nite to each of you.

Shortly after the Air Transport Command (ATC) began hauling supplies over the Hump to China, FDR, in his tenth State of the Union address on 1 January 1943, related details of the hazardous mission:

> Even today we are flying as much lend-lease material into China as ever traversed the Burma Road, flying it over mountains 17,000 feet high, flying blind through sleet and snow. We shall overcome all the formidable obstacles, and get the battle equipment into China to shatter the power of our common enemy.

In the early days of the airlift the Hump operation did not meet the expectation of General Arnold. When he learned that forty-seven planes had been lost in less than two months—sixteen simply disappearing into the mountains—he prescribed two pragmatic stopgap measures:

1. Double the number of crews but retain the same number of operating missions so that the attrition will be distributed over double the number of people.

2. Increase the number of airplanes so that we will always have a standard number of about 250 in operation and in that way our losses will not become so noticeable.

Wartime policy obscured the heavy loss of planes and crews flying the *Aluminum Trail*. Perhaps there was some hyperbole when General Wedemeyer, the commanding officer of the CBI, stated that the Hump operation was "foremost and by far the most dangerous, difficult, and historic achievement of the entire war." The Hump Express motto, "Bring Me Men To Match My Weather," was indicative of the role played by the elements. Day and night, fair weather and foul, the ATC strove to increase the tonnage and keep China in the war. Fuel for the return flight used a portion of the carrying capacity since the route across the Himalayas was a five-hundred mile stretch. To Lyle, the frenzied activity of the airlift was akin to the procession of a column of ants between nest and sugar bowl.

As the war progressed it was no longer relevant whether Japan knew the size and location of the airfields in Assam. After two months in India, Lyle was able to divulge his precise whereabouts.

7 JULY 1945 (SATURDAY). Today they lifted the censoring a little so I can tell you that I am at Misamari, India. You won't be able to find it on the map but it is in the vicinity of Jorhat, Chabua, Ledo, etc, sort of up in that part of India that looks like it should be part of Burma. The

Japs of course have been driven out of part of Assam and Burma so it is very quiet here. Ledo of course is where the Stillwell road starts over the Hump. The foothills of the Himalayas rise up out of the Assam Valley and once in a while we can see some of the snowcaps on a real clear day which is very rare. How would you like to trade places with me? Chuckie would like it of course cause he could hunt tigers, elephants, jackals, monkeys, apes, etc. We have several tame monkeys and a tame ape. They are trying to teach the ape to smoke but not much luck yet.

This evening we are having a bridge game—a couple of the sergeants in the outfit and another fellow. This one graduated from some university in Pennsylvania and was a champion runner and is plenty sharp. This week I was lucky to be near the P.X. when some film came in so I latched on to a roll. Someday I'll borrow a camera and use it up. Last night we saw the show "Suspect" but I can't rave about it. The other late afternoon we had a game of volleyball. Most of the officers are older and kind of slow on their feet but it was fun for a change. It is usually just too hot to do anything like that in the summer months but in the fall and winter we will get some teams organized. Have you heard from the sailors V and V lately? Last I heard they were going to Oakland. As you can plainly see there isn't much news around here so I'll just sign off for a while.

ROWS OF THATCHED HUTS, MISAMARI AIR BASE, INDIA, 1945
OPEN SPACE FOR RECREATION, VOLLEYBALL COURT IN FOREGROUND

In addition to competing in sports in the open space near the rows of thatched huts, the men occasionally staved off boredom by watching a movie on an outdoor screen near the runway.

18 JULY 1945 (WEDNESDAY). Just back from a show—the best I've seen here—"The Royal Scandal," a story of the Czar period in Russia. They show them outdoors and it didn't even rain all during the show. But it has been raining or drizzling about 90% of the time day and night. Nice and fresh and keeps the sun behind clouds. So everything is fine here.

Victory over Europe was a bittersweet time for GIs overseas; most expected to be reassigned to the Pacific theater and many received *Dear John* letters from girlfriends back home, making them members of the *Lonely Hearts Club*.

Lyle wondered about the romance of his sister Irene. While working at the air base in Sioux City she had met Henry Parkhurst, a soldier from Massachusetts. They had exchanged letters while he was serving as a B-24 mechanic with the Eighth Air Force in England. Upon returning to the States to await reassignment, Henry had invited Irene to Boston to meet his family.

Thursday.

Would sure like to be turned loose in your garden for a few minutes. Miss fresh things. Sometimes home seems a long way away and it does right now. But I'm optimistic so I say, Out of the sticks in forty-six. So Dale Korzan joined the Lonely Hearts Club too. The President of the club is the fellow who got dropped hardest. And of course it happens a lot. But that is to be expected. I hope I'm not egotistical enough to expect a girl to sit home and knit for a couple years. Free as the wind, that's me for the duration. I'm very curious as to just how things went with Irene. Haven't heard from her since she went East. I'm sure her interests are in Omaha but she just wanted to make sure. Had a letter from Vivian yesterday. They sure move around. Got a car now too. Does Chuckie really drive now? Why, I never even drove the buggy at his age.

Friday.

Today is a scorcher to be long remembered. But we had it coming cause last week was cooler than normal. Everything is O.K. here though. Am going to play bridge this evening. Worked until midnight last night—sort of comes in spurts. Hope you are all up to snuff. Here is a little clipping from a paper here in this area.

ASSAM SCRAPBOOK ITEM

No cobras or monkeys in this, but no scrapbook of "typical India" shots could be complete from the GI viewpoint without a glimpse of Assam's endless tea fields. C-46s line up beside the tea, others roar overhead, but the changeless work of the tea pickers goes on—and somewhere a professional sipper is probably wondering right now if that slightly different aromatic tinge couldn't be a touch of exhaust fumes.

Time was warped for the troops serving in Assam. The heat and absence of a social life could make a month seem like a year. As a diversion and form of entertainment, as well as to ease his parents' worry and stay connected with the outside world, Lyle wrote letters. And the more he wrote, the more he anticipated in return. During the peak heat one day, he leisurely scrawled:

25 JULY 1945 (WEDNESDAY). A rather quiet afternoon in India with the birds waiting until evening to come out and sing, no touch of breeze, the Indians lying in the shade, and occasionally the drone of a plane coming from or going to China. Only a week left in July which doesn't make me a bit unhappy. That is always the way it is in the army—always marking time. You say, "it will be better in a month when basic training is over," or "gee, I'll be glad when this course is over," etc etc. One could live in a castle in paradise but not enjoy it there because someone is telling you you *must* live there. And when you live with unhappy restless people, you also get unhappy and discontented. Seems like we get all the third rate shows so I don't go very often anymore. We get up a bridge game about once a week and that is always a big occasion. The competition is as keen as one can find anywhere. Finally got a couple letters from Irene when she got back from Boston. Guess she really had a fine time. Irene is not so predictable as she used to be. Her package hasn't arrived yet. I expect it in time for Christmas! Was just thinking if a plane flew straight at 300 miles per hour for two days and two nights without a stop it would reach home. That boat just plowed steadily into the waves for weeks day and night with never a pause. But India now seems less foreign than the Nevada desert cause here we are in the jungle with the native workers living our way of life rather than theirs and it's green here. Why don't you try and get ahold of a 32-volt radio? No news from here. Hope this finds you all feeling tops.

Unexpectedly receiving orders to move to another base, Lyle inventoried the coding materials and signed them over to the lieutenant replacing him at the Misamari station. Together the two officers burned obsolete codebooks in a fifty-five-gallon oil drum, stirred the ashes, and signed the disposal document. Lyle bade farewell, packed his belongings, and caught the next available plane to Tezpur.

TEZPUR, ASSAM, INDIA

At the Tezpur air base, B-24 Liberators labored to lift heavy loads of cargo from the runway before proceeding over the Hump to China. The four-engine bombers, with a flight ceiling of twenty-eight thousand feet and a top speed of 300 mph, flew higher and faster than the C-46 Dumbos and C-47 Gooney Birds used in earlier stages of the Hump operation.

From the code room at Tezpur, not as primitive as the one at Misamari, Lyle informed his folks, "Another chapter has closed."

28 JULY 1945 (SATURDAY). Got a radiogram to transfer here to Tezpur so here I am. This is also in the Assam Valley. Didn't care to leave cause Misamari was just getting to feel like home and now I start all over. It's surprising though how fast you get acquainted in a new place. They were putting me in for a promotion next month at Misamari but of course that is out now. You have to be at a place 3 months to get a recommendation. That was the longest I have stayed any place since leaving Yale. So now I'm attached to a B-24 bomb group. Tezpur, the "City of Blood" in Hindu mythology, is a fairly large town. Every time I drive through an Indian town I'm shocked anew at the poverty and squalor. You have no conception of poverty until you've seen this. Lots of tea plantations here and rice paddies.

Sunday.

A little cooler this morning. This afternoon at 4 o'clock I go to work and finish at midnight. It isn't going to be as nice a working set up here

CODE ROOM, TEZPUR AIR BASE, INDIA, 1945
MACHINE GUNS, BARRED WINDOWS, DOUBLE DOORS, AND CRYPTO MATERIALS IN SAFES

as at Misamari but I like the field just as well. Mail seems to have slowed down a little and moving will hold it back a few days now too. They sure are putting a lot of power over Japan lately. I'm hoping the whole affair will crack open in a few months. August 1 is the anniversary of the air forces and should be a big day over Tokyo.

With the war ended in Europe, the Allies geared up for the final assault on Japan, still a formidable foe. Two Pacific islands taken at great cost in American lives, Iwo Jima and Okinawa, began operating as staging bases for potent B-29 Superfortresses. Equipped with radar and capable of flying more than three thousand miles while carrying heavy bomb loads, B-29s were wreaking havoc on Japanese cities.

Lyle knew the fate of the Japanese people was contingent upon the mind-set of their leaders. Surely, he reasoned, they would recognize the futility of continuing the war and facing the prospect of ground forces invading their home islands. Confident Japan would capitulate within a matter of months, Lyle was failing to take into account profound differences between Eastern and Western thought, so aptly expressed by Rudyard Kipling: "OH, East is East and West is West, and never the twain shall meet."

The troops at Tezpur had no inkling that peace talks were already underway; that Japanese leaders had signaled a willingness to accept the terms of the Potsdam Declaration provided the emperor remained the sovereign ruler of Japan. Allied leaders were adamant, however, that imperial rule be subject to the supreme commander of the Allied occupation force. While Japanese leaders waffled on the emperor issue, B-29 bombers continued to carry out devastating raids on Japanese cities.

Meanwhile, there were matters of life and death at the Tezpur air base. Censorship deterred Lyle from writing about a plane, loaded with a cargo of gasoline, that blew up while taking off for China. But in closing his letter, he alluded to that catastrophic event.

Saw the show "Lake Placid Serenade" last evening. Was enjoying it until something drastic happened. As you can see I have no news so I'll just quit. Don't forget APO 429 Station 214.

At Tezpur, Lyle quickly became friends with his basha mates, two lieutenants with similar interests.

3 AUGUST 1945 (FRIDAY). For some reason I'm just feeling tops tonite—and I hope it's even better with each of you. Somehow I just hope things always stay on an even keel around home—it will be much

easier for us if we come back to something solid—something dependable. We get used to most anything it seems after about so long but there are times when one feels like how swell it would be to have Mommy tuck him in and bring a glass of water when he's sick. It's a lonely feeling like when they fire a volley and a flag wrapped body breaks the stillness of a tropical sea. Although I guess that's a good way to go. Today I had to censor our detachment's mail which is the worst job in the army. I have enough troubles of my own most of the time without hearing other people's too. I work two nights from midnight to eight or nine, two evenings from four to midnight, and a day from eight to four, and then start over again. I'm beginning to like it quite well here. My two bunkies are nice fellows—already it seems like we have known each other for years. Verner Strombom is from Calif. His brother's name is Lyle. His Dad's name is Charlie. Tish, tish. He has an English record player and quite a few good recordings—popular and classical. Oh happy day. But the main spring broke in the drum. So we took it apart and went to a shop and first punched three small holes in each end of the broken steel spring. Then we drilled them a little. No rivits so I cut off short lengths of soft wire and drew them up tight. Then we bent it into a sharper curve to relieve some of the strain and put it back together. It works fine—but we hold our breath when we wind it. We also fixed the automatic shutoff. This fellow (a 2d Louie) is O.K. with mechanics considering he is from the city. He is pretty sharp all around in fact and a lot of fun. He's going to teach me chess sometime or I mean get me started playing. We had some jungle-fresh pineapple at noon and you haven't lived until you have eaten it right out of the husk and ripened by a tropical sun. Tastes good especially after eating canned rations, raw onions, and rice!

When mail redirected from Misamari finally reached Lyle at Tezpur, he happily replied:

Surprise of surprises. Mail caught up with me today and whatcha know, Joe—a letter from Dad and Chuckie. Yes, Irene told me the big news and actually it didn't surprise me too much. I just say "Lucky Guy!" He must have lots of drive cause he sure gave her the rush. When and where? Take one of the checks and get Irene and Henry a wedding present for me if it takes place soon. Dad, you sure wowed me with that "Fee On Say." You should get on Bob Hope's show. But Dad, you just don't understand the situation here. If you so much as glanced at these Indian gals the MPs would toss you in the guardhouse and quick. You see actually you cannot comprehend this country cause you cannot see and smell it. You cannot possibly realize how absolutely positively

LYLE SLADEK IN FRONT OF BASHA, TEZPUR AIR BASE, INDIA, 1945
COLLAR OPEN AND SLEEVES ROLLED UP IN AN ATTEMPT TO COOL OFF

VERNER STROMBOM, LYLE'S BASHA MATE, TEZPUR AIR BASE, INDIA, 1945

LYLE SLADEK HOLDING AN ELEPHANT LEAF, TEZPUR AIR BASE, INDIA, 1945

LYLE SLADEK WITH A GURKHA KNIFE, TEZPUR AIR BASE, INDIA, 1945
DARK SPOTS ON UNIFORM CAUSED BY HEAT AND HUMIDITY DAMAGE TO FILM

it lacks any resemblance to our type of living. Just like trying to tell someone how a carrot tastes. Get me?

My advice to Virginia is to do something that is expansive and preferably go to college this year or next. If I go back to college for a year you might be surprised at the course I take. You guys amuse me— one dance a night isn't enough for you. Oh you lead a hard life.

Powerful engines droned as planes—loaded with gasoline, grenades, canned tomatoes, mortar shells, and other cargo—lumbered off the runway, climbing higher and higher to clear each successive mountain ridge.

Yes, that C-46 picture over the Hump looked natural. While riding the controls through storms I wondered how it would feel to bail out into the dark of the night into the wilds of the world's roughest terrain. Lots have done it—lots don't get a chance to jump. But the life line to China must and will stay open in all weather day and night. August 1 was the anniversary of the air forces. News is good lately isn't it. Got my fingers crossed. Today Verner somehow or other asked me how many pull ups (chins) I could do. Well, I told him I'd want a dollar for each of the first ten, $5 for each of the next five, and $10 for all after that. So he phooed that and said he could do less than ten and he knew he could do as many as I. So I said I figured I could do eleven. He was sure I couldn't. He chinned first and fagged out on 7 and to my surprise 12 didn't completely fag my arms. Hands turned palms away, no kicking, and full drop. So apparently I'm not getting too weak although I have lost weight and am a yellow color. And loose enough to touch palms on the floor with stiff knees. It has rained hourly for the past week so it has been some relief from heat. But you have to dry feet and powder well etc to prevent fungus growth. And envelopes must be strung on thread like beads cause they seal if they touch anything. Great country. Really feeling on top of the world though. Be good.

As anticipated, hundreds of bombers had raided Tokyo on 1 August. Surely, Lyle thought, the devastating firebombing would induce Japanese leaders to admit defeat.

The GIs at Tezpur speculated as to how much longer it would take to subdue the Japanese military. Whereas some were of the opinion the war would be over within a year, others thought that was just wishful thinking. All agreed that sweating out another year or two in the jungle of Assam was an unpleasant prospect. They yearned for the day when they could return to the *good ol'* USA.

A surprise event was in store for the troops at Tezpur.

CHAPTER 16

The Dawn of a New Age

It is a mistake to look too far ahead.
Only one link in the chain of destiny can be handled at a time.
—WINSTON CHURCHILL

THE DAY OF 6 AUGUST began much like others for the troops at Tezpur. The pink hue of dawn and the languid morning air soothed their senses as they shook off the vestiges of sleep. But the men were not deceived. They knew a blazing red sun would soon burst into view, heralding another day with heat so intense it would "make their bloomin' eyebrows crawl." They knew by mid-morning, perspiration would darken their khaki shirts and heat rash would prickle the small of their backs.

Inside the mess hall the rectangular fans suspended from the ceiling stirred the humid air as native boys, seated on the shady side of the building, pulled on ropes. The swaying bamboo flaps cast a hypnotic spell on the men as they consumed a breakfast of canned grapefruit juice, Spam, coarse bread, and an omelet made from powdered eggs.

Quite suddenly, the seemingly ordinary day of tedium and stoicism gave way to awe and wonder. A radio operator had picked up a news bulletin on a shortwave set—something about a powerful bomb dropped on a Japanese city. Soon the whole camp was ablaze with excitement. The men sensed the new weapon, whatever its nature, would hasten the end of the war and the time when they could go home. They eagerly awaited further word of the stunning development.

On the home front, a presidential press release informed the American people:

> Sixteen hours ago an American airplane dropped one bomb on Hiroshima and destroyed its usefulness to the enemy. *That bomb had more power than*

20,000 tons of TNT. It had more than two thousand times the blast power of the British "Grand Slam" which is the largest bomb ever yet used in the history of warfare.

The Japanese began the war from the air at Pearl Harbor. They have been repaid many fold. And the end is not yet. With this bomb we have now added a new and revolutionary increase in destruction to supplement the growing power of our armed forces. . . .

It is an atomic bomb. It is a harnessing of the basic power of the universe. The force from which the sun draws its power has been loosed against those who brought war to the Far East. . . .

The *battle of the laboratories* held fateful risks for us as well as the battles of the air, land, and sea, and we have now won the battle of the laboratories as we have won the other battles. . . .

It was to spare the Japanese people from utter destruction that the ultimatum of July 26 was issued at *Potsdam*. Their leaders promptly rejected that ultimatum. If they do not now accept our terms they may expect a rain of ruin from the air, the like of which has never been seen on this earth. Behind this air attack will follow sea and land forces in such number and power as they have not yet seen and with the fighting skill of which they are already well aware. . . .

The fact that we can release atomic energy ushers in a new era in man's understanding of nature's forces . . . I shall give further consideration and make further recommendations to the Congress as to how atomic power can become a powerful and forceful influence towards the maintenance of world peace.

During ensuing days, sketchy details filtered in to the base at Tezpur. The revelation that Hiroshima had been destroyed by an *atomic* bomb held little meaning for the troops. Few had heard of uranium, isotopes, or atoms. For most of the GIs at Tezpur, knowledge of radiation was limited to watch dials that glowed in the dark and gizmos in shoe stores that pictured greenish images of foot bones. To them, the atomic bomb was just another lethal weapon of war, like jet airplanes and V-2 rockets. There was little soul-searching. The men had been trained to fight a war. In basic training they had sung, "Let's remember Pearl Harbor as we go to meet the foe." Victory and going home was what mattered to them.

When the first atomic bomb failed to bring about surrender, President Truman was advised to deploy the remaining bomb so as to create the impression that many such bombs existed. Beforehand, planes dropped leaflets on Japanese cities. One warning read:

ATTENTION JAPANESE PEOPLE. EVACUATE YOUR CITIES.
Because your military leaders have rejected the thirteen part surrender declaration, two momentous events have occurred in the last few days.
The Soviet Union, because of this rejection on the part of the military, has notified your Ambassador Sato that it has declared war on your nation. Thus, all powerful countries of the world are now at war with you.

Also, because of your leaders' refusal to accept the surrender declaration that would enable Japan to honorably end this useless war, we have employed our atomic bomb.

A single one of our newly developed atomic bombs is actually the equivalent in explosive power to what 2000 of our giant B-29s could have carried on a single mission. Radio Tokyo has told you that with the first use of this weapon of total destruction, Hiroshima was virtually destroyed.

Before we use this bomb again and again to destroy every resource of the military by which they are prolonging this useless war, petition the emperor now to end the war. Our president has outlined for you the thirteen consequences of an honorable surrender. We urge that you accept these consequences and begin the work of building a new, better, and peace-loving Japan.

Act at once or we shall resolutely employ this bomb and all our other superior weapons to promptly and forcefully end the war.

EVACUATE YOUR CITIES.

A second atomic bomb, more powerful than the first, decimated Nagasaki on 9 August. Emperor Hirohito, considered by many Japanese citizens to be a god incarnate, ordered an end to the war. In a recorded radio message he counseled his subjects to accept defeat, to "bear the unbearable." It was the first time the people had heard the voice of their emperor.

When the Allies proclaimed victory over Japan (V-J Day), Lyle was jubilant. Yet he vaguely sensed that the advent of the nuclear age gave rise to problems for which there were no precedents.

14 AUGUST 1945 (TUESDAY). Well today we heard what we have waited 4 years to hear. The atomic bomb certainly changed the situation in a hurry—if only we don't get too swelled up with our own power now. Of course we can't all expect to get back for a while, but I've got a hunch that India is a good place to be located on V-J Day. But it's just a hunch. Seems like I've got enough time in to get out of the army before too long after getting back unless they favor older married fellows. In my case it won't make too much difference. Of course it still seems unbelievable and places other than India seem awfully remote. But I guess now it's just a matter of sweating out a few months—and they will be cooler too. Saw a good show the other night—"Valley for Decision." About the early days in Pittsburgh with Irish people working in a steel mill. Pretty good show as far as shows go. I worked the past two nights and don't go to work again until tomorrow morning. Of course our work must go on for a while yet but should let up before too long. Am I daydreaming or did the war end? Everyone was thinking in terms of 6 months or two years. But I just didn't believe a nation would fight until exterminated cause there is no percentage in that. The handwriting was on the wall.

About this time Mom will say, "Here, it's time for school again. I just don't know where the summer went"—as she says every year. Bet Chuckie isn't too enthused about it. Say, why don't you ask Uncle Sam to bring me right back to teach school?

Still ecstatic, Lyle wrote to Irene:

15 AUGUST 1945 (WEDNESDAY). This is really great isn't it. I just can't realize the war is actually over. The world has waited a long time for this day. And now this eliminates the last objection to a short engagement cause likely Henry will be among the first to get out. So just when? You know that fellow must be a real terror. It seems you goofs have it pretty bad. Say, this world of ours sure looks pretty bright doesn't it. Can you imagine a carefree existence again? And from now on it's, "Hey Bud, don't you know there isn't a war on?" It will be a little rough on lots of us if we have to go to work for a change. But I can tell you are already used to keeping the chips flying. Irene, I've just got a hunch that India is a good place to be at the ending of the war. Just a hunch though. Now it's just a matter of time and I hope a boat back by the Suez. Oh you lucky girl.

My pal Verner is teaching me to play chess. I believe it is a good game. Guess this is all for now so Bye—Love to my Sweet sis.

2d Lt—I've been trying to see you for a week—when can I have a conference with you?

Colonel—Just make a date with my secretary.

2d Lt—I did, sir, and we had a wonderful time but I still want to talk to you.

18 AUGUST 1945 (SATURDAY). Guess I'll just drop in and say "Hello" this evening. Might as well stay up cause I work at midnight. Just as soon work at night cause it's cooler. The mornings about 4 o'clock are getting a little cooler now days. Had to laugh when I opened Mom's letter of August 2 and up in the corner was, "How is your heat rash?" It just so happened that for some reason or other it really came out that day and it was a bit miserable. I'm lucky the worst attack came this late in the season cause it stays pretty much with you until a while after cool weather. Without clothes on it doesn't bother much and it's a good deal better today. It doesn't hurt you any except for making you uncomfortable.

August is moving along pretty fast. I rather like it here. My basha mate is just a year older than I and one of the most interesting and pleasant fellows to be around that I've met. He is giving me pointers on chess and I'm helping him in bridge. I'm sure Dad would like chess cause it's at least as good as checkers. Verner reads chess books on games played by champions like Reubenstein so he is a sharpie. And we still have our record player in operation. Our other occupant is a Signal Corps officer from Arkansas and a graduate of Texas A and M. A nice fellow too. Of course we don't quite know what is in store for us these next few months.

Like others itching to return stateside, Lyle speculated about his standing in the demobilization *point plan* instituted by the War Department. Although aware the criteria were subject to change, he factored in his months of service, overseas time, and marital status before concluding:

I believe I can see the handwriting on the wall that I'll be one of the last to leave here. But that's the way it should be cause I haven't been here long nor do I have many points. As for the point plan, it may be fair enough but it sure doesn't help my cause.

Was surprised at the clipping about Duane Olsen. I feel that my luck should have run out long ago—never anything worse than a sprained ankle. I wonder if fellows like Gerald will still go overseas. This makes 5 months for me since boarding the troopship. I'm just a rookie over here.

Sounds like a good idea to combine the grain. But I can see you had the binder all ready to go too. I sure was glad to get those snapshots of home. Why doesn't this happen more often. But there should have been a picture of Mom feeding the chickens to be complete. Boy, won't the hay go up now with the new stacker. It's funny how a bit of home can come all these miles and look so natural.

ASSEMBLING A HAY STACKER, FAMILY FARM, 1945

Well, what's the dope on Virginia? Somehow if I were doing it I would go to S. D. State for a semester and then make up my mind what to do. I don't believe she should work at all the first semester and I do wish she would take one of my monthly checks for tuition. I don't know why but I'm satisfied that my year at State couldn't have been so good anywhere else. And I've seen a lot of our universities and colleges from Sioux Falls College to U. of Utah to Yale to Okla College for Women. And nowhere will you find such a friendly campus. I hope I'm not prejudiced. I wouldn't consider going back there cause all the kids I knew would be gone and it would never seem right. But I would like to be starting there again as a freshman. How dare you ask? Of course she can use my footlocker. There isn't anything valuable in it anyway. Just pile my stuff in the closet and someday I'll sort it out. Bye.

26 AUGUST 1945 (SUNDAY). It's a pretty nice Sunday morning in India. Early enough to be cool yet, don't work until this evening, and we even had a good breakfast. At 10:30 I'm going to chapel about 4 blocks up the line. The chaplain here is full of vitality and packs them in. He lives a couple doors from here and is usually in on the volleyball games. Last evening we played four games and enjoyed it a lot even though it makes you sweat plenty. The captains, majors, and colonels are a good deal older than my roommate and I so the game is a little slow. We also have a baseball, glove, and mitt. In about another month it will be cool enough for athletics. A nice group of officers in this area.

As the CBI theater began to close down, personnel were shuffled from one base to another to replace soldiers shipping back to the States. Left with fewer diversions after his basha mate was transferred to another base, Lyle, taking advantage of his rank, honed his flying skills.

Tuesday.
Last evening I took an hour of link training. Guess I'll try and get on a regular schedule. That makes 13 hours. It costs up to $20 per hour in civilian life. Blind flying by instruments. The only sad part of the situation is that my roommate, Strombom, got orders to ship out in a hurry so I lost my best friend. Last night I had the satisfaction of beating him in a game of chess—Beat the master himself but couldn't do it very often. It's a good game. He has been a most interesting companion but that's the way it goes. No mail lately. Better be some today. The trouble is on the day you do get mail you think—well, there won't be any tomorrow now. When you don't get mail you are happy to think—there should be some tomorrow. The worst is to expect mail and not get

any. Enough said on the mail situation. Never send any packages—too uncertain over here. Well as you can guess I wish I were home now. But I guess we can sweat out a few more months. I'm in the 6th month now. Not long overseas but plenty long in the army. Guess I can scrape up about 40 points on the readjustment plan. By the way should I hang on to a commission in the Army Reserve like Gerald Korzan and Quinten Evers? It means a couple weeks summer camp yearly—with pay I guess. Or should I get untied entirely? Last year I was home now for 5 days. You know apparently I got by too which is surprising in a deal like that. They can't get me now anymore. I hope. Well has Virginia decided on anything yet? Hope this finds you all well and happy.

Writing on stationery depicting the CBI insignia at the upper left and the Air Force insignia at the upper right, Lyle responded to the expectation of his parents that he would soon be coming home.

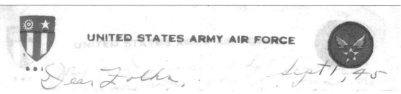

I SEPTEMBER 1945 (SATURDAY). At last mail is coming through again. And lots of news in Irene's and your letters. Your August 9 letter took 22 days and your Aug 17 letter came in just 15 days. Irene's package and your film have not gotten here yet! You folks are more optimistic about us fellows getting back quickly than we are. However, I should get out within nine months which means a maximum of 6 more in India. And there is always a chance of getting a good break too. It is dull and sticky here. People forget that there are no cities for a weekend here, food comes out of cans, and a lousy climate. That's why I felt so bad about fellows being left over here for over 2 1/2 years. That is a lifetime over here. They have left for the States now though. My good friend Staff Sgt Penar of Misamari was one of those who finally got to go home. However, those fellows haven't been in the army much longer than I but they came right overseas. Yes it's really great to have this war over at last. Was glad to hear of V's promotion from ensign to lieutenant. Vernon and I will be Lts for the duration. He can use the extra cash and also he won't get out as soon as I will so it will help him out to be up a grade. I've been in grade [second lieutenant] 14 months in this sad sack outfit. Now I have been in one place long enough to at least theoretically be able to get promoted sometime. Actually it doesn't make

LYLE SLADEK PLAYING CATCH, TEZPUR AIR BASE, INDIA, 1945

any difference. Irene told me all about her visit at home and all the latest around the farm. You are really up with the work this year. I envy you in having something to keep busy with. At last it is a bit cooler and what a relief to have my heat rash ease up. And now we can play volleyball and catch in late afternoon. Less to do now that Verner is gone. He was a good egg. Am anxious to hear what Virginia decides on about school. I can't help feeling she couldn't make a mistake about going to State. I don't agree with you about it being limited to Home Economics and Agri. It has quite a wide range to choose from including a good music dept. But maybe I'm prejudiced and anyway it's none of my business.

Will enclose a couple pictures. Here we have a typical native man and his child. Note the religious symbols around the neck and wrists. Their feet are wide from always going barefooted.

Here is the Taj Mahal—one of the 7 wonders of the world. Many say it is the most beautiful thing ever made by mankind. It is made of white marble and rises to 133 ft. Located at Agra, India, it was finished in 1632. When Mumtaz Mahal, the beautiful wife of Shah Jahan Mahal (the emperor) died, he forced thousands of people to slave for years to build a memorial for her. Later these slave laborers revolted and killed him. They are both buried in the Taj Mahal. I must see it before leaving India. Please save these photos for me. Until later.

TAJ MAHAL, AGRA, INDIA, 1945

As details dribbled in to the troops at Tezpur, they learned hostilities with Japan had officially ended on 2 September with the signing of a surrender document on the deck of the battleship USS *Missouri* in Tokyo Bay.

Under the leadership of General Douglas MacArthur, supreme commander for the Allied powers (SCAP), the United States took control of Japan. MacArthur supervised the writing and implementation of a constitution, assigning to the people political rights previously belonging to the emperor. At a later date, Emperor Hirohito was required to issue a non-divinity proclamation prepared by the Allies to convince the Japanese people he was not a god. The people embraced the democratic form of government and Japan quickly moved into the modern world.

With the ending of the war the Korean Peninsula, under Japanese rule since 1910, became a political vacuum. In the Cairo Declaration of 1943 the United States, Great Britain, and China had promised that "in due course Korea shall become free and independent." The Soviet Union had also subscribed to that pledge. While supervising the surrender of Japanese troops the United States and the Soviet Union agreed that the thirty-eighth parallel would serve to divide Korea into north and south zones of responsibility. To the Soviet Union went the northern portion and to the United States and Great Britain, the southern.

It was not possible to shut down the CBI theater and transport three hundred thousand troops home all at once. Furthermore, the army needed to maintain communication facilities and other support services. While continuing his crypto work, Lyle filled in free time as best he could. In his next letter he enclosed a sketch bearing the notation, "Hindu chopping grass in rain."

Hindu chopping grass in rain
v

9 SEPTEMBER 1945 (SUNDAY). Virginia mentioned that you got a couple pheasants on the way home from town. Dad must be improving all the time—don't tell me it was with the rifle. Does Chuckie do much shooting now days?

Monday.

The other day I drove our jeep for the first time and it was rather embarrassing to find myself heading for a big truck. You see they drive on the left side of the road here and in Australia and it takes a while to get used to it. Got some snapshots from Norma. Here is one of a campus walk at U. of Illinois. Even prettier when there is snow on the trees. Got a V-mail from Kenneth Lunn. He is in Calif near L.A. studying a jet propulsion plane. Got to go to work now. Last night I got to working on a garbled message and it took two hours but it finally came. You can't work too many hours on stuff like that. I feel like I know my job pretty well. Hope you are all in good humor this morning too.

In the press and in everyday conversation, the war just ended had simply been, "the war." On 10 September, President Truman received the following recommendation from the secretary of war and the secretary of the navy:

10 September 1945

The President
The White House

Dear Mr. President: President Wilson, under date of July 31, 1919, addressed a letter to Secretary of War Baker which read, in part, as follows:

"It is hard to find a satisfactory 'official' name for the war but the best, I think, that has been suggested is 'The World War,' and I hope that your judgment will concur."

Subsequently, under date of October 7, 1919, War Department General Orders No. 115 directed:

"The war against the Central Powers of Europe, in which the United States has taken part, will hereafter be designated in all official communications and publications as 'The World War.'"

As a matter of simplicity and to insure uniform terminology, it is recommended that "World War II" be the officially designated name for the present war covering all theaters and the entire period of hostilities.

The term "World War II" has been used in at least seven public laws to designate this period of hostilities. Analysis of publications and radio programs indicates that this term has been accepted by common usage.

If this recommendation is approved it is further recommended that the title "World War II" be published in the *Federal Register* as the official name of the present war. [See 10 *Federal Register* 1188.]

Respectfully yours,
HENRY L. STIMSON,
Secretary of War

JAMES FORRESTAL,
Secretary of the Navy

Approved: September 11, 1945
HARRY S. TRUMAN

Searching for something to do and wanting more flying time, Lyle accompanied a hot pilot in a two-seater plane over the India-Burma border. It caused his mother some anxiety when she received his detailed account:

17 SEPTEMBER 1945 (MONDAY). Just got back from a hair-raising and I do mean "hair raising" flight in an L-5. It's a little plane like the Taylorcraft or Piper Cub but has about twice the horsepower. My typing shows the effects of the ride doesn't it. To start with he took off keeping the plane on the runway just as long as he could to get up lots of speed and all of a sudden he reared back on the stick and we shot up to about 500 feet in a couple seconds. You see these fellows are hot pilots and when they fly a little plane they can practically make it talk—they have better control of it than a bird with its own wings. The countryside was very pretty—so green and the pretty designs of the tea plantations and the paddies and villages. The L-5 is what is known in the army as the Grasshopper. It is used for artillery spotting, evacuating wounded from little clearings in the jungle etc. So the next thing I know we are zooming down to a tiny spot in the jungle and below the treetops and then straight up again in order to get over the trees on the other side. That was tame. But then he gets the idea of flying in the river—just a narrow stream winding between heavy forest growths. So we went down to a few feet over the water just as fast as she would purr and followed the river which meant that in order to turn sharp enough to miss the trees we had to lay it over first on one side and then the other just a working that stick like it was a pump handle. That was a thrill a minute. Sometimes I guess I could have reached out and grabbed a handful of leaves. After doing that for a while he pulled up to a higher altitude again. Just after the most hair-raising maneuver he turned back to me and grinned. "Fun ain't it," he said. The most miserable feeling there is as far as I'm concerned is acrobatics in a plane. Your poor old stomach doesn't know which way to turn and you wish you were dead. I thought he had had enough but he still had another up his sleeve. Whenever he saw a group of natives or water buffalo in a small clearing he would dive down in and buzz them. By that I mean coming in wide open a couple feet off the ground and pulling up a few feet just in time to miss them. Naturally the natives fall flat and almost die of fright. But the fun part of it is that I got more scared than the natives! We buzzed every native and herd of water buffalo in the Assam Valley. I followed through on the dual controls and learned a lot about flying but wouldn't want to do it again. Those pilots go hog wild when they fly a little plane after the lumbering bombers. Our flying reminded me of driving through New York in a Model T Ford with a V-8 engine wide open. I wouldn't

even fly an old secondhand kite the way he flew that plane. Boy I do mean we have some hot pilots. I've seen a P-51 Mustang buzz the field at 400 some odd miles per and do a slow roll at about 500 feet and then pull that thing straight up into the blue. This L-5 had so much power for its size that you can pull it straight up for a long way before it will mush and stall out and you have enough soup on the throttle so you can gun the motor and pull out of most anything. Anyway I got a twenty dollar ride for nothing and another hour of flying in. Still lack a couple of hours of instruction before soloing. No more carnival rides or roller coasters for me—much too tame.

Thursday.

This base is closing now. We may leave Tezpur in a couple weeks. Had a letter from Vernon today. The plane I rode in crashed yesterday. The radiogram sounds like they are in no danger—burns etc. I think they were just making a trip too and not stunting. Lt Eichler, my left hand man, got back from Calcutta.

The bomb group will fly their Liberators home soon. Everything is fine here.

Pilots and crews flying planes back to the States were the first personnel to leave the CBI. Lyle wished he was among them. Mulling over what was in store for the peacetime economy, he predicted runaway inflation once the government dropped wartime price controls. He knew there was a pent-up demand for automobiles, machinery, and homes. The productive capacity of automobile companies had gone toward manufacturing aircraft, jeeps, tanks, and other military wares. Several Brule County neighbors, desperate for transportation, had resurrected abandoned cars or taken to horse-drawn buggies. Many farmers, like his father, had made do with old tractors and worn-out machinery. Much of the lumber coming from the mills had gone into the construction of barracks, boats, and shipping crates. Repair projects had been deferred unless needed to keep the railroads running and the utilities operating. Jobs had been plentiful, but resources and gross national product had flowed into the war effort. Lyle knew the United States faced stiff economic challenges in the months ahead.

22 SEPTEMBER 1945 (SATURDAY). Our country is much more run down than people realize. There has been false prosperity—everyone had their pockets full of currency but couldn't buy new cars, steaks, radios, etc. And all the railroads and roads and lots of homes etc need rebuilding—most farms are run down. Plenty of work to be done. Like in China you can have a basket of twenty dollar Chinese bills and it will only buy a mouldy grain of rice. It has reached the point where they use nothing less than hundred dollar bills. Wages will go down but so

will the cost of living so actually the standard of living will go up now. I hope.

It looks now like those of us in this outfit with less than a year of foreign service are apt to be sent to China or Singapore or some such place. But my work in crypto is fast becoming nonessential so maybe I'll escape. Our bomb group is packing up and will soon convoy to Calcutta. They are flying their B-24s to the States. So our station should close here pretty soon too. Had three booster shots yesterday so my arms are stiff today. Had a little fever last night. I believe they must have used Indian vaccine cause it took ahold.

We just heard a drastic rumor from radio San Francisco about discharges. Seems that someone heard something about two years service getting out after November. I have in two years and seven months so that would be just too good to be true but I don't believe it at all. Here's hoping. If Congress puts on enough pressure on the War Dept maybe they will be forced to loosen up. Until later.

Once the war was over, the parents of servicemen expected their sons, even those overseas, to soon come striding up the walk as if in a Rockwell painting. When that failed to happen, they wrote to their congressmen. Radio commentators and newspaper columnists pressured the War Department to "bring our boys home." Responding to the clamor, General Marshall explained the realities of demobilizing millions of soldiers stationed at hundreds of outposts around the globe. He stated that men who had been overseas for more than a certain number of months would be returned stateside before a specific date, if possible.

24 SEPTEMBER 1945 (MONDAY). This is one of the nicest days we have had here. It rained last night, and this morning clouds are heavy overhead. A cloudy day is different and passes quickly and pleasantly. You get so used to awakening to a brilliant sun, the air is quiet and already warm, and it seems they are pouring huge gobs of sunlight and heat all over you. Everyone shrugs and hardly has ambition to say, "Good morning." I guess that's another reason why the countries in hot climates are backward. It takes changing temperatures etc in order to have a vigorous peoples. Had to chuckle at Mom's suggestion that, "Maybe if you requested it you could get out of the army now." There are 9 million others who want out first as badly as I do. Things are looking very favorable especially since Marshal's statement. I have only 40 points so my only chance of getting out is on two years service. 55 thousand men are leaving this theater in October. I estimate that is 1/4 of all the men in China, Burma, India so it looks good. The main thing is to get back to the US cause then it will be mostly furloughs anyway. Things

are better here now and so we will just take it easy until our turn comes. Only sometimes one gets the feeling, "Time waits for no one, it passes you by." But actually in terms of any college time lost I don't mind that cause this is stuff one can't grasp in college. I'm beginning to doubt if I'll ever actually finish college for a degree. But that's the way it usually goes with me—dabble a little here and putter a little there and never quite finish anything. Would take a couple years.

Nose art—the painting of themes, slogans, and ornamentations on the forward fuselages of planes by aircrew members—was commonplace. One of the best-known images was that of a curvaceous blonde adorning the *Memphis Belle*, a B-17 Flying Fortress. Lyle was complimentary of the men who "kept 'em flying" but acknowledged the risks inherent in being airborne.

Tuesday.

Was surprised to get mail last night. Glad to hear Virginia is getting started at the U. There are good train connections from Vermillion too. Chuckie must be quite a hunter. I'll be afraid to hunt with him around cause he'll laugh when I miss. Those pheasant dinners must be good. We had a good show last night, "Weekend at the Waldorf." Did you get those snaps from Irene yet? Your film arrived a week ago. Irene's package never caught me. By the way the only difference airmail makes is in the States—from N.Y. or Miami it travels by air anyway—except packages. Am sending a couple more snaps of India—please save them for me. We will be a little busier now that the end of the month is near. This work is quite painstaking—Have to be very careful to not lose or expose anything—but a good sort of army job cause no one knows what goes on in here and I'm on my own—Lt Eichler is on the ball too.

The mechanics are busy tuning up the Liberators for flight back to the States—we would say Uncle Sugar—we use phonetics in Air Corps over radio etc. to avoid transmission errors. Most bombers have a large picture painted on the nose. For instance the ship "Cabin in the Sky" has a picture of Lena Horne, the great colored singer I heard in Detroit. Last Roundup, Death Takes a Holiday, Fabulous Fanny, etc all with appropriate pictures. Lots of us in the Air Corps don't have too much trust in flying anymore. Of course safety is not the most considered thing in army flying. I'll always marvel that the Air Corps could keep all these complicated mechanisms in the air and safe on the airways. Our AACS outfit tells them what fields are closed, the weather, etc. We shoot direction finding equipment on them to find their position when lost over the Himalayas and tell them the course to fly out. We regulate the traffic in altitudes and courses so planes do not collide flying blind. We have radio beams all over the world to follow from one field to another. Our control tower regulates traffic landing and taking off and circling the field.

Although recognizing a kernel of truth in John Milton's line, "They also serve who only stand and wait," Lyle did not relish wasting more time at an isolated army outpost. On a clipping from the CBI *Roundup,* he scribbled, "Phooey—3,000 out of 300,000":

FIRST MASS SHIPMENT OF I-B TROOPS HITS NEW YORK CITY
Approximately 3,075 weary but happy India-Burma troops arrived in New York this week aboard the USS *General Greeley* after a 23 day trip from Calcutta.
The men, women—and two babies—who sweated out the Land of Mystery, were greeted hilariously, especially by the afternoon newspapers.
Both the *World-Telegram* and the *Journal-American* printed huge three-column pictures of the first U.S. troops to return en masse from India. They included representatives from such old CBI hands as: the American Kachin Rangers, the Flying Tigers, Merrill's Marauders, the Mars Task Force, Col. Phillip Cochran's Commandos, and the "intellectuals," which is the newspaper term for the men who operated [Army] Airways Communications [System] [AACS] around the Hump and whose average I.Q. is 110.

30 SEPTEMBER 1945 (SUNDAY). Another indifferent day in India. Worked some this forenoon and am pulling a shift this afternoon. The last day of the month is busy—reports to be sent in to headquarters, men to be paid, etc. We are waiting for orders to close down at night cause we are short on personnel and there is very little business at night lately. The latest rumor is that we may go to Indo China or Siam which doesn't make us happy. But we will see what turns up. Looks like they will take about 5 months to evacuate this theater. Actually there probably is not over 300 thousand men in all India, China, Burma so they could get us out faster if they would just loosen up. The men are already restless. The American soldier is noted for his lack of patience. It's pretty dull over here. The bomb group may fly out this week. Wish I were going along. Never saw anything like the way the sun shines here. It just burns out all ambition and beats you right to the ground—from about 9:00 a.m. to 4:30 p.m. The nights are better although a couple this past week were muggy enough to make you sweat until midnight. It rained last night and there are scattered clouds today so it isn't bad. We are farther south than any part of U.S. so the sun still comes almost directly overhead. Not bad if you know enough to stay in the shade in shorts. Seems strange to hear you talk of a light frost already. How is the cane cutting coming? Will be a big job to shock that stuff. Somebody was just trying to sell you a 32-volt radio when he said it would harm the batteries to

tap off 6 volts. Or else he didn't really know any better. It should work good that way. A radio doesn't wear out—if it works at all it's good as new. We sometimes pick up Calcutta, or Kunming, or Honolulu on our radios here at the station but we miss the stateside programs, music, etc. We keep pretty much up on the news though.

Irene said my yellow sapphire was appraised at 25 dollars. At that rate I doubled my money but am still disappointed. I thought it was either valueless or worth a lot. Guess I'll give it to the chickens along with some scratching sand.

The point plan and readjustment deal was in my estimation the biggest psychological mistake of the war. Very few believe it is fair, it caused dissatisfaction to see some get out and the rest stay in, in fact the morale hit a new all time low when that went into effect. Especially when they stopped rotation after two years overseas service.

Glad to hear Virginia got started off to school. Guess the colleges will be full this year. Received the snapshots in your last letter. Everything looked very familiar. Let me know when fellows I know start getting out of the army and navy.

Looks like about ten days or less left here at Tezpur. We are about ready to shut down. I'm ready to move along anytime. Bye.

6 OCTOBER 1945 (SUNDAY). Yesterday a radiogram came in transferring me to Shamshernager and then it was canceled in the afternoon. This station is closing except for a couple minor facilities. My code room is cleared up except for a few things. I may go to H.Q. at Kurmitola in a few days to finish clearing up the books. Now it doesn't seem very likely of shipping to another country in this theater but rather to some other place in India. Sgt Milak came over from Misamari yesterday to see me about some of their problems over there. They are closing now too. I don't have any feeling of being closer to shipping home. Wish they would give us a specific date such as first of January or something cause this way one gets pessimistic and optimistic by turn. The chaplain that I mentioned in the plane wreck got out of the hospital yesterday looking thin and pale but pretty well recovered. They were flying to some point in Burma. At the time of the accident they were somewhere near the India-Burma border in the rugged mountain country. All of a sudden they found themselves in one of those fast-rising cloud formations and couldn't see a thing. When they came out they were about to crash into a mountain so the pilot reared back on the stick and crash landed it very well. But it exploded about as it hit and with one flash of flame just as they were diving out the doors—if they had been a little quicker or later it would have been O.K. The pilot was badly cut in the leg and bleeding badly and the chaplain's hands were

badly burned so he couldn't use them. He had to pretty much slide down the mountain to a stream and then slide down a waterfall to get to the level of the stream. Then they hiked for about six hours before finally coming across natives who guided them four more hours to a village. There they contacted a British ambulance and were taken quite some distance to a little hospital. And of course they were pretty well done up by the time they got there. They both escaped without very bad after affects and really considered themselves fortunate.

Was surprised by a letter from Virginia the other day. Guess she finds college a bit confusing at first. She gave me the details of her course etc and somehow I feel she is wasting a lot of talent. But time will tell. It sounds good to hear you mention frosts and cool weather. Better take it easy on the shocking, Mom, that stuff is too heavy to handle much. I wonder how many times a day the subject comes up of going home. We sure are impatient. Enclosed are a couple snaps taken here. The one is a river ferry and the other is Lt Blake with a tea plantation owners daughter (British). They make lots of money over here on the tea. But I wouldn't live over here for all the money in England. It's hard on one's health for one thing especially of older people. Did Irene send you some of those snapshots? Photographic conditions are not very good over here and one must get the film developed right away. We had a good game of volleyball last evening. One of the group is really muscular but so muscle bound and uncoordinated that he just can't do anything. Really a pity. Comes from too much weight lifting.

I'll send you a new address when I move which shouldn't be many more days. Hope I get out of this Assam Valley. We are far inland but very near sea level.

Lyle marveled at the sight of the mighty mountain chain separating India and China. He contrasted the Himalayas with the Appalachians, the barrier to westward expansion in the early history of the United States. He noted that Mount Mitchell, the highest peak in the Appalachians, was less than a quarter the height of Mount Everest. Likewise, Harney Peak in South Dakota, the highest elevation east of the Rocky Mountains, was a mere hill relative to Mount Everest and many other peaks in the Himalayas.

10 OCTOBER 1945 (WEDNESDAY). Greetings. The mountains are a pretty sight this morning. Over to the north through scattered clouds we can see a brilliant white Mt range with one mountain in particular lifting a symmetrical cone shaped peak high over the world. No wonder they call those Mts the roof of the world. This valley is only a couple hundred feet above sea level and that one Mt is almost 24 thousand feet high so you see it really looks like a Mt. The highest in the Black Hills are about

7 thousand feet and they rise out of a plateau which is considerably above sea level whereas these Mts in a distance of about ninety miles rise from near sea level to twenty-four thousand feet—higher than any in the Americas. One of these days I hope to get closer to them up by one of the resort towns. Mt Everest is a couple hundred miles to the north and east of here. Looks now like I will be here at least two more weeks. Most of my best pals have shipped out now so things are somewhat dull around here. Willet went to Karachi. Got your letter of Sep 26 last night. Surprised to hear Dale Korzan is getting out soon. I believe he has about 3 or 4 months on me—seems to me he went in in the fall. You folks should hire out to the neighbors now that you have the work so far ahead of schedule. How do you do it. Enclosed is a money order for a hundred dollars. Sometime send Irene a five dollar bill—she had a lot of prints made for me etc. Heard a rumor that they are no longer accepting packages for the CBI theater—if that is true maybe they figure on getting us out by the end of the year but I doubt it. January is the earliest I could be home and more likely February and could be even later. All guess work though.

Those B-24s out here on the flight line just about blew me right out of this room right now. One is running up its engines about fifty feet back of here. The bomb group is being held up for some reason or other. They may not get out of here in Oct as planned. There will be more and more trouble as the men get more restless. Not much to do around here and practically no work to do. I have no more codes—it's mostly just a western union now days—wouldn't mind it if we could charge so much per word. Will be sending home another box of junk one of these days. You can believe this or not but just a couple nights ago after laying down to sleep under the mosquito netting drops of perspiration started to run off and this was near midnight too. Not really so hot but the humidity is so high. What luck, just got a letter from Beatrice—don't know how there happens to be mail this morning cause our mail comes in the evening.

Beatrice is stepping out on me these days. Well, there is nothing like competition although twelve thousand miles is somewhat of a handicap. More later.

Now more than a year since the romantic interlude in Detroit, a letter from Beatrice hinting of other suitors fired Lyle's competitive spirit. Restless, and turning twenty-two, he yearned to pursue his dreams.

Rumors flourished in the camp, the optimistic ones circulating the most rapidly. GIs lucky enough to ship out for home gladly crowded into primitive railroad cars for the long, grueling trip across northern India to Karachi,

Returnee Describes Ledo Troop Train Ride

500 Men Make
Trip In Eight Days

By SGT. C. M. BUCHANAN
Roundup Field Correspondent

KARACHI.—Day after day a happy scene is re-enacted as hundreds of jungle troops from outer Assam and Northern Burma leave Ledo by rail for India's west coast port of Karachi. This correspondent, who has sweated out the mud, monsoon and monotony of the forward areas for more than two years, was given as his last assignment the job of covering one of the first mass movements by train across the top of India to a waiting boat at Karachi.

It's a tough trip by all odds, but in comparison to the troop trains that most men endured on their way to Ledo and points beyond, it's a kid's picnic. Griping and grousing is mitigated by the realization that this is the last

Thoughts Of Home
Reduce Griping

for each man. Eight vans of beer were sold to each G.I. and ice put aboard the cars Smart and snappy in colorful uniforms, British soldiers of the Lancashire Fusiliers, one of the several British bands to send off American troops at this station marched the length of the platform playing martial airs

G.I.s spoke of the hospitality displayed here and Col. McCausland, eager to give the troops everything possible, admitted he's had more genuine salutes, full of meaning and appreciation than at any time in his Army service.

WIDE GAUGE

Leaving Lucknow in the late afternoon, the wide-gauge train proved more spacious and com-modious than previous accom-modations. Travelling north-west through the level country of

Forward area men bound for Karachi and points towards America. A skeptical G.I. writes on the side of the first train from Ledo, "We'll believe it when we see it." *(Signal Corps Photo.)*

where they waited to board troopships. In order to increase the capacity of the ships, the men gladly double-bunked (slept in shifts) and ate standing up during the long voyage home via the Suez Canal, Mediterranean Sea, and Atlantic Ocean. Even so, it would take months to transport all of the troops out of the CBI theater. Lyle resigned himself to several more months of Atabrine tablets, tedium, and heat.

14 OCTOBER 1945 (SUNDAY). Maybe at last the weather is breaking. This is a cloudy breezy cool day. Last week was about like July in St. Louis. In fact just a little heat rash appeared on my back. So today one feels like living again. Tomorrow morning I am going to Chabua with some cryptographic stuff as an Officer Courier. Have 5 days temporary duty there which will be nice for a change. Was up there last spring before going to Misamari. Latest rumors seem a bit better. Heard that they plan to clear out this theater by Feb. Guess there are about 200,000 troops here now. At 4,000 to a boat it will take 50 ships. Some of the big ones carry 10,000 troops. My fingers are crossed. Wouldn't be so bad if there was something to do but this way time drags. Plan to play some bridge this evening.

Later.

Had a nice time playing bridge. All packed to go to Chabua tomorrow so more from there.

CHABUA, ASSAM, INDIA

An interlude at Chabua revived Lyle's flagging spirits. He renewed acquaintances with old friends and learned about the production and processing of tea.

The area in and around Chabua played a prominent role during the early stages of the war. Japanese forces moved into Burma shortly after the attack at Pearl Harbor, seized the strategic airfield at Myitkyina, cut off the Burma Road, and halted commerce on the Irrawaddy River from Rangoon to Mandalay. The Japanese army attempted to invade Assam but was repelled. Later, American and Chinese forces, under the leadership of General Stillwell, made a valiant effort to retake Burma but without success.

Although the United States had countered the severing of the Burma Road by transporting supplies over the Hump, it appeared to Lyle that Chiang Kai-shek, titular head of the Nationalist government, was losing control of China. The communist forces of Mao Tse-tung were growing ever stronger, and rumors were rife among the GIs that the supplies reaching China were being split fifty-fifty between the nationalist and communist factions. Sadly, several American soldiers were killed when bandits invaded American bases and made off with war materials.

17 OCTOBER 1945 (WEDNESDAY). Yes, this is Chabua—the crossroads of Asia. Located in the tip of Assam near the border of Burma, China, India near where the Burma road starts its tortuous way to China heading down toward Myitkyina and Mandalay in Burma. Myitkyina (pronounced Mission awe) figured prominently in the news a few months back—one of the biggest battles of Burma. And Mandalay of course is where the "flying fishes play." Eventually the road reaches Kunming which is the area I went to over in Yunnan province of China. That by the way is one of the Communist strongholds and we lost a good deal of equipment etc from attacks by bandit hijackers. They raided a couple of our China fields about 4 months ago and killed some of our men. Seems now that there may not be a revolution in China. In August it seemed about ready to explode. You will find that most of our troops in China don't have much use for the Chinese. They do like the Burmese quite well.

Monday I flew over some secret stuff from Misamari and Tezpur to headquarters here and so now I have a 5 day vacation and I believe per diem of 3 dollars per day. However, it is not the most desirable sort of job even then. That afternoon it rained 4 inches in 1 1/2 hours which is unusual for this time of year. It broke the weather so now it is comfortably cool and do we appreciate it. Who do you suppose I ran into here—Al Richards, a roommate at Yale 20 months ago. He graduated about 3 months before I did. Also quite a few other fellows I know around here. Am living out in a bungalow on an English tea plantation—even has wooden floors, and we have a radio fixed up etc. This morning I walked out in the tea fields. All the plants are trimmed level like a hedge so it's a flat green carpet about 4 feet high. With trees (like elms) spaced at intervals for shade or something. The natives pick the leaves in wicker baskets several times a year. Then it is taken to a roofed drying shed and put in layers to dry. The processing plant is interesting. Two large diesels run a central power system which is taken off to the machines by belts. The tea is washed, sort of ground up, screened, and comes out in boxes labeled "Hattalie Tea Plantation, Ltd" for worldwide shipment. Indians think Cha Pannie teek hi. They like tea water in other words. This is black tea. Yesterday the Hindus finished celebrating their Christmas in some interesting celebrations. Their dance is almost as bad as our jitterbugging. It's a good excuse for them to drink bamboo juice too (liquor, also called jungle juice). Am enjoying

A TEA GARDEN BELLE, AND PRUNING A TEA GARDEN, ASSAM, INDIA, 1945

the change of scenery and cool weather. Should be starting home early in 46—maybe even January. My work is finished it appears to me.

TEZPUR, ASSAM, INDIA

With the opening of Chinese ports to Allied shipping, fewer air bases were needed in India. Upon returning to Tezpur, Lyle learned the field was about to shut down and he was to report to another base. The water echelon, the men responsible for maintaining a potable water supply, would be the last unit to leave Tezpur.

18 OCTOBER 1945 (THURSDAY). This is mostly to give you a new address, APO 433. Am transferring to Kurmitola which is down toward Calcutta. I know some of the fellows there and am glad to have a change. The bombers are leaving here for the States with 7 planes per day. One enthusiastic pilot awakened me very abruptly this morning by buzzing our area at treetop level. Just about blew me out the window. The water echelon will leave in 10 days so then the jungle will soon start reclaiming Tezpur air base. Actually my work is finished but they can't or won't send us back. Latest is that 47 thousand will leave this theater in November. That will still leave 100,000 or more. There are some men with 2 years time here and plenty points who can't seem to get shipped home. Makes us disgusted to hear of cases like that Georgia football player getting out on 41 points through politics—and he had less service than I and no overseas time. But it is looking more favorable all the time. I'm wondering if this restlessness of the past couple years will carry over into civilian life. Maybe it's lack of something to do and not being captain of my own ship. I hate to waste time.

Two letters from you yesterday dated the 3rd and 8th. The Corn Palace looks real fancy this year. I imagine people had plenty cash to spend too. Sounds like Viv and Vernon are expected out there according to Jean. Would be surprised if Vernon were to put out to sea. At least it wouldn't be for over 4 or 5 months and likely at some large port city. Hope he doesn't get shipped out at this time.

You sold quite a bunch of stock didn't you. Beef prices are apt to hold up for a year or two aren't they? So far things seem to be going smoothly enough in reconverting. Pres Truman is doing O.K. for my money. We need good leadership cause I expect one of the biggest crisis in our history. England is of course hardest hit economically. I'm wondering how they will get along in India the next few years. Most of us believe the British have done neither good nor harm to India. I don't believe India can help itself nor can any other country help India. It seems just one of those problems with no answer. The Indians are a rather likable people.

I really don't believe Virginia should be working her first year. And 34¢ is much too little for these times and prices—unless her work is pleasant and educational at the same time. Glad to hear Chuckie is hot with the rifle. Guess we'll have to try him out with a small gauge shotgun next spring. Did you get the washhouse painted, Mom? Boy, I sure could go for some of that fresh food. I believe this canned stuff serves the purpose though. I weighed 187 in suntans the other day so apparently am just as heavy but thinner. Right now I'm wearing trousers they threw at me almost 3 years ago. Sort of a shame how some of the fellows in the army get flabby before they are even 25. When they try to tell you the army builds men they really expect you to be gullible. We won't win the next war if we become a military nation with a huge peacetime army of flabby lazy blubbering idiots. Our army was strong because of its equipment, and of its training on the football fields and in the college laboratories. Just my personal opinion of course. Signing off station Bla Bla Bla until Kurmitola.

In Lyle's view, American GIs had adapted well to technological innovations and fast-changing conditions during the war, perhaps because they were products of a classless society wherein ability, knowledge, and determination counted for more than circumstances of birth.

KURMITOLA, ASSAM, INDIA

After settling in at the Kurmitola air base, Lyle reunited with several friends, including his record-playing buddy, Lt. Verner Strombom. Having replaced a crypto officer who had shipped to the States, Lyle wrote:

28 OCTOBER 1945 (SUNDAY). It is a quiet Sunday evening down here in the station so my work tonite consists of reading and writing letters. There is a big surplus of men in everything now so actually none of us work much. Still working as a security officer but no responsibility now on account of just being an assistant here along with several others. Kurmitola has always been quite a busy base—Headquarters of our AACS Sqdn and Headquarters of the Bengal Wing of the Air Transport Command. Guess it will close in about a month.

Caught a C-47 last Monday to Barrackpore (suburb of Calcutta) in a rather rough four hour ride but not quite rough enough to make me airsick. We flew between the layer of white fluffy clouds below and the grey overcast above in a sort of unreal world up there. At times the sun would break through the overcast above and it was just as though the sun had finally come out after a snowstorm of several weeks in S. Dak which had covered buildings and everything in soft snow. In fact one felt as though he could step out the door and walk away on the snow. At Barrackpore we caught a truck to the Dum Dum air base to try to catch a plane out there but no luck so we went downtown to the Hindustani Building where the army has a Headquarters and were assigned a place to sleep for the night out at Hiallia (racing grounds) Transit tents. We spent the evening eating at an army approved restaurant and shopping for knickknacks before going out to the camp to sleep. The least said about Calcutta the better cause one hardly believes it when he sees it. Always gives me the feeling that I'll be dying with several diseases within a few hours.

We were very fortunate to get a ride up here to Kurmitola the next afternoon in a C-54 Skytrain which is the very nicest ship to travel in. The Presidents always travel in them. They can seat fifty or more and baggage. It was an hours flight up here. The terrain seemed to be composed of lots of little Islands. I believe about half the area is water covered. You see most of the rivers of India come down from the Himalayas and all sort of meet down here in the delta and flow into the Bay of Bengal. The Ganges, the Hooghly, the Bhramaputra etc with their multitude of shifting channels. Even up here a couple hundred miles it is only 24 feet above sea level. Good place for growing rice cause it has to be flooded at intervals during the season. The rice appears to be about ready for harvest. My arrival here was like old home week on account of most everyone I know is now stationed here. My former basha mate at Tezpur with the record player is here too and he is one of the most interesting fellows to live with that I know. Haven't had any mail for two weeks but expect it to be redirected from Tezpur most anytime. Mail is about the only thing that links us up with civilization so it is very important to one's morale. So far it has been very pleasant here and I believe it will continue that way. There are lots of fellows in the same boat as I and with the same interests. No trouble to get up a bridge game etc. We have shortwave radios fixed up in the quarters so we get some good programs from army service stations. Heard "Sentimental Journey" and "Till the end of Time" for the first time here. Already this is month number eight over here and I don't know whether it has gone fast over here or not. It is a sort of different world and time has different value here.

While waiting to ship home, the men at Kurmitola learned that labor leaders were demanding higher wages for union members. The GIs were irked by the news; they were receiving meager army pay and thought strikes at home might delay transportation back to the States.

Unfortunately, some GIs got lost in the shuffle during the demobilization process. Lyle was sympathetic with one soldier who, feeling overdue for returning to the States, solicited help from his congressman.

This was one of the most pleasant days I have had over here. Slept late, played ping pong and a game of chess until noon and then listened to a couple good programs on the radio. Then four of us got in a jeep and went over to the Dhaka Club which is a British club about ten miles from here to see if the rumor about a swimming pool was true. And you know they have an indoor pool that is almost as nice as any in the States with nice clear clean water and open to Americans too. So we swam for a couple hours and came out feeling like a million and resolved to spend many more afternoons there. And we had toast and tea before leaving. The British couldn't function unless they had a spot of tea in the forenoon and afternoon as well as at meals. Their tea is pretty good.

So my hope now is to sweat out the rest of the time here at Kurmitola. Almost like a country club here—just grow fat and lazy. Or at least I keep telling myself. Hope to hear from you tomorrow. Still believe my chances are pretty good of getting out of here about February if not sooner. The transportation seems to be clogged up somewhat. It hurts to read of strikers hissing and booing our soldiers taking over important shipping jobs to keep the ships moving. Labor is getting a bad reputation with the serviceman at that rate, same as the strikes during the war. Don't be misled by my pay—there are four or five million men in this army who only get about 60 dollars a month. Even my pay doesn't average out too high. Some congressman from Florida investigated the deal on some soldier stationed here to see just what the score was. We had to send the radiogram back to him but I wasn't around when it went out so don't know just what it was all about. There are lots of cases of men getting a raw deal. Army red tape can sure snarl up things right. It will be a happy day to get out of its entanglements.

Hope this finds all of you in good health and spirits too. Did the Vs get home? Bye now.

Bored with the humdrum existence at Kurmitola, Lyle and a lieutenant friend finagled a trip to what Lyle thought of as the most exotic country on earth and the ultimate city. On the back of a restaurant tab, he jotted:

N° 68020

存　房　楼　酒

2 NOVEMBER 1945 (FRIDAY). Yes, this is Shanghai with its teeming millions. Just now we are in the 3rd course of a very good dinner at the Hotel Pacific. Our 8th story window looks down on the heart of the city—one should call it the international city—cause there are all kinds of people here from Japs to us to white Russian peoples. Say, maybe you would be surprised at how cute these Chinese waitresses are—wow. Needless to say this is fascinating. We are spending a couple days here before flying back to Kurmitola. Takes about 12 hours flying by way of Kunming to get back. Would like to go back by way of Manila. More later.

The expansion of Japanese influence in Asia had become of concern to the United States government long before the attack at Pearl Harbor. In 1905, when Russian rights in southern Manchuria were transferred to Japan by the Treaty of Portsmouth at the conclusion of the Russo-Japanese war, the integrity of China was threatened. The concern escalated in 1931 when Japanese forces created a new state in Manchuria. Then, in 1937 Japan occupied the coastal region of China (including Shanghai), cutting off access to the West and prompting the Chinese to construct the tortuous 717-mile Burma Road that connected Kunming to eastern Burma.

At the time of Pearl Harbor, Lyle knew little about the East. He pictured Japan as a quaint, colorful land inhabited by characters akin to those portrayed in *Madame Butterfly*. To him, Americans assembled automobiles, skyscrapers, and suspension bridges whereas Japanese people fashioned carnival knickknacks from bamboo and rice paper. That Japan possessed modern planes, skilled pilots, and aircraft carriers came as a rude awakening. His vision of China was based on pictures he had seen in *National Geographic* magazines: terraced rice paddies, men with pigtails, women teetering about on tiny feet. Although Lyle felt no animosity toward the people of Asia, he smugly viewed American culture as being superior. After a few days in Shanghai, his perspective broadened as he encountered industrious people living in a cosmopolitan city.

Safely back to Kurmitola, after "coming in on a wing and a prayer" on the second leg of the return flight from Shanghai, Lyle buoyantly wrote:

4 NOVEMBER 1945 (SUNDAY). Life seems very good this evening— sitting on top of the world. Sort of tired though from the trip of over

.5000 miles—about 25 flying hours round trip. The other day Lt DeLong mentioned something about it would be nice to go to Shanghai. Well, Shanghai has always sounded fascinating to me, so it didn't take me long to get enthused about the idea. We worked out a deal to go on a training flight as 2nd radio operators and talked the chief pilot into taking us along—which is no easy deal to pull. We took off in a C-54 Skytrain about 1:30 in the afternoon and headed across Burma to Kunming, China. It was very pretty over the Mts. The ridges get higher and higher just as though someone with a giant plow terraced a huge slope. We crossed the Irrawady River and arrived at Kunming in the evening. We hauled gas over to Kunming. There we picked up troops and took off about midnight for Shanghai. Gets plenty cold at those high altitudes. As soon as it was getting near dawn we found we were flying just over the highest layer of clouds. And then the fiery red sun appeared over the edge of the fluffy blue clouds and we were just in another world. The prettiest colors you ever did see—an unreal world. Here and there jagged brown peaks first sticking through the clouds. Then as we reached the coastal plain of China the clouds grew thinner and you could see the little villages and the rivers with the hundreds of irrigation ditches. Every inch of land is intensely cultivated and every possible bit of Mt slope is terraced. Then in early morning the tall buildings of Shanghai appeared in the haze and the harbor beyond to the China sea. It was hard to pick out the runway of Kwangwan airfield now occupied by the Allies cause the Japs had camouflaged it very well—but it turned out to be a very well-built field and well dug in as far as air raid shelters etc goes. The Japs had a clever communications center with antenna poles as big as trees set like telegraph poles except with branches left on. It must have been one of their biggest airfields. Guess who we ran into there—none other than Major "Black Mac" McNalley—the terror of cadets at Yale.

Our first thought was to get into town so we caught a gov truck in. In the outskirts as we roared along in our trucks past old looking houses and courtyards it gave me the impression of being as old and immovable as the hills. Old people of the peasant class tilling their tiny fields didn't so much as glance up as we dashed by. I believe their life goes on in a little world and invasions by the Japs, war, the occupation by Americans is hardly noticed—they accept it as inevitably as we accept a cold wave or rainstorm—and they just go on scratching the soil.

Shanghai is everything you have ever heard of it and more. To me it is where the 20th Century met the ricksha—and the outcome is not yet decided. New shiny automobiles go through the streets trying to get through the thousands of rickshas and multitudes of people. You can find the very latest of anything in Shanghai—and also right beside it the old China civilization. Shanghai is sort of an international city ever since it was opened up after the Boxer Rebellion of 1902. There are lots of white people—had dinner with 6 Portuguese girls at the air base just before heading back. The American soldier leaves a good impression most every place he goes. I believe the British will be practically driven out of the Far East in a few years—the American prestige is going up all the time. Seems to me China has a big future. Just a couple days in Shanghai changed my impression of the Chinese. They imitate beautifully our products, they are friendly, courteous, and likable. And clean—and in the cities they are good looking. I thought the girls were attractive— extremely attractive in fact. Nice complexion and features and always a ready smile. Their clothes are beautiful—they walk very nicely and are on the slender order. Their skirts come down about 6 inches below the knee and very narrow but split on each side to the knee. I could go on for hours cause I had a most interesting time. It was amazing the way the stores were stocked etc. There were some Japanese cavalary around. The Japs treated the Shanghai section much better than most. Of course we rode rickshas all over town and haggled with shops to buy things. Of course they start above the price and you start below. Chinese money changes value rapidly and is terrifically inflated. Everything is priced in thousands of dollars. About 2000 sin yen to an American dollar. The minute you go to buy something the Chinese swarm around you like kids at a carnival. And if the Chinese merchant appears to get the best of you in price they are immensely tickled. Sent you a package in the mail from there of silk goods. Mom, you can dispose of them as you see fit— the slip perhaps for Irene. May get there in less than two months—it's insured.

Caught a C-54 out with gas to Liuzhou in the afternoon arriving about dusk at the almost deserted airstrip and unloaded. Then the second leg to Kunming—about a 4 hour flight. But when we arrived there the field was almost closed as far as visibility so they stacked us in the flight pattern at the various altitudes. The field is about 7,000 feet high and in very mountainous terrain. As we droned around and around up there in the overcast awaiting our turn to go down, I realized how life hangs but on a thread. About every minute a plane's light would appear in the murky night—and for one pilot to be flying the wrong let down procedure meant disaster. That is the only time I have seen the crew lay the chutes by the door in ready position. It was a good feeling when our turn came to go down and we broke through the low overcast to see the lights of the field. Then we flew to Calcutta with men for staging shipping areas and then back to here—and glad to get on solid ground again. Three letters waiting when I got back.

This Chinese fortune teller objected very strenuously to having his portrait sketched.

The city has many outdoor eating places like this one. The man with the shovel is roasting walnuts over a charcoal fire.

LAYOUT FROM THE YANK NEWSPAPER SHOWING SKETCHES OF SHANGHAI SHORTLY
AFTER LIBERATION FROM JAPANESE OCCUPATION FORCES

Families live for many generations on these houseboats on the Yangtze River.

This typical peasant girl comes into the city to sell farm goods.

THESE Shanghai sketches show the city shortly after its liberation from the Jap occupation forces. They were made on the spot by Sgt. Joe Stefanelli, YANK staff artist.

A Chinese soldier, doing MP duty in the city, takes some time off to hold a pose.

A side street in the International Settlement. It's healthy for a stranger to walk these streets alone at nig

Parts of the International Settlement are as busy as any city scene back in the U. S. The big building on the right above is the Metropole Hotel.

Looking up the Nanking Road. The triumphal arch here was constructed for the liberation celebration.

MEALTIME, SHANGHAI, CHINA, 1945

LIEUTENANT LYLE SLADEK, SHANGHAI, CHINA, 1945
LYLE'S MOTHER WROTE "SHANGHAI KID" ON BACK

After more than a year in grade as a second lieutenant, Lyle had been stationed at one place long enough to be eligible for a promotion. Learning of his advancement, he replaced his gold bars with *silver*. Once again, Lyle and Vernon held equivalent ranks, army first lieutenant and navy lieutenant. However, the admonition that "everyone should do his best for the war effort" was no longer germane. Mainly concerned with going home, Lyle made no mention of his silver bars.

11 NOVEMBER 1945 (SUNDAY). Am on shift until midnight this evening mostly just putting in my time. Haven't actually done anything for two months now and don't figure on doing anything for the rest of the time in the army. There is not much activity in this theater anymore, and it's a good thing cause no one has the ambition or incentive to do it anyway. There is a rumor of turning this camp into a recreation camp for men awaiting shipment home. The latest dope is that this theater will not be cleaned out completely until next June. Of course morale hit a new low. I still believe there will be enough pressure on to get us back before too long though.

Went swimming again a couple days ago over at the Dhaka Club. They also have a golf course over there which some of the fellows use. This climate is nice in the winter—warm with a bright sun during the day and quite cool at night—about like early September at home. I doubt if it ever freezes here though. Yesterday afternoon the enlisted men beat us in a game of softball by a score of five to four. They play a lot and are pretty good. Guess this must sound like a soft life—well, it is, in fact the big problem is to find things to do. But it certainly is monotonous and it's not a good feeling to watch the months go by completely wasted. Especially when we know there actually is no need for it.

Mail is coming through better lately. Was surprised to hear that Irene and Hank made it home for a few days. Guess some fellows are getting out of the army. Have they made any definite plans yet? Looks now like I might get out before Vernon does. Is Vivian going to stay in Mitchell now? You could be having a big blizzard out there right now couldn't you. One has no feeling that it is late fall here. The grass is green and the leaves still on the trees and the palm trees always look the same. Bought a coconut the other day and devoured it. Also manage to buy some bananas once in a while. But I sure could go for a pheasant dinner with lettuce and milk. Are people cleaning up on them this year? I see where Generals Marshal and Hap Arnold were out there in South Dakota hunting. Are you the school marm these days, Mom? I'm afraid Charlie will probably flunk. Notice how I always type Charles as Charlie. It is a natural reflex from typing Charlie so often in this work. You see, Charlie is phonetic radio talk for the letter C. The alphabet

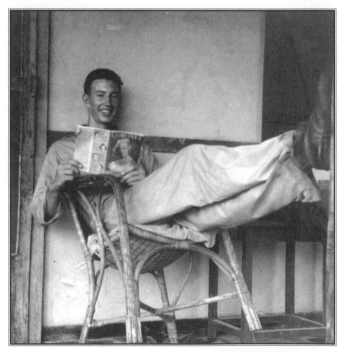

LYLE SLADEK, KURMITOLA AIR BASE, INDIA, 1945
SMOKING A CIGAR AND READING CORONET MAGAZINE

is Able baker charlie dog easy fox george how item jig king love mike nan oboe peter queen roger sugar tare uncle victor william xray yoke zebra. And the numbers are thusly: wun too thuh-ree fow-wer fi-yiv six seven ate niner zero. Voice is hard to understand accurately in army communications so most of the time we use Morse code. Recently my outfit, the fourth AACS wing, was awarded a meritous service plaque for its hump communications. That is the highest award possible for this type of unit. Most of the men in this outfit are the best of the best. And we should have been able to do the job with less men. And the morale in this outfit has always been low for various reasons. Most of the men were radio engineers or mechanics or radio hams in civilian life. So be it.

Monday.

One of the Indians who works for us has invited us to his wedding on the 16th, but it's a days trip by train and river steamer so we won't be able to make it. There is practically no transportation or communications in India. Enclosed is a ten dollar bill. Did I send you two money orders recently? A 100 from Shanghai and a 20 from here? Can't remember having sent you the twenty dollar one. Never mind. I just found the 20 dollar one in a shirt pocket. Bye now.

Lyle was happy to receive a letter with photos, yet he was taken aback by the image of a contemporary wearing civilian clothes.

14 NOVEMBER 1945 (WEDNESDAY). Irene sent me a snapshot of Henry. Seems strange to see a young fellow in a suit. All of a sudden I find out the wedding date has been set and I suppose it will already be past by the time you get this letter. They are fortunate to be getting married in peacetime and with him having a job. Irene said the ceremony would be in Chamberlain. Are you having a dinner at home with all the relatives? Would sure like to be there but it looks like this time I won't make it. The days are slipping by—here it is the middle of November. Will have a little better idea of what the score will be for us. Mail is coming through good lately. Got a letter from Irene in eight days. We usually play a game of softball in late afternoon. We beat the enlisted men yesterday for a change. Still not working very hard. Studying a little Spanish on the side. Guess I'll get this in the mail—don't have too strenuous a time feeding the relatives—and if this should happen to get there in time give my regards to the newlyweds. Our family gets bigger and bigger.

Lyle surmised that a letter he had written a month earlier, detailing his Shanghai sojourn, must have crossed paths with a letter from his mother. Clarifying the time-lapse, he replied:

24 NOVEMBER 1945 (SATURDAY). Five letters caught up with me last night including Mom's letter written Halloween night. It was sure full of news and I could almost hear the rain dripping from the roof and the wind whispering a little. No, I was not out celebrating that night—however, I was gadding about flying high over the hills of China. Glad to hear the corn is good this year and that there is someone around there with enough ambition to pick it. Who shoots the pheasants for you these days? The other day I put in an order for a surplus 12 gauge shotgun—just sort of speculating but I doubt if I'll ever get it.

Sunday.

Today you are likely cleaning up the aftermath of the wedding. Irene told me the latest plans in her letter. Mom and Aunt Anna can really cook so it should have been a big occasion for everyone but the cooks. Vernon said that Hank is quite tall too. Hope you don't forget to have some pictures taken of the affair. November is going fast isn't it. This winter weather is nice here. Cool at night and warm during the day. I'm reviewing some math lately. Have lost the edge of college days but could probably get back in the groove. Just want to find out if I do want to go on in Engineering or not even go to college anymore, or to start something else. Lots of time to decide that yet. Next week Lt Adams and I are entering a bridge tourney. We played together a couple evenings ago and lifted a few rupees off a couple of the fellows. Once in a while we play for some insignificant amount—say a couple annas per hundred points. An anna looks somewhat like our penny but actually it is worth over twice as much so one is apt to spend more here than one realizes. Our decimal system of money in the U.S. is far superior to these English systems. However, their distance and weight systems of kilometers, grams, etc are superior to ours for the same reason. It is on the decimal system. But we are too lazy or ignorant to change from our foot and pound measurements to something better. In science we always use metric system in the laboratories, etc. Vernon in his letter mentioned a funeral in our neighborhood that rather shocked me. Is it so and if so what happened? Seems like you would have mentioned it in this last letter—hope Vernon made some mistake in name or something. Still expect to get out of here in late January—a little more optimistic than most. Nothing we can do about it anyway. Hope you are having nice weather and are all feeling well.

1 DECEMBER 1945 (SATURDAY). Just me again. This was a good day for mail—most everyone received a letter or two. And I rated three including one from you. Seemed strange here in sunny India to hear it was too chilly to finish the field of corn. Is the corn price still pretty good?

Dad should sit in the shade or with his feet in the oven now that Mom is bringing home the bacon. What do you do with *all* that dough, Mom? Didn't you used to say they made pretty good wages teaching school? Guess it's probably just as easy for you to teach the school as to board a teacher and no doubt the pupils rather like the idea too. I suspect Mom can teach the kids something too. But when do you have your morning coffee these days—at recess?? Is it actually December? The months are moving aren't they. Had a letter from the girl I ran around with at the U of Illinois last year at this time. She says college is getting back to normal quite rapidly. Now I regret not having squeezed in a couple more dates during that month. Instead of studying crypto.

Visited a glass factory, a botanical garden, and a museum today at Dhaka. The glass blowing was interesting but their factory setup is ancient and crude compared with ours. For instance the floor is dirt with big holes and rough spots and little kids carry the stuff instead of conveyor belts etc. The museum was full of old firearms and armor of a few centuries ago, and other things like a stuffed Bengal tiger.

Played a cutthroat game of bridge last night and came out on top by a narrow margin of a rupee. (32 cents) Can't make a living that way. Usually we play for fun but sometimes a couple cents per hundred to keep the bidding from getting wild. Have to pick up my pay in the morning.

Latest dope is that only about 3000 men in this theater will be essential after the end of the year so there is a possibility that some of us, if declared surplus, might be sent to Europe. That would be a welcome change from this and also getting near home on govt time. Still feel there is a chance of getting out of here around late Jan or early Febr—but it takes a month to reach the States you know. So you see I won't be making it for Christmas. I believe that there was so much pressure that the army actually is being demobilized about as fast as possible. However, most of us had long ago grown distrustful of the "high up army polices" that even yet we feel that they are out to give us the worst deal they can. Even a dog grows distrustful after getting kicked around enough. So that sort of accounts for some of the bitter letters that occasionally appear in the papers these days. Lots of "hushed affairs" in the army these past years should be investigated and aired out so they'll never happen again. I'm glad to see Gen Eisenhower in as Chief of Staff.

Life is treating me quite well these days—and I hope the same with you.

As additional bases shut down there were more AACS officers than positions to fill. Lyle boarded a C-47 and returned to Chabua.

CHABUA, ASSAM, INDIA

Civil unrest continued to spread throughout India. Seeking independence from British rule, the Congress Party organized a *free India* movement under the leadership of Subhas Chandra Bose. When thousands of Indians of the British army were captured by the Japanese army at the time it overran Malaya, Bose, encouraged by the Japanese, recruited prisoners for his India National Army. Subsequently, those former British soldiers fought alongside the Japanese in Burma. Bose eventually made his way to Japan by way of Germany and, in a broadcast from Tokyo, urged the Indian people to organize an armed insurrection against the British. He formed a provisional government that later declared war on Great Britain and the United States.

On the fourth anniversary of Pearl Harbor, Lyle lamented he was just another cogwheel in the war machine. However, being quartered in a wooden bungalow on a British tea plantation seemed luxurious compared to the thatched huts at Misamari, Tezpur, and Kurmitola.

LYLE SLADEK, CHABUA AIR BASE, INDIA, 1945
INSIDE BUNGALOW ON BRITISH TEA PLANTATION

7 DECEMBER 1945 (FRIDAY). This is from the crossroads of Asia again in the tip of Assam. Don't know what the score is but at least it's a change. It seems that I am one of the first officers in this outfit to be declared surplus in this theater so here I am at some sort of AACS surplus pool. So from now on I'll just be taking it easy here waiting for something to happen. Might be assigned to a station in Europe—or might be sent back to the States—but will likely just sit here for a couple months as army channels slowly grind out my fate. The timing is good—if home newspapers play up the Calcutta riots and potential revolution enough they might send us more ships and get me out of here. They could have every man out of this theater by late January if they wanted to. With my usual good fortune, this might be the break that does the trick. And this is a pleasant place to sweat it out. We are already comfortably settled in good quarters, the food is good, and I know some of the fellows stationed at the base here. It's cooler up here by the mountains and cleaner too.

Jean did a swell job telling me about the big day at home and I do appreciate it. Jean, why don't you get a job as society reporter for the Pukwana Press? And also thanks for getting them a present for me. Bet they received lots of nice gifts.

Here it is almost Christmas again, so of course I'll add my wish of a Merry Merry Christmas for each of you—a season full of the real spirit of Christmas.

Lyle enjoyed the letter from Jean relating details of the wedding of Irene and Henry at a church in Chamberlain the day after Thanksgiving. Virginia was bridesmaid and Dale Korzan, home from Europe, was best man.

When Irene and Henry planned their wedding, the shortage of consumer goods posed obstacles. Unable to find a suitable wedding dress in the Omaha stores, Irene hired a seamstress to sew a gown—only to find it "a complete disaster" when she went for the final fitting. Fortunately, a girlfriend at the office heard of her plight and loaned the perfect gown and veil. Henry encountered no such problem; the blue-serge suit he had worn at his high school graduation in Medfield, Massachusetts, still fit perfectly. But, like most returning veterans, he was unable to find a dependable car on the market. Vivian, temporarily living with her parents in Mitchell, solved the problem by loaning her car for the honeymoon vehicle.

Lyle chuckled when he read Jean's account of two other incidents. The honeymooners were awakened before dawn by the quacking of ducks. Ducks in the Lawler Hotel? No, it was the opening day of hunting season and hunters were practicing their duck calls outside the bridal suite. When the newlyweds returned the car to Vivian, she discovered wedding guests had inadvertently decorated it with a chemical mixture that left lasting marks. Eyebrows raised when Vivian, visibly pregnant, drove about town in her car with the words JUST MARRIED etched on the sides.

7 DECEMBER 1945 (FRIDAY). Dearest Irene,
Jean wrote me a long letter telling all about the big event—including the throwing of rice and the wedding dinner menu. Anyway it seemed to me nicely arranged—neither too formal nor too noisy—but just about the way I would like. I'm depending on you or the folks to send me some pictures that were taken there. The dinner sounded scrumptious. But I guess it could hardly beat a plain winter pheasant dinner of Mom's. And I imagine Hank really appreciates your cooking too after eating in army mess halls. Going to invite me in for dinner one of these days??

Am up in Chabua again. Was declared surplus and flown up here yesterday to the surplus pool. May lay around here a couple months doing nothing, or might go to Europe, or might be heading home in a month or two. At least they have no excuse for keeping me in India. It is nice and cool and sunny up here near the Mts. The chow is quite good and the quarters are nice too—plus knowing lots of fellows here including my Cpl. bridge partner of Tezpur days. So it's a good place to sweat out some more time. The B and A (Bengal and Assam) Railway goes right past my basha. The passenger cars look like the Toonerville Trolley with Indians riding on top, hanging out the windows, and on the sides. The freight cars just have four wheels whereas ours, as you know, have 8 to 12 or more. And that's about the situation right now as I see it. Will let you know of any late developments. Don't forget to write.

12 DECEMBER 1945 (WEDNESDAY). This is sort of a country-club life. We eat plenty, sleep, play softball and bridge, and never do any work. The winter climate up here is hard to beat except that the midday sun burns quite quickly even though we are fairly well tanned. We played a game of softball with the enlisted men the other afternoon and lost 2 to 1. But the next afternoon we took them in a volleyball game. This is just a surplus pool outfit with no work to do so every effort is made to keep the men interested in sports etc. We don't know when we will go or where. We found out all we could from the colonel the other day and it seems that it is just a matter of getting transportation to the States. I believe we may move to a port area in about a month now. And I think there is a good chance of getting home in February. But that is just a guess and could vary either way. Anyway we can sort of see the end in sight now. No mail here yet but expect some today.

Guess you just about have a houseful again with the gals home from school. Are you eating out this year? If it is too cold for you just drop over here for some sunbathing.

16 DECEMBER 1945 (SUNDAY). Guess I'll break down and write a letter even though I haven't received any for a couple weeks. For some reason our mail hasn't been forwarded from Kurmitola yet but may come tomorrow. Things are very quiet here these days and the future seems about the same way. In a week or two the ships leaving India will go to Seattle instead of New York—a trip of 22 days from Calcutta by way of Singapore. That is only a little more than half as long as it took coming over by way of Melbourne.

Played a game of touch football against the enlisted men this afternoon and took a beating. But we had it coming cause we always beat them in volleyball and basketball. A nice bunch of officers around here—and a couple of them are very good in athletics. Can see the end in sight now so a couple weeks one way or the other won't kill us off. Will write more when I hear from you—

Referring to a letter in the *Register,* Lyle concurred with Kenneth Nelson, a former high school classmate stationed in China, that the American government was not leveling with the public about Asian policies. Aware Maoist forces were prevailing in China and knowing firsthand how costly the Hump airlift had been in lives and resources, Lyle had come to view the CBI operation as a tragicomedy. He scolded the government for its failed China policy.

19 DECEMBER 1945 (WEDNESDAY). Finally got some mail today, a couple letters from you forwarded from Kurmitola. Was glad to hear some more about the wedding too. Haven't heard from Irene for a long time but there is probably a couple letters from her in the batch that hasn't caught up with me yet. Just noticed your two letters laying side by side—the APO was right but you had two different station numbers on them. Can't blame you for getting mixed up occasionally on my crazy addresses. The main thing is to get the APO number right. Irene once had Hank's serial number after my name! Dad is doing right well on the corn picking as usual. Pretty good money if the corn price is still up around a dollar per bushel. Seems ironic that Dad should have too much work to do and me just laying around all the time. I found Kenneth Nelson's letter very interesting and accurate. I too feel a bit disgusted with the way things have turned out over here. Our State Dept should have had the backbone to come out and make public our policy in the Orient. If we want to force Nationalism on China and help keep British control in India at the risk of American lives and with American troops at least it could be made public. And now that the war is over the least they could do is pay us for it, that is, if we are forced to stay in the army put it on a commercial basis because we are civilian soldiers, not

volunteers. Don't take this too seriously—just letting off a little steam. At least Nelson is at Shanghai which is paradise after India. But we disagree—the Chinese girls were surprisingly attractive. The Shanghai people have fairer complexions and finer features than the people of north China and inland China.

We have another volleyball game this afternoon. We are still undefeated in the league but almost got took yesterday. The enlisted men would sure like to see us get beat and they really play for all they are worth. Hank and I are entering a bridge tournament tomorrow night just to be doing something. Next door we have a ping pong table and plenty of competition. My game is just about back to its college calibre and improving all the time. As for going home about all I can say for sure is that I feel sure of being back before the end of March. The time for going home doesn't seem to have gotten any closer these past two weeks. Don't know if they are giving us the old run around or what. All I know is that we are helpless and must just sweat it out.

What a laugh—Jean and Wilma playing in Mr. Stone's orchestra. Bet it is really a high class band. It must be a good band with Jean and Wilbur Clutter in it. Well, it's already a year since the nice Christmas vacation of last year. The mistake was in asking for a five day extension. Should have taken it without asking but that might have been stretching my luck a little. Be seeing you one of these days. Will let you know when to stop writing.

A week later, Lyle summed up his third Christmas in uniform.

26 DECEMBER 1945 (WEDNESDAY). We had a rather nice Christmas day here considering. They held short services in the recreation room and then there was a good turkey dinner at the mess hall. In the evening we had a good game of bridge. Had a letter from Vernon the other day. I doubt now that he will be sent out to sea. In fact, I bet he gets out before I do the way things look now. Of course once I get back I'll have over a month of terminal leave coming etc so my army working days are over. Still no late developments on getting out of here. Can't be too long now. Hope everything is O.K. out there. Nothing new to write about so—

30 DECEMBER 1945 (SUNDAY). Another bright, sunny day. Wish you could drop in and see the natives out here trying to sell us jewels. One says he is Tibetan and the others are either Gurkhas or Naga Hills tribesmen. This is the crossroads of Asia and so here you find most every strange tribe of Mongolian, Burmese, Chinese, and Indians with their different dress and habits. These people are short but very strong—

HILLS TRIBESMEN, CHABUA, INDIA, 1945
VISITING CHABUA AIR BASE TO PEDDLE JEWELS

yellow skin and feminine Mongolian features with black hair in a braid, skin hats, beads, and sort of buckskin clothes. Their jewelry looks good to an amateur but actually most of it is poor grade stones, or else made of crystal or glass. A jewelry expert might make some money over here. The mail situation is still pretty bad but should start coming through one of these days. Seems a long time with little news from the outside world. Bet it is cold out there and probably some snowbanks in the usual. Still no idea of when I'll actually leave here. Time is sort of dragging here. By the way I quit taking Atabrine about three months ago and haven't had any attacks of malaria so apparently I was lucky and didn't get it.

New Year's Eve.

Hooray, three letters today but none from you yet. Mail was held up for a week at Casablanca. There are about sixty thousand men in India-Burma now and about twenty some thousand are going out in January so I Feel my turn is about due in February. I feel I have gotten the bad end of this deal but can't complain too much cause most of the time the breaks have come my way in the army. And I guess a month or two one way or the other won't break my back. Well, the New Year starts in a couple hours now. Am looking forward to forty-six.

31 DECEMBER 1945 (MONDAY). Happy New Year—Irene and Hank. You can see this is a pretty tame way to see the New Year in—by writing a letter. At least you can tell that I'm not blue enough to want to go out and get drunk. I for one will be satisfied if the New Year treats us as well as forty-five. At least nothing very bad happened to us. The past year seemed to go very slow for me and yet so lacking in events that looking back it seems to have vanished all at once. I'm certainly looking forward to the coming year and wondering just what is in store for me.

Now you'uns are settled down and can just drift with the current as the future unfolds. Was glad to get your letter of Dec 6 today. Mail has been held up in different places, for instance storms between Africa and India held up first class mail for a week and then it has to be forwarded to my new address so mail has been very scarce for about a month. Sure do miss that mail. Still taking it easy waiting for something to happen. My guess is that maybe in early Feb they will let me climb the plank. Latest rumor is that this AACS pool will be moved to Kankrapara near Calcutta in a short time. Just like the army to keep moving things. Makes no diff to me cause I just don't unpack anymore. The weather has been just perfect up here. In the evening the heavy mists start drifting across the tea plantations leaving cool starry nights. In the morning the bright sun soon dries the dew and warms the air like Sept at home—never a cloud in the sky. We wear suntans during the day and woolens at night. One of my basha mates and I have been playing some checkers lately. He is from St Louis and a good checker player. Of course we have the usual bridge games and occasionally a show. Saw "The Lost Weekend" a few nights ago. A good picture but not too enjoyable in my opinion. Oh yes, I saw "Anchors Away" too and liked it very much. The music, dancing, and colors made it a good show for my money. Sometimes they have for a short subject a "Sing With the Stars" and some of the songs have parts to be sung by the fellows and then a part to be sung by the ladies—and it's always a scream when we sing the ladies parts in high falsetto voices instead of leaving it blank. To say nothing of the caustic comments and catcalls that go with a corney show here.

I guess maybe I am an uncle by now. Vernon may get out before I do the way things are going. But once I get back my time will be mostly terminal leave etc so it won't matter exactly when they give me the important paper. Will land in Seattle and go to the state of Virginia the way it looks. But you know me—will just have to stop off at such places as home, Omaha, Chicago, Detroit, etc. Oh happy day. Goodnight.

Still twiddling his thumbs at the start of a new year, Lyle was cheered by a letter and photographs from home.

3 JANUARY 1946 (THURSDAY). Feels good to have mail coming through again. Your letter of the fifteenth with the snapshots was especially welcome. Certainly a beautiful bride. And whoever took the pictures did a right good job except for a couple where they had to look too directly into the sun to keep their eyes open. The groom looks like he would just as soon get away from being the center of attention. Don't suits have cuffs on the trousers anymore? It's funny how little things hit you all of a sudden—in the picture taken by the table the sugar bowl

IRENE SLADEK AND HENRY PARKHURST, WEDDING DAY, 1945

immediately caught my eye—it's the same blue and white one with white handles. And the glass probably had grape jelly in it. Mom, you look like school teaching is agreeing with you. Looks like a lot of corn in that crib—seems to be sort of in the middle of the yard near the pond. Right? The snow looks cool and crisp. Most afternoons we play volleyball or something outside in shorts but at night we sleep under several blankets. May enter a bridge tournament with Hank this evening. You want to learn to play bridge, Mom? It's a good game for keeping mentally alive when there is nothing else to do. But you certainly aren't missing anything in my opinion. Have been playing some checkers with my other basha mate, Sam. We are quite closely matched. And so it goes. Am feeling swell these days and hope you are too. Bye.

Eight days later Lyle sent word home. He enclosed photos, including one of himself seated inside his bungalow with an intricate stack of checkers piled high on a table and a picture of a movie star pinned on the wall.

11 JANUARY 1946 (FRIDAY). Have about half an hour yet before supper so I might as well drop you a line. We took a few snaps a week ago—I'll send you the negatives—please have a few prints made sometime. The Indian lad is our bearer—that is he works for us—we call him "Ollie." He sweeps the floor, carries our clothes to the "dobhi Wallah" (washer man) etc for a very small wage.

LYLE SLADEK INSIDE BUNGALOW
CHABUA AIR BASE, INDIA, 1945

BEARER OLLIE AND LYLE (WEARING "LIMEY" HAT), CHABUA, INDIA, 1945
OLLIE DID HOUSEKEEPING CHORES FOR A FEW RUPEES A MONTH

Crossword puzzles have been the latest fad here—which proves that we are really hard up for things to do. Have been playing some checkers lately with a fellow named Lt Olmstead. We call him "Bumstead." He seems to be considered checker king around here. He seems to have an edge on me so far. There seems to be quite a stink throughout the world regarding demobilization. I'm not surprised that the lid is finally blowing off the kettle. Gen Eisenhower said all men not needed overseas should be returned home—that's me. Mail is coming through a little better these days—seems to take about three weeks from home now days. Will mail you another package of clothes one of these days. Also sent you a PTA for a 100 dollars last week. Nothing to do, nothing to buy, so we save quite a bit over here. Next month I start drawing longevity pay—old fogey pay for length of service—I believe 5% increase. Pretty good pay for doing nothing. But of course there are lots of privates and not so many 1st Lts—so you see only a few of us are able to save any sizable amount. My army pay still only averages out to about $80 per month. Still hoping to see you soon.

What "soon" meant was still a mystery. Rumors circulated and died.

16 JANUARY 1946 (WEDNESDAY). It seems that at the present time plans call for a shipment of AACS officers and men to Europe—our Headquarters are in Berlin in that AACS Wing. But as I said that is only the present plan and the army starts lots of things it never finishes. So I believe it may blow over. But I hope very strongly to get sent to Europe cause there is no chance of getting out of here for a couple months and Europe would be an interesting, welcome change. Will let you know when and *if* before leaving India. As yet it is just a strong rumor.

This afternoon I took a blanket outside and sunned myself. A bit later a couple snake charmers came along with their baskets of snakes and playing the most fascinating weird music. Laying there half asleep under a tropical sun with the enchanting monotonous music was sort of in another world—a make-believe world. The instruments are wooden pipes with a sort of gourd in the middle and the pitch is about like a Scottish bagpipe. Indian music has a much finer tone scale than ours so it sounds monotonous to our untrained ears. Actually there is nothing exciting about the angry cobras waving their heads in front of the little dark man with the horn. Seems to me like a hard way to make a living. They pass a hat afterwards. Sometimes we get a direct army news broadcast direct from San Francisco. Don't get up too early these cold mornings. Goodnight.

Five months since the end of hostilities and Lyle was still marking time. He scouted out a leather shop on the base and began crafting a calfskin wallet.

21 JANUARY 1946 (MONDAY). A good day today, some mail came through including a couple letters from you. A couple days ago after not getting an expected letter from you I said to myself, "Gee, why don't they write?" But when I stopped to think about it I realized how easy it was for me to say that, laying around here in the sun and never doing anything more strenuous than eating! I forget that out there you may be in the middle of a blizzard, cattle to feed, dinner to cook, and chickens to feed etc. Bet you could use some help. If I were not an officer I would be coming home for discharge now so you see life has its compensations! No news on the Europe deal—heard a rumor they would send a couple planes from there to pick us up. Will be a long cold ride if it comes through which I doubt. Anything to get out of India! Will let you know when something develops. Am getting impatient to get home and also rather anxious to be getting back to Detroit for a spell. We'll be the envy of the town in that Buick! Guess that day will come before too long now. Am sending you a couple more packages. Am cutting my belongings to a minimum in case I fly somewhere and can only take a small weight with me. The clothing you can dispose of as you see fit. Glad those things from Shanghai finally got there. The pieces of cloth should each make a blouse?? That pheasant dinner you told about made me hungry. Glad to hear you are all up and about these days. I've been feeling perfect right along and I believe about the same weight. Am making a belt out of nylon shrouds of a parachute—green and white. A bit loud except for sportswear. Also made a wallet of native leather. Read a book occasionally, work crossword puzzles, play ping pong, etc etc. January will soon be over. Until later.

28 JANUARY 1946 (MONDAY). We just heard a re-read of General Eisenhower's speech to Congress, and it seemed to me that he covered things quite well. He mentioned that too rapid demobilization would paralyze technical units such as the Army Airways Communications System (AACS) but I take issue with him there. I haven't done a thing for four months and the fact is that 60 to 75% of us fellows in AACS haven't had a thing to do here for a couple months. However, I believe his speech is a little late, but will still do a lot of good cause he did put the cards on the table.

Made myself a couple billfolds to be doing something. They turned out quite well—one of them I wouldn't trade for any commercial model cause it's designed for my own likes. You should see my new pajamas. Had an Indian tailor make me a pair out of a cargo parachute—gorgeous rayon material. The catch is that they are bright red or even scarlet—so bright I'll have to wear sunglasses when wearing them. Still haven't heard any news from Mitchell way if I'm an uncle so I'm sweating that out. And so it goes.

Enclosed a snapshot of an Indian snake charmer in front of our basha. In the background a tea field. Note the cobra on the left with flattened head weaving to the music—sounds like Scotch bagpipe.

Next a Naga Hills man—never washes. Note Gurkha knife in belt and charm around his neck.

Although something seemed to be "in the works," Lyle did not want to raise false hopes. In response to a request from his little brother, he gently explained:

4 FEBRUARY 1946 (MONDAY). Awfully sorry Chuckie but I can't bring home a start for your zoo. Because of danger of spreading diseases etc it is not permissible to take any pets to the States. And I'm afraid a monkey wouldn't like S. Dak any better than I like India! A mongoose would make a nice pet but they kill all the birds they get hold of. Actually Chuckie, anything they have in India we have more of and better of in the States.

It seems that the going to Europe prospects are getting hot again. I do know that headquarters here has been negotiating with our headquarters in Berlin regarding a shipment of AACS officers, and the hold up seems to be who will furnish transportation. But I still think it will fall through. Anything to get out of here. Sorry to hear you haven't been hearing from me. It seems storms held up mail for a couple weeks at Casablanca. They took one special ship of mail from there and flew the rest so you should be caught up again by now. Anyway you can expect lots of delays like that these winter months. Mail coming this way has been spotty too but not quite so bad. Last letter from you was Jan 14. Am still waiting for some news from Mitchell way.

A few of us have just gotten back on our feet from a slight food poisoning or dysentary. One fellow went to the hospital but the rest of us had just a light attack. Have been fortunate in being sick only two days here in almost a year. Not even a sniffle of a cold yet. The weather is already noticeably warmer—and it rained the other night. Can just feel the monsoons coming again. I don't believe the temperature gets below 55 at night—the sun is very bright during the days.

Still waiting, waiting. The morale over here is low especially among men with no jobs. I wouldn't complain about being here if there

SNAKE CHARMER WITH COBRA, CHABUA, INDIA, 1945
EARNING RUPEES AT CHABUA AIR BASE

NAGA HILLS MAN, CHABUA, INDIA, 1945
GURKHA KNIFE IN CLOTHING

was absolutely any excuse for it. Redeployment is SNAFU just like everything else in the army. Fellows like "Mr. Shirley Temple" getting out of the army with 26 months service and never been overseas—at the most a miserable 19 points. And they wonder why the morale has collapsed! Oh things aren't really so bad—it's just the indefinite waiting, changes in policy, and sheer boredom of it all. Guess something will happen one of these days, at the most it will be a couple more months.

The British presence on the Indian subcontinent began when ships of the East India Company sailed into the port of Surat in 1608. The company established numerous trading posts and eventually received a royal dictate from the Mughal Emperor exempting it from the payment of custom duties in Bengal. What started as a trading venture became a ruling enterprise after the Nawab of Bengal was defeated at the Battle of Plassey in 1757. A century later, the Sepoy Mutiny marked the start of the *Indian National* movement, the quest to shake off British rule and form an independent India.

Mohandas Gandhi, reverently known as Mahatma Gandhi, became the leader of the Indian National Congress in 1920. As means to achieving political and social goals, he advocated nonviolence tactics such as fasting and boycotts and, when necessary, civil disobedience. Although some Hindus were critical of his philosophy, Gandhi gained a large following. In 1942 he became the leader of the *Quit India* movement. His vision of a united India with Hindus and Muslims living together in peace was shattered during the last stages of the movement. As the British prepared to pull out of India, clashes between Hindus and Muslims resulted in thousands of deaths. Gandhi, the father figure of the independence movement, went on a fast in an attempt to quell the riots.

Lyle, understanding the role of tradition in stable governments and aware of divisions in Indian society (caste, creed, religion), feared immediate independence for India would lead to more bloodshed. Continuing his letter, he remarked:

No particular changes here in India—occasionally a little trouble about the independence movement. Sometimes the nonviolence resistance gets a bit violent. Gandhi still is the big wheel in Hindu politics, and he travels around the country stirring up the people. Actually I don't believe the masses know what it's all about. Too many caste, language, and religious barriers to get well enough organized for entire self-government. The main trouble seems to be that the Indians dislike the British. The British are a strange species by our standards.

Am putting in a piece of an old newspaper that you might find interesting. It's from the Calcutta Statesman. There is some trouble right along down in Burma with Chinese bandits. They are deserters from the Chinese army that helped clean the Japs out of Burma a year ago. They are well supplied with tommy guns.

Hope this finds everybody around the farm feeling swell.

Finally, a week later, Lyle received orders to proceed to Barrackpore, the first step in his journey west.

BARRACKPORE, BENGAL, INDIA

After acknowledging news of the birth of a daughter to the Vs, Lyle elaborated on his own happy prospects.

11 FEBRUARY 1946 (MONDAY). Had a letter from Irene the other day and she of course told me that Carol has arrived. The name seems to fit doesn't it.

It's a bright sunny morning here at the Barrackpore air base on the edge of Calcutta. Quite a conglamoration passes along the road by here—the rickshas, British lorries, oxcarts, women with grey-white saharis carrying baskets on their heads, etc etc. I still think an Indian oxcart is the slowest thing on earth. A sahari is the national dress of the women—it's a strip of cloth about 3 feet wide and about 15 feet long. It is usually a dirty white, but in the upper classes it may be bright silk. Anyhow it is wrapped round and round like some ultra modern evening gowns, and seems to stay on surprisingly enough. The men dress very similar to the women except that one fold comes back loosely between the legs giving a sort of half skirt half trouser appearance. The Indians in the employ of the British of course gradually adopt our style clothes. It's a good deal warmer down here—in fact too warm to suit me. About like June at home except dry and always sunny. April-May in Calcutta just before the monsoon season is the hottest dryest place except for the center of a desert that there is in my opinion. So you see I'm looking forward to getting out of here.

We flew down here a few days ago as the first leg of a long, long trip. By the time you get this letter I may be at Wiesbaden, Germany—a resort town near Berlin. The first group left a couple days ago for Karachi, India, which is the first stop. I am scheduled to leave in a couple days. This should be a trip to end all trips because it will include stops at many important places in the Near East, North Africa, and Europe. So the next few days are critical. Sure hope this comes through cause I want to get out of India. Had expected to get home about now but that seems to be out of the question so this is the next best thing. Now I won't be getting home until late summer. Some of the fellows are getting sent to China which is really a raw deal. At least I am getting two or three weeks closer to home. You can write to my new address:

Hq 5th AACS Wing

APO 633

c/o PM New York

From Wiesbaden it is hard telling where in Europe I'll be assigned. Will write again when I get down the line and it may beat this letter. Boy, I'm sure sweating out these days cause there's always the chance of it falling through. No mail on account of moving so haven't heard from you. Is there a touch of spring in the air yet out there? I sure could go for some good food, namely a meal at home. Our living conditions will be considerably improved now I believe. And near enough so maybe you can send me a box of cookies Mom? Are you getting the packages I sent home? Did I send my watch home in the matchbox with the ivory elephant and gemstones? If I did I may want you to send it to me first class. Never wear a watch here on account of it makes the skin sore, and I never care what time it is. You can do as you like with most of the junk I sent home. Am down to about 70 lbs of bare essentials in the way of clothes and toothbrush. Signing off from India.

The tent camp at Barrackpore on the outskirts of Calcutta was a safe haven from the rioting that had erupted during the trial of an Indian soldier of the British Empire. Captured in Burma by the Japanese army, the soldier was now accused of turning traitor and fighting on the side of Japan.

16 FEBRUARY 1946 (SATURDAY). This is a continuation of the letter a week ago. Our shipments were delayed a few days due to a backlog of air transportation at Karachi. However, a large group went today and I am scheduled to leave Barrackpore tomorrow morning Sunday Feb 17 at eleven o'clock for Karachi. Will hold up on this letter and mail it at Karachi in order to avoid any possible false changes of address.

There has been trouble in Calcutta these days. Reactionary student groups and rabble rousers protesting the trial and sentencing of Capt. Abdul Shasid, an Indian National Army officer who I believe collaborated with the Japs during the Jap attempt to cut off the Assam Valley, have been attacking white people and destroying property and looting business places. 36 American soldiers were injured but only a few hospitalized. About 30 people killed but things are under control now. I was fortunate in being here at camp when it started. Of course immediately Calcutta was placed off bounds and all troops convoyed out to Military bases. I expect there will be a bigger blowout after the

March elections. The mail situation is stinko. Only one planeload from Casablanca to Karachi in two weeks. Will sure be swell to be moving toward home. It's about 9 hours I believe to Karachi. Probably about 40 hours flying time to Berlin in C-54 Skymasters—same as President Truman's plane, the Sacred Cow. Have been picking up a few rupees playing bridge here lately—my luck has been good. I guess AACS is the bridge playingest outfit in the army. Playing among ourselves the games are quite close, but woe to outsiders who don't know too much about the game. More later from Germany.

Upon arrival at Barrackpore, Lyle had struck up an immediate friendship with three officers his age, Hal Segal, Orlo Karstens, and Russ Place. Hal was from a city on the East Coast. Orlo, nicknamed Ollie, was from a small town in Iowa. Russ had been a student at Yale University before the war.

Together the four lieutenants awaited air transportation for the long journey to AACS headquarters in Wiesbaden, Germany. They had no idea of the itinerary or timeline, as the military network did not schedule flights; planes flew when and where needed. The four men had long since ceased to question army ways—they were just relieved to be getting out of India.

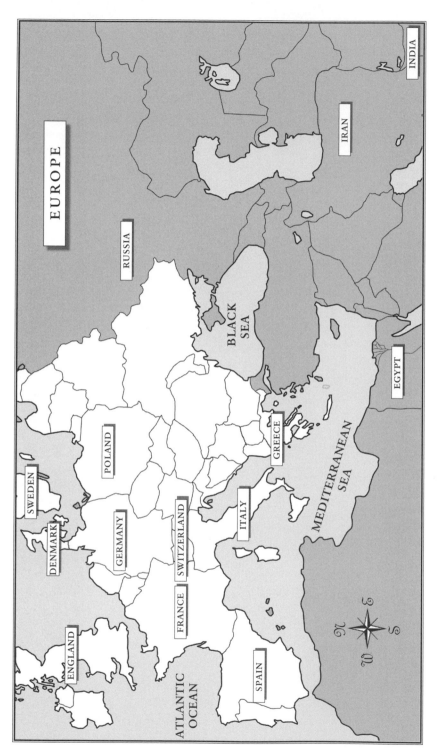

FLYING WEST FROM INDIA TO IRAN TO EGYPT TO GREECE TO ITALY TO FRANCE TO GERMANY

CHAPTER 17

Postwar Duty in Europe

Hope springs eternal in the human breast.
—ALEXANDER POPE

WHILE AT BARRACKPORE awaiting air transportation to the European theater (ETO), Lyle was impatient to continue west. But the waiting was bearable since he was hobnobbing with three lively companions, Hal, Orlo, and Russ. The four buddies looked for interesting things to do. Russ suggested playing a few holes of golf at a nearby course featuring a Hindu temple in the middle of the third fairway, a layout he had read about in Ripley's *Believe It Or Not* column. The men rented clubs and had a hilarious time. Though a rank beginner, Lyle drove a ball the proverbial country mile on the fifth hole.

The next day the men lucked out when a transport plane, due to fly to Karachi nonstop, had room for all four of them. The flight would be the first of many segments on the journey to Wiesbaden, Germany.

Elated when the plane lifted off the runway, Lyle quoted lines from Kipling's *Gunga Din:* "Now in Injia's sunny clime / Where I used to spend my time / A-servin' of . . ."

The plane lacked seats and the cabin was not pressurized, but the men voiced no complaints during the long flight across the subcontinent of India. They found the cold air at high altitudes exhilarating and the loud, steady drone of the four engines reassuring. Spreading a GI blanket on the floor, they engaged in a competitive game of bridge, pausing to snap a photo of the Taj Mahal shining like a jewel in the desert as they passed over Agra at eight thousand feet.

KARACHI, SIND, INDIA (NOW PAKISTAN)

You will yet be the glory of the East;
would that I could come again, Karachi, to see you in your grandeur.
—SIR CHARLES NAPIER, GOVERNOR OF SIND (1843-47)

Debarking at Karachi in the Sind province of India, the men found the desert atmosphere refreshing. They welcomed the change in climate after months in the steamy, languid air of Bengal and Assam.

HAL AND ARAB TRAVELERS, SIND DESERT, INDIA, 1946

LYLE AND ORLO, KARACHI, INDIA, 1946
"CAN WE BUM A RIDE, SAHIB?"

In the morning, rejuvenated after a restful sleep and finding no flights available, the lieutenants explored the surrounding area. Noting a distant object silhouetted against the desert sky, they set out to investigate. As they drew near an immense, barnlike structure they marveled at how it dwarfed other buildings in the vicinity. Curious, they learned it had been built by the British to house a dirigible.

After the German dirigible *Graf Zeppelin* successfully flew around the world in 1929, lighter-than-air travel appeared to be the wave of the future. Great Britain, envisioning regular eight-day flights to the Far East, built an enormous dirigible, *R101,* and erected a hangar at Karachi as a stopover shelter en route to Calcutta. Tragically, the hangar never housed *R101;* while on its maiden voyage toward Karachi, the airship crashed in France. That accident combined with the 1937 disaster of the *Hindenburg,* the pride of the Third Reich, marked the end of the era of gigantic self-propelled dirigibles.

Pacing off the dimensions of the hangar, Lyle was amazed to find it was fifteen times as long and five times as wide as the big red barn at home. Laughing, he related how the whole neighborhood had buzzed with excitement the day they had seen that huge barn, sixty feet long and two stories high, being towed along country lanes by a vintage World War I truck and two tractors. "You could pack three hundred or more such barns into this hangar," Lyle exclaimed.

HANGAR GREAT BRITAIN BUILT FOR DIRIGIBLE *R101,* KARACHI, INDIA, 1946

The next day the four adventurers rented a boat and sailed to an island in the Arabian Sea. Natives looked on as they built a Taj Mahal sandcastle and buried Russ in the sand until he was "up to his neck as usual."

LYLE, HAL, ORLO, AND RUSS, KARACHI, INDIA, 1946
SAILING EXCURSION TO AN ISLAND IN THE ARABIAN SEA

Upon returning to their quarters the four goofs were told a flight would be heading west in a couple of hours and "You'd better be on it."

HAL, RUSS, AND LYLE, KARACHI, INDIA
AT AIRPORT WAITING TO BOARD A C-54 SKYMASTER OUT OF INDIA

CAIRO, EGYPT

Three years to the day of waving good-bye to his family in Chamberlain, Lyle climbed down from a C-54 Skymaster at Payne Field near Cairo. Wow, he thought, here I am in Egypt—fabulous land of Moses, pharaohs, and pyramids.

The food and lodging at Payne Field seemed luxurious; the mess hall served fresh fruit and the beds had mattresses. Relaxing after a fifteen-hour flight from Karachi, Lyle wrote a lengthy letter narrating his sojourn from Barrackpore to Karachi to Abadan to Cairo.

21 FEBRUARY 1946 (THURSDAY, CAIRO, EGYPT). Gee, it's great to be getting back to civilization again—can't hardly realize that at last I'm out of India. This is life again. That waiting waiting humdrum existence was getting on my nerves but now the world seems bright again. Are you surprised to get a letter from Egypt? Guess I might as well start at the beginning and give you a few details of the trip. We left Barrackpore air base about noon on Feb 17 in a C-54 and flew to Karachi via Agra and New Delhi. It was an interesting 7-hour flight and time passed rapidly playing bridge and watching the scenery. At Agra we flew over the Taj Mahal—shining like a jewel in the desert. But one has to see it from the ground to appreciate it. At Karachi on the Sind Desert we found the India we had expected to find in the first place. Much nicer buildings of sandstone, more colorfully clad natives, camels carrying loads across the windswept desert trails, ass carts, and the hot sandy terrain. We stayed three days at Karachi. One hot windy day while gazing out the door of the barracks, this poem I wrote sort of hit me—heat waves were shimmering in the hot desert air and dust was swirling around the legs of the camels—I felt sorry for them.

KARACHI MUSES
Gently blow you desert wind,
Fan the fires of the Sind
Parch the throat of man and beast,
Dry their bones when life has ceased.

Tell me sad-eyed plodding camel,
Moth-eaten, cantankerous mammal
Do you curse fate that says you must
Spend your life in this desert dust??

ARAB CAMEL CARAVAN, SIND DESERT, KARACHI, 1946
SCENE THAT INSPIRED LYLE TO PEN "KARACHI MUSES"

Just outside the Karachi airport is a hangar built by Great Britain to house a dirigible. It is about 150 ft high and 290 steps or 870 feet long. A huge black metal barn. The third day, yesterday, we went to Karachi to the wharf and hired a small fishing sailboat to take us to an island in the Arabian Sea where we swam, sunned, and built a white sand Taj Mahal. The water was clean and cool and the bright sun was just right. We stayed on the beach a little too long and almost sunburned ourselves. It was a very pleasant day. We started to take a nap when we got back out to the air base, but they suddenly informed us we were to leave in a couple hours. So we hurriedly ate and packed and a little after sundown a C-54 loaded with a British general, a 7-month-old snow leopard, mail, and about 30 passengers took off and headed west into the setting sun. Eight hours and ten minutes later at night we arrived at Abadan in Iran (Persia) where we refueled and had a warm meal at a civilian run airport. When our country agreed to withdraw troops from Iran we discharged our soldiers and hired them back as civilians to run a couple airfields. At Abadan (50 miles from Baghdad) is the second largest oil refinery in the world. An hour later we took off for Cairo. Traveling with the sun made the night about 3 hours longer than normal. At sunrise we were flying over the Holy Land. First we saw the Dead Sea where the river Jordan flows into it. Then to Jericho and a few miles farther was Bethlehem and a bit later over in a valley the spires and rooftops of Jerusalem sparkling in the sun. The countryside is quite rough and barren. How quickly we passed over an area so rich in history! A little later we flew along the blue edge of the Mediterranean shore and then over the Suez Canal, the town of Suez, and landed here at Payne Field a ways outside of Cairo. Students in Cairo are on the warpath so we may not get to visit the city right away. Will try to stay here several days before going to Athens and Rome. Will try to get out to the Pyramids too if possible. This is a bit staggering at first—nice brick buildings, ice cream, no mosquitos etc and at breakfast we had some fresh grapefruit, real butter etc. Yes, things are picking up for yours truly. Will probably call you from Germany to give you my new address. Last letter from you was written in early January. Oh yes, my bed here has springs and a thick mattress! Gee it's wonderful to get nearer home. Germany is about 3 weeks nearer home by boat. Will try and send you some snaps of various escapades one of these days.

Am a bit tired after 15 hours in a crowded plane at night—have flown 26 hours so far from Chabua. Next stop Athens, Rome, and on up to Germany. I'm sure lucky to get out of India. Still have to pinch myself to believe it's true. The climate is swell. Cool and sunny. More later from somewhere down the line.

While encamped at Payne Field the travelers visited Cairo and historic sites along the Nile, but they heeded the warning to avoid the city at night due to civil unrest against British rule.

THE TRAVELERS AND PYRAMID TOMB, CAIRO, EGYPT, 1946

ORLO AND THE SPHINX

ORLO AND "PILE OF ROCKS"

ATHENS, GREECE

After several days at Payne Field near Cairo, the lieutenants flew on to Athens. As the men landed at Hassani Airfield they viewed the bomb-damaged runway repaired with a temporary layer of steel mesh. Athens had been hit hard by the war.

HASSANI AIRFIELD, ATHENS, GREECE, 1946
BOMBED RUNWAY REPAIRED WITH STEEL MESH

While viewing ancient ruins and marveling at the Arch of Hadrian and the Parthenon, Lyle pondered, "To the glory that was Greece." He told his companions that if they made it to Rome, he would cite another oft quoted line from Poe's *To Helen.*

ROME, ITALY

As hoped, the next flight took the four officers to Rome. Fortunately, German Field Marshal Kesselring had declared Rome an "open city" when his army retreated to the north in 1944. As per international law, the city was demilitarized, opened to occupation, and its treasures spared from destruction.

Rome cast a magical spell over Lyle and his travel mates as they toured the Pantheon, Forum, and Colosseum. Although Poe had never visited the Eternal City, his words, "the grandeur that was Rome," struck Lyle as profound. He vowed to read *The Development of Western Civilization,* an old history book he had seen at the SDSC library.

ORLO AND COLOSSEUM, ROME, 1946

ORLO AND VICTORY ARCH, ROME, 1946

LYLE AND HAL WITH KING EMANUEL MONUMENT, ROME, 1946

Later on, Lyle marveled at the structural beauty and exquisite ornamentation of Saint Peter's Basilica. He never dreamed of the existence of such a building. While touring Vatican City, the four sightseers posed with American, British, Canadian, and Polish service people for a group photograph.

AMERICAN, BRITISH, CANADIAN, AND POLISH MILITARY PERSONNEL, VATICAN CITY, 1946
LYLE, RUSS, HAL, AND ORLO CENTERED WITH THE DOME OF SAINT PETER'S

A Red Cross canteen in the heart of the city served as a welcome center for soldiers fortunate enough to be in Rome. Still somewhat naive, Lyle lost some lire in a shell game at the foot of the Spanish Steps. He was thrilled to attend a production of *Aida* at the opera house. And while dining in a little café, he sat entranced as a musician played a violin with passion and soul.

RUSS AND SPANISH STEPS, ROME, 1946

LYLE AND FRIEND BY HASSLER HOTEL, ROME, 1946

The stay in Rome was too short. When air transportation became available, Lyle and his three companions flew to Marseilles and on to Paris.

PARIS, FRANCE

The four friends had no idea when leaving India that their travels would take them to *gay Paree*. Landing at Orly Field stirred visions of a famous scene—a crowd of admirers rushing toward the *Spirit of Saint Louis* at the completion of Lindbergh's historic flight across the Atlantic nineteen years earlier.

In compliance with army travel regulations the AACS officers checked in at a hotel run by Allied occupation forces. From the window of his hotel room Lyle looked down on historic Place Vendôme.

Although the French people had suffered greatly during the German occupation, Lyle could see that Paris was recovering rapidly. Already the sidewalk cafés were doing a lively business and the opera house was staging performances. While on a tour of Versailles, the four lieutenants again posed with American, British, Canadian, and Polish military personnel for a group photo. Enjoying their stay, they were less than diligent in seeking a flight to Wiesbaden.

14 MARCH 1946 (THURSDAY, PARIS, FRANCE). We flew in here a couple days ago and plan to leave for Wiesbaden in 3 or 4 days—it's just a couple hours from here. From there we will be assigned somewhere in Europe. There is a rumor that some officers with the longest service and overseas time will be leaving for home soon. I'll be right about on the borderline of making or not making that shipment. As you have probably noticed we have been in no hurry getting to Wiesbaden. Should be a big batch of mail waiting for me there. Yesterday we went on a tour out to Versaille where this picture was taken. It was a damp rainy day but not too uncomfortable. Not so impressive as the similar places in Rome. We visited the du Louvre the other day where we saw the original Le Mona Lisa, the statue Venus de Milo, Whistler's Mother, and famous paintings of Rembrandt and others. We haven't been near Tour Eiffel (Eiffel tower) yet, or Notre Dame Cathedral but we plan to visit them before leaving. The weather is not too cold for March. Paris is a well planned city, wide orderly streets, an efficient subway system, and pretty buildings. The Seine River is walled in on the banks, the parks are clean and pretty, and the shop windows have smart displays. Paris is the prettiest city I've seen but not so interesting as Rome. The fellows around here have had it pretty soft—perhaps too soft. Seems like the army over here is now made up of privates and officers. In my opinion the War Dept has bungled badly in its entire demobilization *program*, if one can even call it that. Maybe they forget that a small organized well

AMERICAN, BRITISH, CANADIAN, AND POLISH MILITARY PERSONNEL, VERSAILLES, 1946
LYLE FIFTH FROM LEFT

VENUS DE MILO, DU LOUVRE, PARIS, 1946

trained group of interested men make a much more effective army than a large number of men who are poorly trained and have no interest in learning. I suppose conditions will start improving pretty soon when the demobilization job is completed. In the meantime I'm just coasting, waiting for the day they let me out.

Mailed a package today containing a tapestry from Cairo. I won't tell you what I paid for it. Those Egyptians are smooth. I had no money in my pocket, and yet they sold me a tapestry which I have no desire to own. Anyway I ended up by borrowing the money and practically shedding tears of remorse at having offered such a low price for "a masterpiece of beauty, a year of hand weaving bla bla"—I'm a hard customer to sell to ordinarily but they could sell me the shirt off my own back and convince me it was a bargain. Maybe it would make a good rug for Skippy's doghouse. Or if anyone admires it, give it to them.

Am anxious to get to Wiesbaden to pick up my mail. The last news from you was in early January. Be sure and tell me the news. Where is Vernon? Have you seen baby Carol yet? I'll write again from Wiesbaden.

Moved by an outing to the surrounding countryside, Lyle wrote:

17 MARCH 1946 (SUNDAY, PARIS, FRANCE). Just a few lines this evening—leaving for Wiesbaden in the morning if the weather is good. Today I went on a Red Cross tour out to Fontainebleau a few miles out of Paris. After we were out in the country a short distance I noticed a peasant woman hoeing out in a field and it struck me that it was just the scene Millet would paint. And to my complete surprise and amazement the guide at that moment pointed to a church and said that it was the church in Millet's "L' Angelus" which hangs in our front room. The steeple can be seen just to the right of the couple. And it was in those fields that Millet *did* paint his "The Gleaners" and "L' Angelus." We visited his studio of a century ago, where artists today still paint in this famous little town in Fontainebleau forrest. To me it means that only a truly great artist like Millet could place a bit of France in our front room—so vividly that even though not even seeing that picture for a couple years it still hit me between the eyes. Maybe I'm not getting across to you how I felt—

We had dinner at a French restaurant, beef, brown bread, beer, custard. Then we visited the castle of the French kings and Napoleon. It was all very interesting. More later.

Things are looking better about getting home.

HAL, LYLE, AND ORLO, PARIS, 1946

RUSS, LYLE, AND HAL, L'ARC DE TRIOMPHE, PARIS, 1946

ORLO AND SEINE RIVER, PARIS, 1946

After weeks of travel, the men boarded a transport for the seventh and last leg of their journey from India to Germany. Not having heard from family and friends during that entire time, receiving letters from home occupied their minds as they stepped off the plane at Wiesbaden, headquarters of the AACS outfit in Europe.

WIESBADEN, GERMANY

Famous for its hot mineral springs and cultural advantages, Wiesbaden had suffered only moderate bomb damage during the war. Hence, unlike industrial centers that lay in ruins, the resortlike city was a suitable site for Allied occupation forces postwar administration in Germany. Still, the men surveyed the barbed wire and German artillery piece that cluttered the front yard of their billet, a stone house on *Theodorenstrasse*.

The Allies faced a monumental task during the reconstruction of postwar Europe. Providing food and shelter for millions of destitute people was the most urgent need. Some of the refugees wanted to return to their homeland, others wished to settle elsewhere. Among the populace were military leaders and government officials suspected of war crimes; it was necessary to identify them and bring them to justice. Governing bodies had to be established for cities and states existing in a political vacuum following the collapse of Nazi Germany. While coping with occupation duties as well as deployment policies and demobilization, the American army shuffled personnel from base to base.

When Lyle and his buddies reported in at AACS headquarters in Wiesbaden they were briefed and given some leeway as to their post locale. Thinking the situation in the Mediterranean region was more stable than in northern Europe, Lyle informed his parents he had opted to go to Naples.

19 MARCH 1946 (TUESDAY, WIESBADEN, GERMANY). Greetings. Looks like we finally got here. Had about a dozen letters waiting—some real old and some quite recent. One from you dated Feb 11 and the other March 2. A later letter from Vernon said you made it to Mitchell to see the granddaughter. Is Vernon really going to get out in April? One would think I'm an important fellow the way they hang on to me. Am going to Naples, Italy, in a couple days to be assigned out there someplace—Italy, or south France, or Hungary, Bulgaria or someplace down there??? I had a choice of staying in the European Theater of Operations (ETO) or going to the Mediterranean T. O. (MTO) so I chose the MTO—it is not an occupation theater so it should let loose of us sooner. Could have stayed up here but England and Scandinavia are pretty well closed up and Germany is not a desirable place to be stationed so I asked to go back down there. What's a few hundred miles one way or another?

HAL AND DUTCH OFFICER, WIESBADEN, GERMANY, 1946
JEEP AND BARBED WIRE IN FOREGROUND

HAL AND GERMAN ARTILLERY PIECE, WIESBADEN, GERMANY, 1946

Germany is a tired country—the people seem to be quite old or very young—a noticeable lack of young people—men especially. Wiesbaden was a health resort and was bombed only once by mistake. They did a pretty good job for a mistake. The rubble of buildings still lie on the sidewalks—parts of buildings still seem undecided as to whether to fall or stand. The people don't seem proud—rather they seem bewildered. At first glance my opinion is that our occupation is going along quite well—but one can't tell what is running along underneath. Naturally the soldiers fraternize with the frauleins which is only to be expected. But otherwise there is no mixing with the Germans. I hold no resentment for their starting the war, but by their crimes against humanity they have forfeited the right to ever be a respected people.

Still don't have any dope on going home, nor can I do anything about it. Certainly am getting rid of the travel bug anyway. Wish some of you could have substituted for me on part of this travel.

A group of Prisoners of War just marched by under armed guard. They certainly aren't the goose stepping conquerors of a few years back.

Learning of the atrocities committed by the Nazi regime and of the trials of accused war criminals taking place in Nuremberg, Lyle reflected on the course of events that had enabled Hitler to mesmerize the German people. Perhaps Hitler had come into power with good intentions; perhaps he had been sincere in his belief that communism was the ultimate evil and that Germany had been treated unjustly following World War I. Once in office he had promoted discipline and instilled pride of country in the German people. But, after gaining a cadre of dedicated followers, he had proclaimed himself Führer. From that time on, no organized opposition had been possible. Just another instance, Lyle supposed, of a dictum espoused by British historian Lord Acton: "Power corrupts, and absolute power corrupts absolutely."

Hitler proceeded to work around the armament sanctions imposed by France, England, and the United States following World War I. By 1937, Germany possessed a modern air force, navy, and highly disciplined army, the most potent war machine in the world. By the time World War II started, Germany had risen from the ashes to become a superpower. In addition to a well-equipped military, German scientists were developing innovative weapons of destruction. In contrast, the United States had a small army (mainly draftees), obsolete fighter planes, and a crippled navy. A strange turn of events, Lyle thought. Now, just four years later, America is the world's superpower. In an age of tyranny, the ideology of a capitalist democracy reigned supreme.

Aware the army and navy had discharged millions of soldiers and sailors from active duty, Lyle contemplated being a civilian again. Although he had readily adapted to army life, he hoped that after more than three years of military culture his transition to civilian life would be as smooth.

23 MARCH 1946 (SATURDAY, WIESBADEN, GERMANY). Just back from taking a hot mineral bath at the Rose Hotel. Sure feel soaked out. Two letters from you yesterday and a letter from Wilma. Sounds like lots of fellows are out of the service now. Guess maybe I could claim to get out for dependency or essential need or something, but I came into this army face forward and might as well go out the same way. Something may break in a month or two. This is month 38 in the army and number 13 overseas so I'm quite high on the list. You see they are short of enlisted men, and they can hold the officers without so much squawk from Congress so they keep swarms of us to do jobs ordinarily done by enlisted men. Do you get the idea? Congress of course is playing politics—they won't lengthen the draft, they want a fast demobilization, they want troops all over the world—those 3 things just won't add up together. And I'm taking the rap. But as long as it turned out this way I'm just traveling around. It doesn't make much difference to me for a while. I'm going to try to go on a tour of Switzerland after getting to Naples. So you see the quicker the army gets rid of me the better off it will be. Keep your ears open on the angles of veterans compensation so you can give me some advice when I get out. College doesn't sound too attractive anymore. Haven't you received the PTA for a hundred dollars yet? I've got the receipt but hate to start the red tape of tracing it. My new address:

Hq 58th AACS Grp
APO 528
c/o PM NYC

That is at Naples, Italy, and is only temporary.

Pending travel orders, Hal, Lyle, Orlo, and Russ took a jaunt to the neighboring city of Frankfurt—bombed to rubble. Stone-faced people, mostly elderly, walked about as if in a daze among remnants of masonry walls and chimneys. Retribution, when it came to Germany, had come with a vengeance. Lyle recalled a phrase attributed to F. Scott Fitzgerald: "The victor belongs to the spoils."

Sunday.
Went to Frankfurt yesterday. It is almost totally destroyed. Have never seen anything similar to it before—it hits you sort of funny. Am

glad to get away from these places. Germany was really hit hard—doubt if it will ever recover in our time.

The weather here is just perfect. Already a few flowers blooming. Went to the Opera "Carmen" the other evening presented by a French Opera Company. Was very good. Sent you a cigar box of ivory insured for $50. It's fragile so be careful if you open it. Cost about 40 dollars for the 3 pieces.

Am enclosing a $5 bill for the first person who opens this letter. Guess it's about time to eat dinner. We have a mess hall in the Gruen Wald Hotel. The few buildings still standing are used by the army. I sleep in a German house on Theodorenstrasse. Strasse means same as our "Street." Sure easy to get lost on these narrow crooked streets. The countryside is similar to Indiana except smaller buildings, smaller fields, and horses instead of tractors. Funny how one can see the storm troopers marching when the Germans play music—the drums are the loud important part of their playing. The Italian musicians play with feeling and warmth and likewise the French. The Germans are cold and stiff in all their actions—they seem to have no emotions. Next stop home or Naples or someplace down the line.

On the move again, Hal, Lyle, and Orlo retraced their route to southern Europe. Russ had opted to stay in northern Europe.

NAPLES, ITALY

With Europe in a state of flux the military sought to cope with myriad problems while preparing contingency plans for unforeseen events. Lyle, cognizant that army postwar duties in Europe were uncharted territory, held no illusions about his role; he merely went along with the flow. Naturally, while awaiting further orders from AACS headquarters in Naples, he, Orlo, and Hal set out to explore the region.

28 MARCH 1946 (THURSDAY, NAPLES, ITALY). Carducci Hotel. Flew down here a couple days ago via Marseille and Rome—about an 8 hour trip in a C-47. Yes, this is sunny Italy—royal palm trees and bright sunny days—organ grinders, donkey carts, and fruit stands on the streets. Naples was hit harder by the war—more wrecked buildings, more crippled people, food and clothing scarcer than in Rome.

Hal, Orlo, and I reported into Group Headquarters here—they are going to Squadron Hq at Rome for assignment—I'm going to Naples Squadron for assignment. Am apt to end up at the air base here or at Athens, Greece. They don't need us anywhere so it's a matter of where we will be the least in the way. Seems to me something is bound to break within a month but so far only rumors.

Yesterday we went out to the ruins of Pompeii in the shadow of volcanic Mt Vesuvius. A few years B.C. the Mt suddenly rumbled and let loose with lava and ashes killing most of the people (those who didn't leave fast enough) and covering Pompeii with ashes. So the city was wiped out and it wasn't until centuries later that the old Pompeii civilization was discovered and excavation begun. It was about the most interesting set up that I have seen—we spent 2 fascinating hours in the city—of course being Tuesday the town was dead!! By the way, it was two years ago exactly that the mountain erupted killing quite a few people.

GLADIATORS HAL AND LYLE, POMPEII, ITALY, 1946

In lieu of more sightseeing, Lyle relaxed and contemplated the monetary state of affairs in Europe. He noted the monies of occupied countries were nearly worthless. Desperate to obtain food and clothing, the German people were selling their jewelry and art objects to obtain American, Swiss, and British currency. In an effort to curtail the black market the occupation government issued special paper money. Like other American army personnel, Lyle received a fraction of his pay in U.S. dollars and the rest in scrip.

Friday.
Hal and Orlo went out to the Isle of Capri for a day. Remember Ray Noble's song in the early 30s—

Twas on the Isle of Capri that I found her,
Beneath the shade of an old walnut tree,
Oh, I can still see the flowers blooming 'round her,
Where we met on the Isle of Capri.

I'm planning to go some weekend. I'm getting so scatterbrained that I can't even scribble anymore. Locked my key inside my footlocker and had to spend an hour fishing for it with a wire! Guess this is just too fast a life for me.

Played bridge last evening and picked up 300 lire. Financial setup over here in Europe is very complex. Seems to me some high up bungled badly in not paying in coupons instead of occupation monies. In that way I believe the black market could have been stopped cold. It is more under control now but about a year ago hundreds of thousands of dollars was cleared by Americans. I don't mean the hijacking black market rings—I mean the small bartering which cannot be eliminated and which is considered "cricket" by everyone. For instance a pack of cigarettes in Italy are equivalent to 300 lire ($1.40 at legal rate of exchange) and will buy about a dollar's worth of Italian products. Worth even more in Germany but there is nothing to buy in Germany. Soldiers have long since bought out German things of value. But finance will not give American money for lire in excess of your credit card showing. You see the American dollar is worth 5 to 1 its legal value here—in France 2 to 1, in Germany 10 to 1 etc. Swiss francs, Am dollars, British pounds, are valued by the world in that order—Swiss francs being entirely 100% backed by gold. Enclosed a 5 bill.

The next day, still free of official duties, Lyle accompanied Hal and Orlo on a weekend excursion to the Isle of Capri. Upon returning, he shared the experience with his family.

1 APRIL 1946 (MONDAY, NAPLES, ITALY). This past weekend was just like opening a National Geographic magazine to some colorful page—and then suddenly finding yourself there. Cause for my money the Isle of Capri is as quaint and colorful as any spot in the world, and so interesting and restful. After a two hour boat trip you dock at Capri harbor at the center of this side where the cliffs give way to a more gradual slope. From the dock one can take a funicular up the very steep hillside. One car goes up as one comes down on the same cable and they pass at the halfway point on a double track. Or you can take the road which contours up the side in S turns. The road is about 12 ft wide between walls and mostly used for walking or carts. We stayed at the rest camp Hotel Quinsanna near the square. The first thing we did was to hire a rowboat to take us out to the Blue Grotto. The ocean has washed huge caverns in the limestone cliffs which rise up 1900 ft out of the sea. The mouth of the Blue Grotto is small so a small rowboat just squeezes in. Then the cavern widens and the light from the sun creates a soft blue in the water and a dark mysterious blue on the

ORLO, ISLE OF CAPRI, ITALY, 1946

BLUE GROTTO, ISLE OF CAPRI, ITALY, 1946

HAL AND FISHERMEN, ISLE OF CAPRI, ITALY, 1946
MENDING NETS, "UNDER HAL'S SUPERVISION OF COURSE!"

walls and ceiling. The water lights up when a paddle stirs it due to the phosphorous. Very impressive. I pulled one oar on the way back and got quite proficient with it. Very good meals with music, cozy atmosphere, friendly people. In the morning we climbed one of the peaks up to Tiberius ruins—a castle and lighthouse on the edge of the cliff where he used to throw people over when he became angry with them. The Isle is very small and has only about 9000 people. The soil parts are terraced and have well tended vineyards and colorful lemon trees with bright yellow lemons on them. The Isle is quite untouched by the war or the world. The people are friendly, clean, and seem very happy. A stroll in late afternoon (especially Sunday) takes one to an enchanted land. The people are out walking dressed in simple bright clothes, the little kids sell bouquets of flowers, you can buy a string of roast chestnuts from the vendor, a little old man, and as you gaze out over the sparkling blue and the sun-kissed gardens and vineyards, you rather envy these people in their simple life. Ran into a Molly McGuire (a Red Cross girl) from S. Dak. She knew Alice and Jimmy Sladek very well and was in same sorority at S.D.U. as Violet Derby. I believe from Dante, S. Dak. A small world, and getting smaller.

Lyle was exasperated when orders came for him to report to the AACS station in Athens. Hostilities had been over for eight months and the bulk of the military had reverted to civilian status. He ached to have his life back. But instead of going toward home, he would be heading in the opposite direction.

> Afternoon.
> A new development. Am going to be assigned in Athens instead of here in Naples as expected. Seems to me I was there about a month ago! What a life. Will be getting there just after the election and in time for the revolution. Don't know yet which side to fight for! Am sending home 3 packages of spare clothes from here—please tell me when stuff arrives. Same old story. Now that the heat is off, demobilization is moving slow again. Too many medium ranking officers "never had it so good" trying to hold on to their empires. And not just hurting fellows like me—it's slowing down the rebuilding and reorganizing of the army on an efficient peacetime basis. The Air Corps is in sad shape these days.

Shortly after retracing their steps to Rome, Lyle, assigned to the cryptographic station at Hassani Airfield, bid farewell to Hal and Orlo and proceeded on to Athens.

ATHENS, GREECE

Upon arrival in Athens, Lyle was billeted at the Hotel Grande Bretagne located on the plaza in the heart of the city. While rubbing shoulders with high-ranking military personnel and diplomats, he was keenly aware that his silver bars dimmed in comparison.

Because of its strategic position, Greece had been the focus of much military action during the war and the people had suffered greatly. When Italy annexed Albania, Great Britain responded by guaranteeing to protect Greece's frontiers. Nevertheless, the German military overran Greece in 1941 and partitioned it into three sectors ruled by German, Italian, and Bulgarian military forces. During the occupation several Greek resistance movements emerged, the strongest being the communist-led National Liberation Front (EAM).

Following the defeat of the Axis powers, gun battles were fought on the streets of Athens in a mini civil war as Greek factions vied for political control of the country. It appeared to be a toss-up as to whether Greece would join the Communist bloc or pursue a more conservative political course. The United States and Great Britain brokered an agreement between the two main factions to hold a plebiscite. Aiming to ensure a fair election, the United States organized the Allied Mission for Observing Greek Elections (AMFOGE) and placed American troops and diplomatic personnel in Greece.

8 APRIL 1946 (MONDAY, ATHENS, GREECE). Seems peaceful enough around here, and yet a few people were killed out in front a few days ago. The "Amfoge" outfit is leaving this week and then there will be just a handful of Americans left over here—less than a hundred in fact. However, there are swarms of British troops here, and further disturbances seem unlikely.

Spent two days in Rome before buzzing down here. Had no desire to come clear back down here—this is only four hours from Cairo—but couldn't talk my way out of it. Guess they will kick me out of this hotel in a day or two and then I'll have to move out to Hassani Field to some lousy quarters. This place was just bubbling over with big brass over the weekend—a three star general, a two star general, and oodles of full colonels and majors. There was a big party including the ambassador to Greece and State Dept officials.

This is a fairly clean modern city but pretty bad off from the war. I believe there is enough food here if it were distributed—but the poor can't afford to pay the price of the black market. I have no respect or sympathy for the people when they can't see to it that the food is shared equally. Perhaps it is this sort of situation that encourages communism. So I guess the Allies must either bring in food—or withdraw troops and let a revolution start. Just my ideas and probably all wet.

A couple of us climbed up to the Acropolis Sunday afternoon and looked over the Parthenon, Temple of Zeus, and other remains of ancient Greece. The white marble ruins look down over the city—it must have been a beautiful sight up there when complete. The guide said it was the prettiest at full moon. So as we say in the army, "I've had this place." One really looks down on history from a place like that. But I'm tired of gazing at the past, I want to start living the present and the future. By the way there is a rumor floating around about officers with 38 months service. I'm completely out of the mood of going back to work so the army had best get rid of me. Anyway my type of work pretty much ended with the war. The Finance Officer almost had a hemorrhage today when I turned in my claim for travel pay—it took me about 45 days to get to Wiesbaden at 3 dollars per day—and quite legal too. I should know my way around after working in the center of these airfields for so long. Mail service down here is pretty much by chance these days—mostly brought from Naples by any of our fellows coming down here. So I probably won't be hearing much from you. Who knows, maybe I'll be dropping in on you in a month or two. Guess it will take almost a month to get home after orders are received cause one has to process at some staging area etc. We will leave from Leghorn, Italy, which is up near Florence and Venice. Will try to go to Switzerland on a tour if they don't get me out of here soon.

The streets below are really crowded this evening as usual. Just across the street is some gov't building of Greece, and then you have the embassy. Also Athens University down the street. My roommate (a major) is a law graduate of Wash U. in St Louis. Guess I'll go out for a little stroll. It's very warm here during the day and quite warm at night too. More later. Hope you have a pleasant Easter.

This is a poor excuse of a letter but—

After two months of travel among European cities, Lyle, feeling little sense of belonging and somewhat disoriented, confided to Irene.

9 APRIL 1946 (TUESDAY, ATHENS, GREECE). Greetings from Hotel Grand Bretagne. Your letter of March 8 caught up with me yesterday surprisingly enough. It's getting so I even have trouble keeping track of myself. This may sound crazy but I woke up in the dark last night and wondered where I was. After what seemed like several minutes

I traced myself to Europe and on around to right here. It was a weird feeling being so lost for a while.

Stopped a couple days in Rome and then came on down here for no good reason. There is nothing for me to do here as per usual—just sweating out a little more time. As soon as they throw me bodily out of this hotel I'll be living out at that run down field. This hotel is probably the best in Athens but nothing to brag about. This Amfoge outfit is sure full of brass. This morning at breakfast there were 3 full colonels and a civilian at my table—next table was a 3 star general, a two star general, and a Lt colonel. Boy, my little silver bars weren't shining very bright just then. Things seem quiet enough now but the day after the election a few people were killed down in front of here. Politics are a little different here than at home. If transportation throughout Greece was improved and the black market stomped out I believe there would be enough food to go around. As is conditions aren't too good. But I haven't actually seen any starvation in Europe like in India.

Irene, the army is making a mistake in hanging on to me. If something doesn't happen soon I'm going to apply for a Swiss tour— they say a week in Switzerland is wonderful. By the way this may sound like the life of Rielly but actually is isn't so hot. These cities are starting to all look alike and I never stay long enough in a place to even get acquainted with people. Very educational but rather tiresome. Anyhow as you know I prefer less congested places and a life of my own. So you can trade places with me if you like. By the way contrary to your letter, I did see the Sphinx and Pyramids. Have been to 5 operas and a ballet so far in Europe!!

Gee, it's almost Easter again. Any April showers yet in Omaha? Rather warm and dry and dusty here. Bye now.

The battleship Missouri arrived at the Athens port today—a symbol of American interests in the Mediterranean.

Shortly after the USS *Missouri* steamed into the harbor at Athens and anchored as a not-so-subtle show of force in support of AMFOGE, Lyle toured the historic battleship. As he read the plaque commemorating the signing of the surrender document by Japanese leaders he wondered whether President Truman, a native son of Missouri, had arranged to exhibit this particular vessel.

A few days later Lyle's hopes for returning stateside were dashed when the demobilization point plan eluded him once again. Upon receiving orders to report to Capodichino Air Base at Naples for duty as Security and Intelligence Officer, he wrote:

15 APRIL 1946 (MONDAY, ATHENS, GREECE). Just got a radiogram transferring me to Naples. Here is the story. A few days ago officers in our outfit wanting release from the army and having 38 months service were declared surplus and are going home. I was short a week of having 38 months so of course I didn't make the list. It is a bit raw cause I have more service points than some of them—in fact a few of these fellows have only a week or two more service and a 1/2 or 1/3 as much overseas time as I have. It's typical of the army—first they use the point system and then they throw that away and use something else—never a definite policy that one can put his foot on. At least so far it has managed to always neatly avoid me. Maybe there will be another group declared surplus and if there is I'll be on that one for sure—unless they decide to use still another basis such as anyone having red hair and three dependents. Anyway now they need a couple more officers at Naples station. I'm glad to go back there cause I want to go on a weeks tour of Switzerland and would have to leave from Naples anyway. Besides there isn't much left here—no regular mail service, poor chow, no P.X. etc. Went aboard the battleship Missouri when it anchored here. It caused quite a stir here in the Middle East sending the Missouri. Saw the surrender plaque etc. They asked me at the final desk at Fort Crook if I wanted army or navy. Maybe I made a mistake?? Is Vernon out yet?

Sent you a P.T.A. from Athens for $200. Let me know if it arrives. I assume you have been getting the allotment check each month for a hundred? Guess it will be quite a shock when it becomes necessary for me to get out and earn my bread. And when the time comes to start paying my own hotel bills and railroad fare. Yes, this is a soft enough life but too soft a life can get boring. And it's a rather pointless and sometimes dreary existence. Athens sounds like a glamorous exciting place when one is gazing out the window at the prairies of South Dakota—South Dakota is an alluring mental paradise when hungry kids beg for ΔΡΑΧΜΑΙ [money], when the wind swirls a cloud of city dust in my face, as trucks and carts rumble along the streets of another strange city, Athens. So—dream of far away places—but don't feel cheated if you never get there. Take my word for it, the other half of the world doesn't live as well as we do. bla bla bla

No mail from you but may have some at Naples   Adios

NAPLES, ITALY

Forty-eight hours after assuming responsibility for the operation of the cryptographic station at Naples, Lyle received a welcome surprise; having had no official leave in more than a year, he was granted a week of R and R.

From Naples, Lyle traveled to Milan where he planned to join a tour group to Switzerland. While sightseeing in Milan he was thrilled at the sight of *The Last Supper* painted by Leonardo da Vinci. But he took no pleasure in visiting the site where revengeful partisans had displayed the bodies of Mussolini and his associates. While conquest was going well, Mussolini had been a hero in the eyes of the people; when the course of the war turned against Italy, Mussolini became the culprit.

Retiring to his room in the Abergo Nord Hotel in Milan, Lyle located writing paper and a pen.

20 APRIL 1946 (SATURDAY, MILAN, ITALY). The military attache plane at Athens was going direct to Naples so I hooked a ride with it. We ran into some turbulent air about an hour out—about as rough as I've seen. When you look out and see the wings flapping like a seagull then you know the air is rough. Didn't have radio contact with Naples so we landed at Bari to check the weather. The weather over the Mts running the length of central Italy was too risky so we went to Foggia air base and spent the night there. We were just a friendly little group—a colonel, two civilian employees of the Embassy, the pilots, and three others of us. So we had a pleasant trip traveling as we pleased. The next morning we made it to Naples where I took over the job as Security and Intelligence Officer at Capodichino air base there. They almost had me cornered into working but I squirmed out by getting a Rest and Recuperation leave to Switzerland! (Seems to be a small fire here at the hotel now—not serious).

So two days after getting to Naples I caught a plane to Rome, Pisa, and then Milan, up here on the Swiss border. Of course I saw the leaning tower of Pisa from the air which makes me feel much better! It's much nicer up here in north Italy. Cleaner and less destroyed by the war, and the people are not so destitute. And there is sort of a feeling of spring up here. Went on a Red Cross tour of the city. Went to the Scala Opera House, the place where Mussolini and 6 others were hung (retaliation for 15 non-facists shot at that spot by Mussolini orders), the third largest cathedral in Europe where they have beautiful stained glass windows (world's largest), and the little church where the original "Last Supper" is on the wall. Rather a coincidence that I should see this masterpiece on Good Friday.

It's getting so people working in the air passenger terminals are beginning to say, "What, you here again—where you going this time?" It would cost a small fortune to pay for all my air travel. This morning we paid $35 for a conducted 7 day tour of Switzerland. That includes train fares, hotels, meals, etc. Also allowed to take $65 Swiss currency into the country etc. Guess I'll buy a watch. We catch a train out at 7:00 a.m. tomorrow. Will get back to Naples about the first of May and I hope by then to be on orders to the States. I should be the first of our outfit to go home if they decide to declare some more surplus. But it could be 4 more months. The War Dept says all officers with two years service will be discharged or aboard ship by 31 August. For some reason or other I am past the stage of being able to do any army mental work or accept any responsibility. If they said go out and dig a ditch or chop some wood I could and would gladly do it. But I can't drive myself to do any paper work. Must be some psychological reason. Maybe it's just lazyness but I doubt it. Primo Canera (former boxing champion) is staying here at Albergo Nord but I haven't seen him. Can already understand a little Italian—it's a lot like Spanish. Life is treating me very well these days— hope you are all mucho Bono too.

The following day Lyle boarded a train and was off to Switzerland with a tour group. A jewel of a country, it seemed an island of sanity in a continent that had run amok. Except for being in uniform, he felt like a civilian again. One evening, while spending a delightful time dancing and socializing, an interesting conversation turned to the Nazi attempt to produce heavy water (deuterium oxide), a possible component of early atomic bombs in which the isotope deuterium replaced the ordinary hydrogen atom. The process required vast amounts of energy, available from the hydroelectric system of occupied Norway. Seeking to curtail the Nazi effort to make an atomic bomb, Norwegian resistance had sabotaged the facility and Allied bombers had attacked the plant from the air.

On stationery from the Bellevue Palace in Bern, Lyle wrote home with renewed hope and joie de vivre.

24 APRIL 1946 (WEDNESDAY, BERN, SWITZERLAND). This is one of the most interesting cities in Switzerland, but not so pretty as Lucerne on the lake. It certainly is refreshing to see these places untouched by the war—young people all out of uniform, no cripples or beggars on the streets, people who have escaped the coarseness and misery that creeps in with a war. And they do realize how fortunate they are—they tell us freely that Switzerland is free today only because America defeated

the Axis. The people here really know how to live. They have to be industrious and scientific to keep a high standard of living in this tiny land of mountains. Yesterday we visited a cheese factory and at the end of the tour they fed us dark bread, beer, and some really good cheese. Cheese exported to America is of the best quality but not aged as much as the Swiss prefer. Then we toured the city and visited the govt buildings, cathedral, beer pits, a centuries old town clock where a rooster crows, the old man time turns an hour glass, another man hammers out the hour on a bell, and bears run around a circle. Quite a sight.

Last night a terrific little orchestra played stateside dance music here at the hotel. There were just a few couples and no extra ladies so we just drooled in our beer. However, a bit later a party of 5 came in so I started dancing with whichever lady was surplus. Then they invited me over to join them—a British general, a British civilian, a British lady who had spent 4 years in the service, and two blondes from Norway. One from Oslo and the other from a place in southern Norway where they produce heavy water for atomic research. I read an article about a month ago about the sabotage there and the bombings to prevent the Germans from producing much heavy water. So we drank wine and had "a jolly good time." The British are quite reserved and may seem dull because of that, but once you get to know them they are very humorous in a dry sort of way, and interesting too. For my money the British are really O.K. Anyway what might have been a dull evening turned out to be pleasant indeed. Am feeling much better after only 3 days in Switzerland—it's sort of my first touch of spring in a couple years.

We go to Lausanne today and tomorrow on to Zurich. Will be back to Naples around the end of the month. Hope you are having a pleasant spring also.

Following one of the most interesting and enjoyable weeks during his entire military service, Lyle made a stopover at Milan on his way back to Naples. On paper from the *salon de correspondance à l'hôtel beau lite Lausanne,* he wrote:

28 APRIL 1946 (SUNDAY, MILAN, ITALY). Back in Italy again feeling much refreshed but still not anxious to get back to work. Our trip was jammed full of adventures plus plenty of wine and night life. At

Zurich I found out that Hal Segal was in the hospital there with yellow jaundice so I visited him. He is one of the original four of us touring the Middle East and Europe. We were allowed to take only 225 francs ($54) into Switzerland but I had plenty American greenbacks from Athens so I invested in a good Swiss watch for about $130 taking about 12% less on the dollar due to currency block between our countries. My watch is a Vacheron-Constantine which is in the top class. It is in a plain stainless steel case and I guess it retails at around $400 in the States if you can get one at all. In other words it is a beautiful watch and should be inexpensive to own. A couple trips to a jeweler and a cheap watch becomes expensive. Of course I paid partly for the trade name.

It's raining today in Milan. Will take a plane to Naples tomorrow if the weather is O.K. They don't fly here unless the weather is good—there was "no weather" over the Hump to China—day and night the planes went over regardless. It amazes me when I think of the machinelike precision of the supply line to China.

If one wants to travel abroad and wants to have a restful vacation (rather than visiting historical spots), Switzerland is definitely the place. But it too would be expensive for civilian tourists. A small group of American soldiers can certainly make a lot of noise in one of the small conservative cities. Soldiers of course in a group are not the quiet individuals of civilian life in the States. The people seemed to like us pretty well even though we did not try too hard to follow their conservative customs. Should be able to find some mail around Naples by now. Haven't had any for over two months now. Also have my fingers crossed on going home. Will write again from Naples.

The next day the weather was suitable for flight. Lyle returned to Naples and resumed responsibility for the cryptographic station. In his next letter, following a diatribe on the world food shortage, he expressed reluctance at being responsible for the code room, especially since he was confronted with a difficult security problem. But, like it or not, he was still an army officer. Setting aside longings for home, he focused on his work; after more than three years of military duties he was not about to mess up now.

30 APRIL 1946 (TUESDAY, NAPLES, ITALY). Thumbed through my snapshots tonight which is a good sign that home is sort of in my mind. At last over a dozen letters caught up with me including the one with your Easter card, and a big surprise—a letter from Dad. If that Egyptian heard you folks call that "hand labor of years, beautiful blending of superb yarn etc etc bla bla" a *rug* he would tear out his hair! Say, have you found any way to get rid of it? Please handle that ivory with care

cause it's quite valuable. Surprised to hear you have chicks already this year. You mentioned the world food shortage several times. Well, there is still an old saying about people "helping themselves" if you know what I mean. In Athens ironically some die of indigestion and some of starvation. In Italy many have too much food while others are hungry. You can feed India and the population will increase even more rapidly, so nature must eventually compensate by a worse famine. But why are we suddenly so interested in food for the rest of the world—for years, for centuries even, people have been starving in the Orient. I believe that only a change in religion can solve the problem—but the Hindus are much more religious than we are. To me it seems a bit queer, but of course the idea of feeding the world is very noble.

Wilma's letter of Feb 18 had a couple snapshots—Virginia, and Jean and Wilma. Also a late letter from Irene. Glad to hear that Vernon got out of the navy, and that the family was out to visit you. I guess they probably still have their car. Bet they will find it a relief to settle down for a bit too. Still nothing in sight for me—it may drag out to the bitter end. The heat is sort of off on demobilization. Today I got back behind the eight ball—had to sign over for secret stuff again—it's a 24 hour responsibility where one can too easily get in trouble. Besides I've been away from it several months—forgotten a lot and had no desire to try to get back in the groove again. But I'm forced to cause in this business they can really slap you for negligence. It's a case too of being between foolish regulations and high ranking brass. I would rather serve out the rest of my time as a Pvt doing K.P. every day. Our organization is so top heavy with headquarters over headquarters that we *create* most of our own work. Like a tractor that can barely pull itself. Too many "little men" who are so blissfully ignorant that they aren't the big shots they think they are. I'm thankful that at least I still realize what a little fish I really am. Army rank is so shallow. I stepped into a job that is really messed up—maybe in a few days things will be smooth. Somehow though I feel that I have had my bit of army life, that maybe someone should be taking my place. These last couple months of travel have compensated somewhat for a year of the monotony of India. It is an altogether different sort of life here in Europe—I don't think there is anything worse than the monotony and heat of a monsoon season unless it's being in prison without labor. American troops have an easy enough life over here. Good night everybody.

Be thinking of you on Mother's Day, Mom.

3 MAY 1946 (FRIDAY, NAPLES, ITALY). Got a letter from you today written 26 April—just seven days—fastest letter yet overseas. Will

answer a couple of your questions before I forget them. No, watches in P.X.s are very rare and when some come in everyone signs up and the lucky people have the privilege of buying one. Same way with cameras, pens, etc. All P.X. goods are rationed. If I could go to Switzerland again I could pick up good watches for the girls but that is out. As I said before we are limited to $65 dollars worth of Swiss francs for the week's tour of *outside* expenses and spending money. I blew twice that much for my watch. Mom, you have first chance on that tapestry—if you don't want it please give it to the Vs with my compliments. It may be worth something in the States cause it missed export taxes etc. The large ivory statue is the Hindu God of Love (80 rupees). The little African (deer??) I thought were cute. I think I paid 2 pounds for the two of them—I only wanted to buy one but those Egyptian salesmen are smooth—he reduced his price a bit and sold me two of them??

Ran into Lowell Nelson from Chamberlain the other day. He is in one of my higher headquarters, a corporal. My top Sgt is from South Dakota—Mobridge to be exact. A very steady slow type—just the sort of fellow I *need* in this work. It's rare to even meet anyone from S.D. so this is rather a coincidence. Everything is getting well under control now in my hideout. One can't be too careful with crypto stuff.

May try to smuggle home an old German rifle just to be doing something. My chances are good of being home in June but that is still a guess. We are starting to wear suntans now instead of woolens.

I was at Casserta (20 miles from Naples) yesterday—exactly 1 year after the surrender in Italy was signed there. Southern Italy is in bad shape.

4 MAY 1946 (SATURDAY, NAPLES, ITALY). Dear Irene,
Am starting to sweat out these next couple weeks cause there is a chance of getting orders home before long. Can't count on it though. Southern Italy seems extra dark and dirty after a week in Switzerland. In fact the green cleanliness of Switzerland was sort of shocking—it doesn't seem possible that India and Switzerland could be in the same world. For a pleasant restful vacation Switzerland is undoubtedly tops. Of course it lacks the historical interests of Italy. We went bicycling in the cities, rowing on the lakes, took guided tours to places of interest, and shopped in the neat little stores. Our tour included Luzern, Bern, Lausanne, and Lugano—and some of us also went to Geneva for a couple hours to look around the League of Nation's grounds. We saw the beautiful lone peacock mentioned in April 29 Time magazine. Swiss beer is tops, and they also have pretty good wine. We are limited to $65 worth of francs on the tour so we had to be conservative on the buying, or be broke socially.

Gee, it's good to be getting mail again. Mom said Virginia was down to see you at vacation time. How is college treating her? School will almost be out by the time you get this letter. By the way, how much longer will your job hold out?

Monday.

Looks like things are breaking my way again. Am keeping my hopes down in case something should go wrong—but I guess you might as well stop writing to me here. Don't forget Sis you promised me a meal sometime—and you didn't limit the number of calories. Be seeing you'uns.

6 MAY 1946 (MONDAY, NAPLES, ITALY). It looks like that old Sladek luck is still with me. I won't make any rash predictions, but things are looking extremely favorable for me at the moment. Naturally I'm all keyed up so the next few days will probably go quite slow.

Guess I'll send home another box of junk—my old pair of G.I. shoes etc. Am down to a bare minimum of personal belongings.

Found out that this Sgt from Mobridge also went to SD State College—a few years before my time though. We know some of the same people etc. It's been a pleasure working with him, he is typical of the conscientious Sgts who are the backbone of this army.

Guess you might as well stop my mail until further notice. Will likely be moving from this address in a couple weeks or less. I've seen lots of about faces in this army so I'm keeping my hopes down. More later.

P.S. Don't forget Mom, you promised to take some more driving lessons!

Three was Lyle's lucky number. After three months in Europe and three years and three months in the army, he received the long-awaited order to proceed to the Zone of the Interior, army lingo for the United States of America. After years of hurry and wait and army turnabouts, he could barely believe he was going home.

After signing over the cryptographic material to his replacement officer, Lyle was free to catch a flight to Leghorn, a port on the Ligurian Sea west of Tuscany.

LEGHORN (LIVORNO), ITALY

While waiting to board a troopship at Leghorn, there was time for one last excursion to a neighboring city. Ascending the steps to the top of the Leaning Tower of Pisa, Lyle, full of high hopes for the future, climbed the flagpole on the roof and paid homage to all the stars in the heavens.

Shortly before setting out across the Mediterranean Sea and the Atlantic Ocean, the last leg of a globe-trotting odyssey, the South Dakota farm boy wrote his last letter as a soldier in the World War II army.

18 MAY 1946 (SATURDAY, LIVORNO, ITALY). My orders came May 14 to proceed to the Zone of the Interior for discharge, so I got rid of my codes and caught a special plane up here to the Leghorn Port of Embarkation. The USS General Muir arrived here today and will leave on or about May 23 for New York, with *me aboard*. The voyage will take approximately ten days so we will hit NY the first week in June. My separation center will likely be Camp McCoy, Wisconsin, but not too sure. Needless to say I have been sweating these days out—time is dragging now. One is always sweating out something in the army. As yet I have no feeling of going home, but I guess one of these days I'll find myself there. Somehow I didn't think I'd ever get home from India.

Yesterday my buddy and I went over to Pisa. We climbed to the very top of the leaning tower, looked around in the cathedral etc. Some fellows went to Florence today on a sightseeing tour. We were too lazy to go. Had a typhus shot today—my last shot in the army I guess. Am going to try to get a German rifle barrel through the customs inspection—sent the stock home by mail—it may not get through the mail either. These next days will really go slow. Have no plans of any sort for the future so it's hard telling what will develop. Of course home is my first objective, and too there is a certain party in Detroit whom I haven't seen in almost two years. Two years is a long time, one can change a lot. May call you long distance from Wisconsin or someplace in that vicinity so don't be surprised. This is a poor excuse of a letter.

So I'll be seeing you. Just one thing—in an otherwise rather hectic world, the quieter my return into the old channels the better I will like it. Sometimes wish I had kept a day by day diary these past few years. But I guess most important observations are tucked away in some corner of the mind.

There is properly no history, only biography.
—RALPH WALDO EMERSON

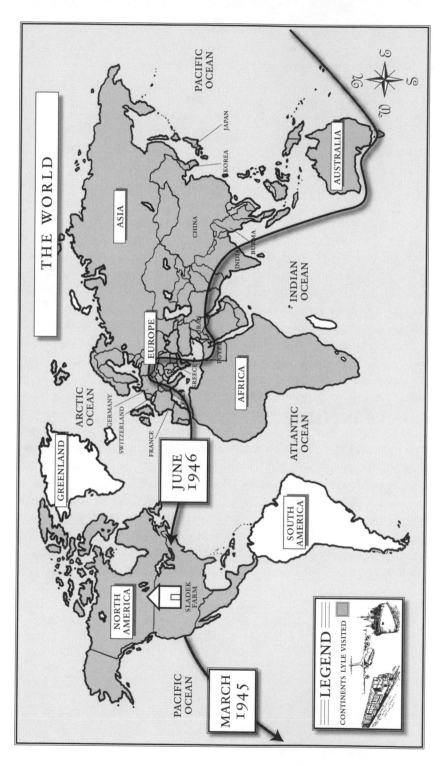

WOLRD WAR II DRAFTEE LYLE SLADEK CIRCLED THE GLOBE BY LAND, SEA AND AIR, 1943-1946

Love and Laughter and Peace Ever After

All the world's a stage,
And all the men and women merely players;
They have their exits and their entrances.
—SHAKESPEARE

FRANKLIN ROOSEVELT AND ADOLF HITLER walked onto the world stage in early 1933, voiced their lines, and then made their exits in April 1945—Roosevelt dying of natural causes and Hitler by his own hand.

Following the deaths of those key players, Harry Truman, Winston Churchill, and Joseph Stalin played the leading roles in the waning months of the war. Truman, quite suddenly thrust into the presidency, encountered two strong personalities when he met with Churchill and Stalin at Potsdam, Germany, in July 1945. Moreover, as the conference opened, President Truman received word that an atomic bomb had been successfully detonated at a test site in New Mexico.

While at Potsdam the Big Three discussed postwar arrangements for Germany. They agreed to partition the ravaged country into four occupation zones—American, British, French, and Russian—with each section to include a portion of Berlin. They also issued an ultimatum to Japanese leaders to surrender unconditionally or bear swift and absolute destruction to their country.

When the Japanese government failed to comply, the Allies faced the prospect of a land invasion of the home islands, an operation projected to cost hundreds of thousands of casualties, military and civilian. After consulting with his advisors, President Truman made the momentous decision to employ atomic bombs as weapons of war.

The American people, at home and abroad, rejoiced when the curtain fell on the most widespread and destructive war in history. They had endured nearly four years of anxiety and sacrifice while awaiting the longed-for day, "when the war is over." Celebrating V-J Day, they envisioned the utopian future promised in Nat Burton's wartime song:

> There'll be blue birds over
> The white cliffs of Dover,
> Tomorrow, just you wait and see.
>
> There'll be love and laughter
> And peace ever after
> Tomorrow, when the world is free.
>
> The shepherd will tend his sheep,
> The valley will bloom again
> And Jimmy will go to sleep,
> In his own little room again.

Dreams of a free world and lasting peace soon faded. The advent of nuclear weapons, with the potential to destroy civilization, ushered in an era of fear and suspicion between the communist and democratic countries. Stalin, still rankled from the long delay in the opening of a second front from the west, questioned American and British intentions. He reminded Truman and Churchill that the Soviet Union, in bearing the brunt of the land war, had accounted for nearly 90 percent of all German casualties and that twenty million Soviet soldiers and civilians had died repelling the German invasion of their homeland.

At the same time, American and British leaders were apprehensive that the marxist philosophy espoused by the Soviet Union would envelop an impoverished Europe. Another issue arose when Stalin, seeking to replenish the gutted industry of his country, began transporting machinery and industrial material from Germany to Russia. General Clay, President Truman's representative in Europe, warned that "Germany would starve unless it could produce for export and that immediate steps would have to be taken to revise industrial production."

Still caught up in the euphoria of V-J Day the American people were unaware of growing tensions abroad, until Churchill traveled to Fulton, Missouri, and delivered a stunning speech at Westminster College. He alerted the free world of an insidious *iron curtain* falling across the landscape of Europe. Alluding to secrecy and lack of cooperation, Churchill warned that whole regions of eastern Europe, whether their citizens approved or not, were being drawn into the Soviet sphere of influence:

The United States stands at this time at the pinnacle of world power. It is a solemn moment for the American Democracy. . . . It is my duty however . . . to place before you certain facts about the present position in Europe.

From Stettin in the Baltic to Trieste in the Adriatic, an iron curtain has descended across the Continent. Behind that line lie all the capitals of the ancient states of Central and Eastern Europe. Warsaw, Berlin, Prague, Vienna, Budapest, Belgrade, Bucharest and Sofia, all these famous cities and the populations around them lie in what I must call the Soviet sphere, and all are subject in one form or another, not only to Soviet influence but to a very high and, in many cases, increasing measure of control from Moscow.

Churchill's speech heralded the start of a new and strange kind of event, the *cold war*, a phenomenon that was to plague the world for decades to come.

Still in Europe and fretting to go home, Lyle, a mere pawn in the war's endgame, was disheartened by the dissension among former allies. How ironic, he thought, that it may have been Hitler's abhorrence of bolshevism that induced him to order the invasion of Poland, triggering a global conflict. In light of Churchill's Iron Curtain speech, Lyle realized it was naive to think he had been involved in the last war of the twentieth century.

At Leghorn, Italy, Lyle waited to board the USS *General Muir* for the voyage back to the States. Long conditioned to army ways and not wanting a last-minute disappointment, he braced himself for the possibility of a change in orders or to further delays. Neither happened. On 23 May he boarded the ship for home.

Unlike the passage to India, the voyage through the Mediterranean and across the Atlantic was comfortable and nonthreatening; the ship was not crowded, the seas were calm, and there was no submarine menace. Other than shaking hands with a former heavyweight boxing champion, with fists as big as cantaloupes, and participating in a songfest on deck one evening, Lyle retained no memory of the homeward bound trip.

Seeing the Statue of Liberty come into view invoked thoughts in Lyle of his birthright. Though his grandparents had arrived at the land of the free before the welcoming edifice had been erected, he thanked God they had come to America. He contemplated Mahatma Gandhi's words: "Freedom is like birth. Til we are fully free, we are slaves."

There was no welcoming scene when the USS *General Muir* entered the harbor at New York. No fireboats were present to send plumes of water into the air. No band was playing "It's Been a Long, Long Time" as the ship docked. No newspaper reporters were on hand to photograph the returning troops. Nearly a year had elapsed since the end of hostilities; the country had turned its attention to peacetime activities.

The following days passed in a blur. At Fort Dix, New Jersey, Lyle satisfied his craving for fresh, cold milk while seated at a long table in a mess hall. After two days he traveled by train to Camp McCoy, Wisconsin, where he was processed by the numbers and discharged. An army officer one minute, a civilian the next, he removed the bars from the shoulders of his uniform.

Once again Lyle was his own man. Eager to renew acquaintances with Beatrice and her parents, he elected to take a side trip from Chicago to Detroit. Although it had been nearly two years since their parting at the railroad station, he was warmly welcomed. Impatient to greet his family, however, he lingered just a day. Promising to return, he boarded a train for the long ride to South Dakota.

LYLE AND BEATRICE, DETROIT, MICHIGAN, 1946

The family farm again became the center of the universe for Lyle. Vernon and Vivian, along with baby daughter Carol, motored in from Aberdeen. Irene and Henry, soon to become parents, arrived from Omaha. Virginia was home from the University of South Dakota and Jean and Wilma from high school in Chamberlain. Chuckie, reveling in a summer of freedom from school, was intrigued by the metal parts of the Mauser rifle that had accompanied Lyle through customs. When the wooden stock arrived by parcel post, he eagerly helped Lyle assemble the German gun. "Did anyone ever get shot from this gun?" Chuckie asked.

Seeing the look in Chuckie's eyes, Lyle told him that many American soldiers had died—more from accidents, disease, and other military perils than from combat.

"The worst things that happened to me," Lyle continued, "were a broken finger and a sprained ankle—and those were from playing sports. All the stars were in the right alignment for me—many GIs were not so fortunate. I hope and pray you'll never know war."

While Henry, Vivian, and baby Carol looked on, the nine family members gathered on the front steps for a photograph. Lyle was still clad in his army uniform—minus the bars. The mail-order house was filled with love and laughter. Lyle shared with his mother lines written by Robert Browning: "God's in his heaven / All's right with the world!"

SLADEK FAMILY REUNITED, JUNE 1946
VERNON, IRENE, CHUCKIE, CHARLES, JEAN, WILMA, EMMA, VIRGINIA, AND LYLE

Initially Lyle welcomed the seclusion afforded by the family farm. After years of moving from one army post to another, he appreciated the sense of place and quiet routine of farm life. Replacing his father on the neighborhood threshing crew and doing other physical labor helped him unwind as he contemplated his future. But after two months he grew restless. The dearth of social opportunities began to pall. Few women his age resided on the neighboring farms or in the nearby towns since many, seeking career opportunities, had gravitated to the cities during the war years. Lack of transportation was another problem. Although some cars were trickling off the assembly lines, most ended up on the black market. Used cars were either repainted taxicabs from Chicago or old wrecks retrieved from junkyards.

One morning in August, Lyle told his parents he was going to Detroit.

"You can take the Dodge if you want to," his father offered.

"Thanks, but you wouldn't have a car at home. Just drop me off at the corner of Highway 16 near Kimball and my thumb will get me there."

Lyle rode with a variety of interesting people as he made his way across South Dakota, Minnesota, and Wisconsin, arriving two days later at Manitowoc on the western shore of Lake Michigan. While on the overnight ferry passage across the lake, he made the acquaintance of a man who offered him a ride all the way to Detroit.

Urban blight contrasted sharply with the lush green of upstate Michigan. Debris swirled about on the downtown streets. Men loitered on the sidewalks in front of the Cadillac Hotel and Hudson's department store. It was evident Detroit was suffering from unemployment and social unrest; factories that had operated around-the-clock to produce tanks and airplanes had shut down when the war ended.

Tired from the long trip, Lyle checked into a seedy hotel, showered, and telephoned Beatrice. After hiking to Gratiot Avenue he boarded a streetcar. The ride out to Cedargrove bore little resemblance to the jolly hour ride romanticized by Judy Garland in the "Trolley Song." The screech of steel wheels grinding on steel rails, the slamming of tram doors, and the blaring of automobile horns was anything but musical. A country boy at heart, Lyle began to realize he was out of his element in the city.

Had Detroit been Lyle's hometown he would have faced fewer obstacles in making the transition to civilian life. Upon returning home from a year and a half of overseas duty he would have tossed his duffel bag on the front porch, greeted his family, called Beatrice for a date, borrowed the family car, and proceeded to get on with his life. As it was, he had no place to live, no car, and no prospects for earning a living—a dreary situation. After two days of trying to rekindle the excitement that wartime circumstances had ignited, peacetime reality became apparent. Realizing they had divergent interests, Lyle and Beatrice parted amiably. Making his way to the Michigan

Central Railroad Station, Lyle purchased a coach ticket and returned to South Dakota.

Back home again, Lyle decided to take advantage of the Servicemen's Readjustment Act (GI Bill of Rights). Congress, cognizant of the Soldier's Bonus fiasco following World War I, had enacted the GI Bill of Rights in 1944. Lyle enrolled at South Dakota State College (SDSC) where he had begun the study of engineering five years earlier. Like other veterans, many of whom never expected to pursue a college education, he was eligible for free tuition and a living allowance. To accommodate the flood of veterans, SDSC converted Quonset huts to classrooms and apartments.

Service and travel experiences had broadened Lyle's view of the world. Some aspects of the college scene now seemed juvenile and some of the lectures pedantic and mundane. Finding it would take less time to acquire a degree in mathematics than in engineering, due to the college credits he had acquired in the service, he switched his major. At the same time, he resumed his interests in debate, drama, extemporaneous speaking, and card games.

LYLE SLADEK AND COLLEGE BUDDIES, SDSC, 1947
PLAYING CARDS AND PRANKS

The following year, when Wilma joined Lyle, Virginia, and Jean at SDSC, *The Collegian* featured:

COLLEGE BECOMES FAMILY AFFAIR
FOURSOME FEEL THEY NEVER LEFT HOME

One freshman whose chances of getting homesick are less than the ordinary is Wilma Sladek, the youngest member of the most adequately represented family on State's campus. Sixteen years old and lacking only 1½ credits from high school, she decided to follow the rest of the family and come to State as a special student. She is interested in music and is taking piano and bassoon lessons. Hailing from Chamberlain, Wilma attended high school there as did her brother Lyle and her two sisters, Virginia and Jean.

Jean, a sophomore, and Virginia, a junior, are both English-Journalism majors and are interested in music in the way of band and chorus.

The only masculine representative of the Sladek family is Lyle, a senior mathematician and member of Pi Kappa Delta. Lyle spent four years in the service, the majority of which time he was in India.

One of the few disadvantages of coming to college is leaving the family fireside. It is not so in the case of the Sladek family; they bring the family right along.

"STATE COLLEGE'S MOST REPRESENTATIVE FAMILY CASUALLY DISCUSS THEIR LATEST LETTERS FROM HOME OVER THE FUNNIES IN A CORNER OF THE UNION LOUNGE" LYLE, VIRGINIA, JEAN, AND WILMA SLADEK, 1947

One September evening, Lyle noticed a striking blonde dining in the cafeteria. "I remember you," he said, as he placed his tray on the table. "You played the violin at my cousin Walter's wedding last summer."

"Yes, that's right. The bride and I became friends at nursing school."

Patricia Knotts had interrupted her education at the University of South Dakota to enter the wartime Cadet Nurse Corps and, after three years of service, had become a registered nurse. Wishing to complete a bachelor of science degree she had enrolled at SDSC that fall. On weekends she worked at the city hospital in Brookings, receiving fifty cents an hour, meals while on duty, and laundry service to keep her uniforms stiffly starched.

PATRICIA KNOTTS, 1947

Despite a ten o'clock curfew and just one telephone per floor at the women's dormitory, Lyle arranged many dates with Patricia. A romance blossomed as fall turned to winter and winter to spring. In June, Lyle graduated with a bachelor of science degree in mathematics and a minor in electrical engineering.

LYLE SLADEK, COLLEGE GRADUATION, 1948

That summer, Lyle and Chuckie tended the family farm so Emma and Charles could accompany Irene, Henry, and baby Curtis to the East Coast. Henry drove the fluid drive Dodge to Boston and then on to the Parkhurst summer cottage at Old Orchard Beach in Maine. While enjoying the Atlantic seashore Emma and Charles stuck their toes in the "little salty pool," as facetiously described by Lyle when stationed at Miami Beach.

Three decades earlier Emma had written to Charles of her "pipe dream" to visit New York. Dreams do come true. Taking their first airplane ride, Irene escorted her parents from Boston to New York for a tour of the "big city." It was the highlight of a summer to remember.

Upon returning home Emma and Charles learned Patricia and Lyle had set September twelfth for their wedding date.

LYLE SLADEK AND PATRICIA KNOTTS, WEDDING DAY, 1948

VERNON AND VIVIAN, LYLE AND PATRICIA, HENRY AND IRENE, 1948

Since Patricia needed more credits to complete her bachelor's degree and
Lyle aspired for a master's in speech, they enrolled at the University of South
Dakota. The influx of veterans had created a severe shortage of housing in
Vermillion, so the newlyweds spent a cold, snowy winter in a home-built
trailer and shared a community bathhouse with other married veterans in a
city park.

As the postwar years unfolded, the war continued to exert a strong
influence on the Sladek family saga. While training at a satellite base near
Mitchell before deploying to England, Henry had remarked to a buddy,
"This would be a good place to live someday." That day came in 1948 when
Irene, Henry, and baby Curtis moved there from Omaha. Chuckie joined
the Parkhurst household in order to attend high school in Mitchell. Lyle and
Patricia, upon completing their degrees, decided to settle there. Wishing to
retire from the farm and be near their children, Emma and Charles leased
their land to neighbors, disposed of their farm machinery, and bought a
house in that same city.

Patricia resumed her nursing career at Methodist State Hospital while
Lyle, like his father before him, built a house for his bride.

CHARLES SLADEK, LYLE SLADEK, AND HENRY PARKHURST
MITCHELL, SOUTH DAKOTA, 1949

HOME OF LYLE AND PATRICIA SLADEK, MITCHELL, SOUTH DAKOTA, 1953

After completing the family home, Lyle signed on to teach mathematics at Mitchell Senior High School. His effort to make Plane Geometry meaningful to the students received attention in the local newspaper:

TEACHER AT MITCHELL HIGH SCHOOL REVIVES INTEREST IN GEOMETRY WITH MODEL HOUSE

Interest in geometry, one of the least popular classes for many students, has recently increased at Mitchell High School.

The classes, traditionally interesting to only the mathematical-minded students, are now drawing the interest of all students. . . .

The revival of interest and popularity in the mathematical studies at the high school has been motivated by a simple model house built to scale.

The model house has proven so popular that students who formerly shunned the classrooms after hours, and even sometimes during regular class hours, have been found lingering after the dismissal of classes to shower the instructor with further questions. . . .

Sladek first devised the idea for the structure one day last summer while working in his basement workshop. He realized a need for a practical emphasis of his mathematic courses. . . .

"This wood structure, modeled after a $12,000 family home . . . is large enough to see the practical applications of geometric figures. . . .

"The study of geometry," Sladek said, "is the study of the sizes, shapes and positions of all manmade things about us. The buildings, bridges, machines, roads, instruments, art, drawing, maps, furniture, toys, and communications that we use every day make up the subject matter for geometry."

LYLE SLADEK TEACHING WITH MODEL HOUSE, MITCHELL HIGH SCHOOL, 1953
NOTE DOLL ON TOP OF LADDER

Sladek points out to his classes that everyone uses the simplest principles each day in their work and play. . . .

He is married and . . . is now faced with the problem of constructing another model house—this one as a doll house for his oldest daughter.

Sladek concluded by saying that although many other figures could be used to illustrate principles of geometry in the classroom, a model house was chosen as the visual aid because it is familiar to all boys and girls.

The family circle widened following the wedding celebrations of "the girls." Virginia married Don Jensen, a navy veteran who had survived kamikaze attacks in the Pacific. Jean married Richard Rindels, an army veteran who had been involved in the retaking of the Philippines. Wilma married Robert Smith, a marine veteran who had served on tiny Johnson Island in the Pacific.

Dreams of a peaceful postwar world were shattered in June 1950 when the North Korean People's Army crossed the thirty-eighth parallel into South Korea with the aim of reuniting Korea under communist rule. The invasion triggered a response from the United States and the conflict escalated under the umbrella of a fledging United Nations. Along with other veterans, Lyle and Henry were called to register for the draft a second time.

"How can this be, Henry? I haven't even finished wearing out my GI shoes!"

"Beats me, Lyle. Who would've dreamed of another war so soon!"

Although neither Lyle nor Henry were called to serve in the Korean War, Chuckie became involved. Shortly after beginning the study of engineering at SDSC, he was drafted and served as an aircraft mechanic in Korea. Upon returning to the United States he was hospitalized with kidney failure. A last resort blood transfusion—or a miracle—enabled Chuckie to survive. He functioned for several years before having to endure kidney dialysis. Although he bore the affliction with courage and grace, his suffering cast a pall over the entire family.

CHARLES (CHUCKIE) SLADEK IN UNIFORM, KOREA, 1956

By 1956 Lyle and Patricia had become the parents of four daughters, Susan Kay, Ann Louise, Laura Rebecca, and Karen Margaret. During those baby boom years, Vernon and Vivian, Irene and Hank, Virginia and Don, Jean and Richard, and Wilma and Robert also welcomed offspring into the family.

SUSAN, ANN, PATRICIA, LYLE, KAREN, AND LAURA SLADEK, 1957

SLADEK FAMILY GATHERING, MITCHELL, SOUTH DAKOTA, 1957
AUTHOR KAREN SLADEK FRONT CENTER

EMMA AND CHARLES SLADEK AND SEVEN CHILDREN:
JEAN, CHUCKIE, IRENE, LYLE, WILMA, VERNON, AND VIRGINIA
CIRCA 1957

As the cold war escalated during the 1950s, the United States and the Soviet Union vied for world leadership. With the Soviet Union making rapid advances in science (such as *Sputnik,* the Russian satellite that moved into orbit in October 1957), American leaders recognized the need to bolster science education in the United States. Lyle received an invitation to study at Stanford University in the summer of 1956:

MITCHELL TEACHER EXPLORES MATH FUTURE

Lyle V. Sladek, Mitchell High School math instructor is one of 30 science and mathematics teachers from throughout the country currently exploring the future in their fields at Stanford University. . . .

"We have picked some of the finest science and mathematics teachers in the western United States for this study, the Shell Merit Fellowship Program," said Dr. Hurd, who is co-ordinator of the program. "It is the longest and most intense study of its type ever held in this country and the teachers are not letting us down. They are most serious about the study."

Over the next two decades, while other family members were busy with careers and children, Chuckie's health gradually deteriorated. One day in the spring of 1977 an administrator at the Veterans Administration Hospital in Minneapolis called Lyle and his sisters and asked, "Would you be willing to donate a kidney to your brother Charles should you be found to be a suitable donor?" Eventually, Lyle received a letter of notification:

> We have chosen you to be the best candidate for a donor for your brother Charles at the present time. . . . If you should be found healthy and an acceptable donor, your next admission would be for the nephrectomy (kidney removal) which takes approximately 3 weeks of in-hospital time and then a return home with limited activities.

Following a series of physical examinations and a psychological screening, Lyle received a confirmation letter from the transplant coordinator:

> The transplant for your brother, Charles, has been scheduled for December 29th. It will be necessary for you to be admitted to 4AW on December 26, 1977. The length of this hospitalization will be about two weeks. In preparation for your surgery you should increase your fluid intake by 4-5 glasses on December 25.
> Please call us if you are unable to be admitted December 26, 1977. Thank you for your cooperation.

Upon arrival at the hospital, Lyle learned Chuckie had contacted a viral infection, delaying the transplant operation for a week. In the end, however, the kidney transplant was successful.

2 FEBRUARY 1978 (VA HOSPITAL, MINNEAPOLIS, MINNESOTA).
    Dear Lyle,
    Not much going on here since you left. Hope your yard didn't grow up to weeds what with all the rain. It has remained cold here but not much more snow.
    The blood chemistries continued to improve since you left and are all *very* good now. I am still eating like a horse and have gained a little weight already. I hope you are continuing to make steady progress in re-gaining your strength.
    Lyle, I will always be in gratitude for your selfless sacrifice and the graciousness you displayed throughout your prolonged stay. I hope you will never find cause to regret it. Only you could have done it with the style you did.
    Elmer Nelson and the two other transplantees are gone on pass much of the time so only the nurses and I are here some of the time. I get out of the ward for exercise now though.
    Enjoy your FREEDOM, Lyle! Love, Charles

2 JANUARY 1980 (MITCHELL, SOUTH DAKOTA).
    Dear Lyle,
    I got back from Minneapolis last Friday eve. All the tests were fine.

The hospital wasn't too full; seems people don't get sick around the holidays. . . . I picked up a bug in Mpls. and my brains are in low gear today. . . . January 6th will mark two years since you crawled on the operating table, Lyle. I wish to again express my deep gratitude for your gift which was beyond the call of duty. I hope you are fine and will continue so. You have made my life much better.

Best wishes to you and yours for 1980!

With love, Charles

Chuckie, conscientious about taking antirejection medicine, lived another thirteen years. At the time of his death the kidney was still functioning well.

For more than a quarter century the Mitchell home of Emma and Charles was the scene of frequent family gatherings. During those years, twenty-seven grandchildren munched on Emma's cookies, listened to Charles play the violin, and engaged in competitive games of checkers. Those pleasant times ended abruptly in 1974 when Emma died suddenly at home and, five months later to the day, Charles passed away while tending the garden.

Following the memorial service for their father, the children gathered at the family home. Vernon, now the family patriarch, read the Last Will and Testament. The reading completed, the children set about disposing of the possessions their parents had accumulated over a period of six decades. It was a heartbreaking task. Memories of years gone by overwhelmed them.

Some of the keepsakes their parents had treasured found a new home. Others were consigned to the trash heap.

"Does anyone want this old Chinese checkerboard?"

"Yes, I'll take it for my children."

"How about these books by Harold Bell Wright?"

"Not me."

"Then toss 'em."

The contents of a shoe box were emptied onto a table in the dining room.

"I remember that little green booklet. My teacher gave it to me when I was in the first grade."

Along with faded newspaper clippings and picture postcards, *Stephenson's Graded Classical Poems* had survived several moves and many housecleanings. A fuzzy image came into focus for Lyle, faded, and then sharpened again. An elderly man, stern but with a twinkle in his eye, was hovering over his schoolroom desk. "You can read it," his kindly teacher was saying. "Just sound out the words."

"I'm glad Mother saved my little book of poems. Maybe someday I can pass it along to grandchildren with the hope that they, too, will grow up with an appreciation of poetry."

A cardboard box, carefully bound with twine, was lifted down from a closet shelf.

"Look at this! Mother saved all the letters I wrote while in the army. I had no idea. I'll take them home to read when I get time."

VINCIT OMNIA VERITAS

Except for the framework skeleton of the Sears, Roebuck and Co. mail-order house and the foundation stones of the homestead house, the dwelling places of three generations of Sladeks are no more. But the homestead land cherished by Vencel and Josephine Sladek belongs to the fourth generation.

A portion of the prairie land remains untouched by the plow. In the spring, meadowlarks find a safe haven for their nests midst the undergrowth of buffalo grass. On summer days, bumblebees seek out the blossoms of wild roses growing among long-stemmed grasses. During Emma's "Golden Autumn Days," purple thistles and goldenrods dot the prairie with splashes of color. Raging blizzards cover the land with snow as it rests through the winter until the growing season returns and, in nature's endless cycle, thunderstorms again refresh the soil.

In 1975, Lyle and his siblings were astonished and thrilled to learn that the John Deere tractor lived on in all its splendor. Whereas most of the outdated farm machinery had ended up as scrap metal when Emma and Charles moved to Mitchell, the old green-and-yellow poppin' Johnny had found a home on a farm in Davison County. It was prominently displayed on the midway during the Mitchell Corn Palace festival. It carried this sign:

1931 G.P
WIDE TREAD
JOHN DEERE'S 1ST ROW
CROP TRACTOR
ORIGINAL OWNER
CHARLES SLADEK
PUKWANA

ACKNOWLEDGEMENTS

THE AUTHOR IS INDEBTED to her mother and father. They made this book possible and shared in the journey of its creation. Much gratitude goes to the author's husband, family, and friends for their contributions, encouragement, and patience. Many thanks to *Lucky Stars and Gold Bars* editors for their guidance.

REFERENCES

Although God cannot alter the past, historians can.
— SAMUEL BUTLER

IN THE INTEREST OF historical "truth," the author aimed to draw upon a firsthand account and primary sources. Extensive interviews with her father supplement the letters he wrote during the war years. His archives include magazine and newspaper clippings, some of foreign extraction. Several clippings lack headings, dates, or page numbers. The Internet and other sources were accessed merely to substantiate dates and quotes derived from dialogue with her father, someone who was there.

PREFACE: A BOX OF LETTERS

Those who cannot remember   48129. Santayana, George. The Columbia World of Quotations. 1996. Bartleby.com. 28 October 2002.
    <http://www.bartleby.com/66/29/48129.html>.
There is always inequity   John McNair at The University of Tennessee, Knoxville, Division of Information Infrastructure. The University of Tennessee, Knoxville. 15 May 2001.
    <http://www.ns.utk.edu/-mcnair/>.

1 HOME SEEMS A LONG WAY AWAY

Only mad dogs   Dog Proverbs. DogQuotes.com. 27 February 2002.
    <http://www.dogquotes.com/dogproverbs.html>.
bloomin' eyebrows crawl   Gunga Din. Rudyard Kipling. Modern British Poetry.
    Bartleby.com. 16 April 2002.
    <wysiwyg://4/http://www.bartleby.com/103/48.html>.

2 NO PLACE LIKE HOME

It takes a heap o'livin'   Edgar A. Guest (1881-1959) HOME. University of Toronto.
    21 May 2002.
    <http://www.library.utoronto.ca/utel/rp/poems/guest11.html>.
The Homestead Act. American Memory Library of Congress. 16 July 2001.
    <http://memory.loc.gov/ammem/today/may20.htm>.
The archbishop claimed a prior lien   Jennewein, J. Leonard. Dakota Panorama. Dakota Territory Centennial Commission, 1961.

3 RUMBLINGS OF WAR

Power corrupts   Quoteland.com. 27 August 2001.
    <http://161.58.184.85/qldb/author/65?qlSess=b54d72aa0d01deb4f55417d2aedcb961>.

I will employ my strength   The Rise of Hitler – Jan. 30, 1933 Hitler Named Chancellor of Germany. The History Place. 21 May 2002.
<www.bofhlet.net/tasteless/13/named.htm>.

Happy days are here again   Happy Days Are Here Again, Jack Yellen and Milton Ager 1929. 26 June 2002.
<http://www.utu.fi/hum/historia/yh/scarry/USDocuments/HappyDays.htm>.

Prosperity cannot be restored   Herbert Hoover 31st President (1929-1933) The Engineer President In His Own Words. The American President. 21 May 2002.
<www.americanpresident.org/kotrain/courses/HH/HH_In_His_Own_Words.htm>.

I am certain that my fellow Americans   Franklin D. Roosevelt First Inaugural Address March 4, 1933. 23 July 2001.
<http://www.nationalcenter.org/FRooseveltFirstInaugural.html>.

I see a great nation   Franklin D. Roosevelt: Second Inaugural Address. U.S. Inaugural Adresses. 1989. 23 February 2003.
<http://www.bartleby.com/124/pres50.html>.

The Munich Agreement of 1938. 13 July 2001.
<http://sorrel.humboldt.edu/~rescuers/book/Chlup/chluplinks/munich.htm>.

We, the German Fuhrer and Chancellor   Peace For Our Time by Neville Chamberlain. 9 July 2001.
<http://library.byu.edu/~rdh/eurodocs/uk/peace.html>.

I shall give a propagandist reason   The psychology and development of Adolph Hitler Schicklgruber – abelard. 15 May 2001.
<wysiwyg://127/http://www.abelard.org/hitler/hitler.htm>.

This nation will remain   Address of the President From the White House September 3, 1939. 15 May 2001.
<http://www.mhrcc.org/fdr/chat14.html>.

Without victory   Winston Churchill Blood, Sweat and Tears. The History Place Great Speeches Collection. 15 May 2001.
<wysiwyg://90/http://www.historyplace.com/speeches/Churchill.htm>.

I expect the battle of Britain   Their Finest Hour – Winston Churchill. 22 August 2001.
<http://www.winstonchruchill.org/finestc.htm>.

My friends: This is not a fireside chat   Speeches by Franklin D. Roosevelt: The Arsenal of Democracy. 15 May 2001.
<http://www.tamu.edu/scom/pres/speeches/fdrarsenal.htm>.

4 SWEPT INTO THE MAELSTROM OF A GLOBAL CONFLICT

Older men declare war   Lesson Plans Library Children of War. 6 June 2001.
<http://school.discovery.com/lessonplans/activities/childrenofwar/>.

I found my thrill   Words and music by Al Lewis, Larry Stock and Vincent Rose, recorded by Glenn Miller, reached #1 in 1940. Blueberry Hill. 21 May 2002.
<www.edict.com.hk/music/blueberryhill.htm>.

Yesterday, December 7, 1941   Franklin D. Roosevelt's Pearl Harbor Speech (December 8, 1941). 3 January 2003.
<http://bcn.boulder.co.us/government/national/speeches/spch2.htm>.

Now it is impossible   Survivors. Pulitzer Prize for history-quote made by Mr. Kennedy. 21 May 2002.
<www.ussblockisland.org/cve21survivors.htm>.

On the morning of December 11   U.S. Declarations of War. Message from the President. 5 June 2001.
<http://www.ibiblio.org/pha/77-1-148/77-1-148.html>.

Washington's Birthday   Roosevelt's Famous Washington's Birthday Speech @ bentutner.com. 7 January 2003.
<http://benturner.com/theirs/roosevelt.php>.

Japanese ancestry   Japanese-Americans Internment Camps During World War II. From the Special Collections Department, J. Willard Marriott Library, University of Utah, and Private Collections. 21 June 2002.
<http://www.lib.utah.edu/spc/photo/9066/9066.htm>.

Whereas the successful prosecution　War Relocation Authority Exhibit – Text of Executive Order No. 9066 Authorizing the Secretary of War to Prescribe Military Areas. 21 May 2002.
　　<dizzy.library.arizona.edu/images/jpamer/execordr.html>.
global war　Diane Rabson, NCAR archivist. It Happened Here: The Invisible Ally. SN Monthly, October 1998. 5 June 2001.
　　<http://www.ucar.edu/communications/staffnotes/9810/here.html>.

5　YOU'RE IN THE ARMY NOW, YOU'RE NOT BEHIND A PLOW

You're in the Army now　Composed by Isham Jones, lyrics by Till Taylor and Ole Olsson. You're in the Army Now. 1 May 2001.
　　<http://www.acronet.net/~robokopp/usa/armynow.htm>.
We defend and we build　The Quotations Home Page – Alphabetical by Topic-Series 21. 29 May 2001.
　　<http://www.geocities.com/~spanoudi/topic-a3.html>.
I should like to see　Address Delivered by President Roosevelt to the Congress, May 16, 1940. 20 June 2002.
　　<http://www.mtholyoke.edu/acad/intrel/WorldWar2/fdr16.html>.
Billy Mitchell Bombing of Ostfrieland and Court-Martial. University of Wisconsin-Milwaukee Golda Meir Library. 20 June 2002.
　　<http://www.uwm.edu/Dept/Library/arch/mitchell/introl.htm>.
Doolittle Tokyo Raiders. 11 May 2002.
　　<http://www.wpafb.af.mil/museum/history/wwii/dtr.htm>.
Selective service, in U.S. history, term for conscription. Electric Library Presents Encyclopedia.com. 11 June 2001.
　　<http://www.encyclopedia.com/printablenew/11664.htm>.
History of the Draft, Background of Selective Service. 11 June 2001.
　　<wysiwyg://197/http://usmilitary.about.c...tary/library/milinfo/bldrafthistory.htm>.
We live in fame　The Army Air Corps Song. 12 July 2001.
　　<http://www.geocities.com/pentagon/6179/airforce.html>.

6　ART DECO BARRACKS AND BRONZED GODS

Moon Over Miami　Eddy Duchin – words by Edgar Leslie, music by Joe Burke. Moon Over Miami. 6 May 2001.
　　<http://www.summer.com.br/~pfilho/html/lyrics/m/moon_over_mimai.tx>.
The best hotel room is none too good　Florida in WWII – Historic Sites and Resources – Miami Beach Hotels. 21 May 2002.
　　<dhr.dos.state.fl.us/wwwii/sites.cfm?PR_ID=139>.
On the Banks of the Wabash　Written by Paul Dresser, composed by Paul Dresser. Official Song of the State of Indiana. On the Banks of the Wabash, Far Away. 3 May 2001.
　　<http://www.50states.com/songs/indiana.htm>.
Hold-the-line　Guide Introduction: Minutes of the Executive Council of the American Federation of Labor. LexisNexis Academic & Library Solutions. 21 May 2002.
　　<www.lexisnexis.com/academic/guides/ labor_studies/afl/afla.htm>.
I am speaking tonight　americanpresidency.org – FDR Fireside Chats. Franklin D. Roosevelt – Fireside Chats. 46 Fireside Chat. May 2, 1943. The American Presidency Project, University of California, Santa Barbara. 14 March 2002.
　　<www.americanpresidency.org>.

7　MEET ME IN ST. LOUIS

Meet me in St. Louis　Lyrics by Andrew B. Sterling. Music by Frederick Allen "Kerry" Mills. "Meet Me In St. Louis, Louis." 21 May 2002.
　　<www.usgennet.org/~ahmostlu/louislyrics.htm>.
Per Veritatem Vis.　1904 Olympics and Francis Field Today. 20 June 2001.
　　<http://www.virtualworldfairs.com/stl/1904olympics.htm>.
Don't sit under the apple tree　Words and music by Lew Brown, Charlie Tobias, and Sam H. Stept. Don't Sit Under The Apple Tree. 21 May 2002.
　　<www.geocities.com/Nashville/1761/appltree.html>.

My fellow Americans   americanpresidency.org – FDR Fireside Chats. Franklin D. Roosevelt
– Fireside Chats. 86 Fireside Chat. July 28, 1943. The American Presidency Project,
University of California, Santa Barbara. 14 March 2002.
<www.americanpresidency.org>.

Waco glider   AviationCrashes.Com Military Photo Gallery: US Army Air Force Waco
CG-4A. 4 May 2001.
<wysiwyg://59/http://www.aviationcrashes.com/photo/military/1aug1943.htm>.

8 FAMILIAR FACES AND WIDE-OPEN SPACES
The cultivators of the earth   Bill Clinton, June 23, 1998, Quote of the Week. 30 May 2001.
<http://www.fccouncil.com/public2/news/quotes/062398clinton.htm>.

9 THE CHANGING WINDS OF WAR
In an unreliable world   The Statesman. 28 July 1943.

die for Mussolini and Hitler   Churchill and FDR joint appeal. From: UNITED STATES
ARMY IN WORLD WAR II, Special Studies: CHRONOLOGY, 1941-1945, compiled by
Mary H. Williams, Office of the Chief of Military History. 6 June 2001.
<http://www.ibiblio.org/pub/academic/history/marshall/military/wwii/4307.txt>.

July 25: Mussolini Deposed. 11 June 2002.
<http://www.yad-vashem.org.il/about_holo.../1942-1945/1943/chronology_1943_20.htm>.

Be pleased to inform Their Lordships   GI – World War II Commemoration. 6 June 2001.
<http://gi.grolier.com/wwii/wwii_8.html>.

Today, it is announced   Franklin D. Roosevelt's September 8, 1943 Fireside Chat.
Historical Document Index, The Political Resource Page. 3 January 2003.
<www.politicalresource.net>.

God Bless America   God Bless America – Song Lyrics. ScoutSongs.com Virtual Songbook.
11 October 2001.
<http://www.scoutsongs.com/lyrics/godblessamerica.html>.

The Star Spangled Banner   Francis Scott Key. The National Anthem of the United States of
America "The Star Spangled Banner". 12 September 2001.
<http://usacitylink.com/usa/ssb.html>.

IO CAROLINA IN THE MORNING
Carolina, in the Morning   Words by Gus Kahn, music by Walter Donaldson. Magic
Shadow Shapes – Lyrics "Carolina". 21 May 2002.
<members.tripod.com/~f_fly/Carolina.html>.

SJAFB. 27 June 2001.
<http://www.seymourjohnson.af.mil/4fw/sjafb.htm>.

Oh! How I Hate   Oh How I Hate To Get Up – Song Lyrics. ScoutSongs.com Virtual
Songbook. 1 May 2001.
<http://www.scoutsongs.com/lyrics/hatetogetup.html>.

Stars and Stripes   American Patriotic Song Lyrics and Words – Stars and Stripes Forever.
27 November 2001.
<http://www.theromantic.com/partitoiclyrics/starsandstripesforecer.htm>.

The Road Not Taken   The Road Not Taken. Frost, Robert. 1920. Mountain Interval.
Bartleby.com Great Books Online. 27 February 2002.
<wysiwyg://4/http://www.bartleby.com/119/1.htm>.

On this Christmas Eve   Franklin D. Roosevelt's December 24, 1943 Fireside Chat.
Historical Document Index, The Political Resource Page. 3 January 2003.
<www.politicalresource.net>.

Oh! What a Beautiful Morning   Oh What a Beautiful Morning – Song Lyrics.
ScoutSongs.com Virtual Songbook. 30 April 2001.
<http://www.scoutsongs.com/lyrics/beautifulmorning.html>.

Be Strong!   1943 service program: SERVICE FOR CADETS Aviation Cadet Pre-Technical
School Chapel No. 4, Seymour Johnson Field, N.C. 10 A.M.

To be especially watchful   Eleven General Orders. U.S. Coastguard. 29 April 2001.
<http://www.uscg.mil/reserve/pubs/helmsman/eleven.htm>.

Lienhard, John H. <u>No. 470: The Japanese Zero</u>. 20 May 2002.
  <http://www.uh.edu/engines/epi470.htm>.
Laurie, Clayton D. <u>Anzio 1944</u>. U.S. Army Center of Military History. 27 February 2002.
  <http://www.army.mil/cmh-pg/brochures/anzio/72-19.htm>.
Army Subsistence History. <u>Subsistence and Army Cooks History Page</u>. Quartermaster
  Museum, Quartermaster Foundation. 30 June 2002.
  <http://www.qmfound.com/army_subsistence_history.htm>.

                    11 FOR GOD, FOR COUNTRY, AND FOR YALE
Technical School, AAFTTC (pamphlet). <u>Aviation Cadets Yale University</u>. Yale
  University, New Haven, Connecticut.
School Days   Words by Will D. Cobb and music by Gus Edwards (1907). <u>School Days Sing
  Along Nostalgic MID…g, With Lyrics, 1907 Public Domain Song</u>. 15 May 2001.
  <http://www.melodylane.net/schooldays.htm>.
My only regret   <u>Lingg – Famous Quotes, Who Spoke Them, Their Circumstances</u>.
  1 June 2001.
  <http://www.columbia-center.org/bllingg/jtl/quotes.html>.
<u>Marinship 1942-1945 Exhibit</u>. 27 June 2002.
  <http://www.baymodel.org/marinship.htm>.
<u>Rosie the Riveter Trust, A History of the Richmond Shipyards</u>. 27 June 2002.
  <http://www.rosietheriveter.org/shiphist.htm>.
Ac-cent-tchu-ate the positive   Music by Harold Arlen. Lyrics by Johnny Mercer. <u>The Music
  of Homefront</u>. 3 March 2003.
  <http://www.geocities.com/Hollywood/Highrise/7502/mjusic.htm>.
Never in the field of human   <u>Winston Churchill Quotes</u>. 22 September 2001.
  <http://www.winstonchurchill.org/sdquotes.htm>.
<u>Alton Glenn Miller, Major, United States Army</u>. 17 December 2001.
  <http://www.arlingtoncemetery.com/agmiller.htm>.
<u>Military District of Washington – Fact Sheet: Glenn Miller</u>. 29 June 2001.
  <http://www.mdw.army.mil/fs-p37.htm>.
The alert young men / Sanitation at the Army Air Forces   <u>Excerpt from New Haven Dept.
  of Health,…Protecting the Health of the Air Cadets</u>. Document was digitized 1999 as part
  of the New Haven Health project. 3 May 2001.
  http://info.med.yale.edu/newhavenhealth…ments/historical/monthly,aircadets.htm>.
Yesterday on June fourth, 1944   <u>Franklin D. Roosevelt's June 5, 1944 Fireside Chat</u>.
  Historical Document Index, The Political Resource Page. 3 January 2003.
  <www.politicalresource.net>.
The Great Crusade / OK, let's go   <u>D-day, 1944</u>. National Archives and Records
  Administration. 3 March 2002.
  <http://www.nara.gov/exhall/american_originals_iv/sections/nonjavatext_d-day.html>.
Of course, there are always pessimists   <u>americanpresidency.org – FDR Fireside Chats.
  Franklin D. Roosevelt – Fireside Chats. 43 Fireside Chat. June 12, 1944</u>. The American
  Presidency Project, University of California, Santa Barbara. 14 March 2002.
  <www.americanpresidency.org>.
ALLIED AIR SUPPORT of the French invasion   <u>The Beaver</u>. 16 June 1944.

                    12 AN OFFICER AND A GENTLEMAN
What is outside yourself   <u>Charles Daney's Quotation Collection. Clothing and the lack
  thereof</u>. 5 May 2001.
  <http://www.best.com/~cgd/home/quotes.htm>.
<u>Nellis History</u>. 1 March 2002.
  <http://www.nellis.af.mil/history/default.htm>.

                    13 DON'T FENCE ME IN
Oh, give me land, lots of land   <u>Don't Fence Me In</u>. 1 May 2001.
  <http://www.kcmetro.cc.mo.us/pennvalley/biology/lewis/crosby/DontFence.html>.

The Battle of the Bulge. 30 June 2002.
  http://helius.acomp.usf.edu/~dsargent/bestbulge2.htm>.
unsinkable aircraft carrier   Radio Days – Iwo Jima – the unsinkable aircraft carrier.
  21 May 2002.
  <http://www.otr.com/iwo_jima.html>.
Iwo Jima – The Picture. 16 March 2002.
  <http://www.iwojima.com/raising/rasingb.htm.>

14 PASSAGE TO THE UNKNOWN
Wardlow, Chester. The Transportation Corps: Movements, Training and Supply. In
  USAWWII series. Washington D.C: Office of the Chief of Military History, Department
  of the Army, 1951.
Roll on, thou deep   The Sea, Byron, George Gordon, Lord (1788-1824). 30 June 2002.
  <http://www.ac.wwu.edu/~stephan/webstuff/poetry/Bryon-TheSea.html>.
U.S. Senate Historical Minutes: Churchill Addresses Congress, December 26, 1941.
  8 March 2002.
  <http://www.senate.gov/learning/min_5haah.htm>.
V-Mail "Victory" Mail from World War II. 8 March 2002.
  <wysiwyg://4/http://www.si.edu/postal/learnmore/vmail.htm>.
World War Two Advertising History – V-Mail [Ad*Access]. 8 March 2002.
  <http://scriptorium.lib.duke.edu/adaccess/vmail.htm>.
McDonald, James. British Open 'V' Nerve War; Churchill Spurs Resistance. 8 March 2002.
  <http://www.nytimes.com/learning/general/onthisday/big/0719.htm>.
Where the flyin'-fishes play   Poetry of Rudyard Kipling, full-text; Rudyard Kipling's poems.
  Everypoet.com. 20 May 2001.
  <http://www.everypoet.com/archive/poetry/Rudyard_Kipling/kipling_mandalay.htm>.

15 FLYING THE HUMP, SUPPLYING CHINA BY AIR
This is a solemn but a glorious hour   Truman Library - Public Papers. Broadcast to the
  American People Announcing the Surrender of Germany. 20 September 2003.
  <http://www.trumanlibrary.org/ww2/veday.htm>.
tossed aircraft   Costello, John. The Pacific War 1941-1945. New York: Rawson, Wade,
  1981.
we are flying as much lend-lease   Franklin Roosevelt's 10th State of the Union Message.
  5 June 2001.
  <http://www.presidency.ucsb.edu/sou_pages/froosevelt10su.html>.
Double the number of crews   Hap Arnold. Coffey, Thomas. HAP, The Story of the U.S. Air
  Force and the Man Who Built It. New York: Viking Press, 1982.
Aluminum Trail   What Was Known As The "Aluminum Trail" During World War II.
  3 May 2001.
  <http://www.museumofaviation.org/avi_trivia/alum_trail.htm>.
foremost and by far the most dangerous   China National Aviation Corporation (CNAC).
  11 March 2003.
  <http://www.cnac.org/>.
Bring me men to match   Support Planes and Missions, Pilots. 4 May 2001.
  <http://www.southernoregonwarbirds.org/sup2.htm>.
OH, East is East   Poet's Corner – Rudyard Kipling – Selected Works. The Ballad of East
  and West. 17 May 2001.
  <wysiwyg://33/http://www.geocities.com/-spanoudi/poems/kiplin01.htm>.
prompt and utter destruction   Potsdam conference. AAHM Gallery Tour – Decisions:
  Dropping of "The Bomb" Exhibit. 26 June 2002.
  <http://www.airpowermuseum.org/trdecisn.htm>.

16 DAWN OF A NEW AGE
It is a mistake to look   Winston Churchill Quotations. 21 May 2002.
  <webpages.ainet.com/gosner/quotationsarch/ quotations1/author/Churchill.htm>.

Japan Surrenders, Peace At Last. 27 June 2002.
    <http://library.thinkquest.org/CR0215466/japan_surrenders.htm>.
American Experience / Truman / Primary Sources/ White House Press Release
    Announcing the Bombing of Hiroshima, August 6, 1945. 15 March 2002.
    <wysiwyg://24/http://www.pbs.org/wgbh/amex/truman/psources/ps_pressrelease.htm>.
Attention Japanese People   American Experience / Truman / Primary Sources / Leaflets
    Dropped On Cities in Japan. 15 March 2002.
    wysiwyg://21/http://www.pbs.org/wgbh/amex/truman/psources/ps_leaflets.htm>.
Emperor Hirohito. 27 June 2002.
    <wysiwyg://15/http://www.expage.com/page/wwiigen31>.
bear the unbearable   Nagasaki. The National Atomic Museum. 30 June 2002.
    <www.atomicmuseum.com/tour/dd5.dfm - 10K>.
Assam Scrapbook Item   Hump Express.
in due course Korea   Cairo Conference 22 – 26 November 1943. 5 June 2001.
    <http://www.taiwandocuments.org/cairo.htm>.
United States. Department of State. The Naming of World War II, September 11, 1945.
    Washington. GPO, 1945.
    .....<http://www.ibiblio.org/pha/policy/post-war/450911a.html>.
First Mass Shipment of I-B Troops Hits New York City.   Roundup. October 4, 1945.
They also serve who   On His Blindness. J. Milton. The Golden Treasury. Bartleby.com
    Great Books Online. 17 May 2001.
    <wysiwyg://15/http://www.bartleby.com/106/71.htm>.

17 POSTWAR DUTY IN EUROPE

Hope springs eternal   Alexander Pope (1688-1744). An Essay on Man in Four Epistles:
    Epistle 1. University of Toronto. 9 July 2001.
    <http://www.library.utoronto.ca/utel/rp/poems/pope10.html>.
Now in Injia's sunny   Poetry of Rudyard Kipling, full-text; Rudyard Kipling's poems.
    Everypoet.com. 20 May 2001.
    http://www.everypoet.com/archive/poetry/Rudyard_Kipling/kipling_gunga_din.htm>.
You will yet be the glory of the East   DAWN Special Report On South Asian Century;
    Karachi's quotable quotes. 13 April 2002.
    <http://www.dawn.com/events/milleninium/43.htm>.
Graf Zeppelin. 13 April 2002.
    <http://www.interlog.com/~reevans/zeps/lz127mdf.htm>.
A Nazi Perspective on the Fall of Rome. German Propaganda Archive. Calvin College.
    4 February 2002.
    <http://www.calvin.edu/academic/cas/gpa/rome.htm>.
CIN – Pius XII's Defense of Jews and Others: 1944-45 - Rome, 'Open City'.
    4 February 2002.
    <wysiwyg://44/http://www.cin.org/p12-4.htm>.
the glory that was Greece / the grandeur that was Rome   Edgar Allen Poe: The Complete
    Works. To Helen by Edgar Allen Poe. 21 May 2002.
    <eserver.org/books/poe/>.
There is properly no history, only biography   Ralph Waldo Emerson Quotations.
    6 June 2001.
    http://webpages.ainet.com/gosner/quotationsarch/quotations1/author/Emerson.htm>.

EPILOGUE: LOVE AND LAUGHTER AND PEACE EVER AFTER

All the world's a stage   William Shakespeare – The Academy of American Poets – All the
    Worlds' a Stage. 30 June 2002.
    <http://www.poets.org/poems/poems.cfm?prmID-1714>.
There'll be blue birds over   There'll be blue birds over the White Cliffs of Dover.
    1 May 2001.
    <http://www.acronet.net/~robokopp/english/therellb.htm>.

The United States stands at this time at the pinnacle   Complete Speeches of Winston Churchill. Sinews of Peace, March 5, 1946, Westminster College, Fulton, Missouri. 5 May 2001.
  <http://www.winstonchurchill.org/sinews.htm>.

Germany would starve   Partnership: Potsdam. 10 June 2002.
  <http://members.nbci.com/_XMCM/cfmorgan/potsdam.htm>.

God's in his heaven   Quotations Pages – Series 12 – Quotes from Poetry B. 13 September 2002.
  <http://www.geocities.com/~spanoudi/qfp.b.html>.

College Becomes Family Affair   South Dakota Collegian, South Dakota State College, 1947.

LYLE SLADEK lives with his wife Patricia in California. A multitude of experiences while in the Army Air Corps during World War II profoundly shaped his life. He treasures memories of the wonderful people he met during those years and would like to renew acquaintances. "It was my good fortune," he says, "to orbit with so many outstanding individuals during that time. It is my hope and prayer that the intervening years have been as kind to them as they have been to me."

Now Professor of Mathematics, Emeritus, at California Lutheran University, Lyle peddles his bicycle around the campus, frequents the college library, and shares stories with friends. He retains his penchant for puns, poetry, and language as well as music, history, and writing. One room of his home is cluttered with puzzles and posers as well as artifacts that illustrate concepts of mathematics and physics. Along with tending a garden, tinkering in his workshop, and playing pool or bridge with his buddies, he stands ready to help friends and neighbors with house repairs.

Although Lyle has been the recipient of many honors and awards, he has kept the down-to-earth traits of his early upbringing in the heartland of America. Along with his biographical sketch in *Who's Who in America* is this tribute to his parents: "I have sought to return full measure to society for all the opportunities and joys of life that have come my way. I learned from my parents during the dust bowl years that adversity often can be overcome through patience and determination."

Should you stop by for a visit, bring a dictionary because Lyle will likely ask for your help in solving the daily newspaper crossword.

LYLE SLADEK, BRULE COUNTY WWII MEMORIAL, SOUTH DAKOTA, 2000

MILITARY

Cryptographic Security Officer, WWII Army Air Corps (1943-1946):
China-Burma-India (CBI); Pacific theater of operations (PTO)
European theater of operations (ETO)
Mediterranean theater of operations (MTO)

PROFESSIONAL

Professor of Mathematics, Emeritus, California Lutheran University
Shell Merit Fellow, Stanford University
Recipient Meritorious Achievement Award in Education
National Science Foundation (NSF) Fellow
Fulbright Lecturer
National Science Foundation (NSF) Lecturer

EDUCATION

Ph.D., Mathematics Education, UCLA
M.A., Mathematics Education, Stanford University
M.A., Speech and English, University of South Dakota
B.A., Mathematics, Electrical Engineering, South Dakota State University

OTHER

Subject of biographical record, *Who's Who in America*
Contributor of short stories/poems to newspapers and magazines
Speaker on World War II topics

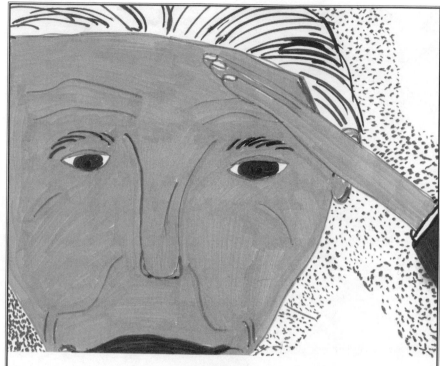

MY HERO

My hero is my grandpa. His name is Lyle Sladek. He is a brilliant mathematician, and before he retired, he taught math at Californian Lutheran University. One time I went to visit grandpa Lyle, and he introduced me to his class.

Grandpa Lyle is also a very good handyman. Last time I went to see him he built my brother and me a car. It had a steering wheel, brakes, seat, and even a horn. In the evening rode down hills in it.

I also think grandpa Lyle is very brave. When he was about eighteen he fought in World War II.

That is why he is **my hero**!

LYLE SLADEK
DRAWN BY GRANDAUGHTER NATASHA SLADEK PALEWICZ (FOURTH GRADE)
NOTE LEFT-HAND SALUTE